CW01671609

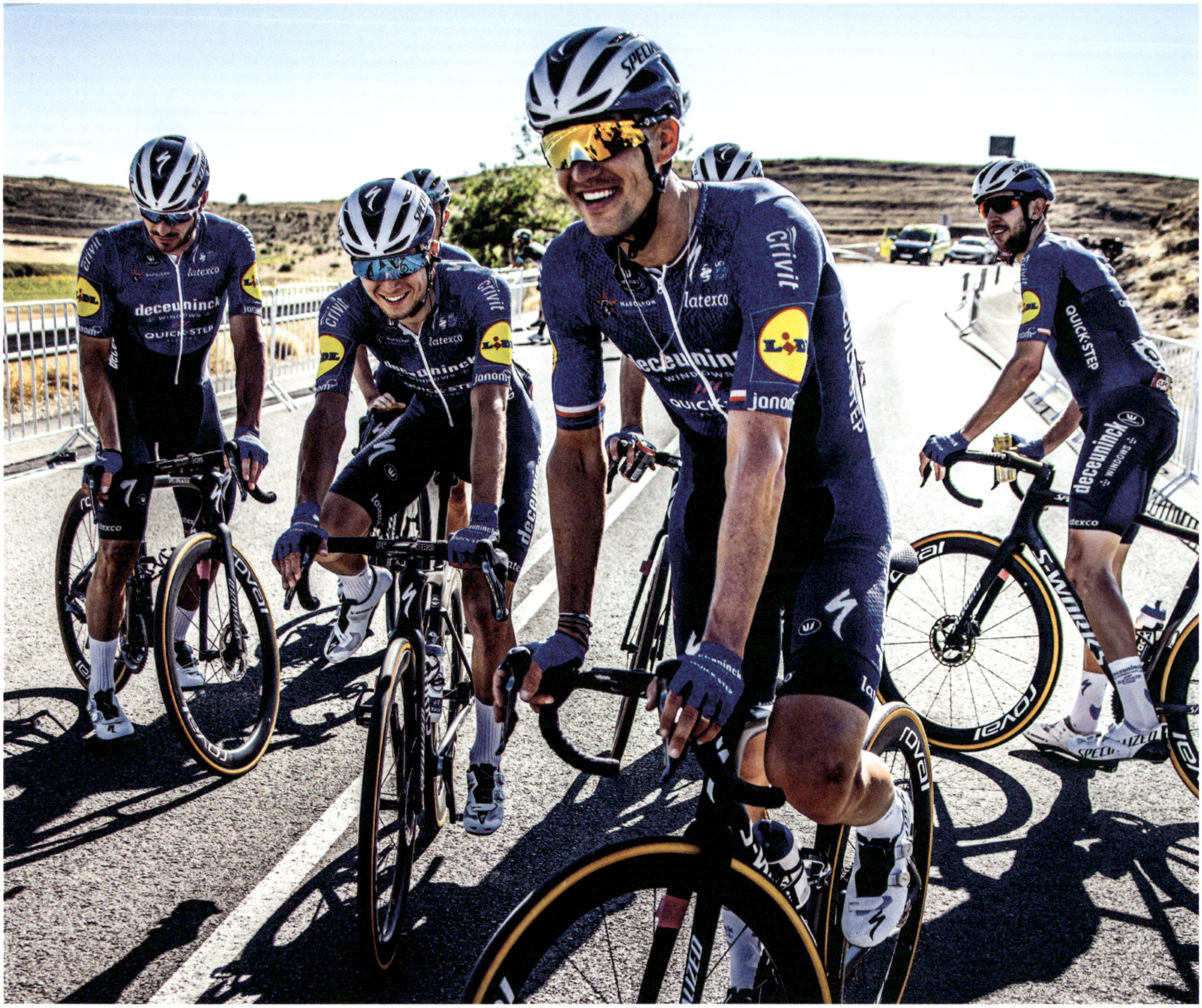
deceuninck
WINDOWS
QUICK-STEP
latexco
Crivit

WOUT BEEL
GEERT VANDENBON

THE WOLFPACK WAY

WINNING IS AN ATTITUDE.
AND HARD WORK.

Lannoo

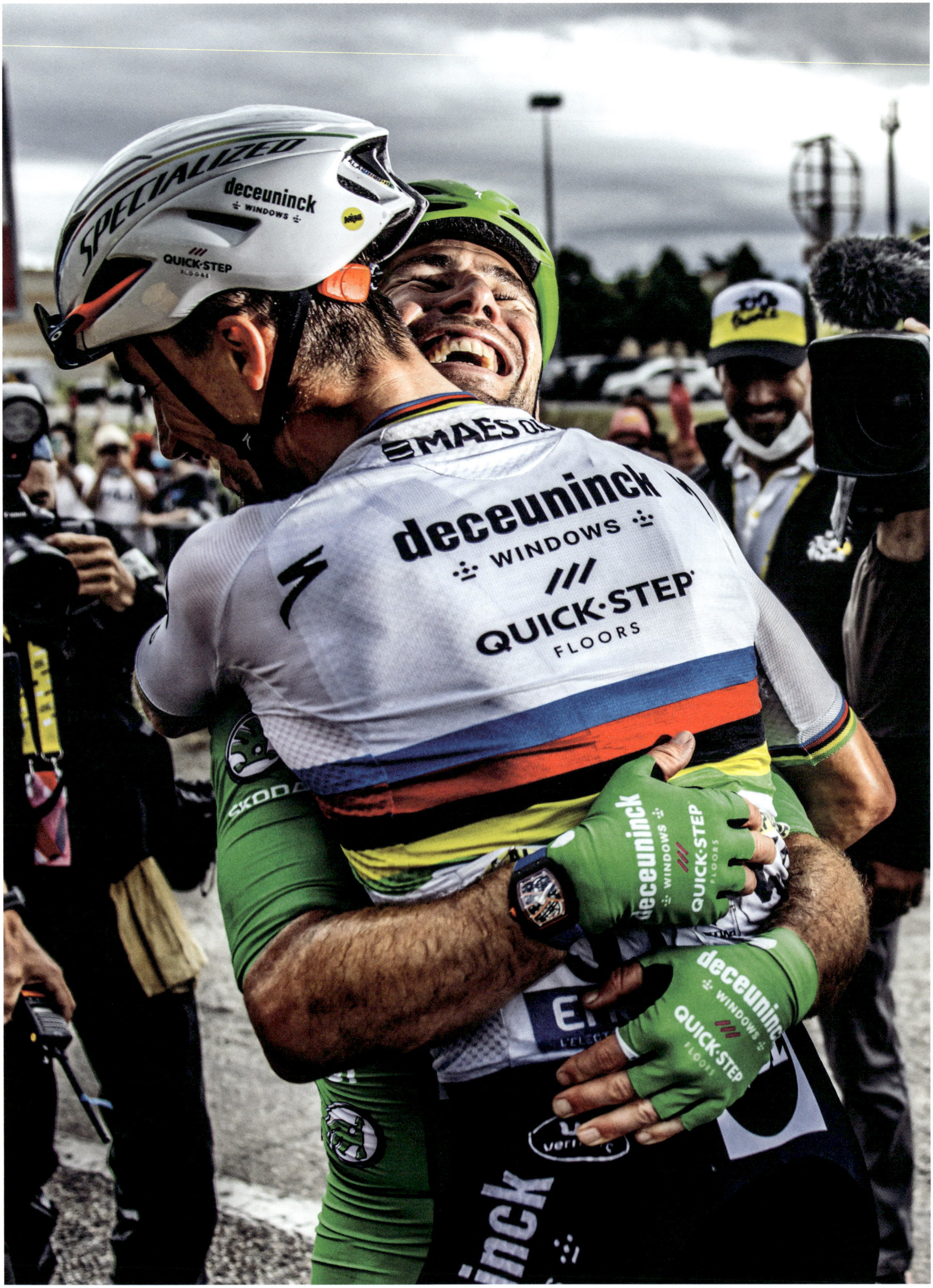
SPECIALIZED
deceuninck
WINDOWS
QUICK-STEP
FLOORS
MAES
deceuninck
WINDOWS
QUICK-STEP
FLOORS
SKODA

INDRUKWEKKEND

Het wielerjaar 2021 was indrukwekkend. Hier zouden we er een punt achter kunnen zetten en jullie – lezers, fans, sympathisanten, renners, staf en sponsors van het Deceuninck – Quick-Step Team – alleen nog foto's laten zien. Prachtige, unieke beelden van huisfotograaf Wout Beel.

Maar het seizoen 2021 was té indrukwekkend om er niet een klein snufje duiding aan toe te voegen. Een beetje extra peper bij die heerlijke, warme soep. Eten én drinken was het, met op gepaste tijden een fijn glas champagne erbovenop. Dat was 2021 voor The Wolfpack.

VERBLUFFENDE CIJFERS

Cijfers. 284 koersdagen, altijd op twee en soms drie fronten. Van begin februari tot midden oktober. En dan werden de januarikoersen op het zuidelijk halfrond nog geschrapt ten gevolge van de coronapandemie. Een profploeg is een logistiek wonder. Een bonte bende karakters die samen één sterke en toch soepele machine vormen. 30 profs onder contract en een staf van 54 medewerkers. Een lange ketting met dik 80 schakels, altijd klaar voor de koers, altijd bereid om samen, met de juiste spirit én professionaliteit, lastminuteobstakels aan te pakken. Elk schakeltje is belangrijk. Samen op pad, kriskras over de aardbol. Samen vreugdevol bij winst, samen sterk bij verlies.

Een roedel Wolven.

EEN RENNER IS EEN TEAM

Nog cijfers: 65 zeges. The Wolfpack behaalde 65 overwinningen, een wonderbaarlijk cijfer. Cijfers waar andere teams niet van durven dromen. Van de eerste rit in de Tour de la Provence met Davide Ballerini op 11 februari tot Remco Evenepoel in de Coppa Bernocchi op 4 oktober.

Remco Evenepoel. De naam zal vaak vallen in het boek. Maar ook die van Mark Cavendish, Kasper Asgreen, João Almeida, Rémi Cavagna, Yves Lampaert of Julian Alaphilippe, natuurlijk. Maar... een renner is een team. Steeds weer, elke dag. Niemand wint alleen. Elke winst is teamwinst.

Meer cijfers. Vlaanderen kreeg de eer de honderdste editie van het WK te organiseren, dat al voor de tiende keer in België werd gehouden. Het werd een uniek event, een uitbarsting van vreugde na achttien donkere coronamaanden. Het WK op de weg in Leuven overtrof de stoutste verwachtingen. Met Wolfpack-lid Julian Alaphilippe als superieure winnaar. Misschien nog indrukwekkender voor The Wolfpack: van de 194 profs uit 45 landen die aan de start kwamen, behoorden niet minder dan 16 coureurs tot de DQT-stal. Ze reden voor 8 landen.

ACHTER DE CIJFERS

Het was een indrukwekkend jaar. Dat zal blijken uit de selectie van prachtige beelden die dit boek rijk is. De opsomming van glorierijke momenten is lang. Een voorsmaakje: de klassieke zeges van Kasper Asgreen, de verbluffende Tour de France van Mark Cavendish, de tweede regenboogtrui van Julian Alaphilippe, de comeback van Remco Evenepoel, de verrijzenis van Fabio Jakobsen, de zeges van Sam Bennett, de bevestiging van João Almeida, Rémi Cavagna, Florian Sénéchal, Mikkel Honoré en Davide Ballerini, het delirium van Yves Lampaert op het BK tijdrijden. Ook Jannik Steimle, Josef Cerny, Mattia Cattaneo, Andrea Bagioli en Mauri Vansevenant pikten bloemen mee. Al waren die bloemen nu eens een worst dan weer een beker.

Achttien verschillende winnaars, waaruit de sterkte van het team in de breedte blijkt. Maar de verdienste van de ploegmaten die niet in het lijstje staan, is er niet minder om. Iljo Keisse trok 74 keer zijn koersplunje aan, Tim Declercq maalde 11.118 kilometers af en Michael Mørkøv haalde als lead-out 13 keer de top 10. Patrick Lefevere: 'Ik heb nooit het belang onderschat van de renners die lager in de hiërarchie staan. Ze beïnvloeden de toppers, houden ze wakker en zorgen voor dynamiek en sfeer in de groep. Ook als er op meerdere fronten wordt gestreden. Almeida die wint op 12 augustus in Polen en Evenepoel op dezelfde dag in Denemarken. Dat geeft een boost!'

Geniet van de beelden! We hopen dat ze een stukje inkijk geven in de ziel van de Wolvenroedel, in hoe The Wolfpack functioneert. Meer dan tachtig professionals die samen on the road gaan om te koersen, te strijden en te winnen. Meer dan tachtig karakters die, samen met elkaar, van en voor de koers leven. Een heel jaar lang. En volgend jaar opnieuw. Als een perpetuum mobile.

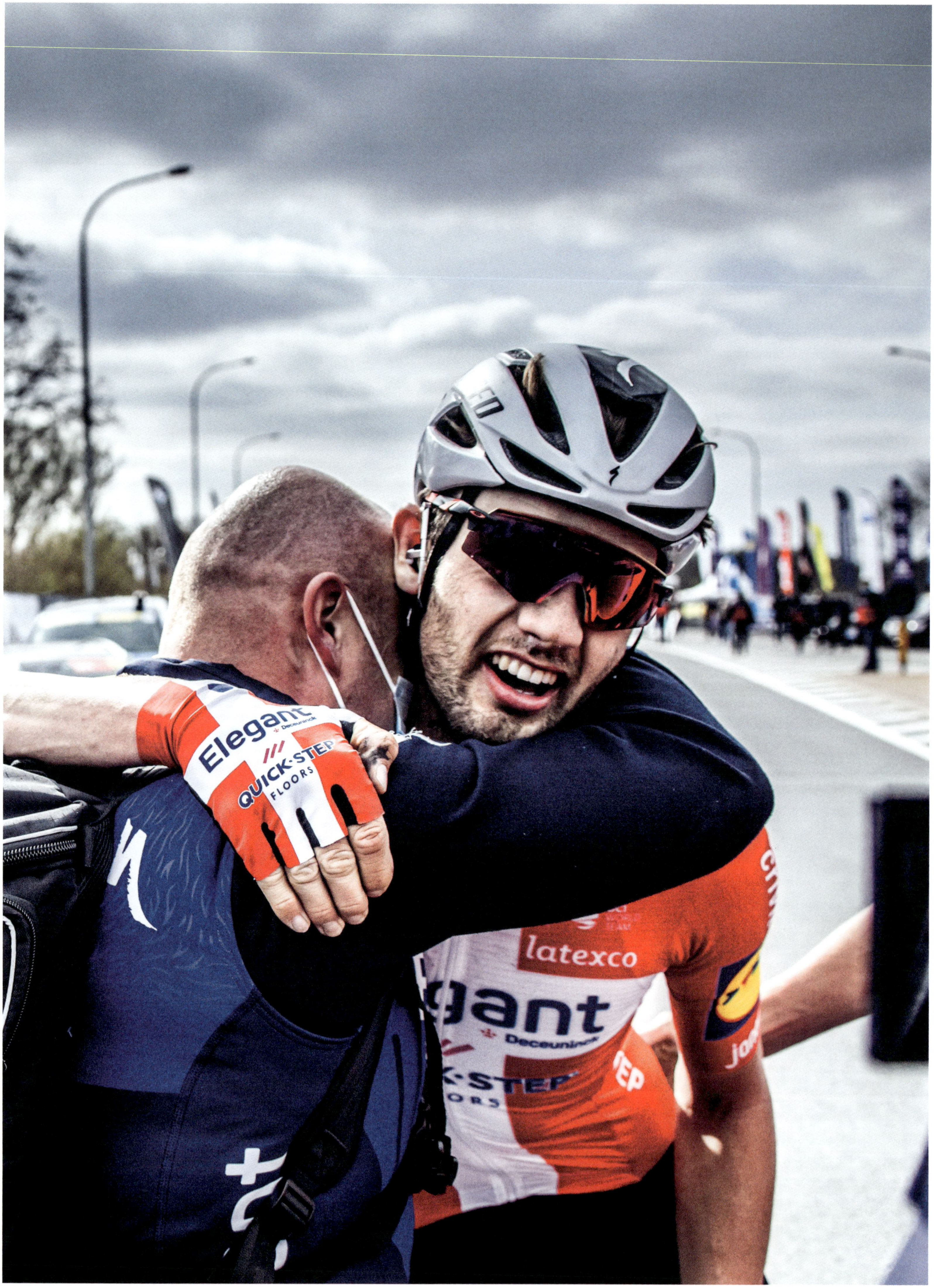
Elegant
QUICK-STEP
FLOORS
latexco

IMPRESSIVE

The 2021 cycling year was impressive. We could simply show you – our readers, fans, supporters, riders, staff, and sponsors of the Deceuninck – Quick-Step Team – some nice photos. Beautiful, unique images captured by team photographer Wout Beel.

However, the 2021 season was too impressive not to add some contextual storytelling. An extra pinch of pepper to that delicious, hot soup. And, along with a season as fantastic as a multi-course gourmet meal, at opportune moments we've been able to celebrate with a glass of fine champagne. That was 2021 for The Wolfpack.

STAGGERING FIGURES

By the numbers: 284 race days, always on two and sometimes on three fronts. From early February to mid-October. The January races in the southern hemisphere were cancelled due to the COVID-19 pandemic. A professional team is a logistical miracle. A bold crew of different characters that together form one strong and yet flexible machine. Thirty professionals under contract, and a total staff of 54 people. A long chain with over 80 links, always ready for the race, always prepared to tackle last-minute obstacles together – all with the right spirit and professionalism. Each link matters. Together on the road, crisscrossing the globe. Ecstatic when we win, strong and supportive when we lose.

A wolfpack.

A RIDER IS A TEAM

More figures: Sixty-five victories. The Wolfpack has achieved 65 victories, a prodigious figure. These are numbers that other teams wouldn't even dare to dream of. From the first stage in the Tour de la Provence with Davide Ballerini on February 11, to Remco Evenepoel in the Coppa Bernocchi on October 4.

Remco Evenepoel. His name will be mentioned often in this book, along with Mark Cavendish, Kasper Asgreen, João Almeida, Rémi Cavagna, Yves Lampaert, and Julian Alaphilippe, of course. But... a rider is a team. Every day, again and again. Nobody wins alone. Every win is a team win.

More figures. Flanders had the honor of organizing the 100th edition of the World Championships, the tenth time Belgium hosted the event. It became a unique event, an outburst of joy after 18 dark months of the pandemic. The Road World Championships in Leuven exceeded the wildest expectations, with Wolfpack member Julian Alaphilippe taking gold. Perhaps even more impressive for The Wolfpack: of the 194 professionals from 45 countries who came to the start, no fewer than 16 riders, competing for 8 different countries, were members of the DQT family.

BEHIND THE FIGURES

It was an impressive year, as you'll see in the selection of beautiful images that appear in this book. The list of glorious moments is long: the classics victories of Kasper Asgreen, the stunning Tour de France of Mark Cavendish, the second rainbow jersey of Julian Alaphilippe, the comeback of Remco Evenepoel, the resurrection of Fabio Jakobsen, the victories of Sam Bennett, the confirmation of João Almeida, Rémi Cavagna, Florian Sénéchal, Mikkel Honoré, and Davide Ballerini, the delirium of Yves Lampaert at the Belgian Time Trial Championship. Jannik Steimle, Josef Cerny, Mattia Cattaneo, Andrea Bagioli, and Mauri Vansevenant also earned accolades. We've quite clearly done it all.

Eighteen different winners demonstrate the multi-faceted strength of the team. Still, the merit of those teammates who are not on the list is no less. Iljo Keisse donned his racing kit 74 times, Tim Declercq covered 11,118 kilometers and Michael Mørkøv reached the top 10 as a lead-out man 13 times. Patrick Lefevere: "I've never underestimated the importance of the riders lower in the hierarchy. They influence the top riders, keep them awake, and add a great dynamic to the group. Even when we're competing on several fronts, such as Almeida winning on 12 August in Poland and Evenepoel on the same day in Denmark. It just gives us all a big boost!"

Enjoy these images! We hope they provide a glimpse into the soul of the Wolfpack, into how it functions and comes together. More than 80 professionals go on the road together to race, fight, and win. More than 80 characters who live because of and for the race, together with each other. For an entire year. And again, next year. Like a perpetual motion machine.

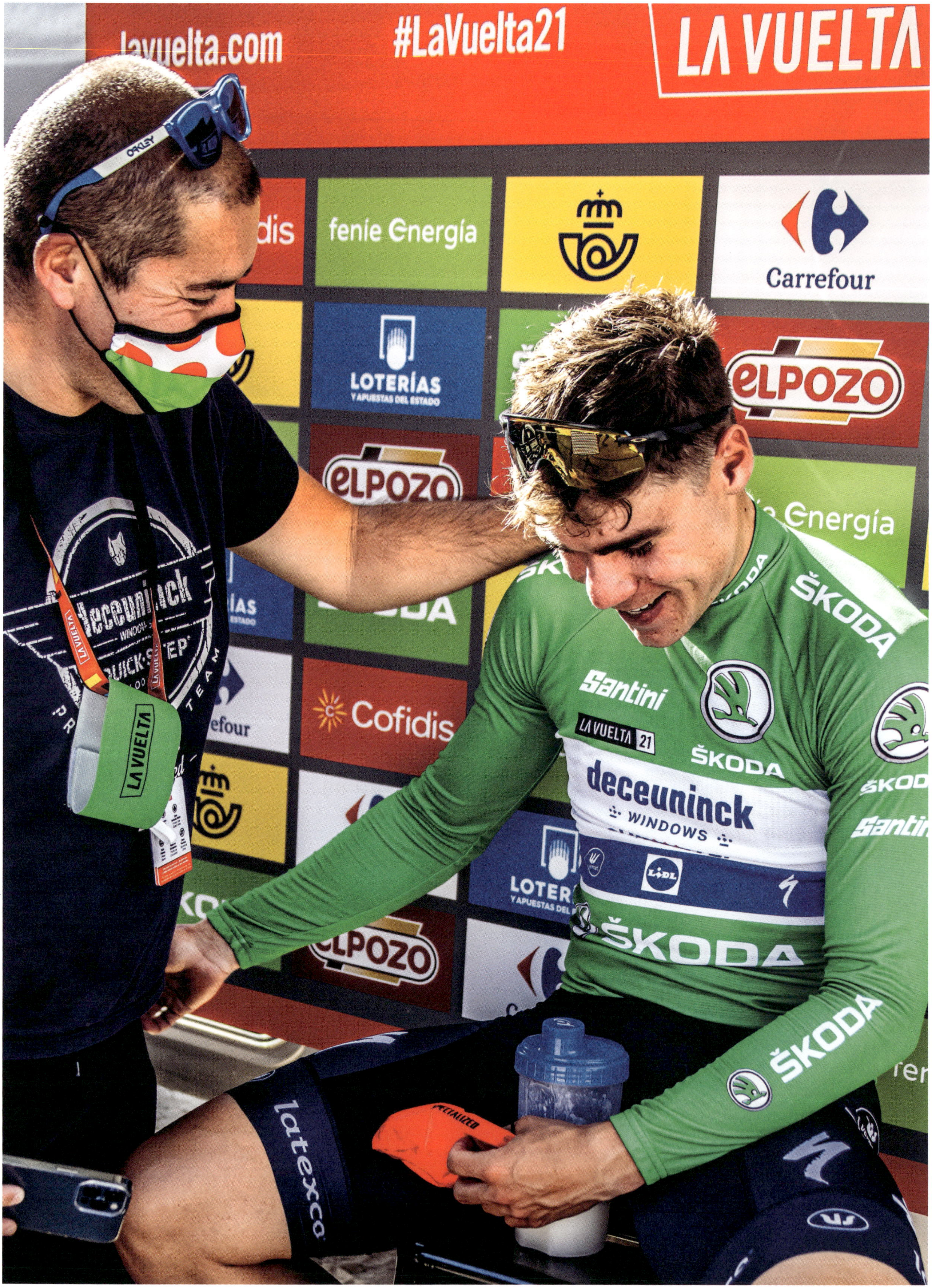

lavuelta.com
#LaVuelta21
LA VUELTA
fenie Energía
Carrefour
LOTERÍAS
Y APUESTAS DEL ESTADO
elpozo
Cofidis
Santini
LA VUELTA 21
ŠKODA
deceuninck
WINDOWS
LIDL
latexco

GRANDIOSE

L'année cycliste 2021 a été grandiose. Nous pourrions nous contenter de cette phrase et vous montrer – à vous, lecteurs, fans, supporters, coureurs, membres du staff et sponsors de l'équipe cycliste professionnelle Deceuninck – Quick-Step Team – les photos et rien d'autre. De superbes clichés de Wout Beel, le photographe attitré de l'équipe.

Mais la saison 2021 a été tellement exceptionnelle qu'on a voulu y ajouter un petit quelque chose. Un peu plus de poivre comme touche finale à une délicieuse soupe maison. Un repas des plus chaleureux accompagné d'un verre de champagne bien mérité. Pour le Wolfpack, c'était ça, l'année 2021.

DES CHIFFRES STUPÉFIANTS

Des chiffres. 284 jours de course, toujours sur deux et parfois trois fronts. De début février à mi-octobre. Et puis soudainement, au mois de janvier, les courses dans l'hémisphère sud ont été annulées à cause de la pandémie de Covid-19. D'un point de vue logistique, une équipe professionnelle performante tient du miracle. La réunion de personnes hétéroclites qui, ensemble, forment une machine solide et pourtant flexible. 30 professionnels sous contrat et un staff comprenant 54 personnes. Une longue chaîne de plus de 80 maillons, toujours prête pour la course, toujours prête à affronter ensemble les obstacles de dernière minute, avec la bonne attitude et le professionnalisme que cela implique. Chaque maillon est important. Ensemble sur la route, à sillonner le monde. Là pour se féliciter après les victoires et se serrer les coudes en cas de défaite.

Une meute de loups.

UN COUREUR EST UNE ÉQUIPE

Encore des chiffres : 65 victoires. Le Wolfpack a décroché 65 victoires, un chiffre miraculeux. Un chiffre qui fait à coup sûr rêver d'autres équipes. De la première étape du Tour de la Provence avec Davide Ballerini, le 11 février, au triomphe de Remco Evenepoel lors de la Coppa Bernocchi, le 4 octobre.

Remco Evenepoel. Ce nom apparaîtra souvent dans ce livre. Tout comme celui de Mark Cavendish, Kasper Asgreen, João Almeida, Rémi Cavagna, Yves Lampaert ou Julian Alaphilippe, bien sûr. Mais... un coureur est une équipe. Encore et toujours et tous les jours. Personne ne gagne seul. Chaque victoire est une victoire d'équipe.

Plus de chiffres. La Flandre a eu l'honneur d'organiser la 100e édition des Championnats du Monde sur route de l'UCI, pour la dixième fois en Belgique. C'est devenu un événement unique, une lueur d'espoir après dix-huit mois lugubres de pandémie. Les Championnats du Monde sur route à Louvain ont dépassé les attentes les plus folles. Avec Julian Alaphilippe sacré Champion du Monde de cyclisme. Un fait peut-être encore plus impressionnant pour le Wolfpack : sur les 194 professionnels de 45 pays qui se sont présentés au départ, pas moins de 16 coureurs appartenaient à l'écurie DQT. Ils représentaient 8 pays.

DERRIÈRE LES CHIFFRES

C'était une année spectaculaire. Les photos sélectionnées pour ce livre vous le prouveront. La liste des instants mémorables est longue. Un avant-goût : les victoires sur les classiques de Kasper Asgreen, le Tour de France époustouflant de Mark Cavendish, le deuxième maillot arc-en-ciel de Julian Alaphilippe, le retour de Remco Evenepoel, la résurrection de Fabio Jakobsen, les victoires de Sam Bennett, la confirmation de João Almeida, Rémi Cavagna, Florian Sénéchal, Mikkel Honoré et Davide Ballerini, Yves Lampaert Champion de Belgique du contre-la-montre. Jannik Steimle, Josef Cerny, Mattia Cattaneo, Andrea Bagioli et Mauri Vansevenant sont aussi rentrés avec la victoire en poche. Même si le symbole de ces victoires était parfois un trophée, parfois de la saucisse.

Dix-huit vainqueurs différents, ce qui montre la force de l'équipe dans son ensemble. Cependant, les coéquipiers dont le nom n'apparaît pas dans cette liste ont tout autant de mérite. Iljo Keisse a enfilé sa combinaison 74 fois, Tim Declercq a parcouru 11 118 kilomètres et Michael Mørkøv a atteint le top 10 treize fois en son rôle de poisson-pilote. Patrick Lefevere : « Je n'ai jamais sous-estimé l'importance des coureurs en bas de la hiérarchie. Ils poussent les meilleurs coureurs, les maintiennent en alerte et assurent la dynamique et l'ambiance du groupe, que ce soit sur un ou plusieurs fronts. Almeida vainqueur le 12 août en Pologne et Evenepoel le même jour au Danemark. Ça motive vraiment ! »

Profitez bien des photos ! Nous espérons qu'elles vous aideront à comprendre ce qui anime et unit le Wolfpack. Plus de quatre-vingts professionnels qui prennent la route ensemble pour courir, concourir et gagner. Plus de quatre-vingts protagonistes qui vivent de la course et pour la course, les uns avec les autres. Durant toute une année. Et qui recommenceront l'année prochaine. Animés d'un mouvement perpétuel.

Het Deceuninck – Quick-Step Team last elk jaar opnieuw diverse trainingsstages in. Dit was tijdens het voorjaar 2021 niet anders. Integendeel. De eerste rittenwedstrijden op het zuidelijk halfrond (Australië, Zuid-Amerika) en ook in Spanje en Italië werden afgelast, of uitgesteld vanwege de coronapandemie. Dus moest de conditie van de toppers op een alternatieve manier worden opgebouwd. Dan maar op stage naar het Zuiden.

Het Wolfpack-trainingskamp in de buurt van het stadje Altea, tussen Benidorm en Calpe, is een vast gegeven. Renners vinden aan de Costa Blanca alles wat ze nodig hebben voor de perfecte conditieopbouw: de juiste temperaturen in een mild voorjaarsklimaat, vlakke, brede wegen en nijdige beklimmingen. Altea ligt zo'n 60 kilometer ten zuiden van Valencia, en die wereldstad biedt dan weer prima pisteaccommodaties. In de Luis Puig-velodroom wordt op wetenschappelijke wijze geschaafd aan snelheid en tijdrittechniek.

Every year, the Deceuninck – Quick-Step Team organizes several training camps. Spring of 2021 was no exception. The first stage races in the southern hemisphere (Australia, South America) and in Spain and Italy were cancelled or postponed due to the coronavirus pandemic. The top riders had to optimize their fitness in a different way. As a result, we embarked on a training trip to the south.

The Wolfpack training camp near the town of Altea, located between Benidorm and Calpe in Spain, is a familiar event. The Costa Blanca offers cyclists everything they need to get into perfect shape. Ideal temperatures in a mild spring climate, flat, wide roads, and steep climbs. Altea is located about 60 km south of Valencia, which in turn offers excellent accommodations. In the Luis Puig velodrome, speed and time trial techniques are honed with the help of scientifically proven methods.

Chaque année, la Deceuninck – Quick-Step Team participe à plusieurs camps d'entraînement. Le printemps 2021 n'a pas fait exception. Les premières courses par étapes dans l'hémisphère sud (Australie, Amérique du Sud) ainsi qu'en Espagne et en Italie ont été annulées ou reportées à cause de la pandémie de Covid-19. Les cyclistes de haut niveau ont donc dû trouver d'autres moyen de rester au top et ont donc participé à un stage cycliste dans le Sud.

Le camp d'entraînement du Wolfpack près de la ville d'Altea, entre Benidorm et Calpe, est un classique. Sur la Costa Blanca, les coureurs disposent de tout ce dont ils ont besoin pour atteindre des performances de pointe : les températures idéales d'un printemps doux, des routes plates et larges et des montées raides. Altea se situe à environ 60 km au sud de Valence, une ville aux infrastructures sportives idéales. Dans le Palais vélodrome Luis Puig, les loups peuvent travailler leurs techniques de contre-la-montre et leur vitesse à l'aide de méthodes scientifiquement prouvées.

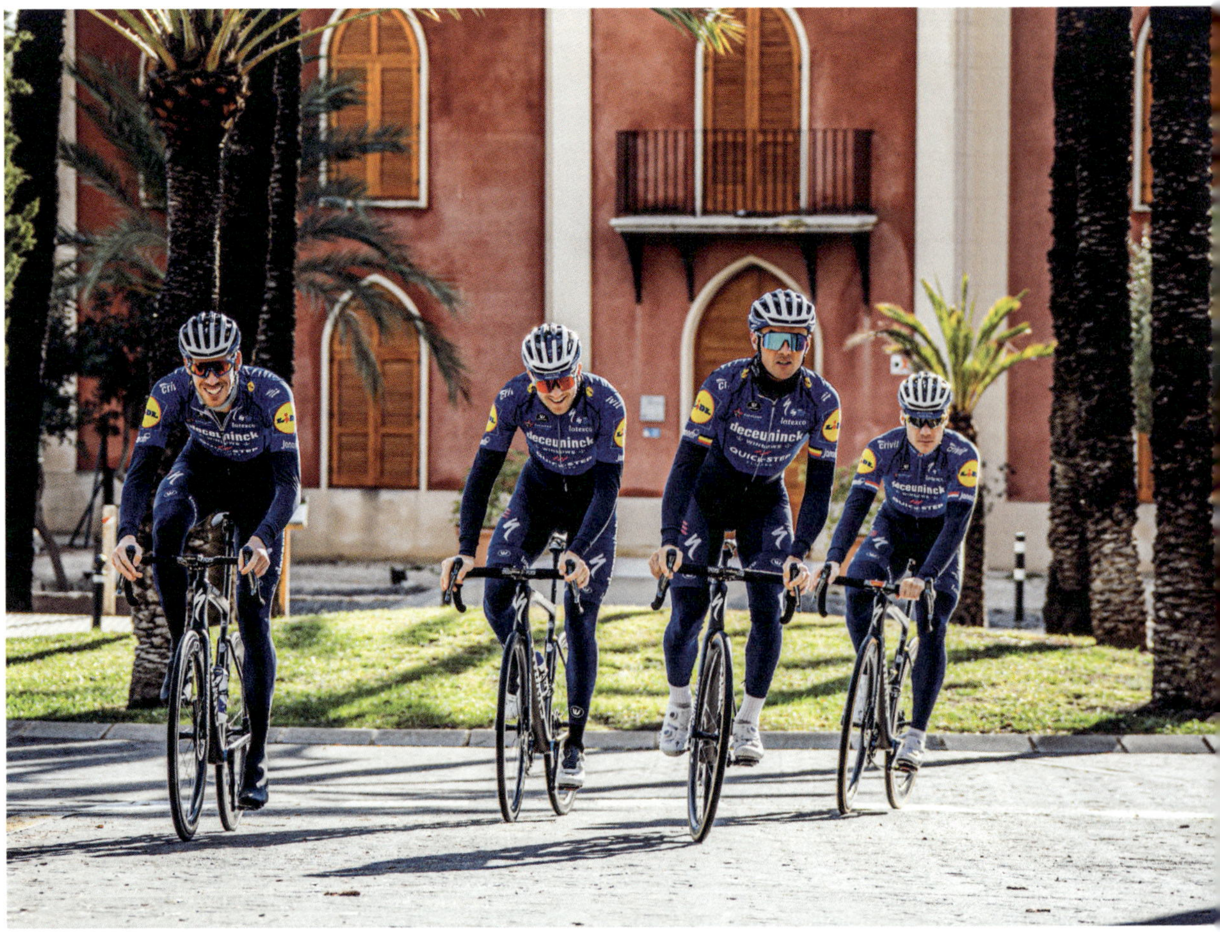

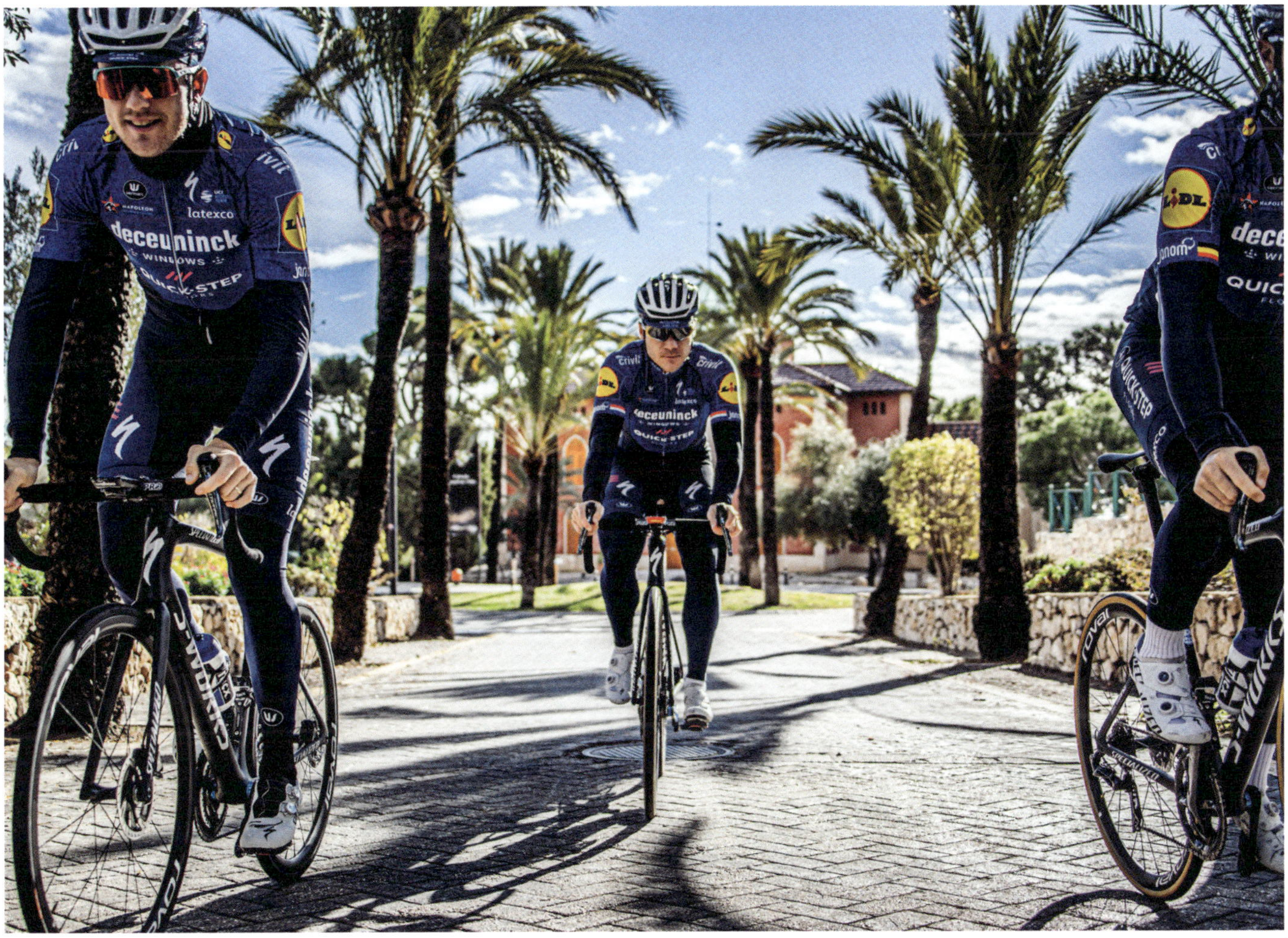
deceuninck
WINDOWS
QUICK-STEP
latexco
crivit

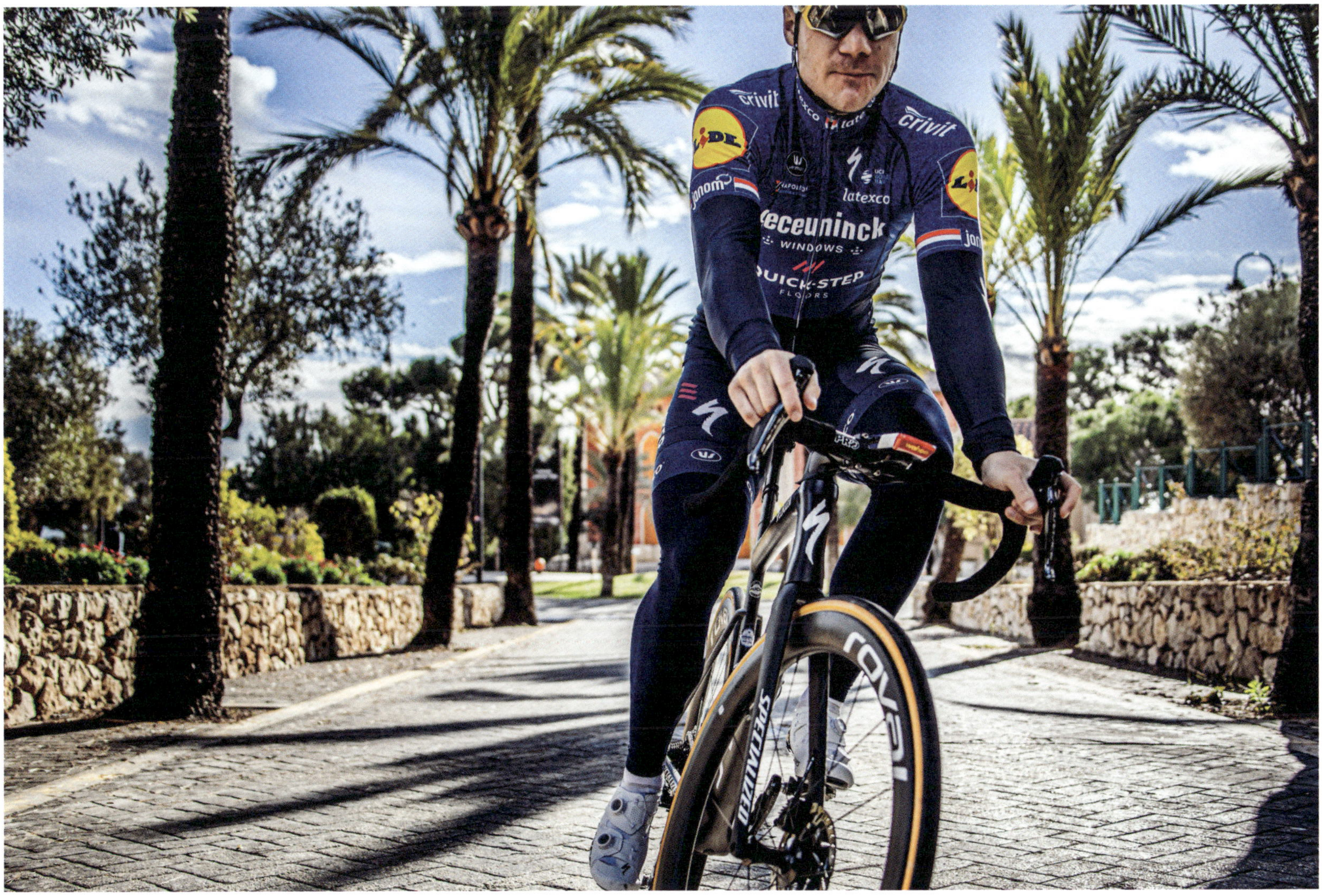
crivit
latexco
deceuninck
WINDOWS
QUICK-STEP
FLOORS
roval
SPECIALIZED

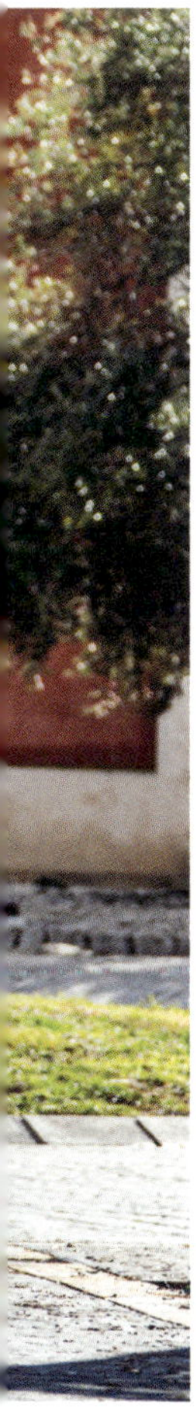

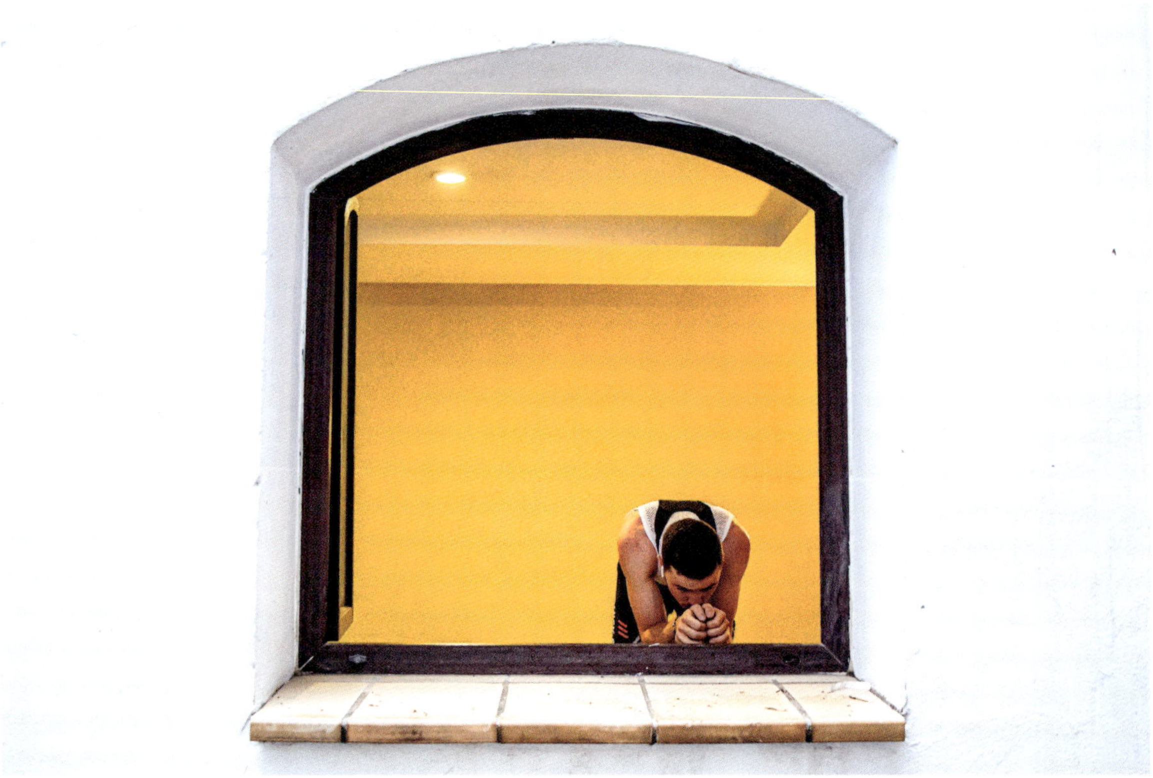

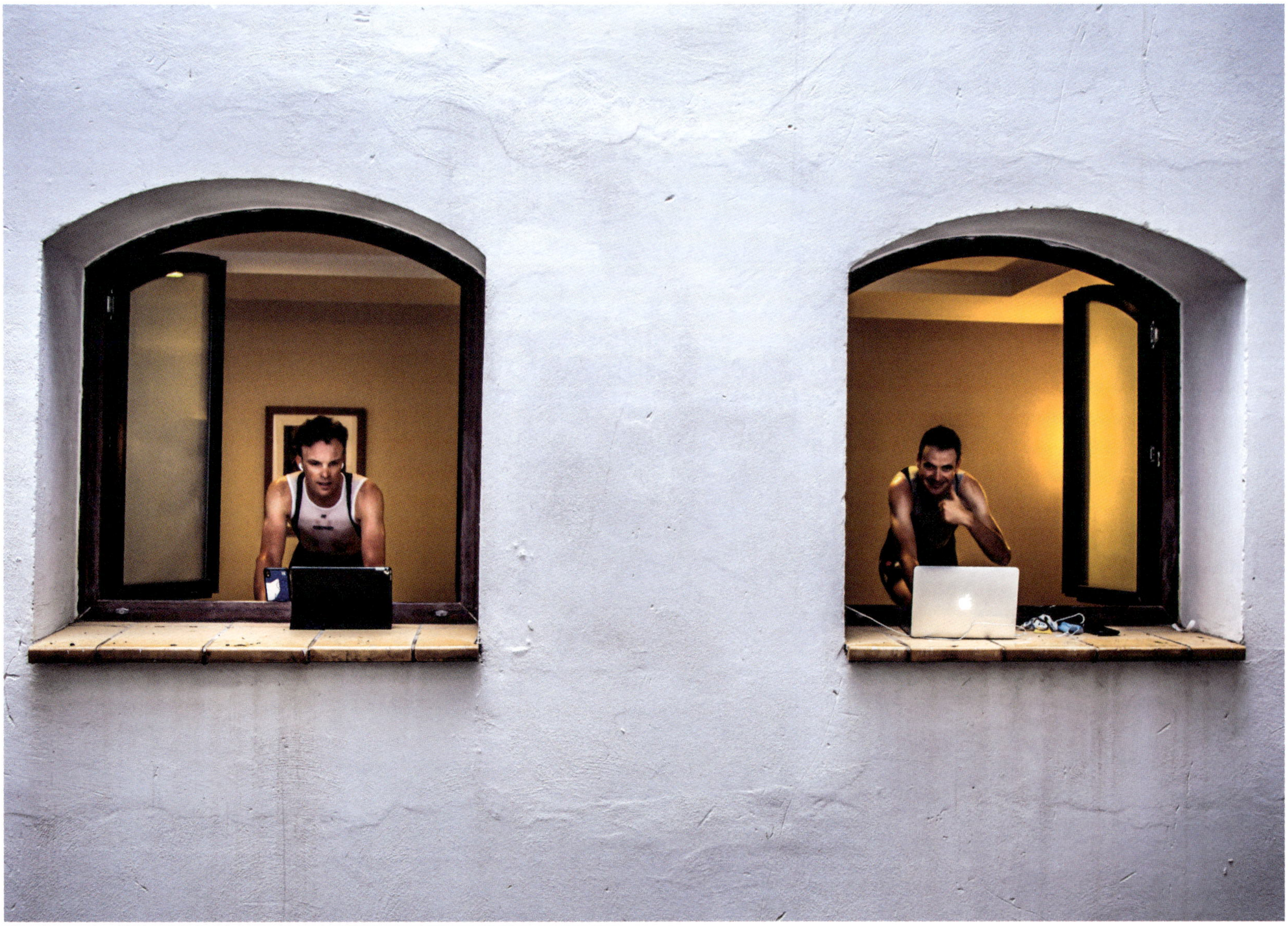

ALTEA, 07.01.2021

Uitkijken naar het seizoen. Met open venster. Rémi Cavagna, Mark Cavendish, Iljo Keisse en Pieter Serry.

Looking forward to the season. An open window. Rémi Cavagna, Mark Cavendish, Iljo Keisse and Pieter Serry.

En route pour la prochaine saison. La fenêtre ouverte. Rémi Cavagna, Mark Cavendish, Iljo Keisse et Pieter Serry.

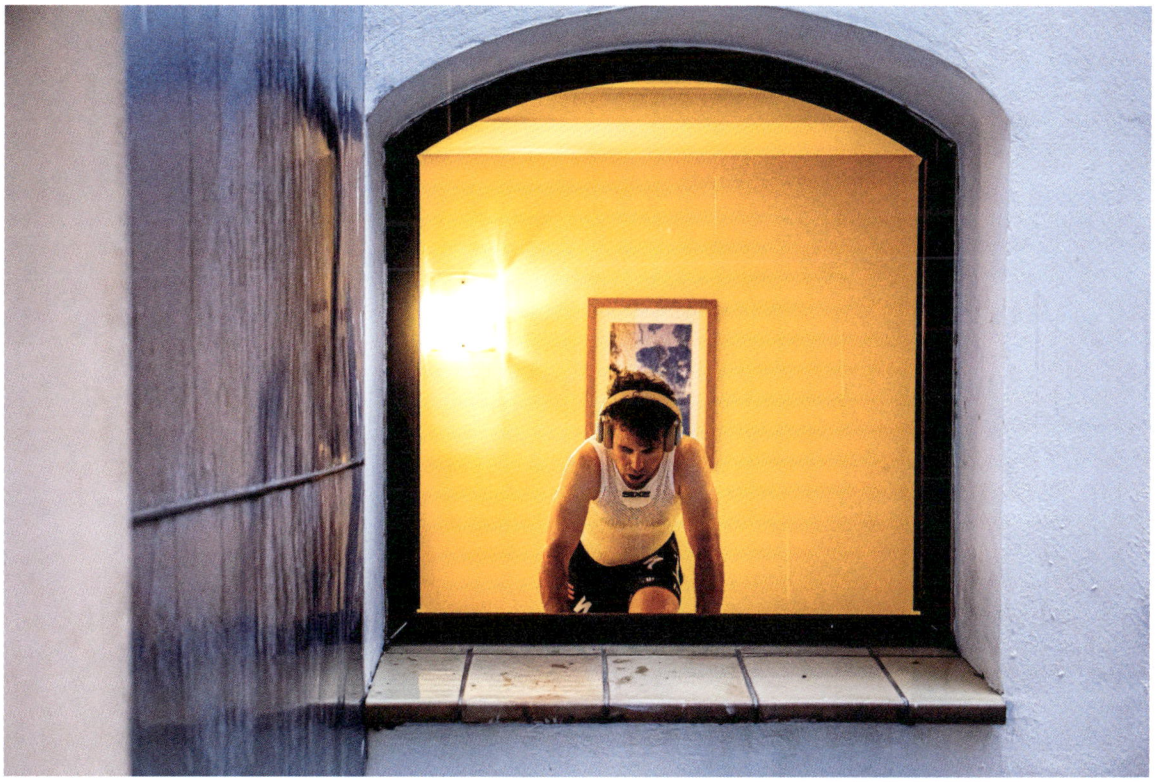

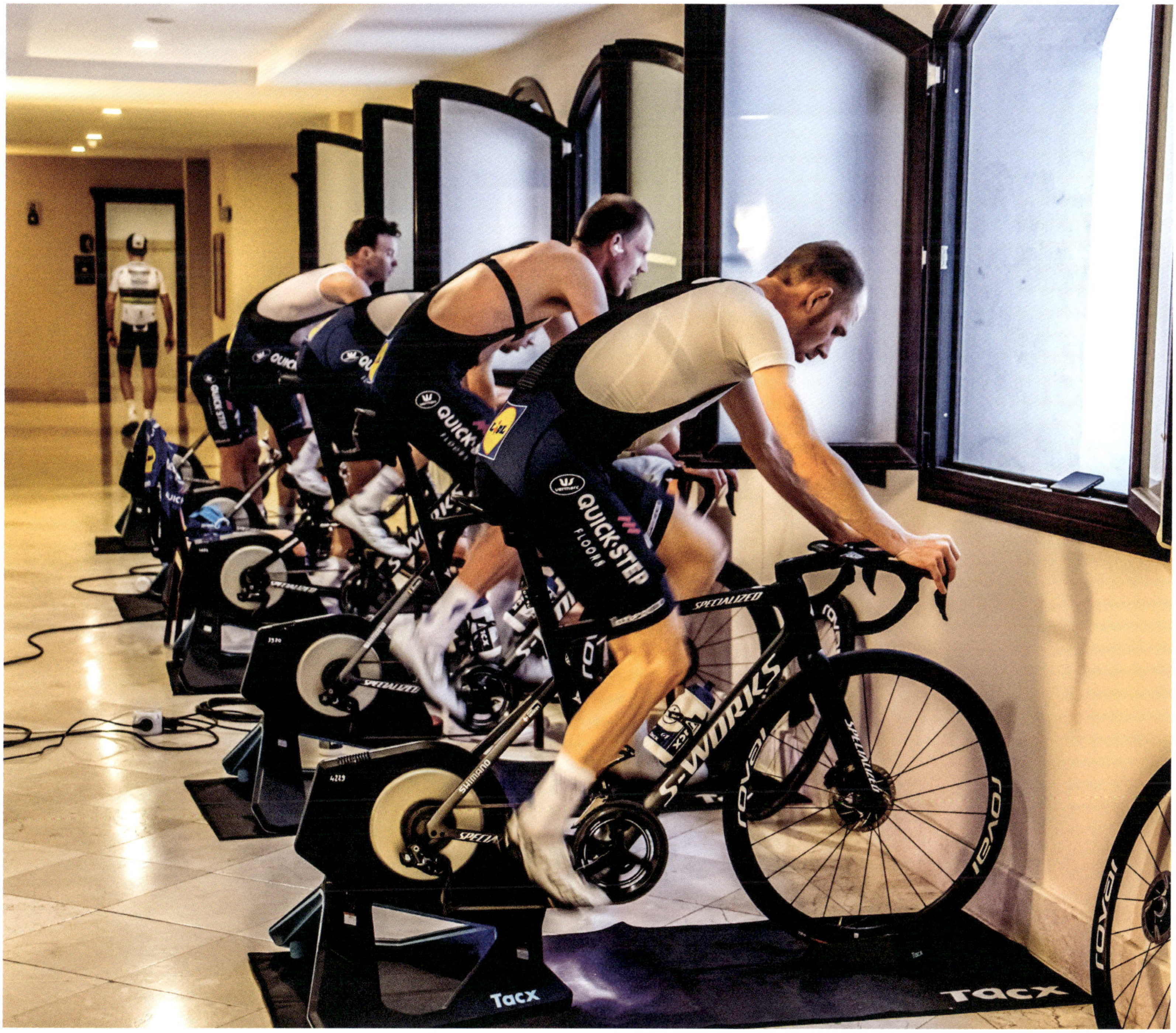
QUICK-STEP
FLOORS
SPECIALIZED
S-WORKS
roval
Tacx
Tacx

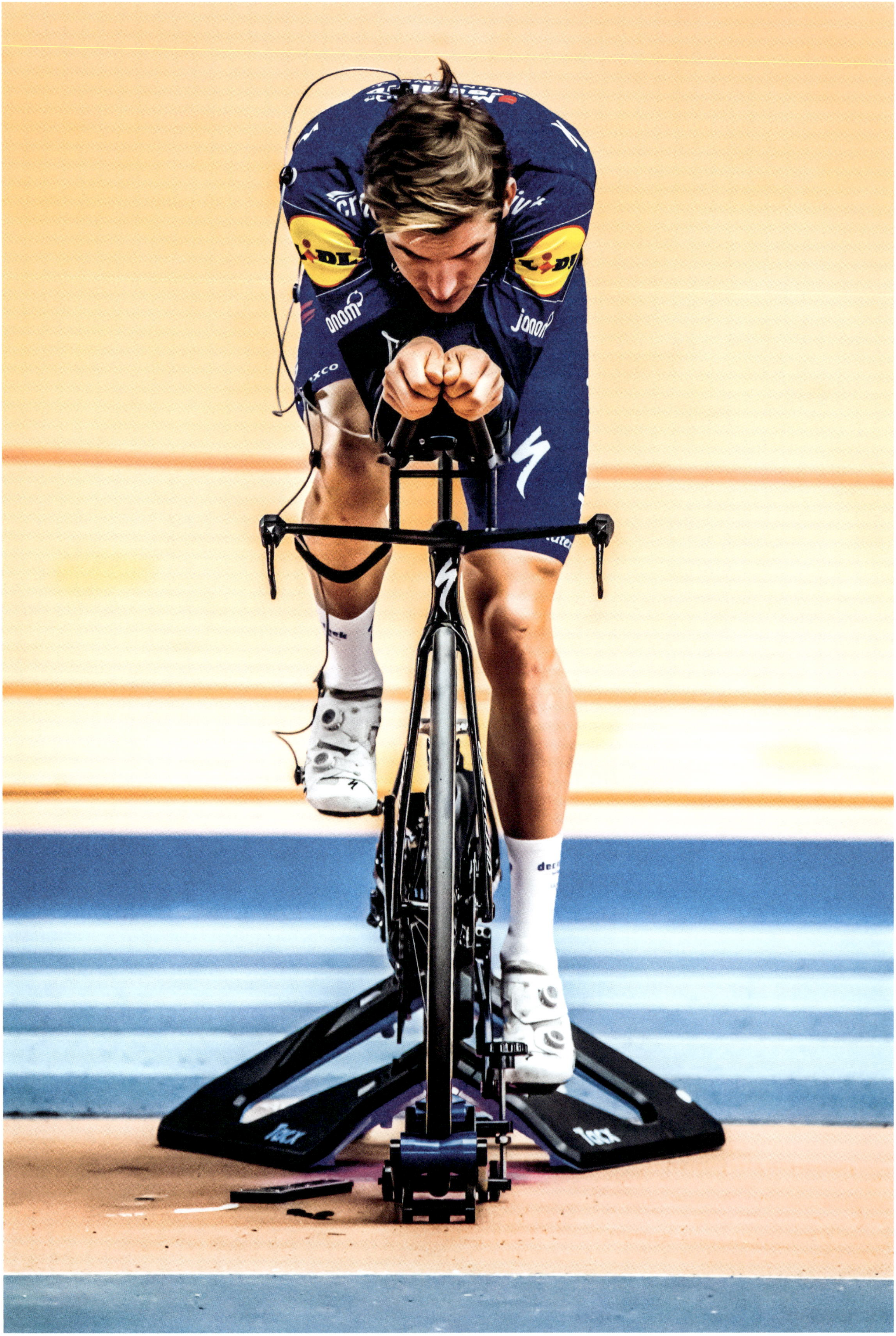

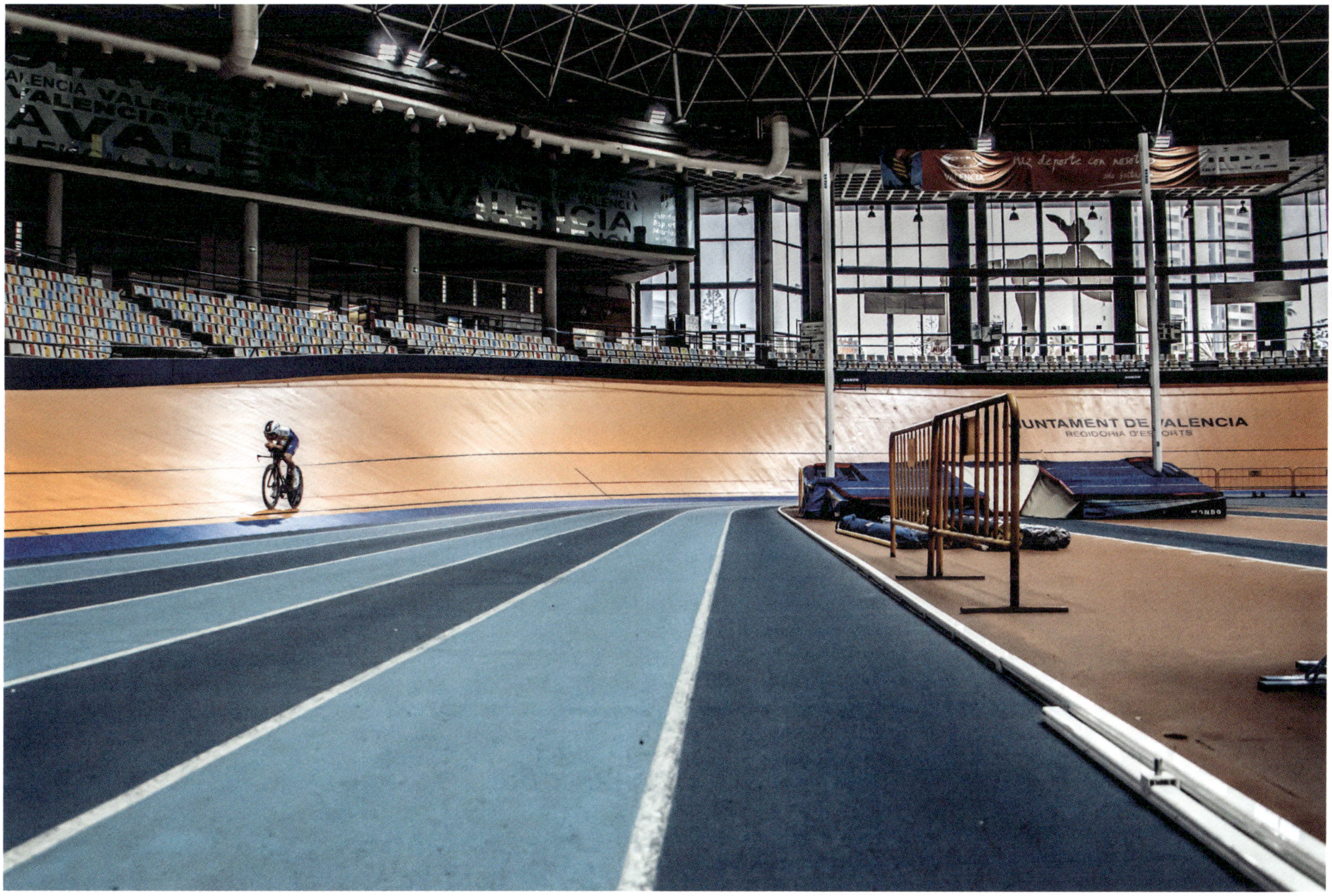

VALENCIA, 07.01.2021

Mikkel Honoré op de tijdritfiets.
James Knox als een lone rider.

Mikkel Honoré on the time trial bike.
James Knox as a "lone rider".

Mikkel Honoré sur son vélo de contre-la-montre. ◀
James Knox en coureur solitaire. ▲

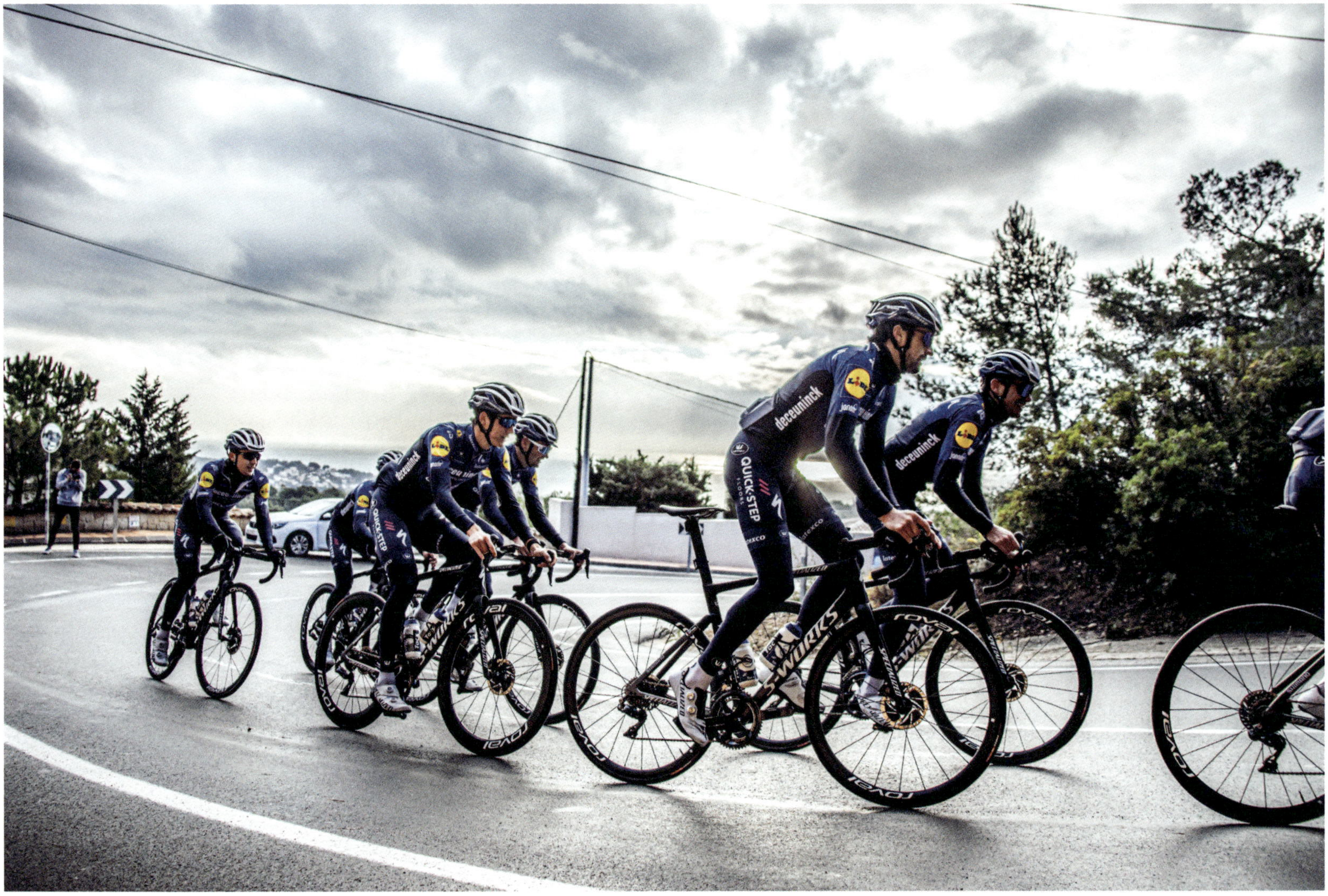
deceuninck
QUICK-STEP
S-WORKS
deceuninck

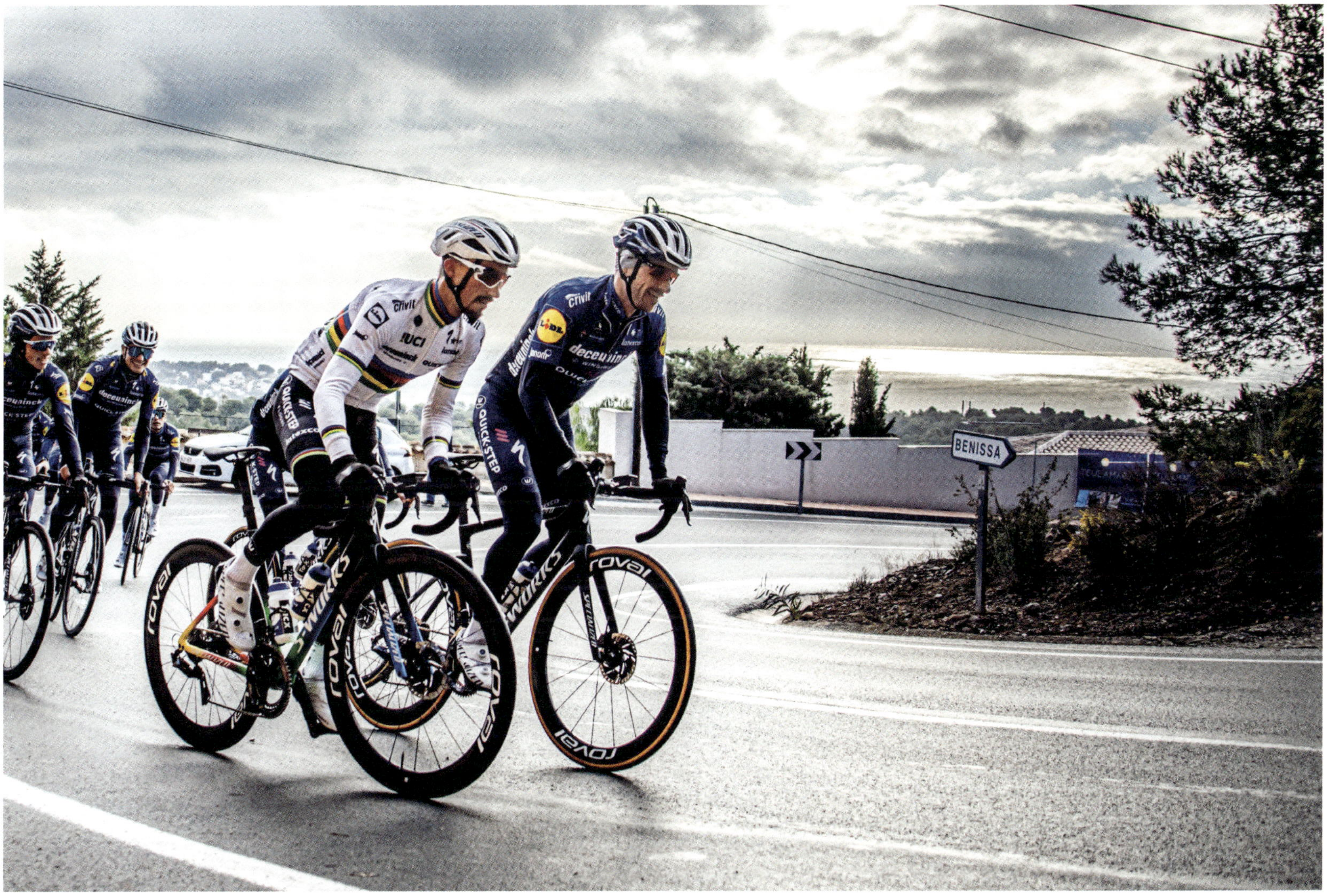

ALTEA, 11.01.2021

Tijd voor de buitenlucht. Wereldkampioen Julian Alaphilippe en kompaan Dries Devenyns nemen enkele lengten voorsprong, ten dienste van de fotograaf.

Time for some fresh air. World Champion Julian Alaphilippe and his companion Dries Devenyns get a few lengths ahead, ideal for the photographer.

Il est temps de prendre l'air. Le Champion du Monde Julian Alaphilippe et son coéquipier Dries Devenyns ont une petite longueur d'avance, pour le plaisir du photographe.

ALTEA, 11.01.2021

Michael Mørkøv
& Sam Bennett

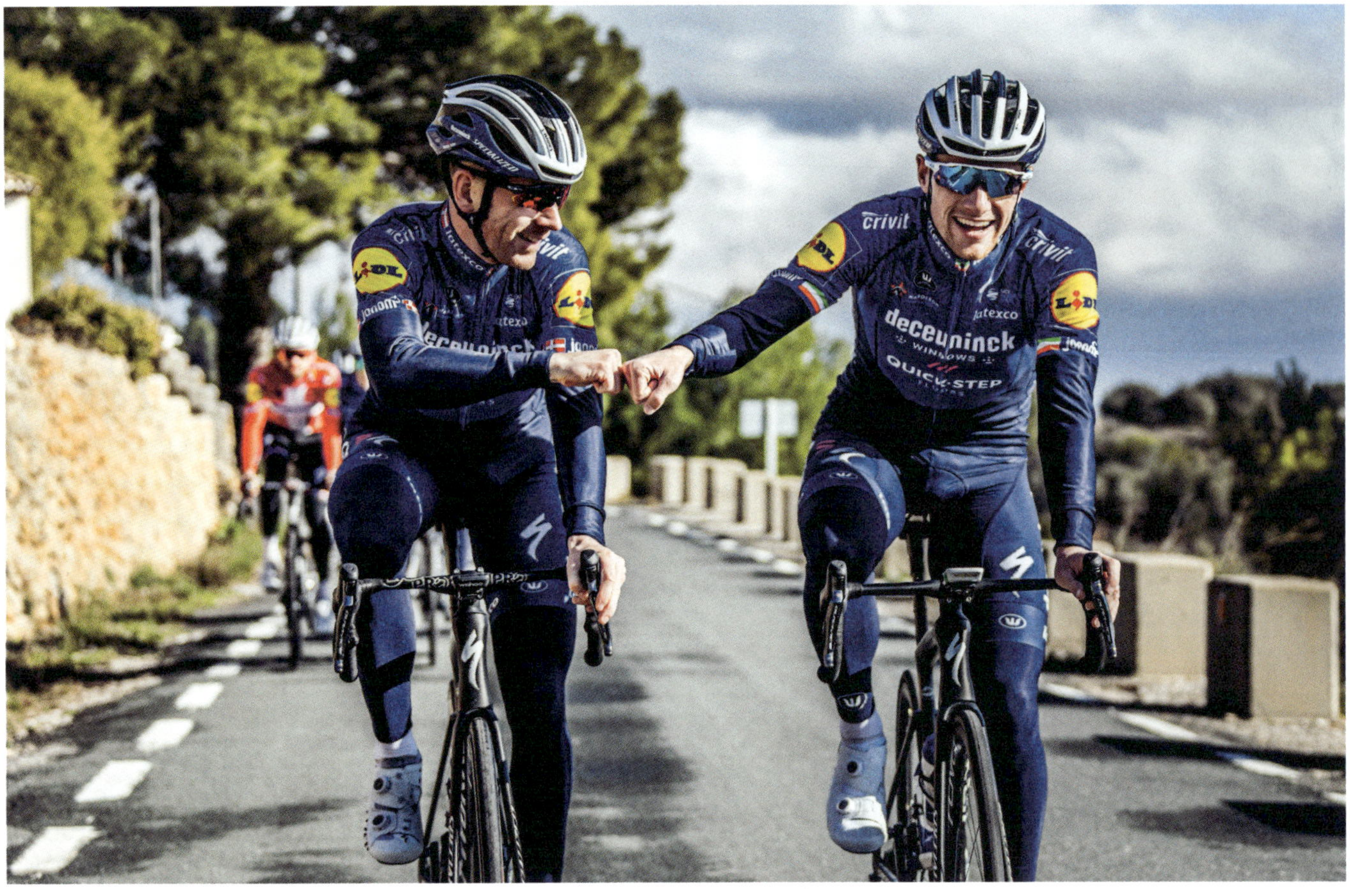

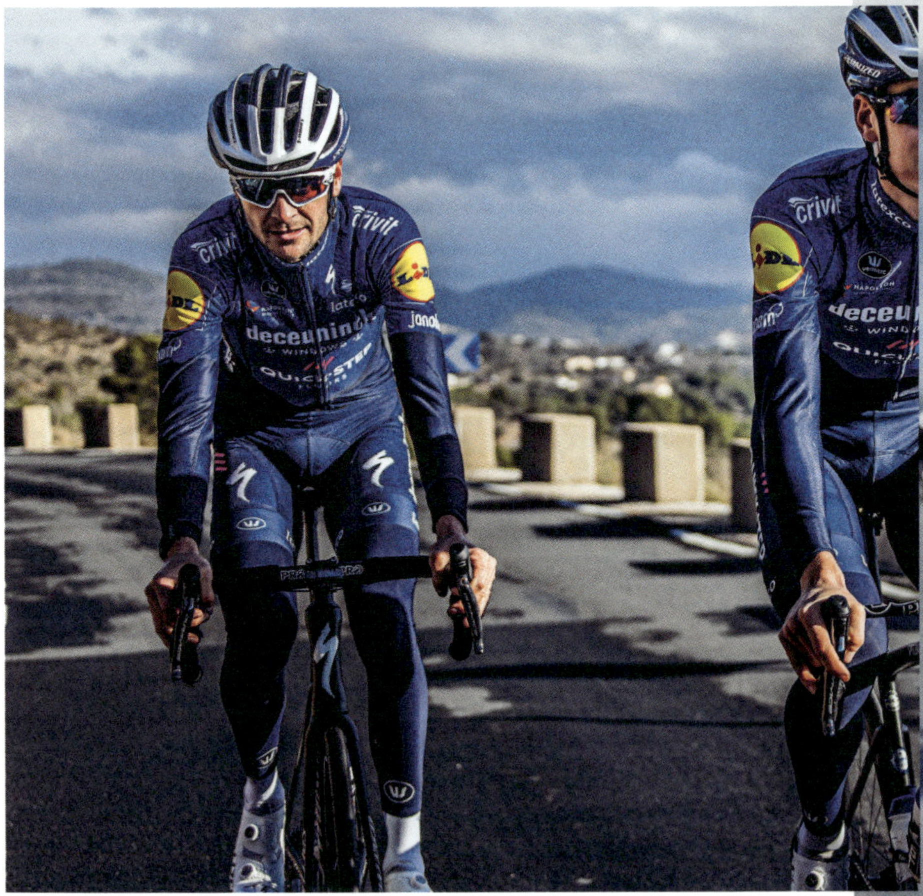

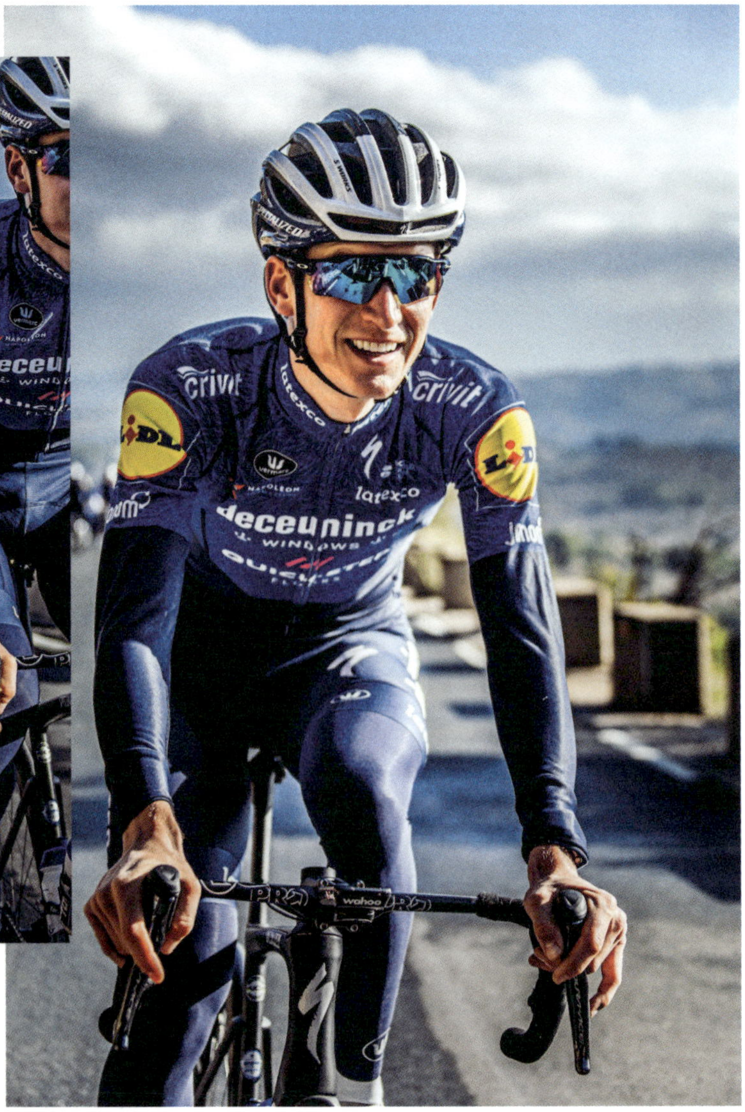

Pieter Serry &
Mikkel Honoré

Mauri Vansevenant
& Andrea Bagioli

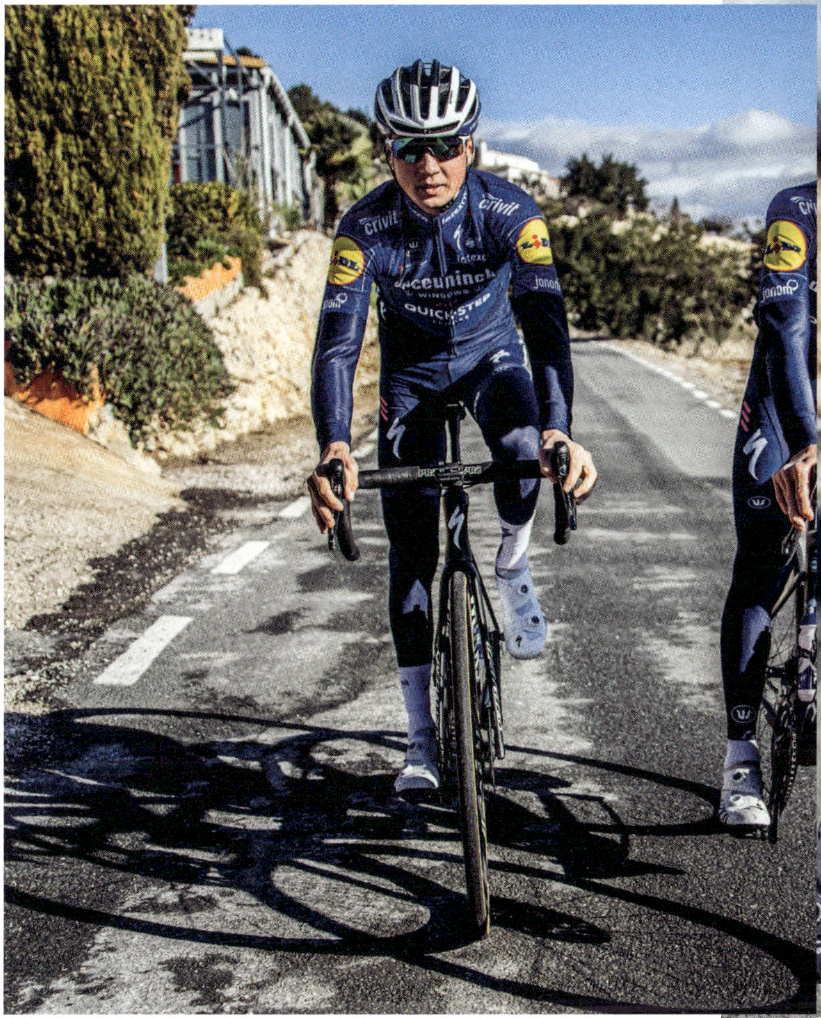

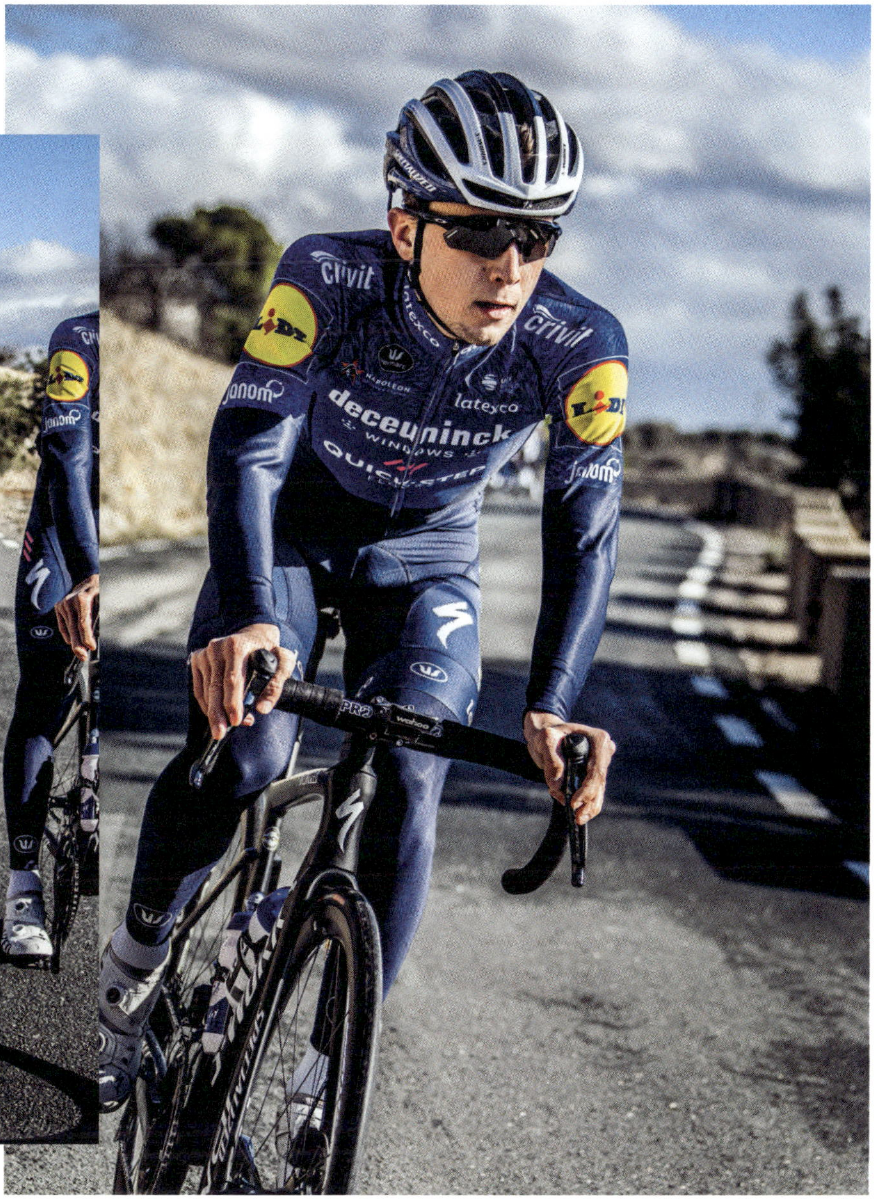

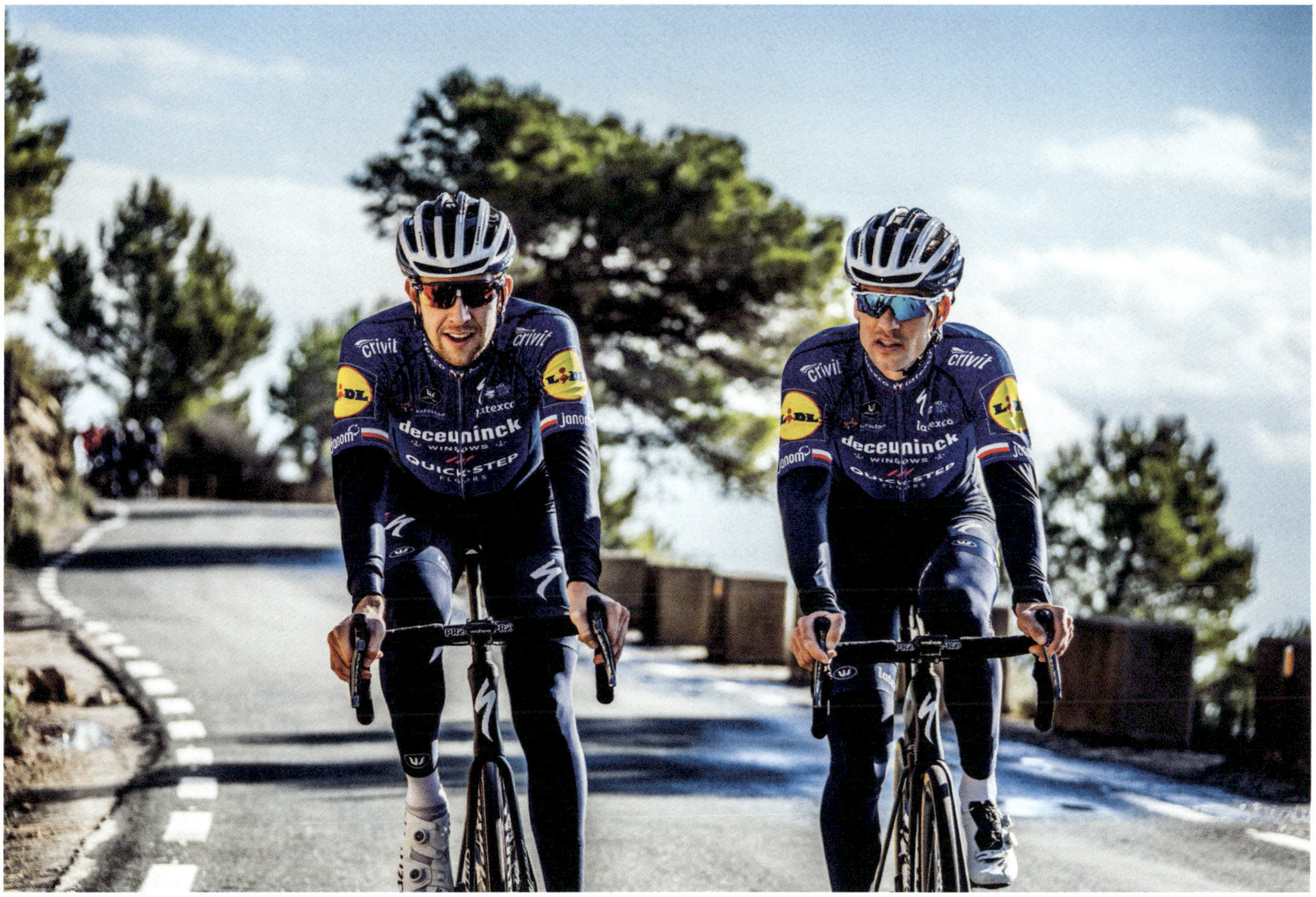

Josef Cerny &
Zdenek Stybar

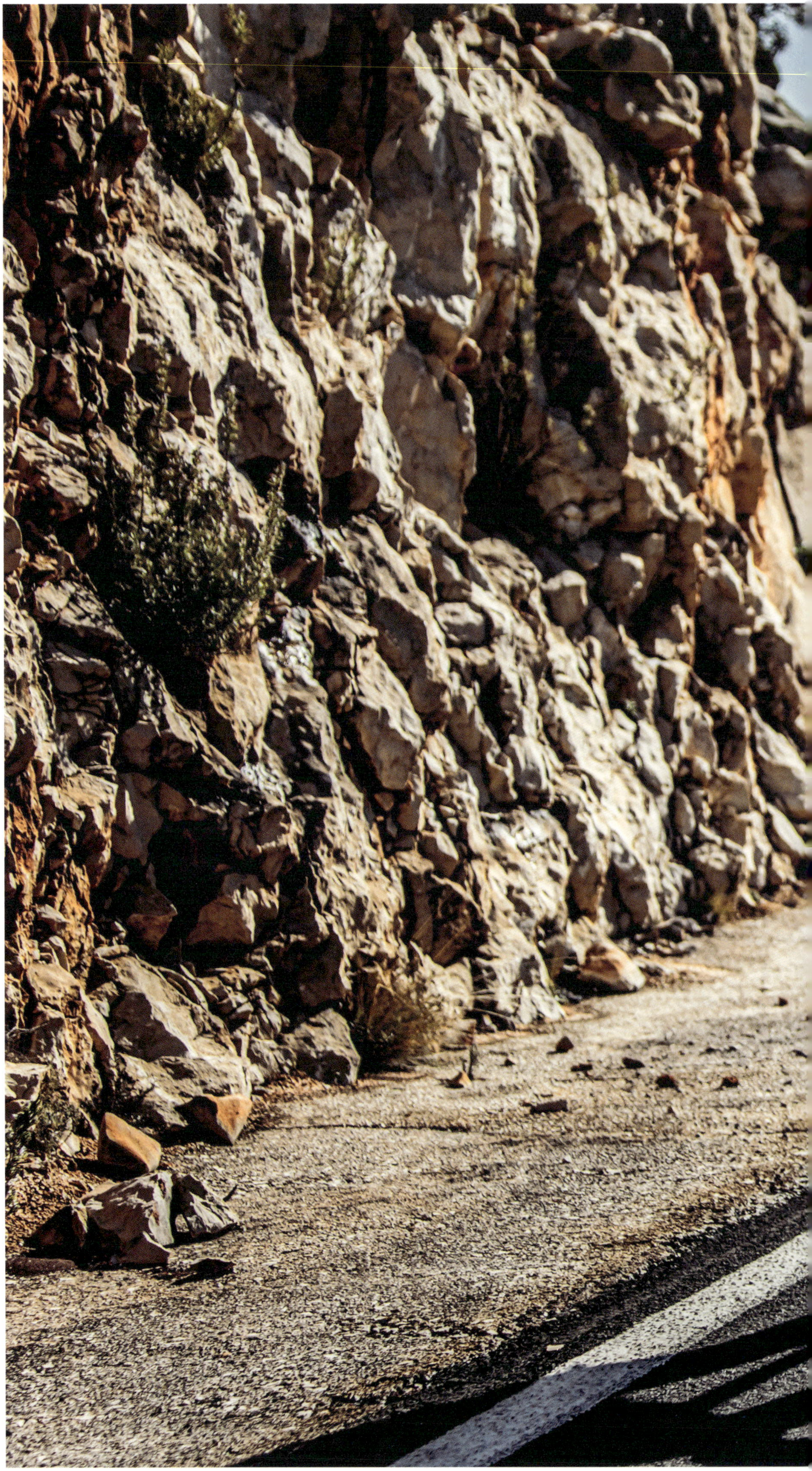

ALTEA, 11.01.2021

Rémi Cavagna en Jannik Steimle trekken gekke bekken. Op de achtergrond El Peñon de Ifach, of de rots van Calpe.

Rémi Cavagna and Jannik Steimle making funny faces. Shown in the background: El Peñon de Ifach, or the Calpe Rock.

Rémi Cavagna et Jannik Steimle font des grimaces. En arrière-plan, on reconnaît le Peñón de Ifach de Calp.

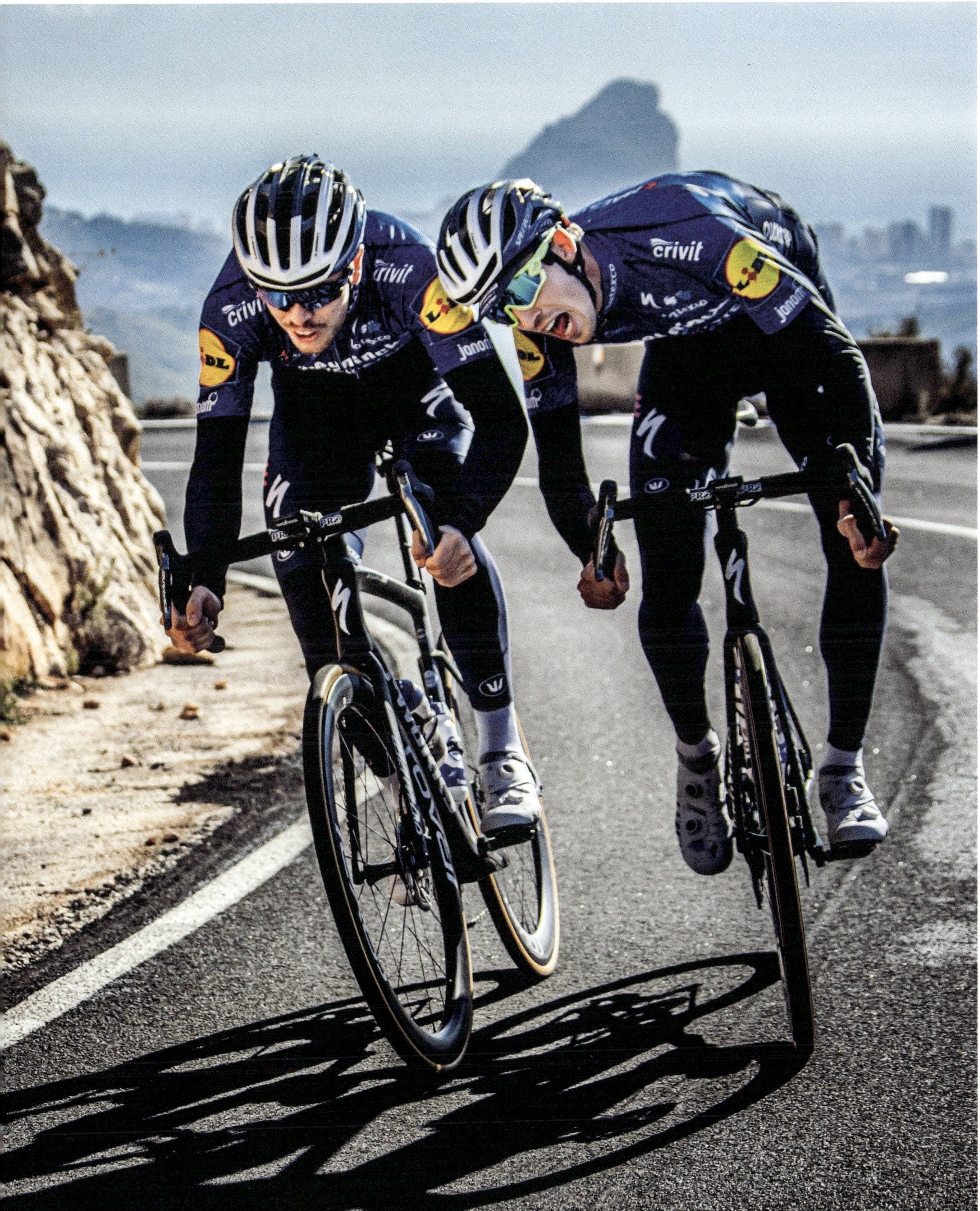
crivit
crivit
crivit

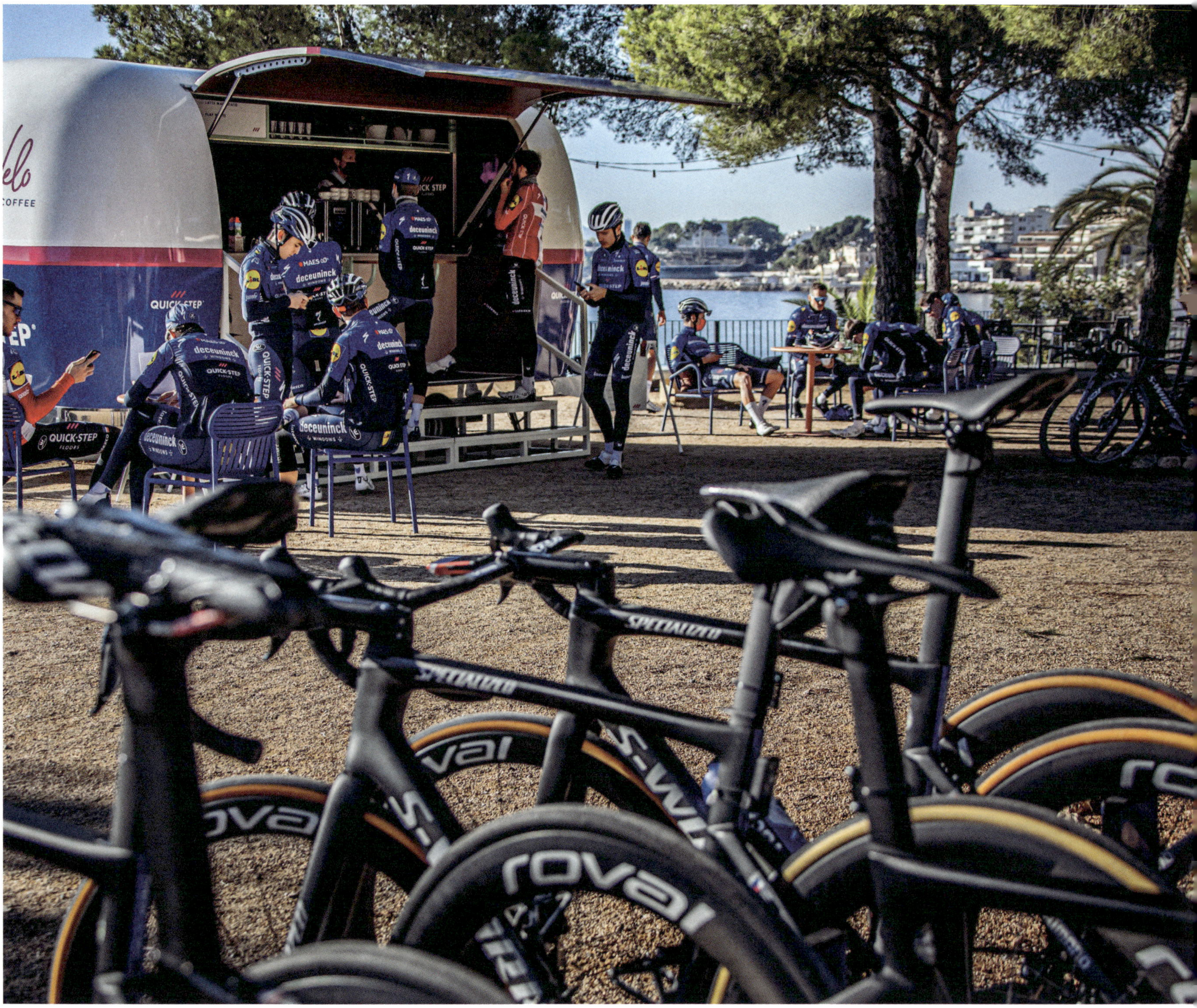

ALTEA, 13.01.2021

En dan is er koffie. Coureurs en koffie, het is een bijzonder huwelijk. Met hoog bezoek vandaag: de Bar Vélo van sponsor Quick-Step. Het plaatje lijkt zo weggeplukt uit een reclamespot voor het zwarte goud.

Jawel, koffie. Ook Tom Steels weet hoe lekker het is.

And then there was coffee. Riders always seem to have a special bond with it. Today's treat: the Bar Vélo from sponsor Quick-Step. This image looks to have been taken from an expensive advertisement.

Once again, coffee. Tom Steels enjoys it too.

Jamais sans café. Les coureurs ont une relation spéciale avec le café. Le Bar Vélo du sponsor Quick-Step, particulièrement populaire aujourd'hui. Cette image semble tout droit sortie d'une publicité pour une grande marque de café. ▲

Du café. Aussi Tom Steels peut l'apprécier. ▶

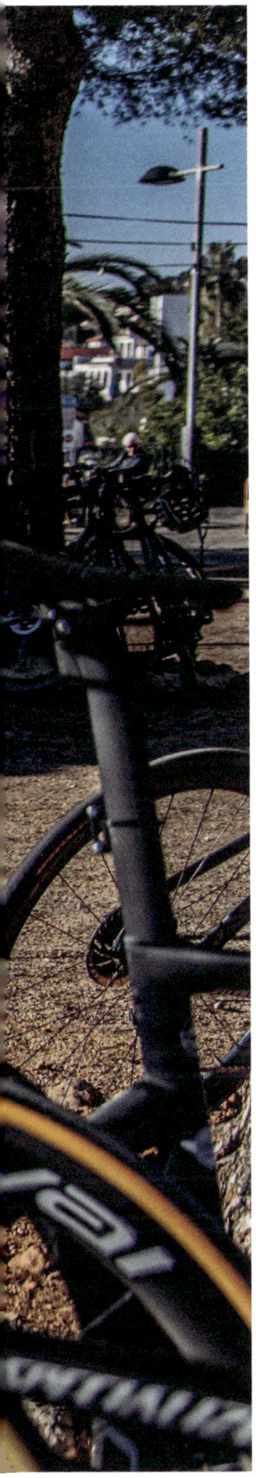

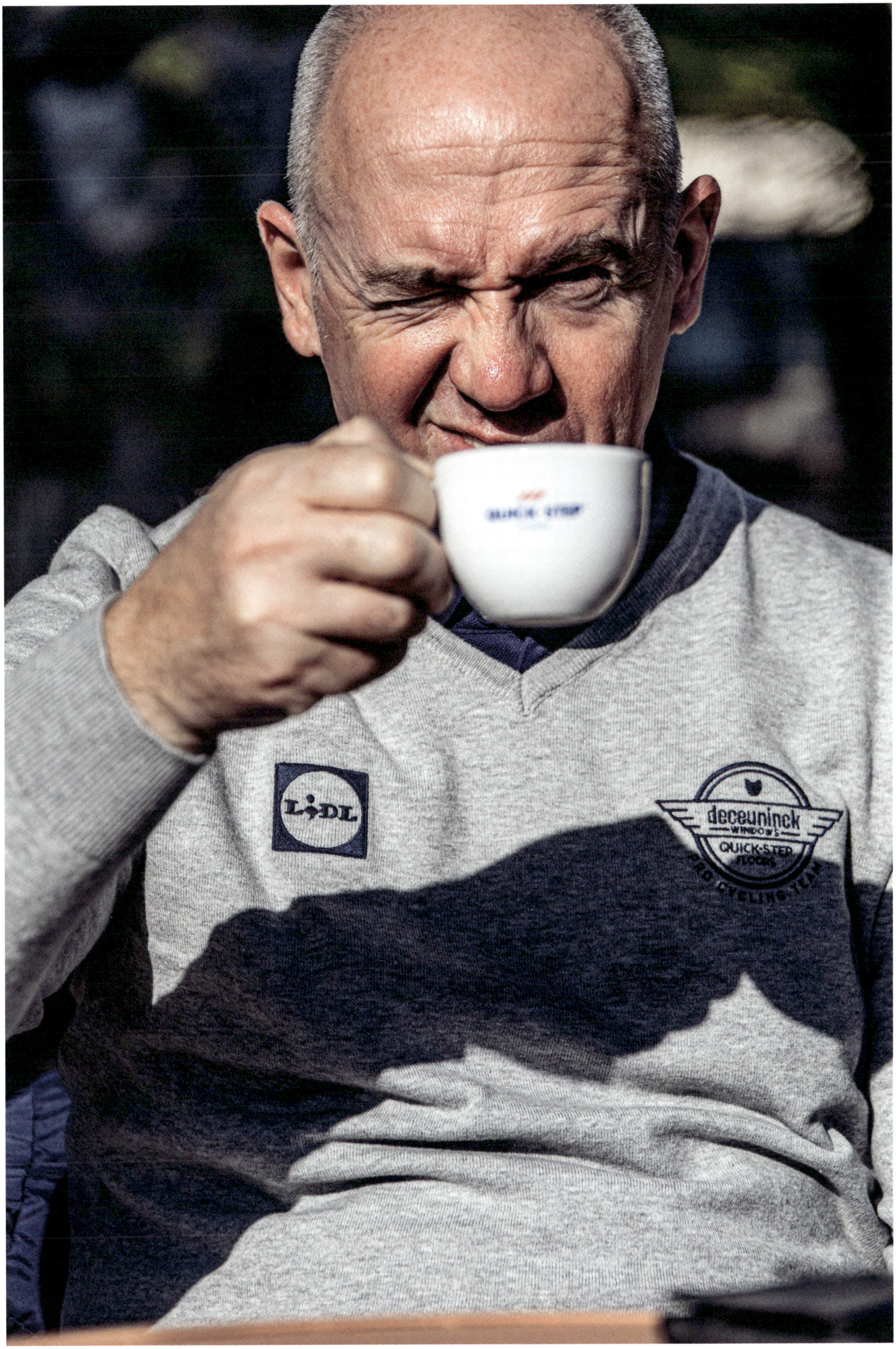
LIDL
deceuninck
WINDOWS
QUICK-STEP
FLOORS
PRO CYCLING TEAM

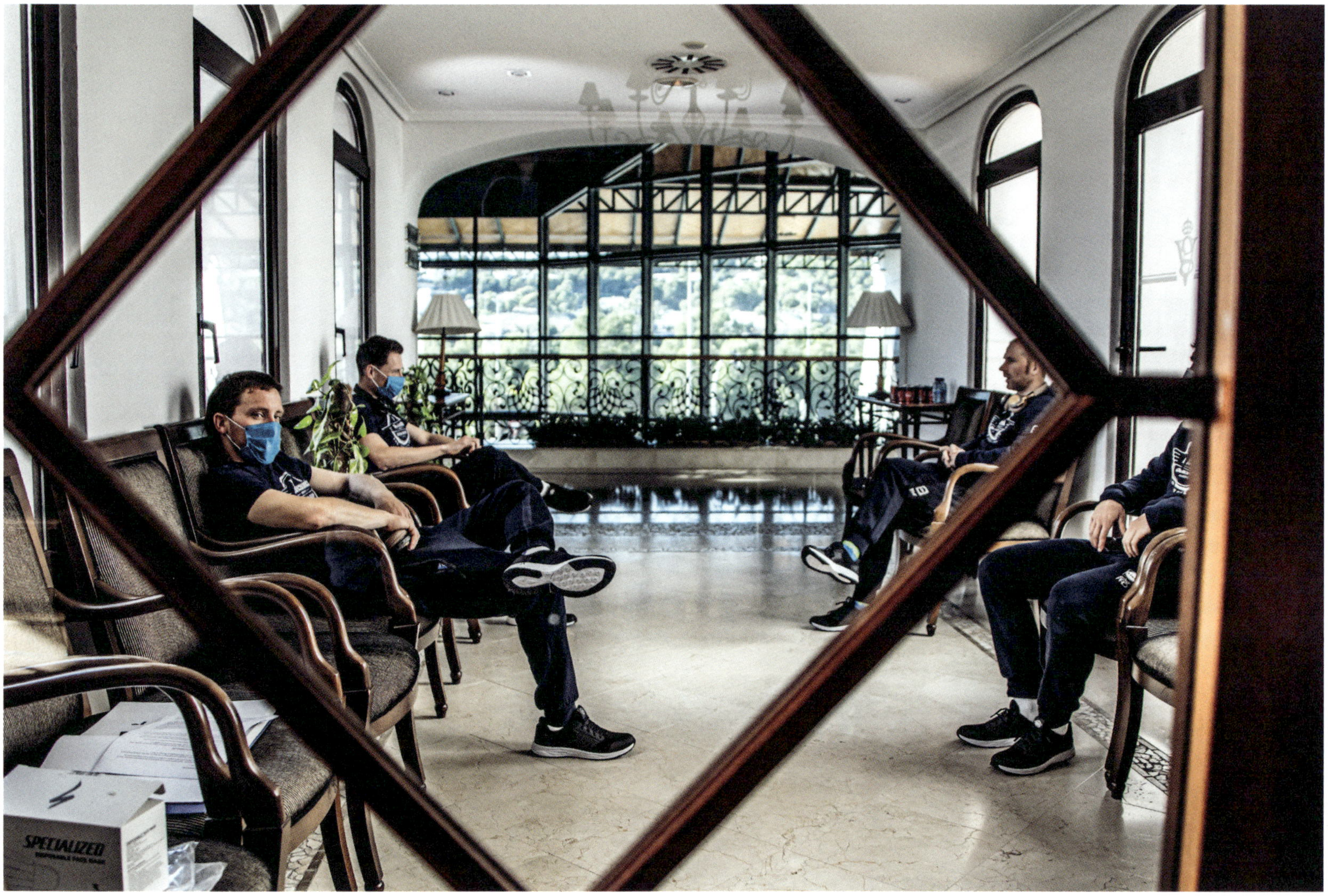

ALTEA, 13.01.2021

V.l.n.r.: Shane Archbold, Sam Bennett, Michael Mørkøv en Fabio Jakobsen wachten hun beurt af voor de digitale persbabbel tijdens het trainingskamp.

FLTR: Shane Archbold, Sam Bennett, Michael Mørkøv and Fabio Jakobsen wait their turn for the digital press chat during training camp.

Dgàd : Shane Archbold, Sam Bennett, Michael Mørkøv et Fabio Jakobsen attendent leur tour pour la conférence de presse numérique pendant le camp d'entraînement. ▲

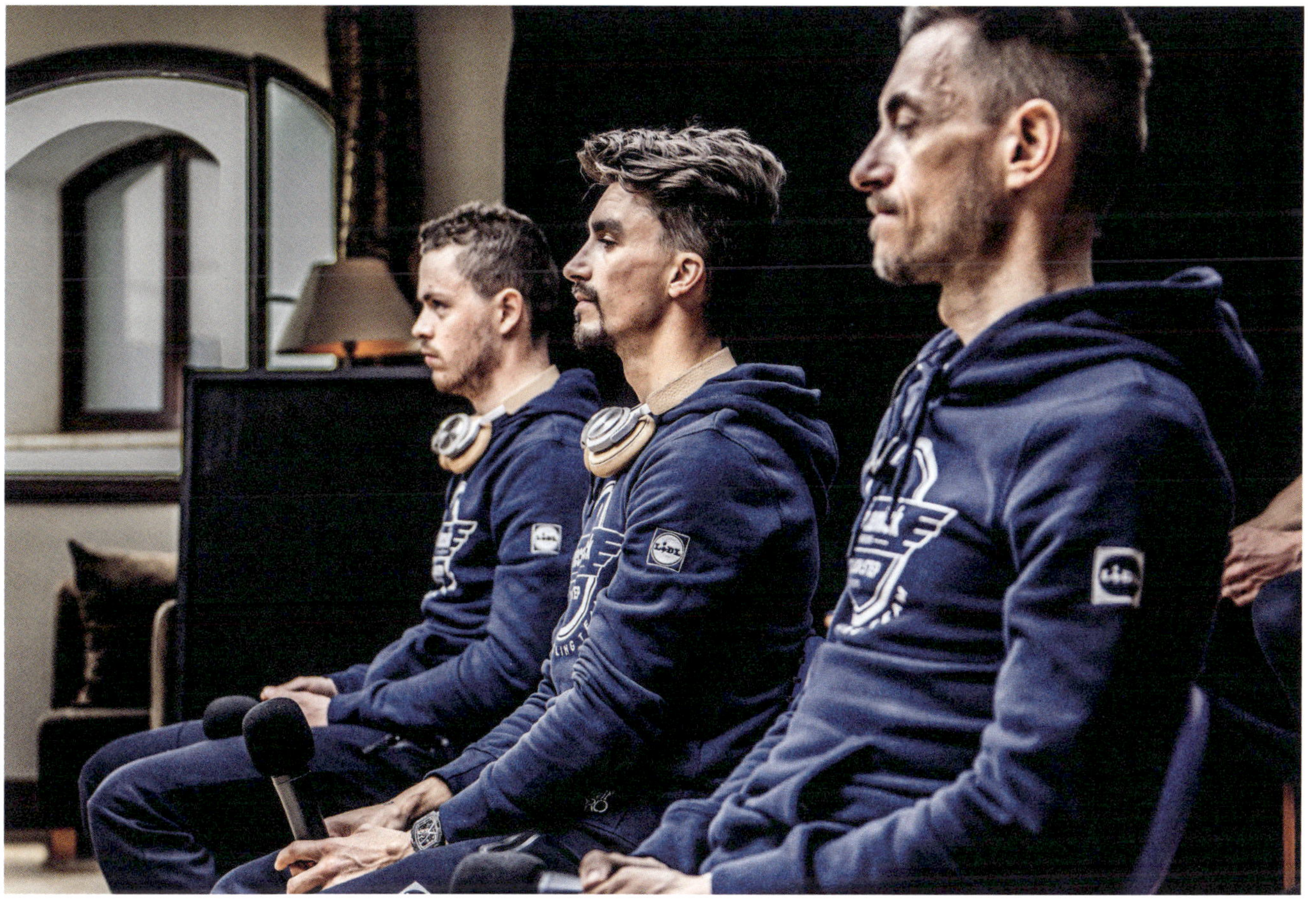

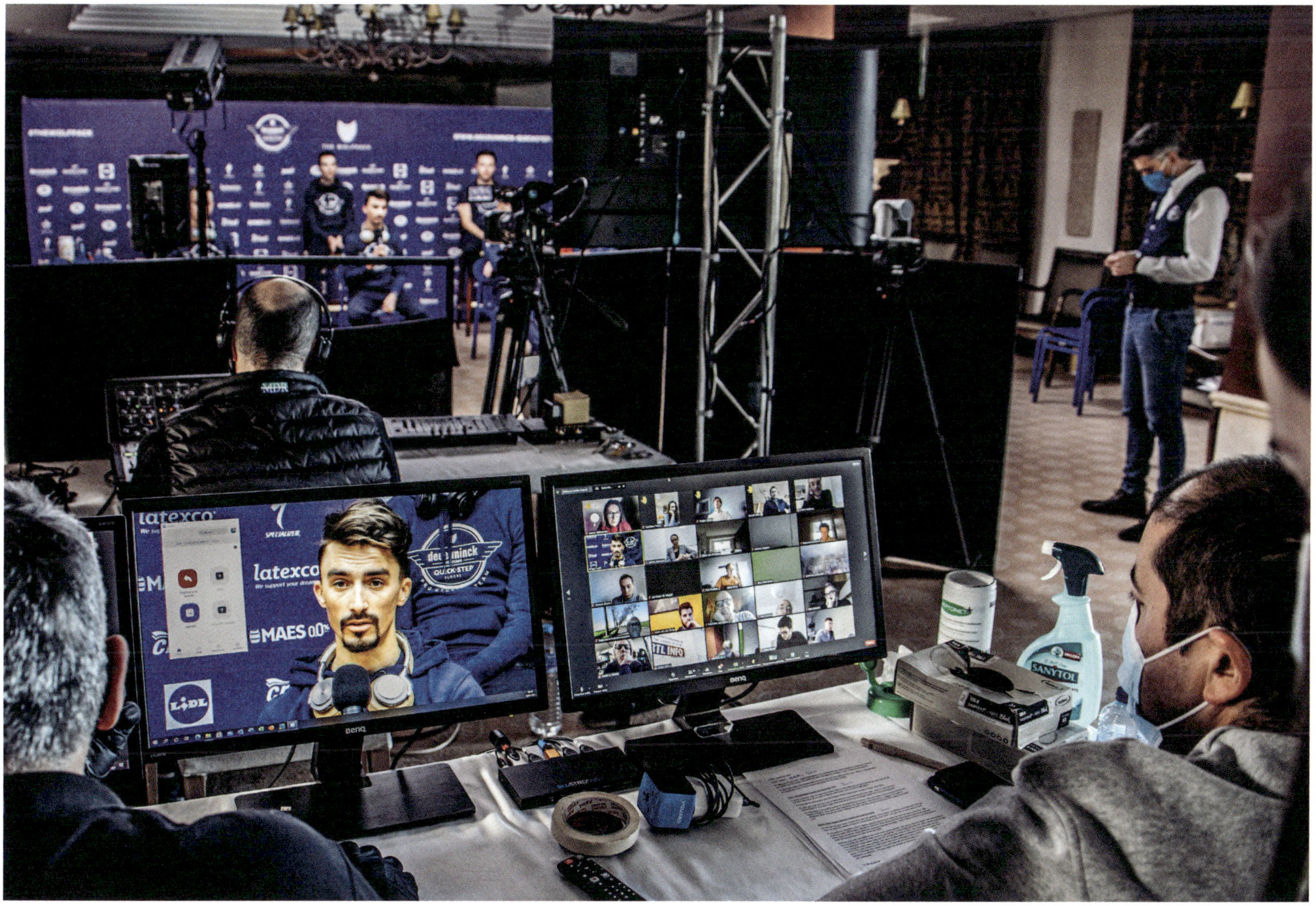
latexco
SANYTOL

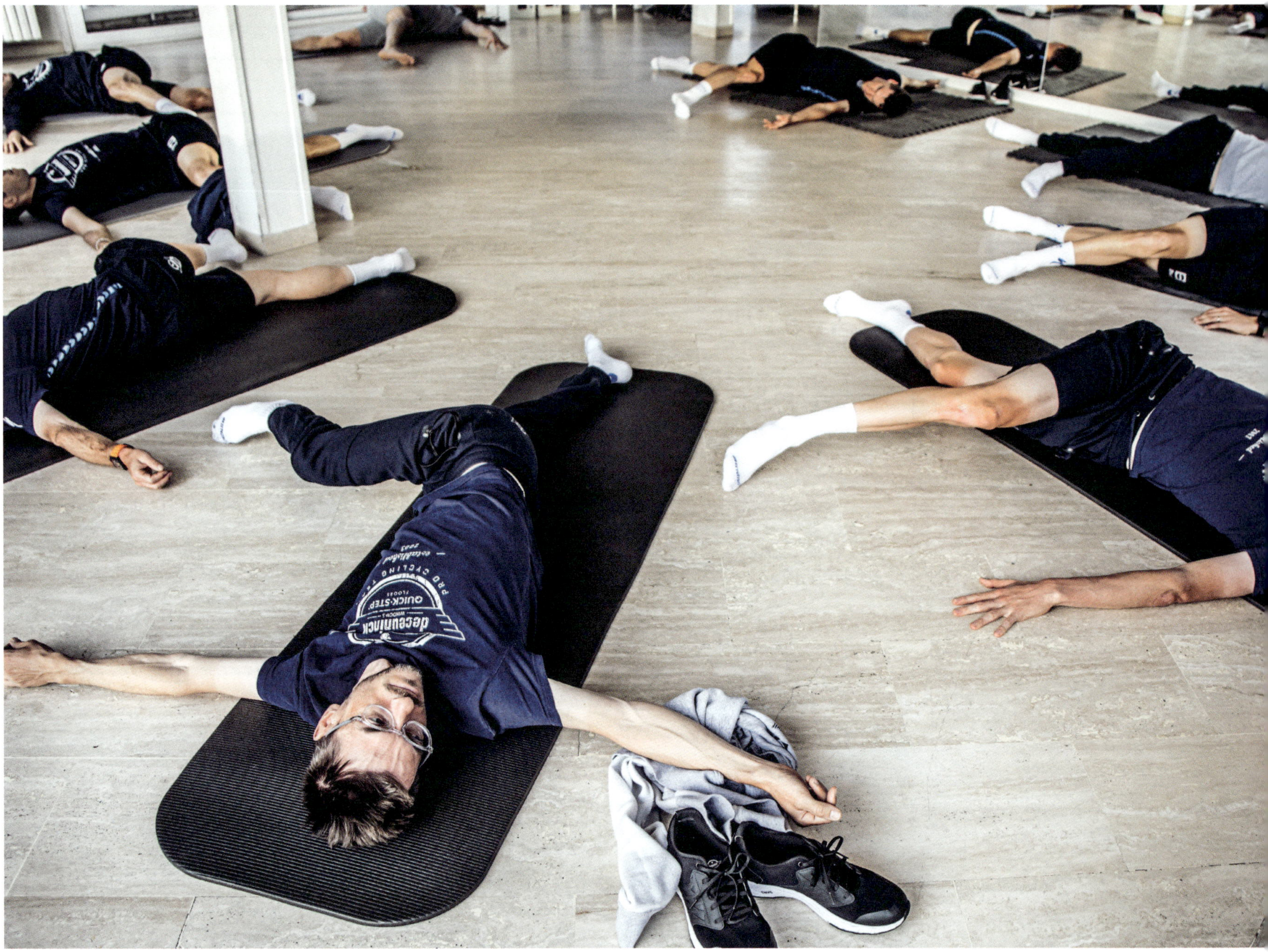

GIRONA, 15.02.2021

Oefeningen in lenigheid, opgelegd door fysiotherapeut Steven Vrancken, als voorbereiding op het klassieke voorjaarswerk in maart en april.

Aan de kaarttafel: tijd voor ontspanning, maar wel op het scherpst van de snee. Topsporters willen altijd winnen. Links vooraan: Tim Declercq twijfelt, Ian Garrison wacht af. Aan de overkant van de tafel v.l.n.r.: Dries Devenyns smeedt een plan, Florian Sénéchal en Jannik Steimle kijken toe, en Bert Van Lerberghe peilt naar de strategie van Tim.

Álvaro Hodeg aan het kaartspel. Let op zijn linkerhand.

Physiotherapist Steven Vrancken helps the team improve their flexibility in preparation for the spring classics in March and April.

Fun at the card table; it's time for some relaxation, yet the team stays focused. After all, top athletes always want to win. In the front left, Tim Declercq hesitates, while Ian Garrison waits his turn. On the other side of the table, Dries Devenyns is making a plan, Florian Sénéchal and Jannik Steimle are watching, and Bert Van Lerberghe is guessing Tim's strategy.

Álvaro Hodeg playing cards. Note his left hand.

Exercices de souplesse, imposés par Steven Vrancken, kinésithérapeute, en vue de préparer les épreuves de printemps, en mars et avril. ▲

À la table de jeu, un moment de détente, mais rempli de tension. Pour les sportifs de haut niveau, perdre n'est jamais une option. À l'avant, à gauche, Tim Declercq hésite, Ian Garrison attend. De l'autre côté de la table, de gauche à droite, Dries Devenyns mijote quelque chose, Florian Sénéchal et Jannik Steimle observent et Bert Van Lerberghe essaie de deviner la stratégie de Tim. ◥

Álvaro Hodeg en plein jeu de cartes. Notez sa main gauche. ▶

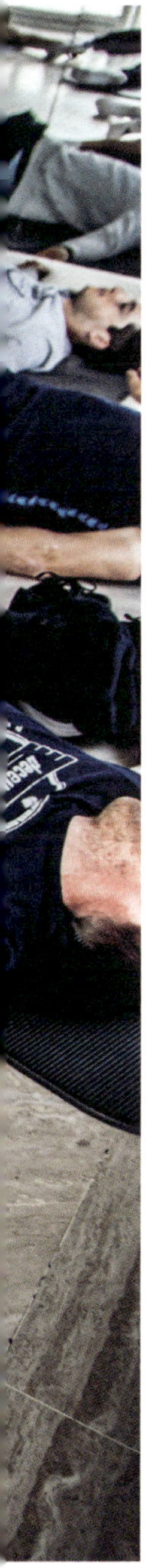

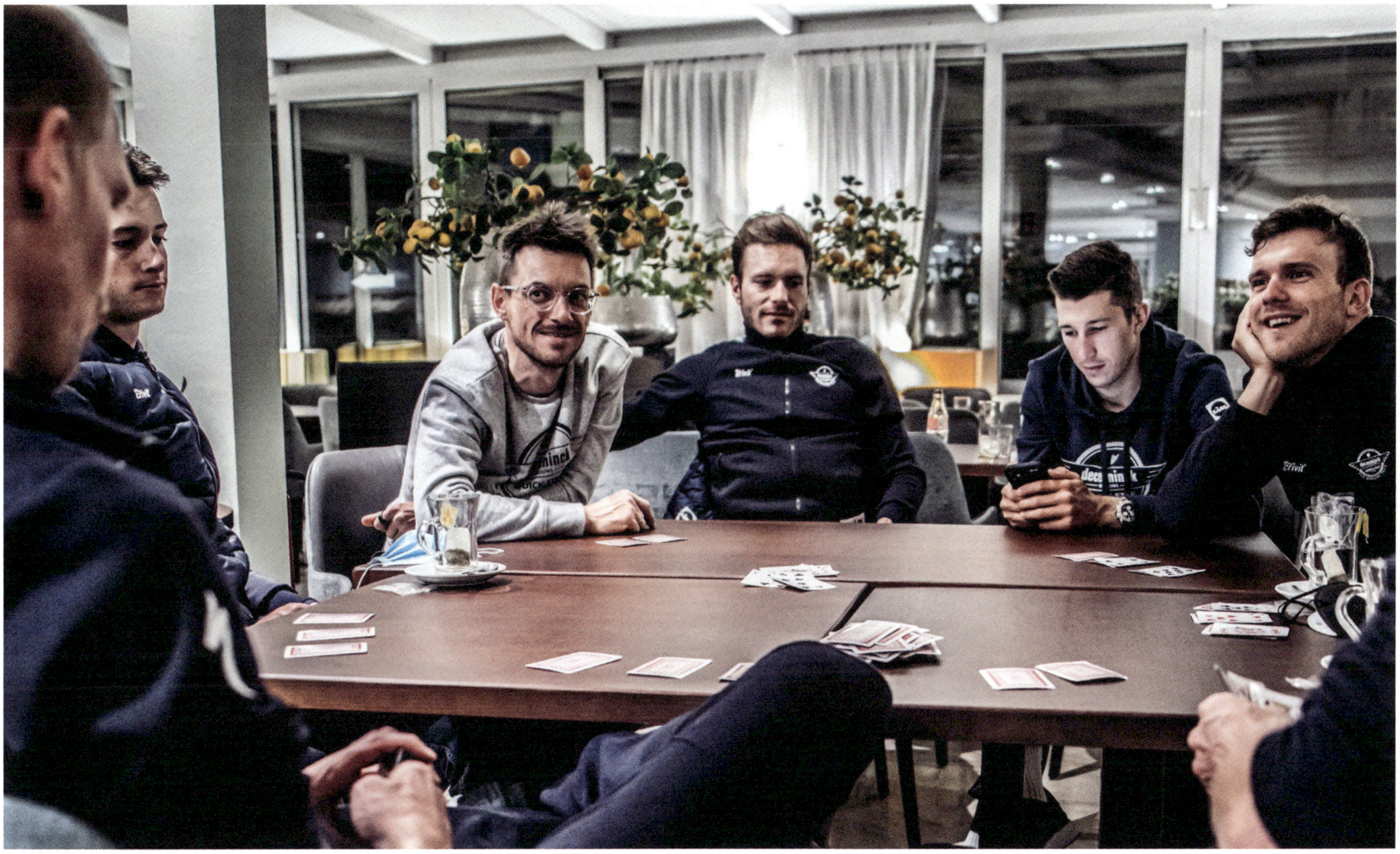

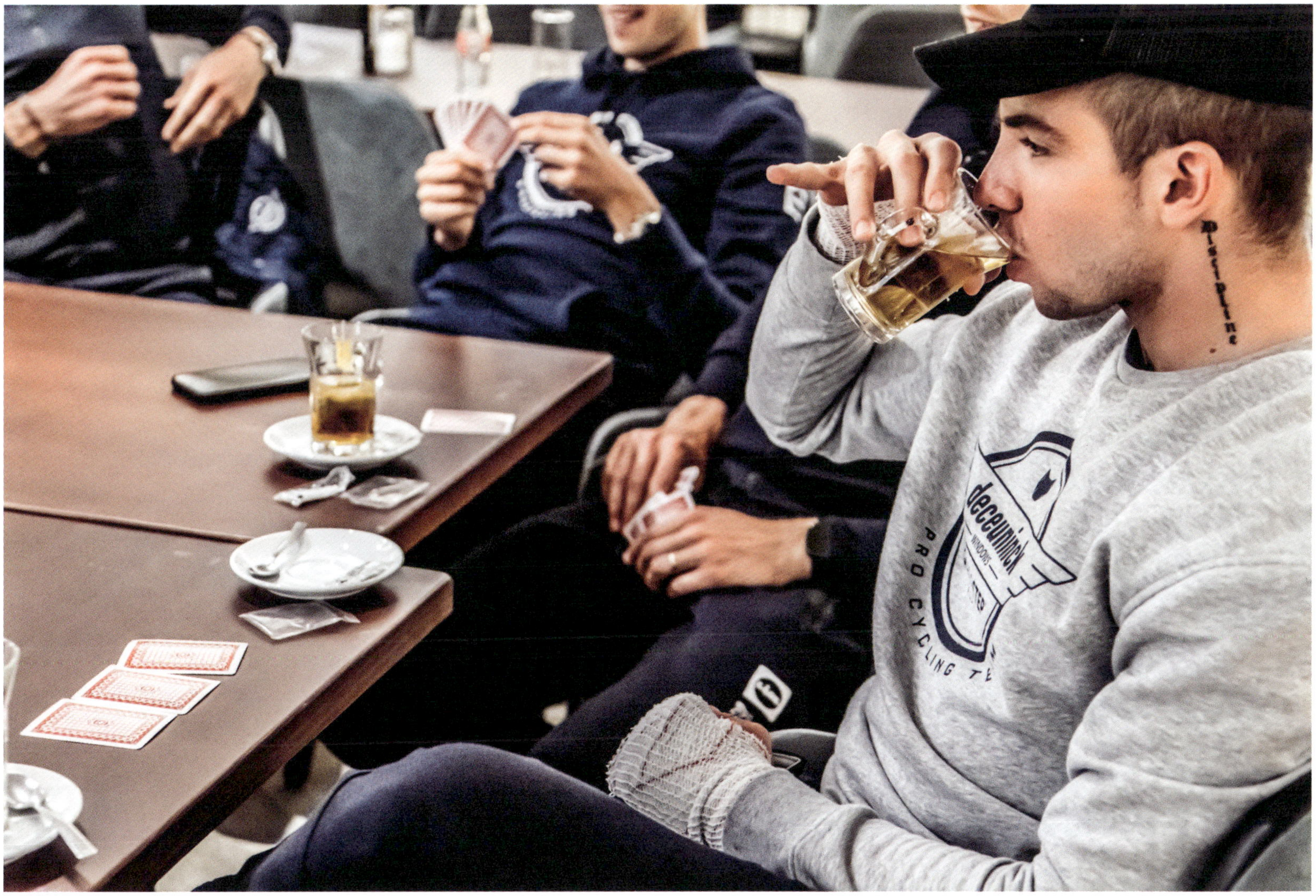
deceuninck

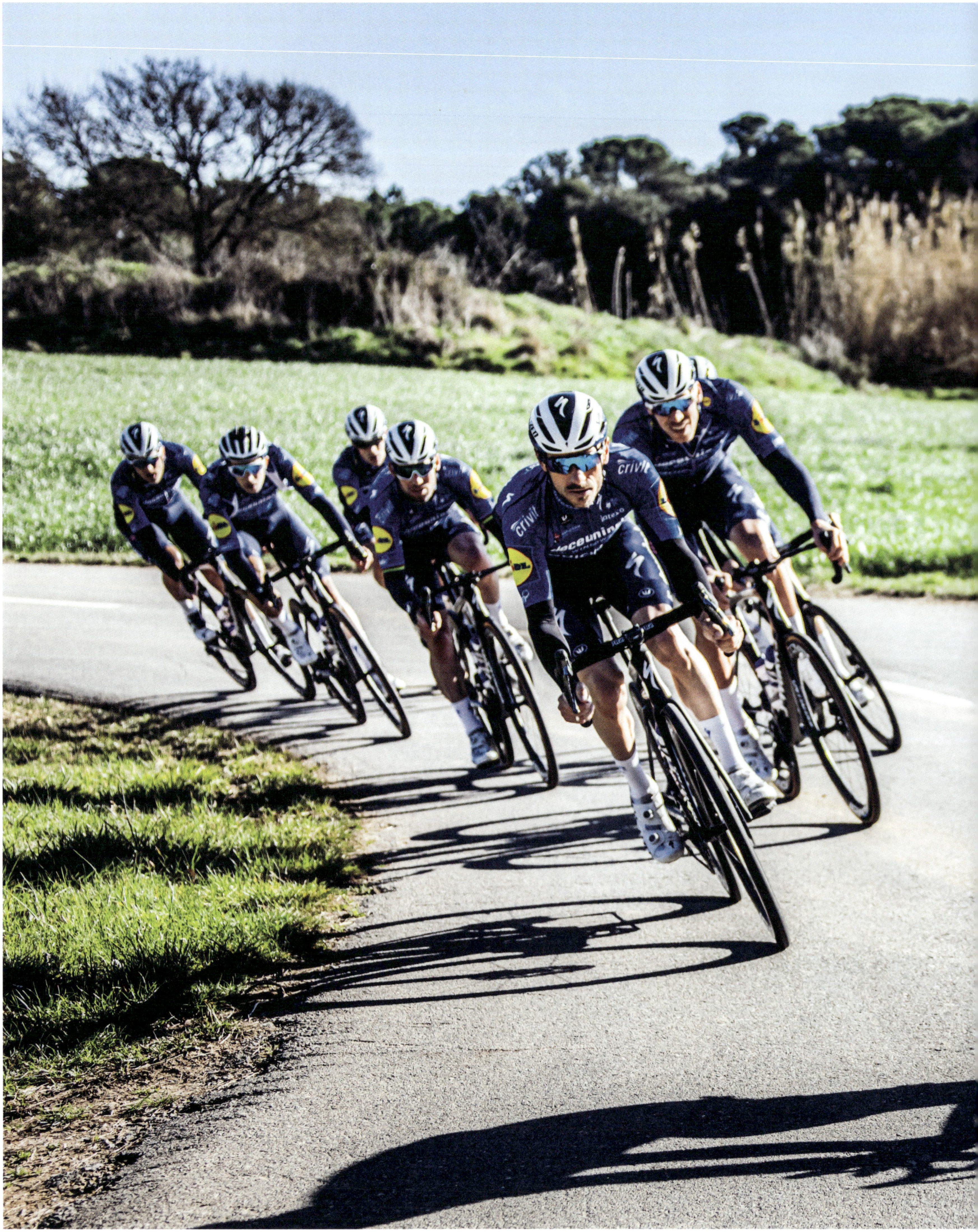
crivit

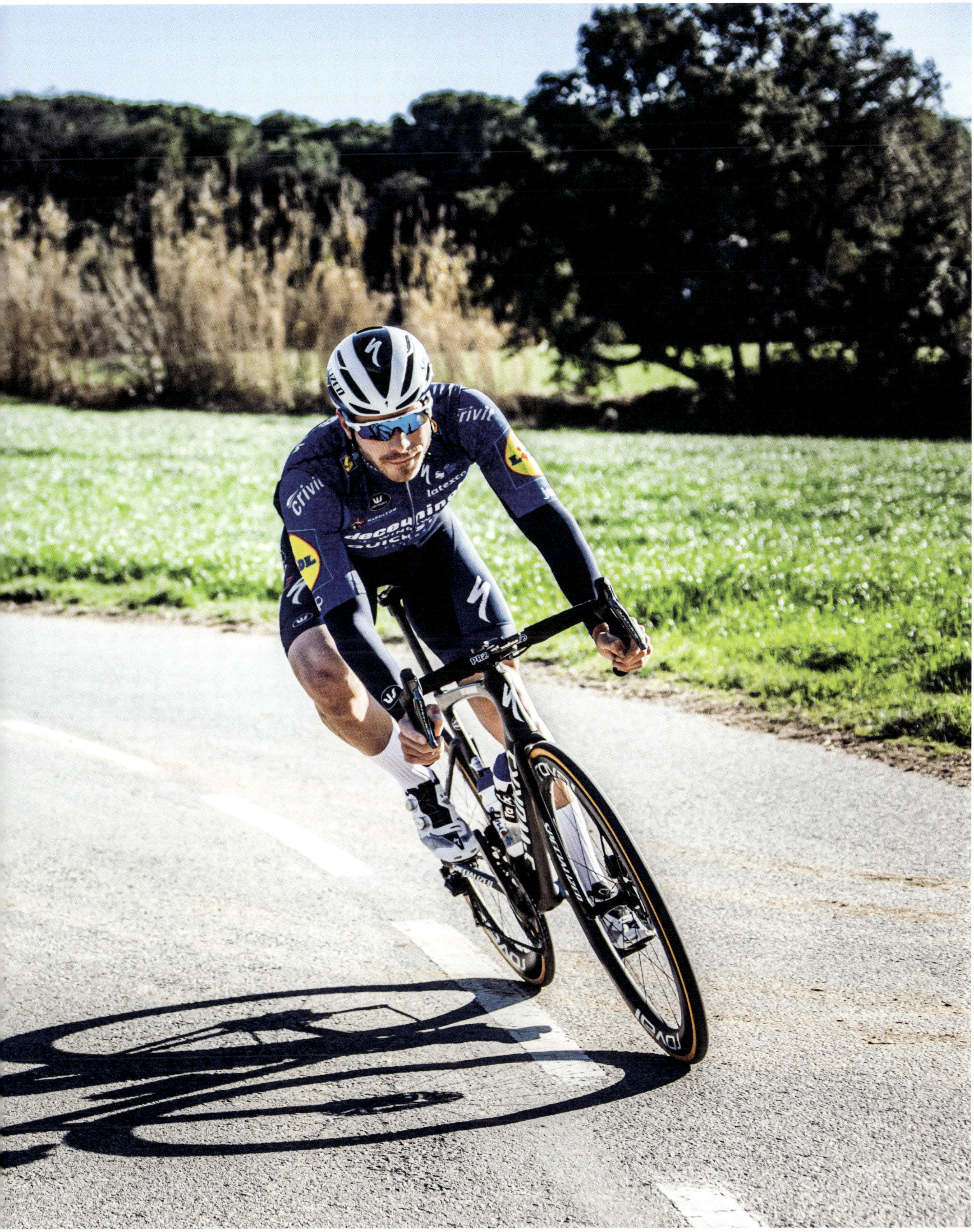
latexco
crivit

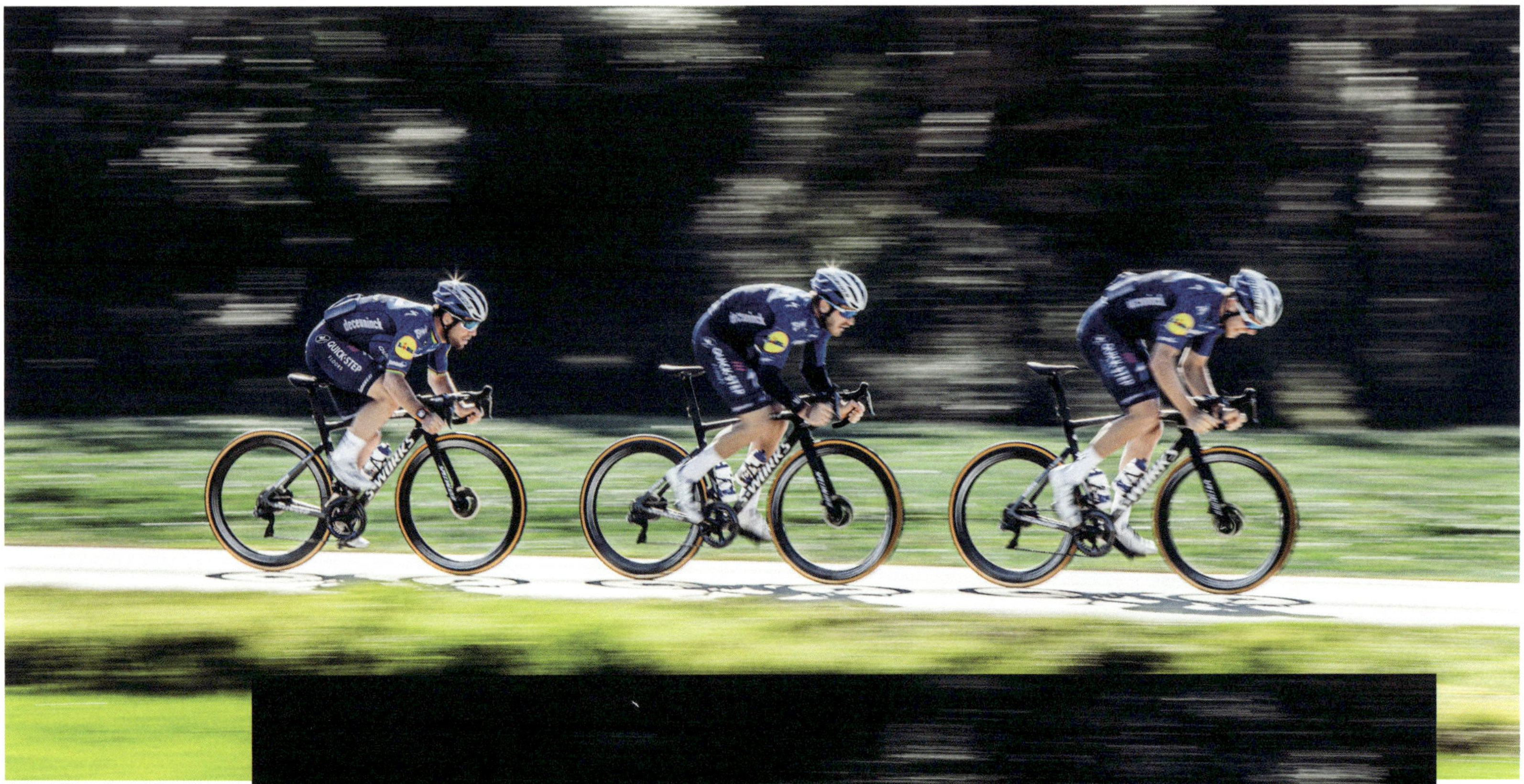

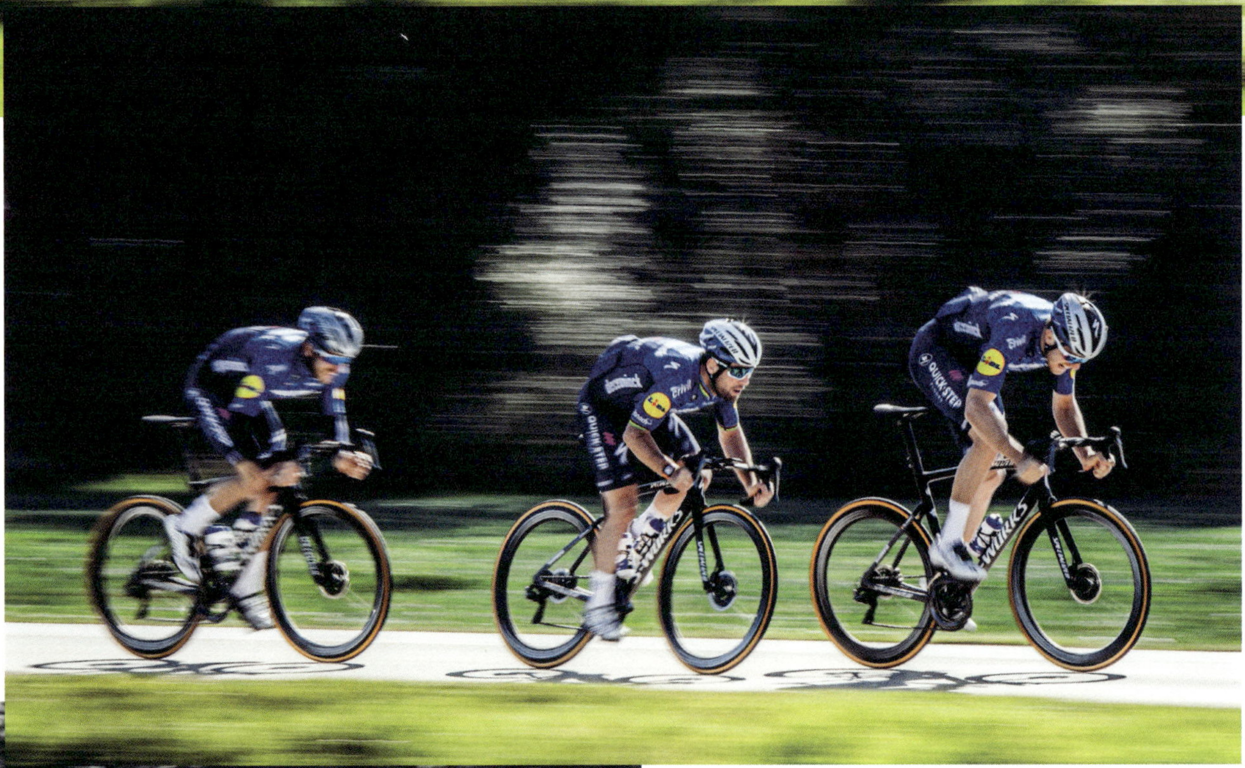

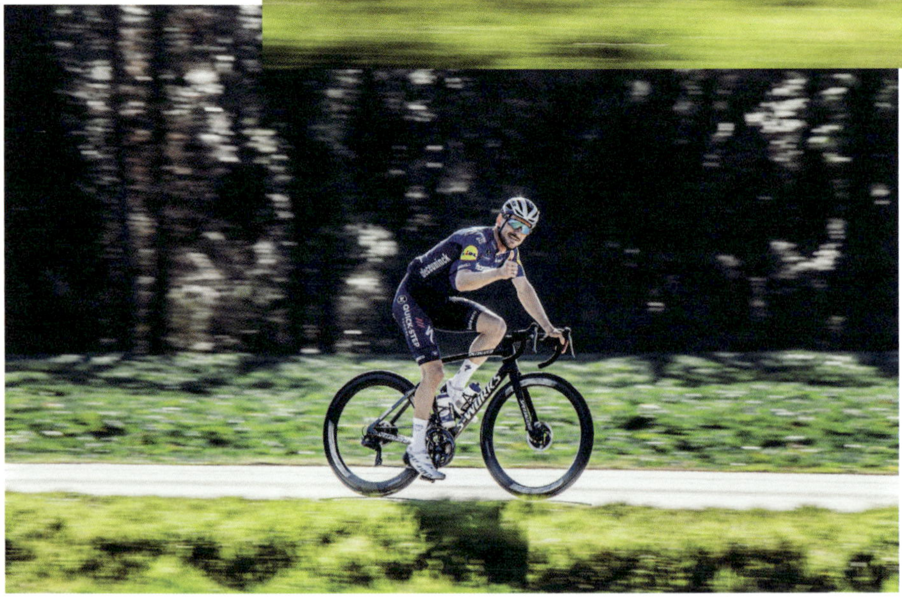

GIRONA, 17.02.2021

Lead-outtraining in Girona. Bert Van Lerberghe neemt Mark Cavendish en Florian Sénéchal op sleeptouw.

Lead-out training in Girona. Bert Van Lerberghe takes Mark Cavendish and Florian Sénéchal in tow.

Entraînement au sprint à Girona. Bert Van Lerberghe joue les poissons-pilotes pour Mark Cavendish et Florian Sénéchal.

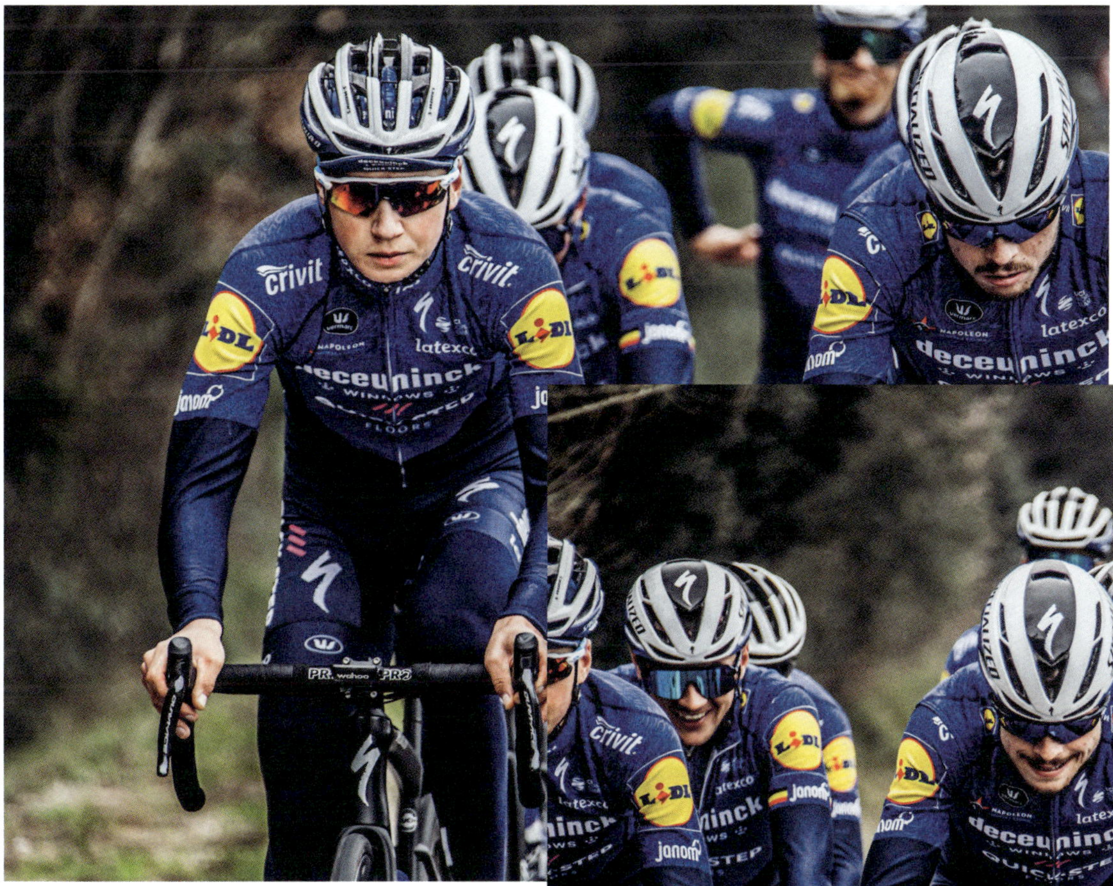

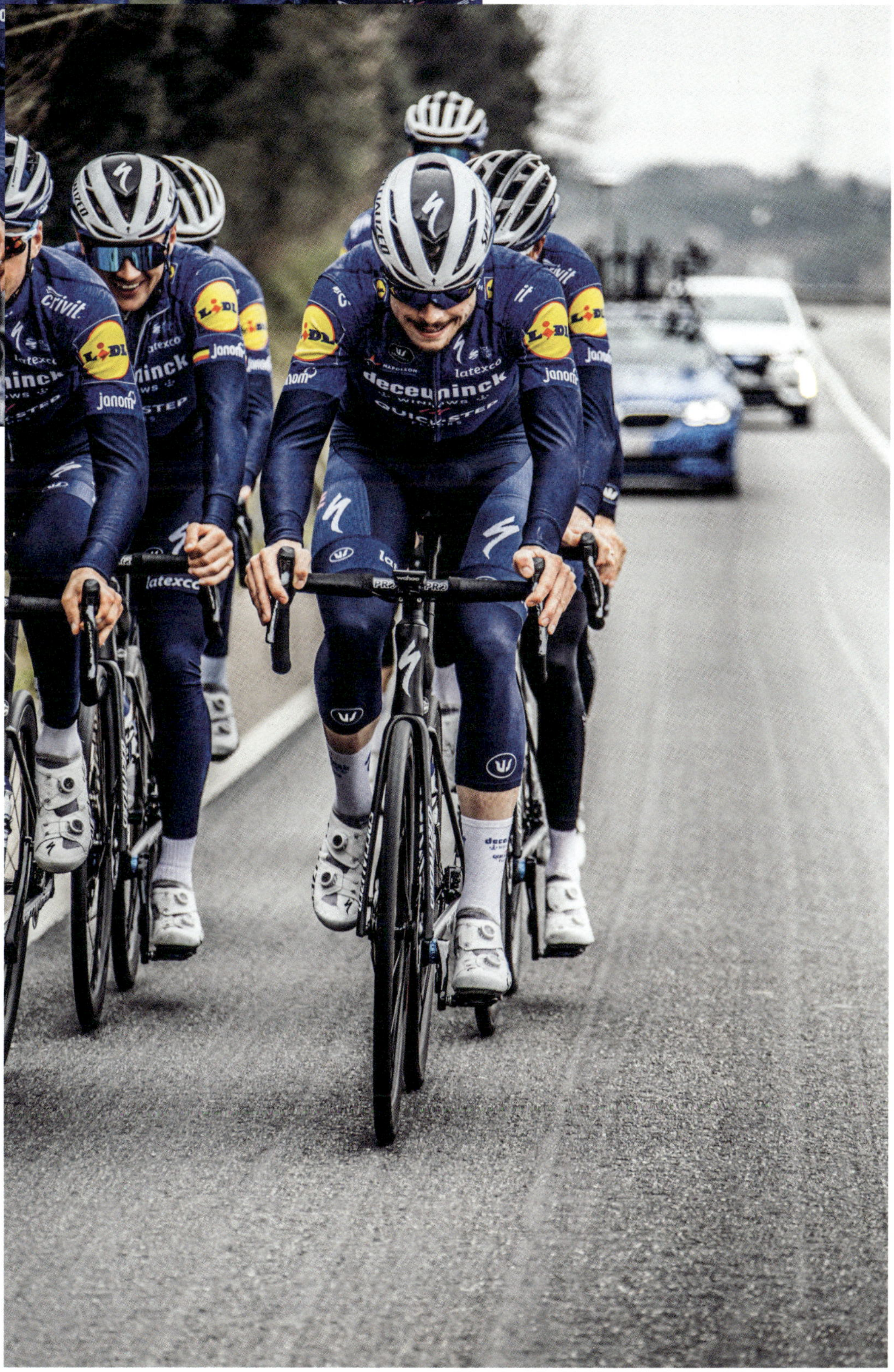

GIRONA, 18.02.2021

Mauri Vansevenant
& Rémi Cavagna

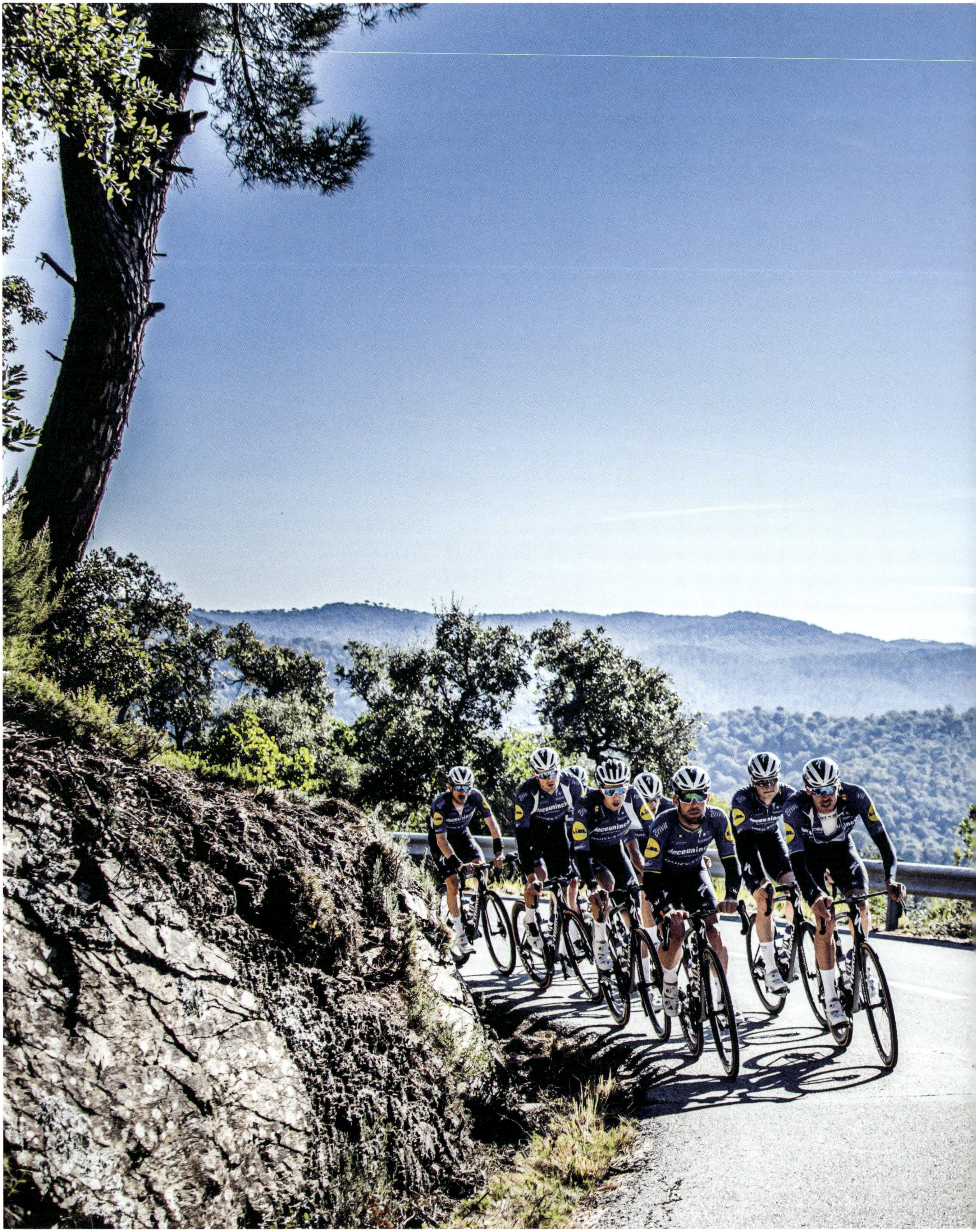

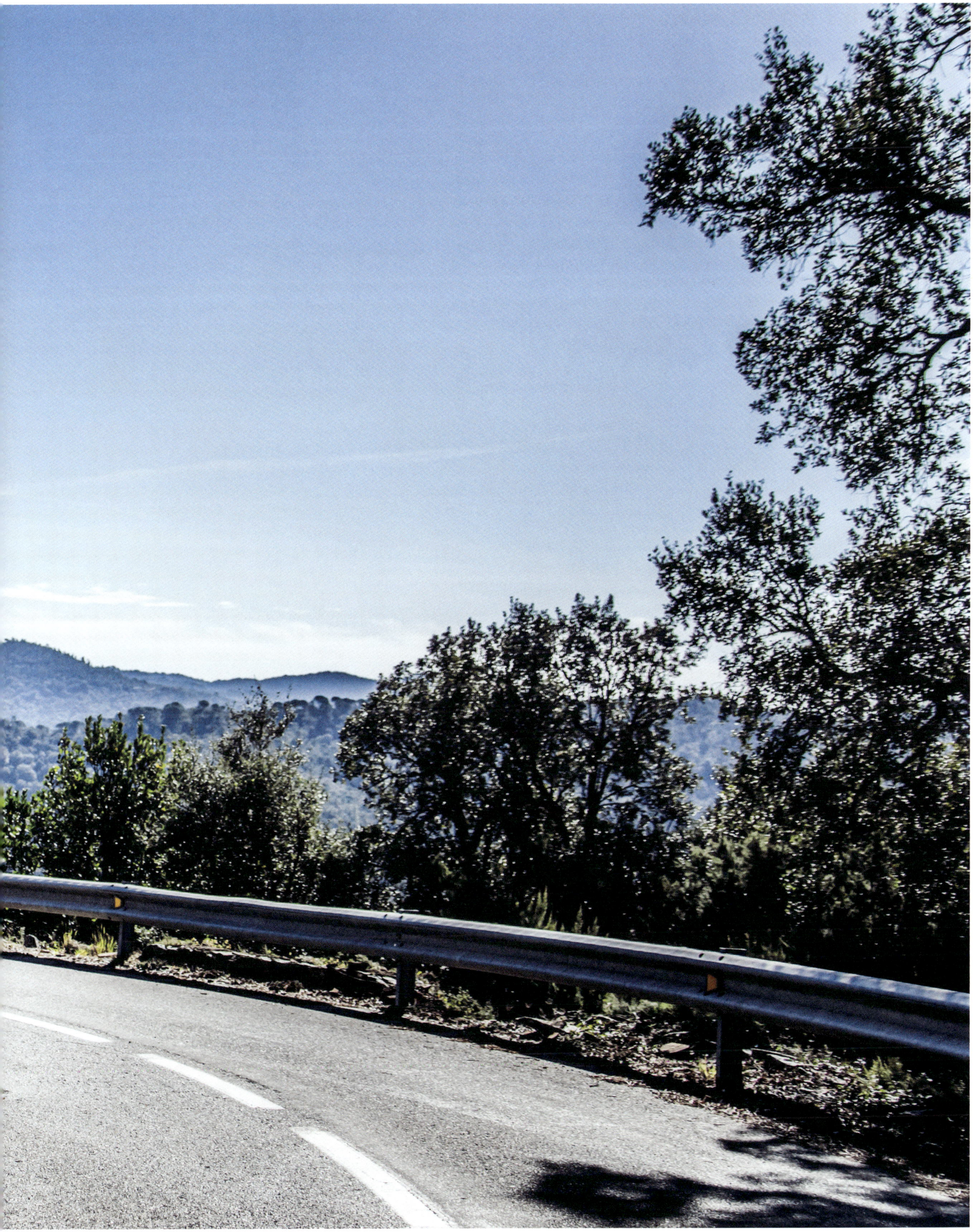

OMLOOP HET NIEUWSBLAD 27.02.2021

De Omloop Het Nieuwsblad vormt sinds mensenheugenis de openingswedstrijd van het klassieke wielerseizoen in België, in tandem met Kuurne-Brussel-Kuurne, natuurlijk. De eerste op zaterdag, de tweede op zondag. Het was direct 'bingo' voor het Deceuninck – Quick-Step Team: winst met Davide Ballerini in Ninove. In Kuurne strandde Bert Van Lerberghe op een negende plaats.

Omloop Het Nieuwsblad has always been the opening race of the classics season in Belgium – of course in tandem with Kuurne-Brussels-Kuurne. The first takes place on Saturday, the other on Sunday. It was an instant win for the Deceuninck – Quick-Step Team, with Davide Ballerini in Ninove. In Kuurne, Bert Van Lerberghe finished in ninth place.

Depuis des temps immémoriaux, le Omloop Het Nieuwsblad est la course d'ouverture de la saison cycliste classique en Belgique. Conjointement avec Kuurne-Bruxelles-Kuurne. La première, le samedi et l'autre, le dimanche. Le week-end a été une belle réussite pour l'équipe Deceuninck – Quick-Step avec une victoire de Davide Ballerini à Ninove. À Kuurne, Bert Van Lerberghe a terminé à la neuvième place.

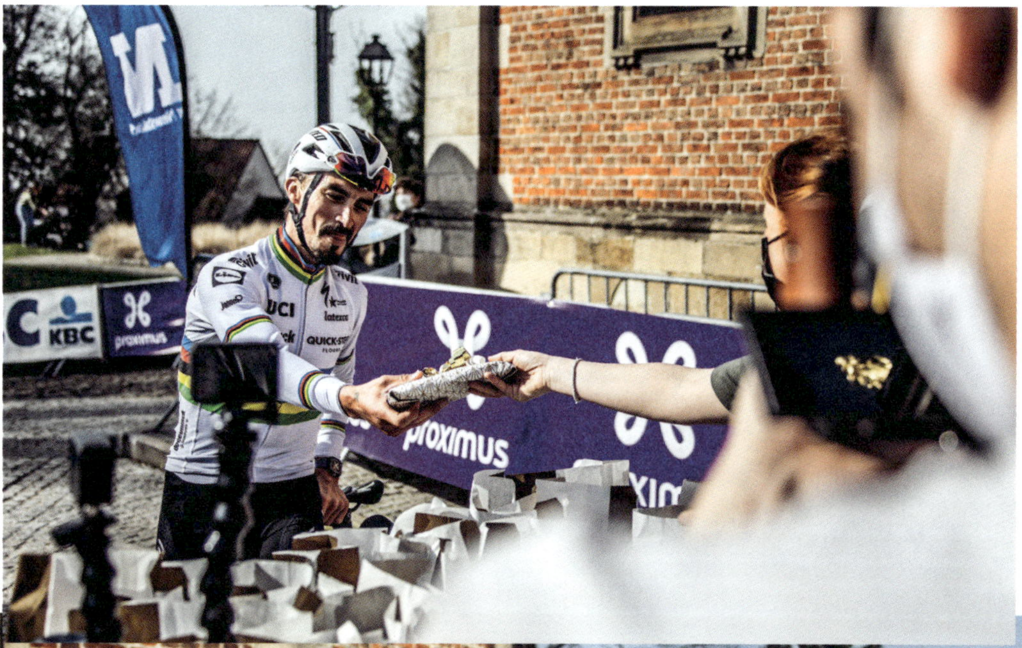

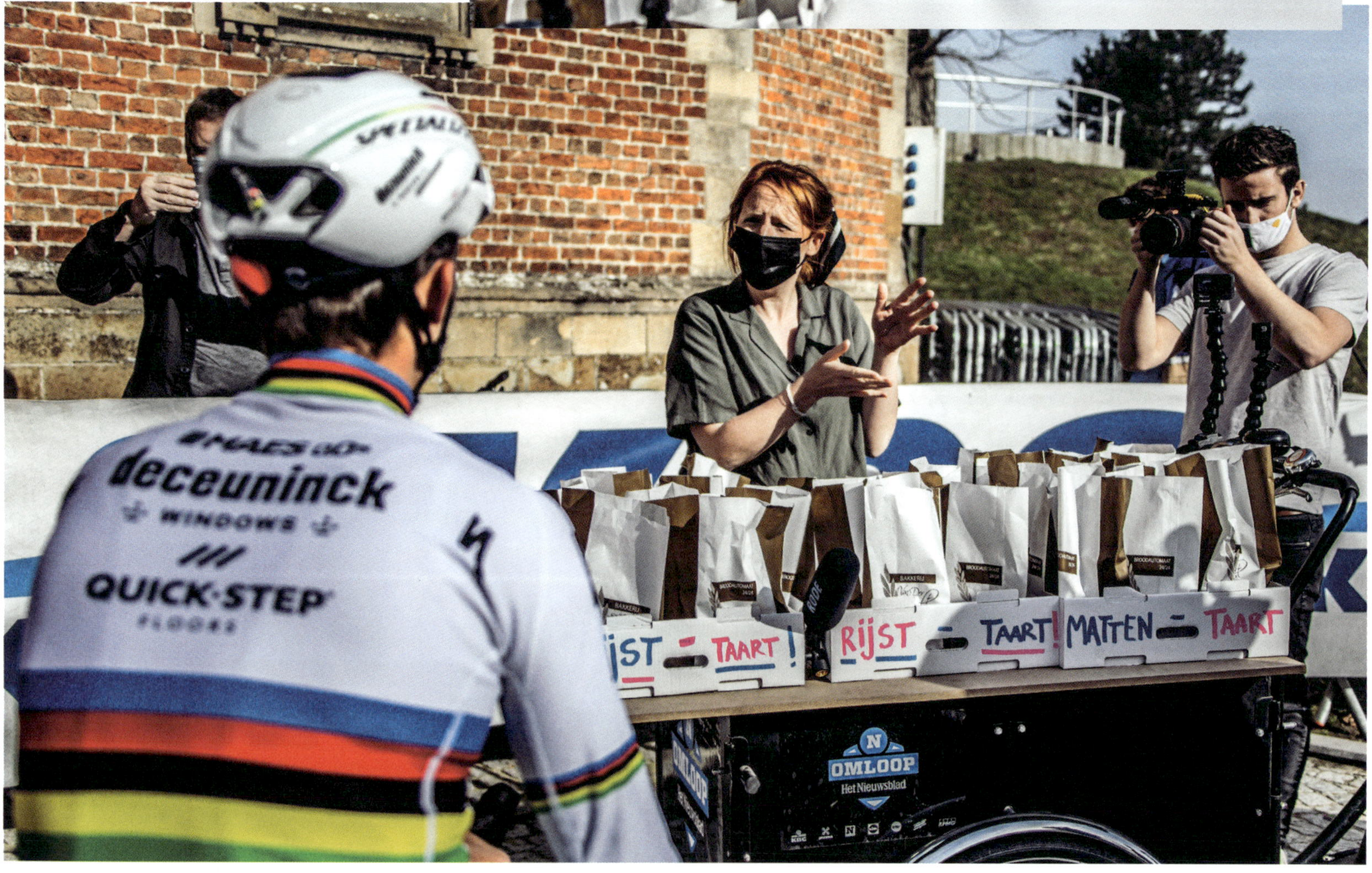

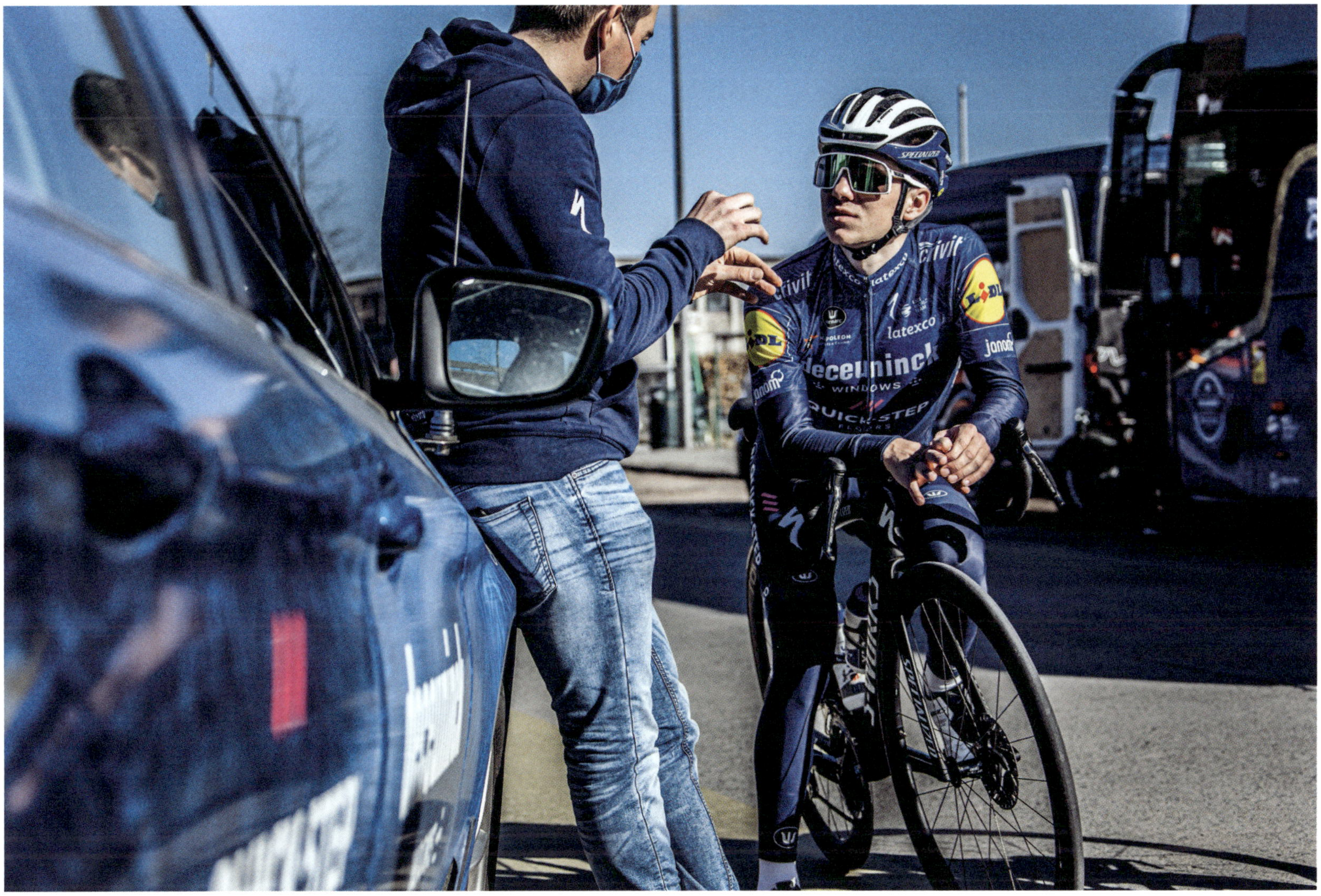

RECON OMLOOP HET NIEUWSBLAD, 24.02.2021

Julian Alaphilippe houdt halt aan de kapel boven op de Muur van Geraardsbergen. Ook radiozender Studio Brussel was het belang van het openingsweekend niet ontgaan. Om de renners een hart onder de riem te steken verraste grande dame Linde Merckpoel het rennersgild tijdens de verkenning van de Omloop. Ze deed dat met het lekkers dat de streek te bieden heeft: rijsttaartjes en natuurlijk de onvolprezen mattentaart, coronaproof verpakt in aparte pakketjes.

Misschien was het voor Remco een kleine fietstocht vanuit Schepdaal naar zijn ploegmakkers op verkenning, het was een mijlpaal in zijn genezingsproces na zijn val in Il Lombardia op 15 augustus 2020. Op woensdag 24 februari 2021 klom hij de fiets op, voor een bezoek aan zijn ploegmakkers in volle voorbereiding op het openingsweekend. Op de foto: Remco Evenepoel in gesprek met mecanicien Nicolas Coosemans.

Julian Alaphilippe stops at the chapel on top of the Muur van Geraardsbergen. The importance of the opening weekend had not escaped Flemish radio station Studio Brussel either. In order to encourage the riders, grande dame Linde Merckpoel surprised them during the reconnaissance of the Omloop. She did this with the delicacies that the region has to offer: rice cakes, and of course the unsurpassed mattentaart, both safely packed in separate packages. Covid-proof.

While it may have been a quick bike ride from Schepdaal to meet up with his teammates on reconnaissance, but it certainly was a milestone in his healing process after his fall in Il Lombardia on 15 August 2020. On Wednesday 24 February 2021, he took his bike to visit his teammates in full preparation for the opening weekend. Shown: Remco Evenepoel talking to mechanic Nicolas Coosemans.

Julian Alaphilippe s'arrête à la chapelle au sommet du Mur de Grammont. L'importance du week-end d'ouverture n'a pas échappé à la station de radio flamande Studio Brussel. Afin d'encourager les coureurs, Linde Merckpoel, la célèbre présentatrice radio, a surpris les coureurs au sommet du Mur de Grammont et leur a offert des spécialités de la région. Des gâteaux de riz et l'inégalable mattentaart, la spécialité flamande, le tout emballé dans des paquets individuels, bien sûr, Covid-19 oblige. ◀

Pour Remco, même si le trajet à vélo de Schepdael pour rejoindre ses coéquipiers en reconnaissance était assez court, c'était une étape importante dans son processus de récupération après sa chute lors d'Il Lombardia le 15 août 2020. Le mercredi 24 février 2021, il est monté sur son vélo pour rendre visite à ses coéquipiers en pleine préparation du week-end d'ouverture. Sur la photo : Remco Evenepoel en pleine discussion avec le mécanicien Nicolas Coosemans. ▲

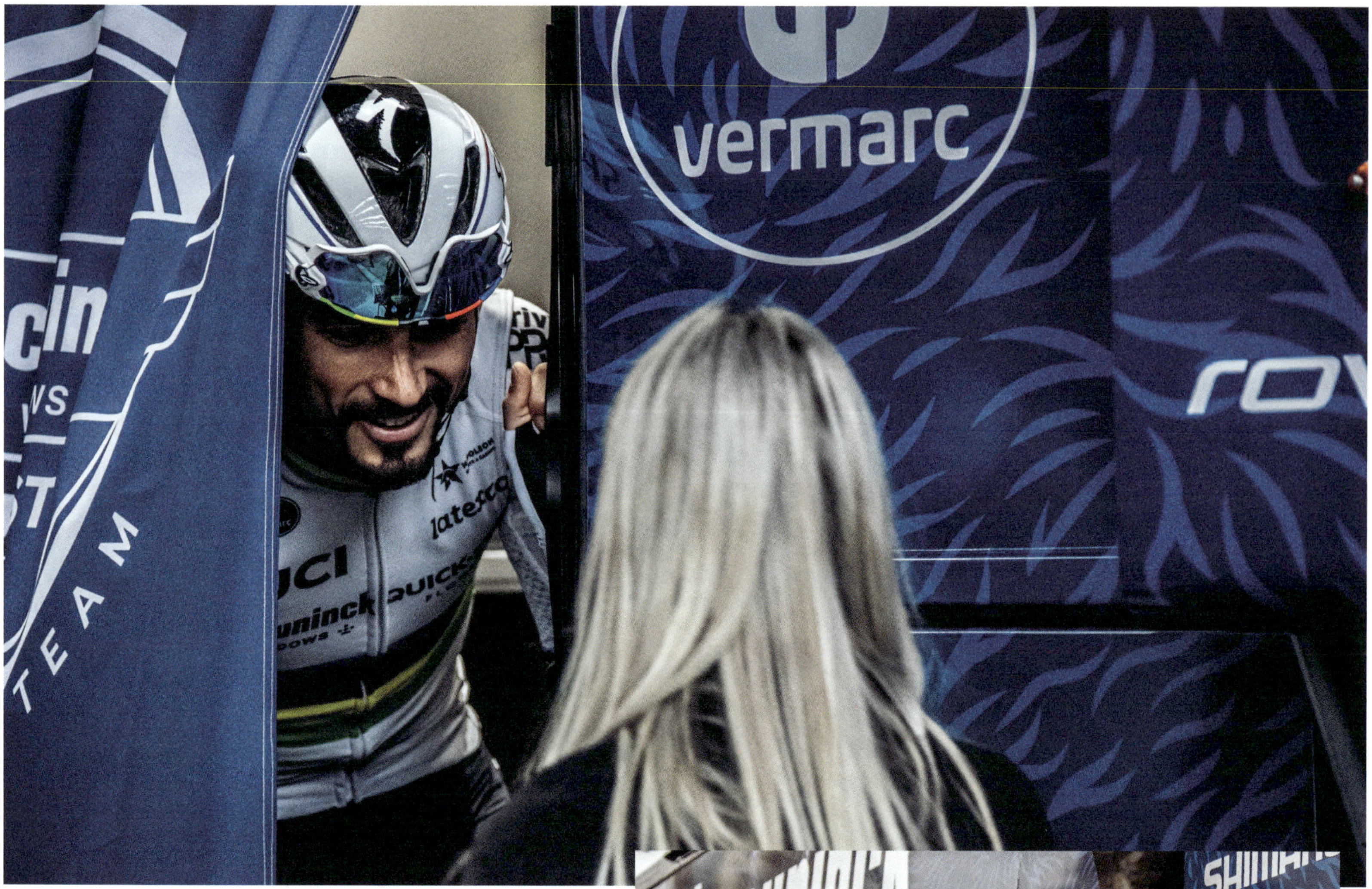
vermarc
TEAM

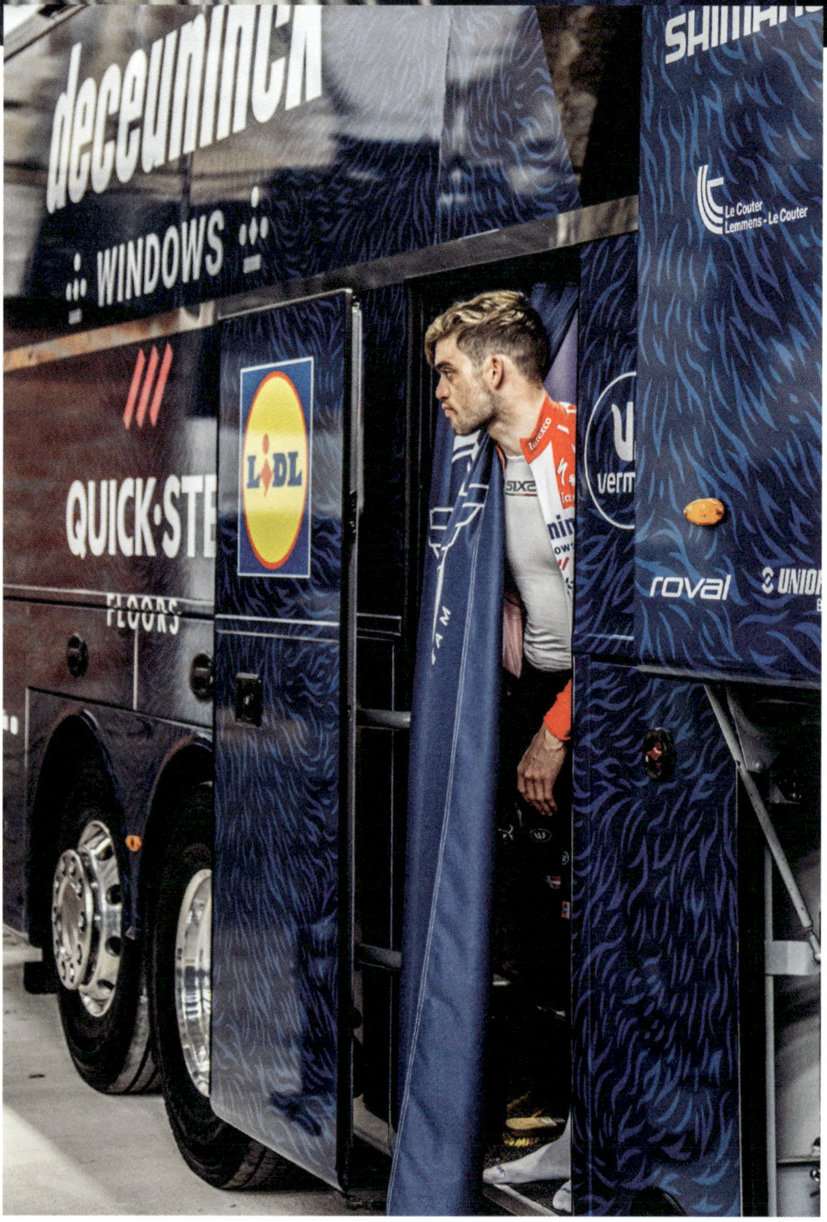
WINDOWS
LIDL
roval

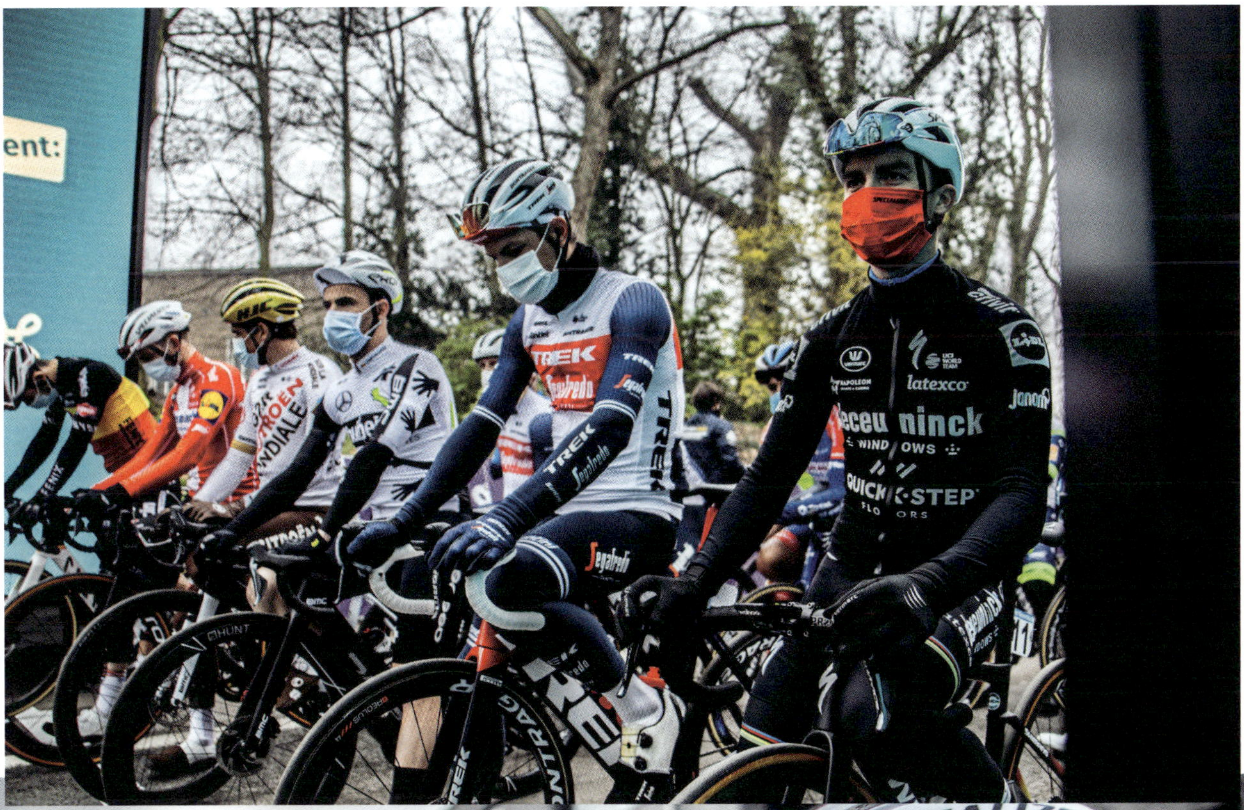

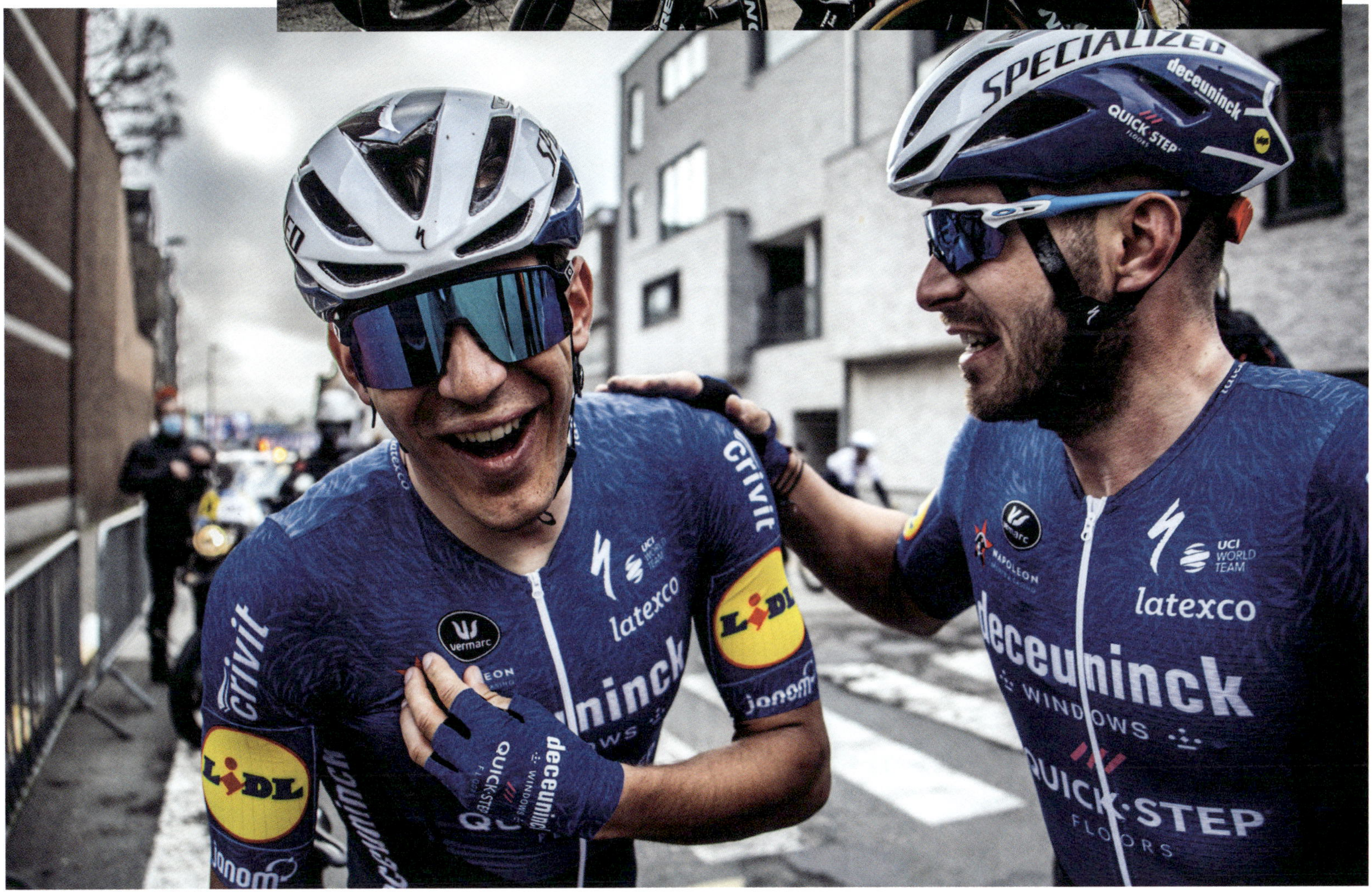

NINOVE, 27.02.2021

Nadat hij op 11 en 12 februari al de eerste twee ritten in de Tour de la Provence heeft gewonnen (met de puntentrui erbovenop), plukt hij ook de bloemen in de Omloop Het Nieuwsblad. Hij is de snelste van het hele pak in aankomstplaats Ninove. Links winnaar Davide Ballerini, rechts Florian Sénéchal, die de lead-out mende en zelf zevende werd.

After winning the first two stages in the Tour de la Provence on 11 and 12 February (in addition to the points jersey), he also comes out on top in the Omloop Het Nieuwsblad. He proves to be the fastest of the whole pack in arrival at Ninove. On the left winner Davide Ballerini, on the right Florian Sénéchal who provided the lead-out and finished in seventh place.

Après avoir remporté les deux premières étapes du Tour de la Provence les 11 et 12 février (et le maillot de classement par points), Davide Ballerini s'est également imposé au sprint sur le Omloop Het Nieuwsblad. Il est le plus rapide du peloton à l'arrivée à Ninove. À gauche, Davide Ballerini, le vainqueur, à droite, Florian Sénéchal, son poisson-pilote qui a lui-même terminé septième. ▲

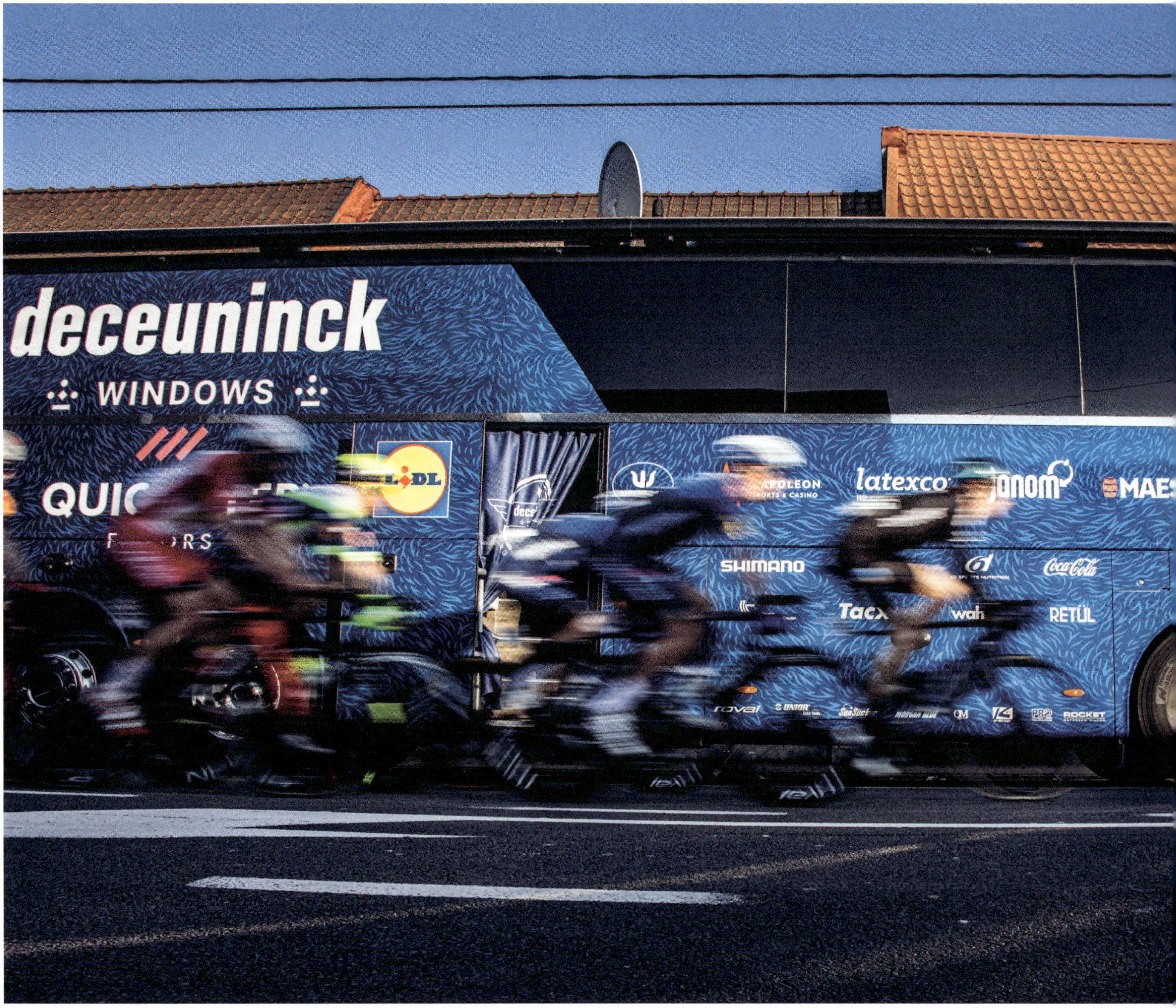
deceuninck
WINDOWS
LIDL
latexco
SHIMANO
Coca-Cola
Tacx
wahoo
RETÜL

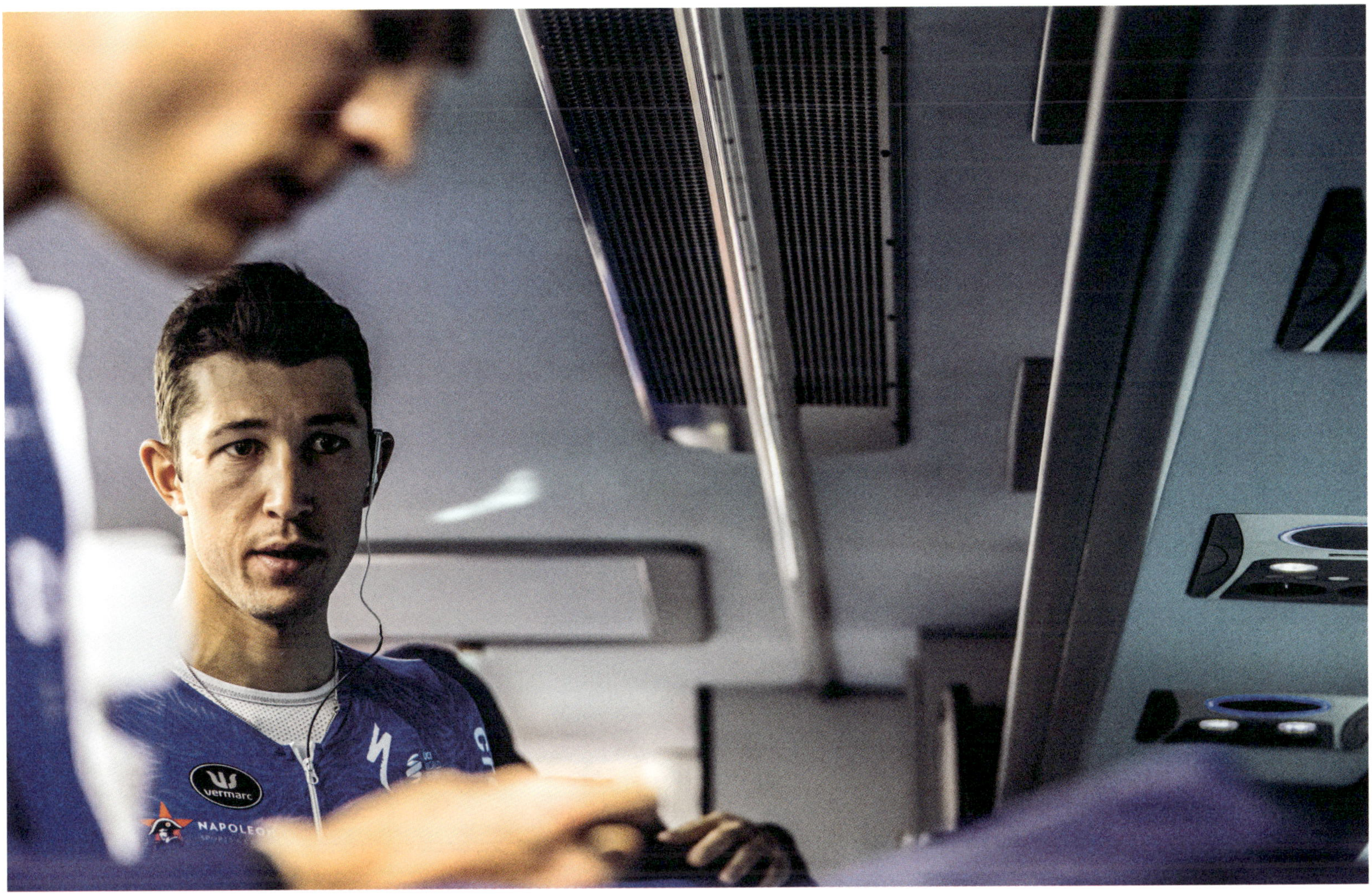

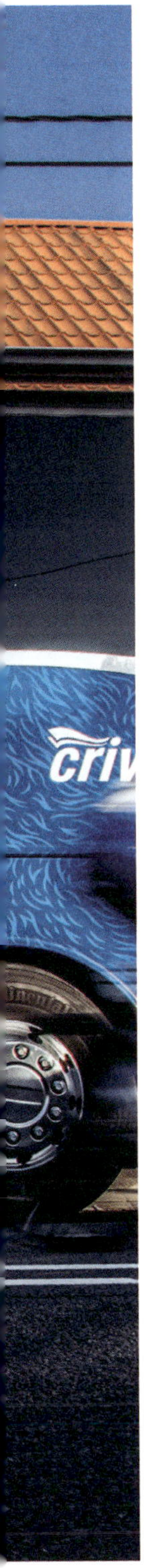
crivi

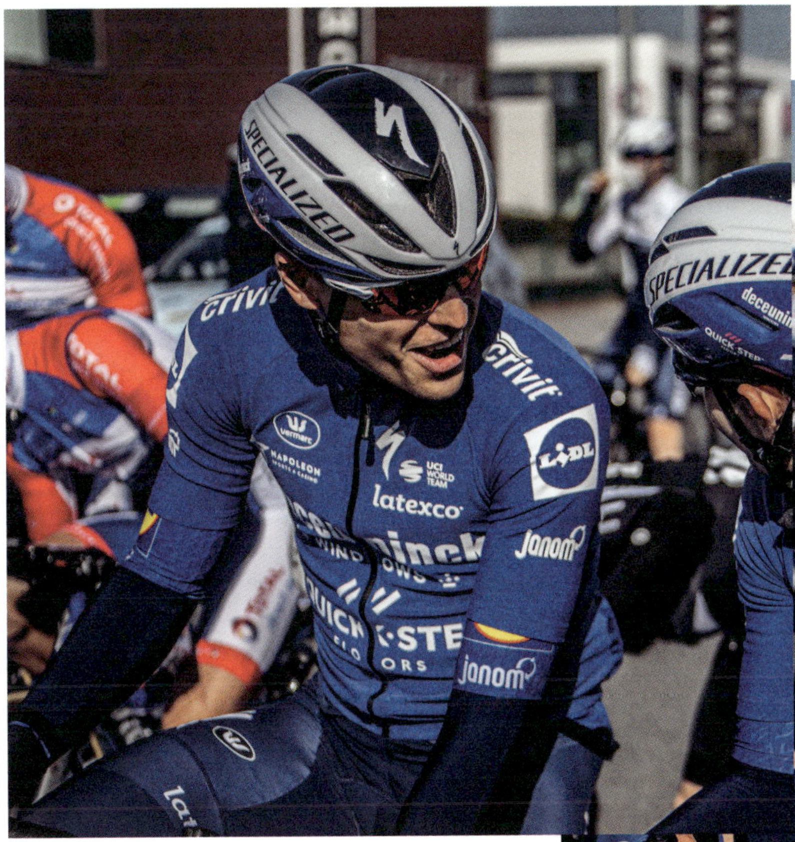
SPECIALIZED
crivit
latexco
janom

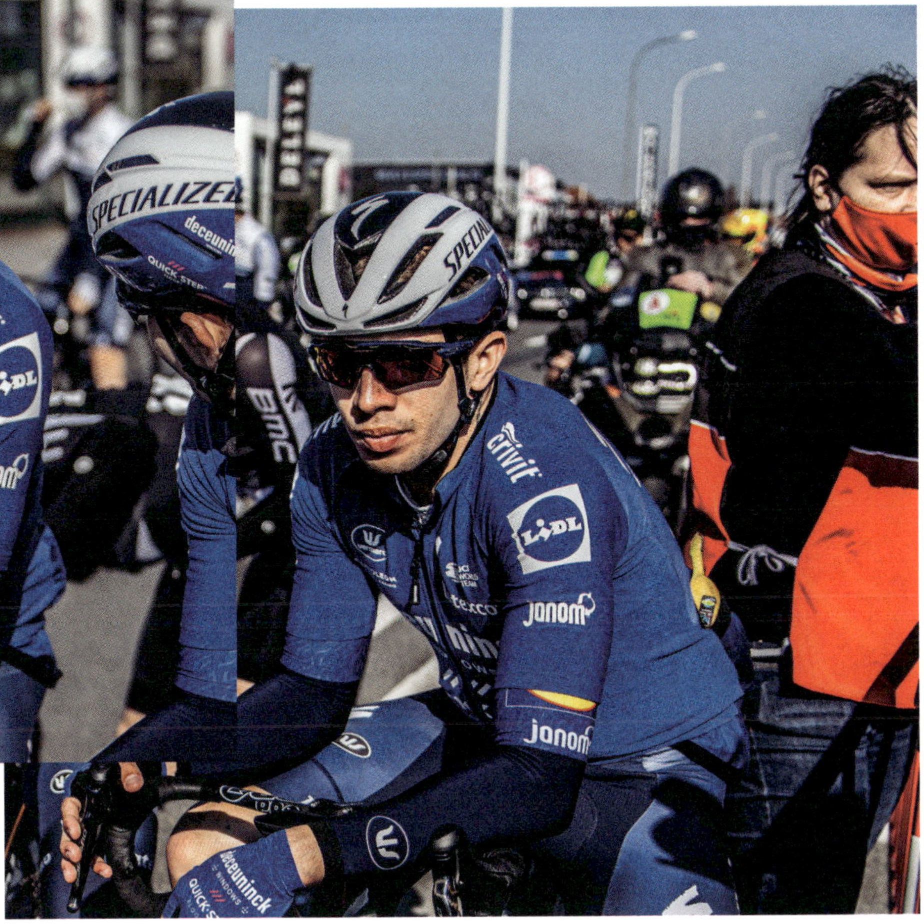
SPECIALIZED
crivit
LIDL
janom

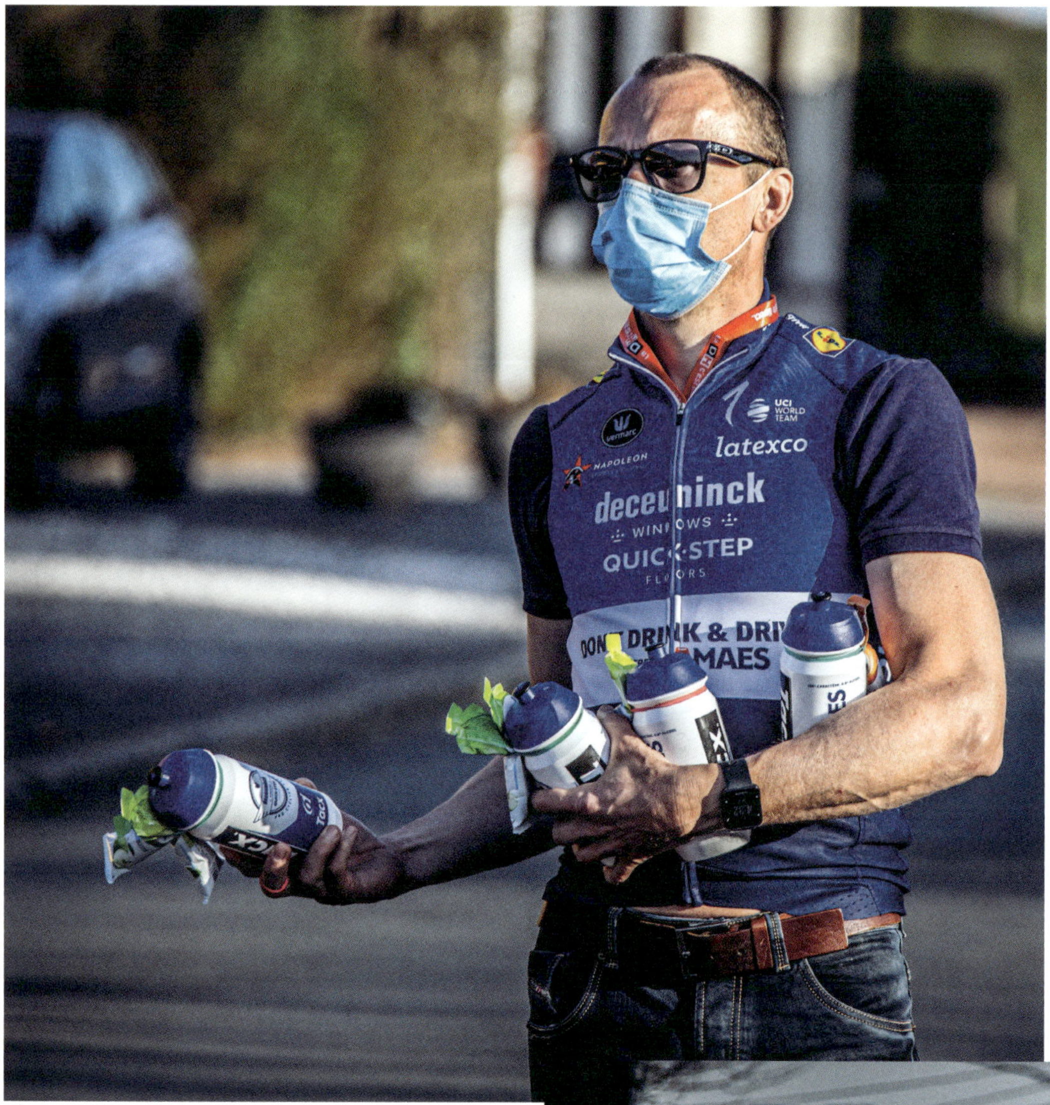

DOUR, 02.03.2021

Ter gelegenheid van Le Samyn bracht The Wolfpack de 0.0%-campagne 'Don't drink and drive - powered by Maes' onder de aandacht met speciale shirts. Goede burgerzin is geen loze kreet bij de ploeg van Patrick Lefevere.

On the occasion of Le Samyn on March 2, The Wolfpack brought the 0.0% campaign Don't drink and drive - powered by MAES to the public with custom T-shirts. Good citizenship isn't an empty slogan for Patrick Lefevere's team.

À l'occasion du Samyn, le 2 mars, le Wolfpack a fait passer un message puissant : « Don't drink & drive - powered by Maes ». Le maillot de l'équipe était pourvu du slogan de la campagne 0,0 %, traduisant l'esprit civique de l'équipe de Patrick Lefevere.

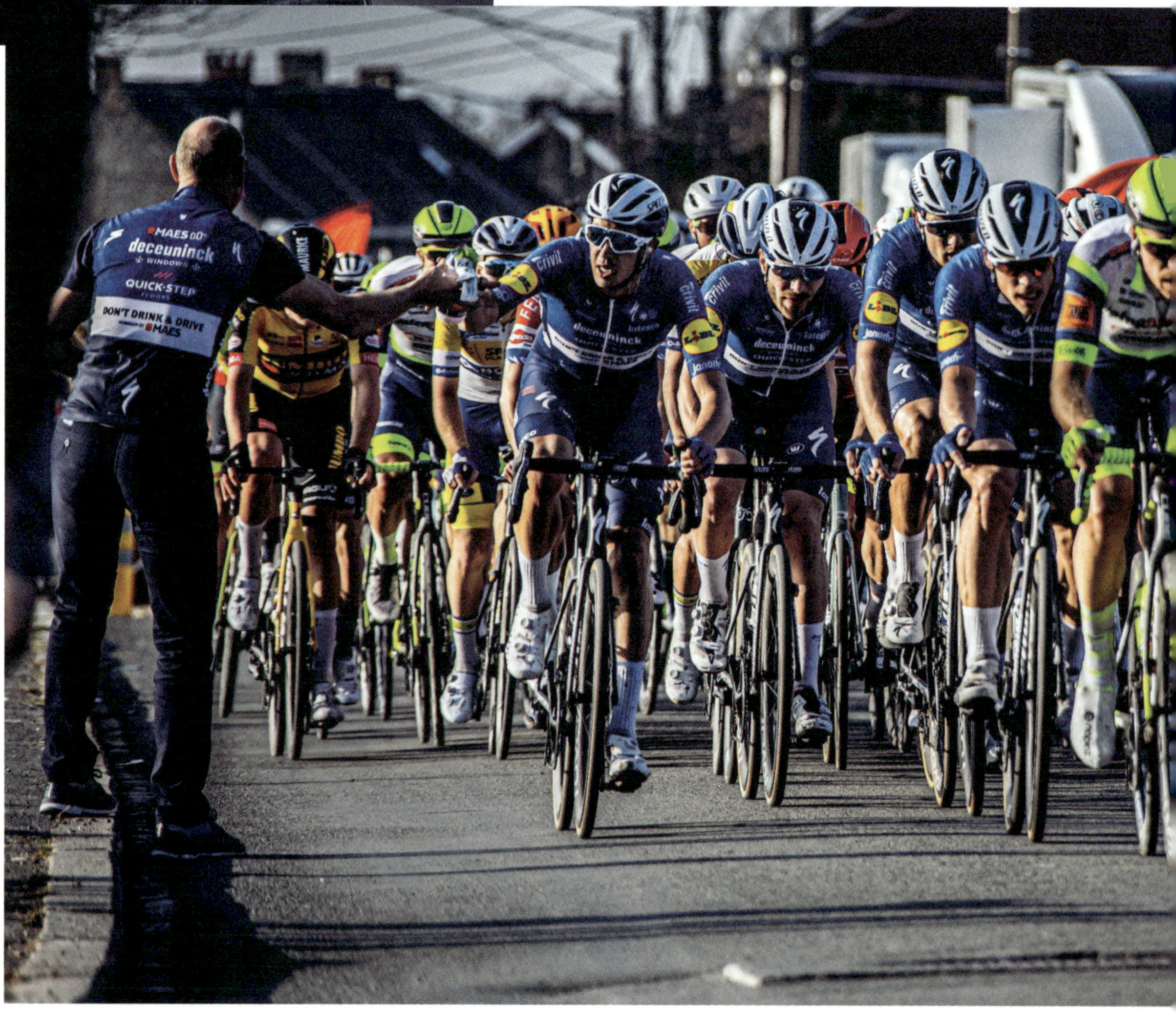

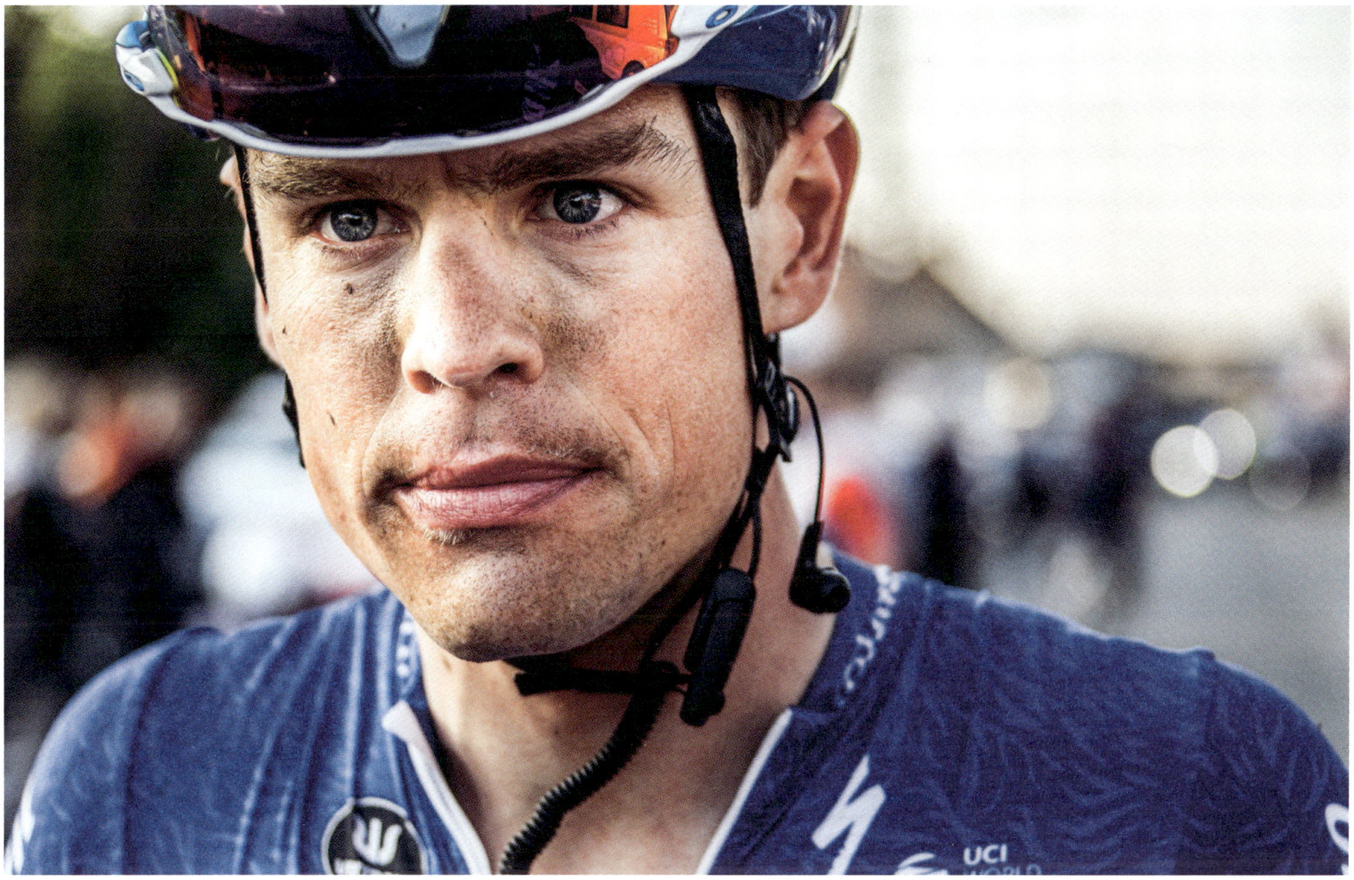
UCI

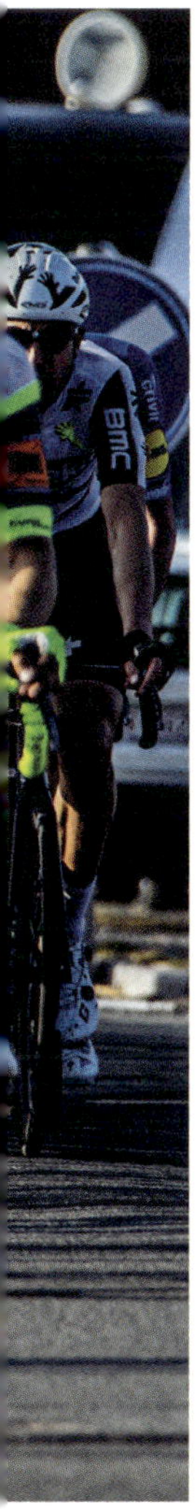

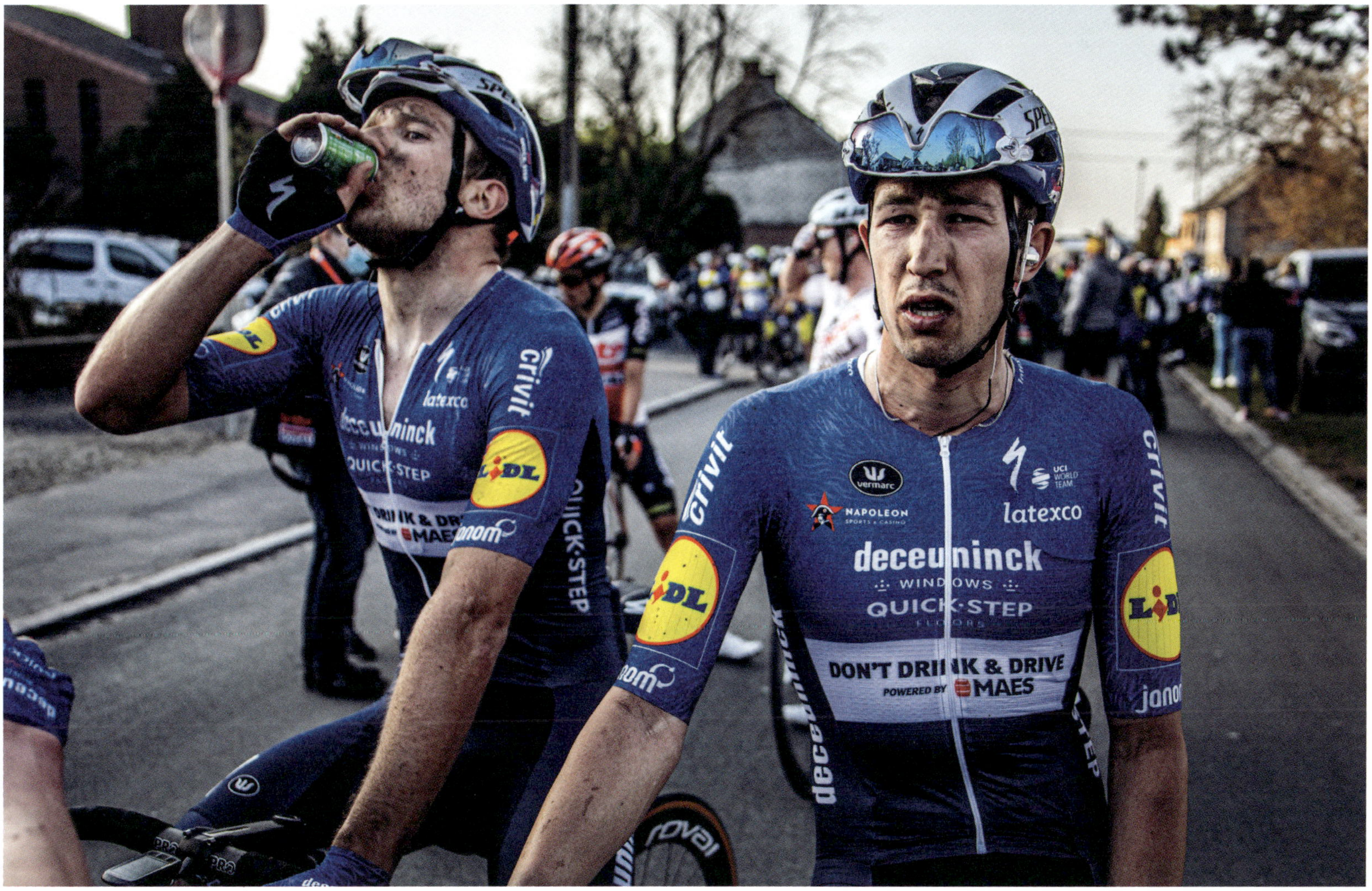
latexco
QUICK·STEP
crivit
NAPOLEON
vermarc
POWERED BY MAES

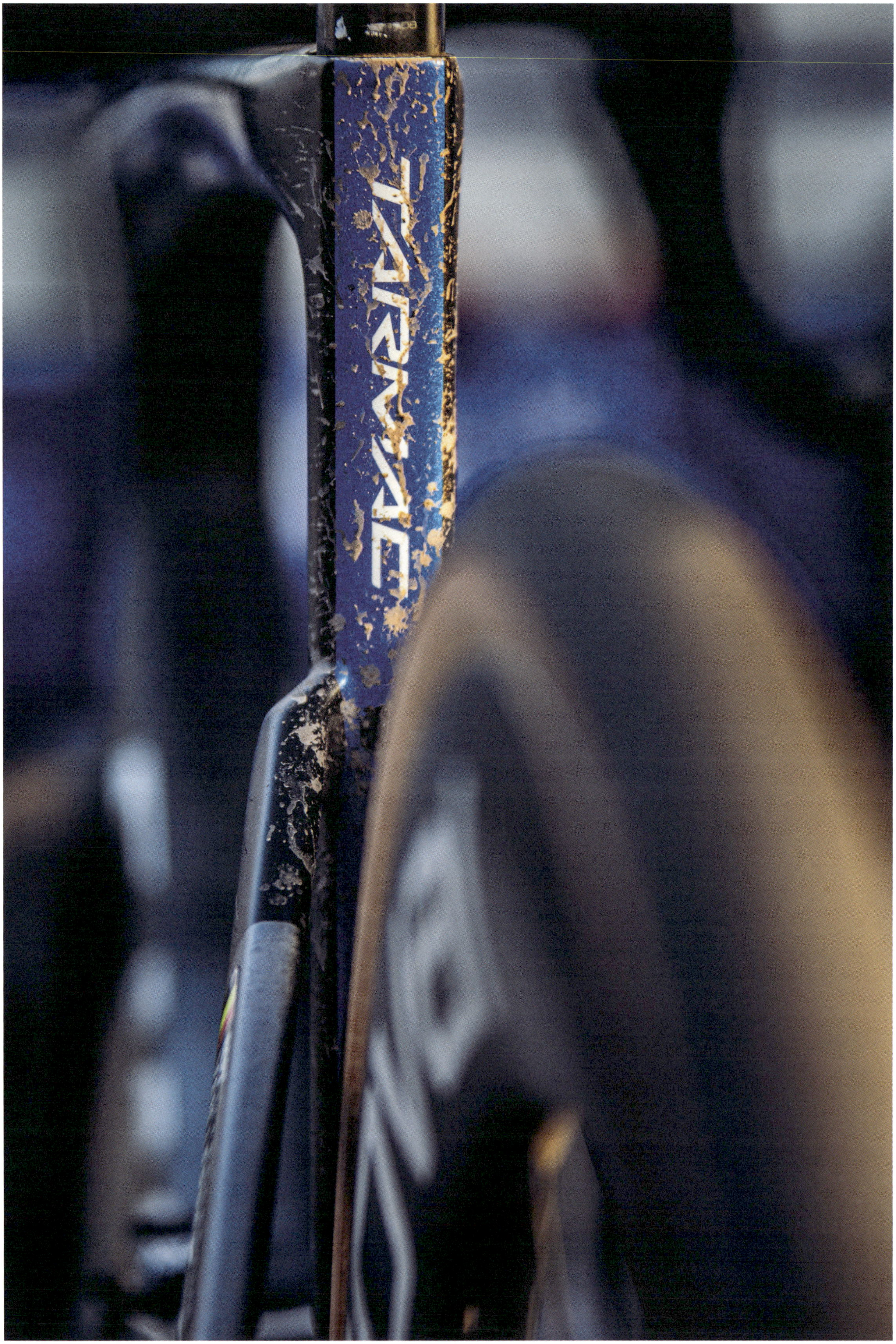
TARMAC

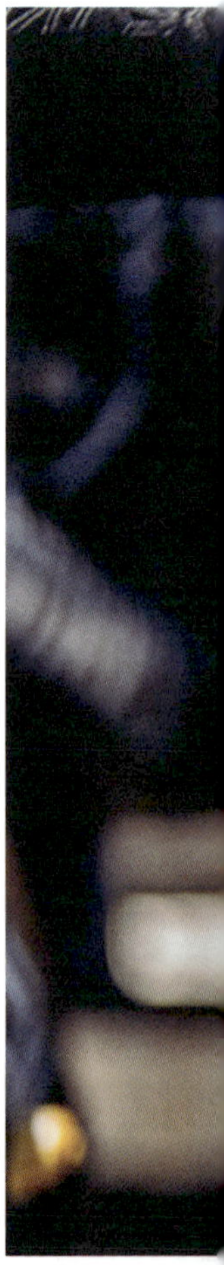

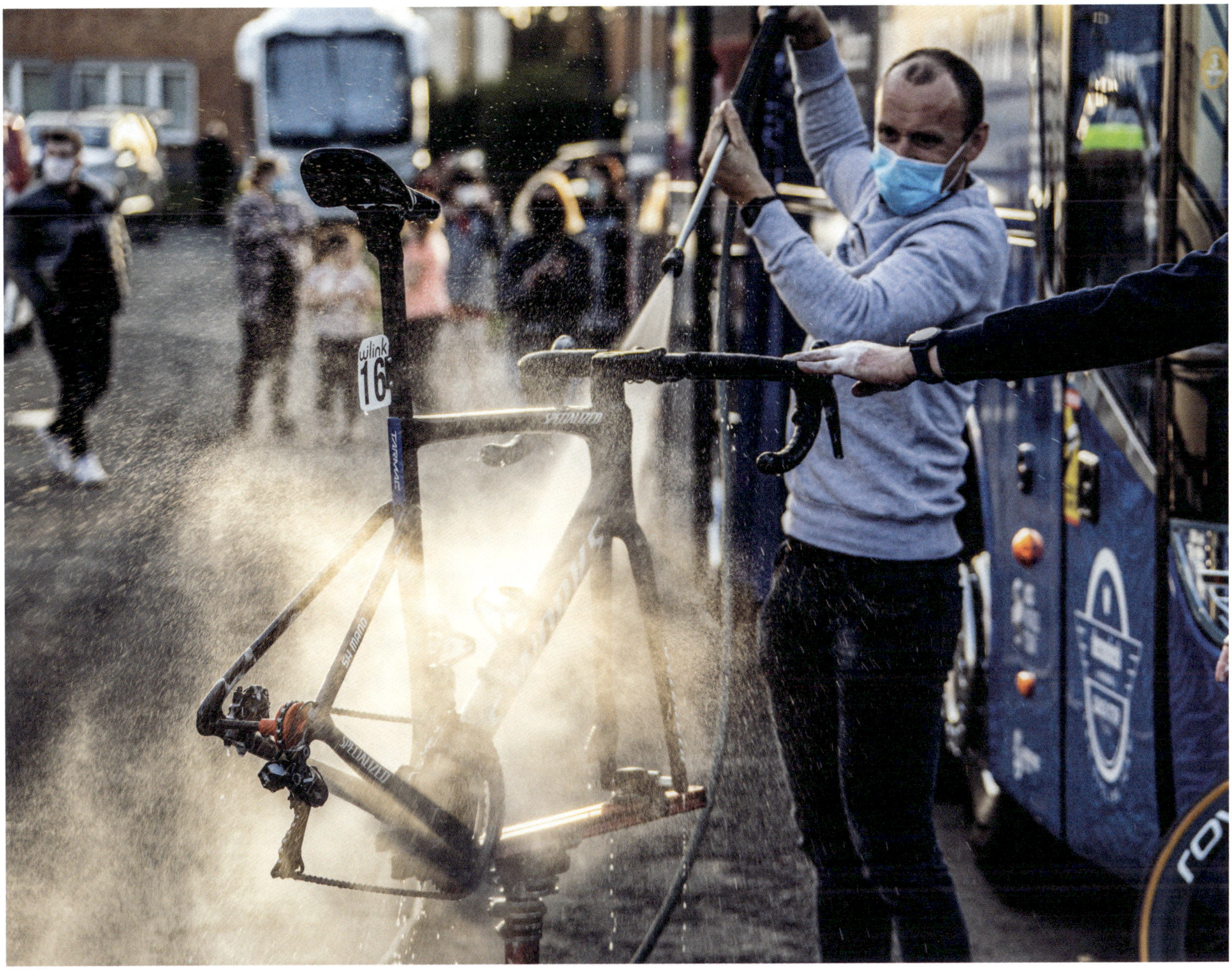
wilink
16
SPECIALIZED

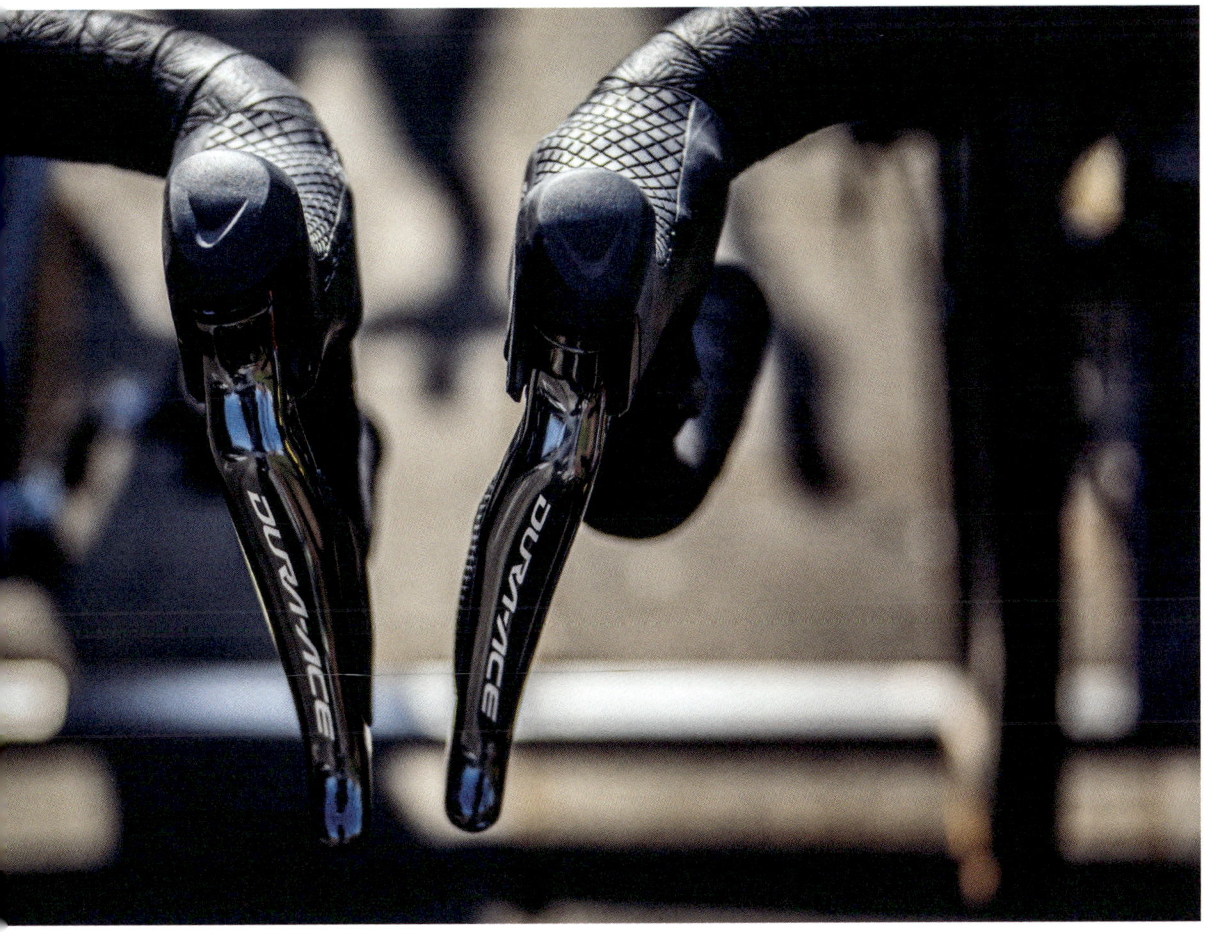
DURA-ACE
DURA-ACE

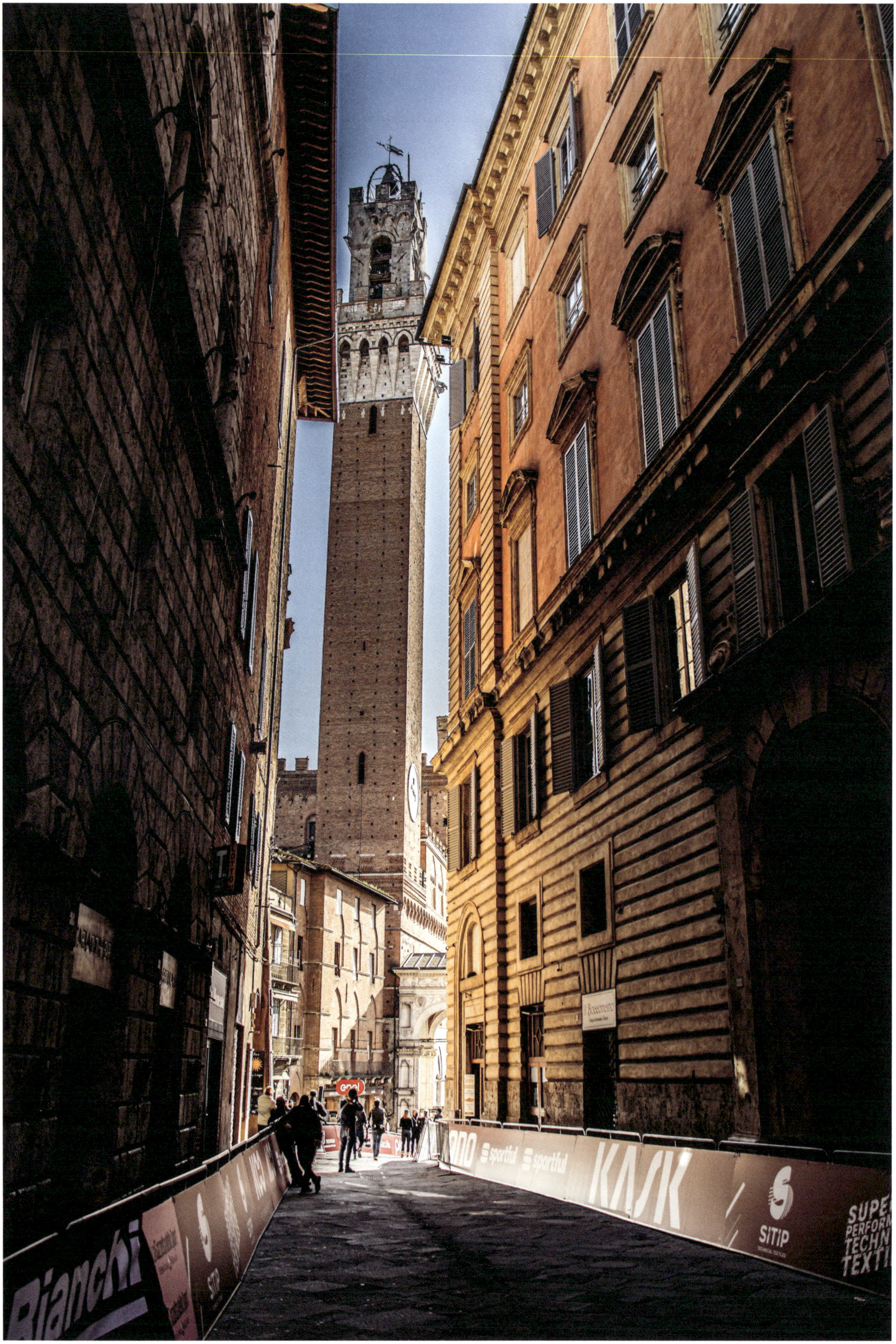
Bianchi
sportful
sportful
KASK
SITIP

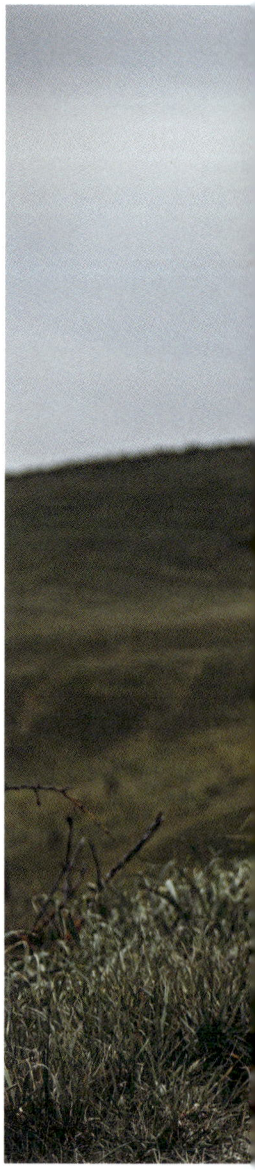

Wordt deze wedstrijd het zesde klassieke wielermonument? In de hoofden van de renners is dat al een tijdje zo. De Strade Bianche in het wondermooie Toscane, met start en aankomst in Siena. Relatief kort (184 kilometer) en zonder grote beklimmingen. Maar nooit vlak, wel met enkele pittige hellingen. En vooral elf iconische gravelstroken, in het vakjargon *sterrati* genoemd. Alsof dat nog niet volstaat, is de laatste klim naar het Piazza del Campo in Siena van een goddelijke schoonheid, maar o zo zwaar. Dat was op zaterdag 6 maart 2021 niet anders.

Will this race become cycling's sixth Monument? In the minds of the riders, it has been for some time. The Strade Bianche takes place in beautiful Tuscany, with its start and finish in Siena. Relatively short (184 km) and without big climbs. But it's never flat and features some tough challenges. Above all, it offers 11 iconic gravel stretches, officially called *sterrati*. As if that wasn't enough, the final climb to Siena's Piazza del Campo is divinely beautiful... but very hard. This was no different on Saturday 6 March 2021.

Cette course deviendra-t-elle le sixième monument du cyclisme ? En tout cas, dans l'esprit des coureurs, elle l'est déjà depuis longtemps. Les Strade Bianche ont lieu en plein cœur des superbes paysages de Toscane, avec départ et arrivée à Sienne. C'est une course relativement courte (184 km) et sans grandes montées. Le parcours n'est cependant jamais plat et compte quelques passages assez difficiles, mais surtout onze chemins de graviers et de terre blancs emblématiques, appelés *sterrati* dans le jargon. Et pour ajouter à tout cela, la montée finale vers la célèbre Piazza del Campo de Sienne est d'une beauté à couper le souffle, mais extrêmement difficile. Cela s'est encore une fois vu le samedi 6 mars 2021.

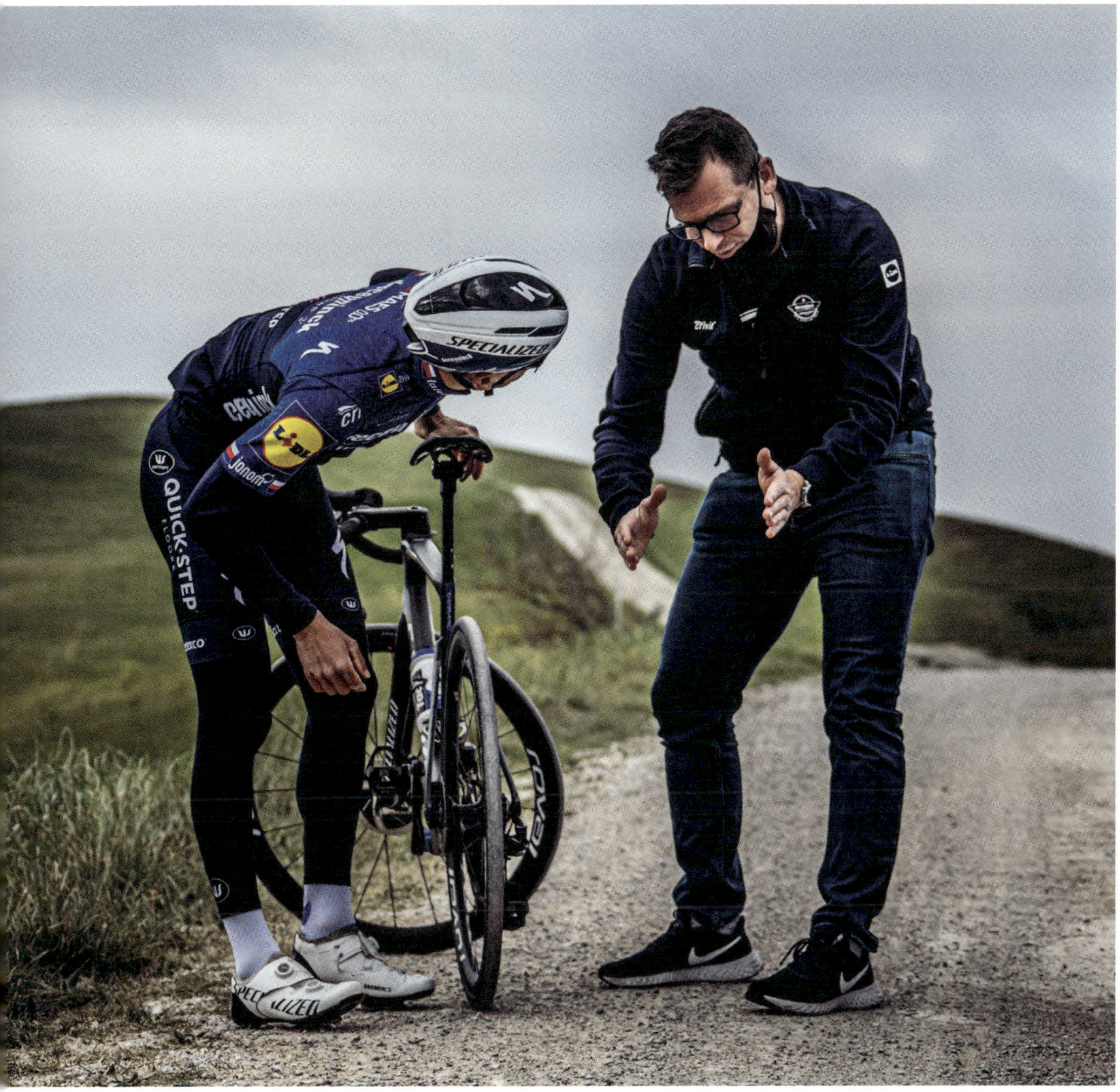

Zdenek Stybar overlegt met mecanicien Kurt Roose.

Zdenek Stybar consults with mechanic Kurt Roose.

Zdenek Stybar discute avec son mécanicien Kurt Roose. ◀

Zicht op de Torre del Mangia, de klokkentoren die heerst over het mythische Piazza del Campo, de iconische finish van Strade Bianche.

View of the Torre del Mangia, the bell tower that reigns over the mythical Piazza del Campo, the iconic finish of Strade Bianche.

Vue de la Torre del Mangia, le clocher qui surplombe la mythique Piazza del Campo où est installée la ligne d'arrivée iconique des Strade Bianche. ◀◀

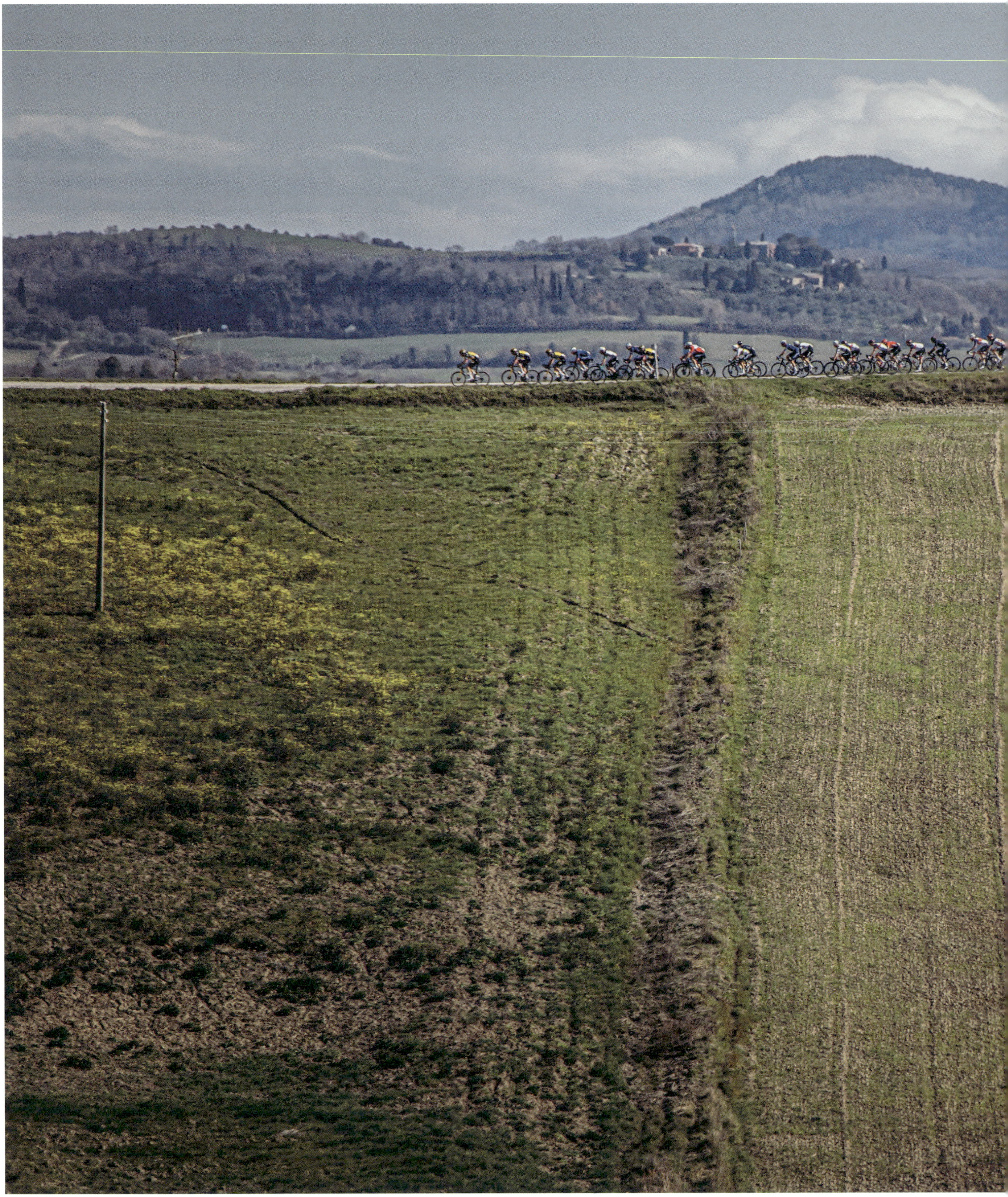

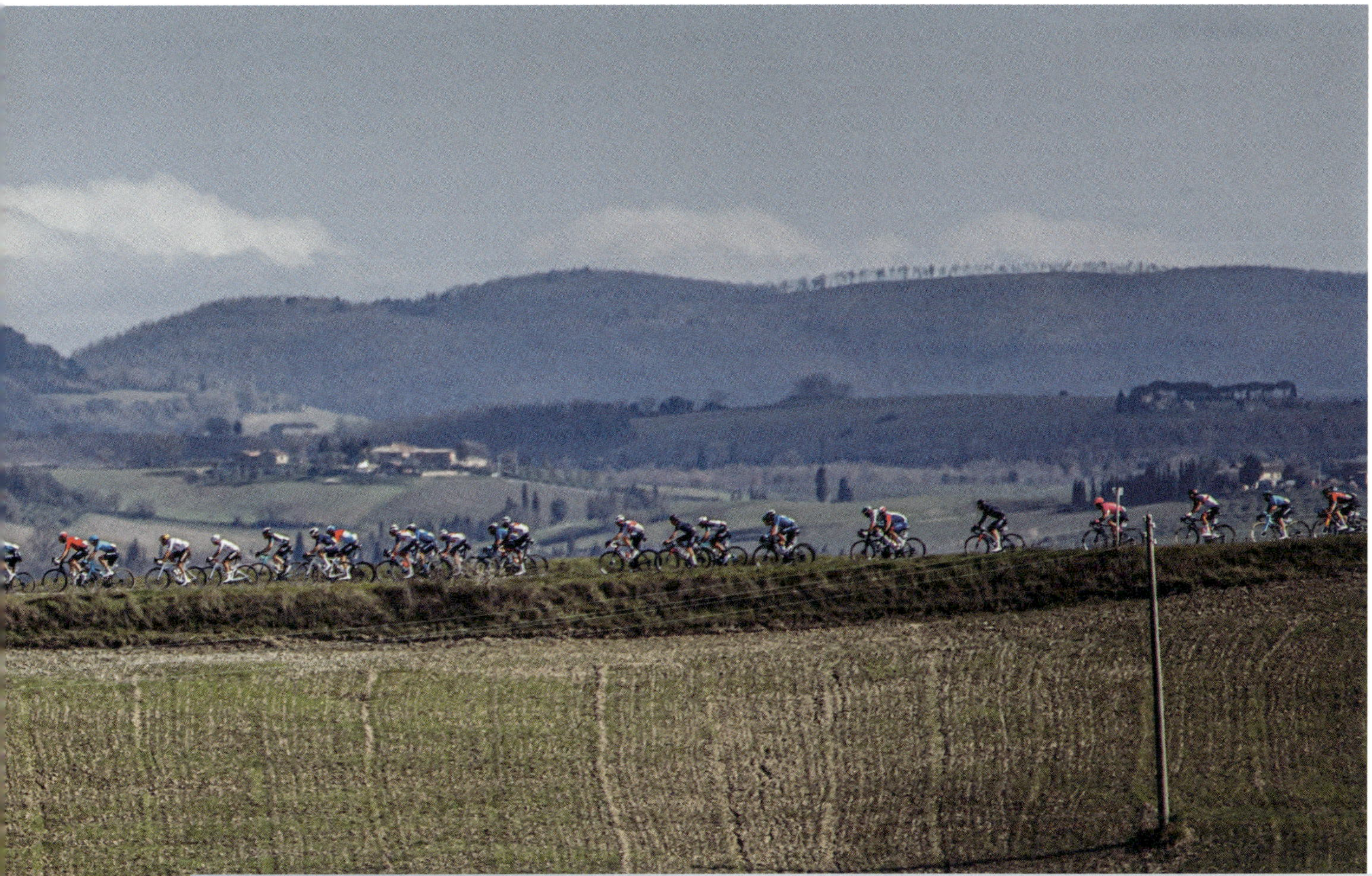

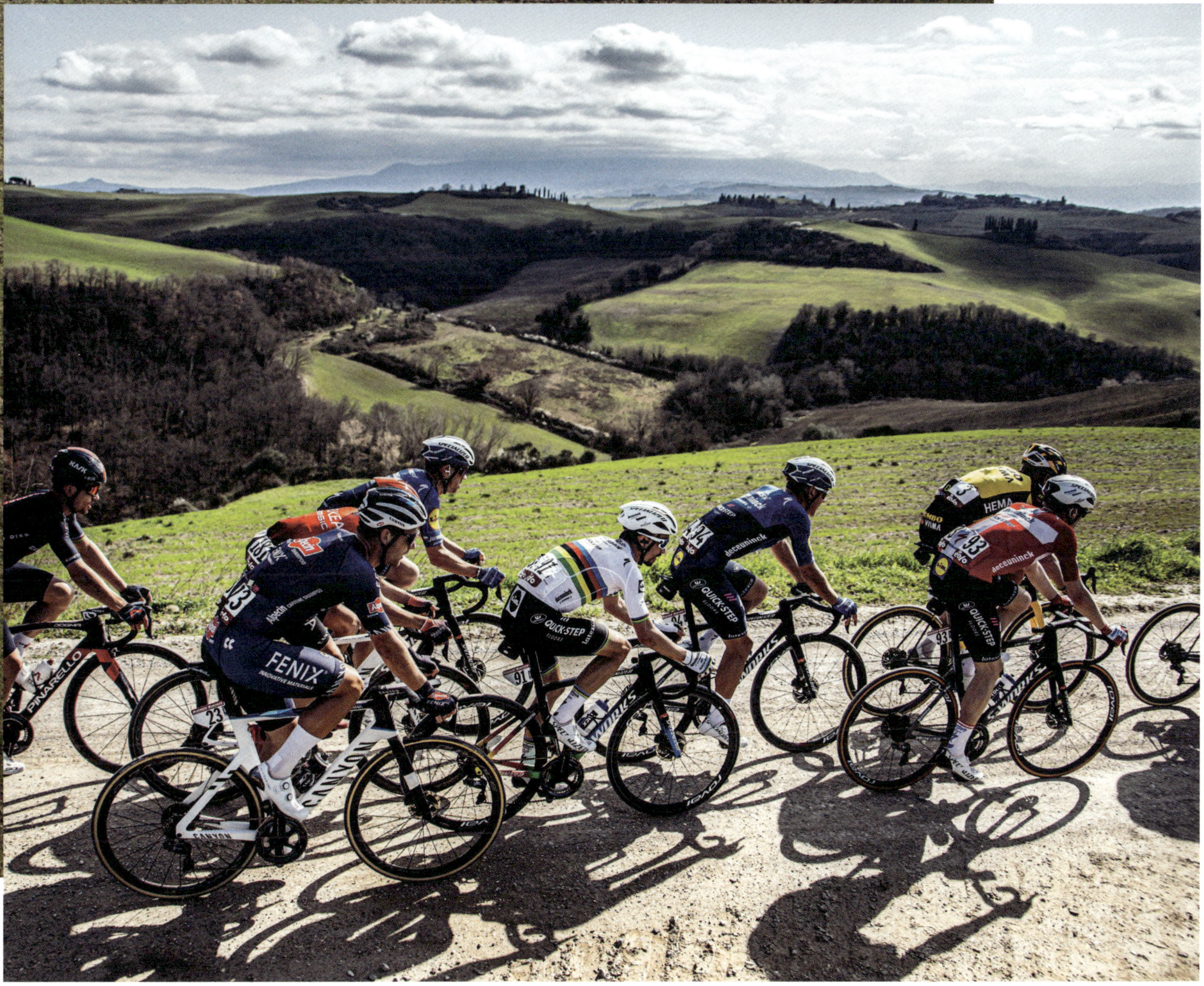
FENIX

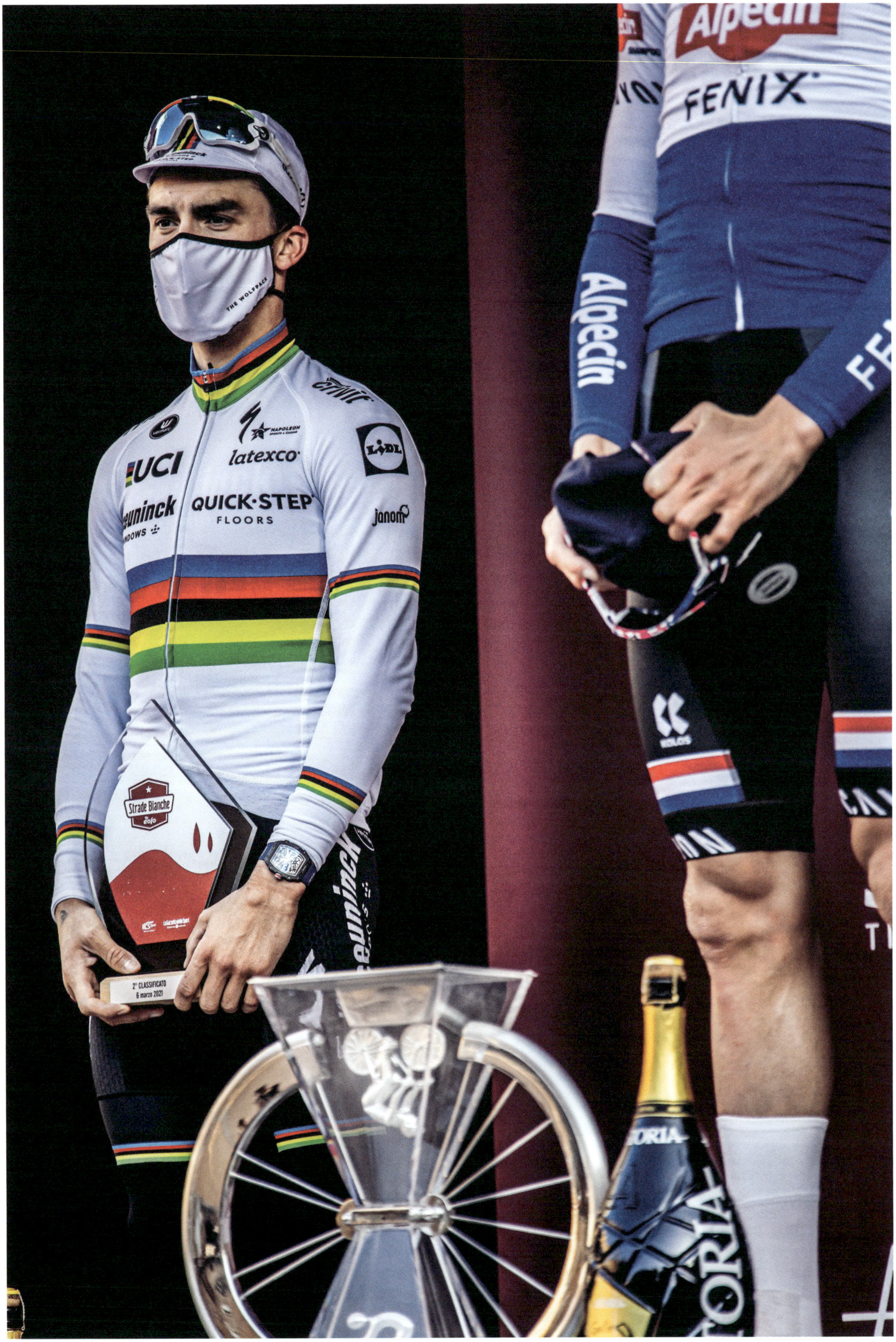
UCI
latexco
QUICK-STEP
FLOORS
janom
Alpecin
FENIX
Alpecin
Strade Bianche
2° CLASSIFICATO
6 marzo 2021

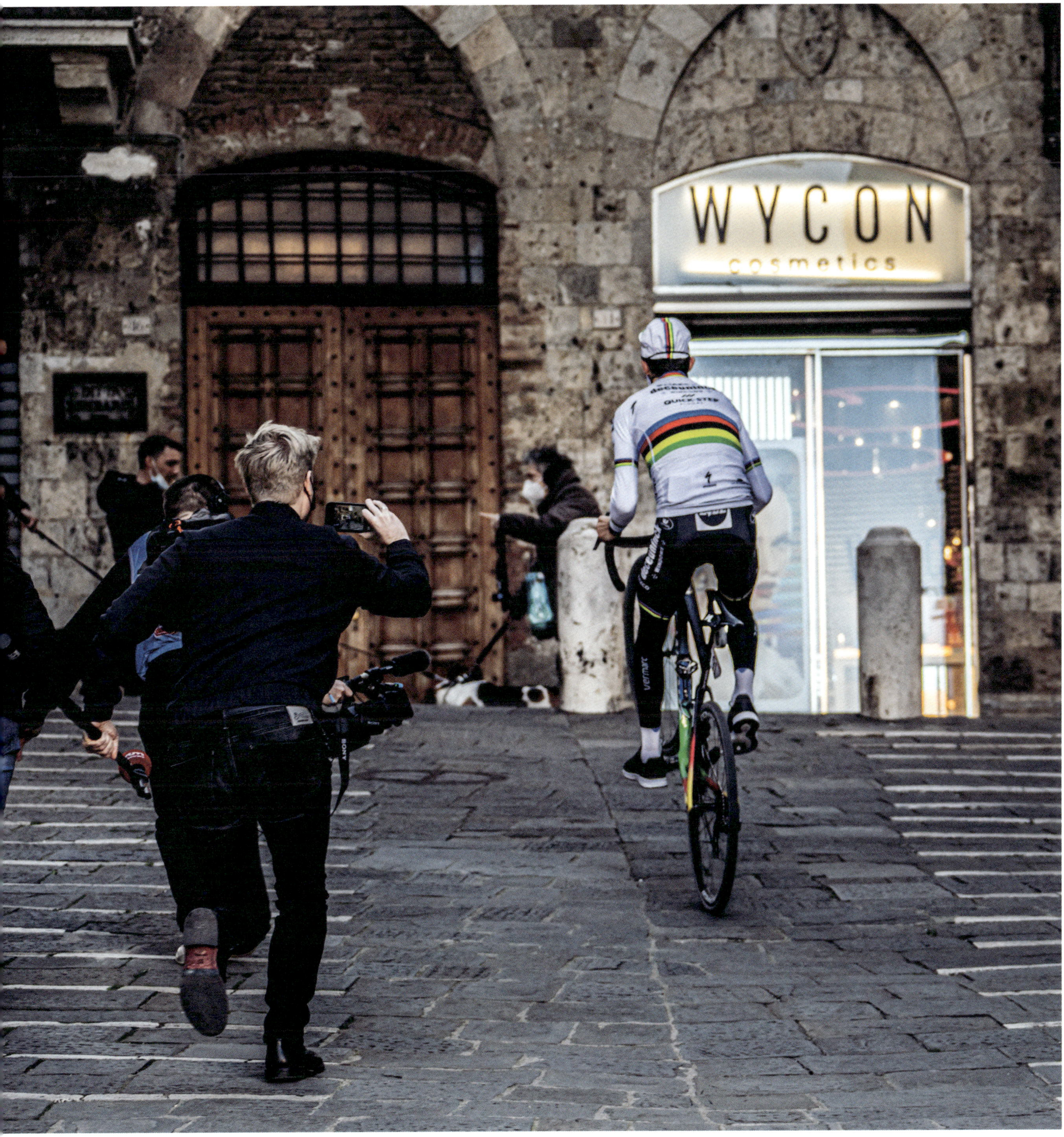

SIENA, 06.03.2021

Julian Alaphilippe lijkt weg te dromen bij zijn tweede plaats. De laatste push van Mathieu van der Poel snoerde sterke Julian de mond. Hij werd tweede op 5 seconden van MVDP.

Julian Alaphilippe seems to be dreaming away at his second place. Mathieu van der Poel's final push silenced a strong Julian. He finished runner-up, 5 seconds behind MVDP.

Julian Alaphilippe perdu dans ses pensées après être arrivé deuxième. Le sprint final de Mathieu van der Poel a eu raison de lui. Il a terminé deuxième, 5 secondes derrière MVDP. ◀

GP INDUSTRIA & ARTIGIANATO 07.03.2021

Wat een fijne verrassing! Mauri Vansevenant troeft grote namen als Bauke Mollema, Mikel Landa en Nairo Quintana af in de sprint van de GP Industria & Artigianato in Larciano, Centraal-Toscane.

'Komaan, broere, riêjen!'

Het is een quote van zus Steffi Vansevenant. Ze schreeuwde vanuit de ouderlijke living broer Mauri naar zijn eerste profzege. De zoon van ex-prof Wim Vansevenant keerde met een bijzondere prijs terug naar de teambus: 14 kilogram mortadella.

What a pleasant surprise. On Sunday, 7 March 2021, Mauri Vansevenant beats big names such as Bauke Mollema, Mikel Landa, and Nairo Quintana in the sprint of the GP Industria & Artigianato in Larciano, right in the middle of Tuscany.

"Komaan, broere, riêjen!"

In the words of Steffi Vansevenant, Mauri's sister: "Come on, brother, ride!" From their parents' living room, she cheered her brother Mauri towards his first professional victory. The son of former pro Wim Vansevenant returned to the team bus with a special prize: 14 kg of mortadella.

Quelle agréable surprise ! Mauri Vansevenant a devancé des grands noms comme Mollema, Landa et Quintana dans le sprint du GP Industria & Artigianato ou « Grand Prix de l'industrie et de l'artisanat » à Larciano, en Toscane centrale.

« Komaan, broere, riêjen! »

Ces mots sont ceux de la sœur du coureur, Steffi Vansevenant : « Allez, frangin, pédale ! » Elle les a criés depuis le salon familial pour encourager son frère Mauri à remporter sa première victoire professionnelle. Le fils de l'ex-coureur professionnel Wim Vansevenant a regagné le bus de l'équipe avec un prix spécial : 14 kg de mortadelle.

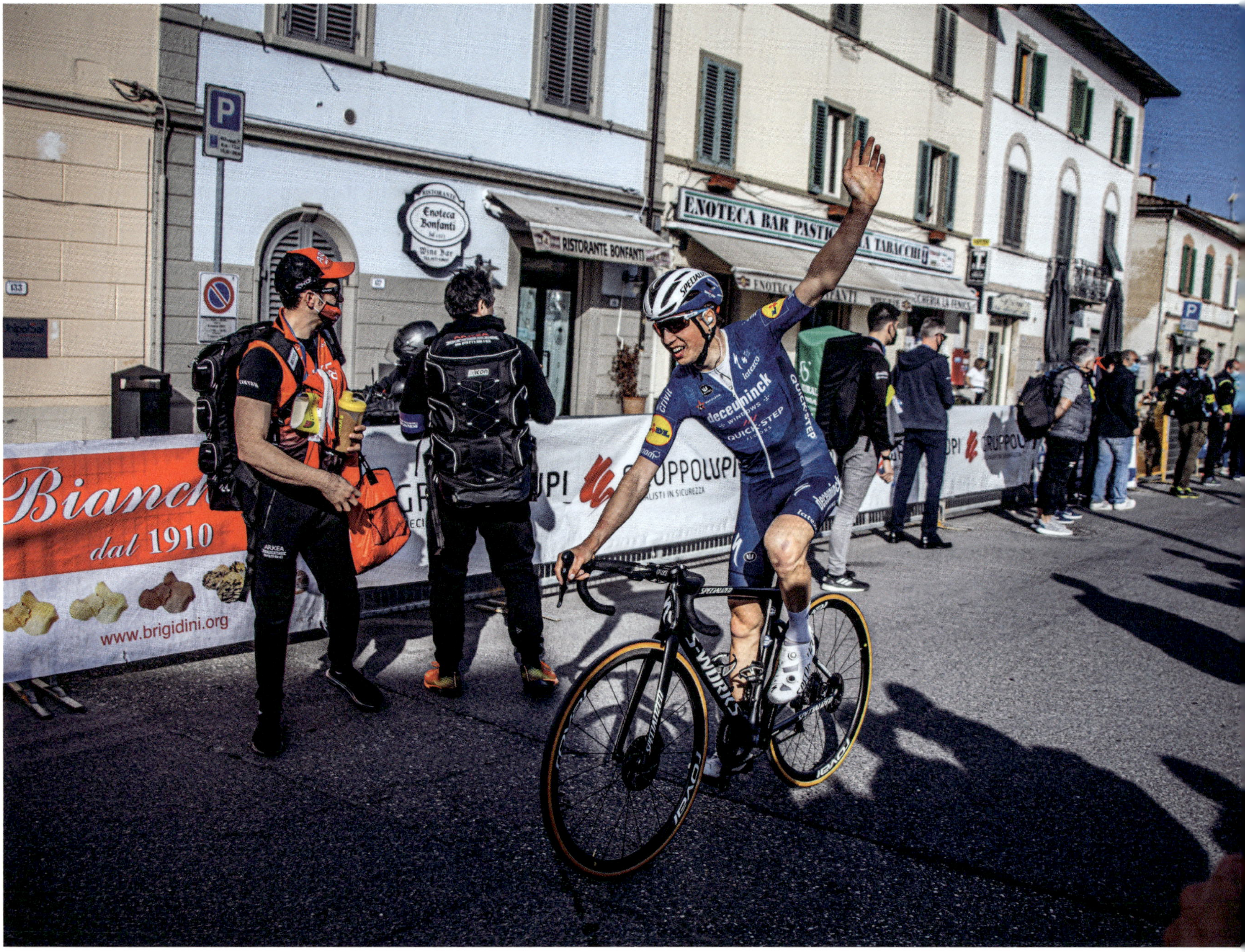

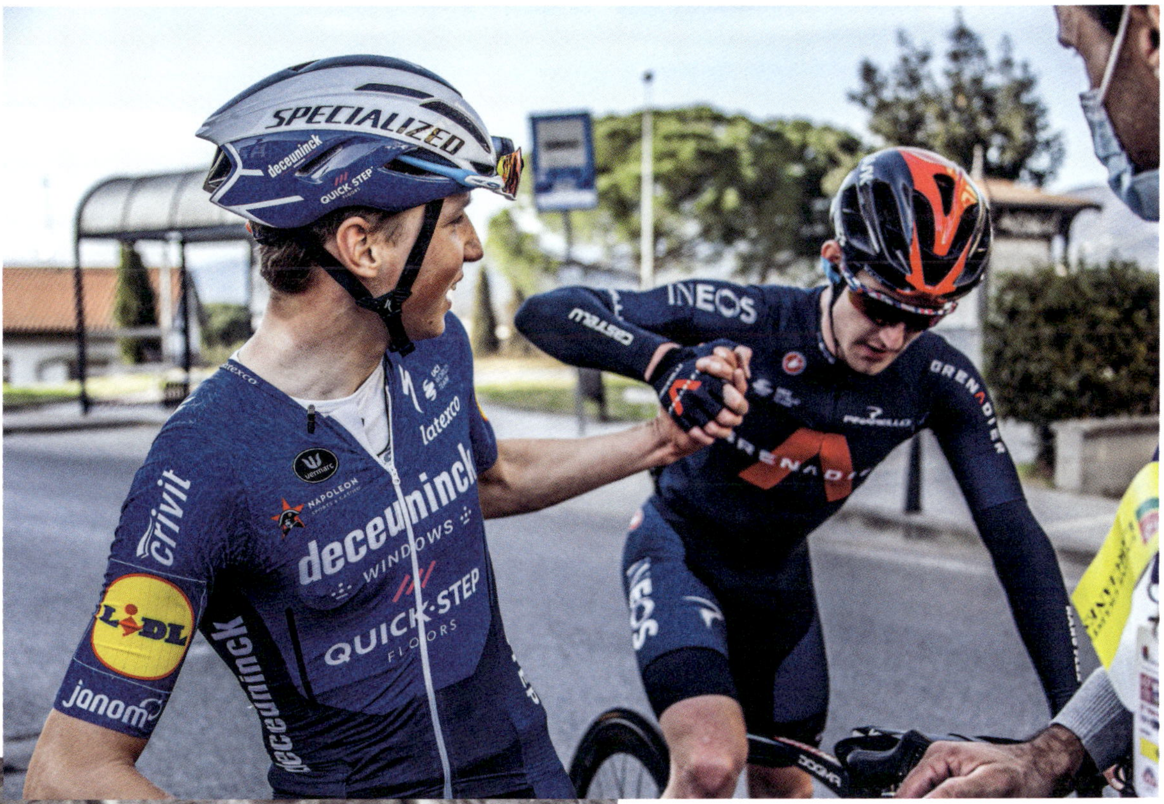

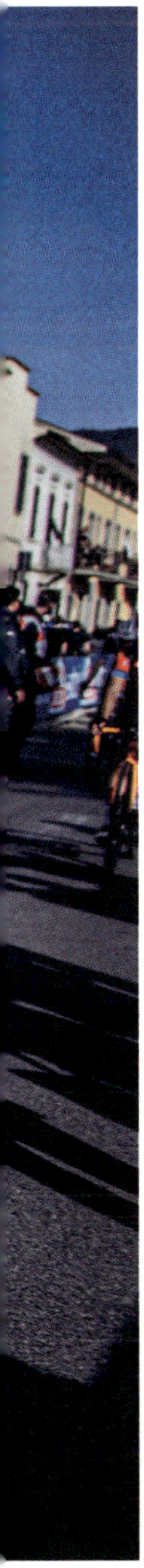

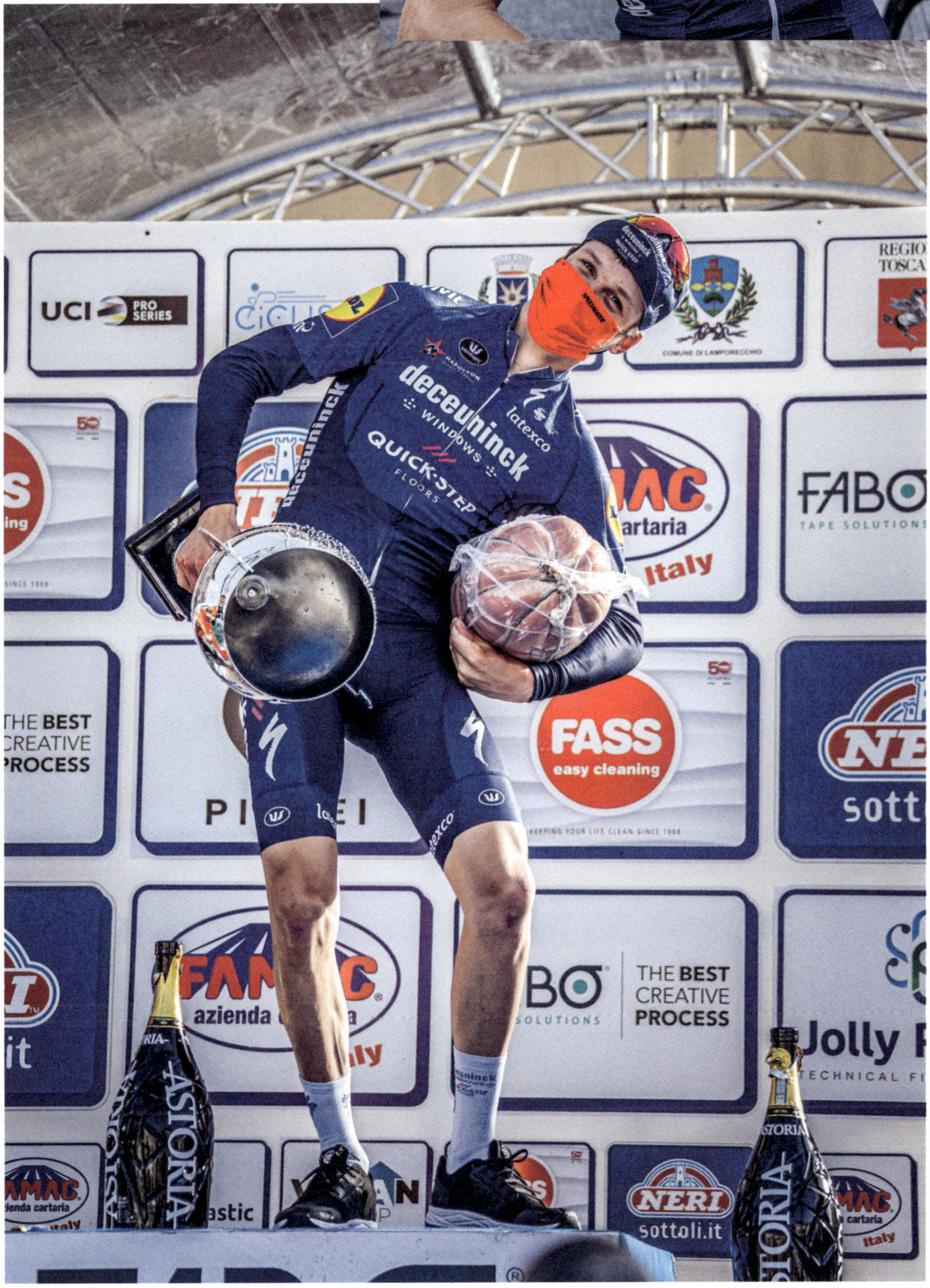

Koersen winnen, dat is lastig. Maar trofeeën torsen, dát is pas een karwei. In zijn rechterhand de veel te grote zegebeker. Niettemin klein bier in vergelijking met de mortadella in zijn linkerhand: 14 kilogram lokale salamispecialiteit. Naar verluidt heeft de ploeg er drie maanden van gegeten.

Winning races is difficult. But carrying trophies, that's a real chore. In his right hand, the oversized trophy – a small weight to carry compared to the mortadella in his left hand. No less than 14 kg of local salami. The team is said to have eaten from it for three months.

Remporter une course est difficile. Mais soulever un trophée l'est encore plus. Il tient la coupe bien trop grosse dans sa main droite, mais ce n'est rien à côté de la mortadelle qu'il tient dans sa main gauche : un salami de 14 kg, la spécialité locale. Il paraît que l'équipe en a mangé pendant trois mois. ◀

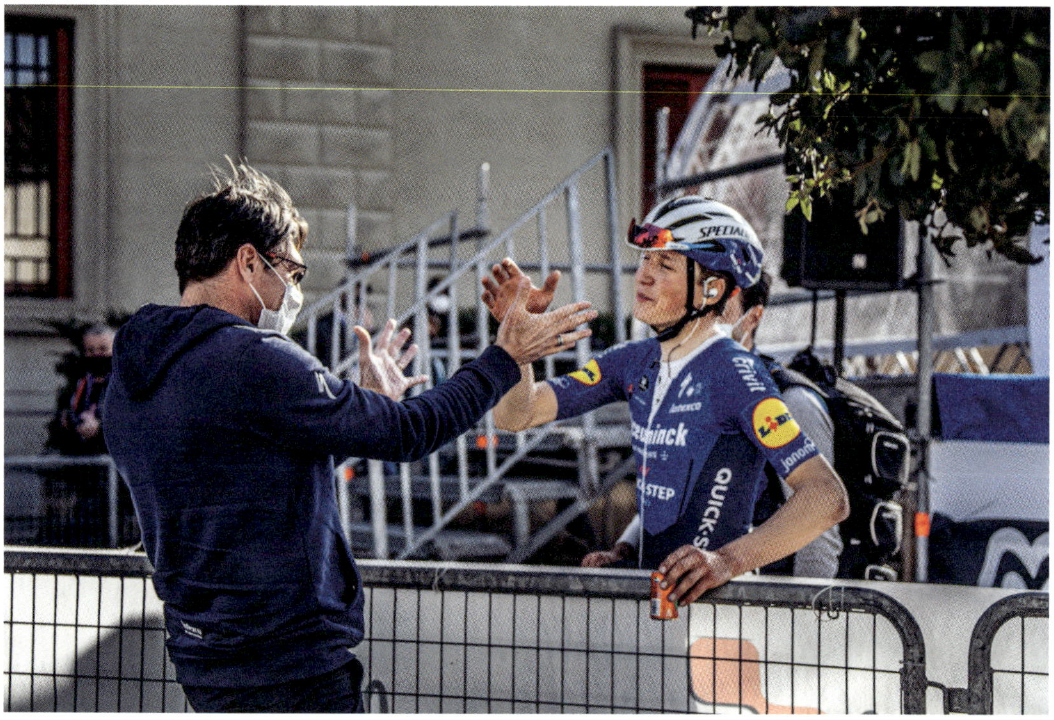

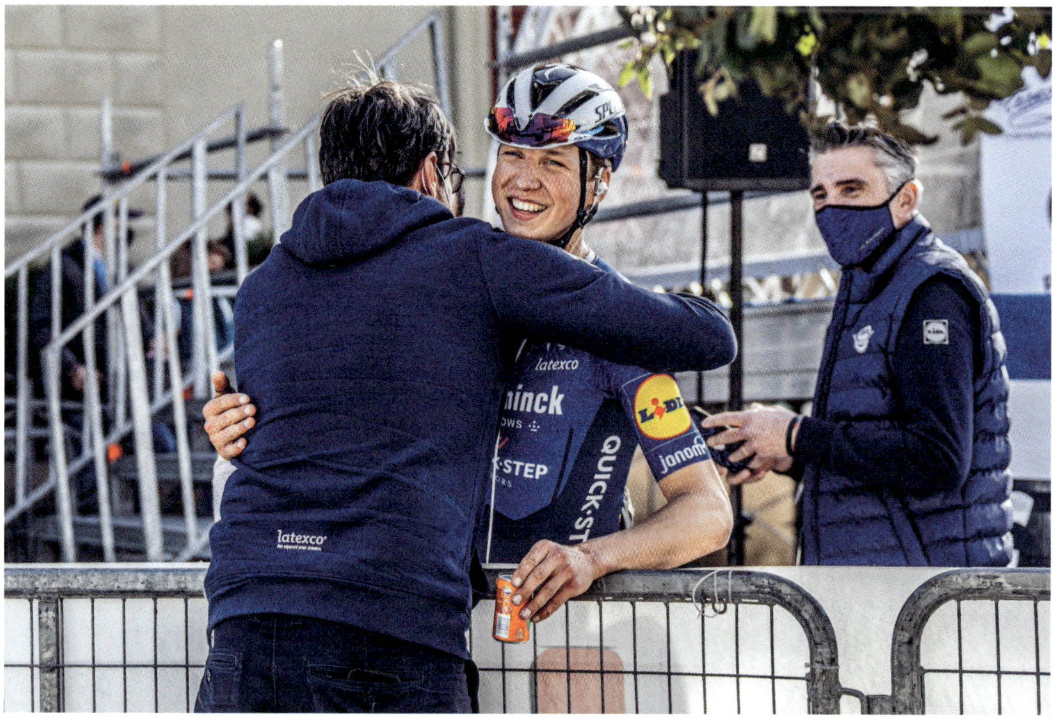

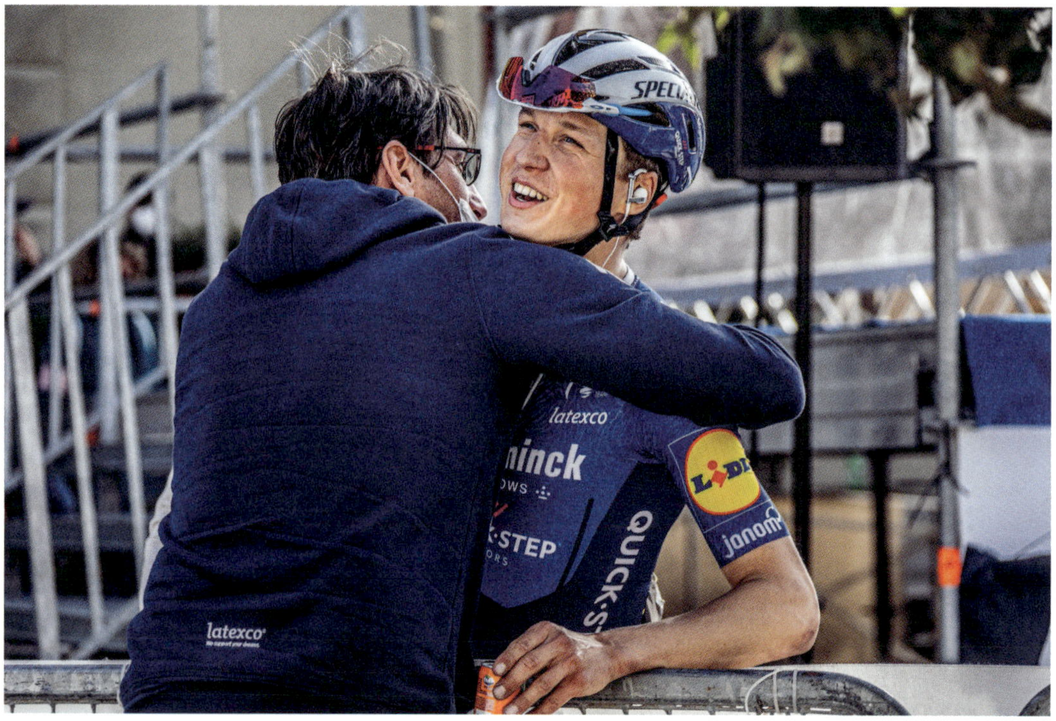

Mauri Vansevenant straalt. Davide Bramati toont zijn blijdschap met een innige knuffel. En Alessandro Tegner geniet van het plaatje.

Mauri Vansevenant is shining. Davide Bramati shows his joy with a heartfelt hug. Alessandro Tegner enjoys the sight.

Mauri Vansevenant rayonne. Davide Bramati montre sa joie en le serrant dans ses bras. Et Alessandro Tegner se réjouit de la photo.

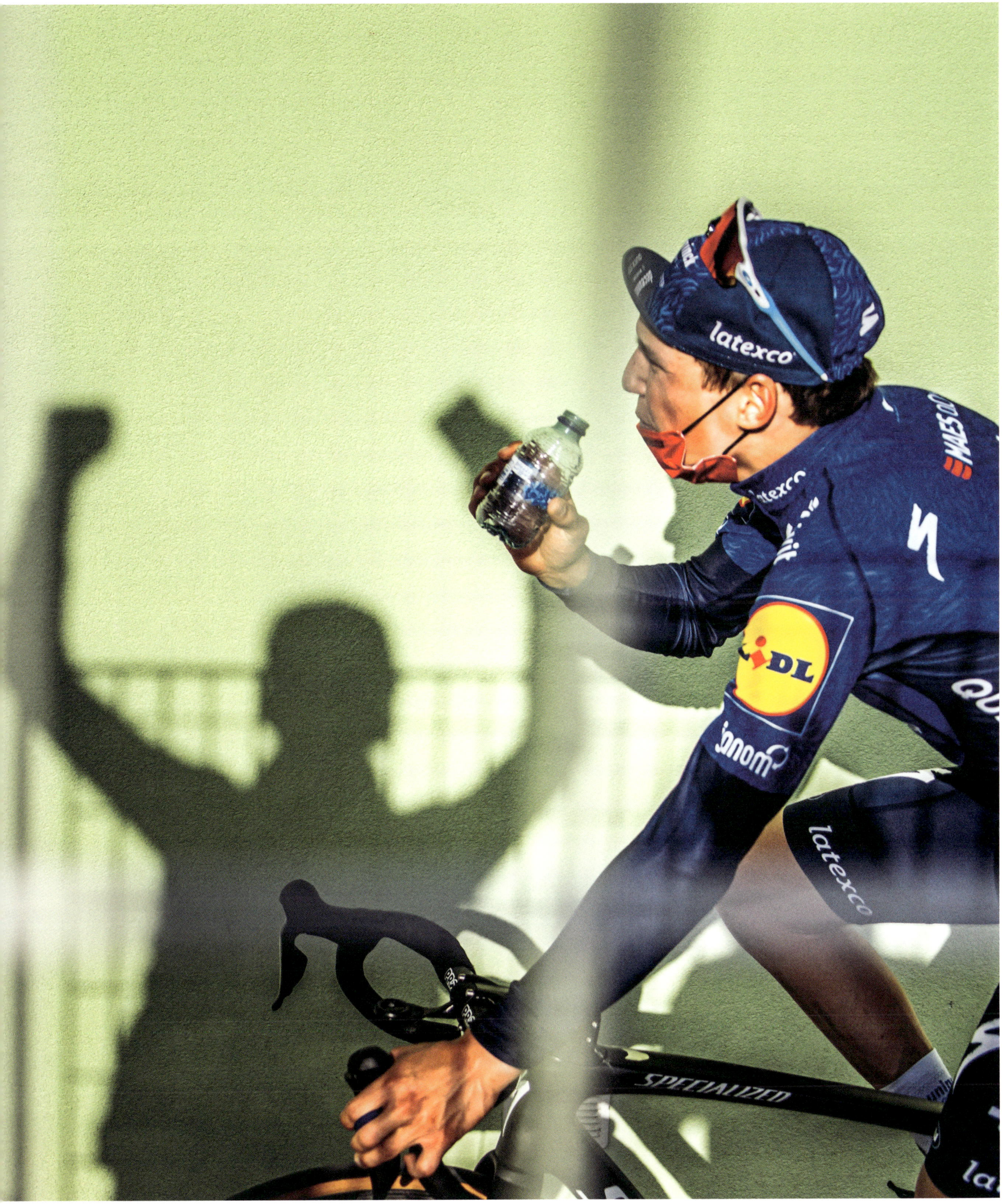
latexco
latexco
SPECIALIZED

TIRRENO-ADRIATICO
10.03 - 16.03.2021

De vloek van de regenboogtrui, daar heeft Julian Alaphilippe geen last van gehad dit seizoen. In de tweede rit van de Tirreno-Adriatico opent hij zijn rekening. Hij klopt op 11 maart 2021 Mathieu van der Poel, Wout van Aert, Tadej Pogacar en het hele pak in een massaprint.

The curse of the rainbow jersey has not affected Julian Alaphilippe this season. In the second stage of the Tirreno-Adriatico, he opens his account. On 11 March 2021, he beats Mathieu van der Poel, Wout van Aert, Tadej Pogacar, and the entire pack in a bunch sprint.

Cette saison, Julian Alaphilippe n'a pas été victime de la malédiction du maillot arc-en-ciel. En effet, il s'impose à la deuxième étape du Tirreno-Adriatico. Le 11 mars 2021, il bat Mathieu van der Poel, Wout van Aert, Tadej Pogacar et les autres dans un sprint du peloton.

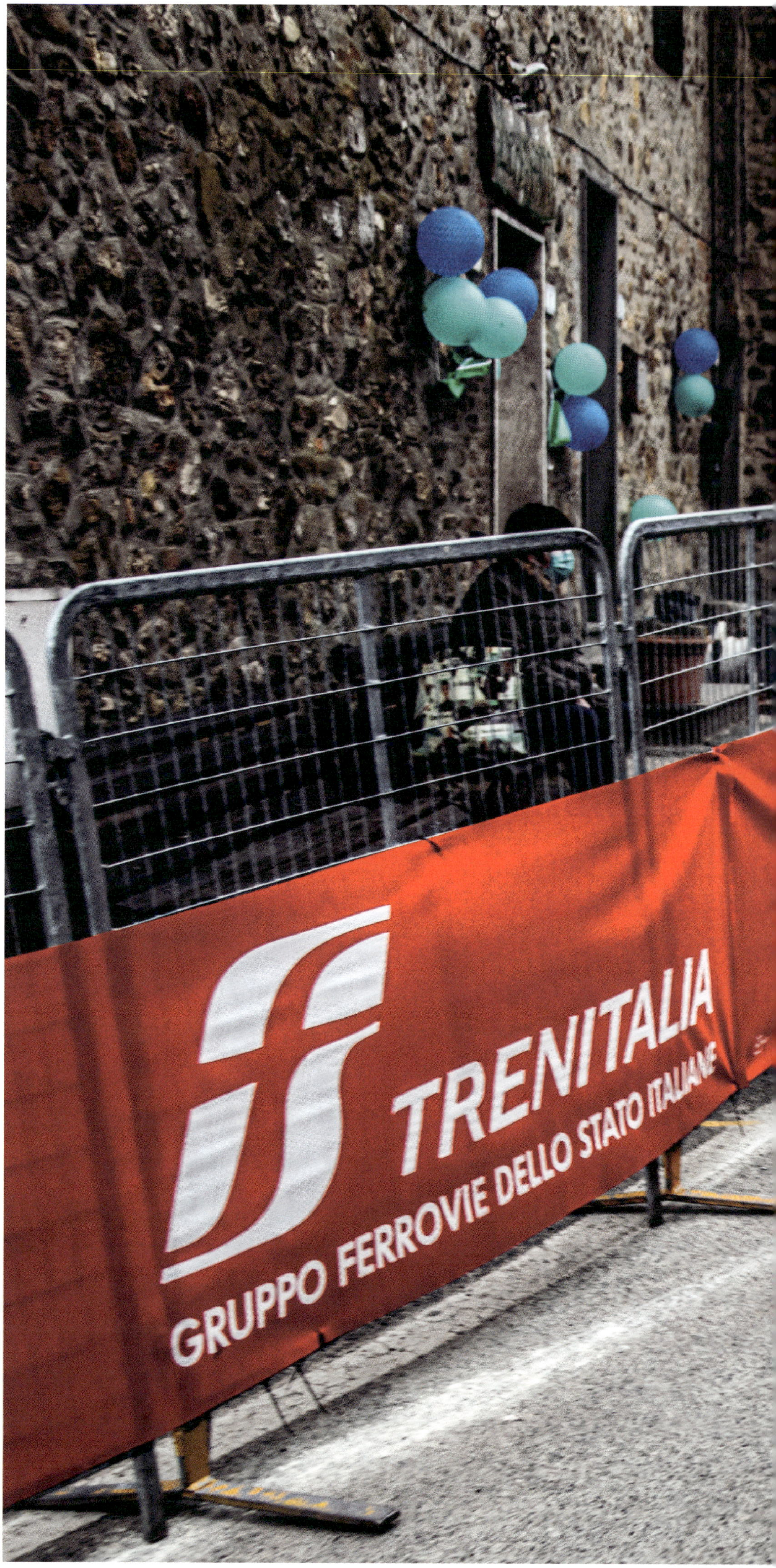

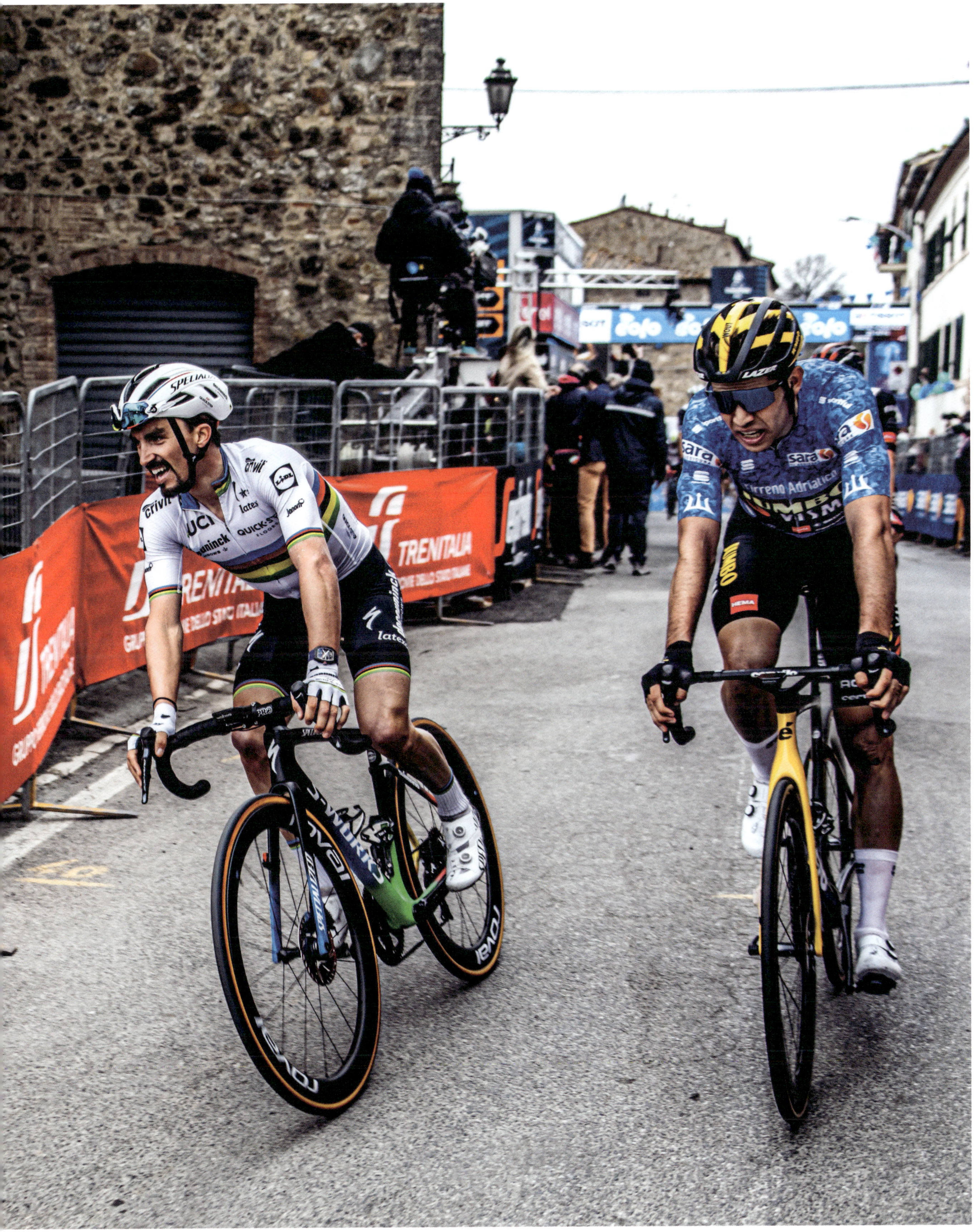
TRENITALIA

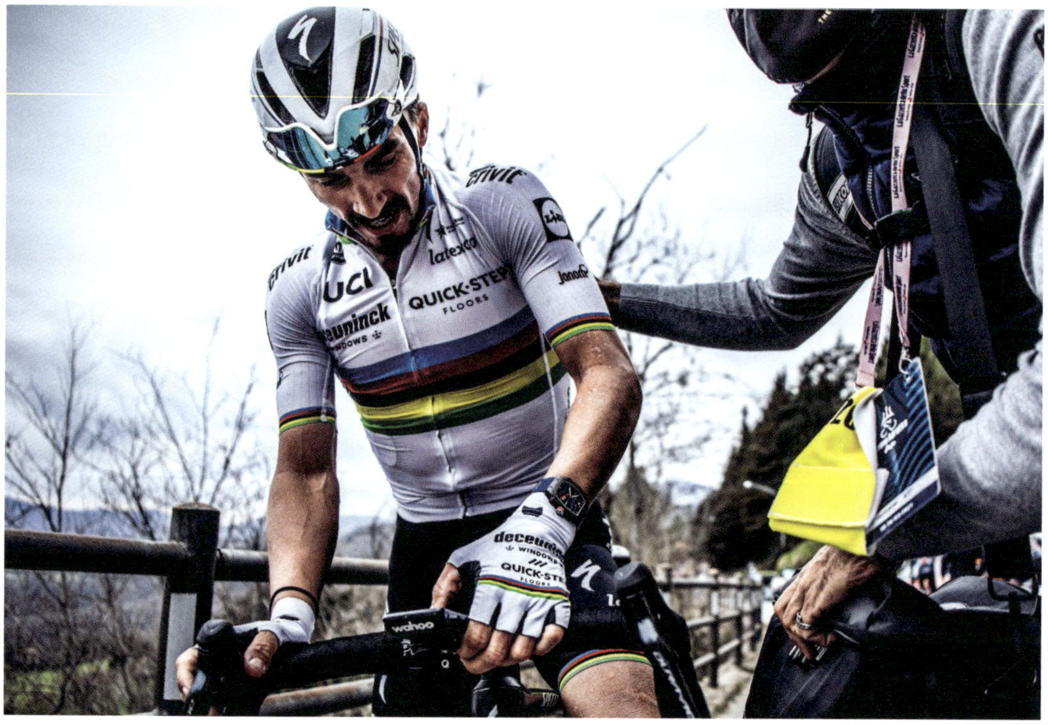
UCI
QUICK-STEP
FLOORS
latexco
wahoo

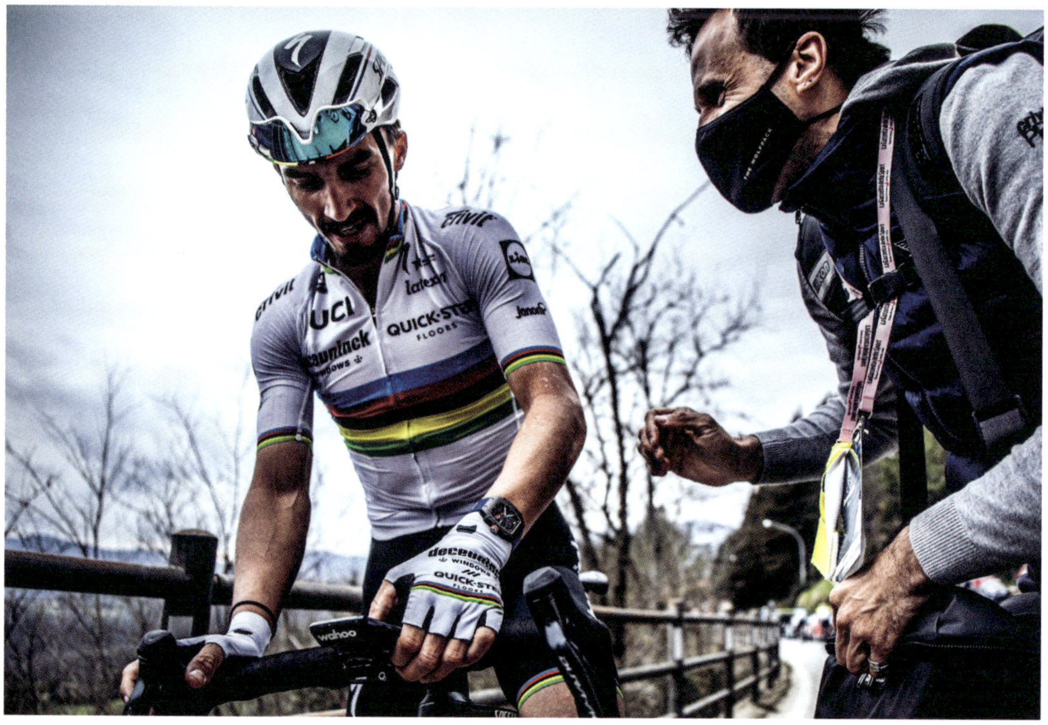
UCI
QUICK-STEP
FLOORS
wahoo

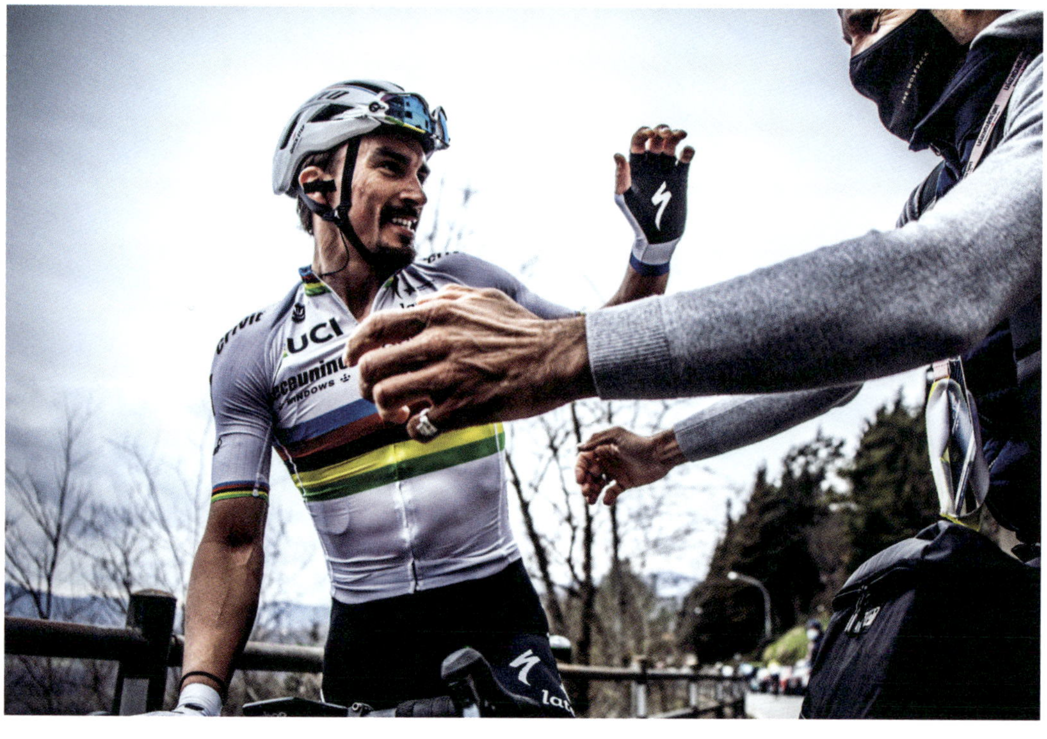
UCI

CHIUSDINO, 11.03.2021

Julian Alaphilippe hijgt uit in de armen van masseur Yankee Germano, die zijn euforie nauwelijks kan verbergen achter zijn mondmasker.

Julian Alaphilippe gasps in the arms of masseur Yankee Germano, who can hardly hide his euphoria behind his mask.

Julian Alaphilippe, à bout de souffle, dans les bras du masseur Yankee Germano, qui a du mal à cacher son euphorie derrière son masque.

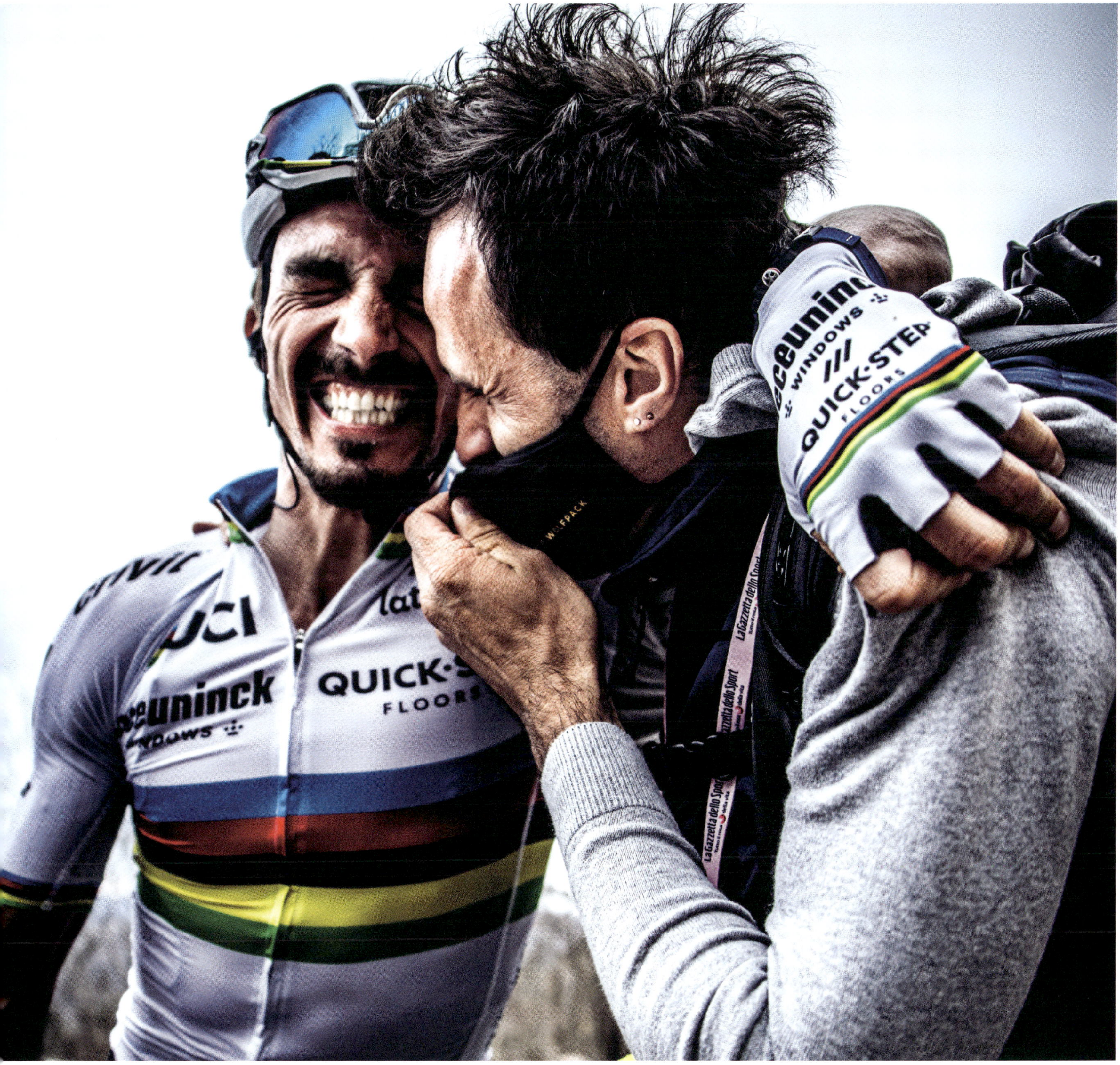

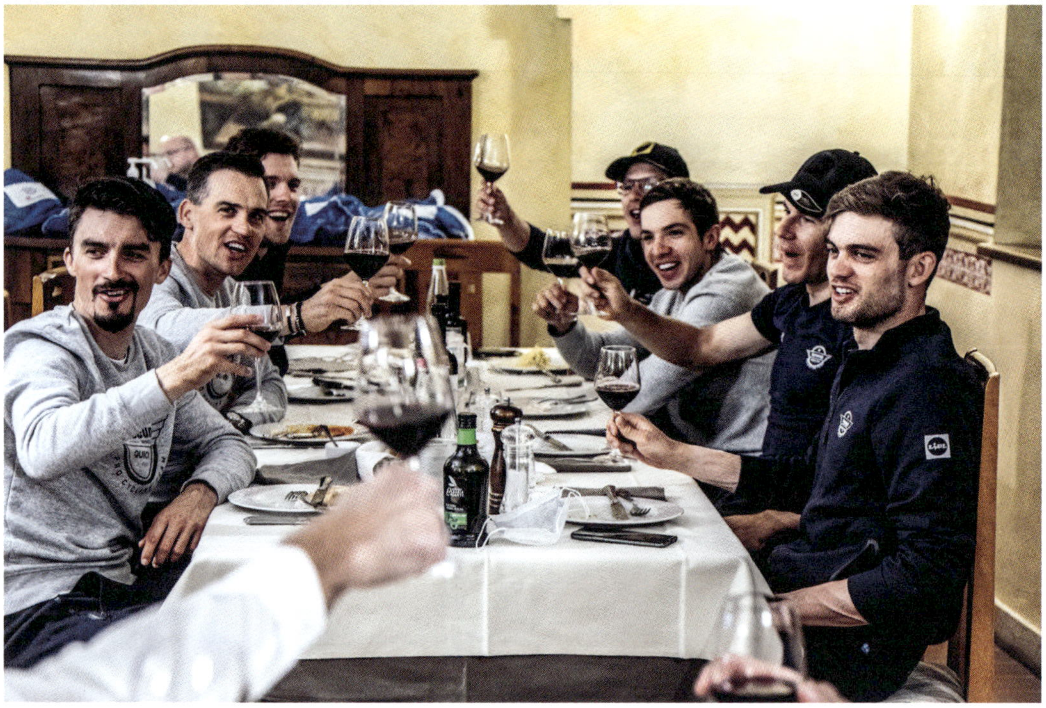

Feest aan tafel. En daar hoort een zuinig glas goede rode wijn bij. V.l.n.r.: Julian Alaphilippe, Zdenek Stybar, Bert Van Lerberghe, João Almeida, Álvaro Hodeg, Davide Ballerini, Kasper Asgreen.

Party at the table. And that includes a glass of quality red wine. FLTR: Julian Alaphilippe, Zdenek Stybar, Bert Van Lerberghe, João Almeida, Álvaro Hodeg, Davide Ballerini, Kasper Asgreen.

Un véritable festin. Sans oublier un bon verre de vin rouge. Dgàd : Julian Alaphilippe, Zdenek Stybar, Bert Van Lerberghe, João Almeida, Álvaro Hodeg, Davide Ballerini, Kasper Asgreen. ◀

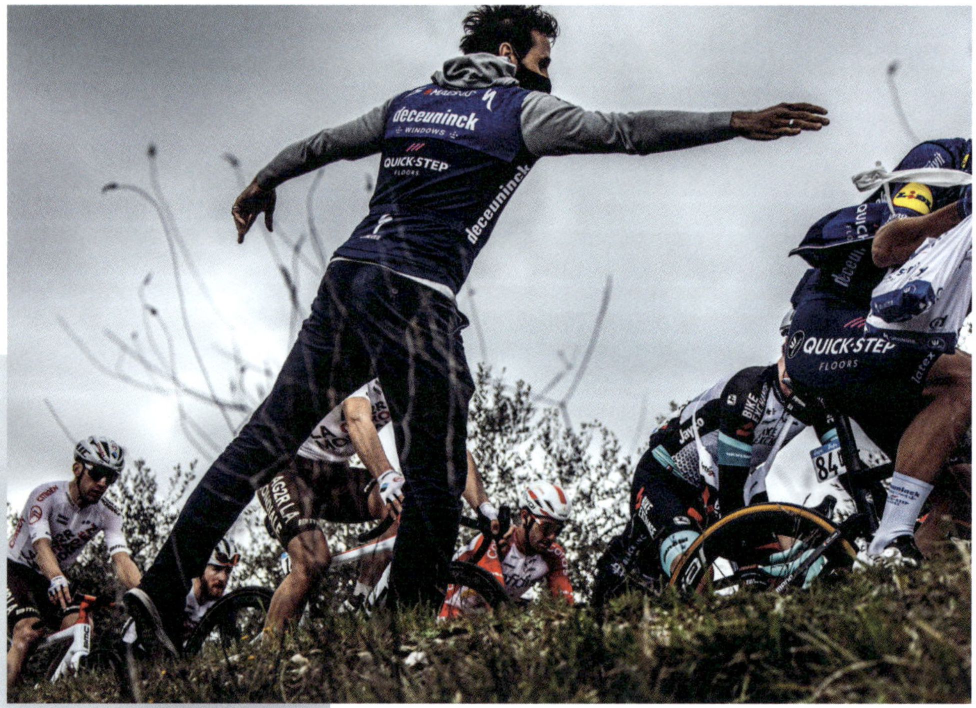

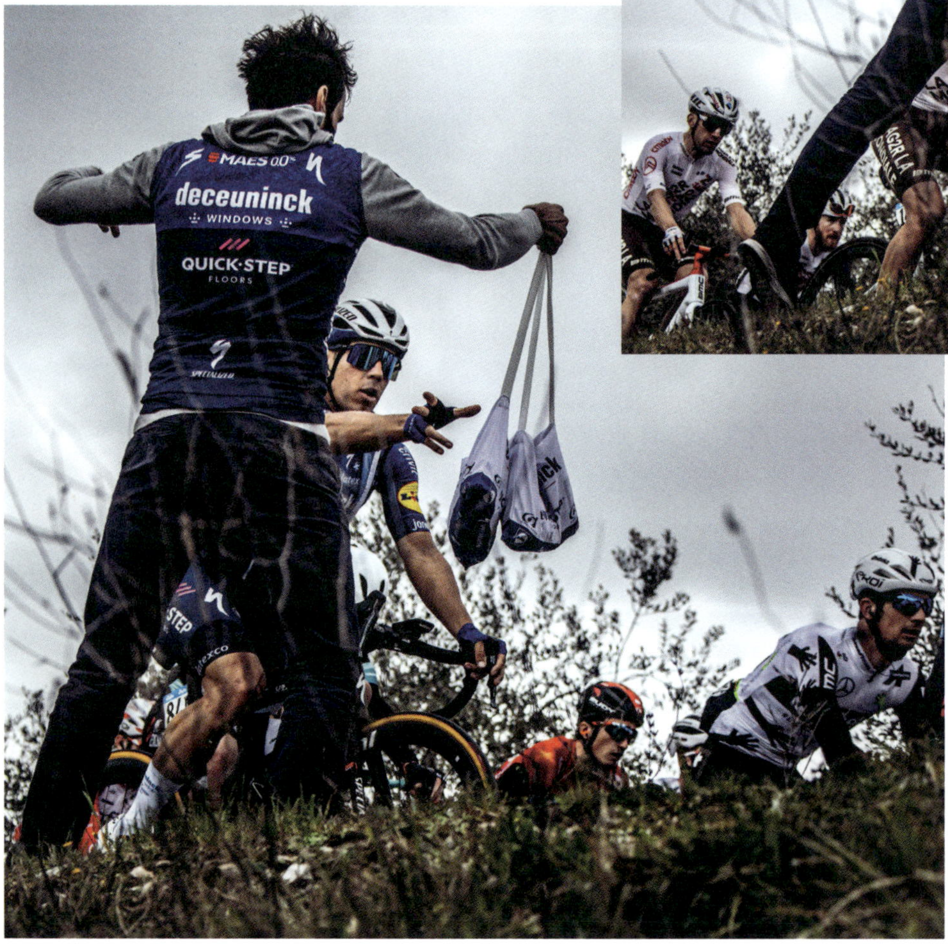

Na de derde etappe in de Tirreno-Adriatico: Zdenek Stybar en João Almeida balen. Ze speelden gangmaker voor Davide Ballerini, maar Mathieu van der Poel was die dag de snelste. Davide werd derde.

After stage 3 of Tirreno-Adriatico, Zdenek Stybar and João Almeida are disappointed. They were leading Davide Ballerini, but Mathieu van der Poel was the fastest that day. Davide finished third.

Après la troisième étape de la Tirreno-Adriatico : Zdenek Stybar et João Almeida sont dépités. Ils ont tenté de porter Davide Ballerini, mais Mathieu van der Poel a été le plus rapide ce jour-là. Davide a terminé troisième. ▶

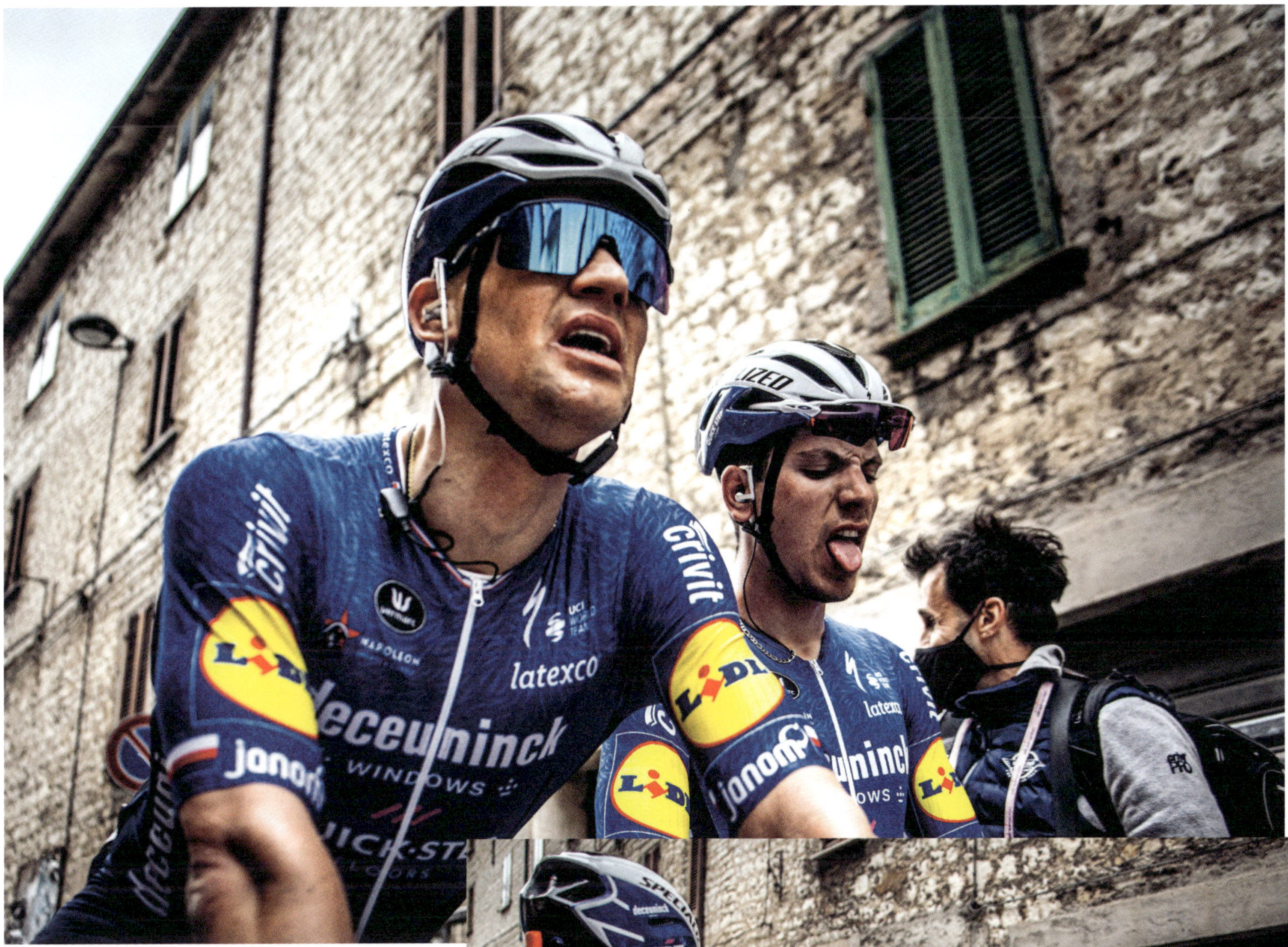
Crivit
latexco
deceuninck
WINDOWS

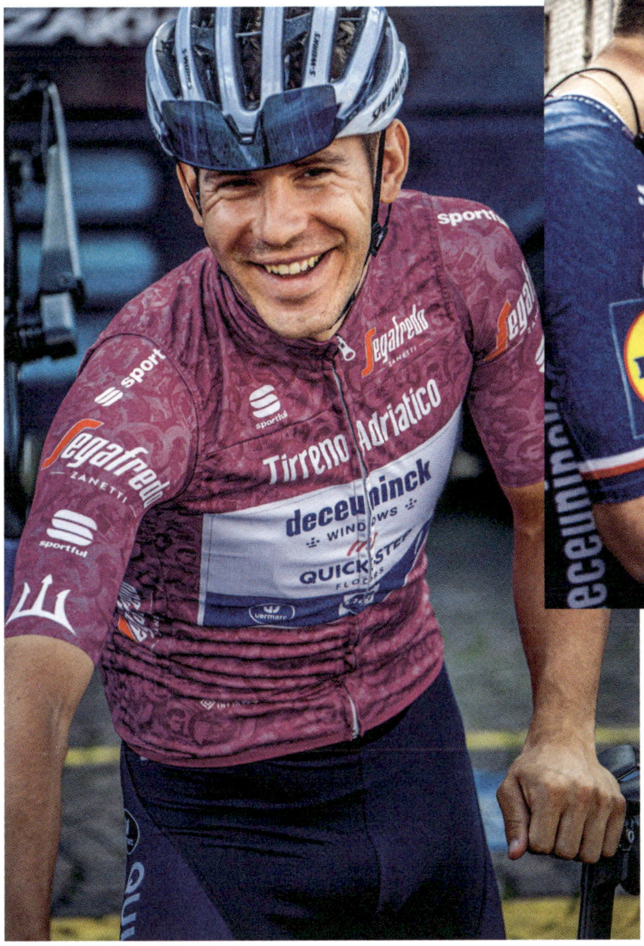
Tirreno Adriatico
deceuninck
QUICK-STEP
Segafredo

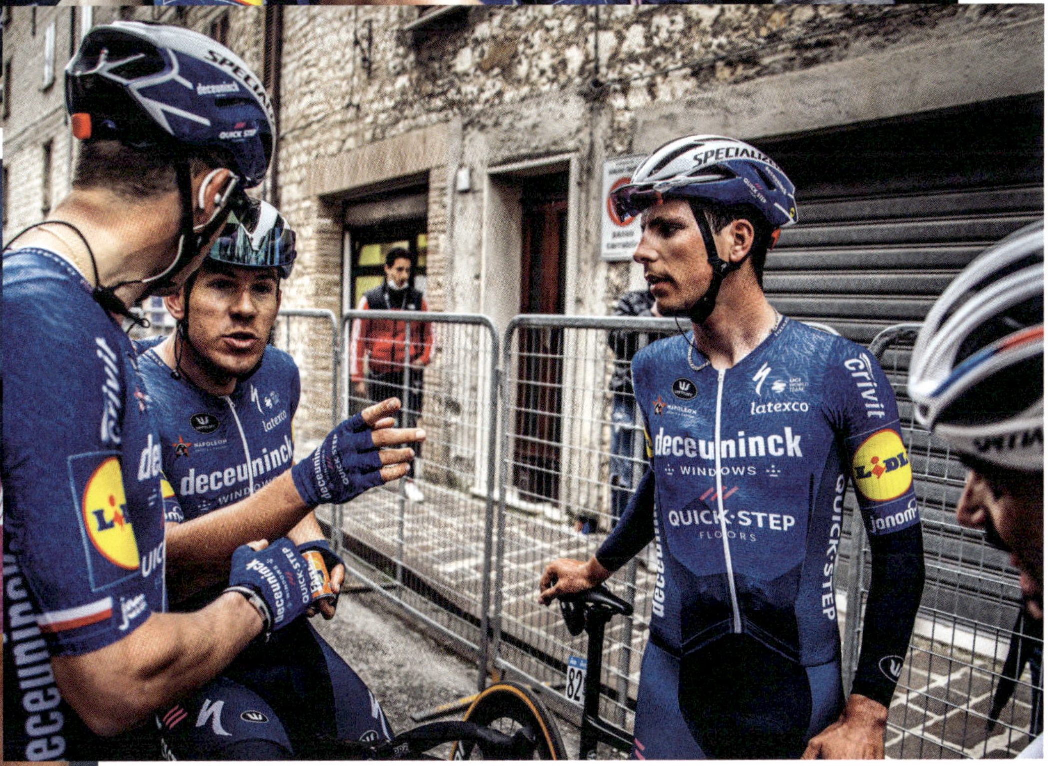
deceuninck
latexco
QUICK-STEP
FLOORS

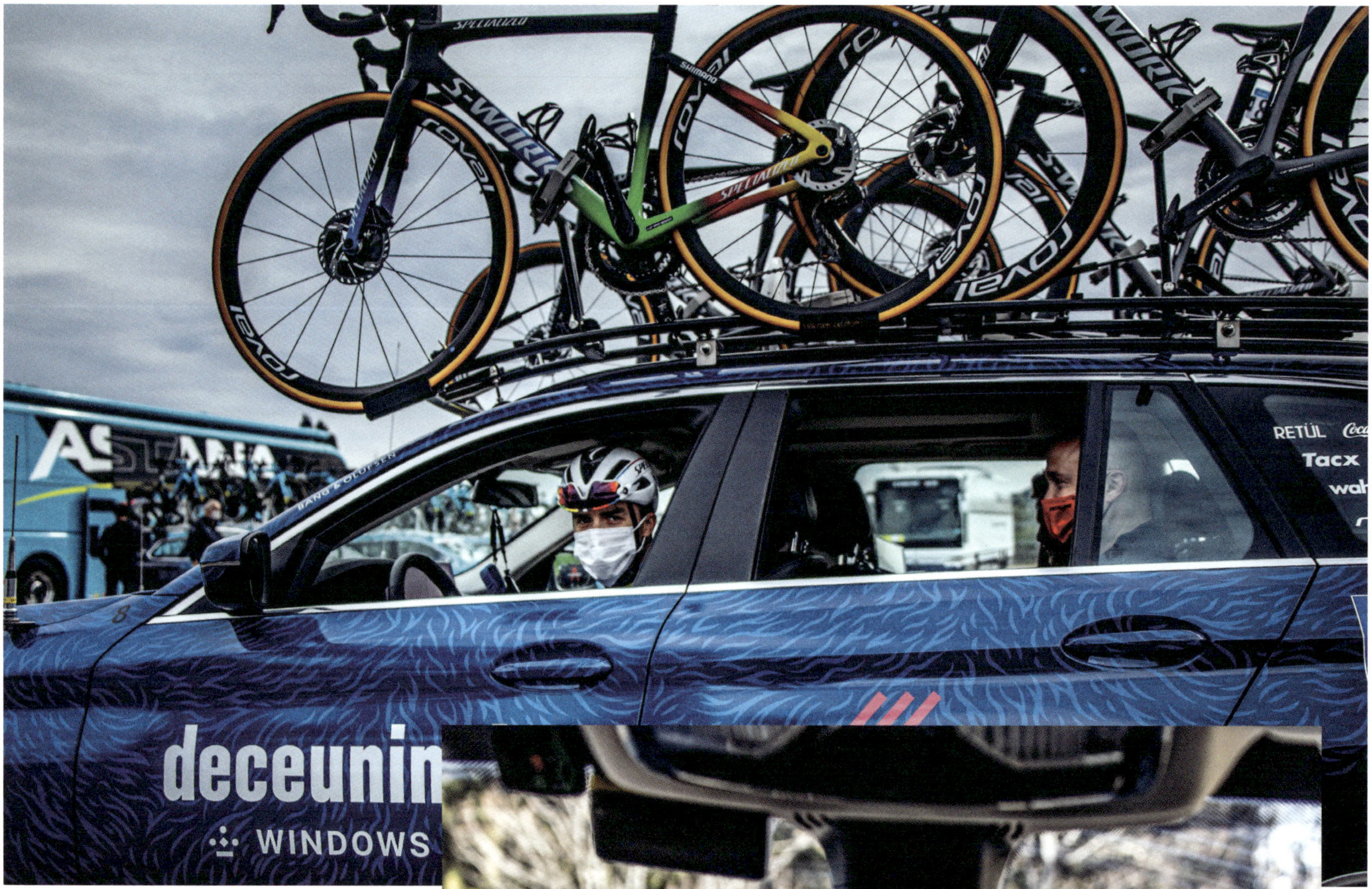
RETÜL
Tacx
deceunin
WINDOWS

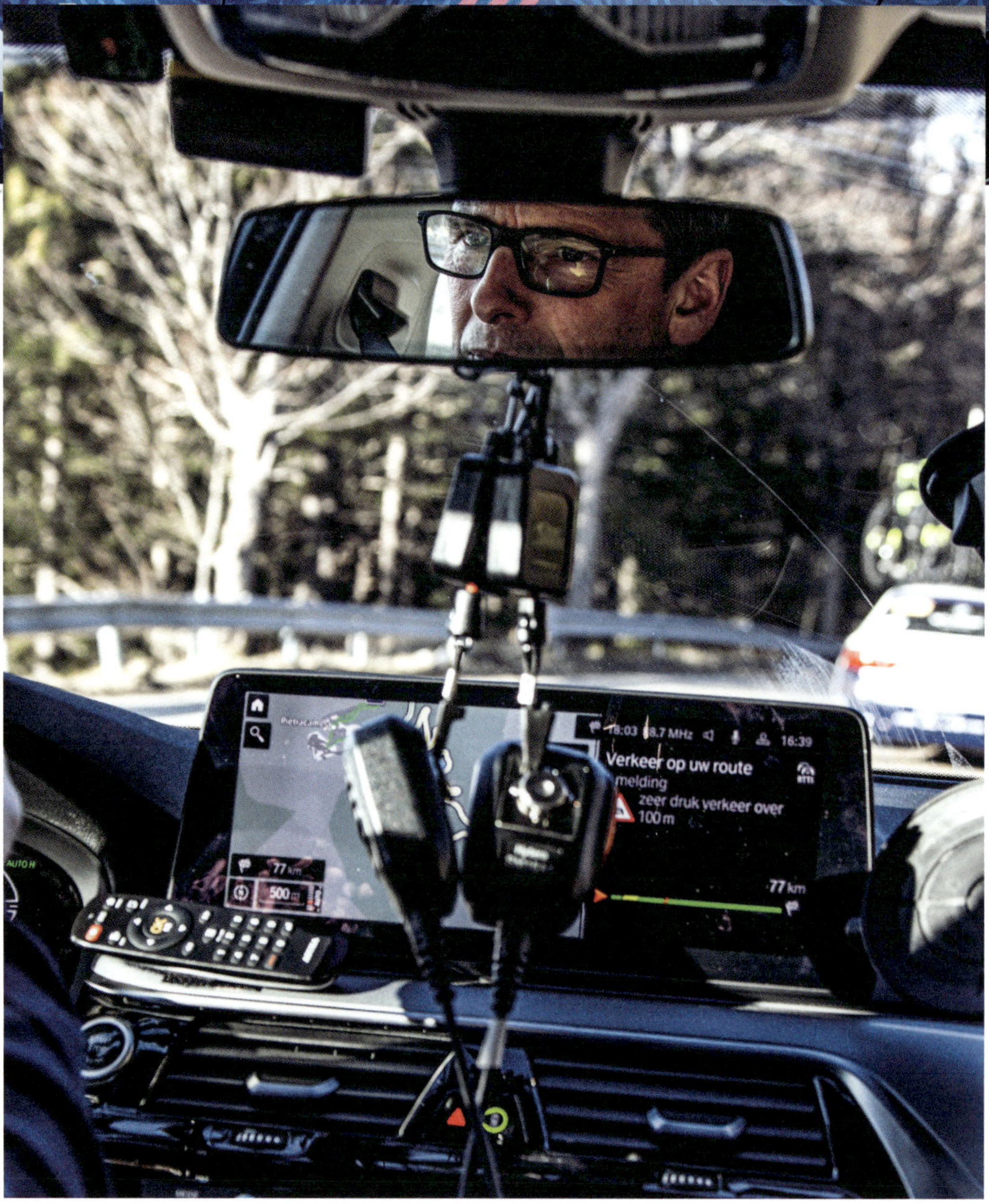
Verkeer op uw route
melding
zeer druk verkeer over
100 m
77 km

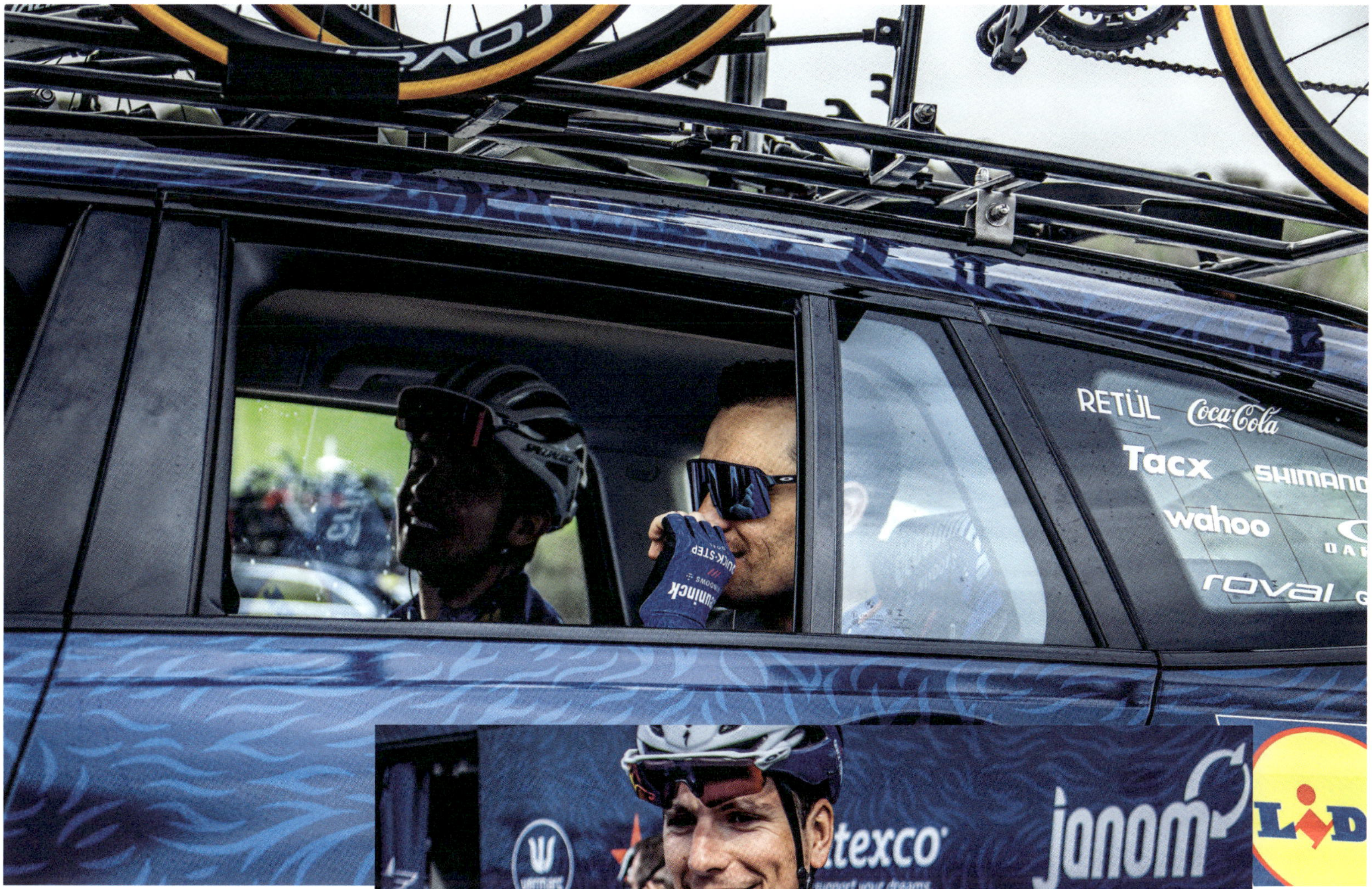
RETÜL
Coca-Cola
Tacx
wahoo
roval

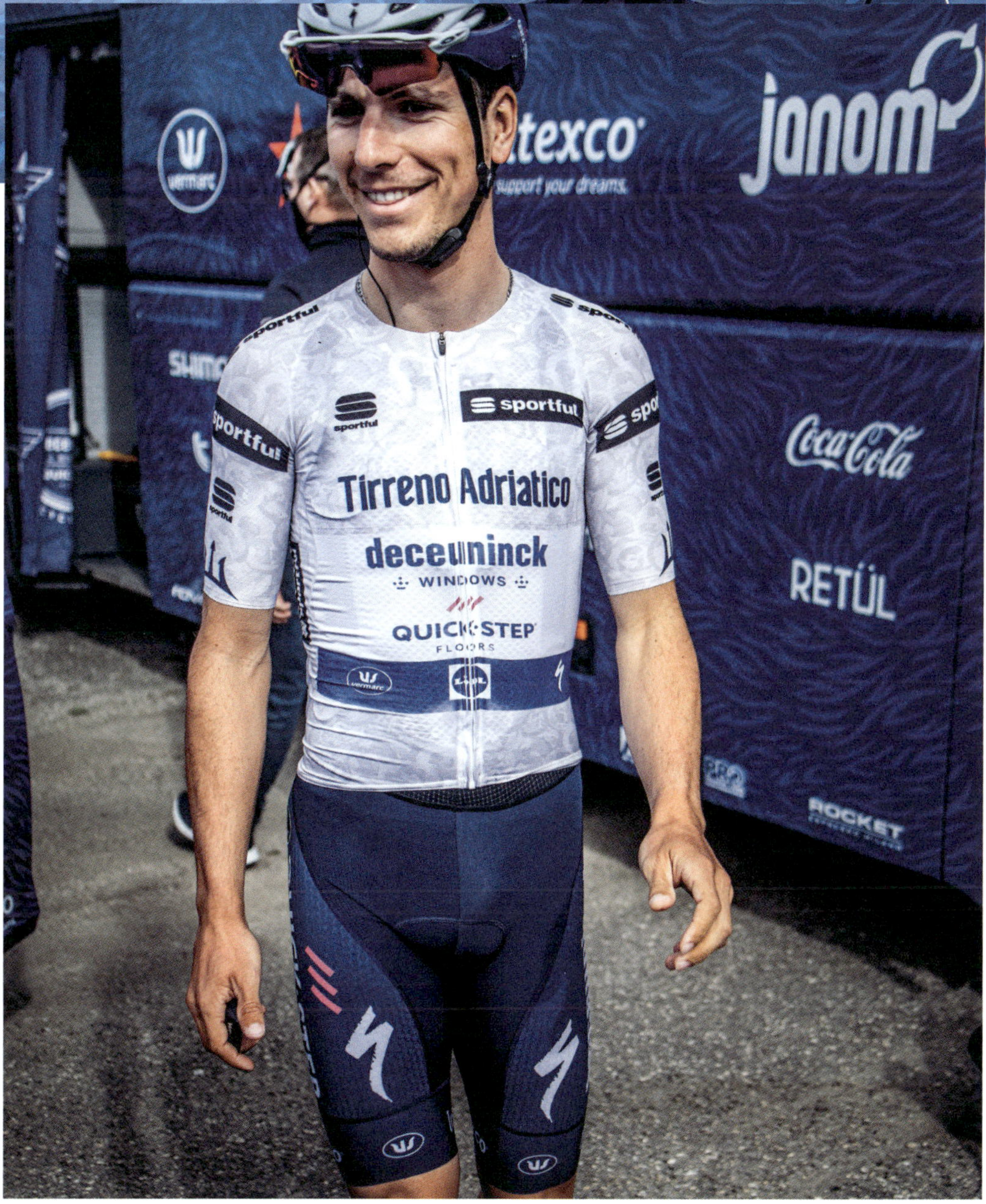
Coca-Cola
RETÜL
sportful
Tirreno Adriatico
deceuninck
WINDOWS
QUICK-STEP
FLOORS

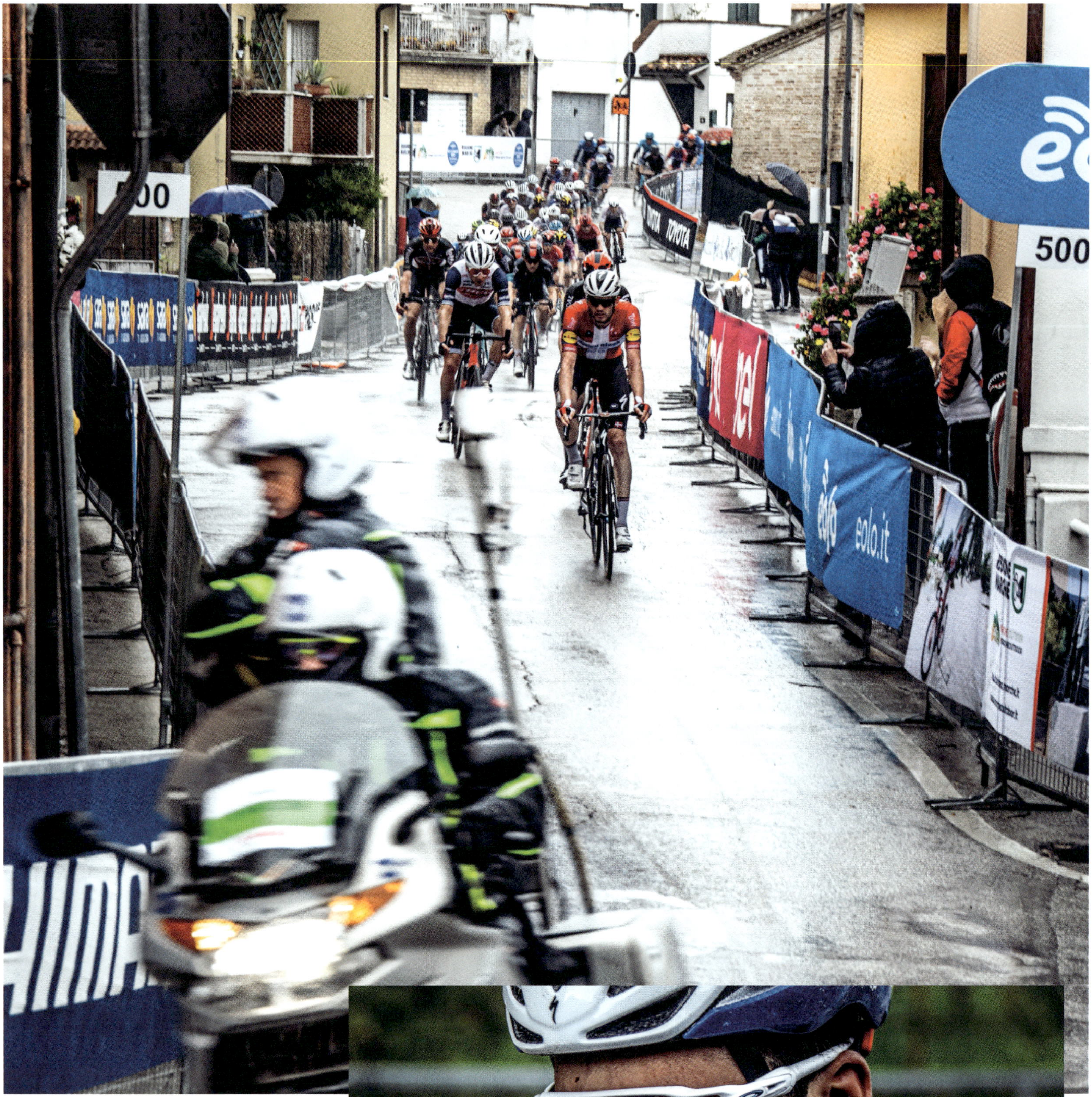
500
TOYOTA
eolo.it
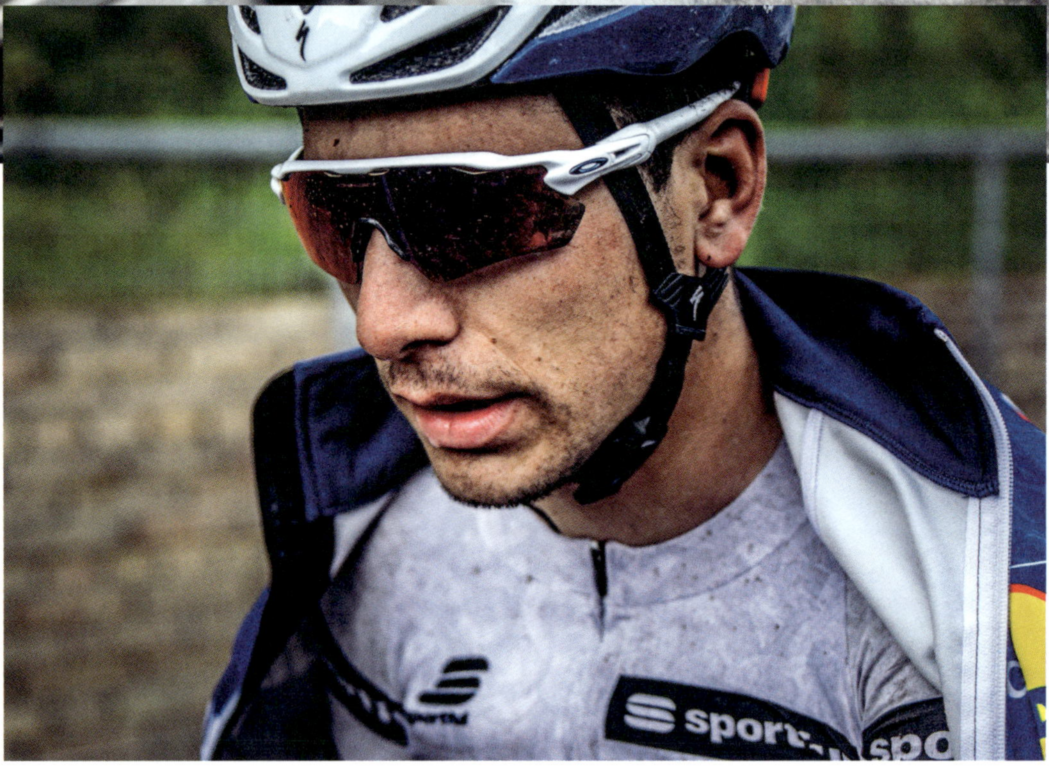
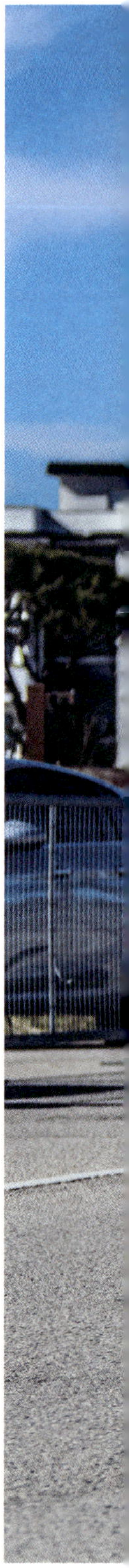

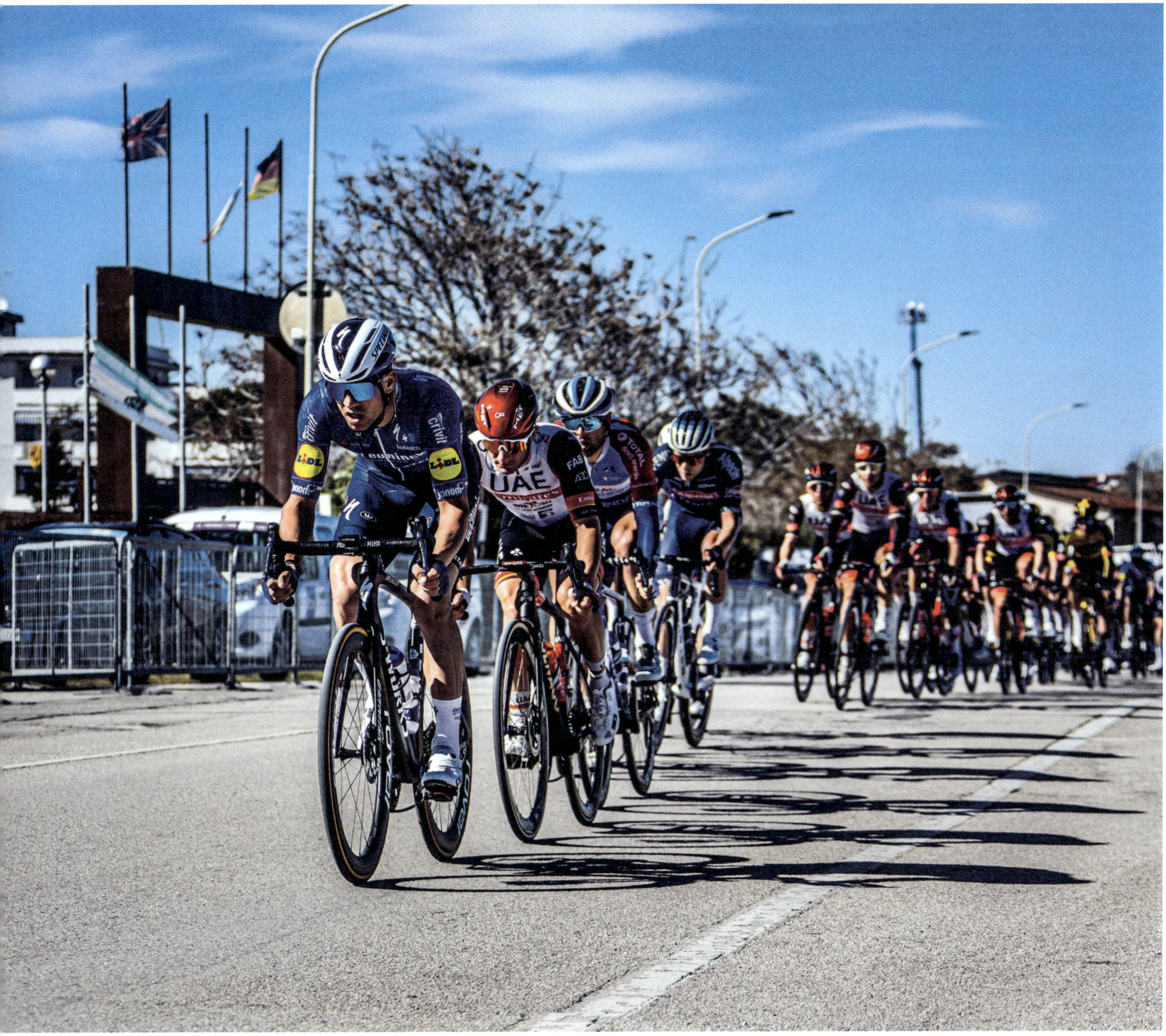

LIDO DI FERMO, 15.03.2021

De zesde etappe van de Tirreno-Adriatico. Zdenek Stybar leidt de achtervolging op zes ontsnapte renners.

Stage 6 of Tirreno-Adriatico. Zdenek Stybar leads the pursuit behind the six escapees.

La sixième étape de la Tirreno-Adriatico. Zdenek Stybar à la tête du peloton en chasse de six échappés.

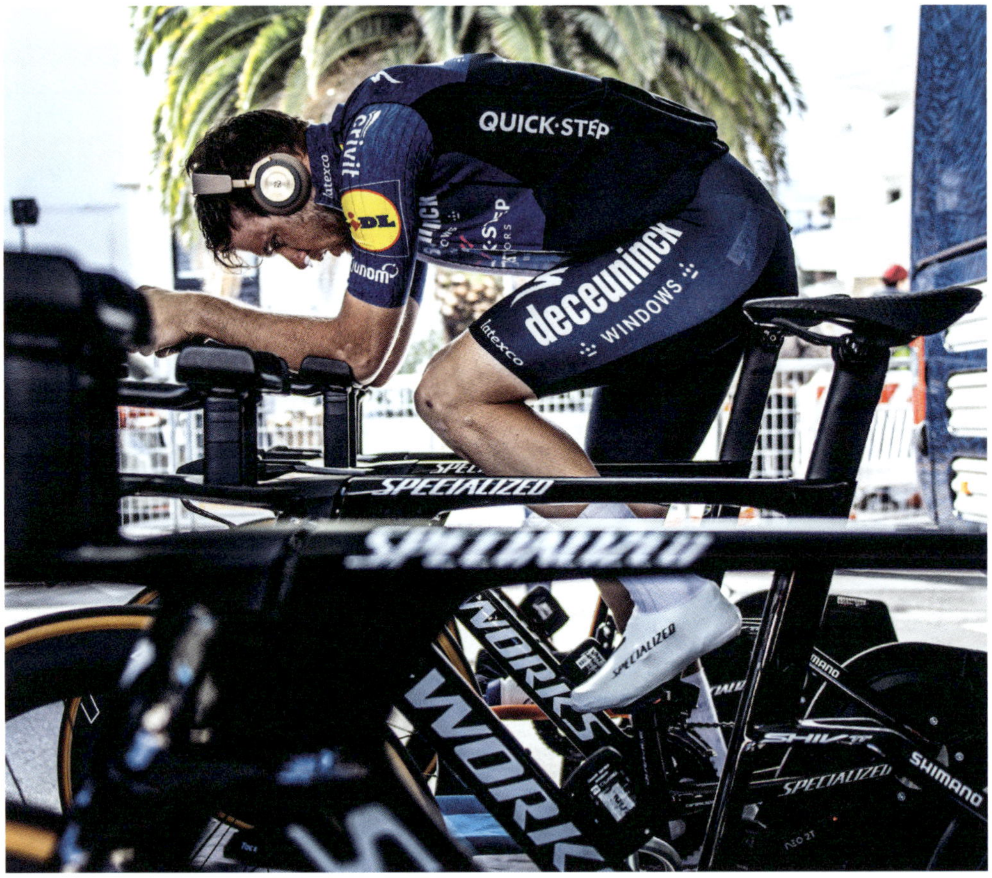

João Almeida krijgt de zegen van dokter Philip Jansen tijdens de opwarming voor de afsluitende tijdrit in San Benedetto del Tronto. João eindigde zevende, Kasper Asgreen achtste.

João Almeida gets the blessing of doctor Philip Jansen during the warm-up for the final time trial in San Benedetto del Tronto. João finished seventh, Kasper Asgreen eighth.

Le docteur Philip Jansen donne sa bénédiction à João Almeida pendant l'échauffement pour le contre-la-montre final à San Benedetto del Tronto. João a terminé septième, Kasper Asgreen huitième. ◢

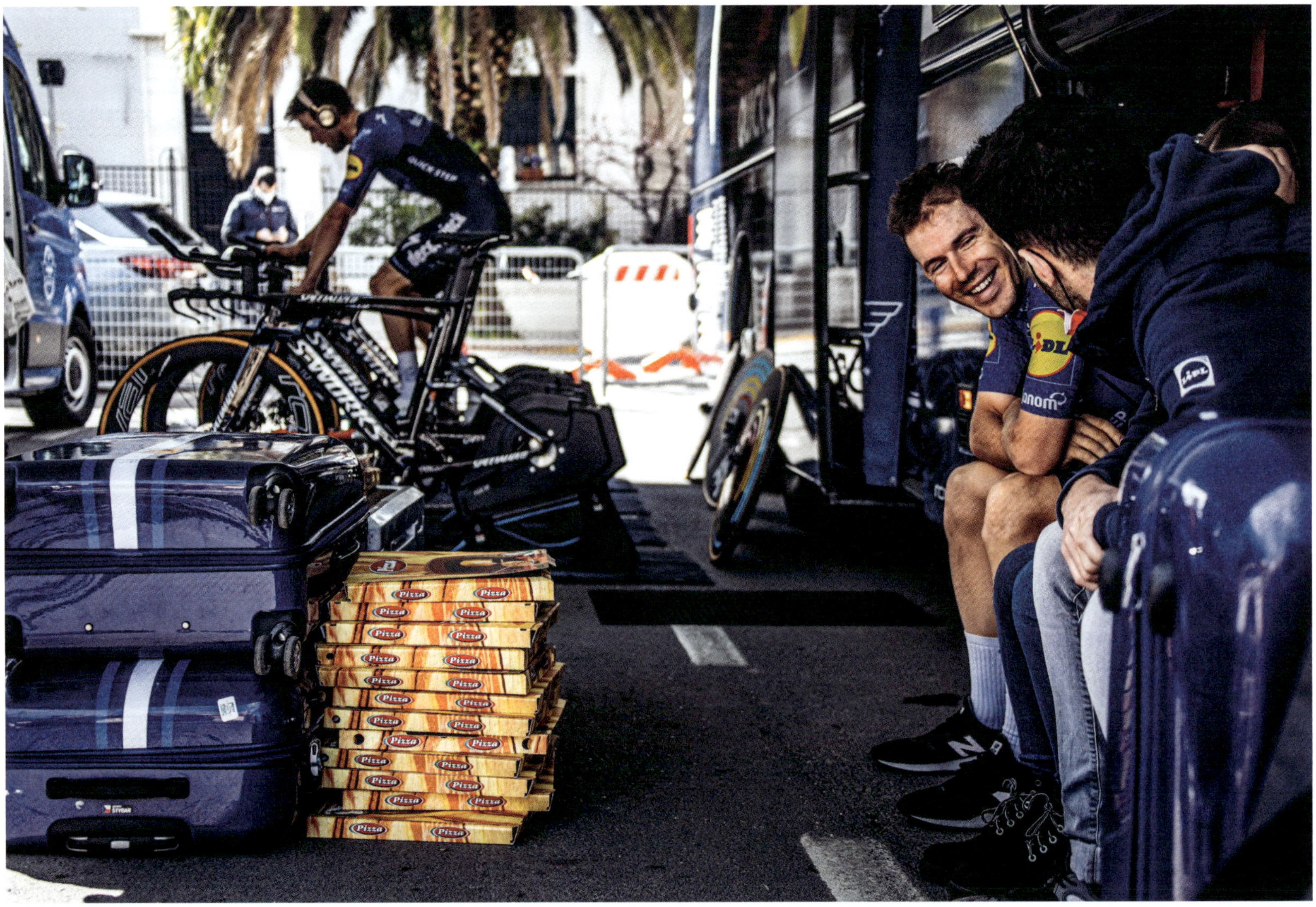

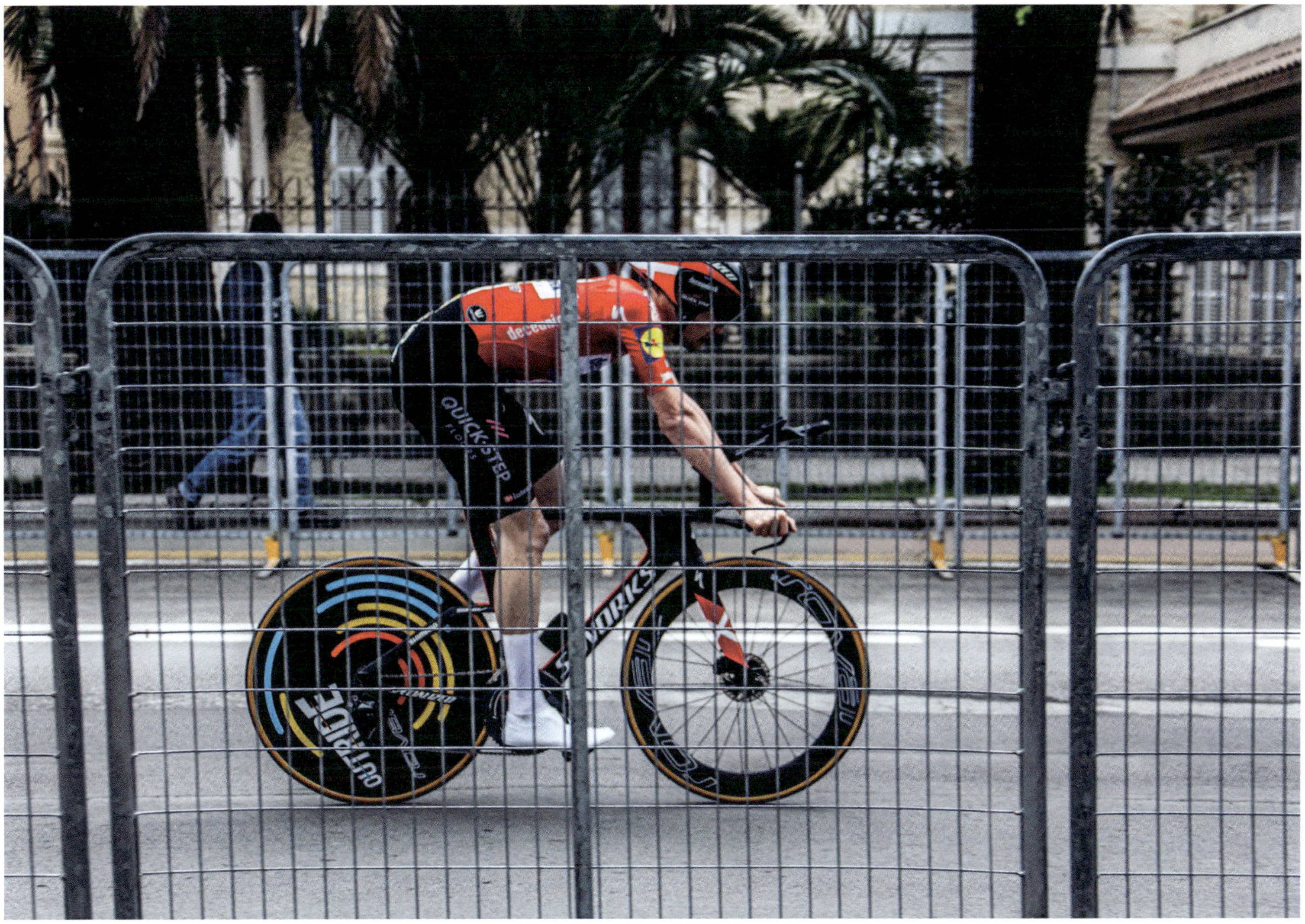
QUICK-STEP
OUTRIDE

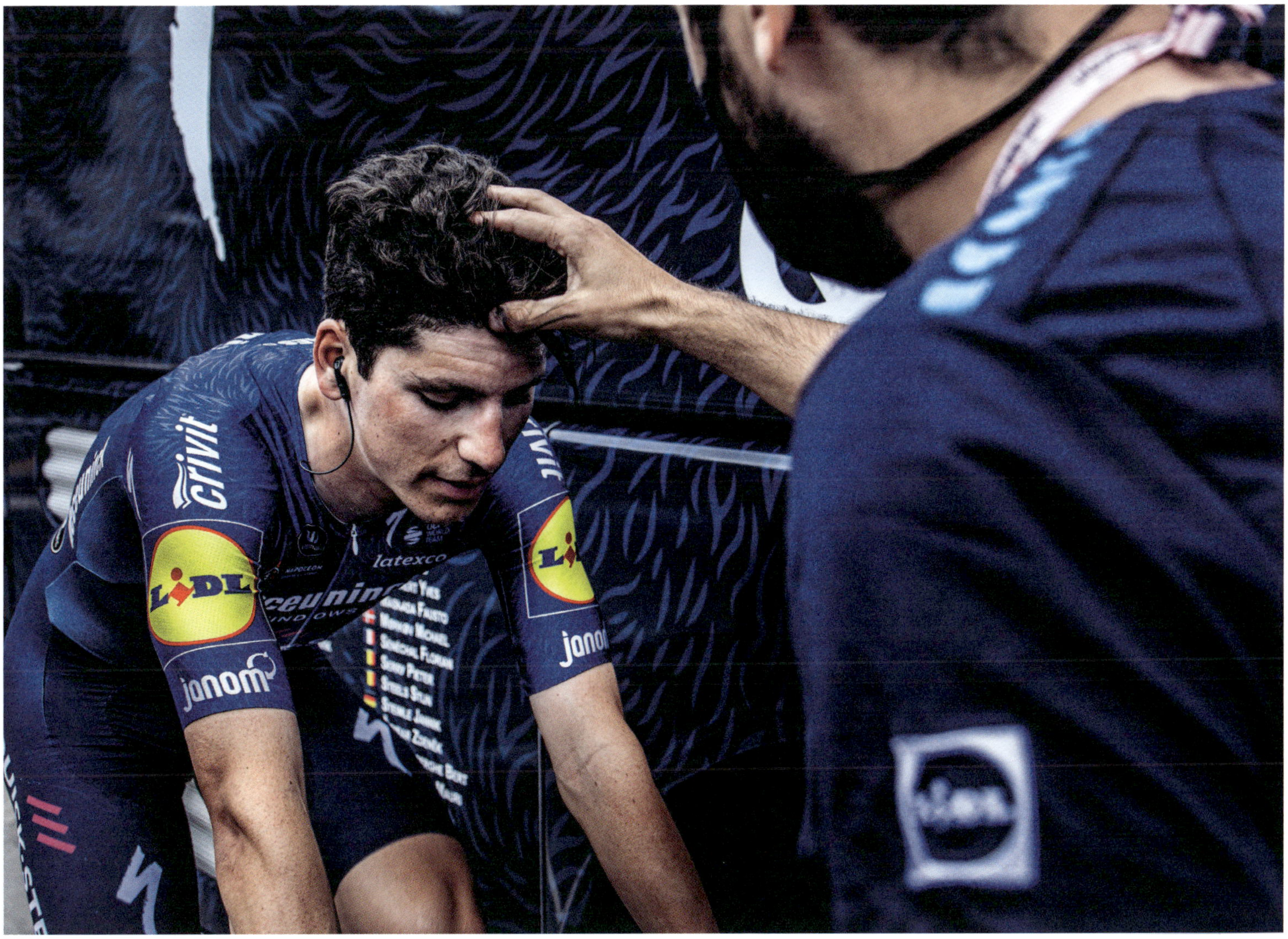
crivit
LIDL
latexco

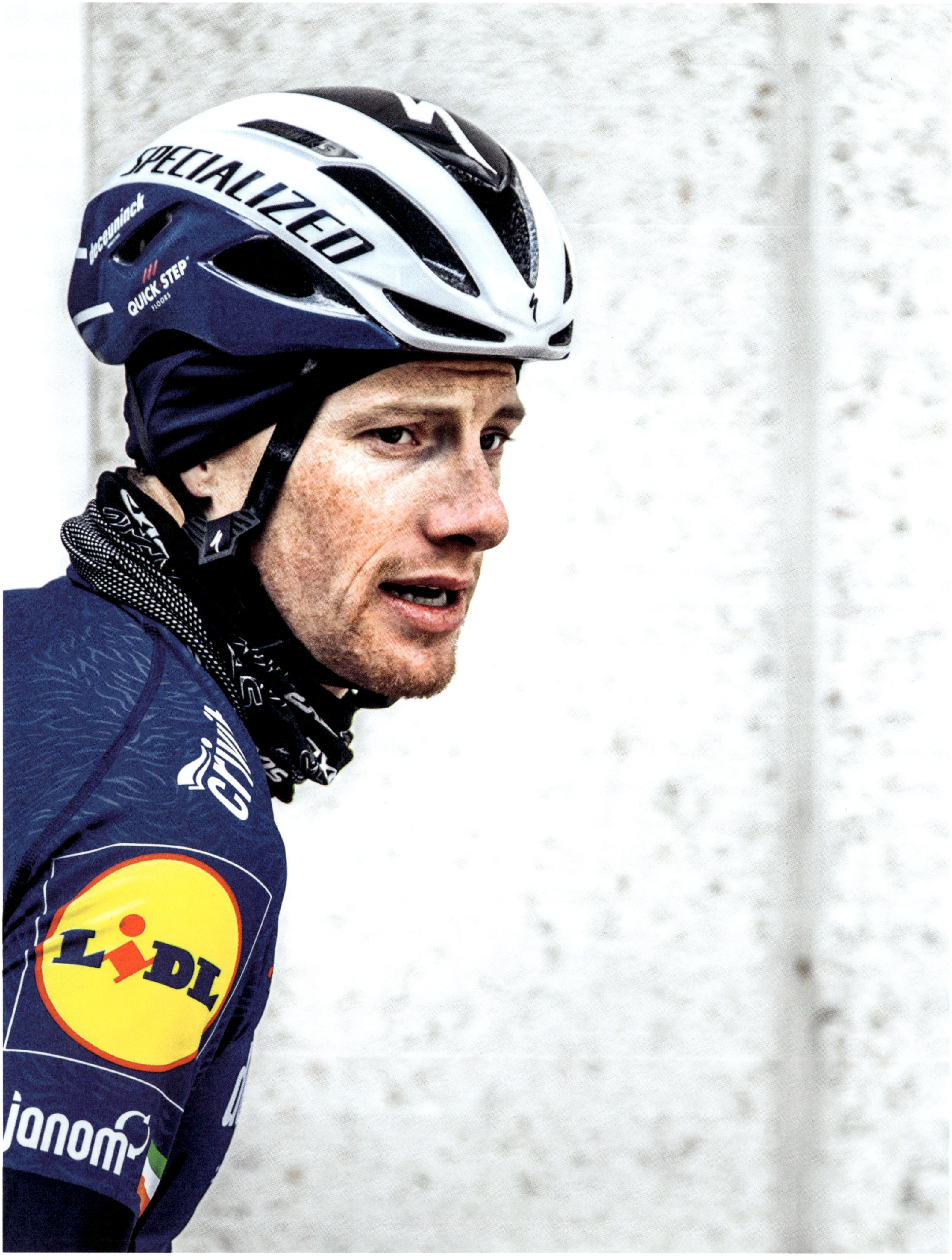
SPECIALIZED
deceuninck
QUICK STEP
LiDL

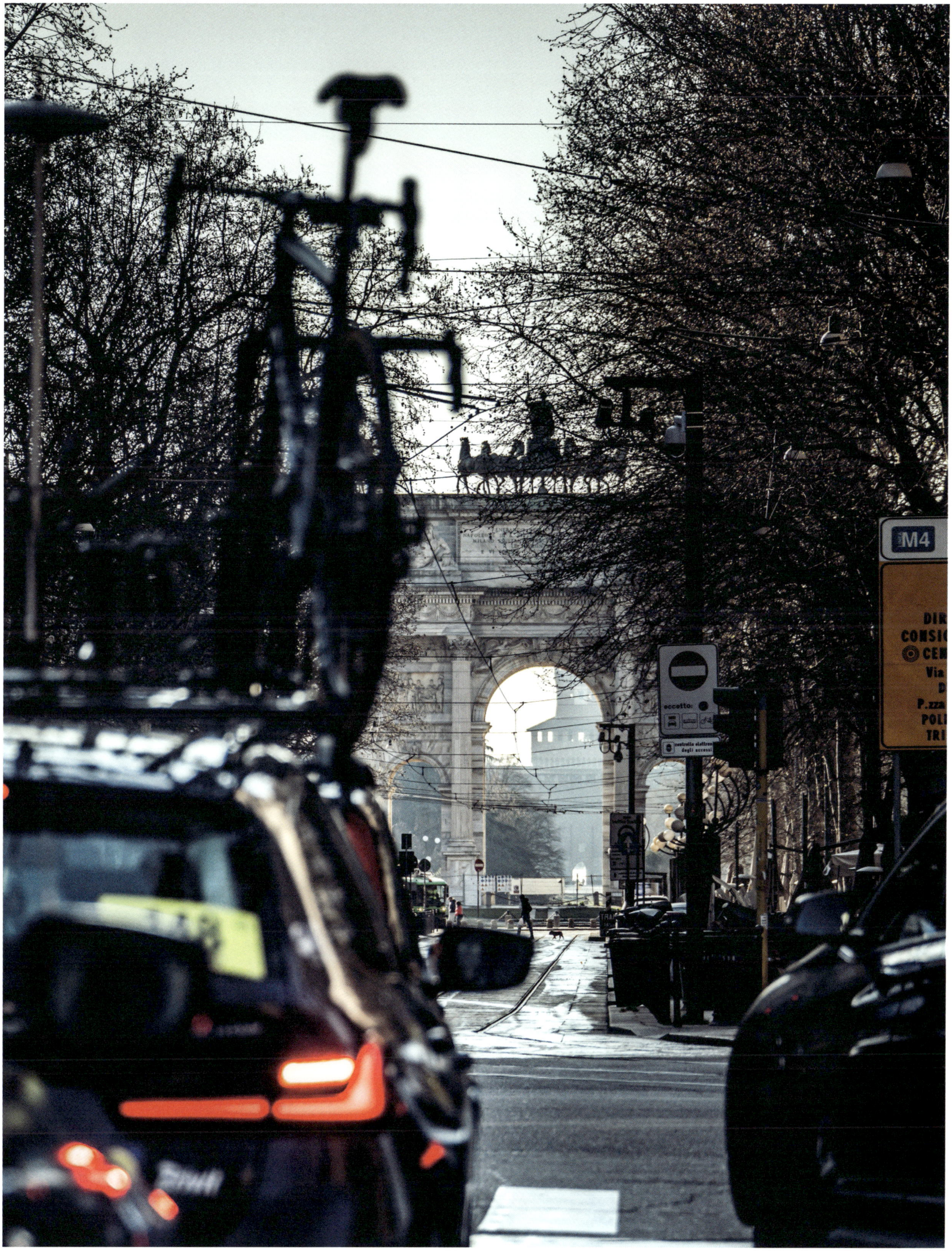
M4
eccetto

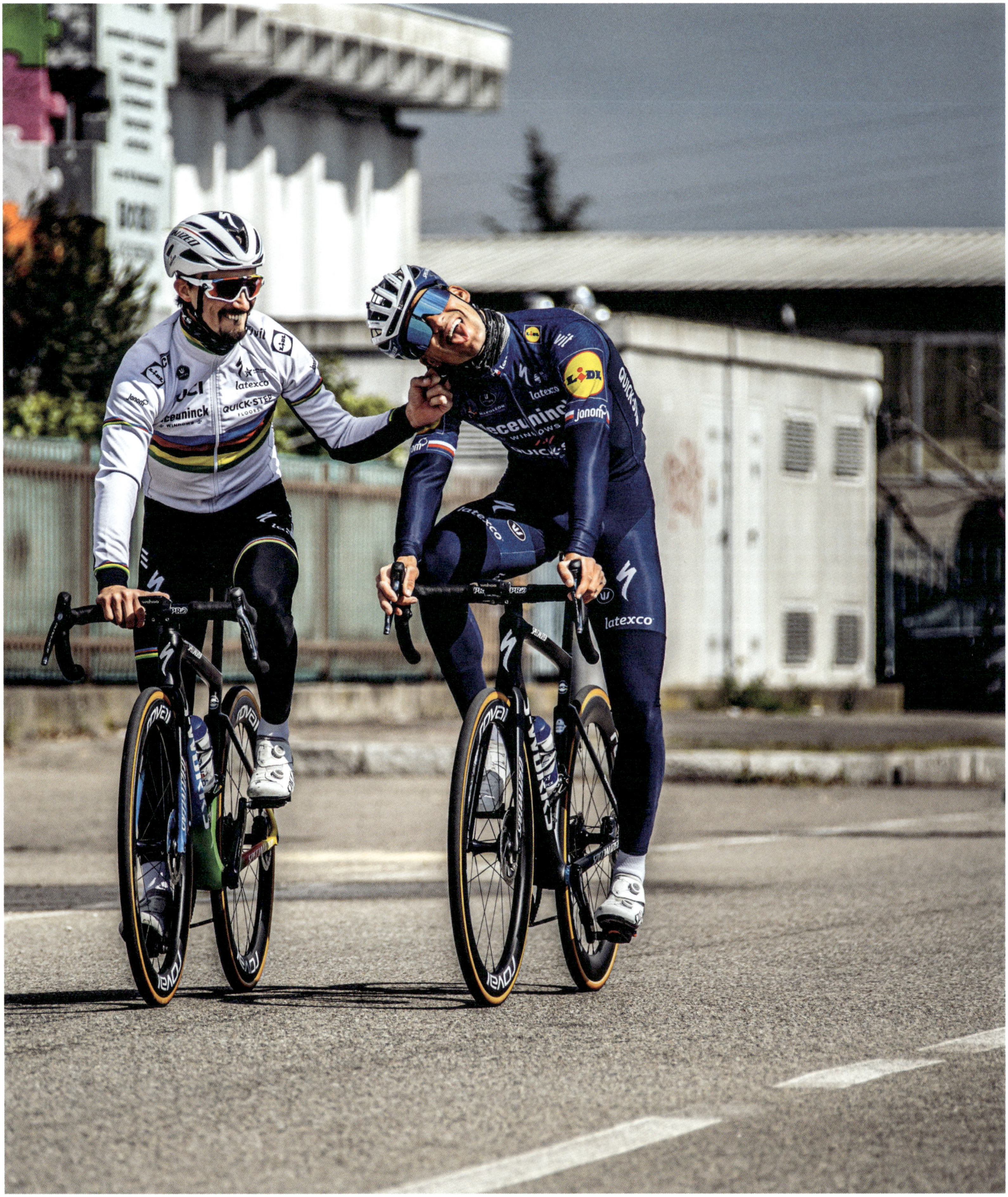
latexco
janom
latexco

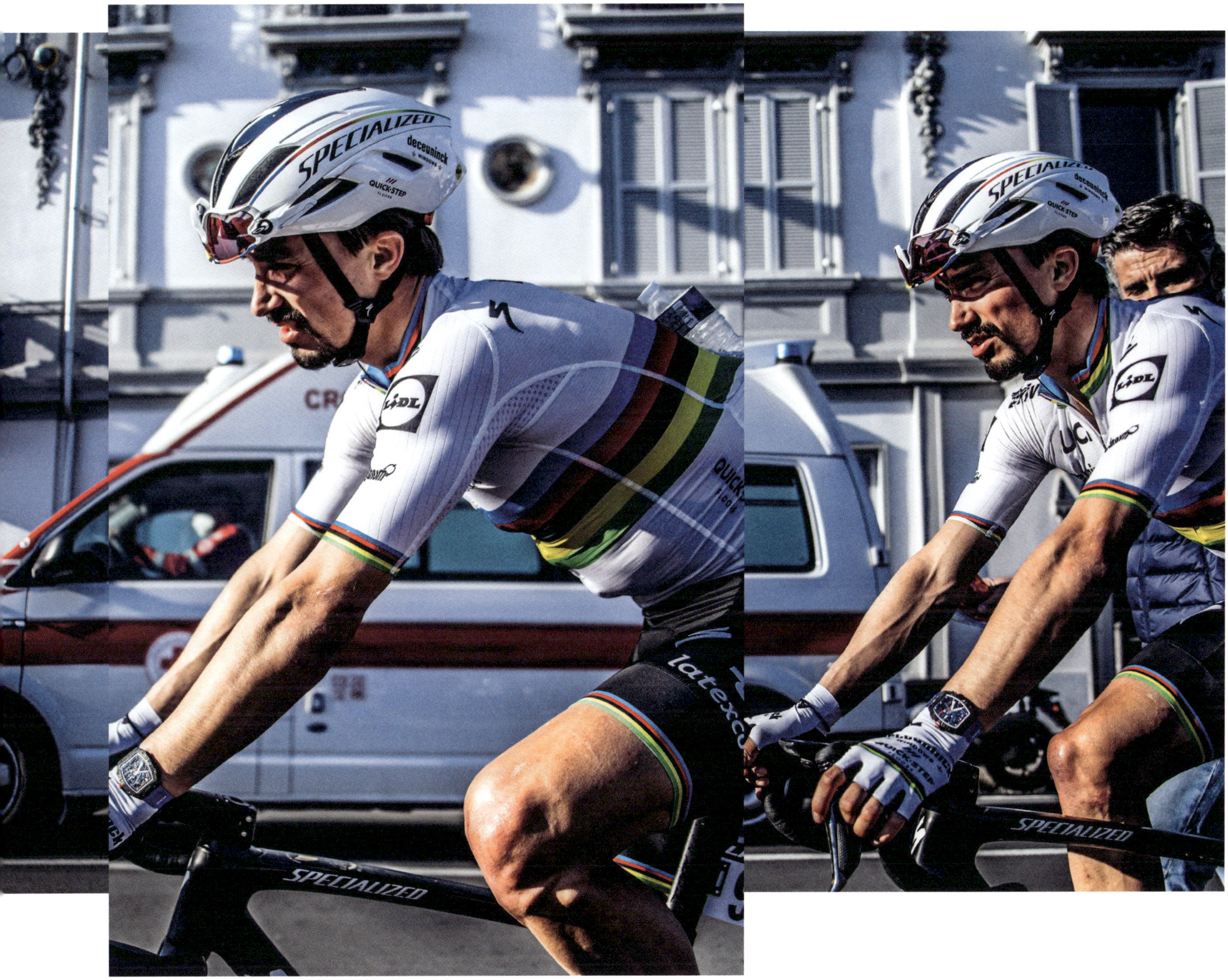

Julian Alaphilippe houdt Zdenek Stybar bij de les, maar dan wel op zeer onorthodoxe wijze.

Julian Alaphilippe keeps Zdenek Stybar on his toes, but in a very unorthodox way.

Julian Alaphilippe aide Zdenek Stybar à garder le rythme, mais d'une manière peu orthodoxe.

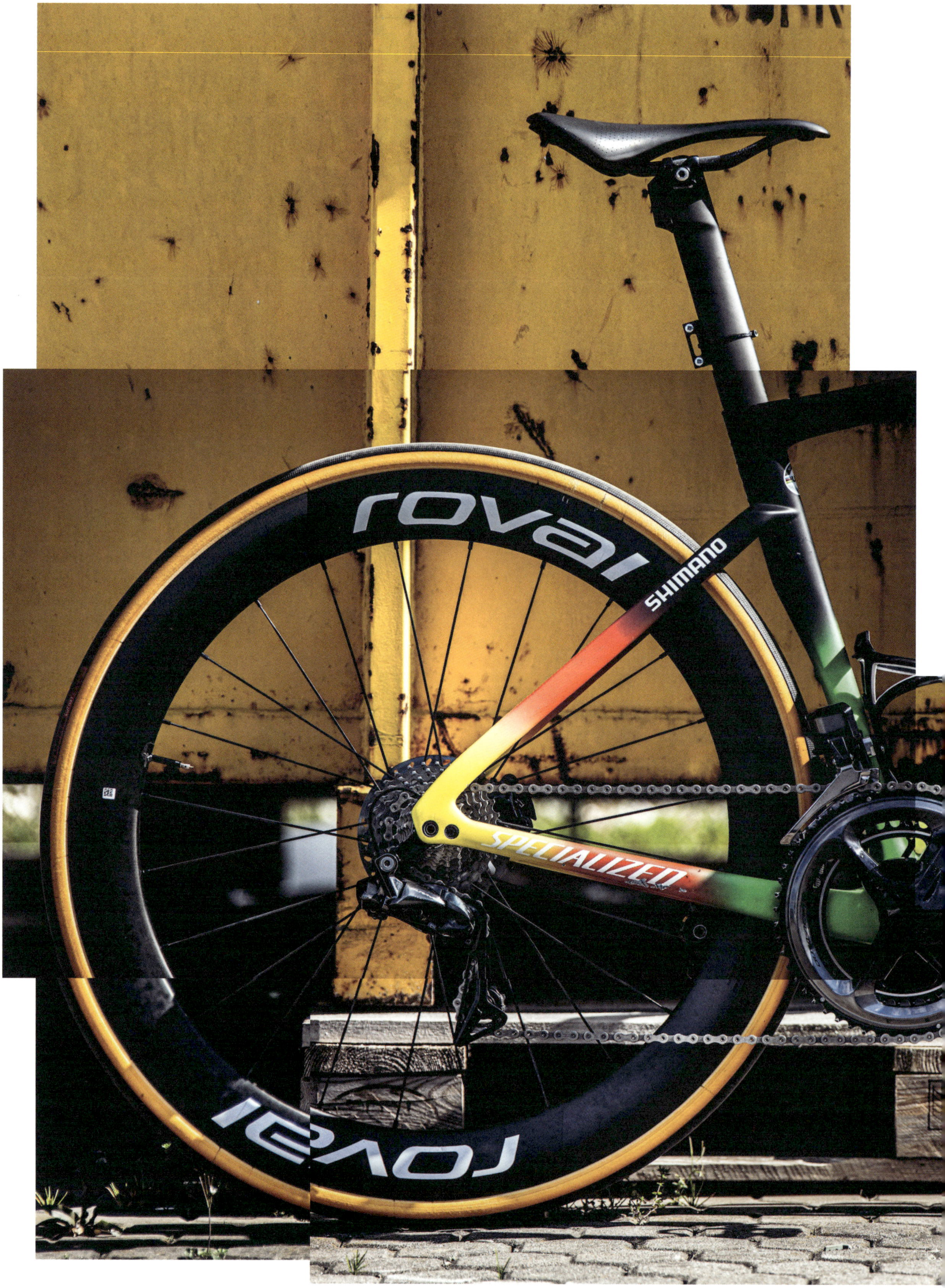
roval
SHIMANO
SPECIALIZED

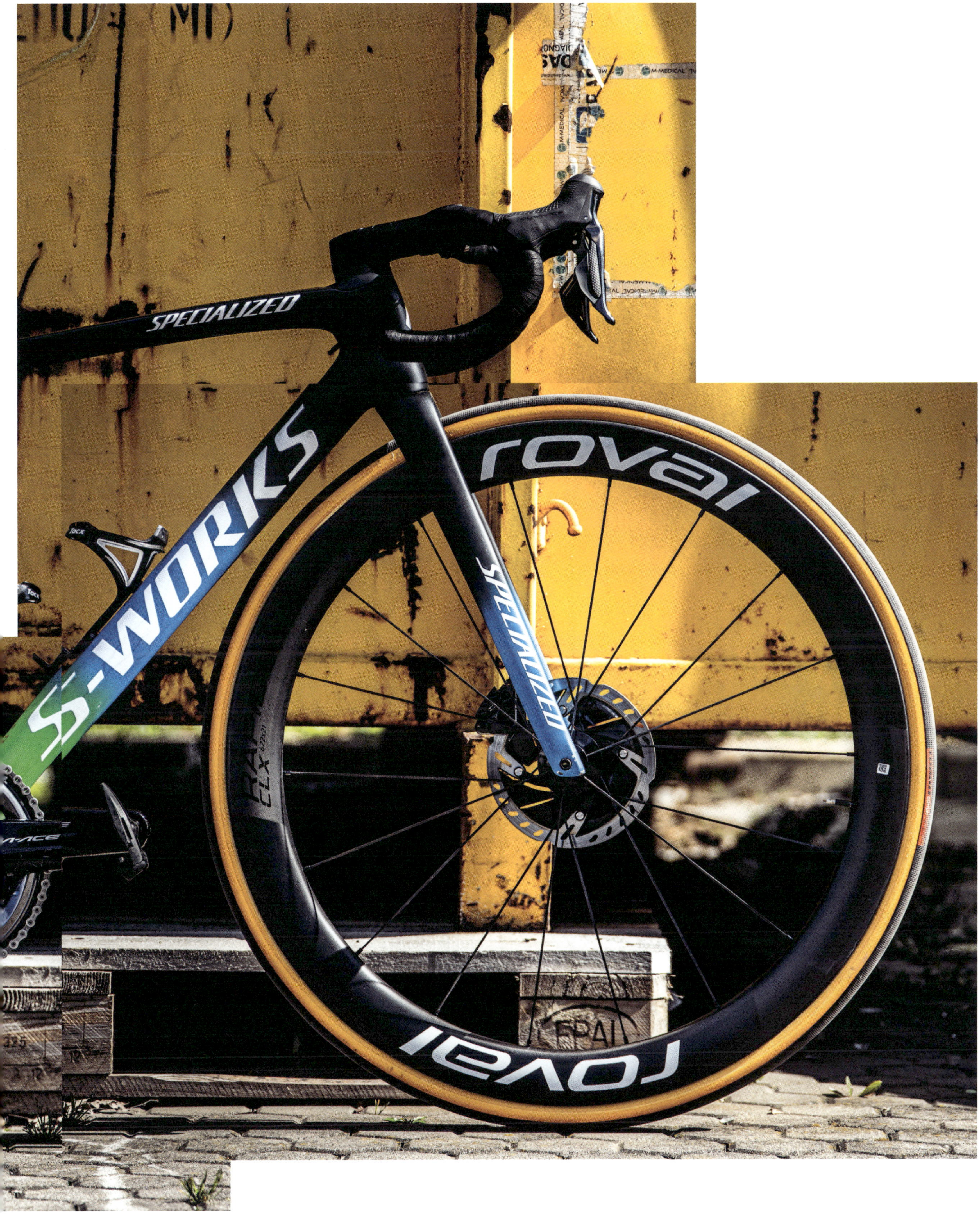
SPECIALIZED
S-WORKS
roval
SPECIALIZED
roval

OXYCLEAN CLASSIC BRUGGE-DE PANNE
24.03.2021

Sam Bennett pakt de winst in de Oxyclean Classic Brugge-De Panne op woensdag 24 maart. Het was zijn vijfde overwinning van het seizoen. Eerder, eind februari, boekte hij twee sprintzeges in de UAE Tour.

Sam Bennett takes the win in the Oxyclean Classic Bruges–De Panne on Wednesday 24 March. It was his fifth win of the season. Earlier, at the end of February, he scored two sprint victories in the UAE Tour.

Sam Bennett a remporté la victoire de l'Oxyclean Classic Brugge-De Panne, tenue le mercredi 24 mars. Il s'agissait de sa cinquième victoire de la saison. Un peu plus tôt, à la fin du mois de février, il a remporté deux victoires au sprint lors du UAE Tour.

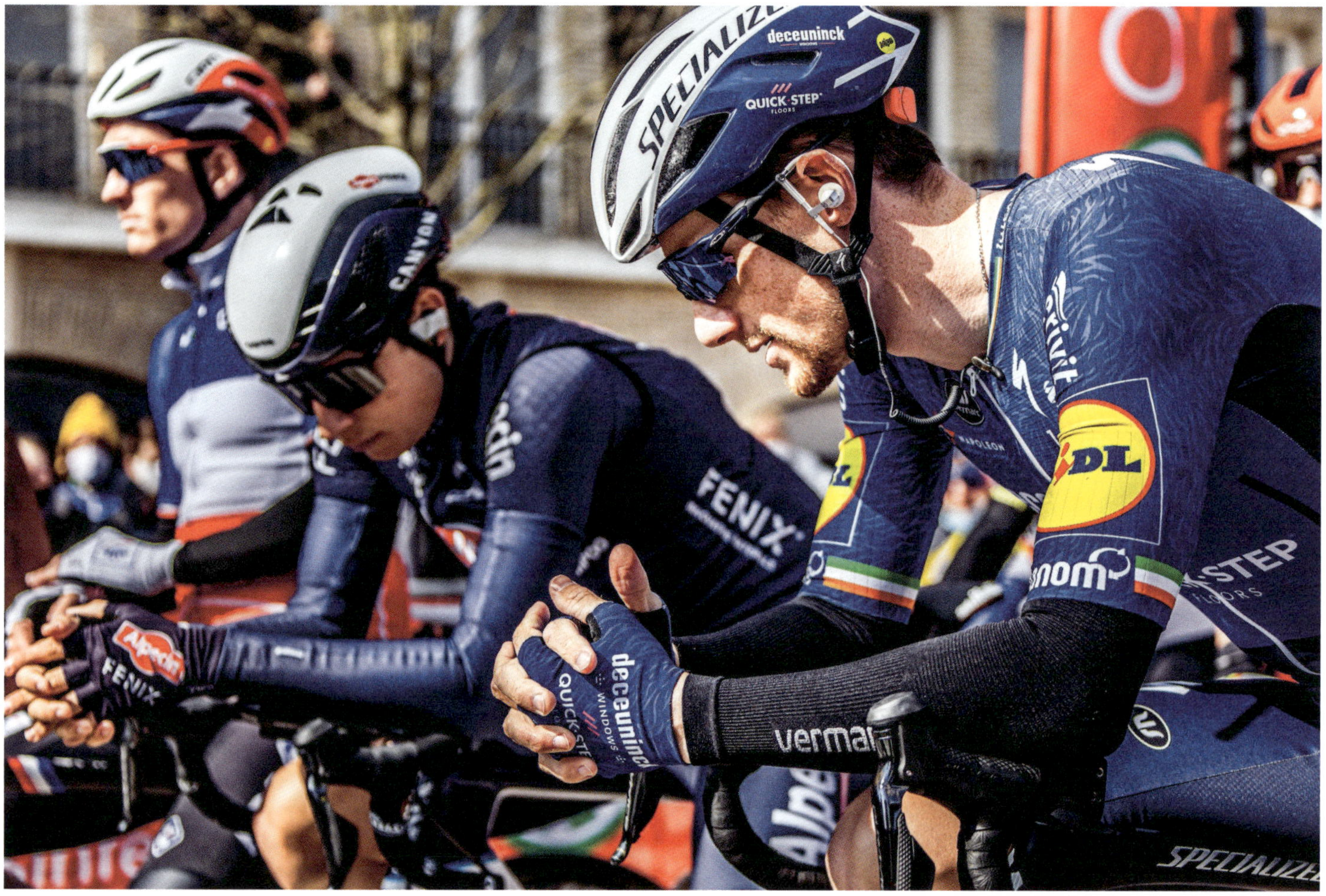

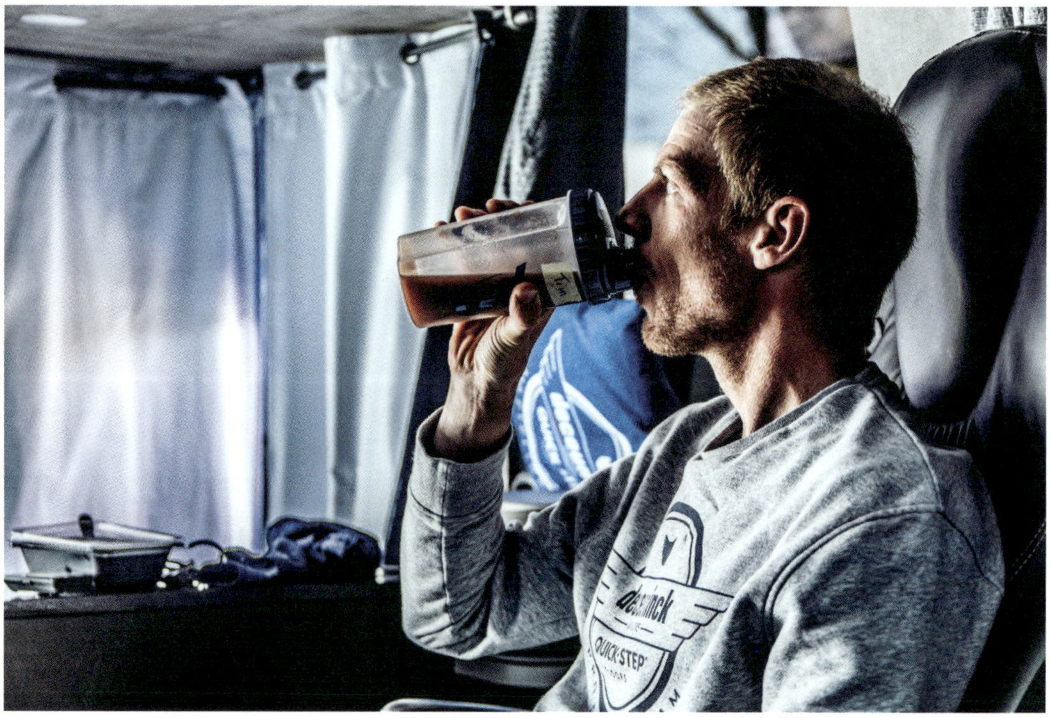

Een vuistje als uiting van blijdschap. Onze Ier Sam Bennett na zijn winst in De Panne.

A fist-bump expresses his joy. Our Irishman Sam Bennett after his win in De Panne.

Le poing serré et le sourire aux lèvres. Notre Irlandais Sam Bennett après sa victoire à La Panne.

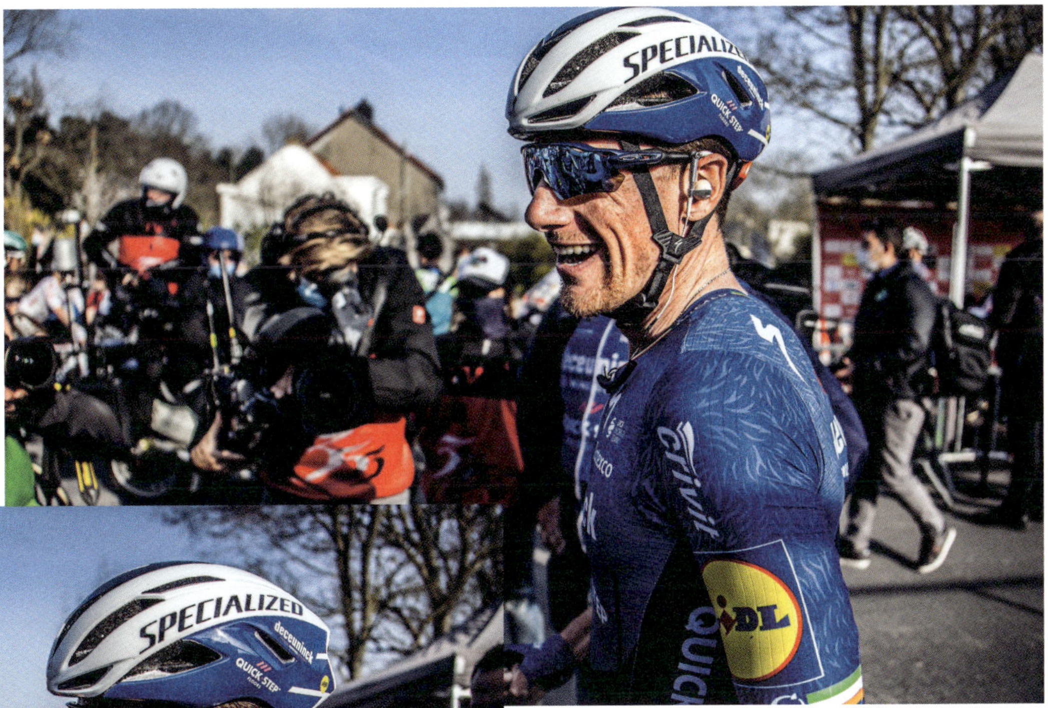

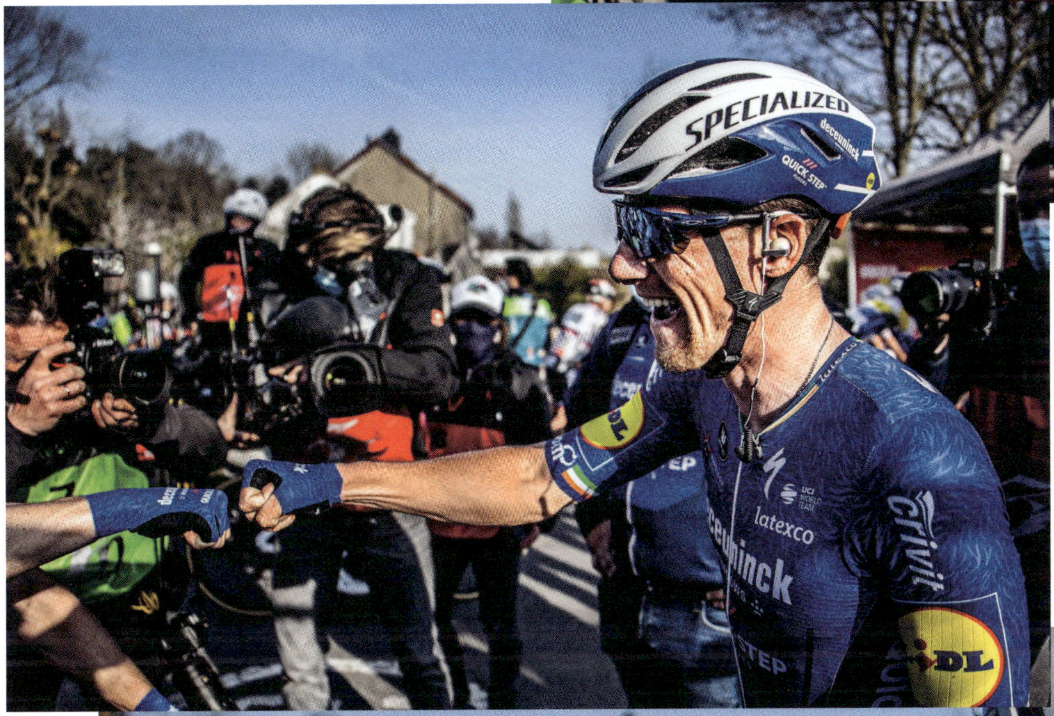

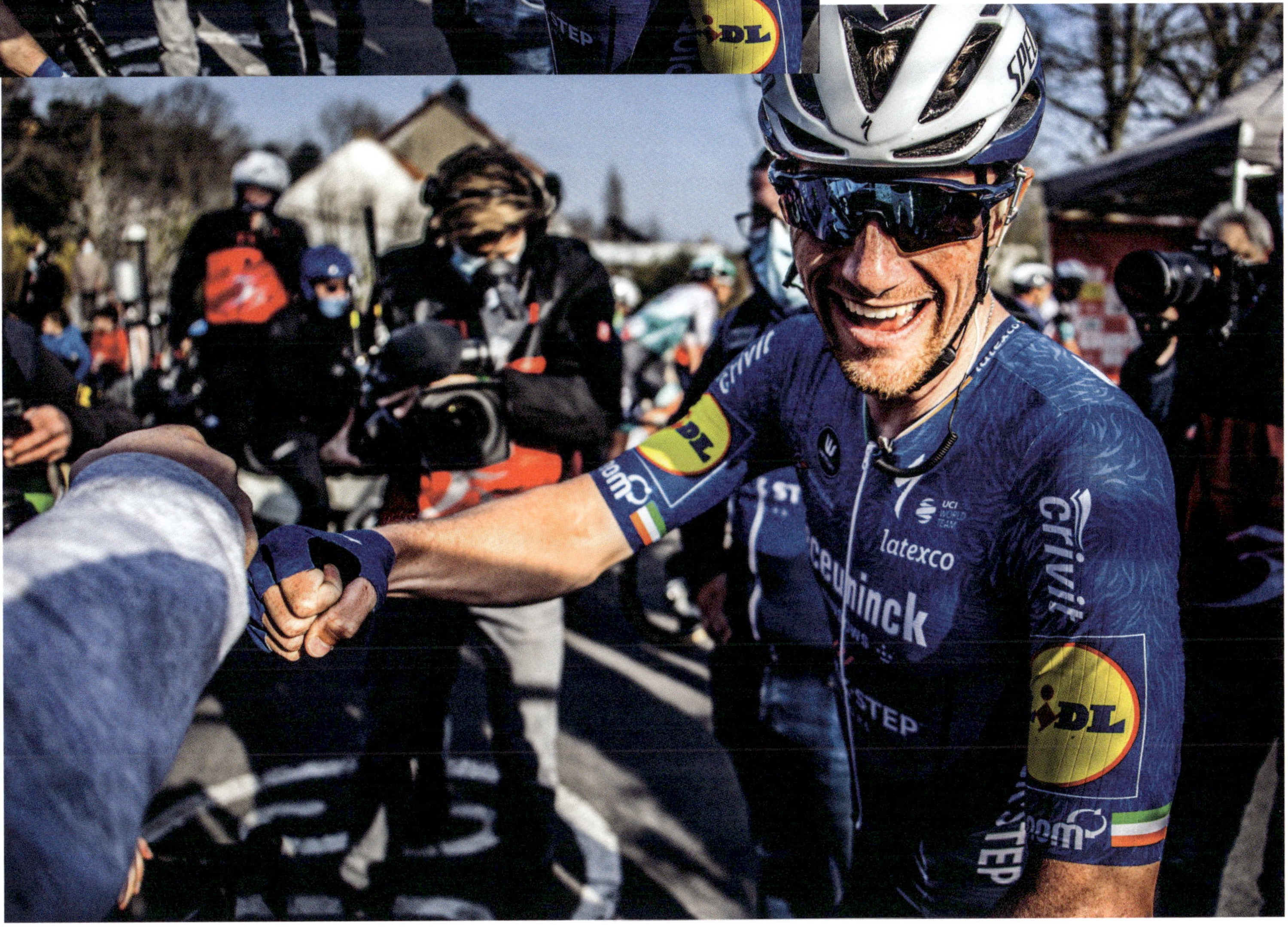

E3 SAXO BANK CLASSIC
26.03.2021

En daar is Deens Kampioen Kasper Asgreen. Na DQT-winst met Zdenek Stybar in 2019 haalde Asgreen op verbluffende wijze de E3 binnen, op 26 maart 2021. Hij kneep er op 70 kilometer van de meet solo tussenuit, werd bijgehaald door een keurgroep, maar sloeg op 5 kilometer van de aankomst in Harelbeke opnieuw toe. Dubbel feest voor de ploeg van Patrick Lefevere, want Florian Sénéchal eindigde tweede. En ook dat volstond nog niet, want Stybar finishte vijfde. En toen moest de Ronde van Vlaanderen nog komen...

And there's Danish Champion Kasper Asgreen. After DQT's win with Zdenek Stybar in 2019, Asgreen enjoyed a stunning E3 win on 26 March 2021. He attacked solo at 70 km from the finish, was caught by a small group but struck again at 5 km from the line in Harelbeke. Double celebrations are in order for Patrick Lefevere's team, as Florian Sénéchal finished second. And as if this wasn't enough: Stybar finished fifth. The Ronde van Vlaanderen was still to come.

Cette fois-ci, c'est le Champion Danois Kasper Asgreen qui l'emporte. Après la victoire de la DQT grâce à Zdenek Stybar en 2019, Asgreen a remporté l'E3 de manière spectaculaire, le 26 mars 2021. Il s'est imposé en solitaire à 70 km d'Harelbeke, avant d'être rejoint par un petit groupe, pour finalement placer une accélération décisive à 5 km de la ligne à Harelbeke. Doubles célébrations pour l'équipe de Patrick Lefevere, car Florian Sénéchal a terminé deuxième. Mais ce n'est pas tout : Stybar a terminé cinquième. Le Ronde van Vlaanderen était encore à venir...

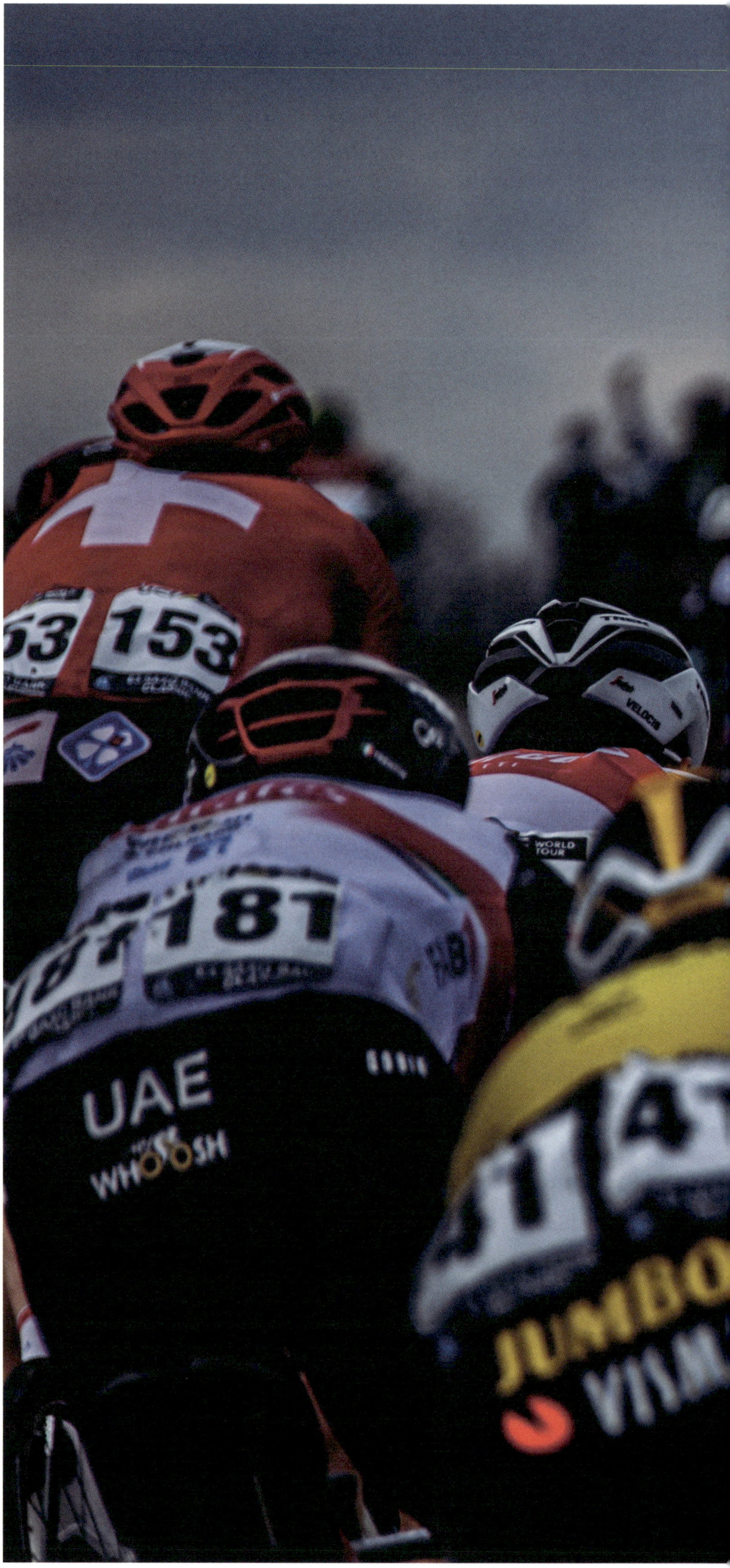

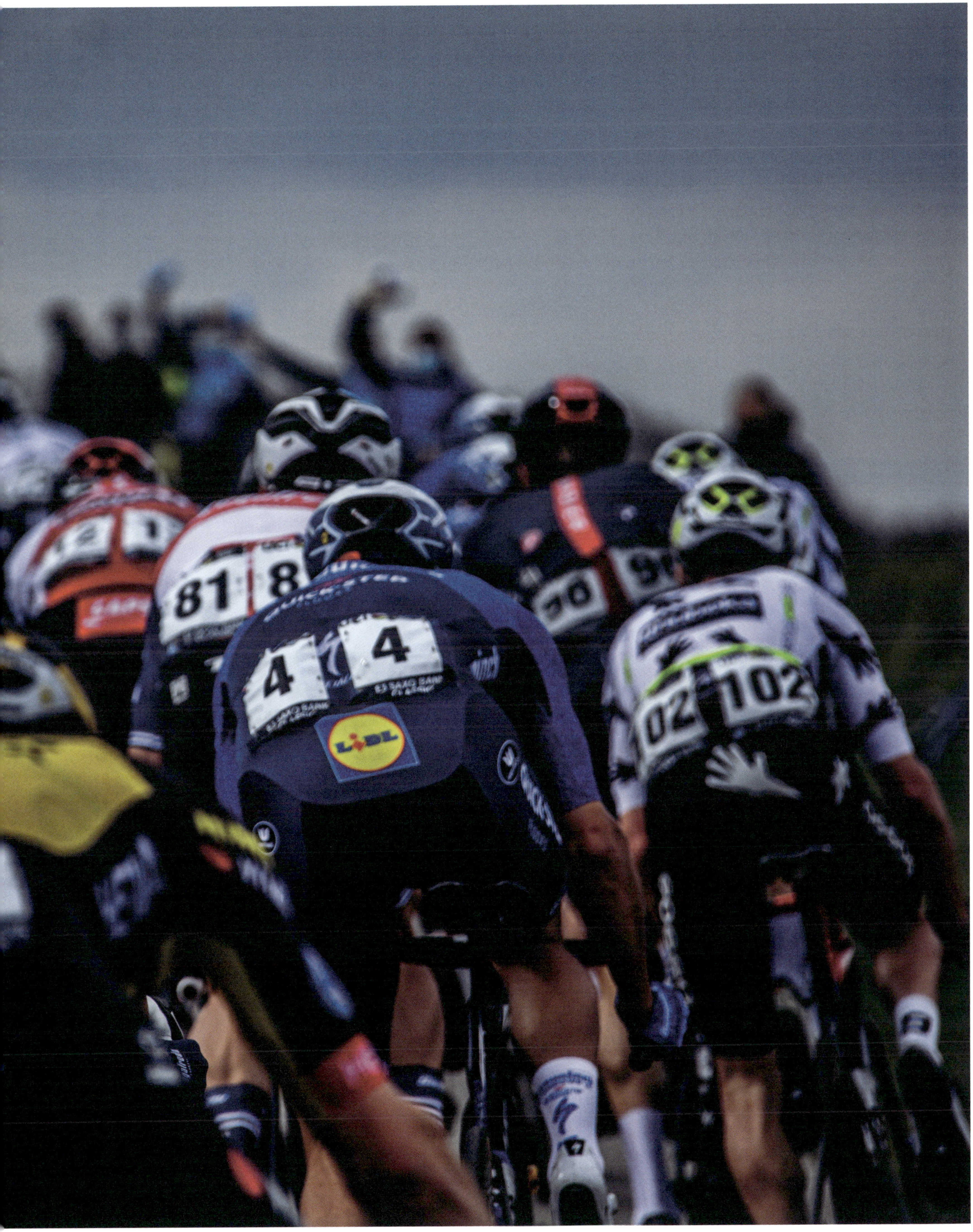
81
4
4
102

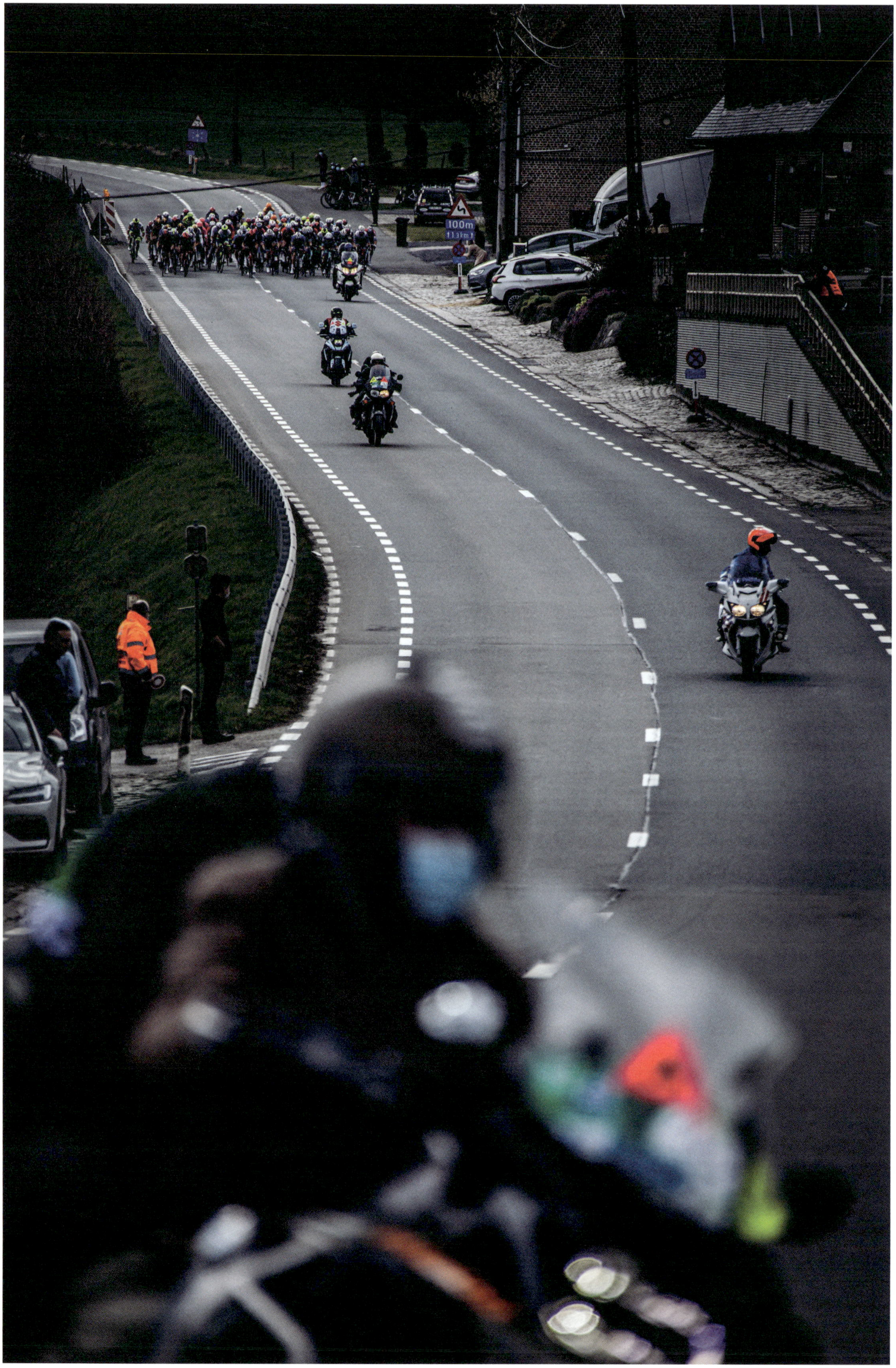
100m

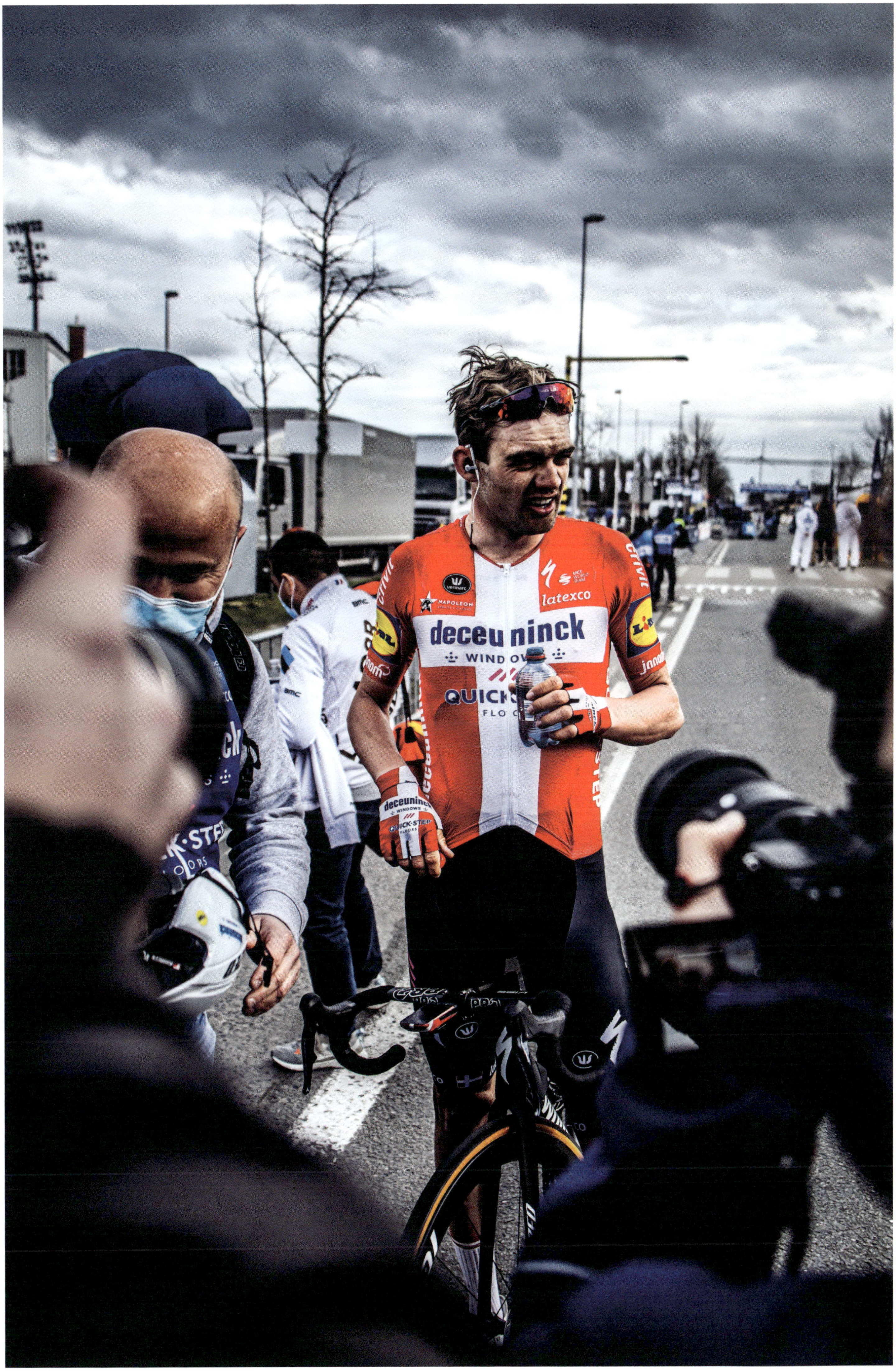
latexco
deceuninck

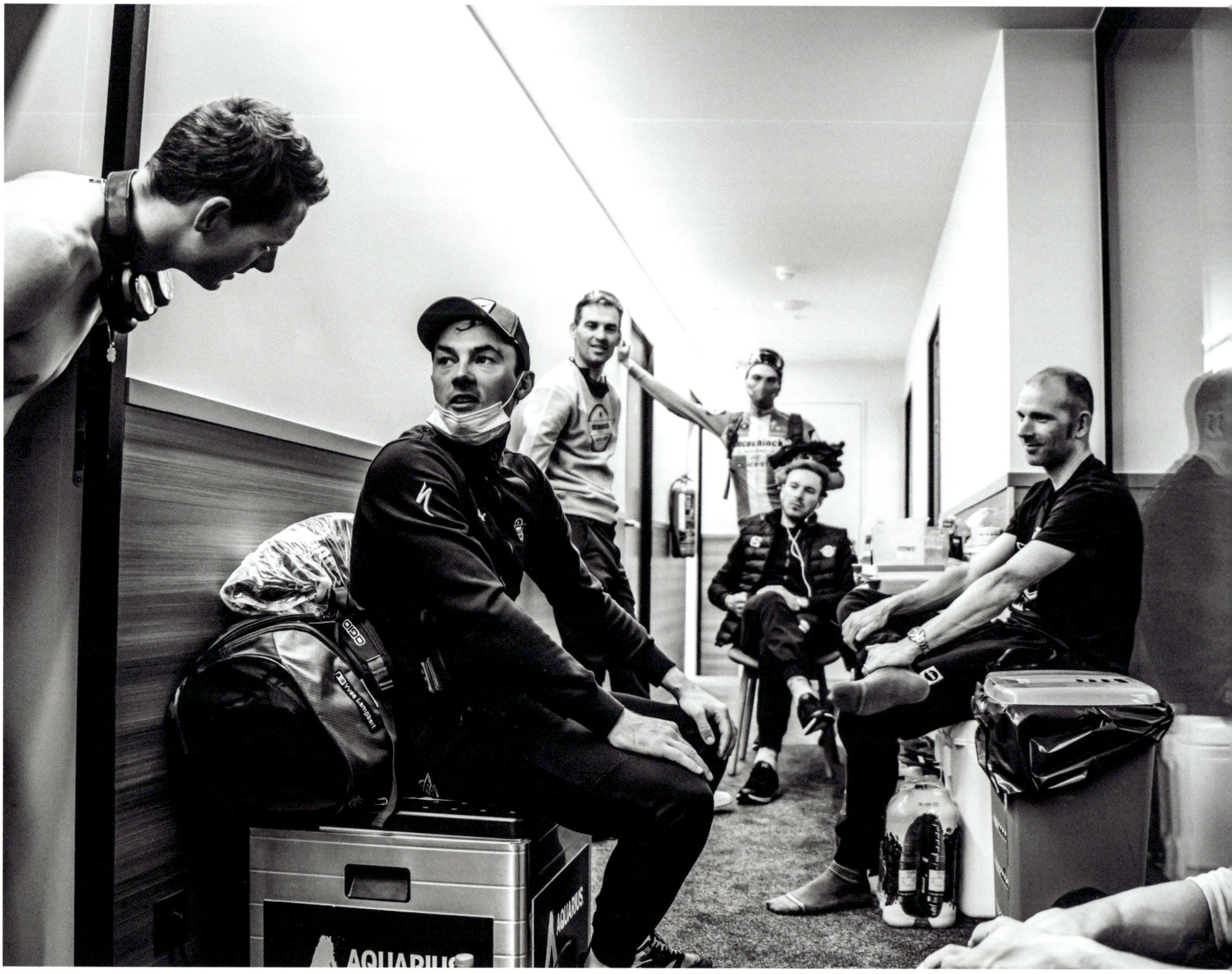

TIELT, 26.03.2021

Een naakte Sam Bennett – enkel getooid met een hoofdtelefoon – steekt zijn hoofd door de deur, tot jolijt van Yves Lampaert, Zdenek Stybar, Kasper Asgreen, Florian Sénéchal, Michael Mørkøv en Stijn Steels.

Coffee time, barista time! Zdenek Stybar loert, observeert en keurt de fameuze 'Rocket Espresso'. Op zoek naar het allerbeste kopje. Steeds weer opnieuw.

Sam Bennett – in the buff except for his headphones – sticks his head through the door, to the amusement of Yves Lampaert, Zdenek Stybar, Kasper Asgreen, Florian Sénéchal, Michael Mørkøv, and Stijn Steels.

Coffee-time, barista-time! Zdenek Stybar is watching, observing, and judging the famous `Rocket Espresso'. Always looking for the tastiest cup.

Sam Bennett est nu et ne porte rien d'autre qu'un casque autour du cou. Il passe la tête par la porte, au grand amusement d'Yves Lampaert, Zdenek Stybar, Kasper Asgreen, Florian Sénéchal, Michael Mørkøv et Stijn Steels. ▲

Coffee time, barista time! Zdenek Stybar regarde, observe et inspecte le fameux « Rocket Espresso ». À chaque fois. ▶

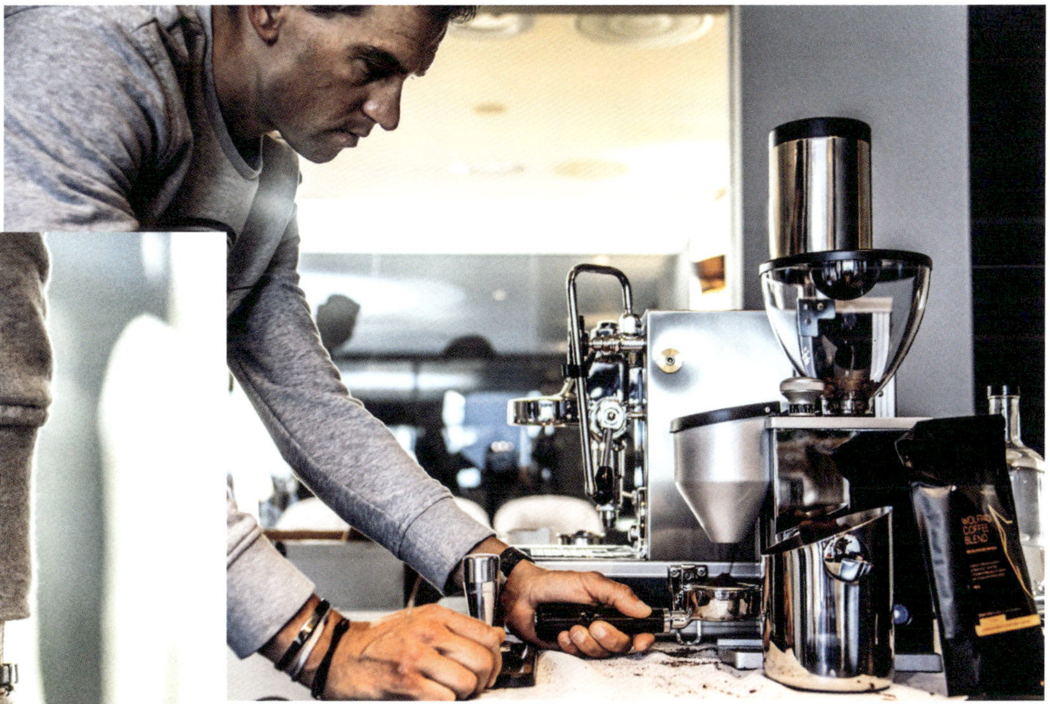

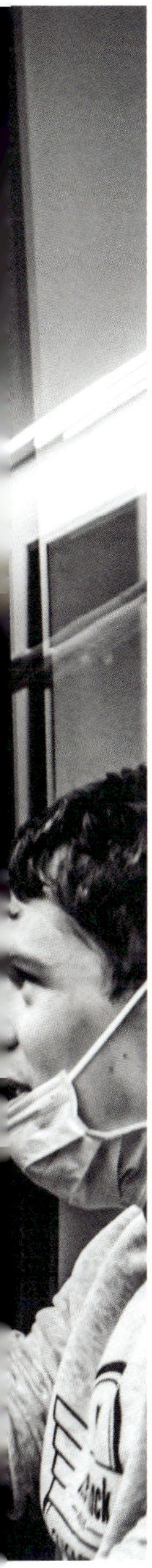

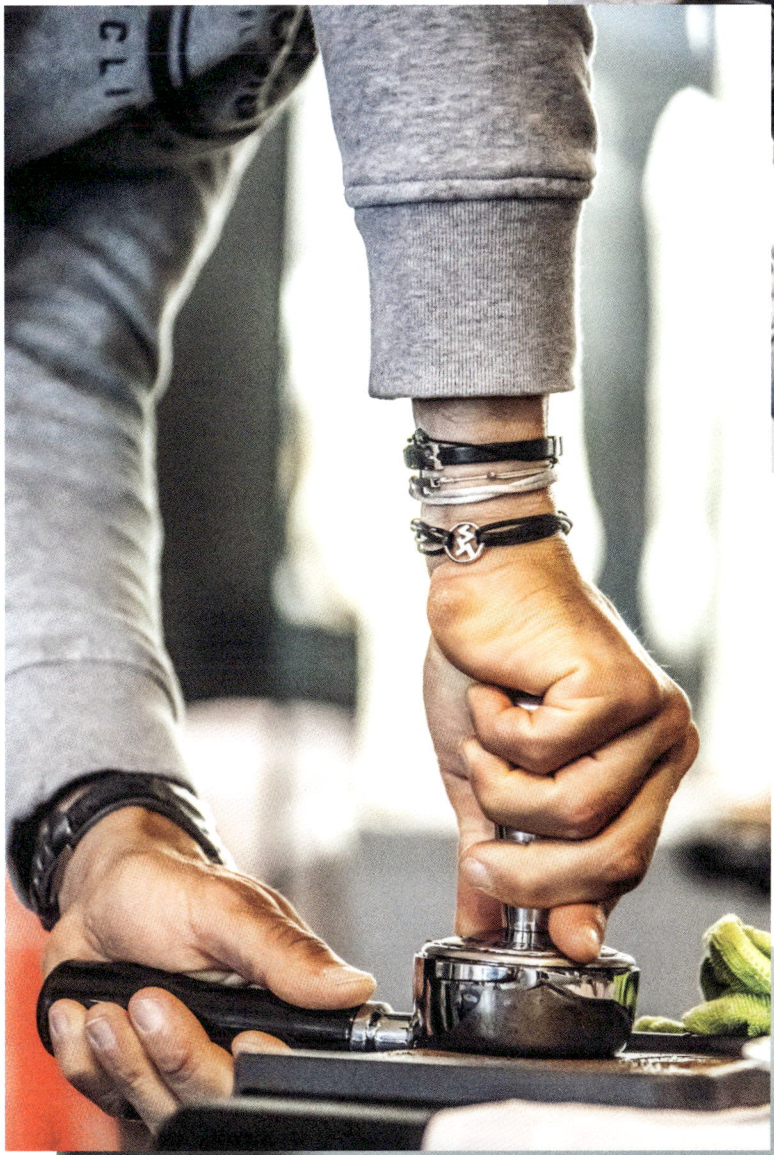

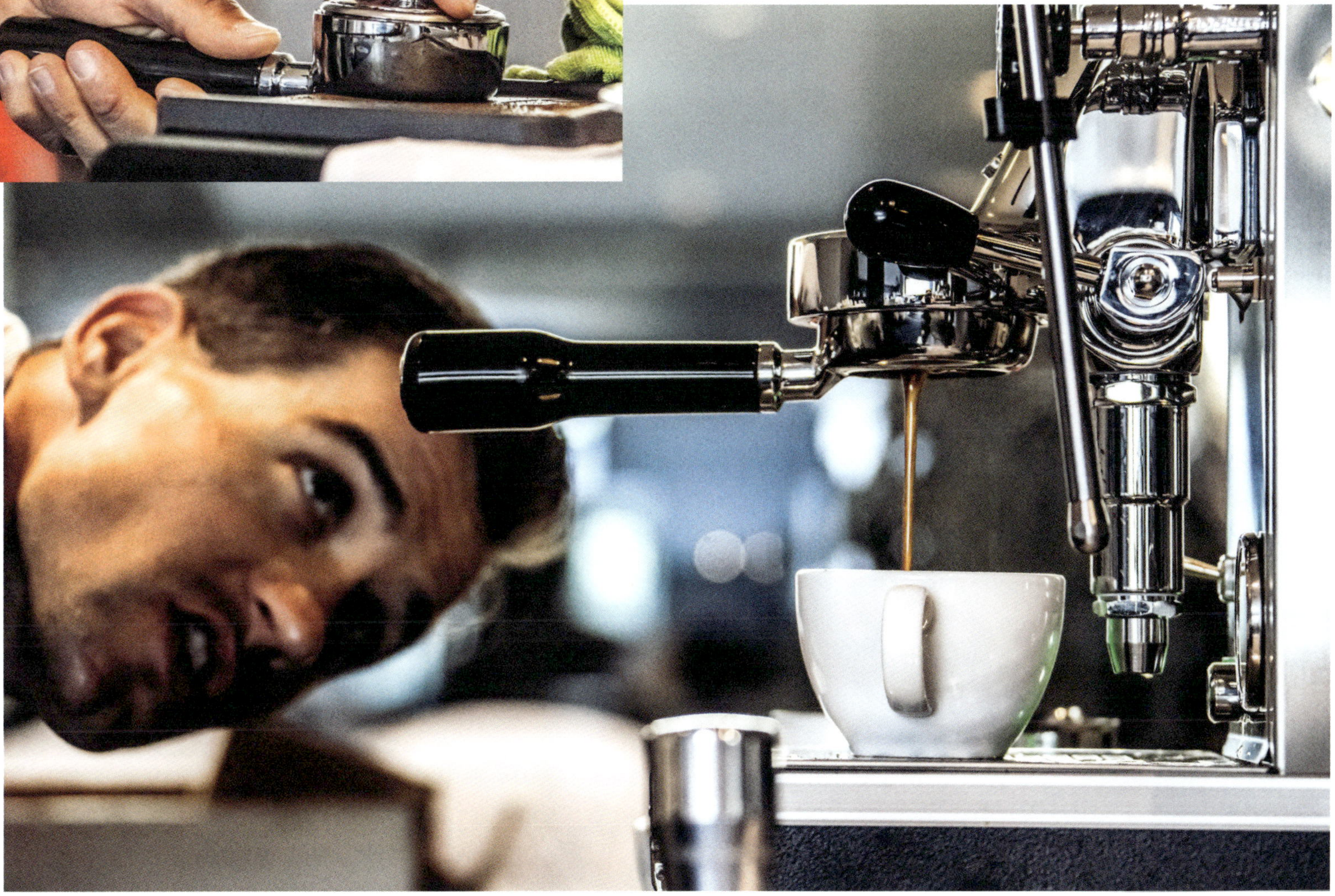

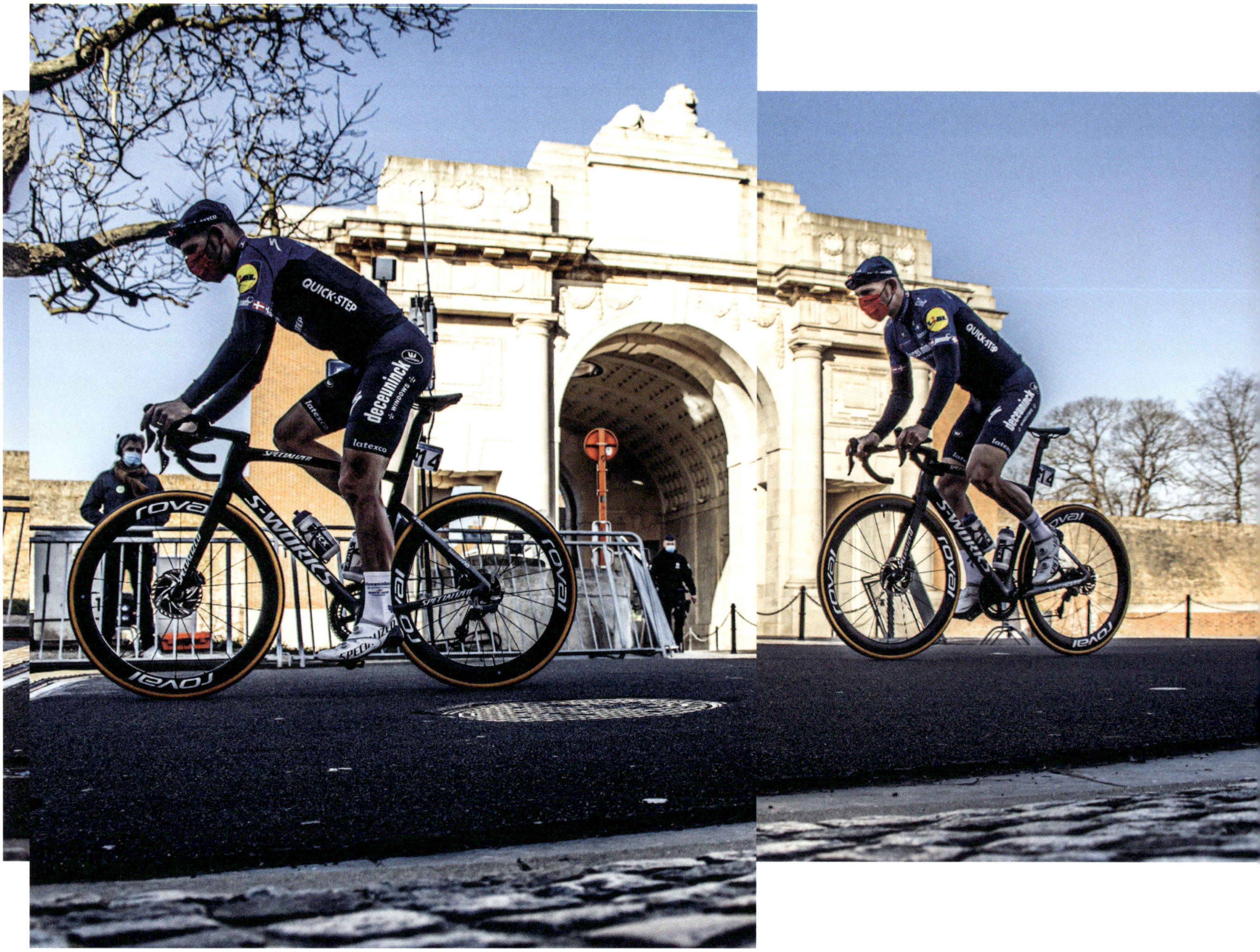

KEMMELBERG, 28.03.2021

Mecanicien Dominique Landuyt (midden) stapt voor de laatste keer als DQT-mecanicien naar de top van de Kemmelberg. Na dit seizoen neemt hij afscheid van de professionele wielersport, die hij sinds 1991 diende. Hij werkte voor de ploeg sinds 2008.

Het echte werk op zondag 28 maart. Zdenek Stybar bestormt de Kemmel, in het hart van Flanders Fields. Uiterst rechts en half verborgen, Davide Ballerini. Na de klassieker onderging Zdenek een ablatie, wat leidde tot enkele maanden inactiviteit (ook na een pinkbreuk). Pas in de Vuelta kon de Tsjech weer over al zijn troeven beschikken.

Mechanic Dominique Landuyt (center) climbs to the top of Mount Kemmel for the last time as a DQT mechanic. After this season, he says goodbye to the sport of professional cycling which he has served since 1991. He started working for the team in 2008.

The real work on Sunday 28 March. Zdenek Stybar storms the Kemmel, in the heart of Flanders Fields. On the far right, half hidden, is Davide Ballerini. After this classic, Zdenek underwent an ablation procedure, which led to several months of inactivity (also after a small finger fracture). It wasn't until the Vuelta that the Czech was able to use all his assets again.

Dominique Landuyt (au centre) atteint le sommet du mont Kemmel, c'est sa dernière fois en tant que mécanicien de la DQT. Après cette saison, il fera ses adieux au monde du cyclisme professionnel, dans lequel il travaille depuis 1991. Il travaille pour l'équipe depuis 2008.

La vraie épreuve, le dimanche 28 mars. Zdenek Stybar prend d'assaut le mont Kemmel, au cœur des fameux Champs des Flandres. À l'extrême droite et à moitié caché, Davide Ballerini. Zdenek a subi une ablation après la classique. En raison de cette procédure, mais aussi d'une petite fracture du doigt, il a dû observer plusieurs mois de repos. Il a fallu attendre la Vuelta pour que le Tchèque puisse à nouveau démontrer ses talents.

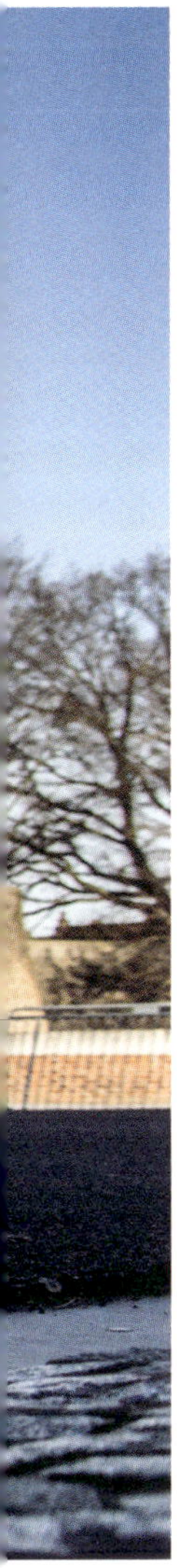

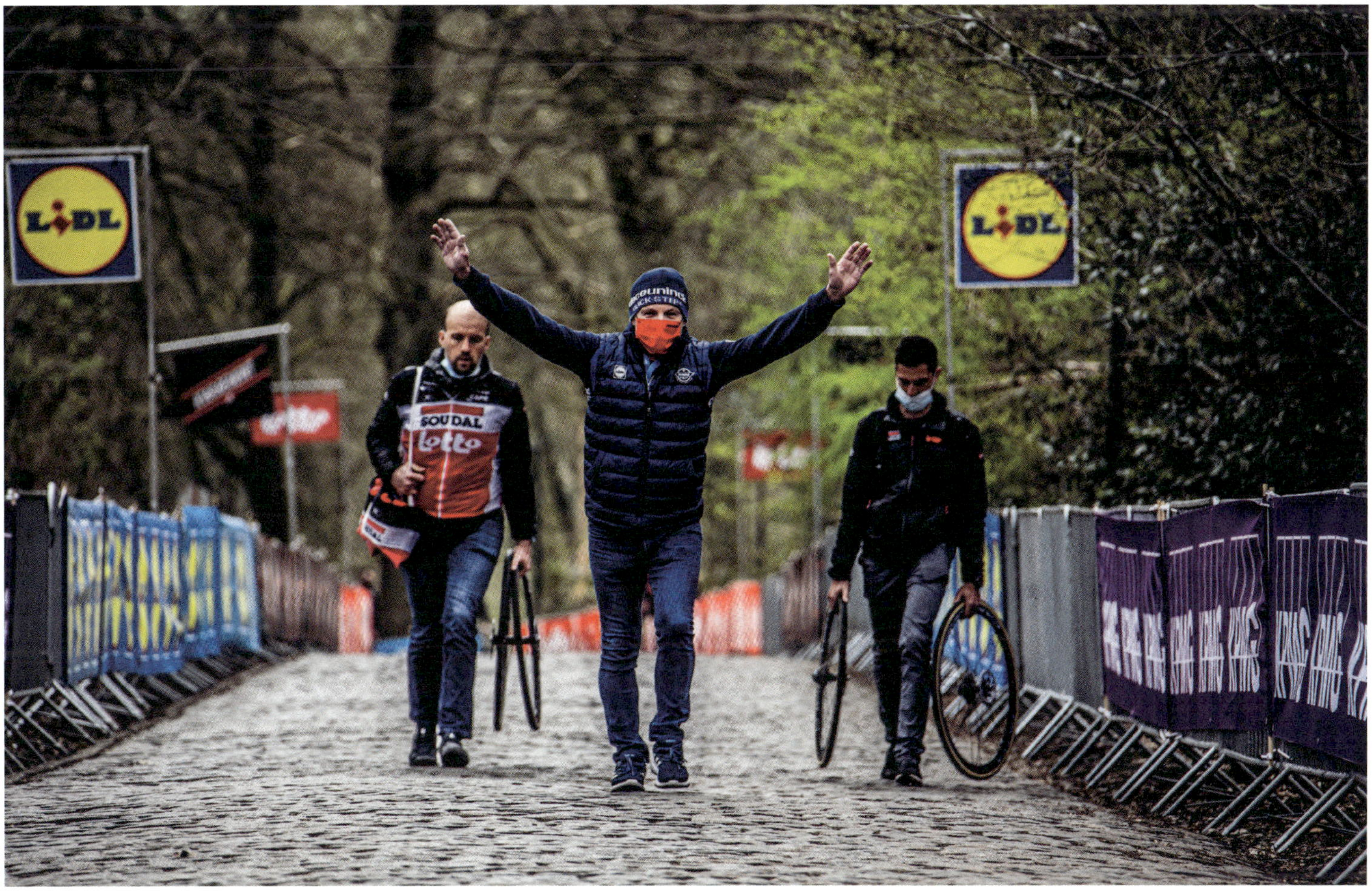
LIDL
LIDL
SOUDAL
lotto

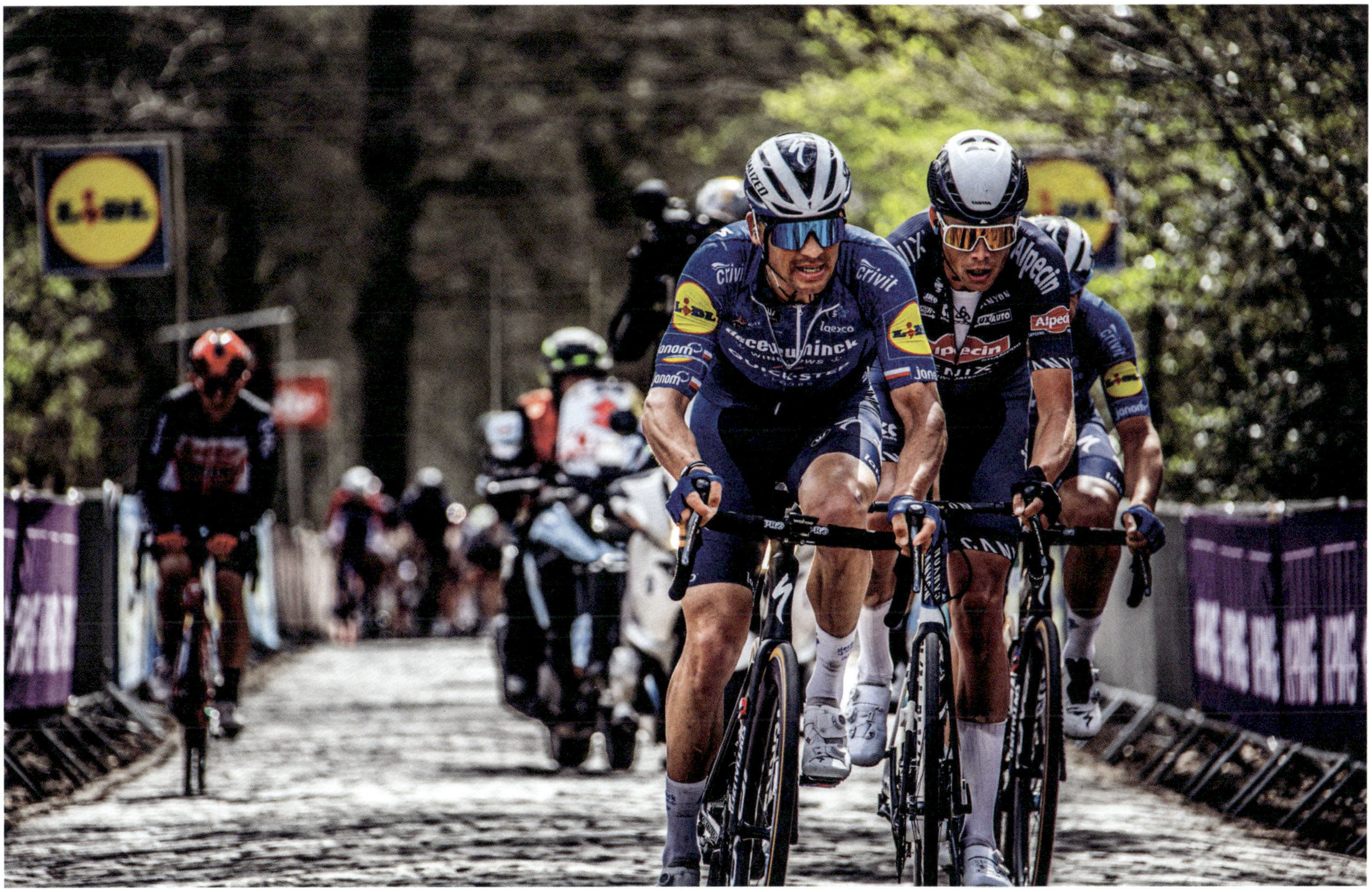
LIDL
crivit
Alpecin

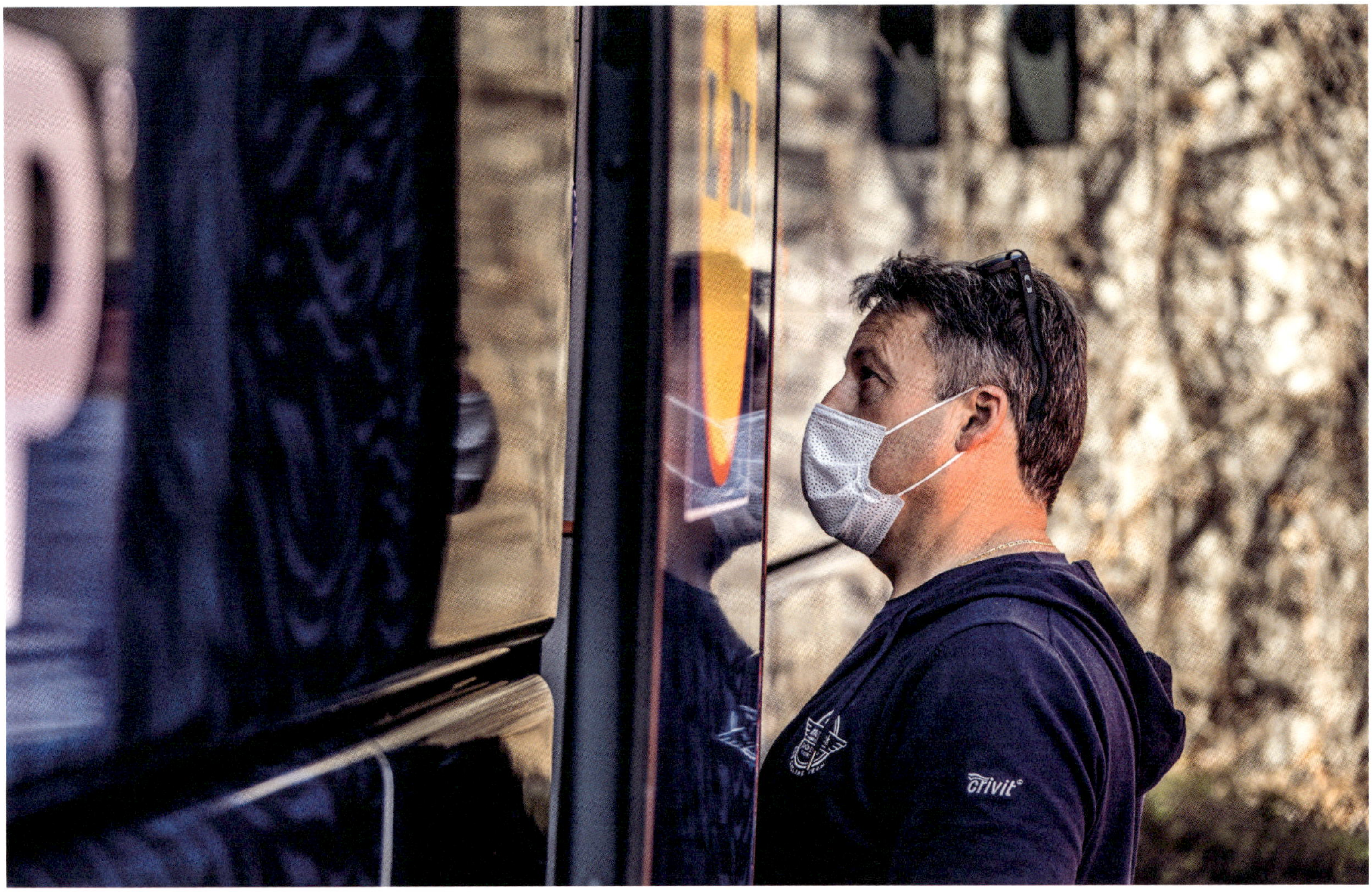
crivit

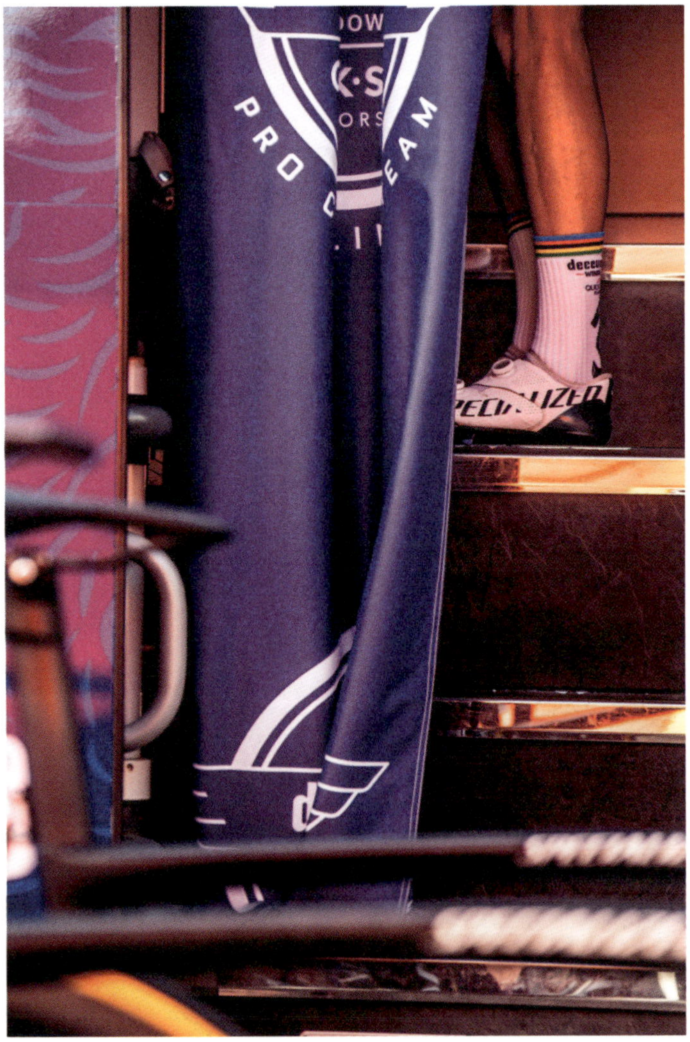

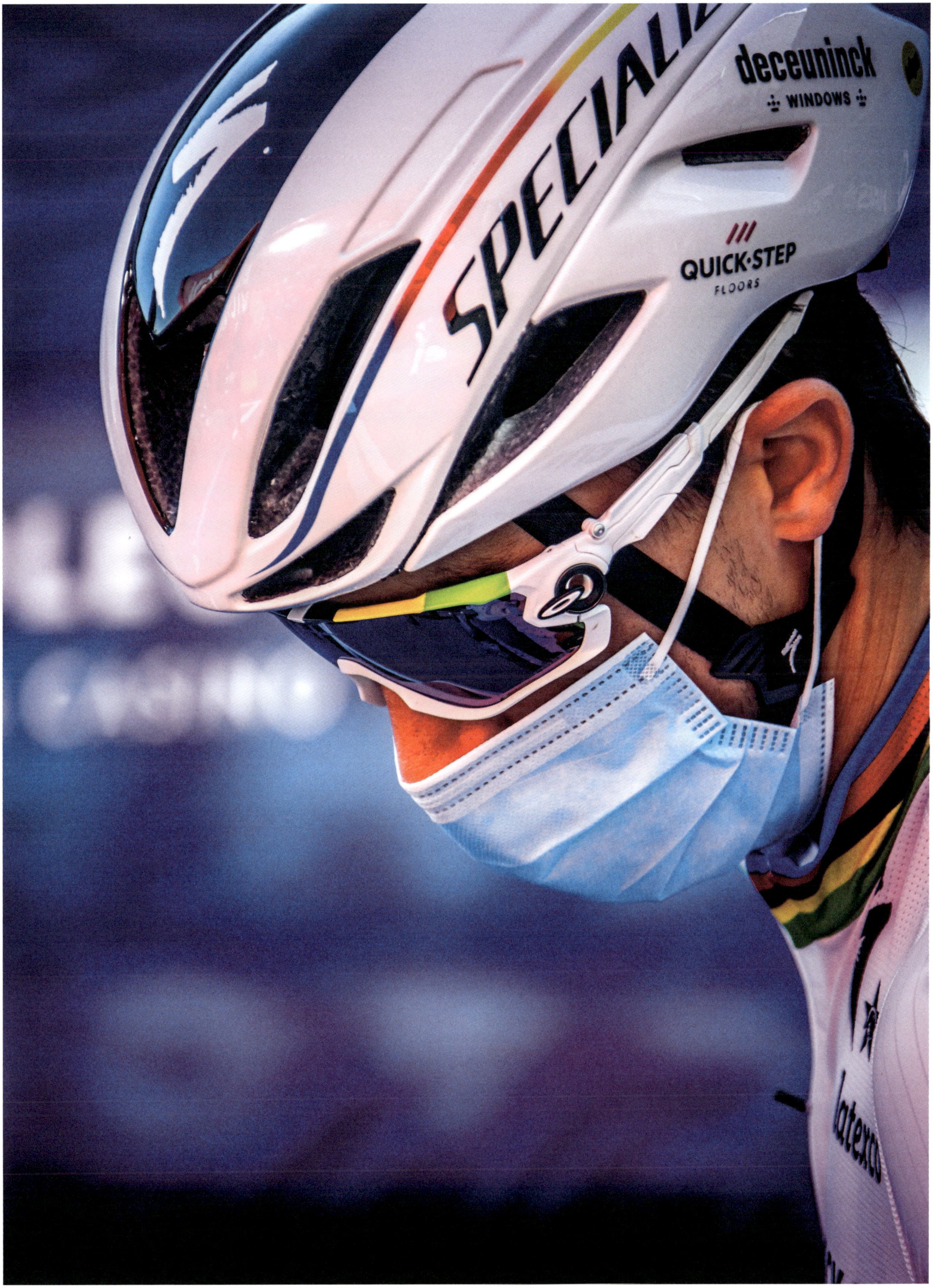
deceuninck
WINDOWS
QUICK·STEP
FLOORS
latexco

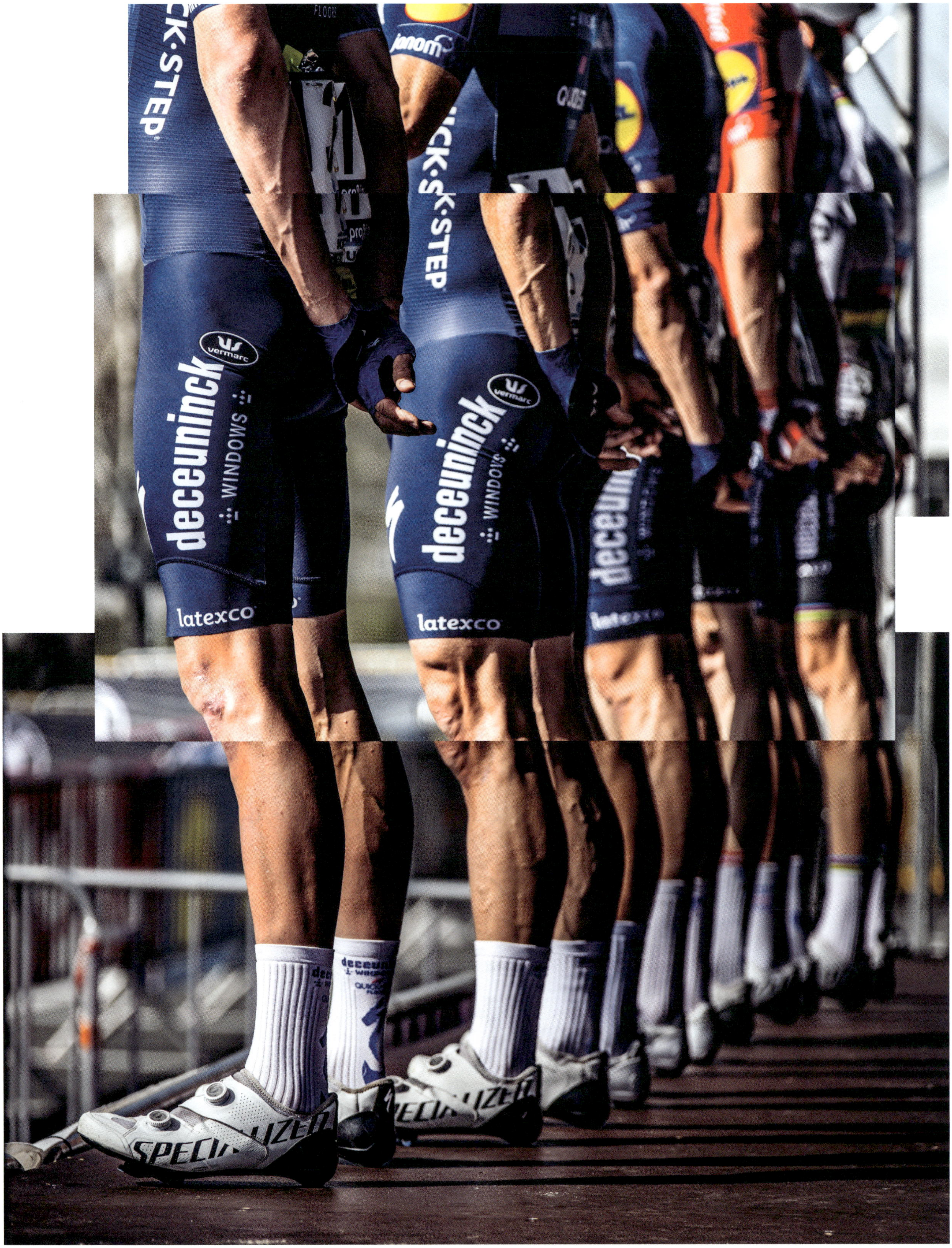
deceuninck
WINDOWS
vermarc
latexco

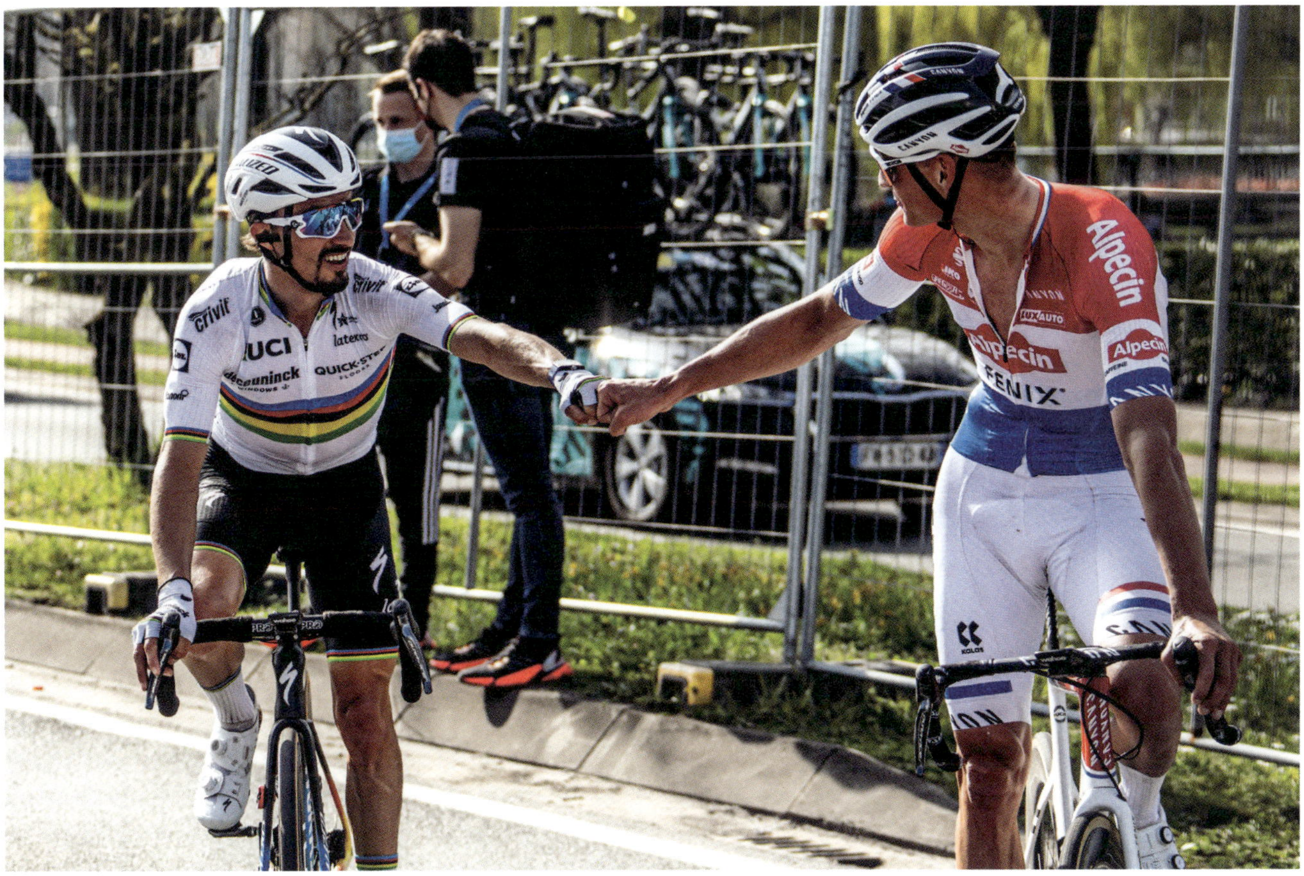
crivit
UCI
latexco
QUICK-STEP
Alpecin
FENIX
Alpecin

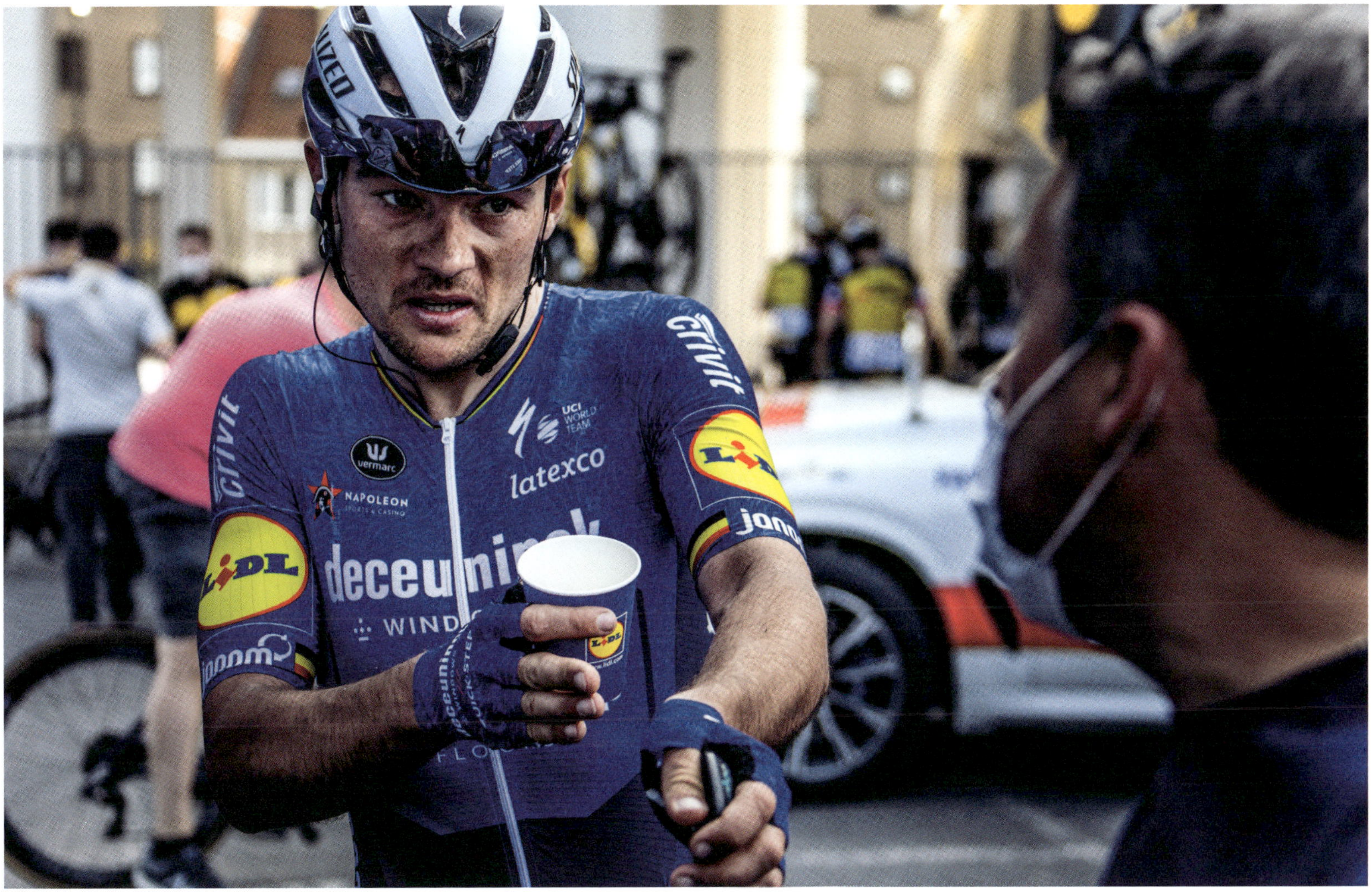
crivit
UCI
WORLD
TEAM
vermarc
latexco
NAPOLEON
LIDL
crivit
LIDL

RONDE VAN VLAANDEREN
04.04.2021

Een van de mooiste zeges van het jaar voor het Deceuninck – Quick-Step Team. De Deense Kampioen Kasper Asgreen schrijft op 4 april 2021 de 105de Ronde van Vlaanderen op zijn naam. Hij verslaat Mathieu van der Poel na een bloedstollende sprint met twee.

One of the most beautiful wins of the year for the Deceuninck – Quick-Step Team. Danish Champion Kasper Asgreen wins the 105th Ronde van Vlaanderen on 4 April 2021. He beats Mathieu van der Poel in a nerve-racking two-up sprint.

L'une des plus belles victoires de l'année pour l'équipe Deceuninck – Quick-Step. Le Champion Danois Kasper Asgreen a remporté la 105e édition du Ronde van Vlaanderen le 4 avril 2021. Il a dominé au sprint le tenant du titre Mathieu van der Poel.

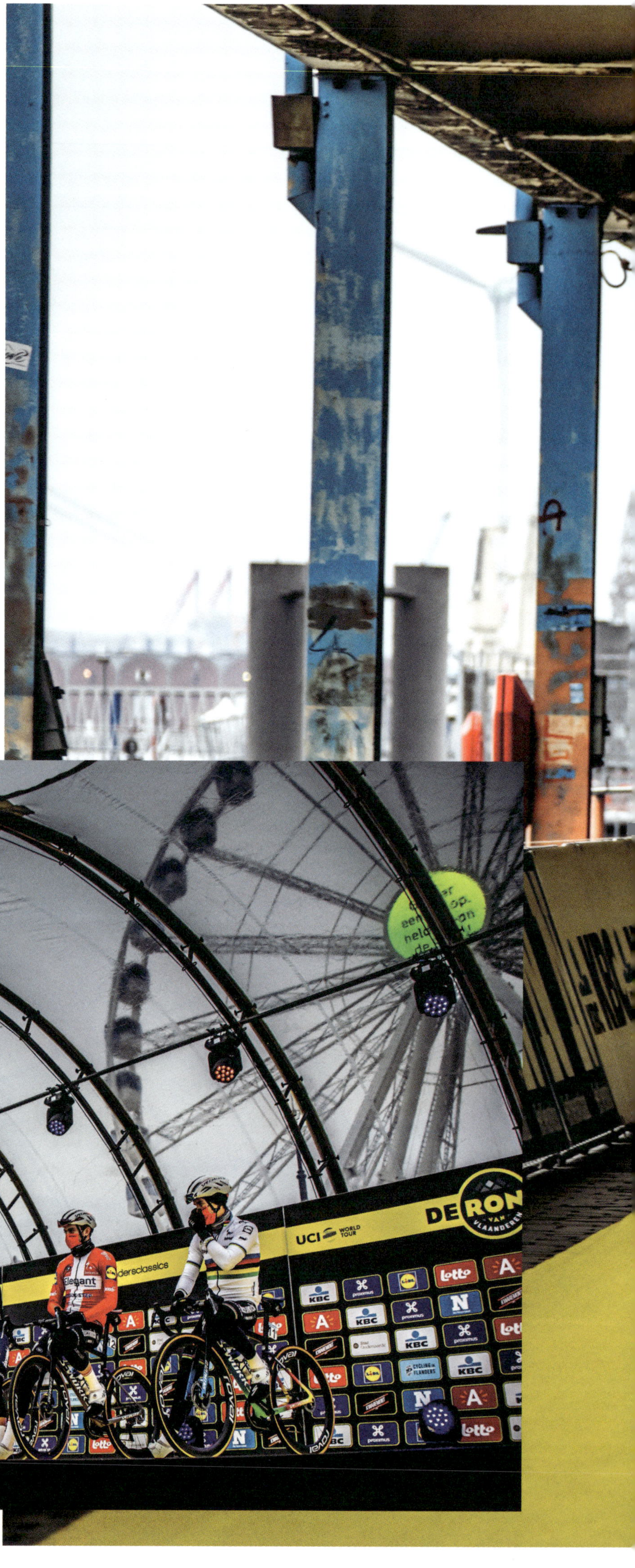

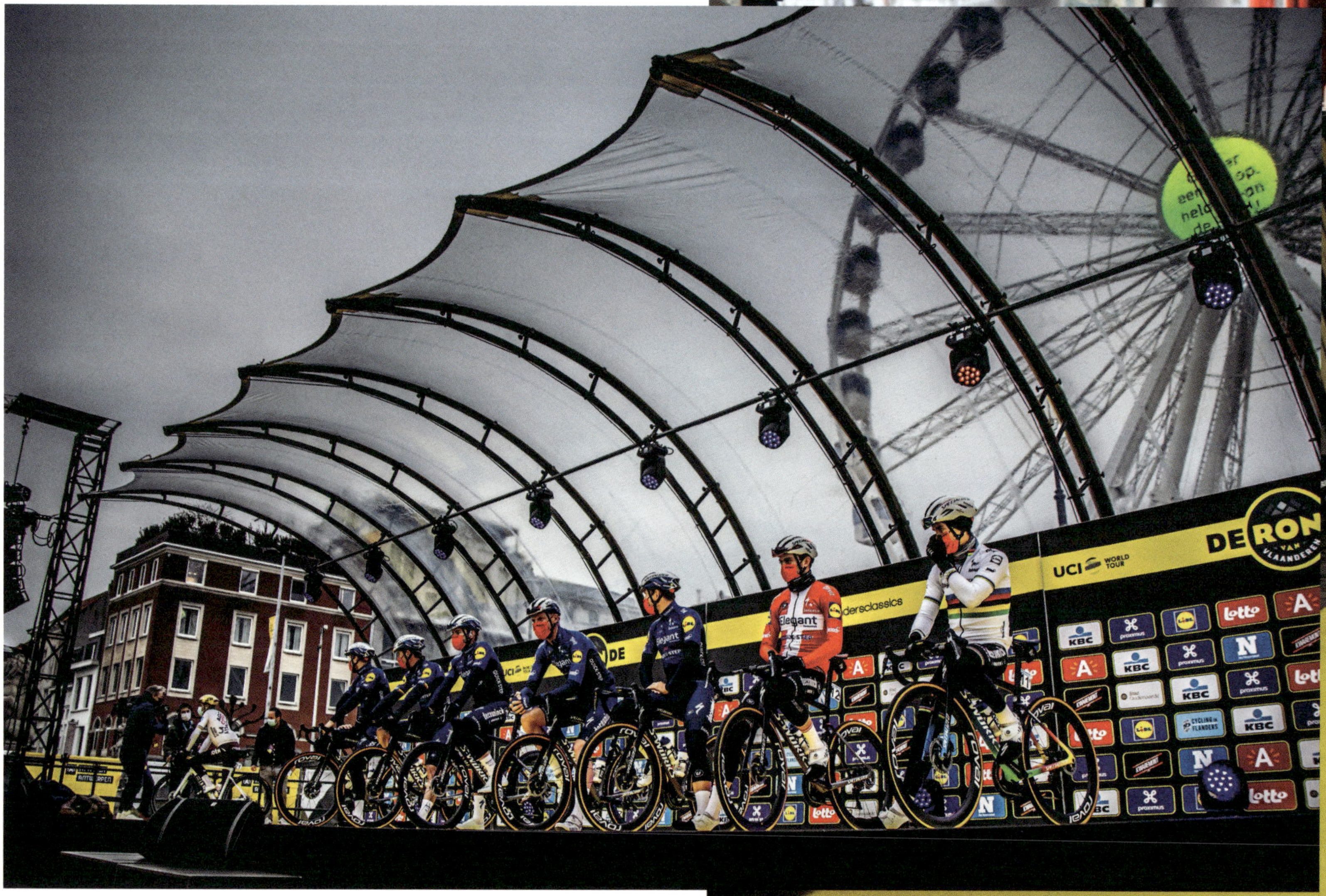

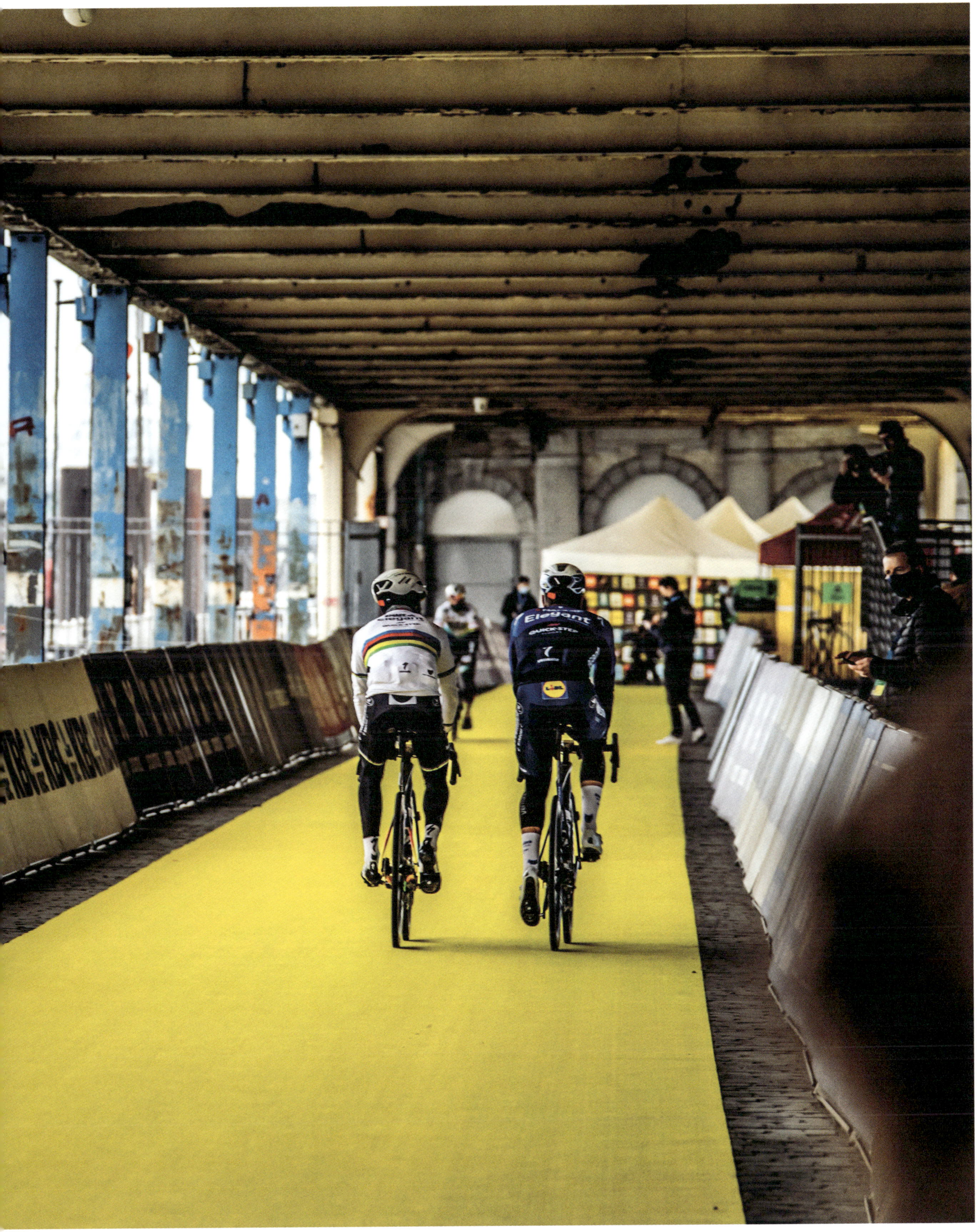
Elegant
KBC

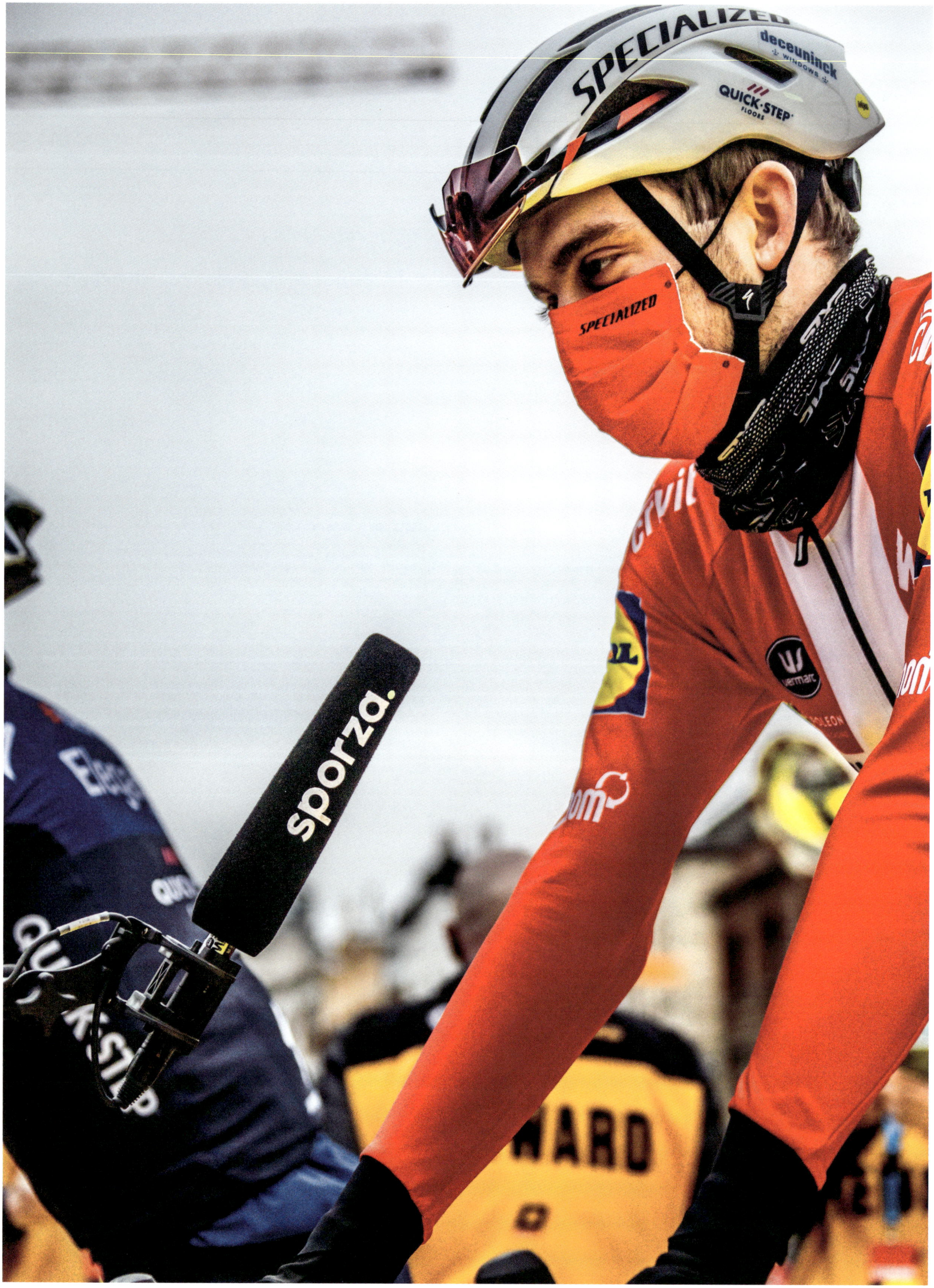
SPECIALIZED
deceuninck
WINDOWS
QUICK·STEP
FLOORS
SPECIALIZED
sporza.

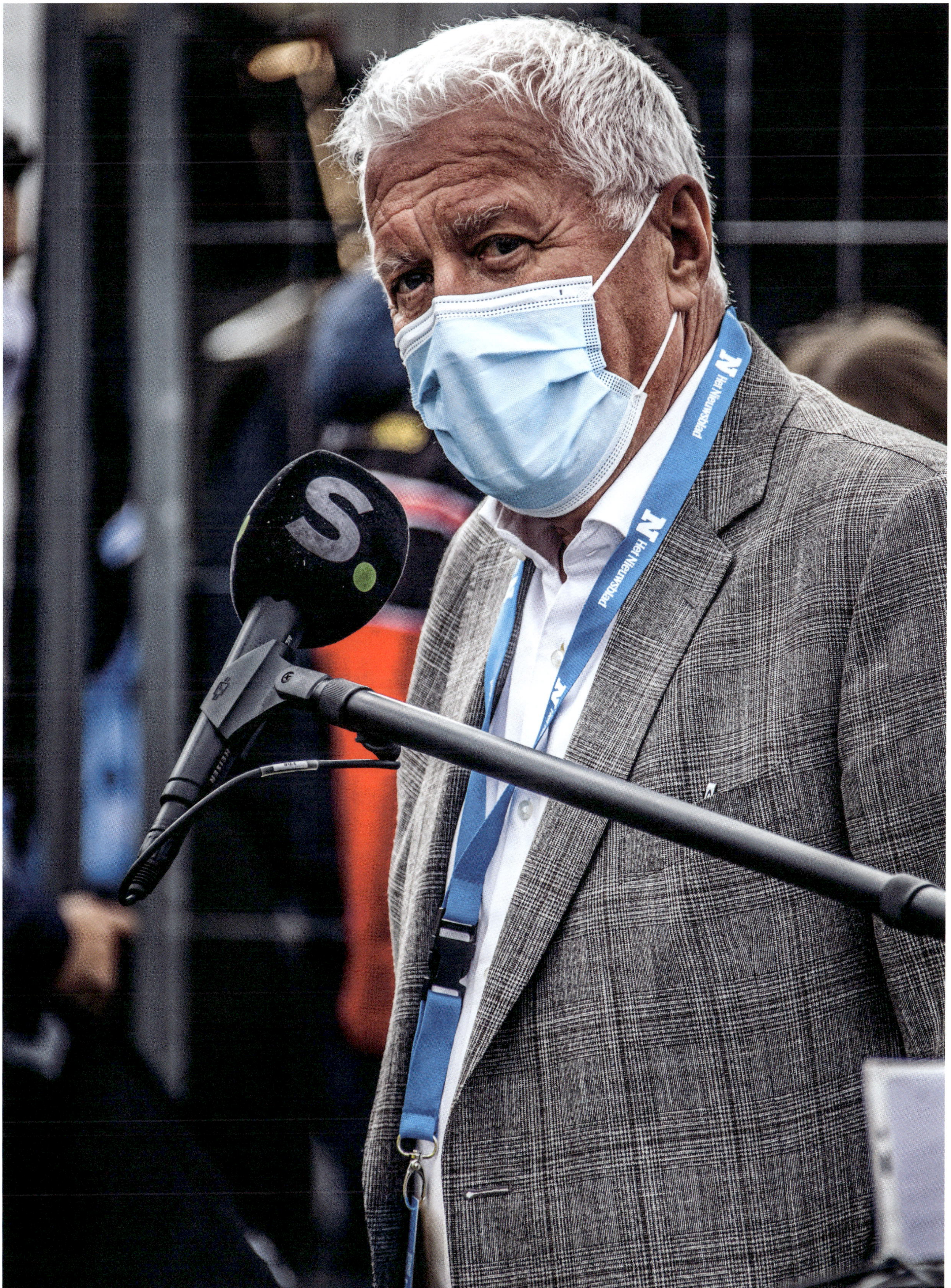
Het Nieuwsblad

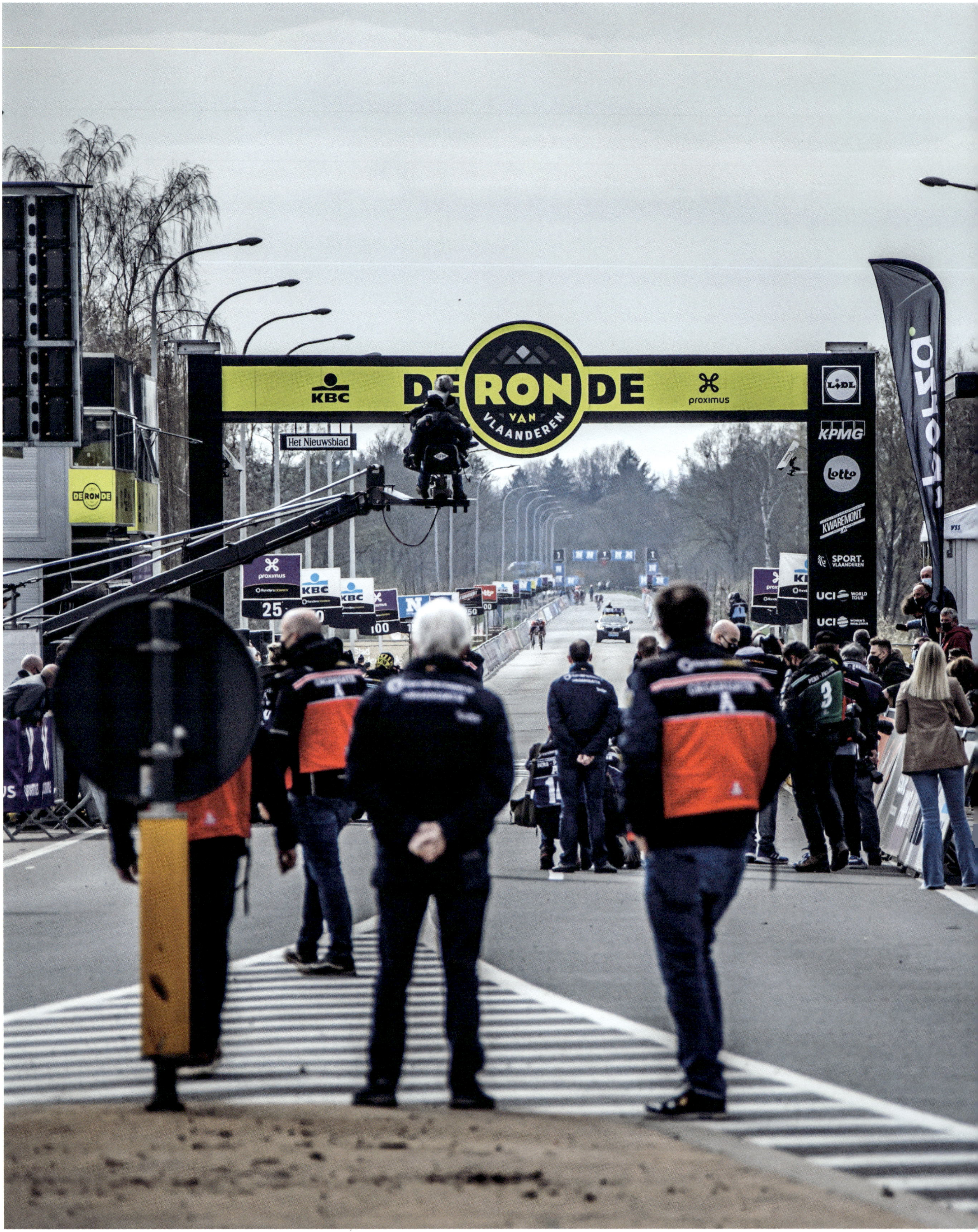
KBC
DE RONDE VAN VLAANDEREN
proximus
LIDL
KPMG
lotto
KWAREMONT
SPORT. VLAANDEREN
UCI WORLD TOUR
Het Nieuwsblad

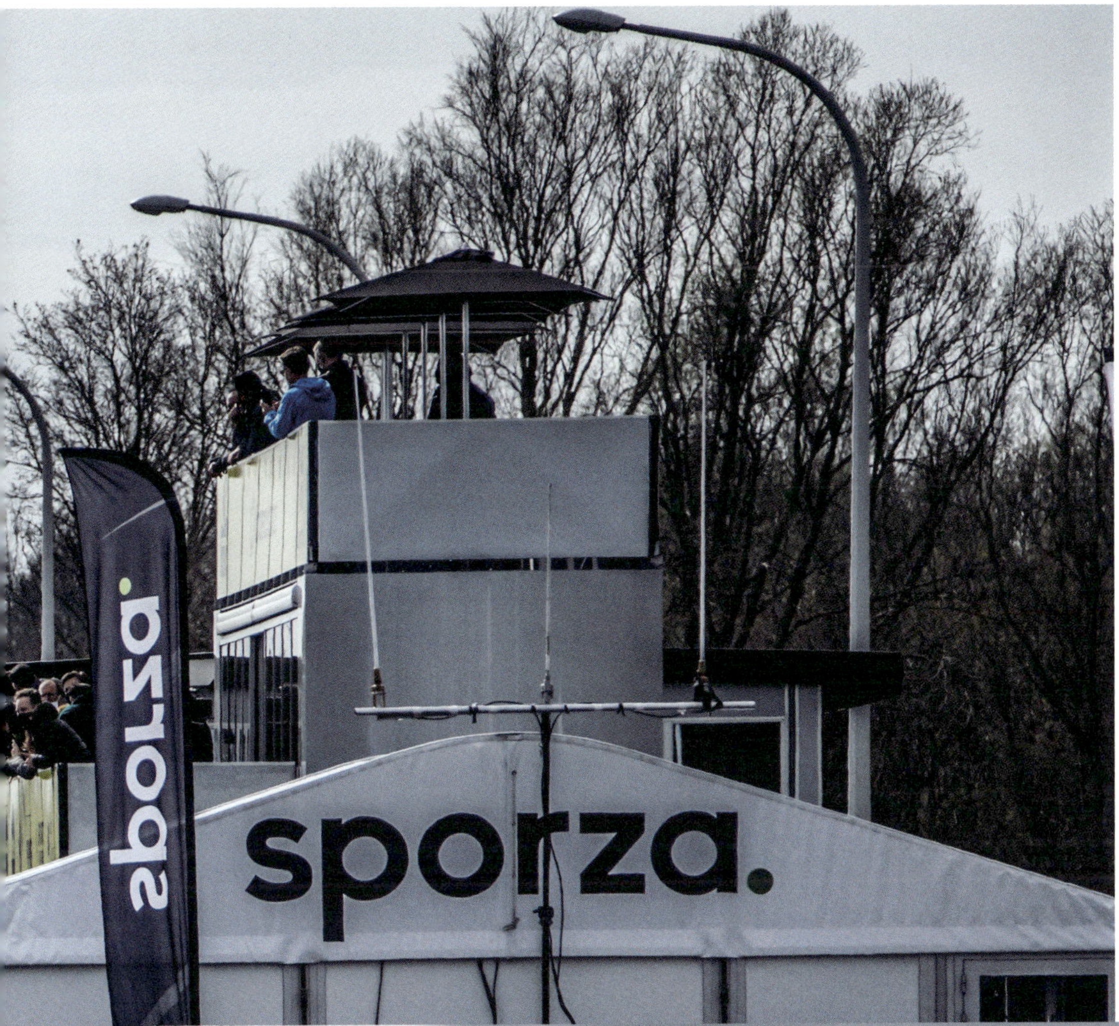
sporza.
sporza.

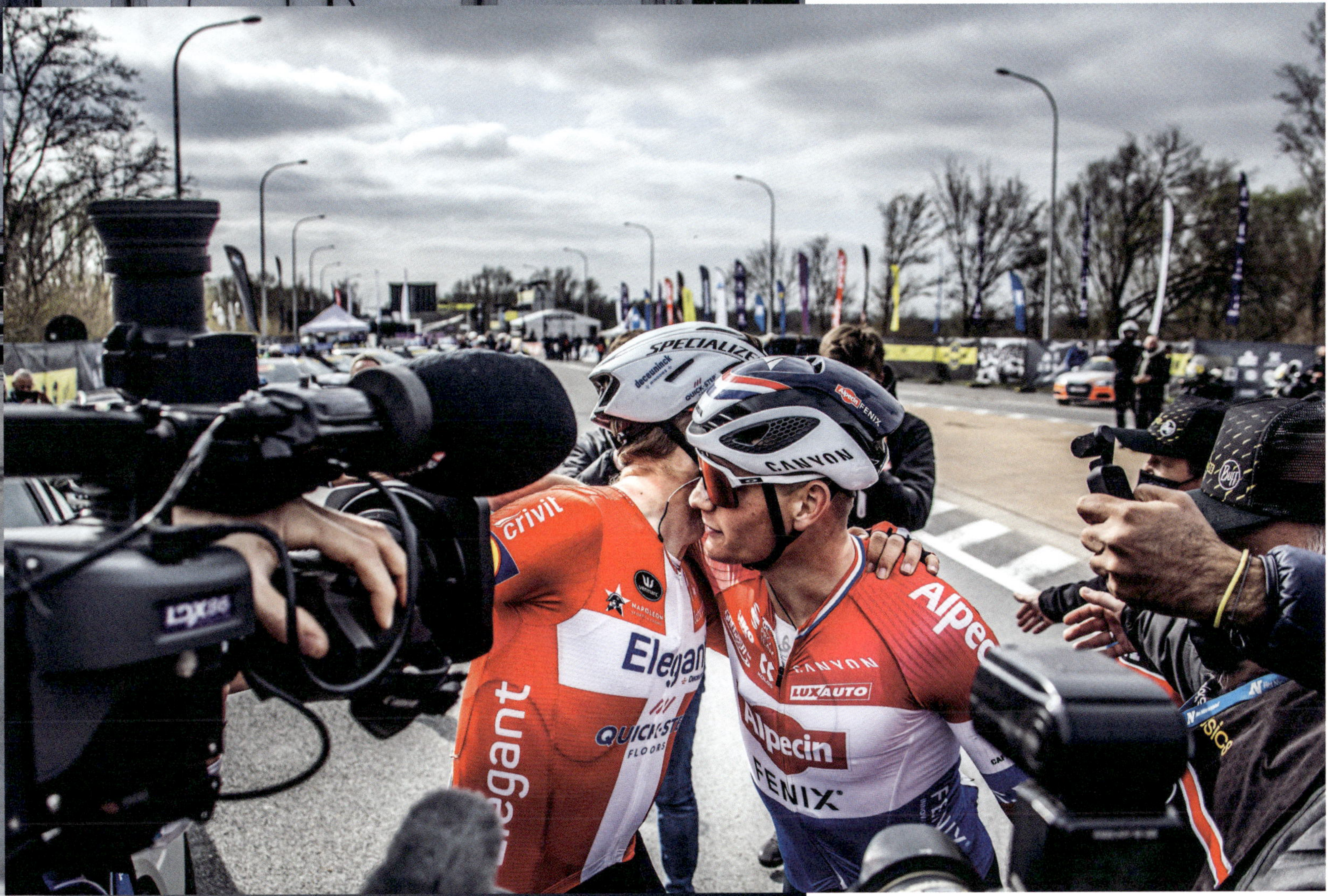
crivit
Elegant
elegant
QUICK-STEP
FLOORS
CANYON
CANYON
LUXAUTO
Alpecin
FENIX

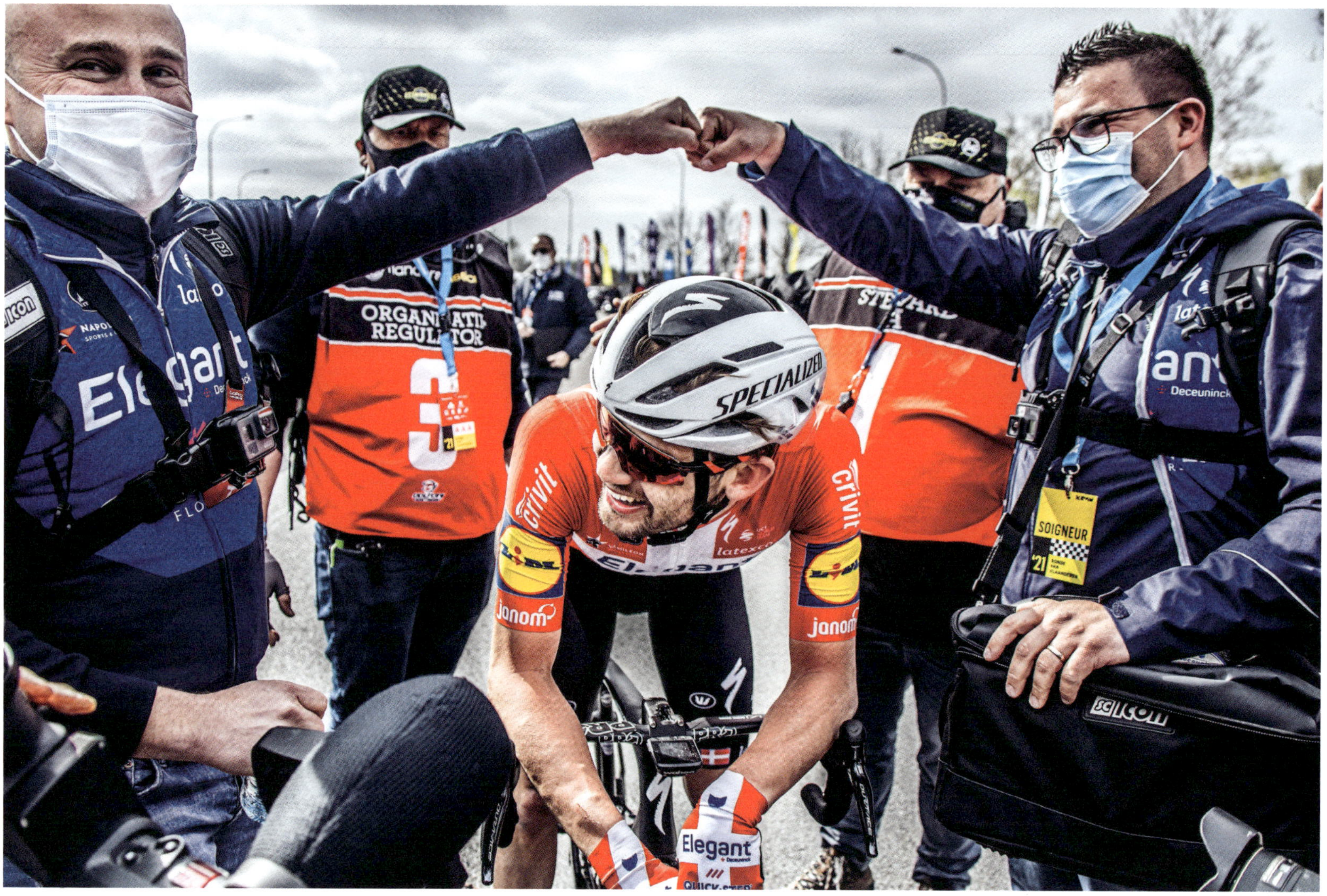

OUDENAARDE, 04.04.2021

De vuisten van fysiotherapeut Steven Vrancken en masseur Kevin Verstaen vormen een triomfboog voor Kasper Asgreen. Die hijgt nog even na, maar zijn lach zegt alles. Hij is de winnaar van Vlaanderens Mooiste.

Stel je voor: nadat alle verplichtingen achter de rug zijn – medische controle, tv-interviews, persconferentie – staat de laureaat van Vlaanderens Mooiste erop zijn fiets eigenhandig op het dak van de volgwagen te zetten. Op naar het avondfeest.

The fists of physiotherapist Steven Vrancken and masseur Kevin Verstaen form a triumphal arch for Kasper Asgreen. He's still panting, but his smile says it all. He's the winner of *Vlaanderens Mooiste*.

Imagine this: after all the obligations have been fulfilled – a medical check-up, TV interviews, press conference – the winner of *Vlaanderens Mooiste* insists on putting his bike on the roof of the car with his own hands. On to the evening party.

Les poings du kinésithérapeute Steven Vrancken et du masseur Kevin Verstaen forment un arc de triomphe pour Kasper Asgreen. Il n'a pas encore repris son souffle, mais son sourire en dit long. Il est déclaré vainqueur de la Ronde. ▲

Vous y croyez ? Après avoir remporté la course ET rempli toutes ses obligations – visite médicale, interviews télévisées, conférence de presse – Kasper insiste pour fixer lui-même son vélo sur le toit de la voiture suiveuse. Et maintenant, la soirée ! ▶

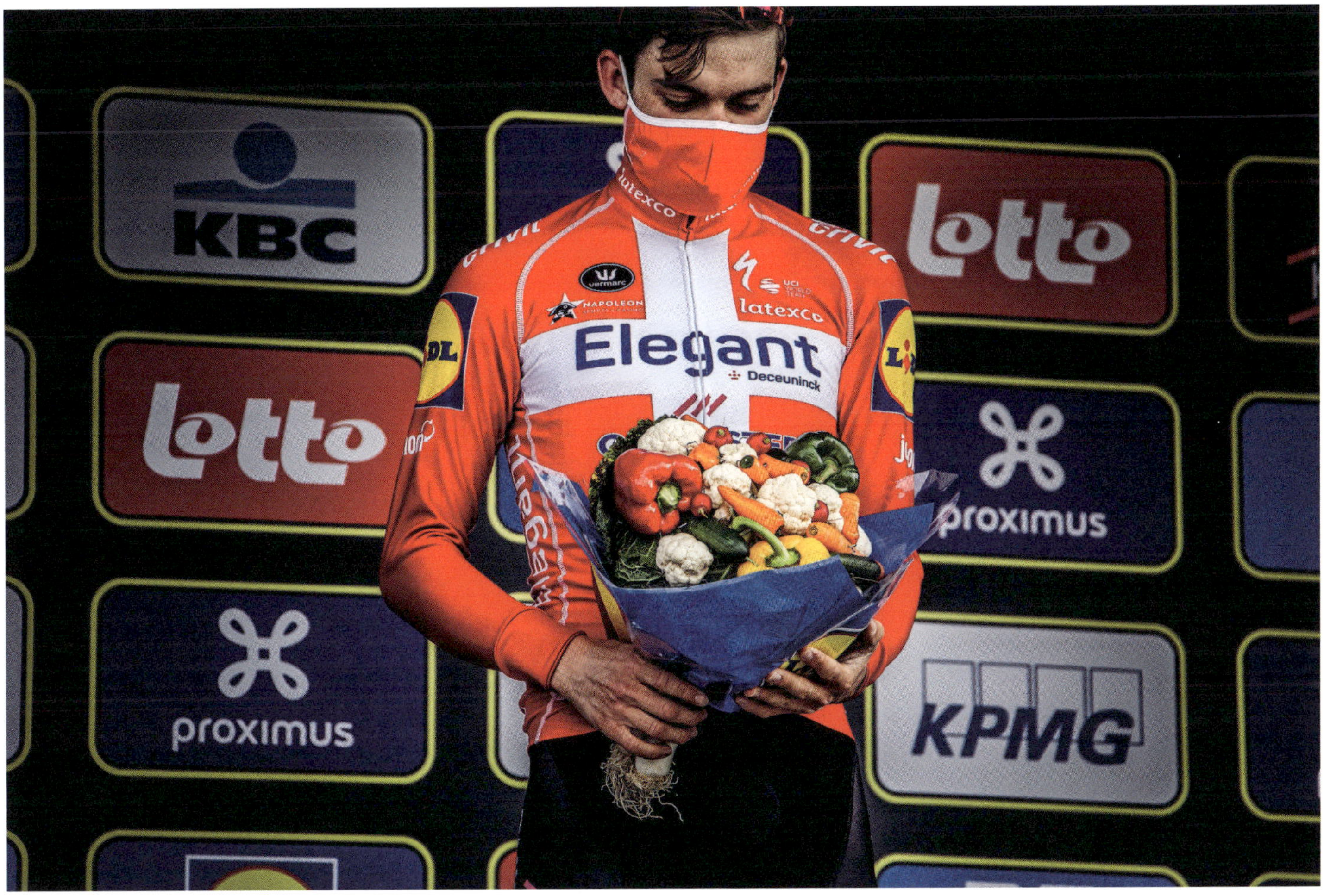
KBC
lotto
lotto
proximus
proximus
KPMG
Elegant
Deceuninck
latexco
crivit

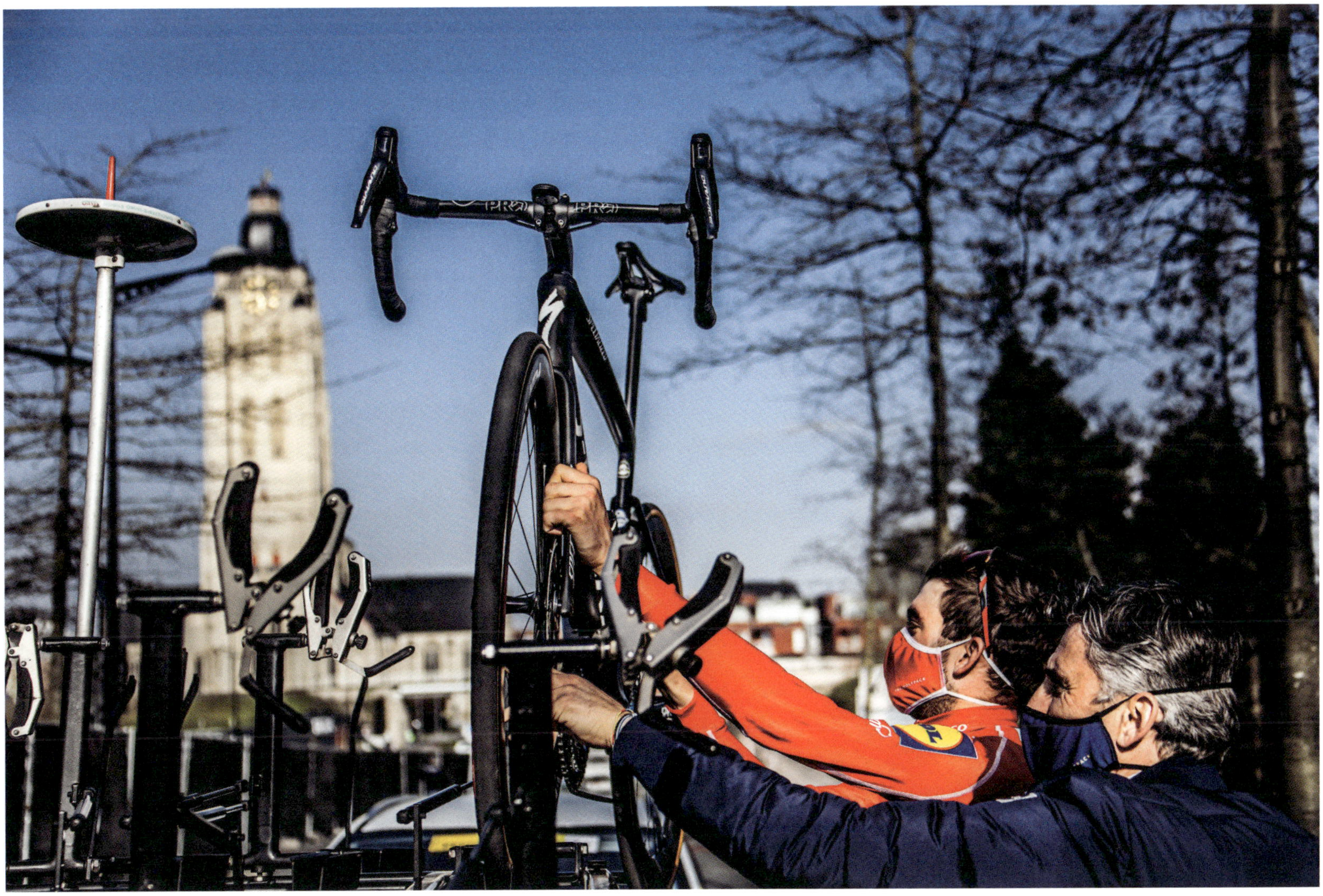

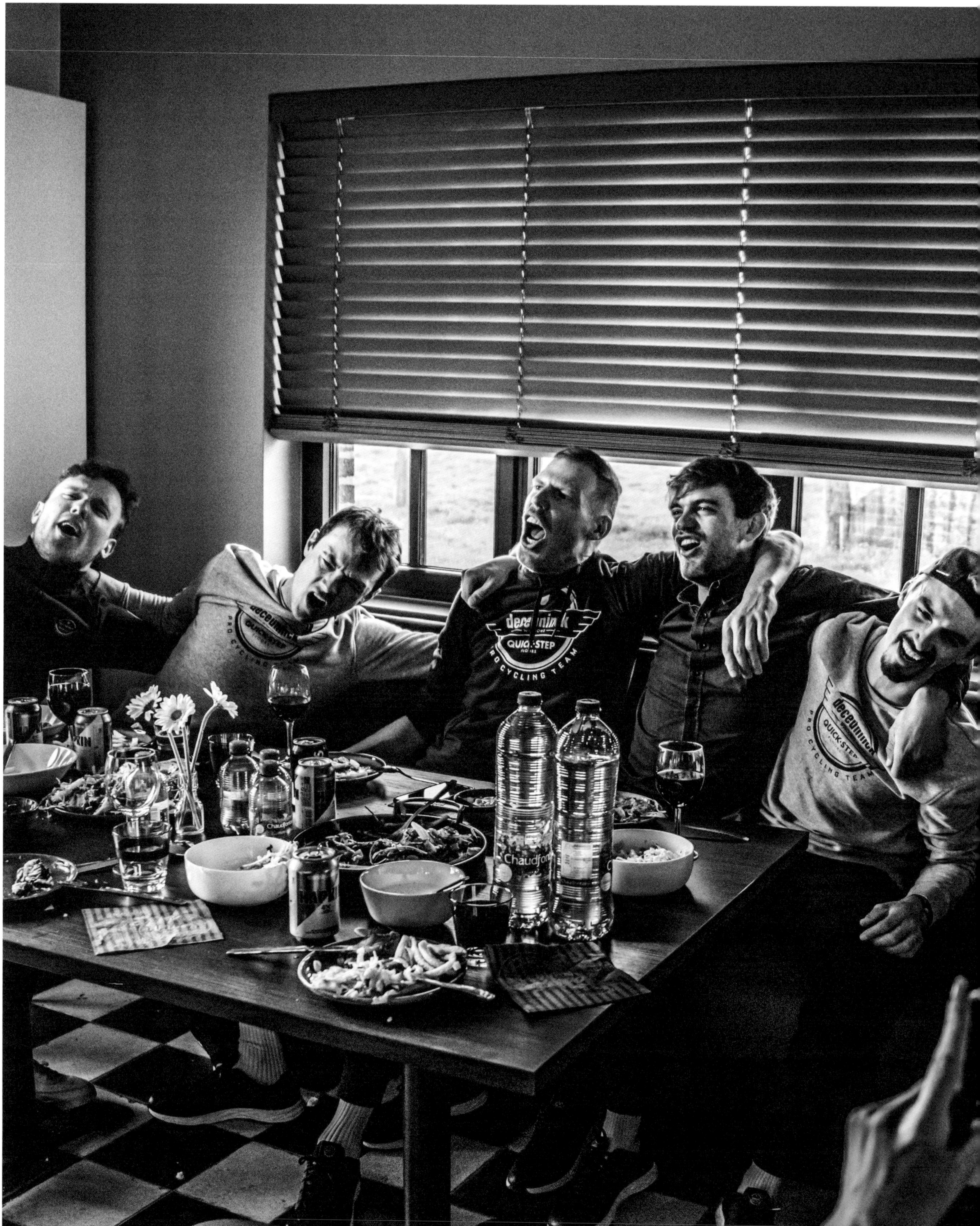
QUICK·STEP
PRO CYCLING TEAM

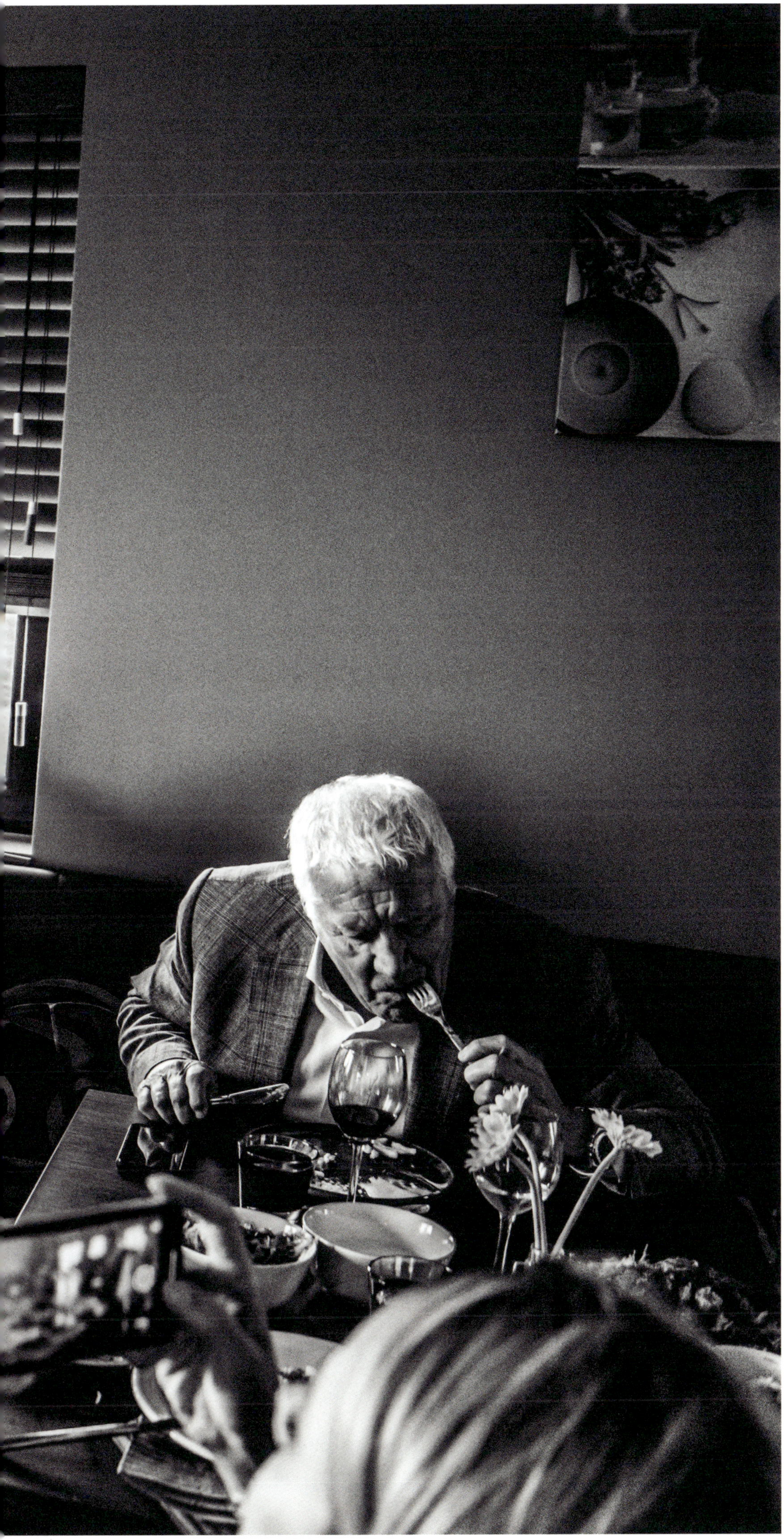

Feest en plezier. The Wolfpack-spirit in zwart en wit. En of het verdiend was. V.l.n.r.: Bert Van Lerberghe, Yves Lampaert, Tim Declercq, Kasper Asgreen en Julian Alaphilippe op zoek naar de hoogste noten. In de zevende hemel zijn ze al. De borden leeg, de glazen nog eventjes vol. Rechts zit een meneer onverstoord zijn maaltijd te verorberen. Hij ziet de roedel in extase, maar eet rustig verder. Ooit zei Hennie Kuiper: 'Wielrennen is eerst het bord van de ander leegeten, voor je aan je eigen bord begint.'

Partying and fun, in the Wolfpack spirit. Much deserved. FLTR: Bert Van Lerberghe, Yves Lampaert, Tim Declercq, Kasper Asgreen, and Julian Alaphilippe reaching for the highest notes. Their night is already a success. Plates empty, glasses still full. On the right, a gentleman is calmly eating his meal. He saw the pack in ecstasy, and simply continued eating. Hennie Kuiper once said: "Cycling is all about eating the other rider's meal before starting your own."

Joie et célébrations. L'esprit du Wolfpack en noir et blanc. Des célébrations bien méritées. Dgàd : Bert Van Lerberghe, Yves Lampaert, Tim Declercq, Kasper Asgreen et Julian Alaphilippe qui sont tout sauf silencieux. Ils sont déjà au septième ciel. Les assiettes vides, les verres encore pleins. Les chants de la meute ne semblent pas déranger le monsieur à leur droite. Il continue à manger comme si de rien n'était. Hennie Kuiper a dit un jour : « Le cyclisme consiste à manger l'assiette de l'autre avant de commencer la sienne. »

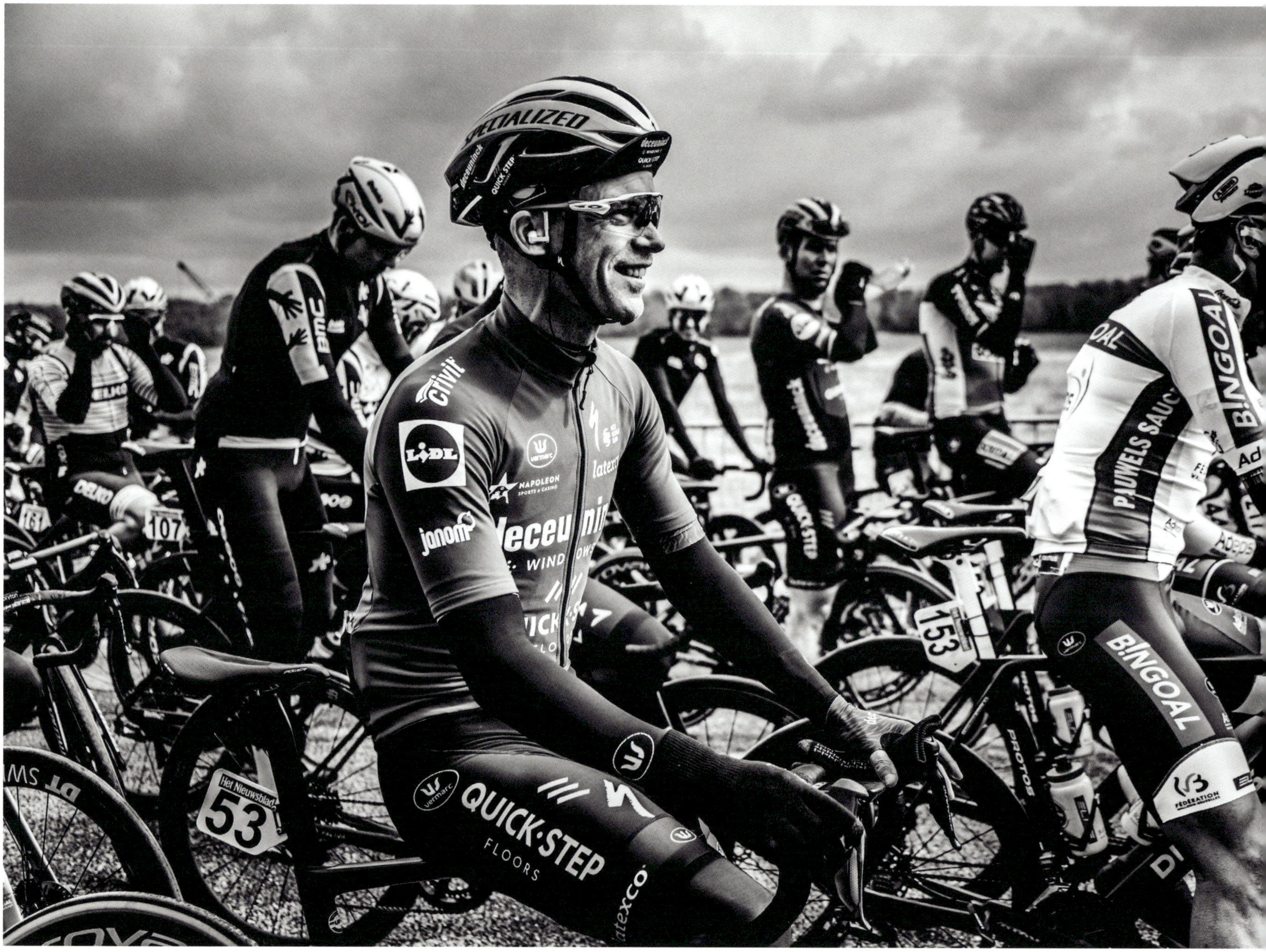
SPECIALIZED
LIDL
QUICK-STEP
FLOORS
BINGOAL
Het Nieuwsblad
53
107
153

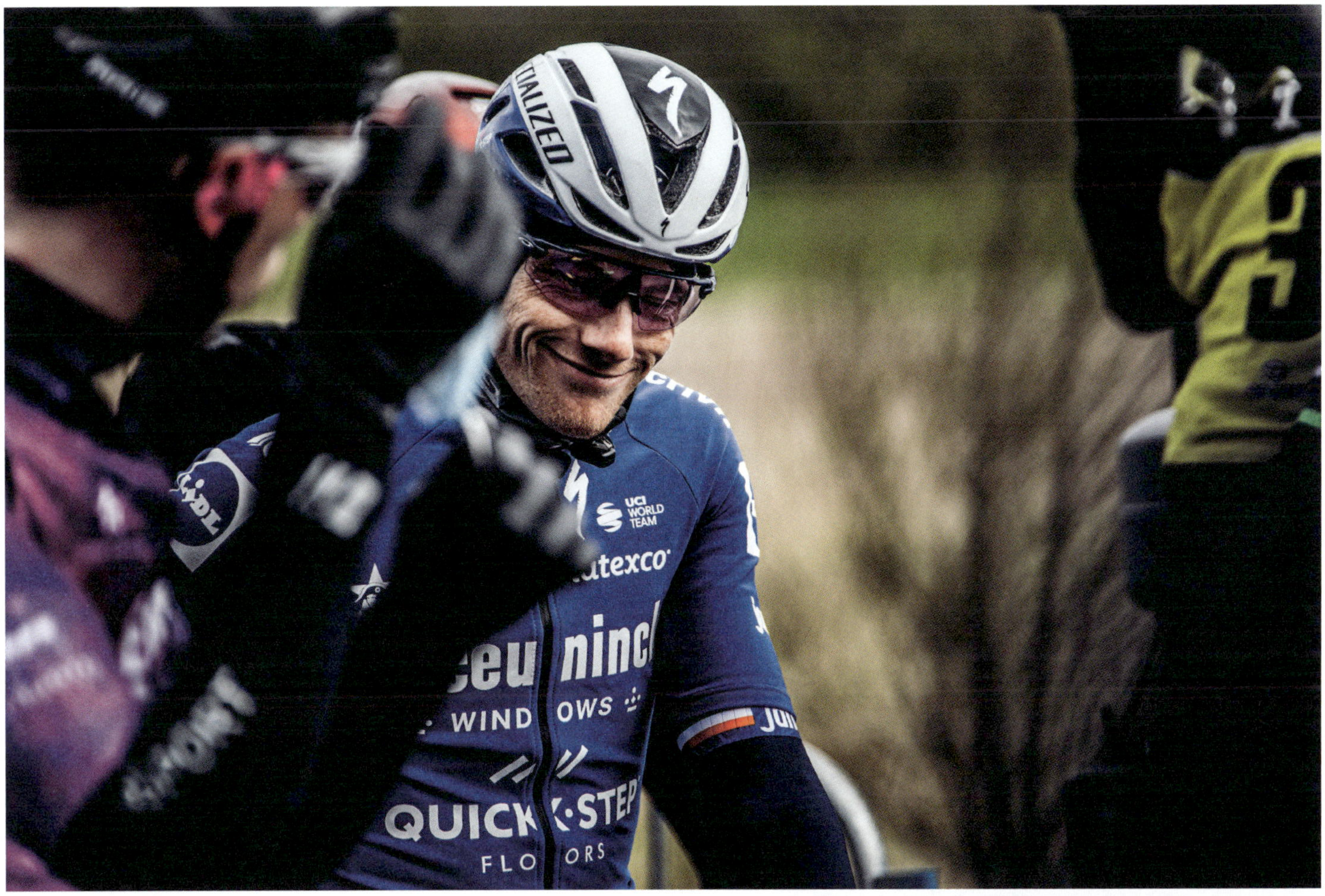
UCI
WORLD
TEAM

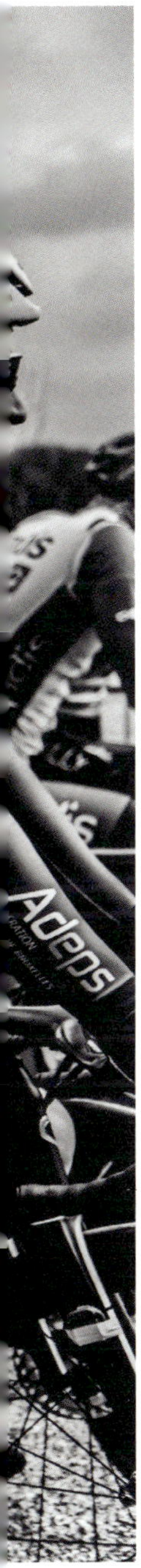
Adeps

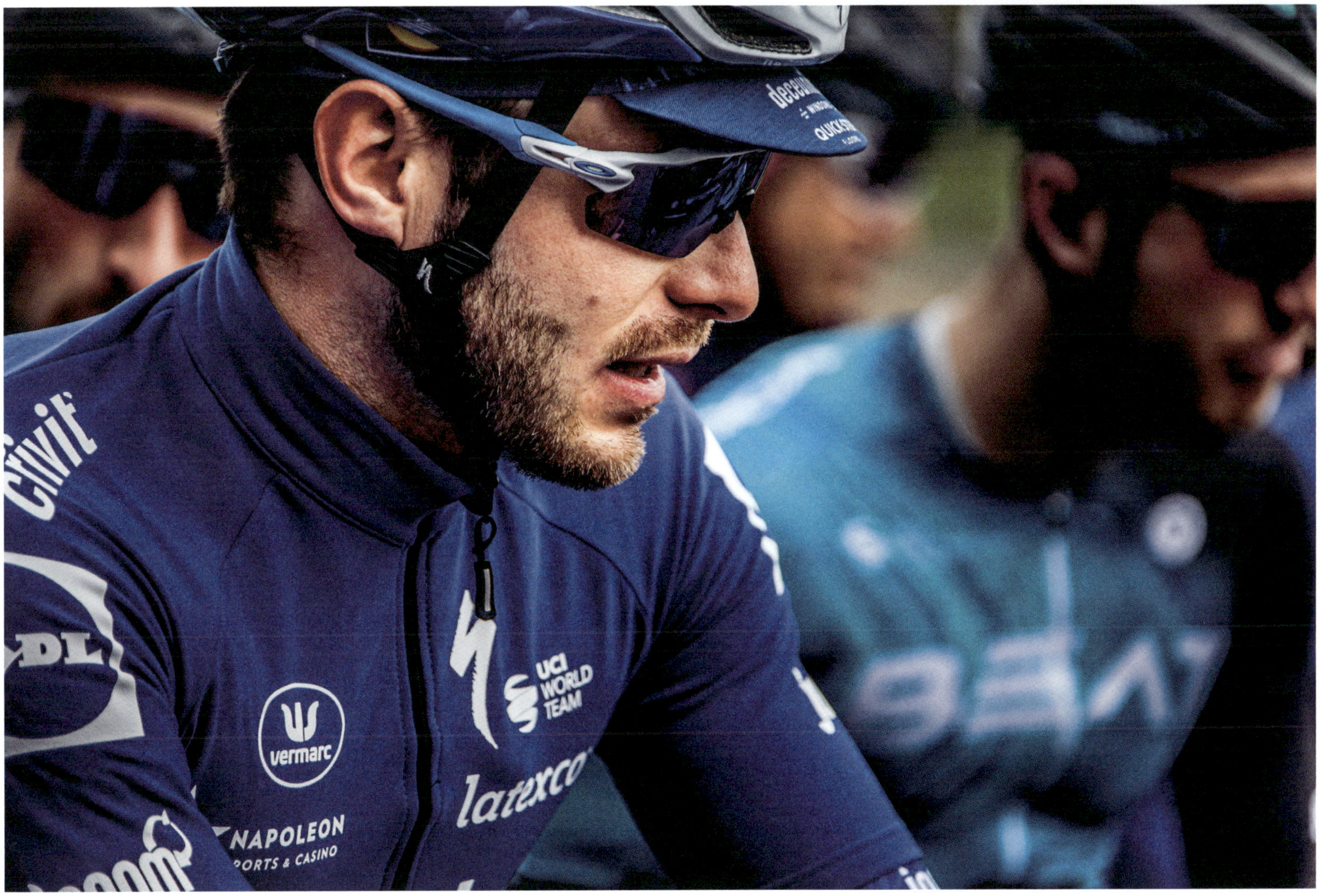
UCI
WORLD
TEAM
vermarc
latexco
NAPOLEON

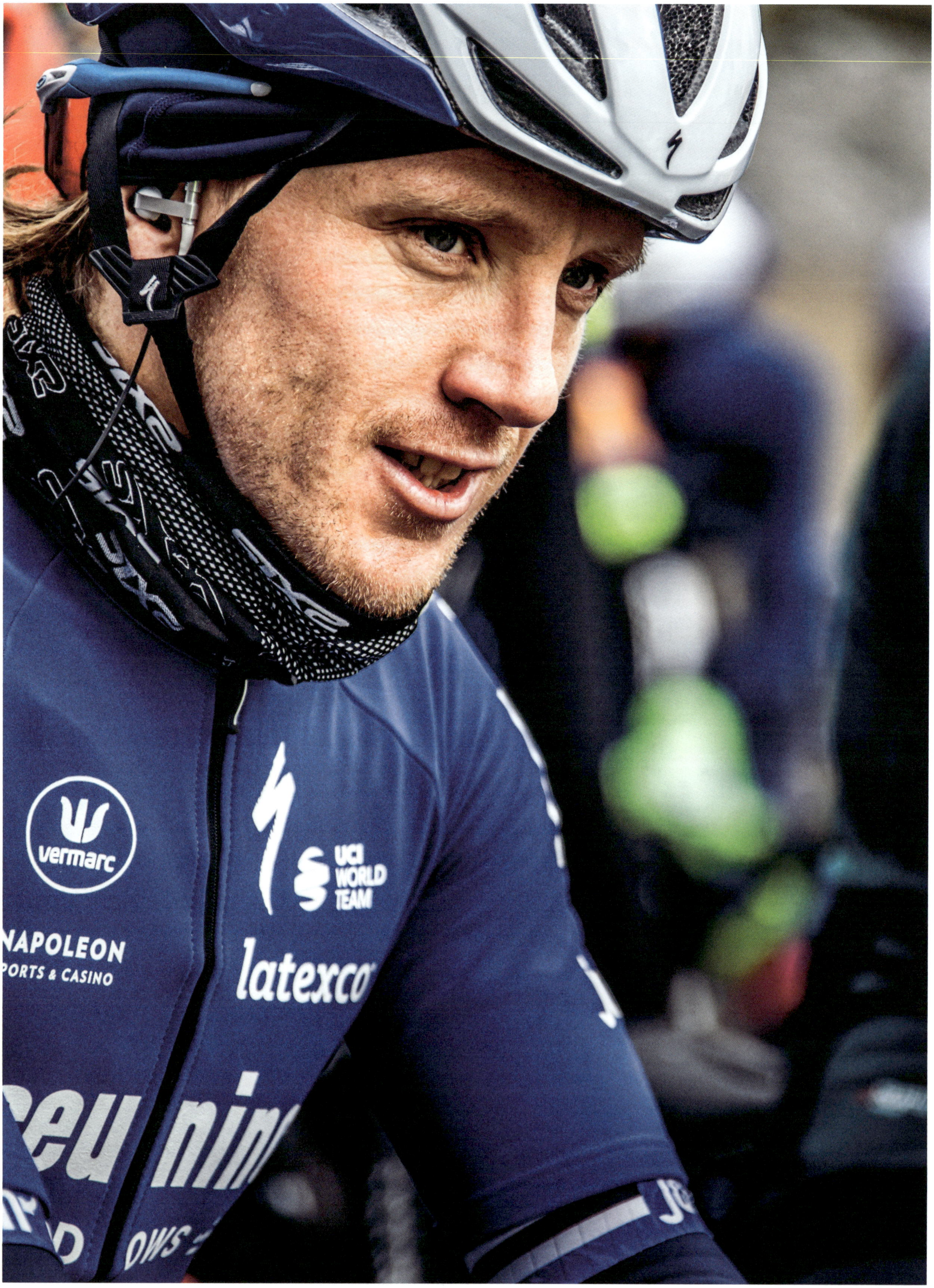
vermarc
NAPOLEON
UCI WORLD TEAM

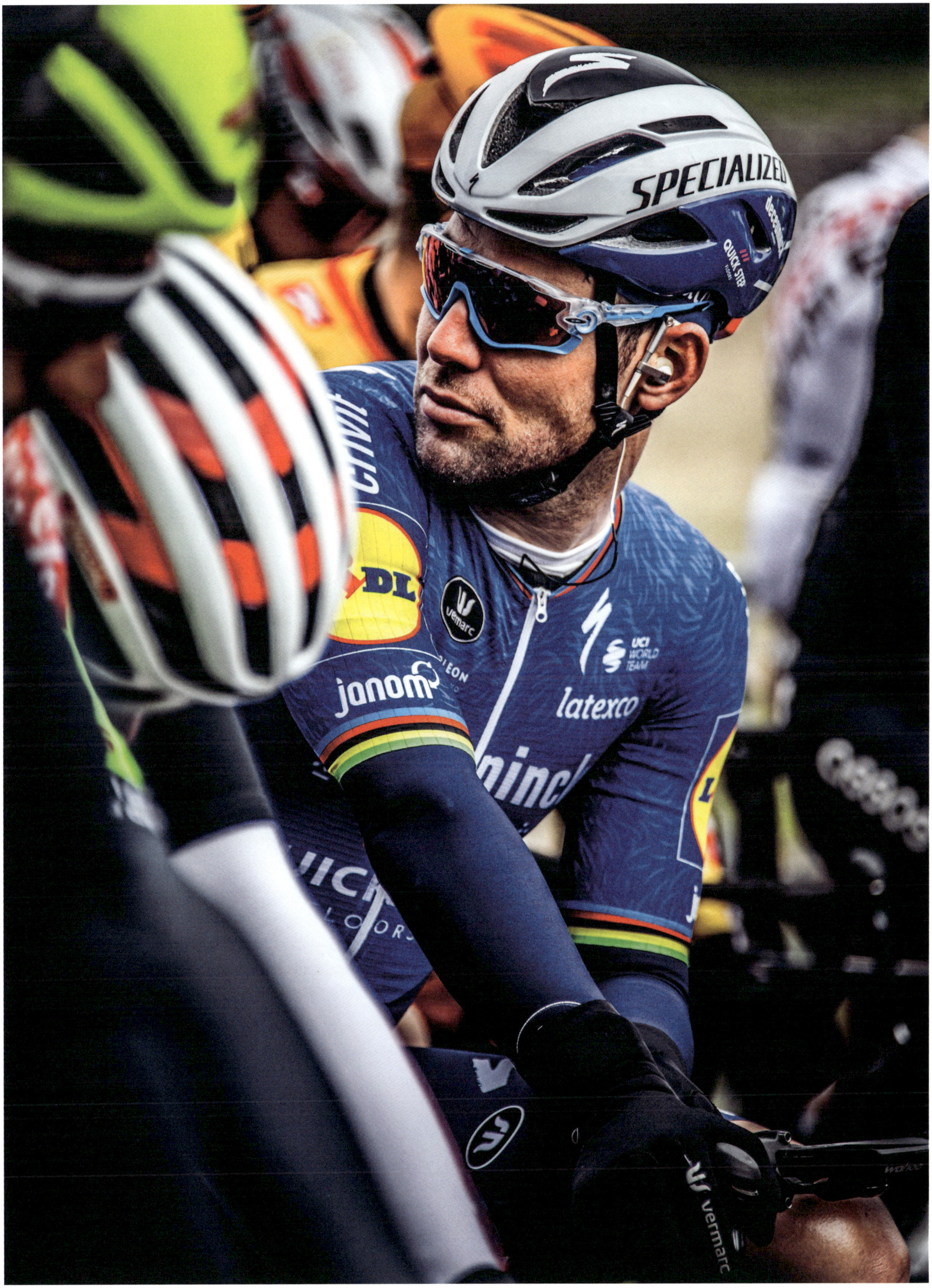
SPECIALIZED
latexco
UCI WORLD TEAM
vermarc

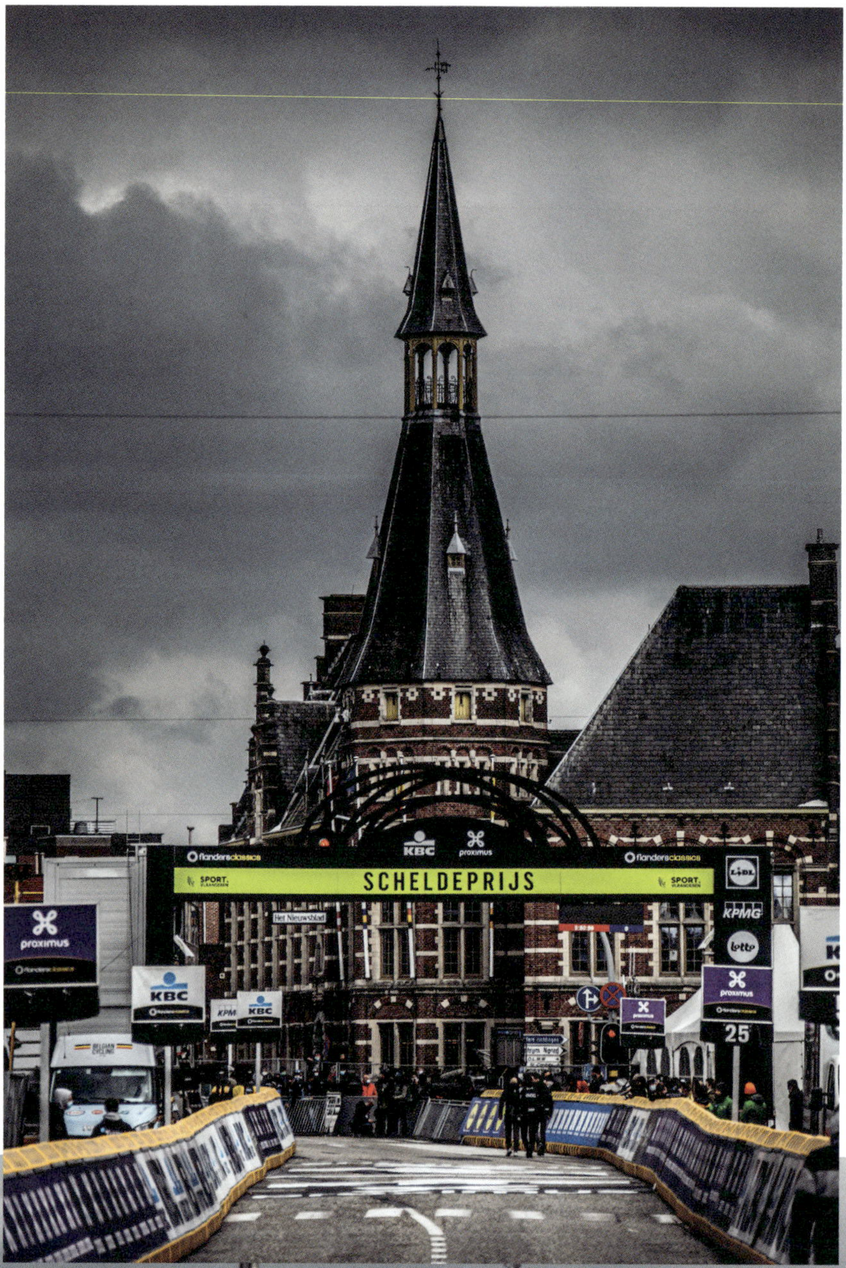
SCHELDEPRIJS
KBC
proximus
KPMG

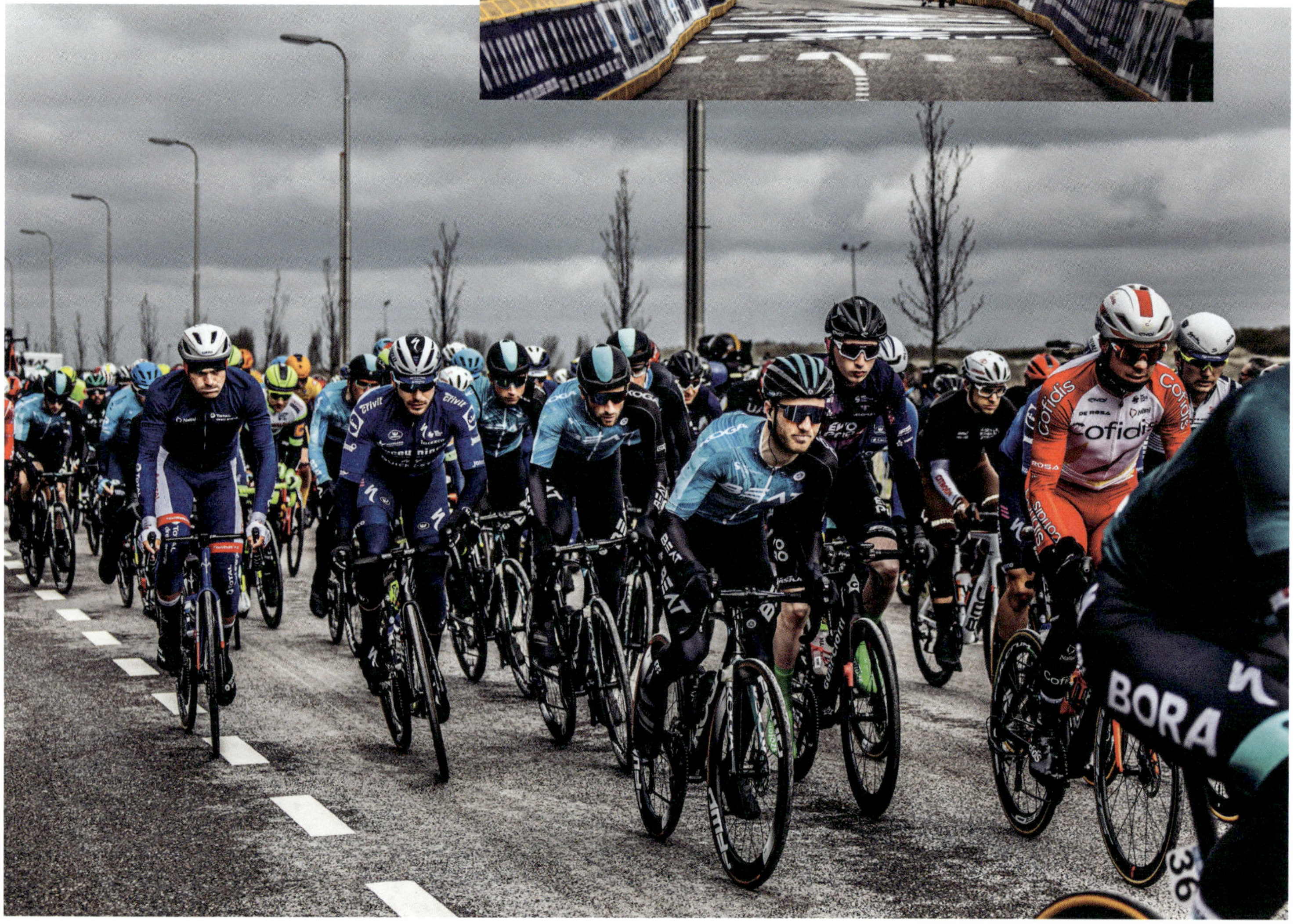
Cofidis
BORA

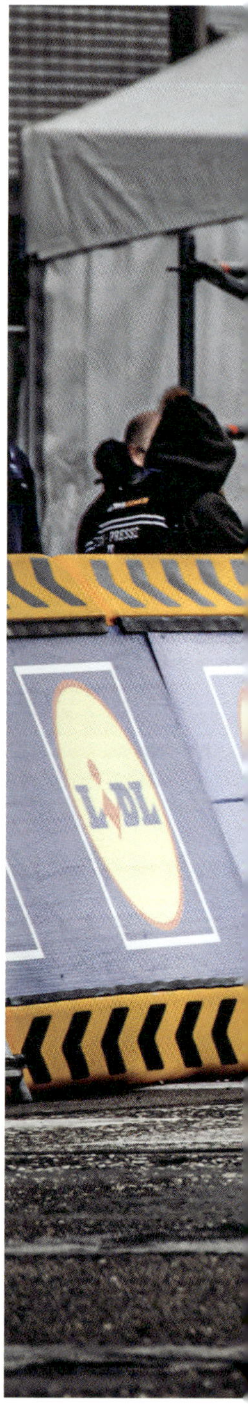
LIDL

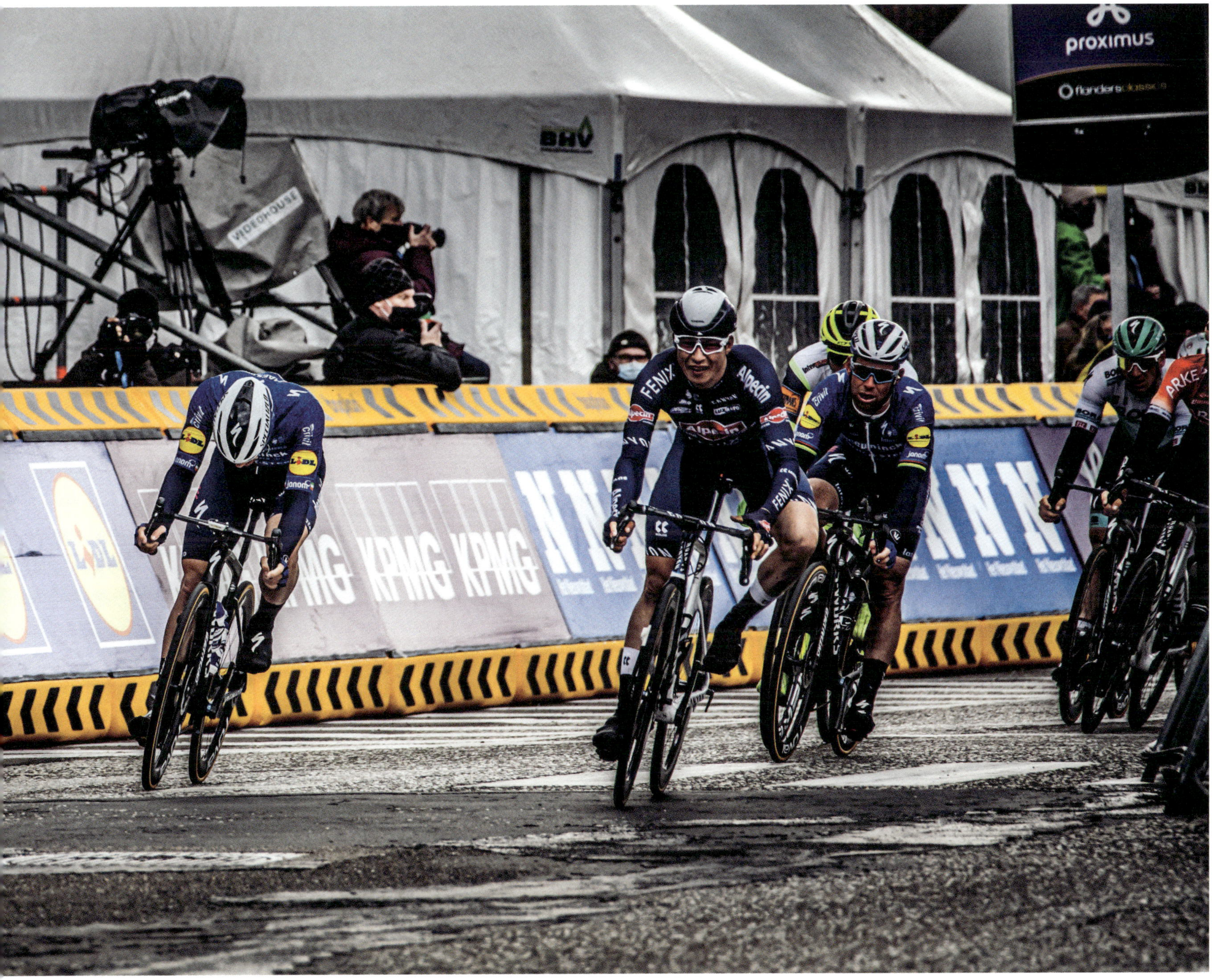
proximus
flanders classics
BHV
VIDEOHOUSE
KPMG KPMG KPMG
FENIX
Alpecin
LIDL

BRABANTSE PIJL
14.04.2021

Na de euforie van de Ronde van Vlaanderen volgde tien dagen later een lastige Brabantse Pijl, ten dele op het parcours van het WK. Hoe sterk de plannen ook waren, een massale valpartij op 38 kilometer van de meet maaide de ambities van The Wolfpack weg. Yves Lampaert, Pieter Serry, Florian Sénéchal en Mikkel Honoré gingen tegen de vlakte.

Zeker jammer voor Mikkel Honoré, die aan een sterk voorjaar bezig was. Hij won de vijfde rit in Settimana Coppi e Bartali op 27 maart en de vijfde rit in de Ronde van het Baskenland op 9 april. Daar reden twee Wolfpackers samen naar de meet: Josef Cerny en Mikkel Honoré. Waarna de minzame Tsjech de bloemen liet aan zijn Deense ploegmaat. Meer Wolfpack kan het niet zijn.

Ten days after the euphoria of the Ronde van Vlaanderen, a difficult Brabantse Pijl followed, part of it on the course of the World Championships. The prospects were good for a strong performance, yet a massive crash 38 km from the finish shattered The Wolfpack's ambitions. Yves Lampaert, Pieter Serry, Florian Sénéchal, and Mikkel Honoré took a bad fall.

It was a real disappointment for Mikkel Honoré, who was riding well this spring. He won the fifth stage in Settimana Coppi e Bartali on 27 March, and the fifth stage in the Vuelta al País Vasco on 9 April. There, two Wolfpack riders rode together to the finish – Josef Cerny and Mikkel Honoré. The affable Czech left the flowers to his Danish teammate. A true testimony to the Wolfpack spirit.

Dix jours après l'euphorie du Ronde van Vlaanderen, c'était au tour de la Flèche Brabançonne, une épreuve assez difficile qui se déroule en partie sur le parcours des Championnats du Monde. Malgré la préparation de ses coureurs, une grosse chute collective à 38 km est venue ruiner les plans du Wolfpack. Yves Lampaert, Pieter Serry, Florian Sénéchal et Mikkel Honoré se sont retrouvés au sol.

C'est dommage pour Mikkel Honoré qui réalisait un bon printemps jusque-là. Il a remporté la cinquième étape de la Settimana Coppi e Bartali le 27 mars et la cinquième étape du Tour du Pays basque le 9 avril. Au cours de cette dernière course, deux coureurs de la meute, Josef Cerny et Mikkel Honoré sont arrivés ensemble sur la ligne d'arrivée. Après ce joli doublé, l'honorable Tchèque a laissé la victoire à son coéquipier danois. Quoi de plus Wolfpack que ça ?

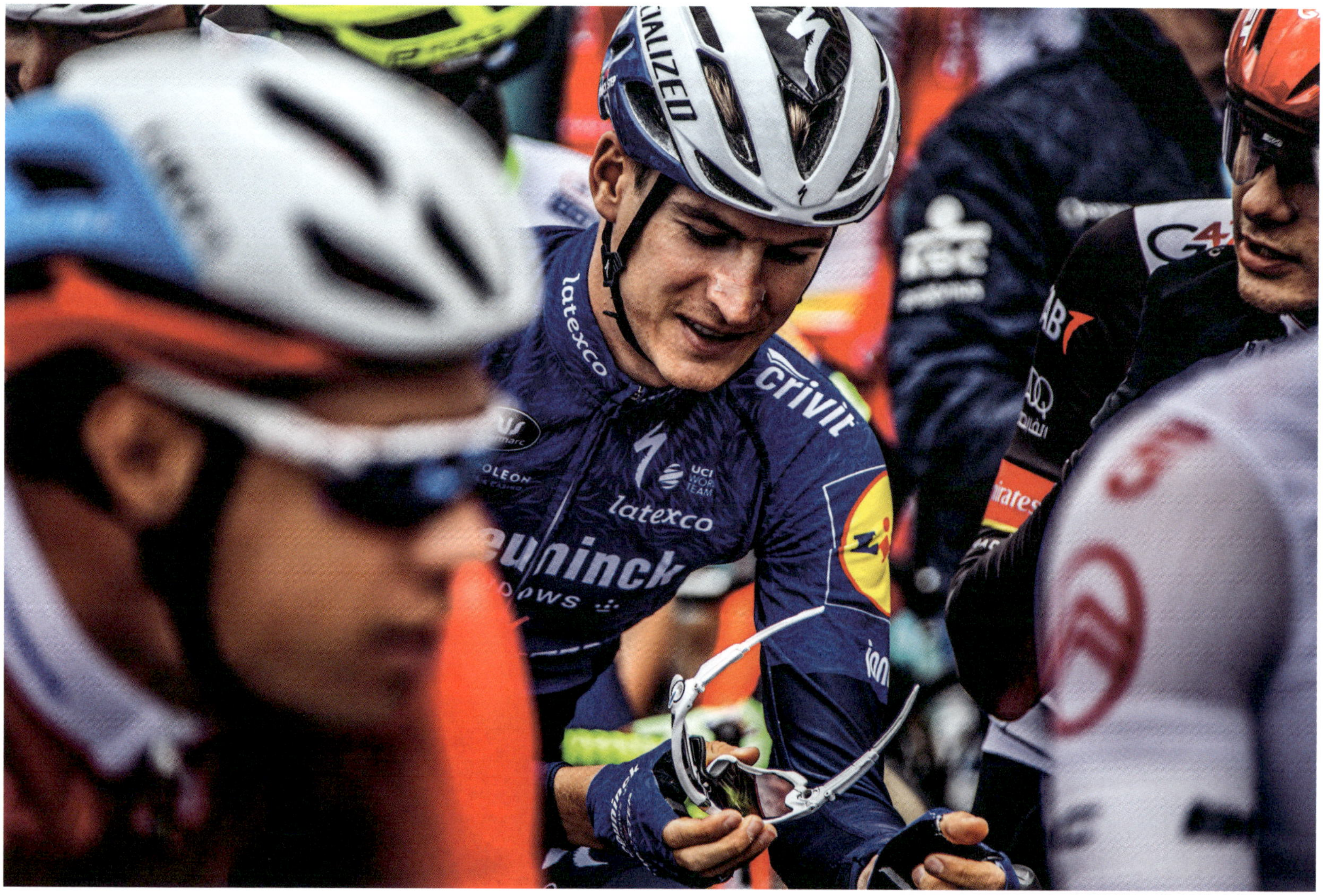

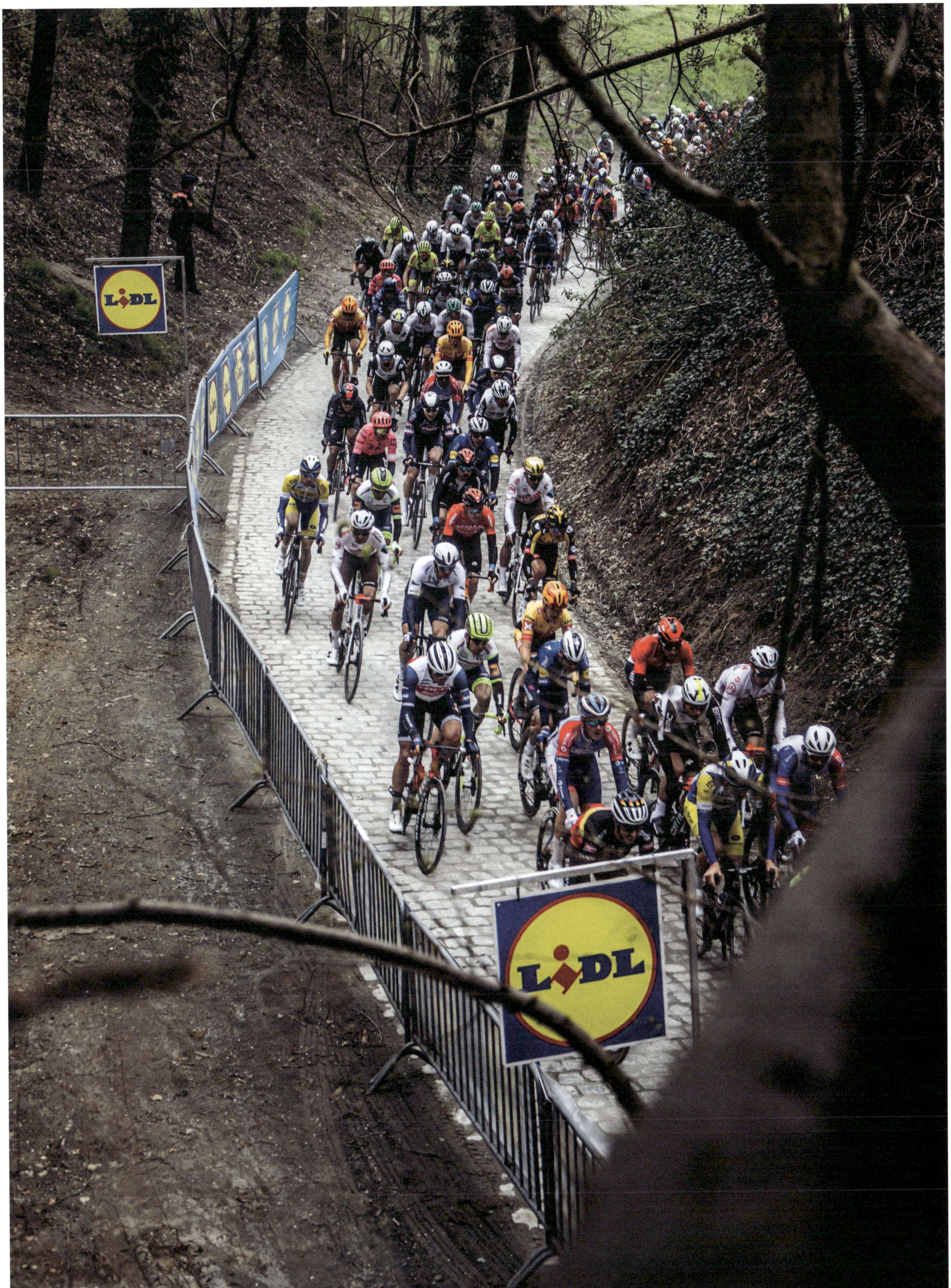
LIDL
LIDL

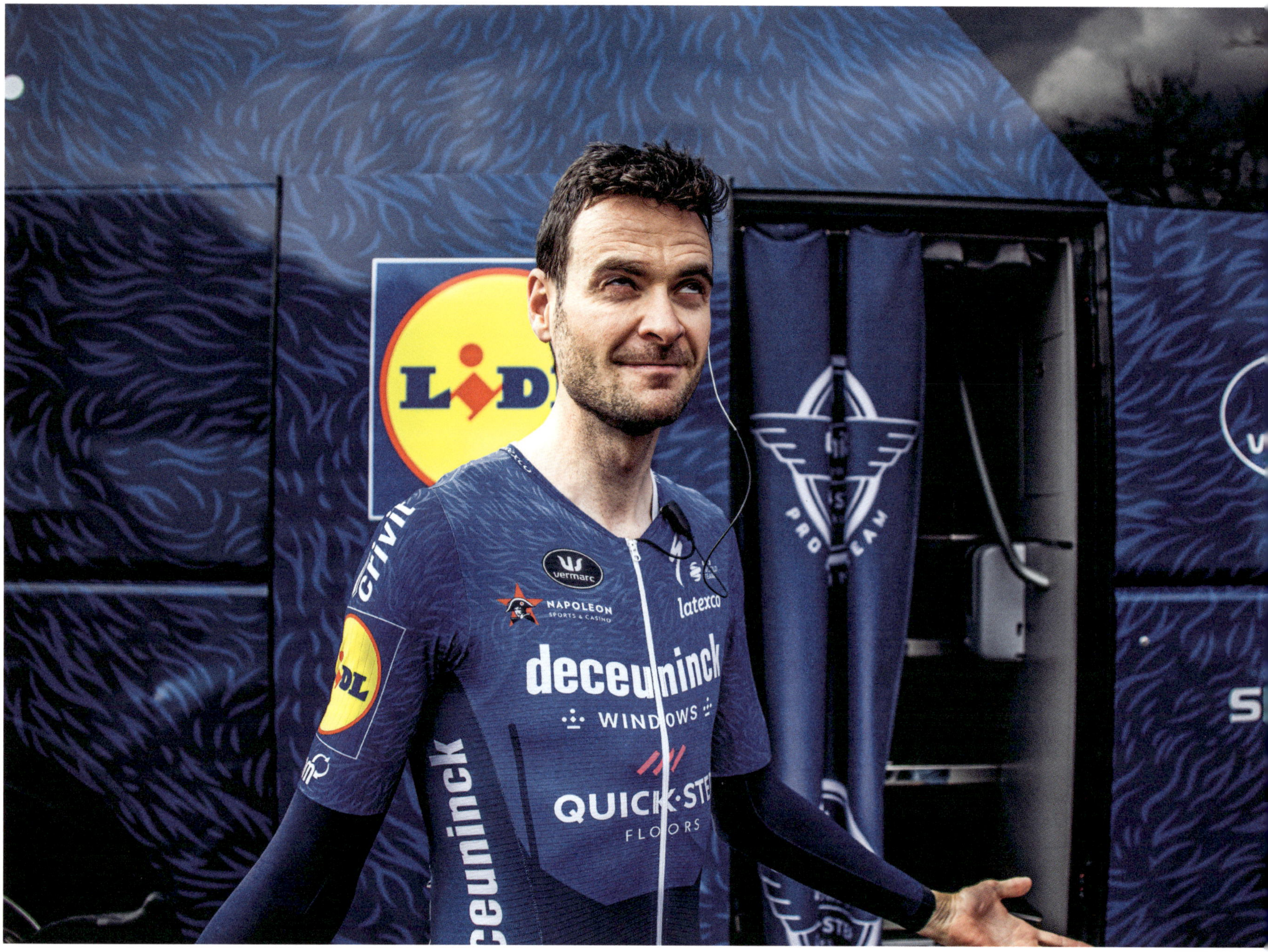

OVERIJSE, 14.04.2021

Na de Brabantse Pijl toont Yves Lampaert zijn geschaafde schouder aan verzorger Marc Patry. Links wijst Pieter Serry op nog meer averij.

After the Brabantse Pijl, Yves Lampaert shows his scraped shoulder to soigneur Marc Patry. On the left, Pieter Serry points out more damage.

Après la Flèche Brabançonne, Yves Lampaert montre son épaule au soigneur Marc Patry. À gauche, Pieter Serry lui fait remarquer d'autres dégâts. ▶

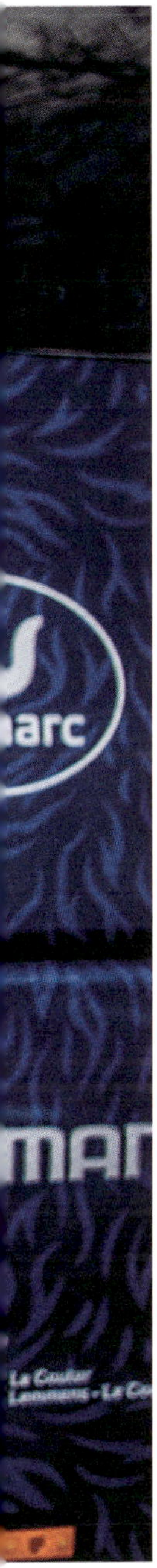

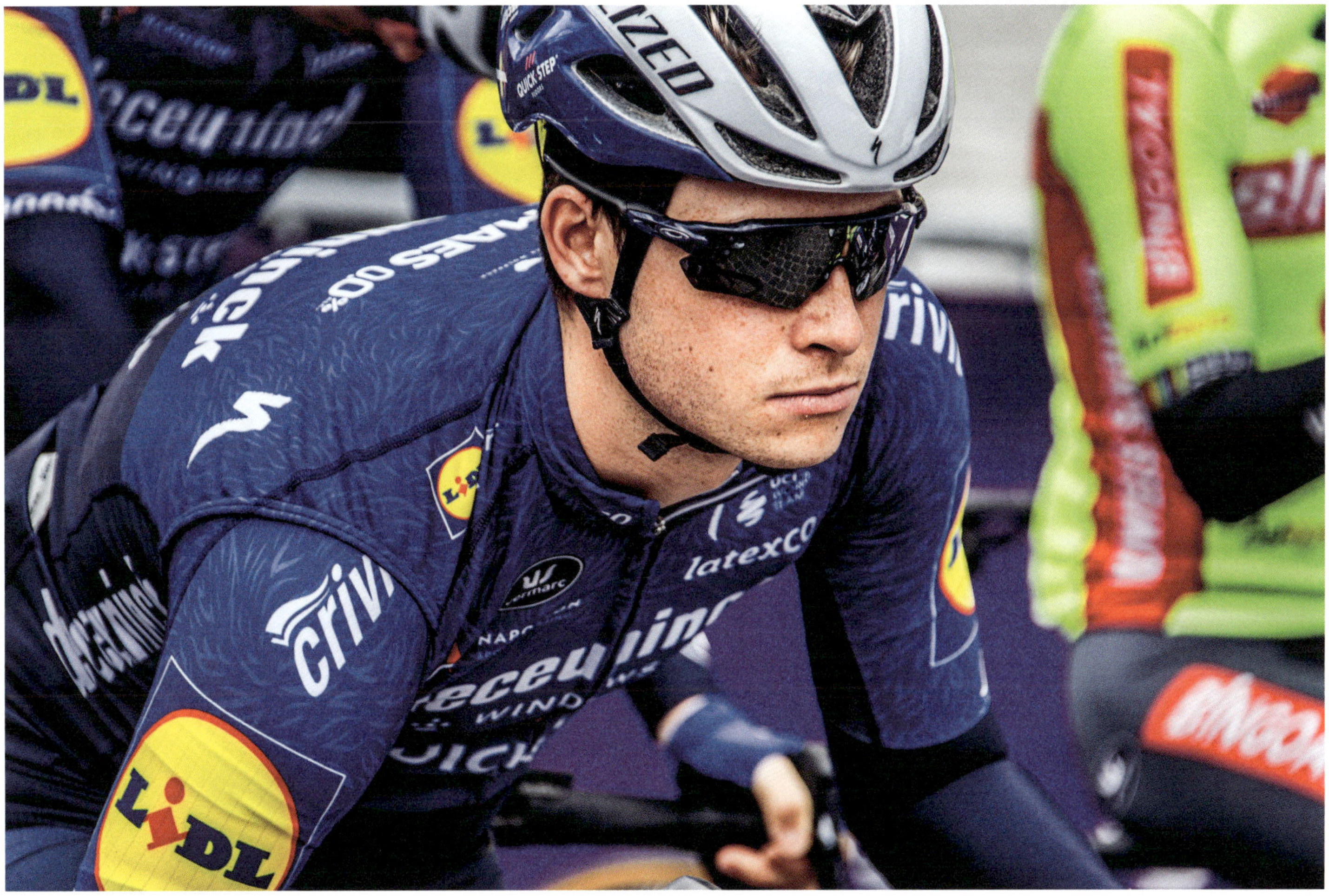
crivit
LIDL
latexco

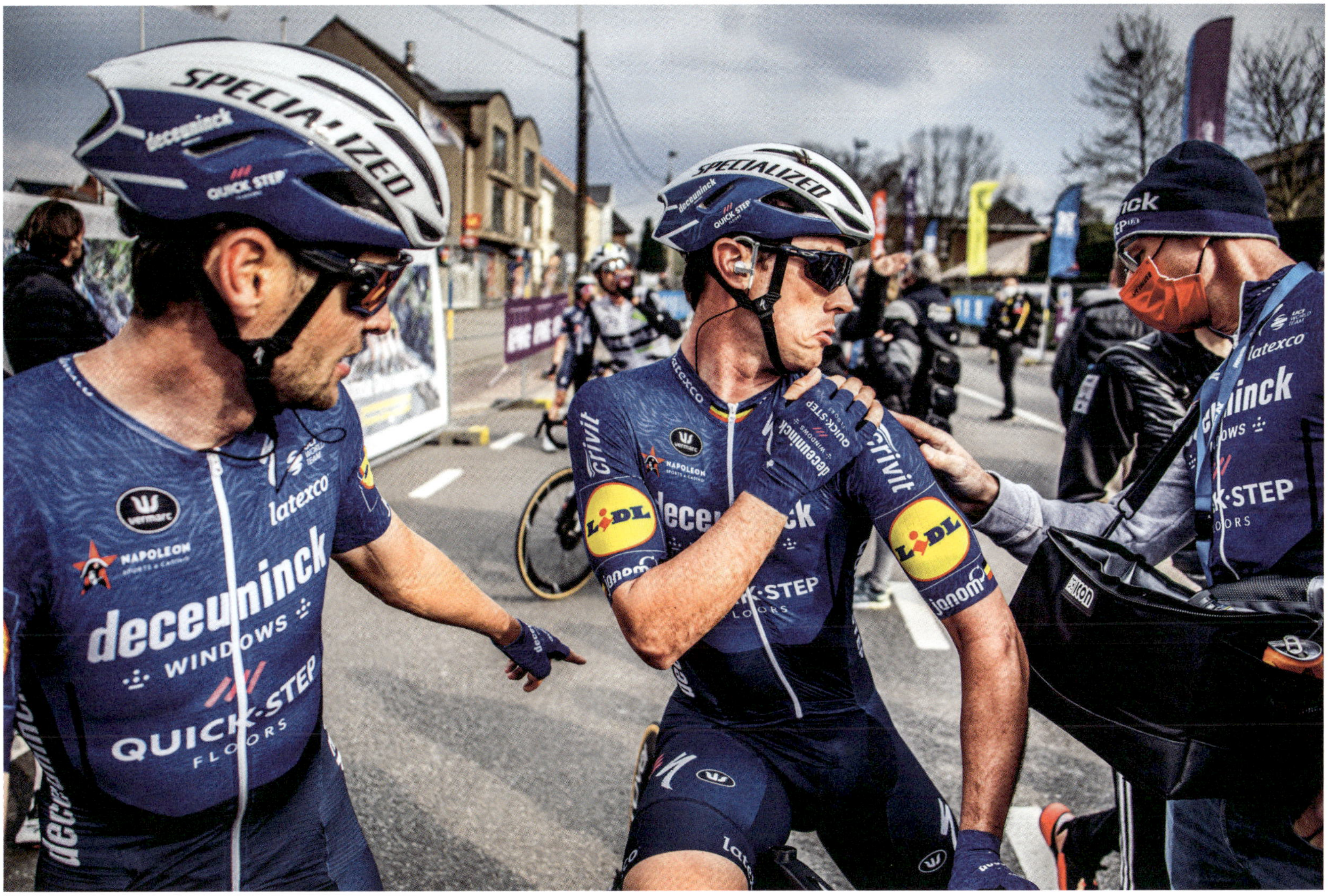
SPECIALIZED
QUICK-STEP
latexco
NAPOLEON
deceuninck
WINDOWS
QUICK-STEP
FLOORS
crivit
LIDL

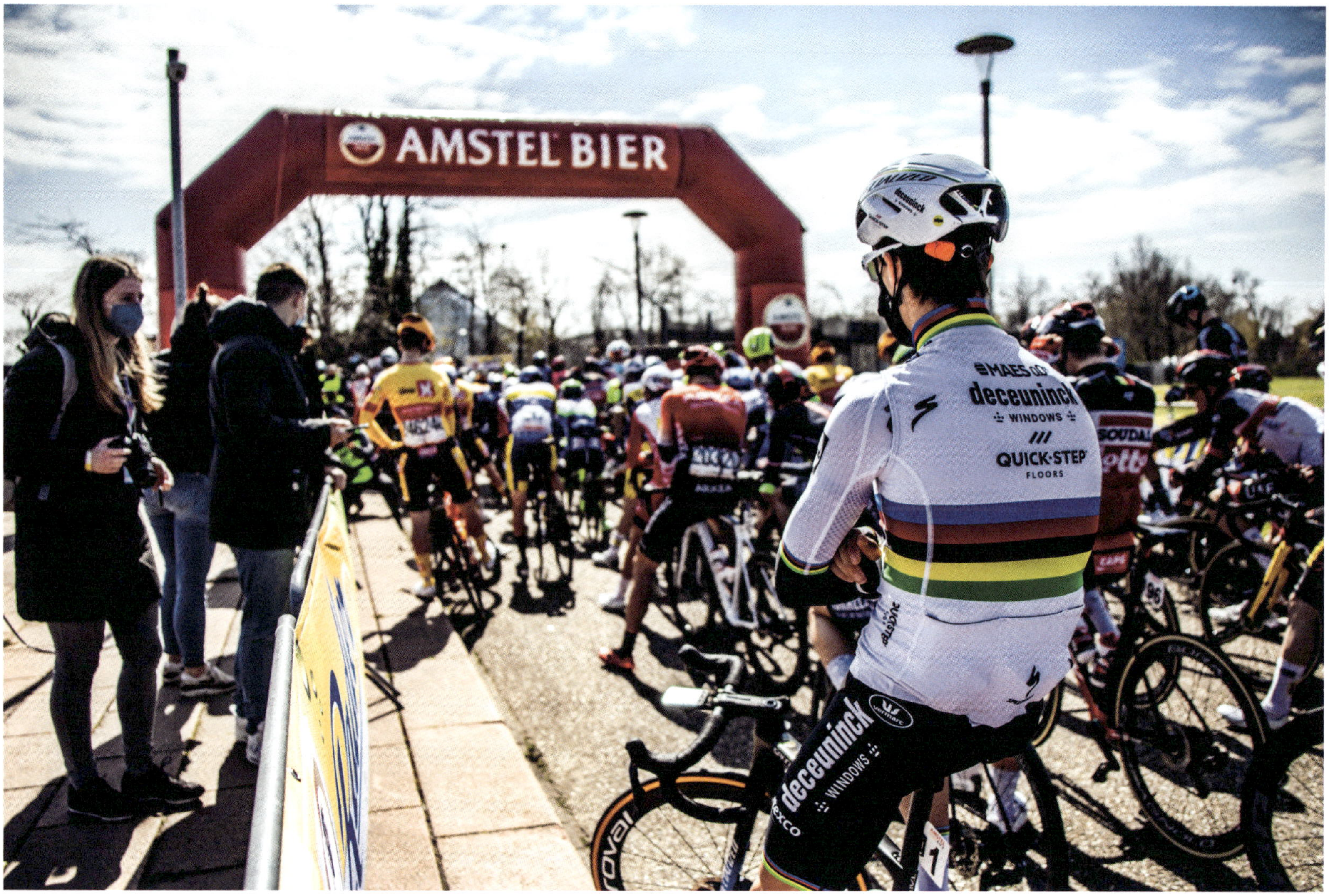
AMSTEL BIER
deceuninck
WINDOWS
QUICK-STEP
FLOORS

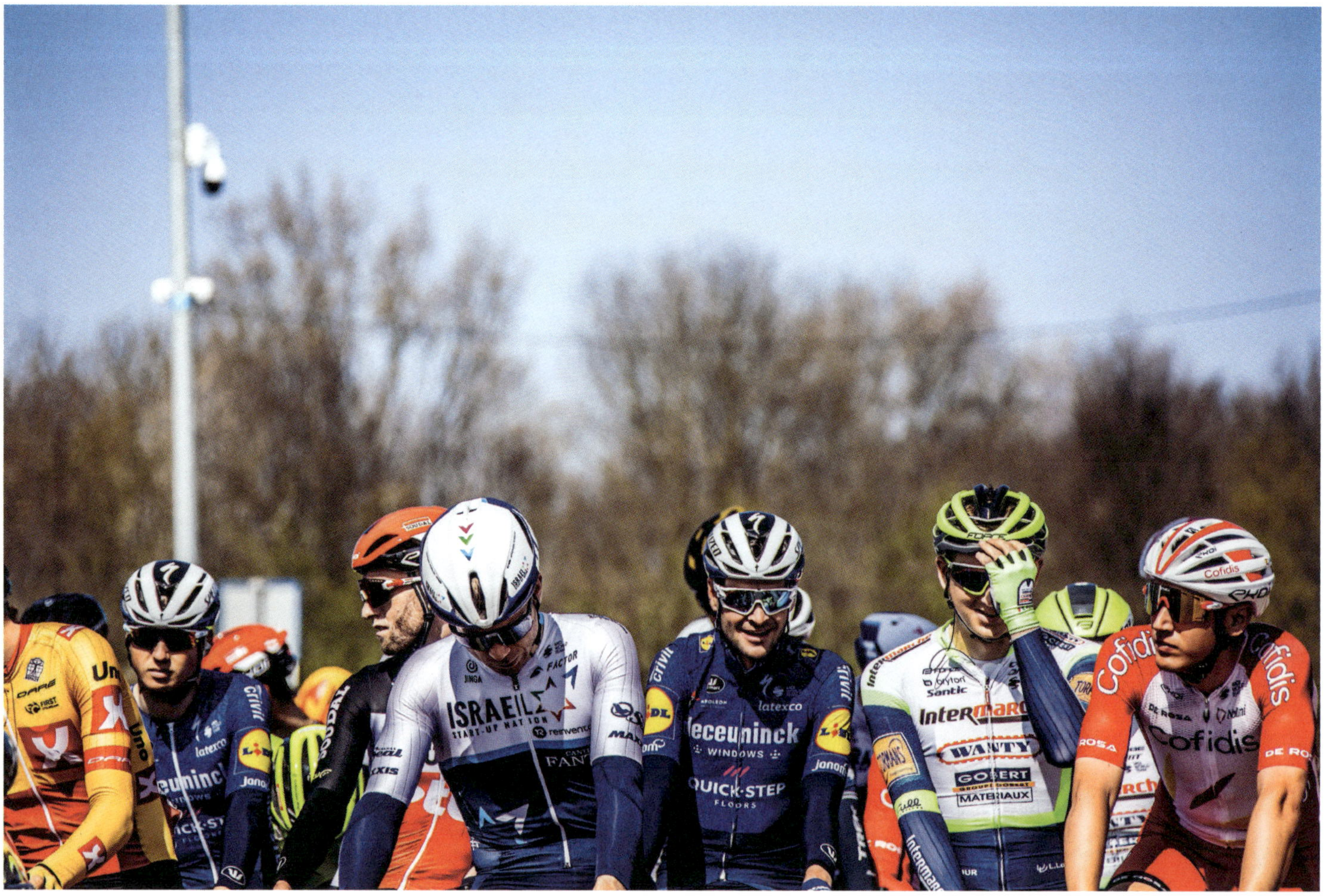
ISRAEL
START-UP NATION
deceuninck
WINDOWS
QUICK-STEP
FLOORS
Intermarché
WANTY
GOBERT
MATÉRIAUX
Cofidis

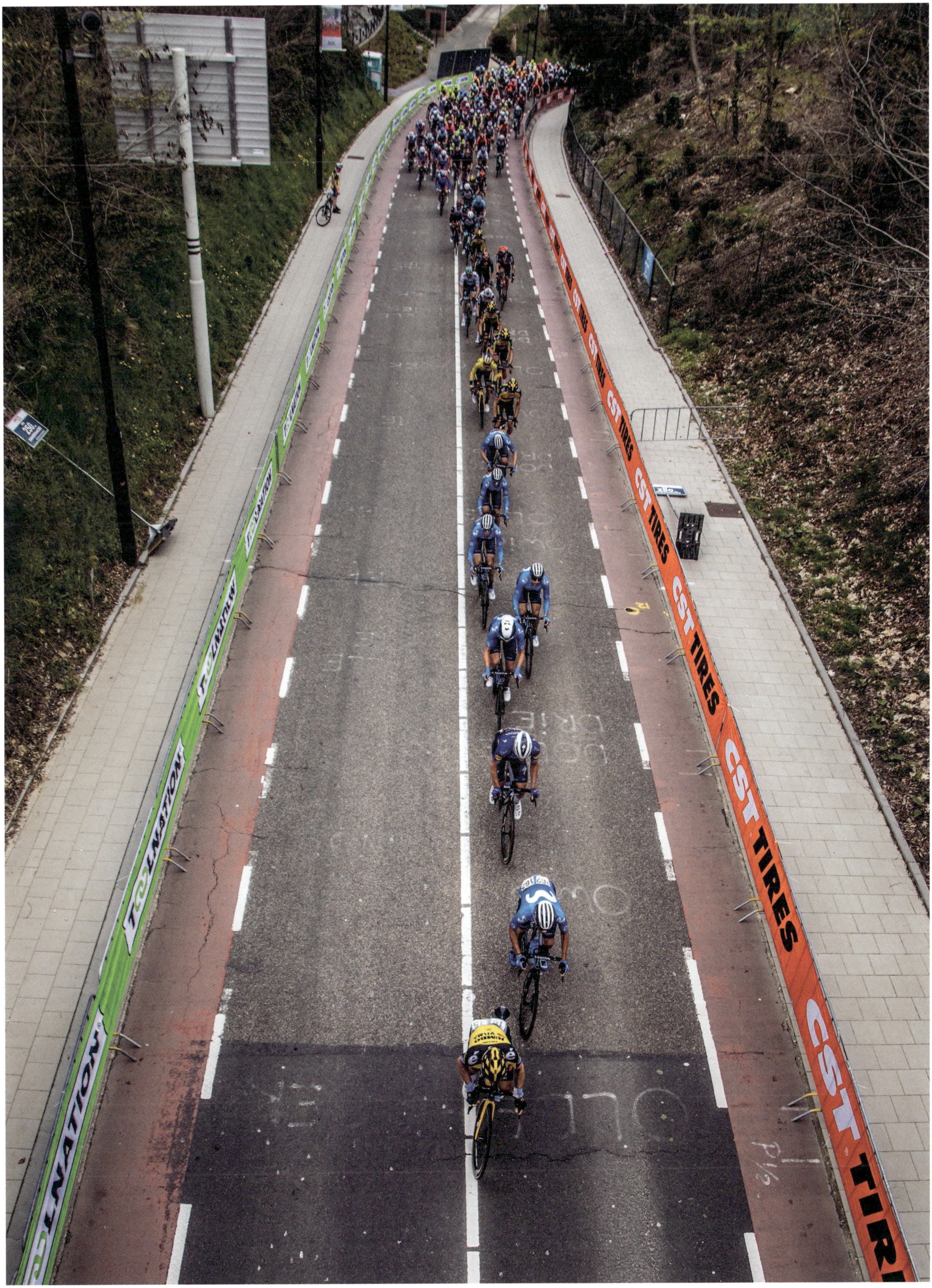
CST TIRES

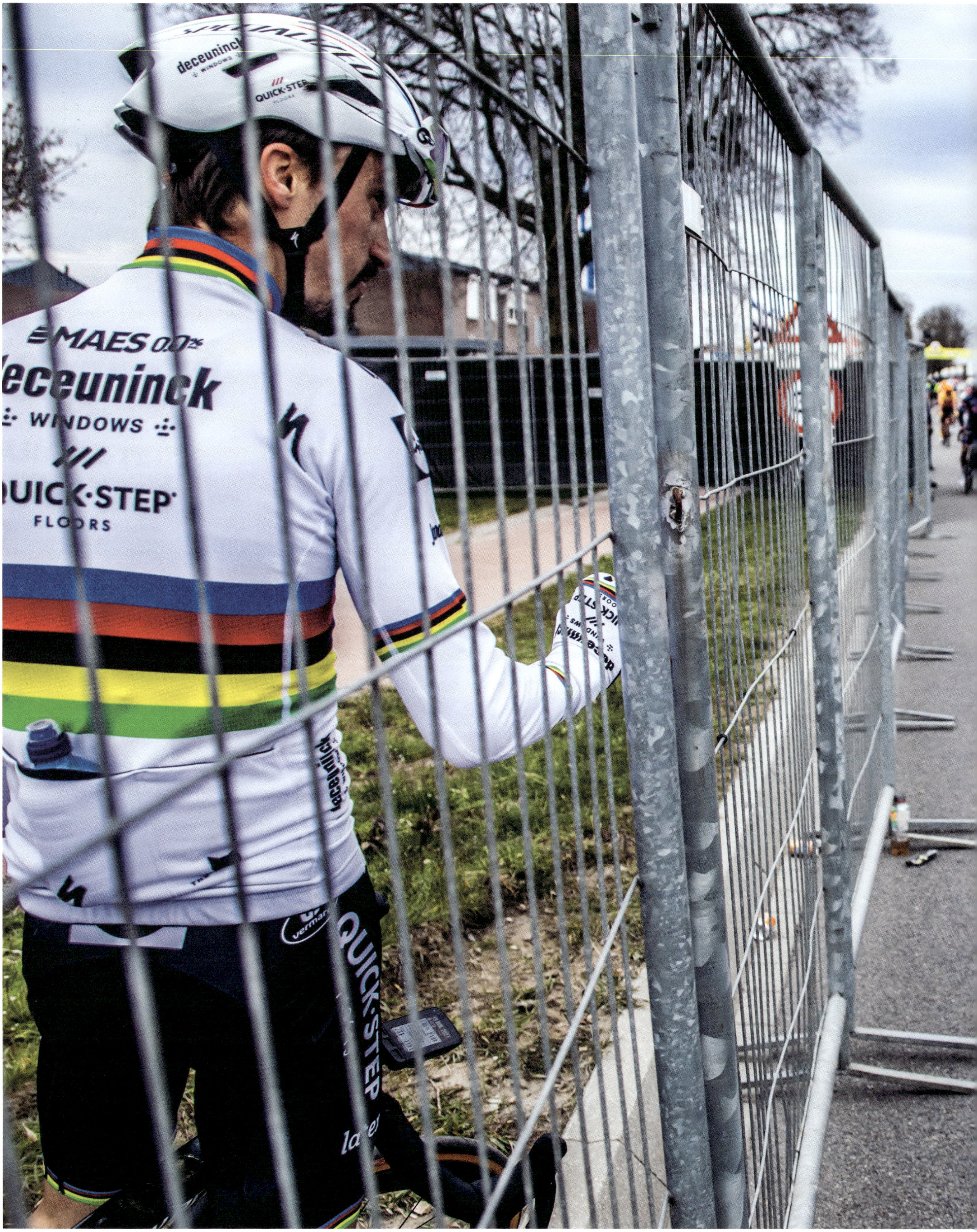
deceuninck
QUICK·STEP
MAES 0.0%
WINDOWS
FLOORS

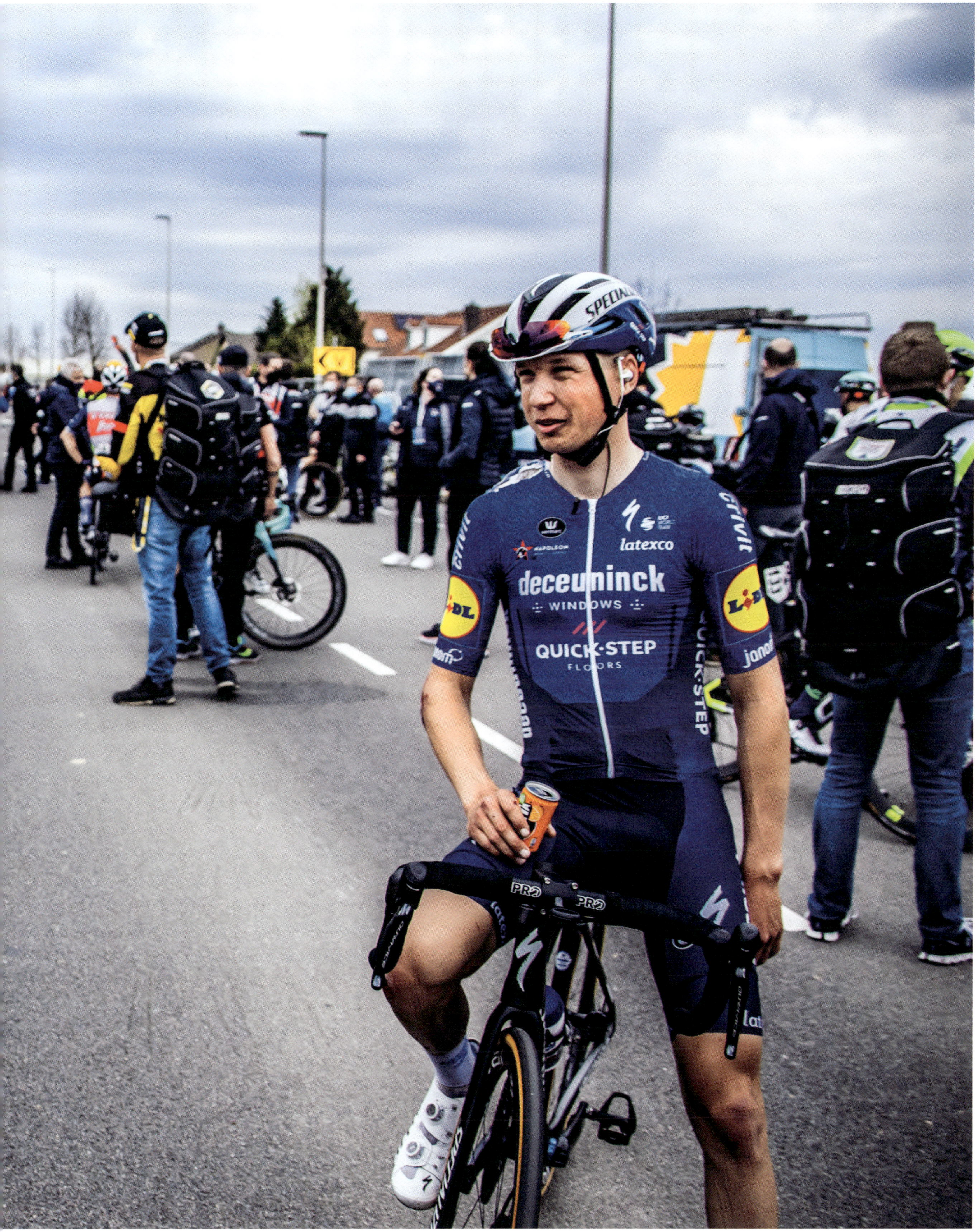
deceuninck
WINDOWS
QUICK-STEP
FLOORS
latexco
LIDL

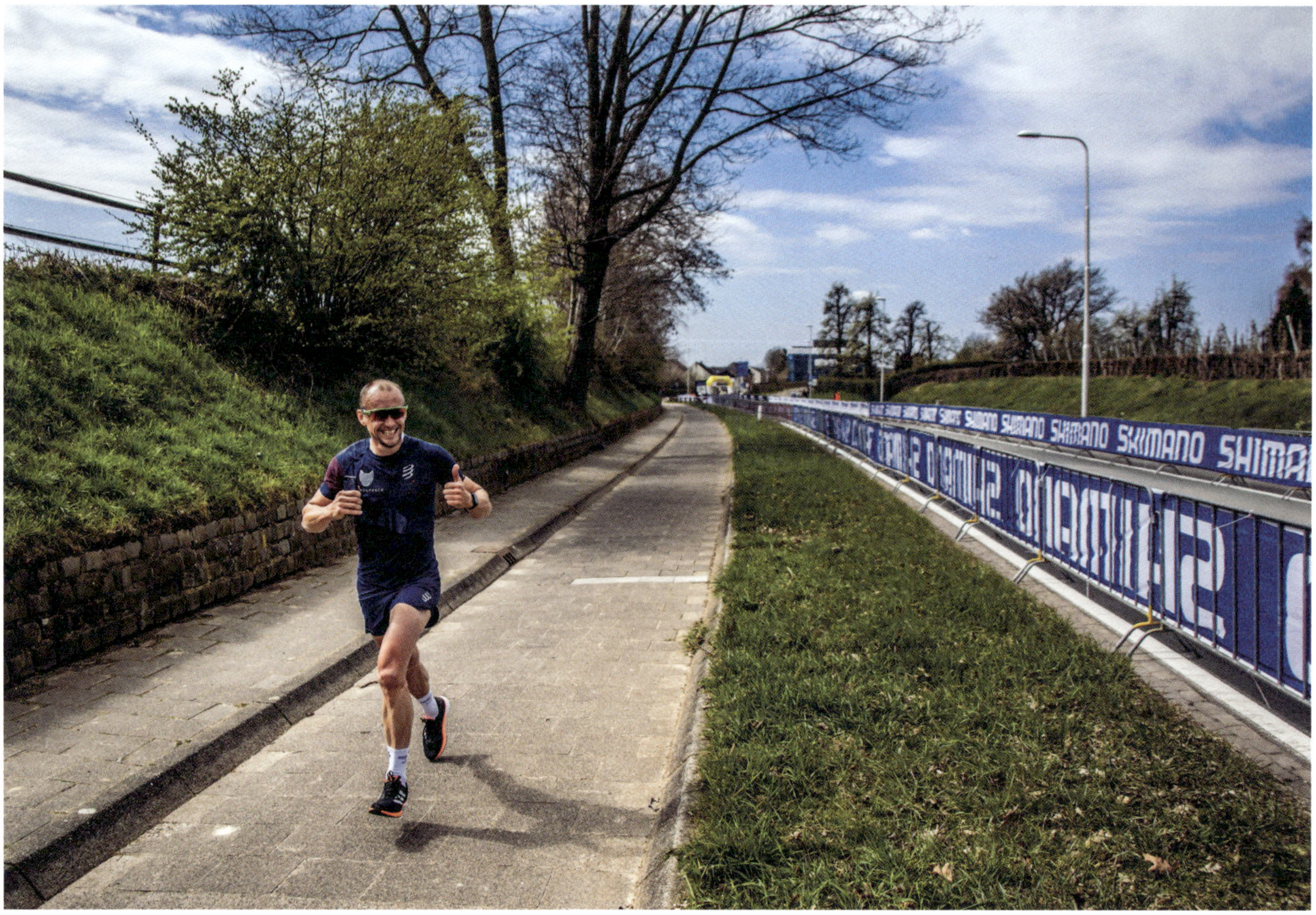
SHIMANO

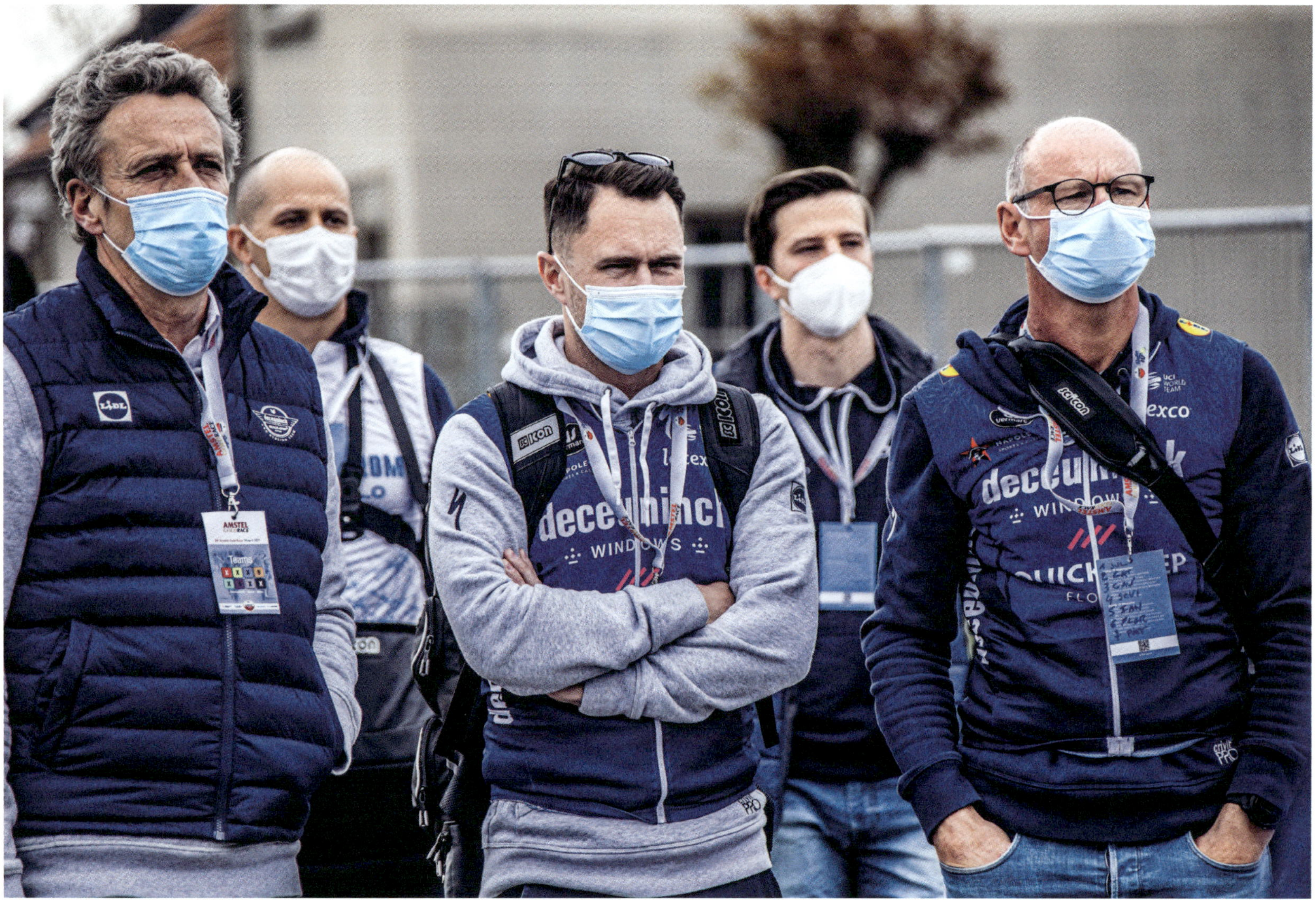
WINDOWS

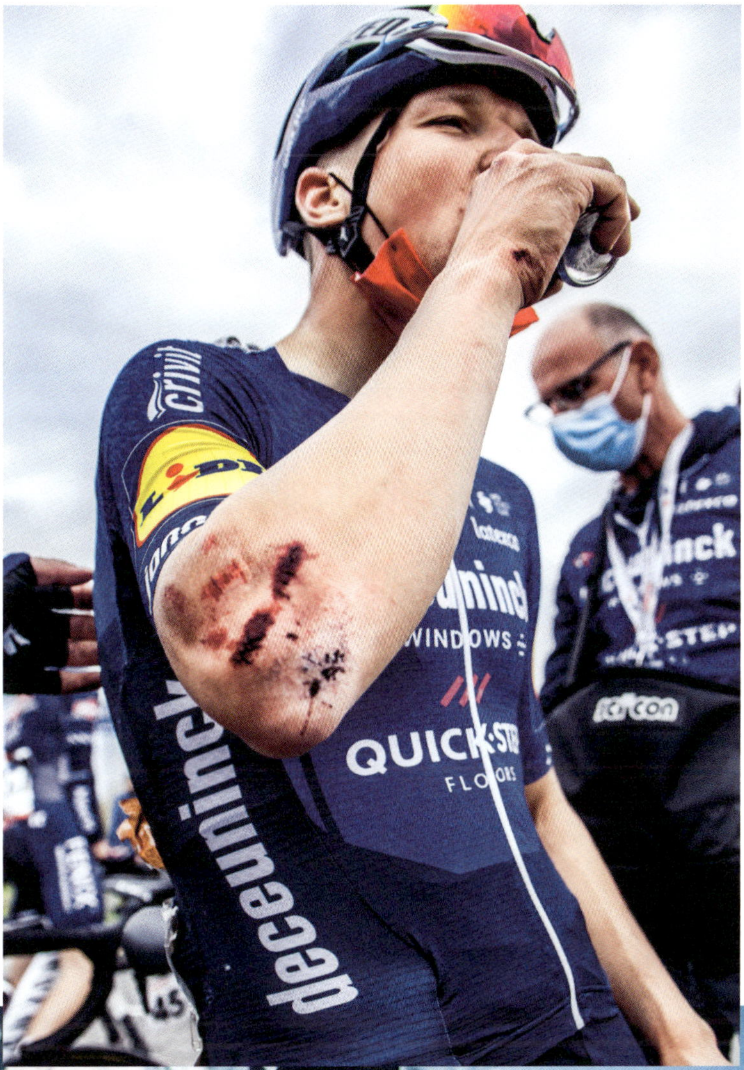

VALKENBURG, 18.04.2021

Als de teambus goed en wel in de buurt van de aankomst staat opgesteld, gaat chauffeur James Vanlandschoot 10 km lopen.

Once the team bus is set up near the finish line, driver James Vanlandschoot runs 10 km out and back again.

Une fois qu'il a garé le bus de l'équipe près de l'arrivée, James Vanlandschoot, le chauffeur, en profite pour faire un petit jogging de 10 km. ◀

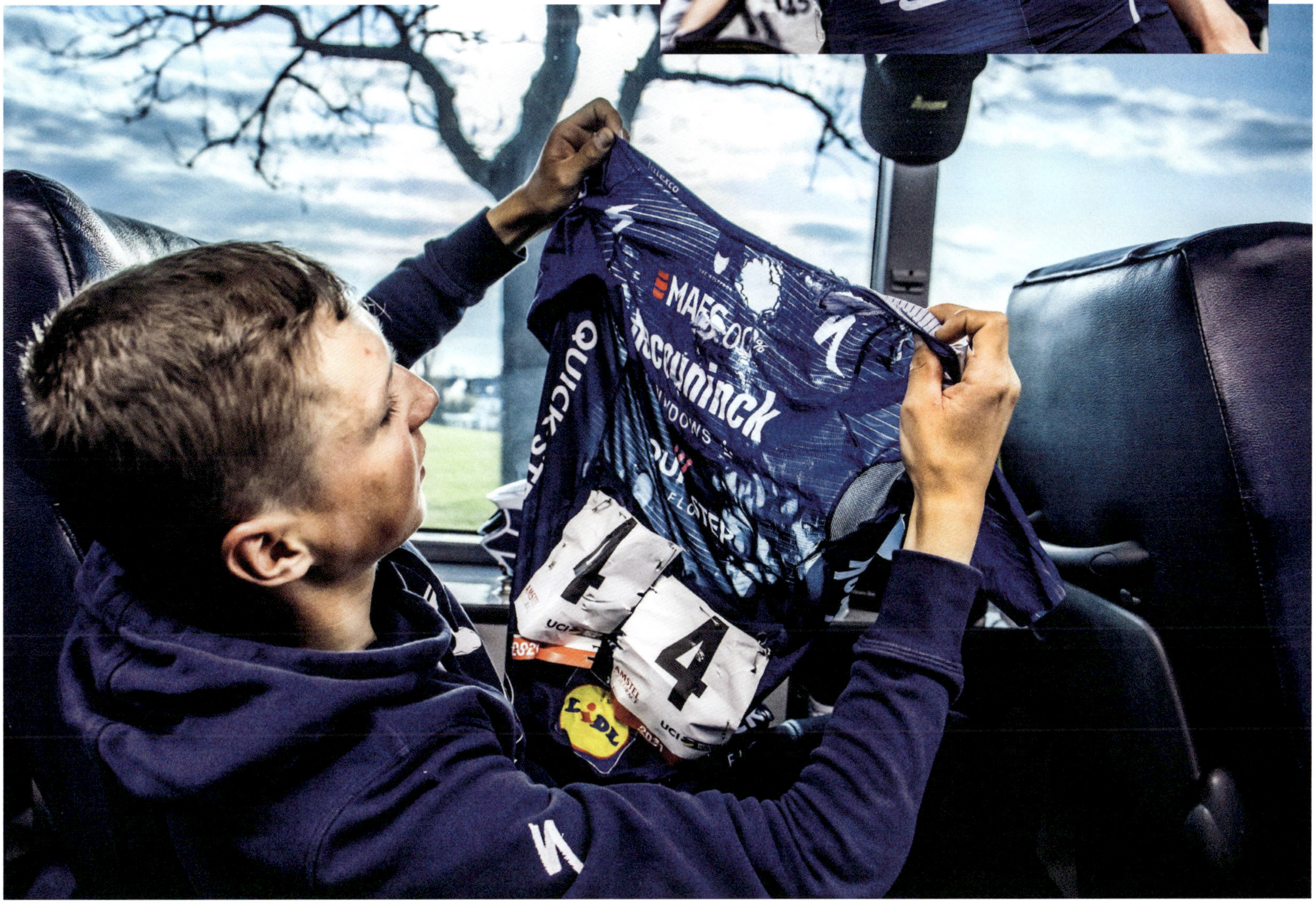

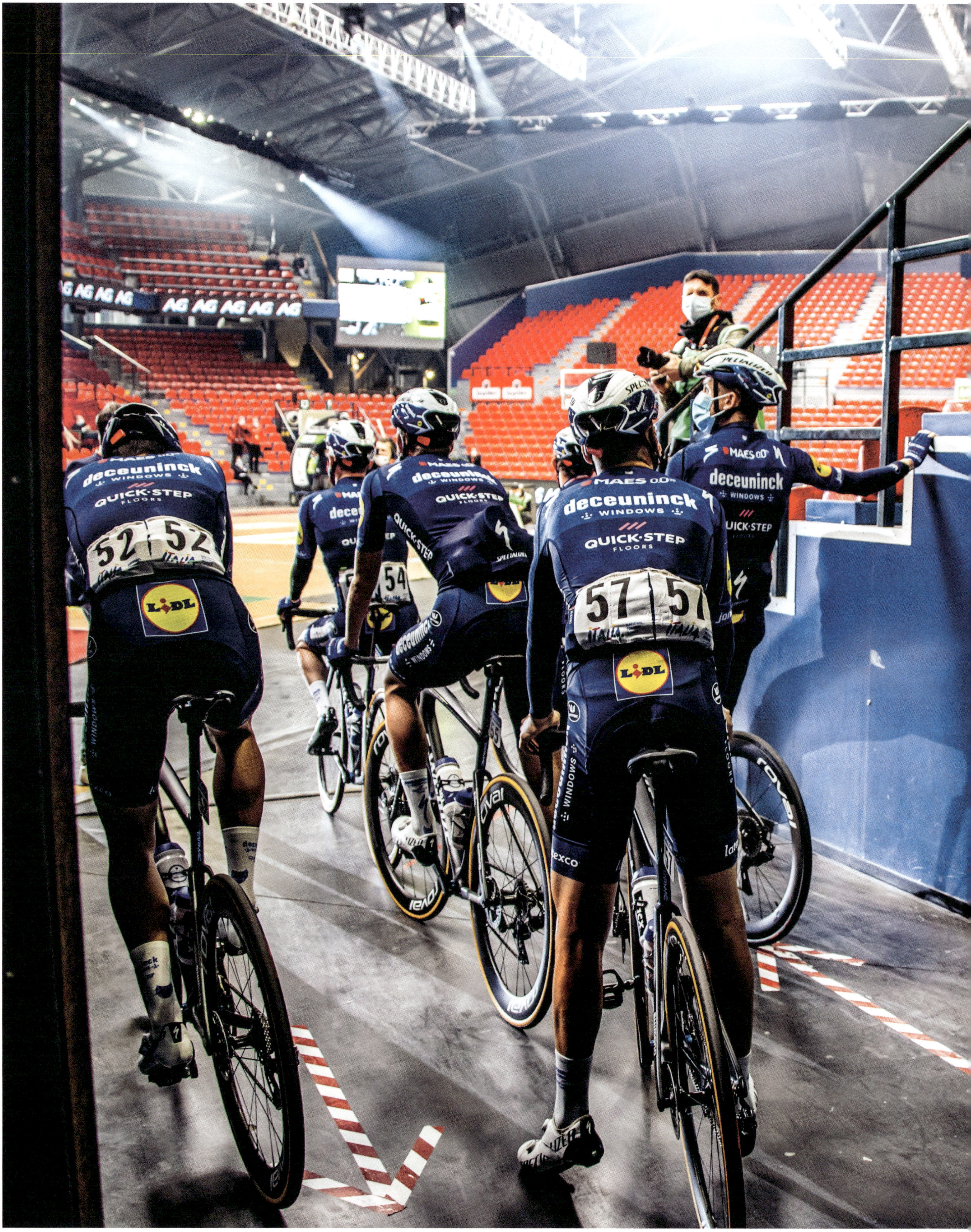
AG AG AG AG
AG AG AG AG AG
MAES 0.0
deceuninck
WINDOWS
QUICK·STEP
FLOORS
52 52
54
57 57
LIDL

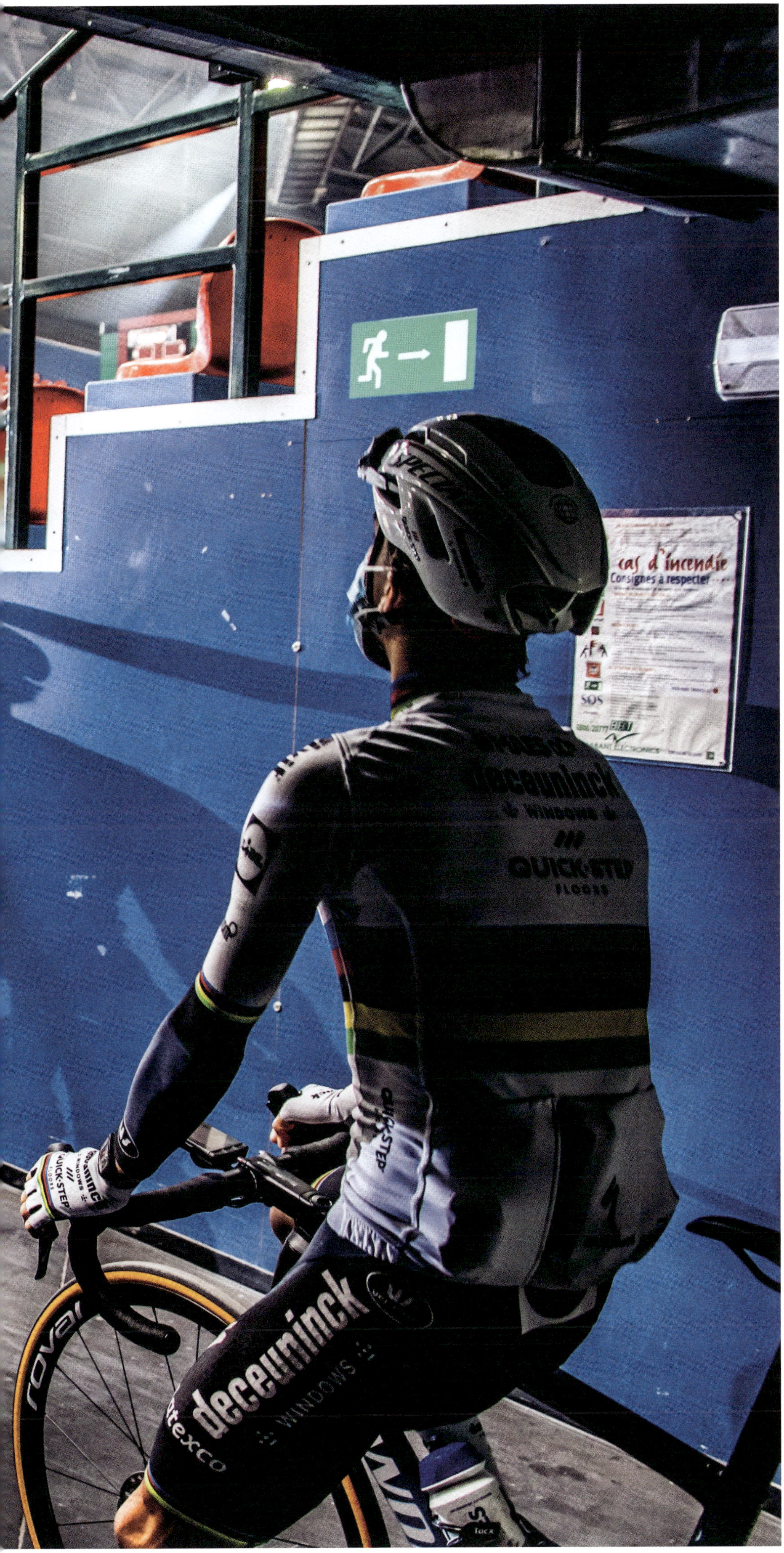

FLÈCHE WALLONE
21.04.2021

De Waalse Pijl is een van de lievelingswedstrijden van Julian Alaphilippe. Hij won er op 21 april 2021 voor de derde keer op vier edities. Al heeft hij zijn hart en zijn dromen verpand aan Luik-Bastenaken-Luik, vermoedelijk de meest 'Franse' Belgische wedstrijd. Hij werd er twee keer tweede. Dat Julian van 'dubbels' houdt, zullen we ook in Leuven zien op 26 september.

The Flèche Wallonne is one of Julian Alaphilippe's favorite races. On 21 April 2021, he won it for the third time in four editions. However, his heart is set on Liège-Bastogne-Liège, probably the most "French" Belgian race. He came in second twice. We'll see that Julian likes "doubles" in Leuven on 26 September.

La Flèche Wallonne est l'une des courses préférées de Julian Alaphilippe. Il l'a remportée le 21 avril 2021 pour la troisième fois en quatre éditions. Mais son objectif reste Liège-Bastogne-Liège, probablement la course belge la plus « française ». C'est la deuxième fois qu'il termine deuxième. Et les doubles (victoires), ça le connaît, comme nous l'avons vu à Louvain le 26 septembre.

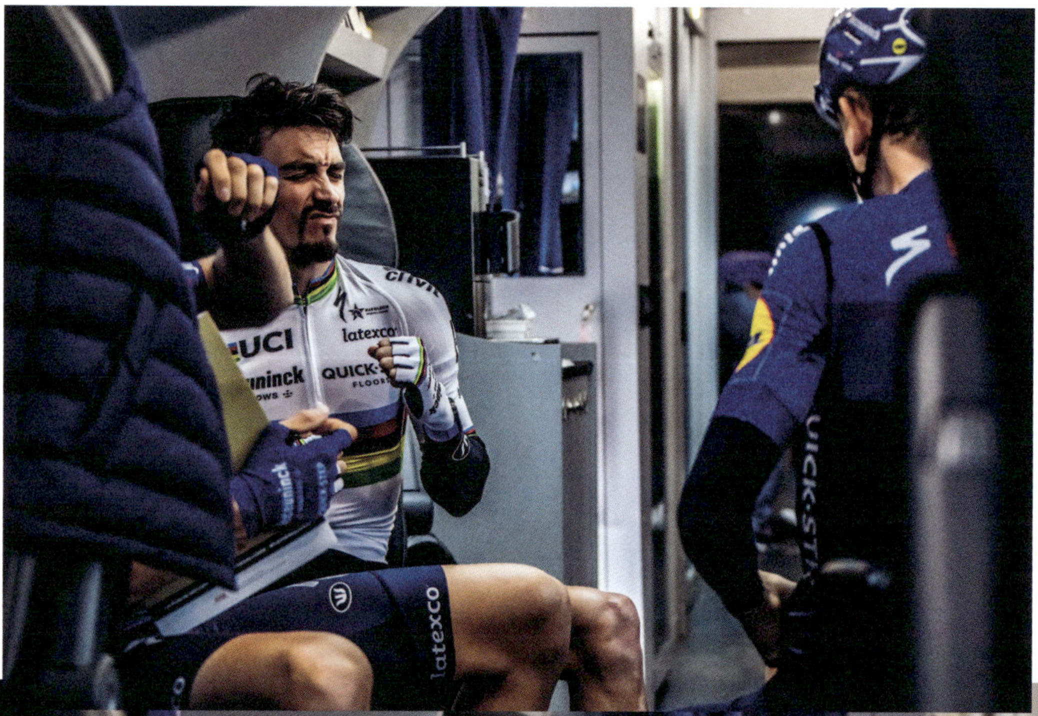

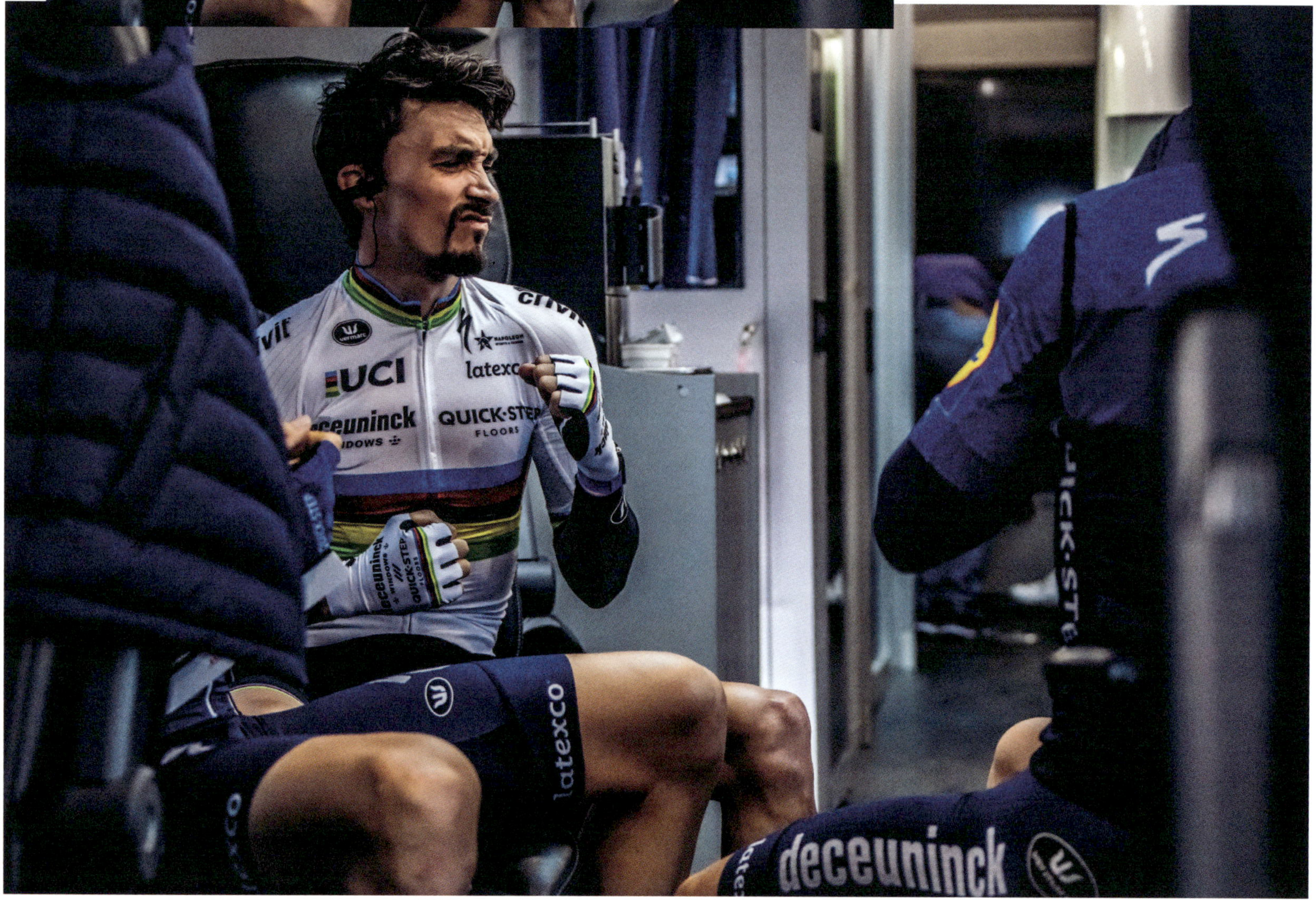

Julian Alaphilippe in de Wolfpack-bus op weg naar de start van de Waalse Pijl in Charleroi. De motivatie op scherp zetten met de juiste muziek. Op naar de zeven kapelletjes op de Mur de Huy.

Julian Alaphilippe in the Wolfpack bus on his way to the start of the Flèche Wallonne in Charleroi. The right music gets him motivated. On to the seven chapels on the Mur de Huy.

Julian Alaphilippe dans le bus du Wolfpack, en route pour le départ de la Flèche Wallonne à Charleroi. De la bonne musique pour se motiver. Direction les sept chapelles du Mur de Huy.

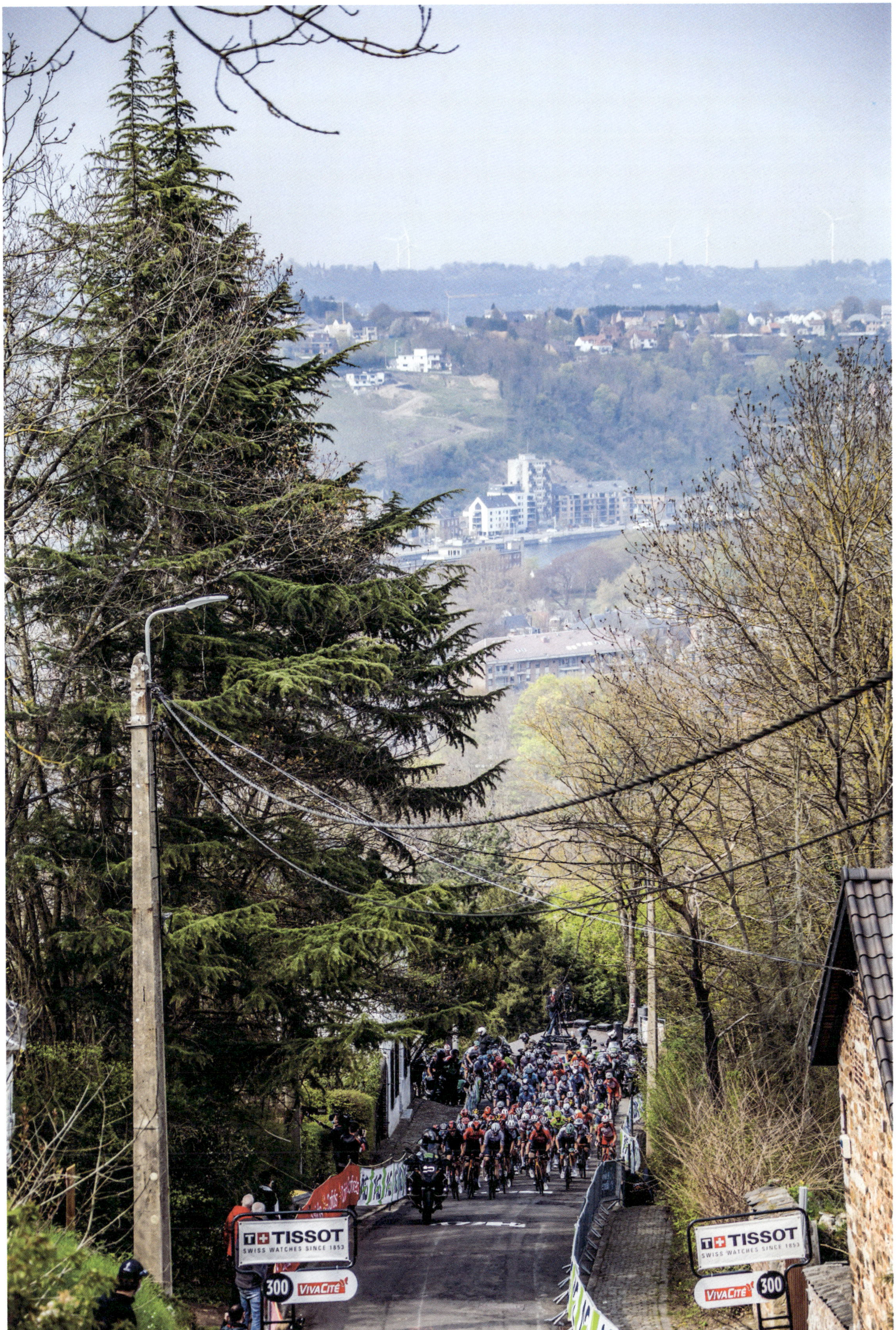
TISSOT
SWISS WATCHES SINCE 1853
300
VivaCité
TISSOT
SWISS WATCHES SINCE 1853
VivaCité
300

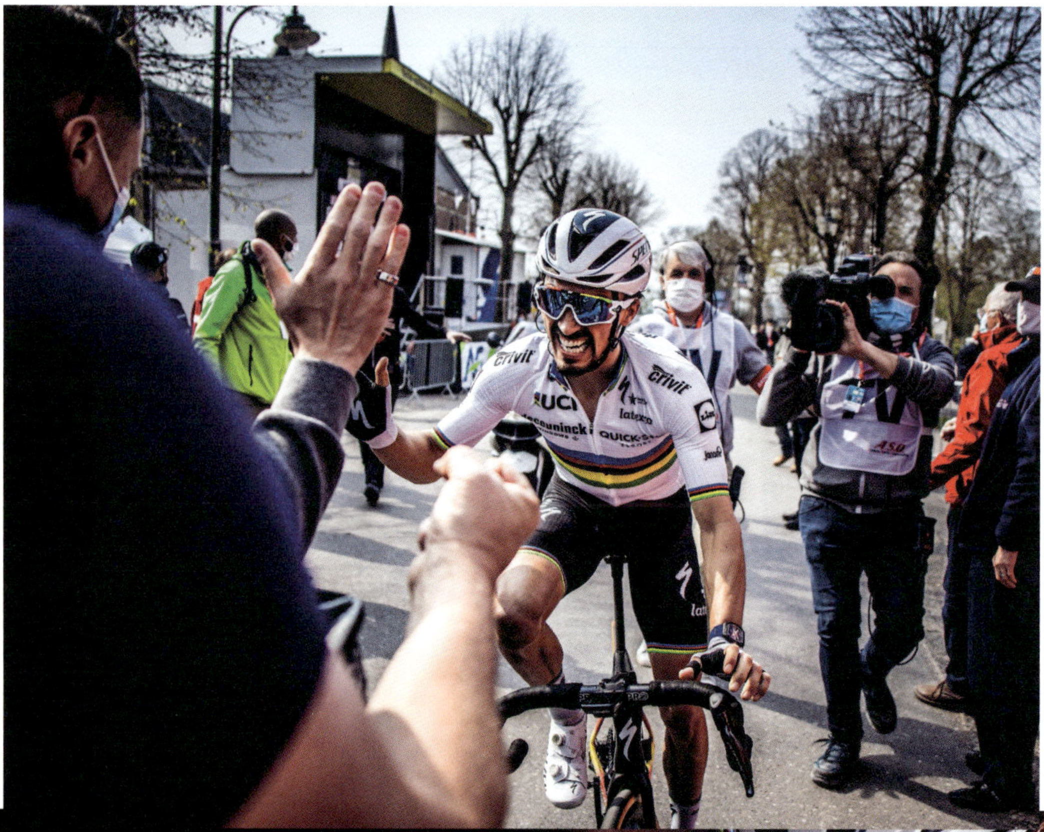

Julian Alaphilippe enkele meters na de meet van de Flèche Wallonne. Nog voor hij uitgehijgd is, dankt hij via de teamradio zijn ploegmakkers die hem tot aan de voet van de klim brachten. Een mooi gebaar van een groot mens, een groot kampioen.

Julian Alaphilippe just past the finish line of the Flèche Wallonne. Before he even stopped to take a breath, he thanked his teammates via the team radio for bringing him to the foot of the climb. A beautiful gesture from a great man, a great champion.

Julian Alaphilippe quelques mètres après l'arrivée de la Flèche Wallonne. Avant même de reprendre son souffle, il utilise la radio de l'équipe pour remercier ses coéquipiers qui l'ont porté au pied de la montée. Un beau geste pour un grand homme, un grand champion.

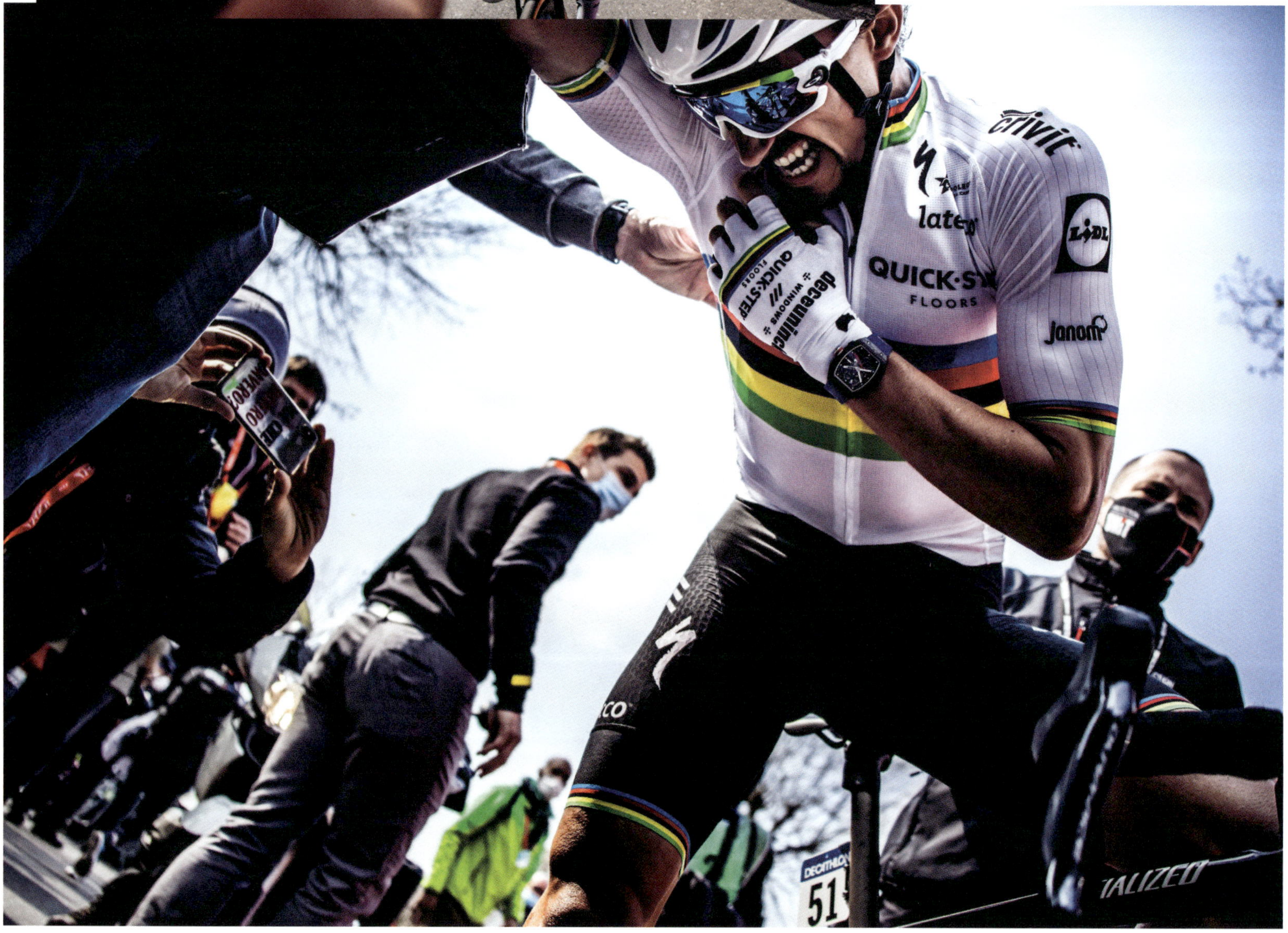

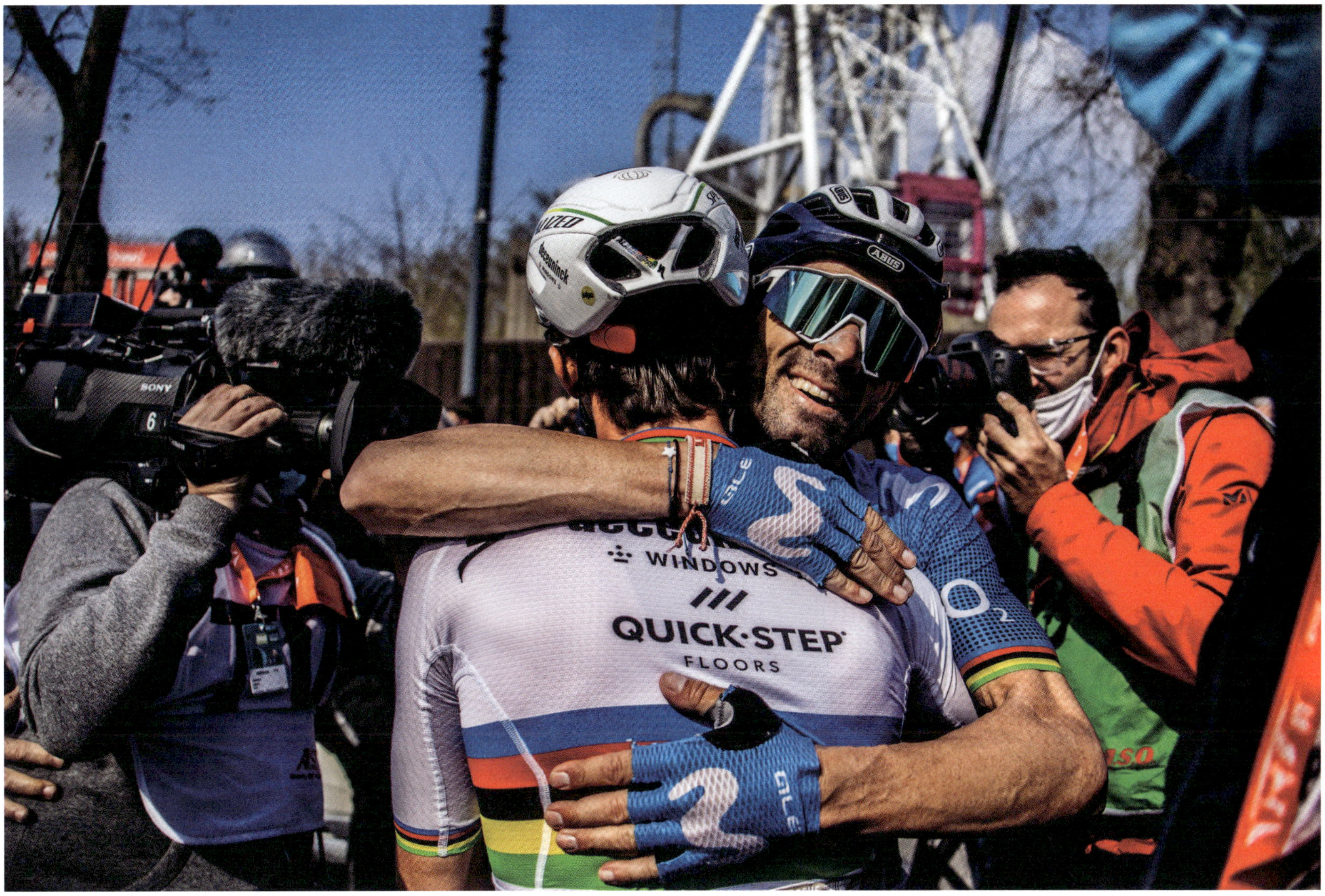

HUY, 21.04.2021

Julian Alaphilippe en Alejandro Valverde in een innige omhelzing. Het toont het respect van grote kampioenen voor elkaar. Valverde finishte derde op 6 seconden in de Waalse Pijl.

Julian Alaphilippe and Alejandro Valverde in a close embrace. It shows the respect that great champions have for each other. Valverde finished third at six seconds in the Flèche Wallonne.

Julian Alaphilippe et Alejandro Valverde en pleine étreinte. Cette photo illustre le respect que les grands champions ont les uns pour les autres. Valverde a terminé troisième à 6 secondes. ▲

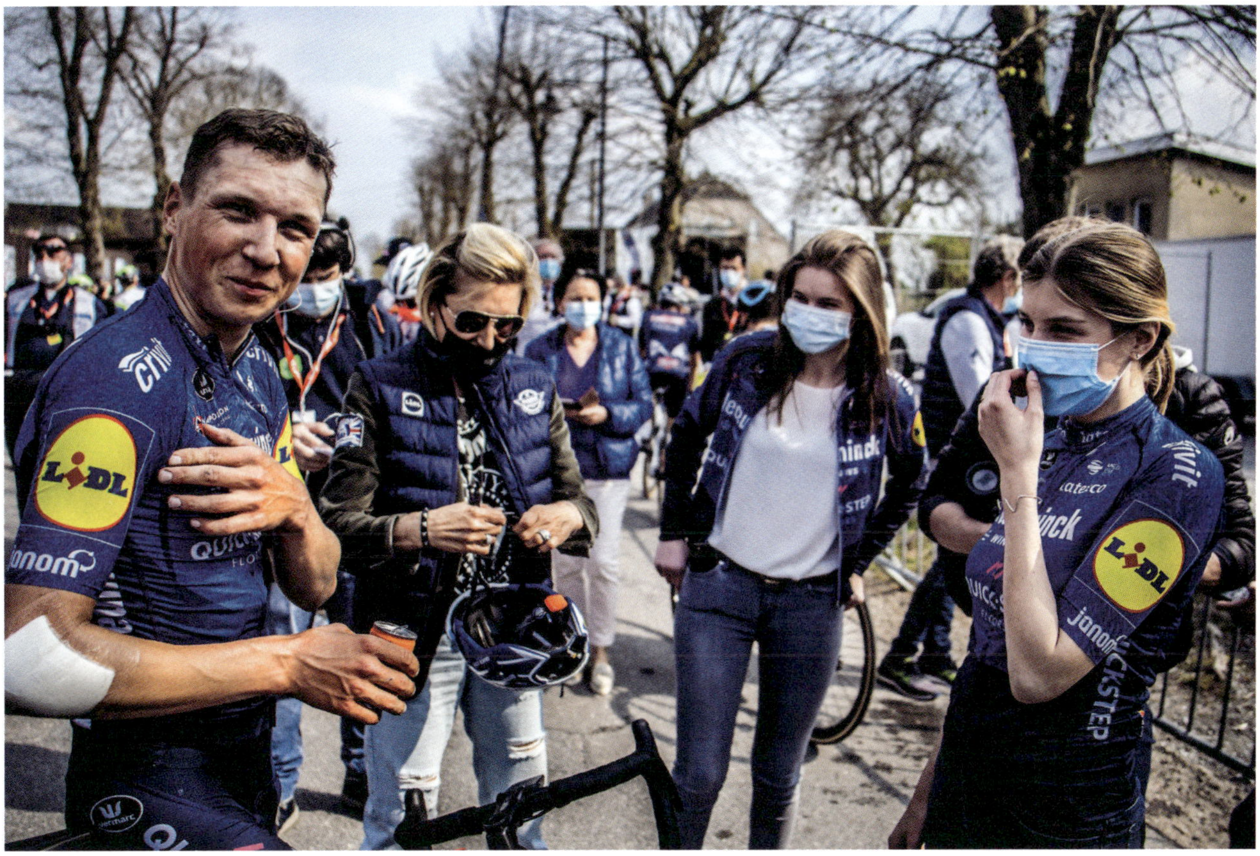

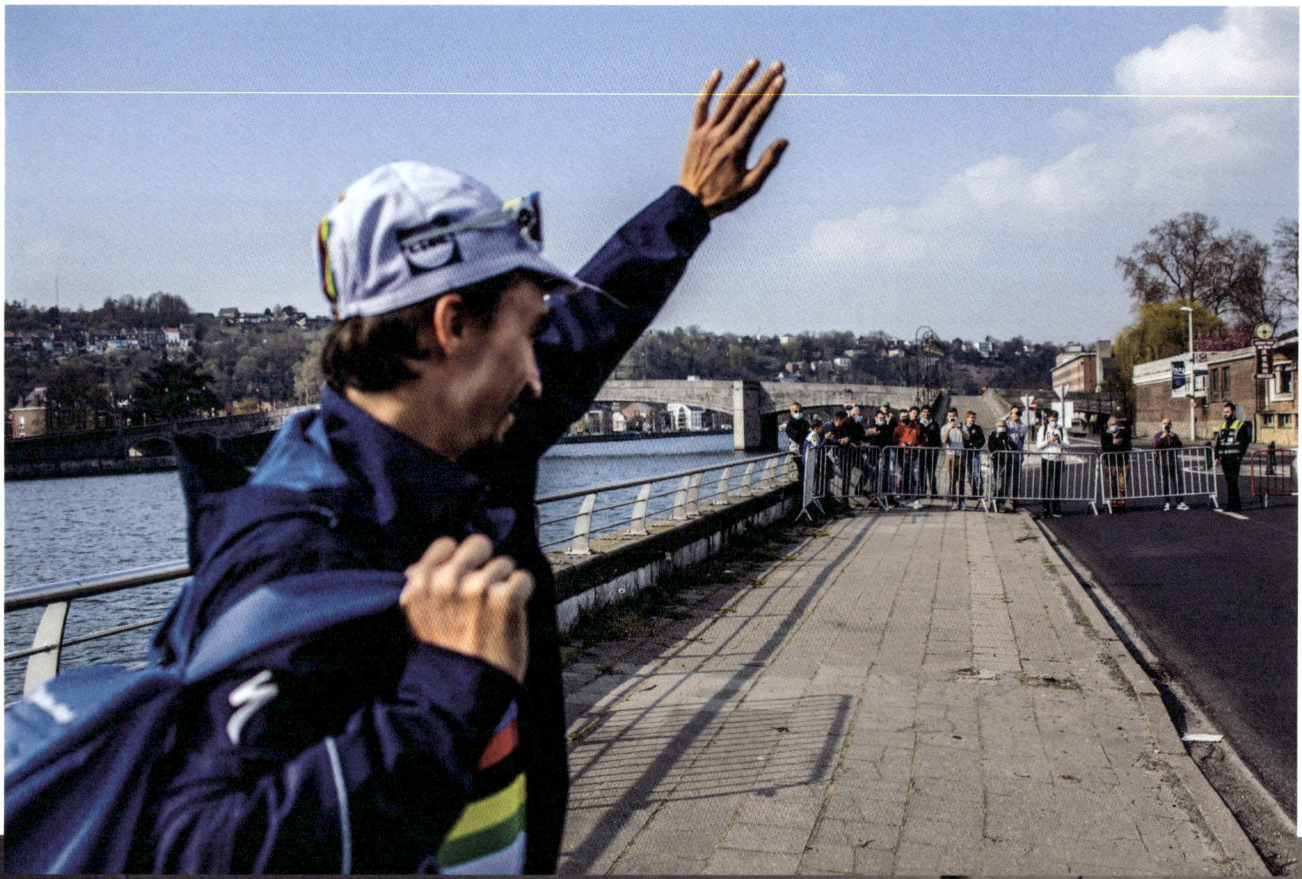

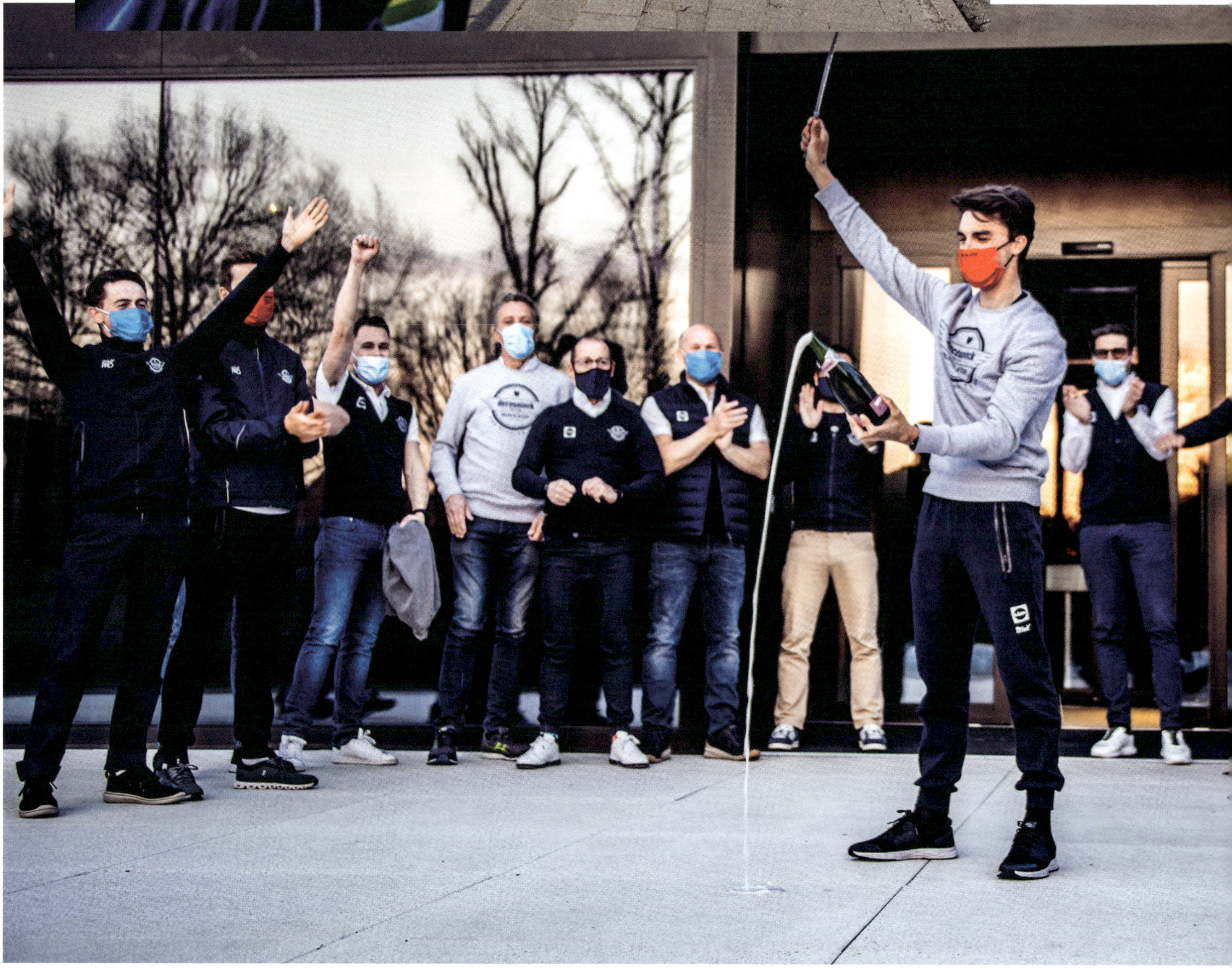

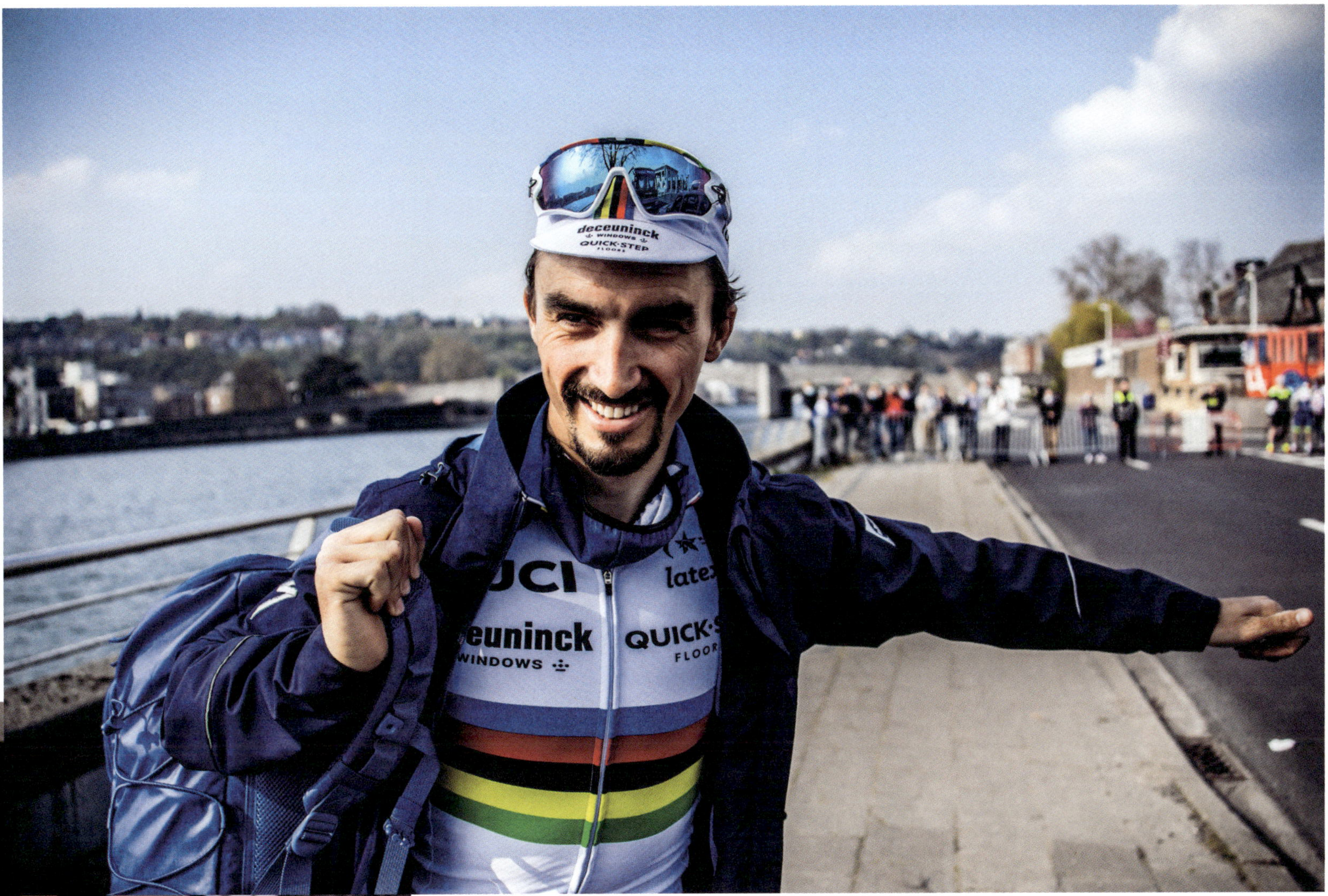

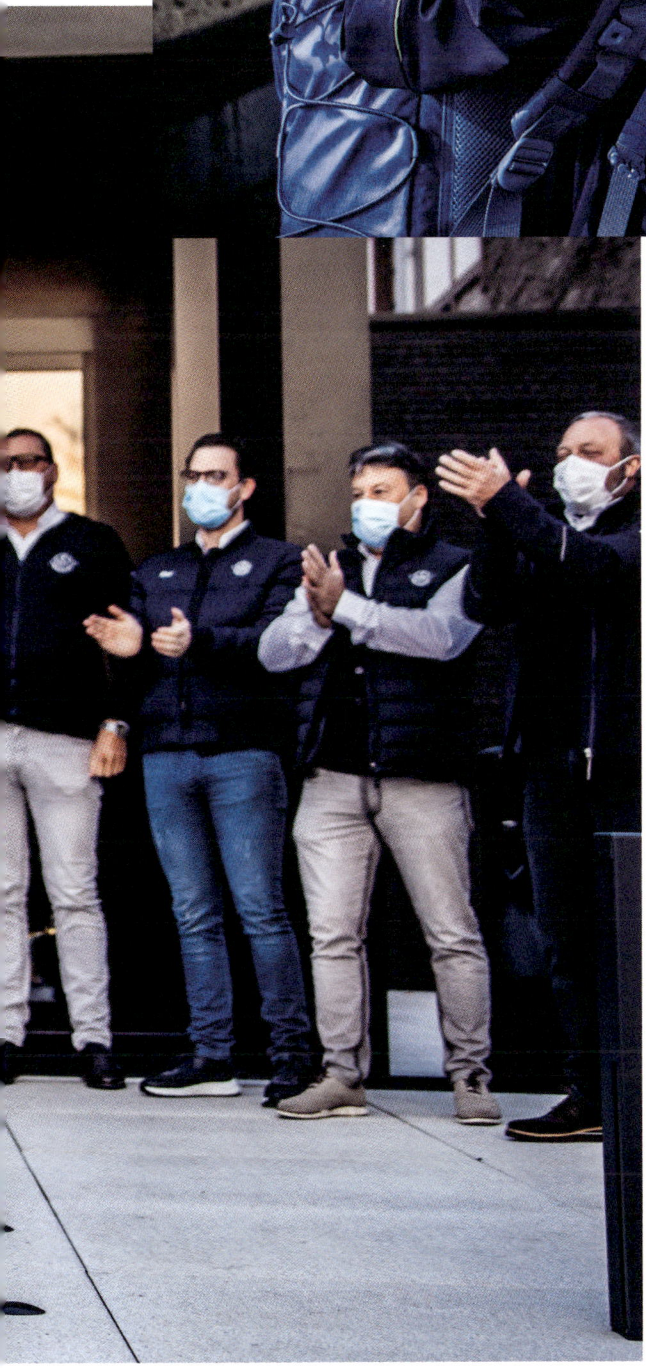

De truc met het sabel. Teamspirit is belangrijk. De ploeg slaagt er wonderwel in om het evenwicht te vinden tussen inspanning en ontspanning. Na een stevige overwinning mag er een glaasje worden gedronken. En dat verloopt nooit zoutloos. Zoals na de zege van Julian Alaphilippe. Als een volleerd sabelvechter opent Julian de eerste fles champagne die wordt gekraakt. En of het verdiend was.

The trick with the sabre. Team spirit is important. The team manages to strike a balance between effort and relaxation. After a solid victory, a drink is in order. It never goes without the necessary celebrations. A celebration is certainly called for following Julian Alaphilippe's victory. Julian opens the first bottle of champagne like an accomplished swordsman. Much deserved.

Sablons le champagne. L'esprit d'équipe est important. L'équipe réussit toujours à trouver un équilibre entre effort et détente. Après une belle victoire, un verre s'impose. Et la meute fête toujours bien ça, comme cette fois-ci, pour la victoire de Julian Alaphilippe. Tel un professionnel, Julian ouvre la première bouteille de champagne et la casse. Des célébrations bien méritées.

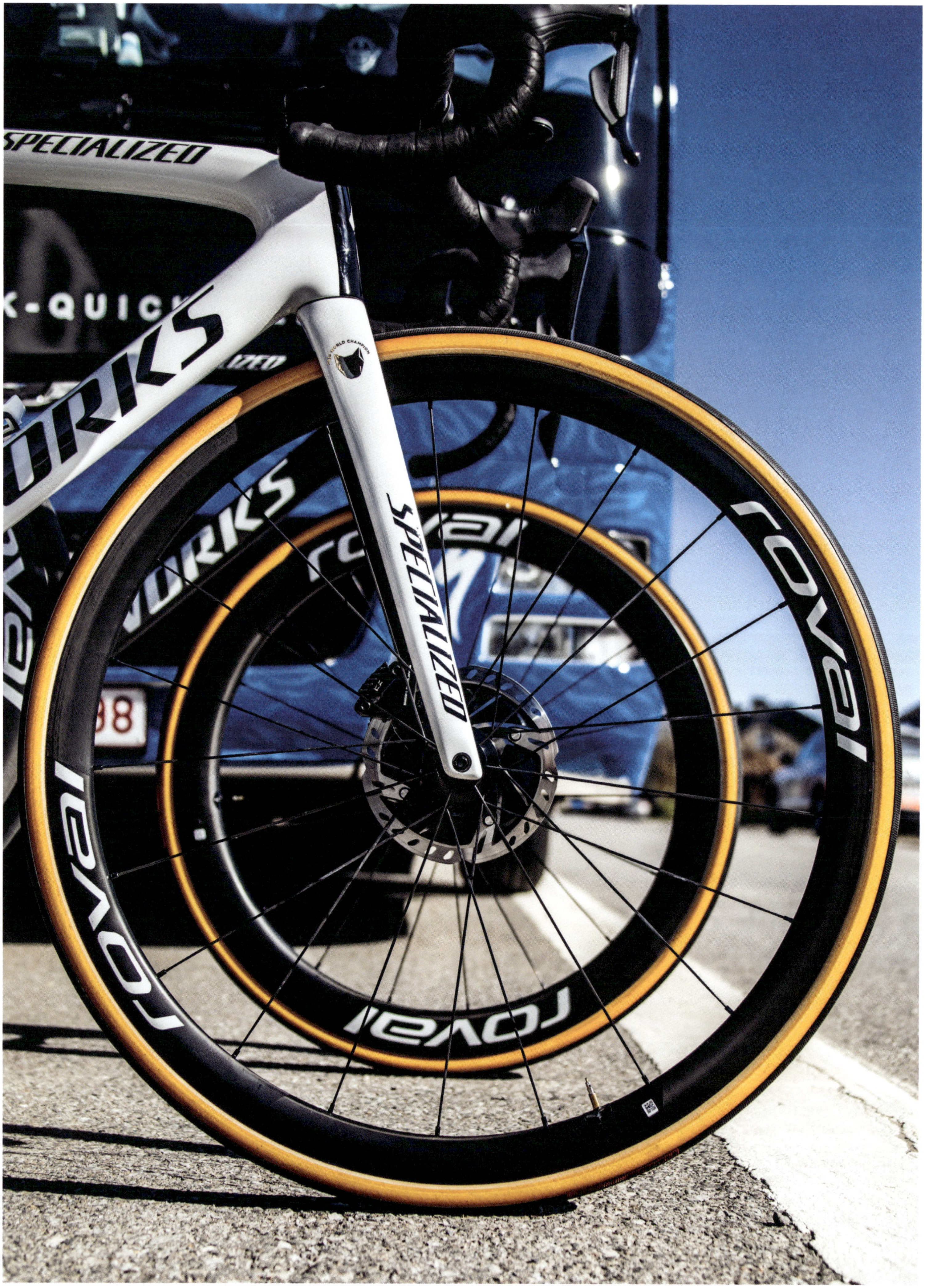

SPECIALIZED
SPECIALIZED
roval

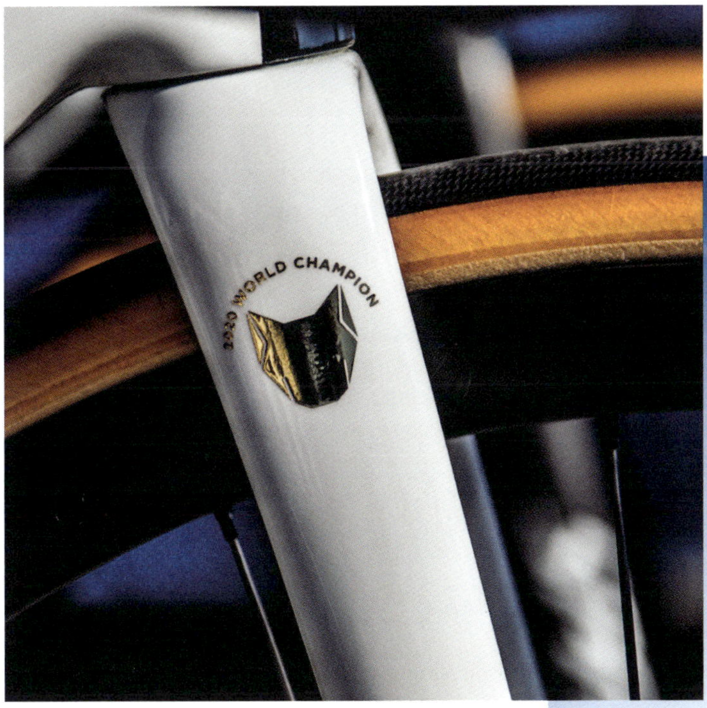

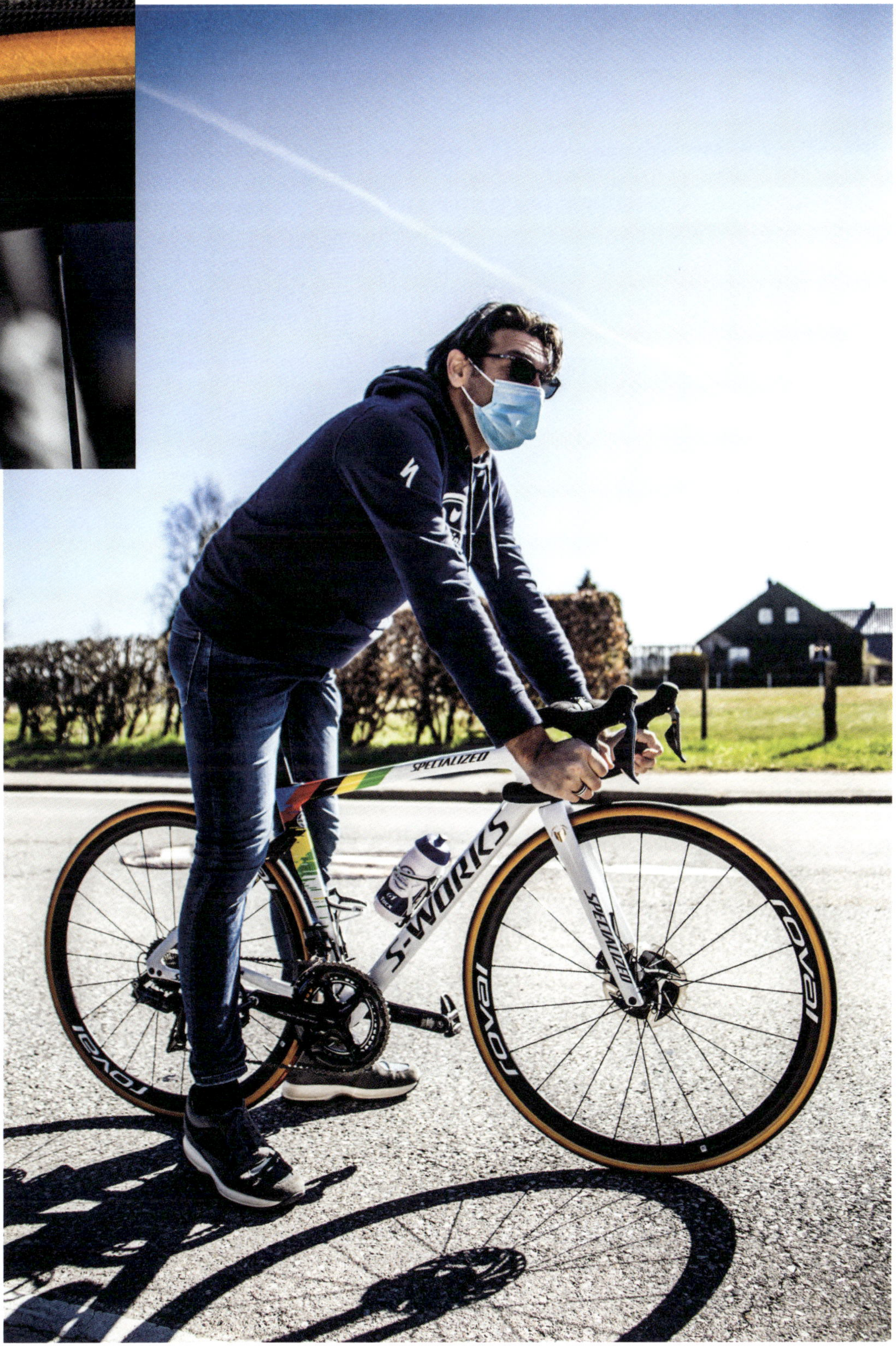

Luik-Bastenaken-Luik volgde naar jaarlijkse gewoonte vier dagen na de Waalse Pijl. Het DQT Team was uiterst gemotiveerd, zowel de renners als iedereen die bij de ploeg betrokken is. Zo stond er een mooie verrassing te wachten op Wereldkampioen Alaphilippe. Voor het eerst fietste hij op zijn 'witte' Wereldkampioenenvehikel. Wat een parel. Van Specialized, natuurlijk.

As usual, Liège-Bastogne-Liège followed four days after the Flèche Wallonne. An extremely motivated DQT Team. Motivation is strong among both the riders and everyone involved in the team. A nice surprise awaited World Champion Alaphilippe. For the first time, he rode on his "white" World Champion's bike. What a gem. From Specialized, of course.

Comme d'habitude, Liège-Bastogne-Liège a eu lieu quatre jours après la Flèche Wallonne. Toute l'équipe DQT était particulièrement motivée, aussi bien les coureurs que le staff. Une belle surprise attendait le Champion du Monde Alaphilippe. Pour la première fois, il a pédalé sur son vélo « blanc » de Champion du Monde. Quel éclat. De Specialized, bien entendu.

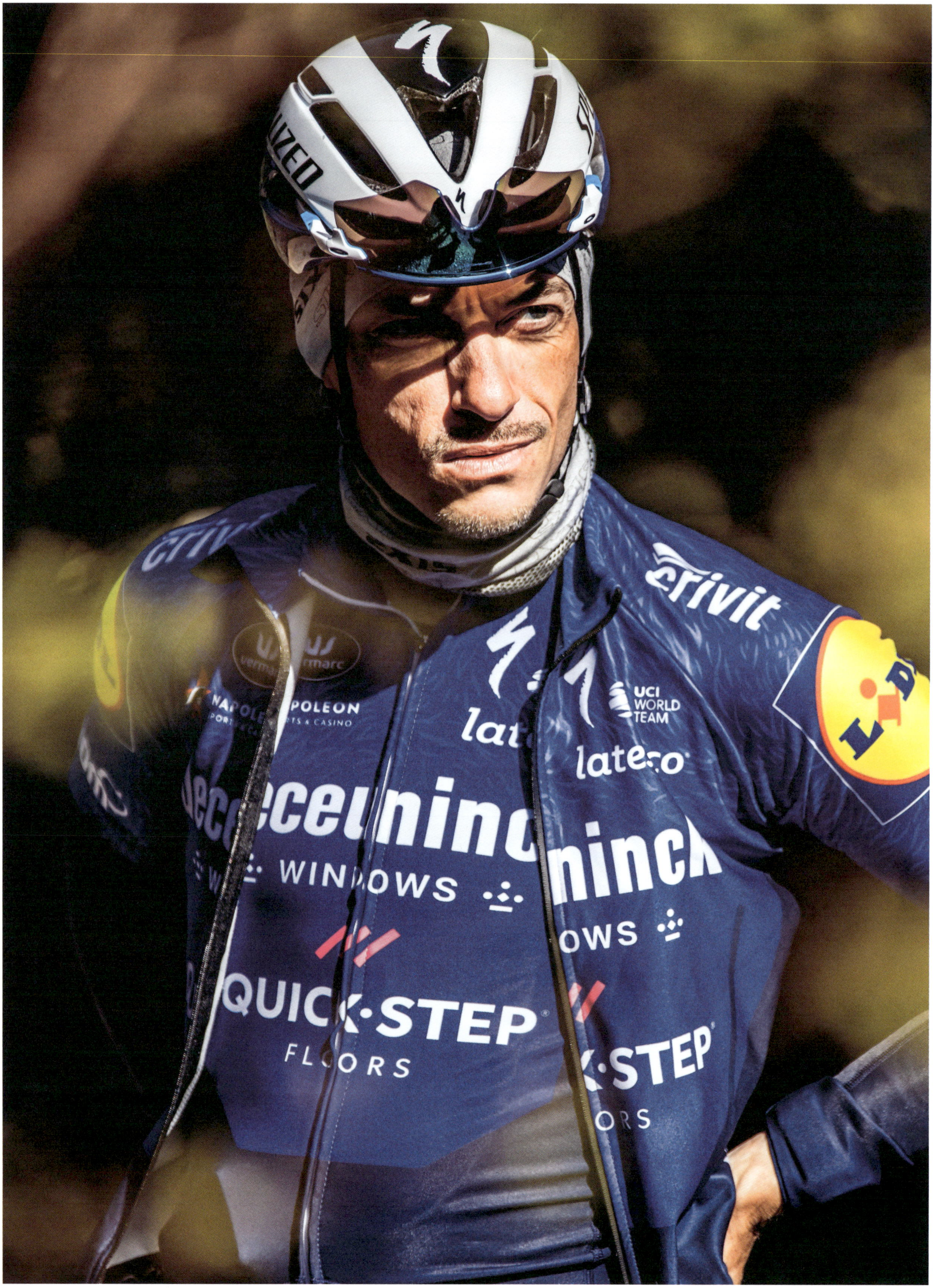
crivit
UCI
WORLD
TEAM
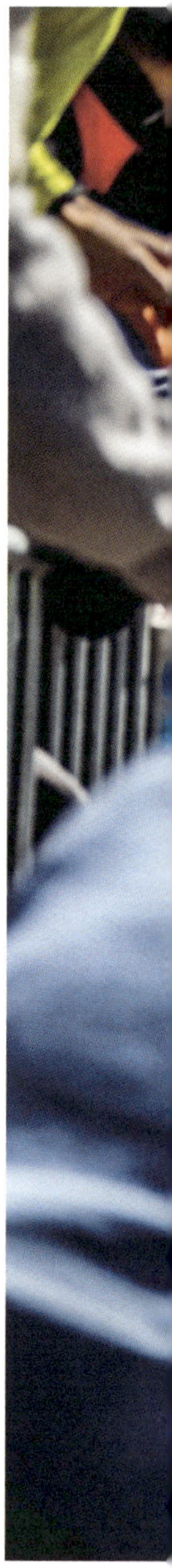

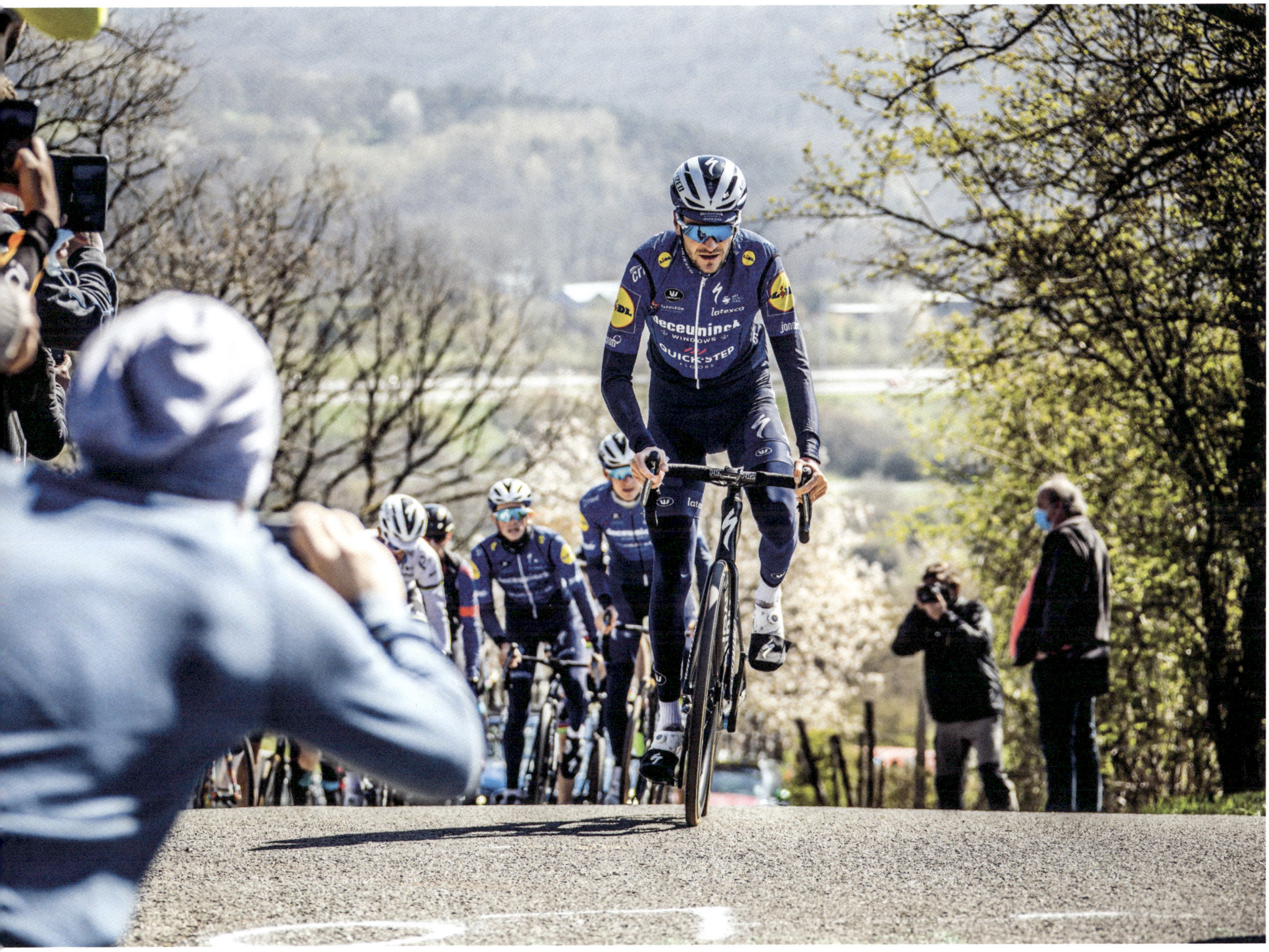

AYWAILLE, 23.04.2021

Verkenning van Luik-Bastenaken-Luik. Pieter Serry overwint de befaamde helling van La Redoute in de gemeente Sougné. In zijn spoor volgen de andere Wolven.

Exploring Liège-Bastogne-Liège. Pieter Serry conquers the famous climb of La Redoute in the town of Sougné. Other wolves follow in his tracks.

En reconnaissance à Liège-Bastogne-Liège. Pieter Serry conquiert la célèbre côte de la Redoute à Sougné-Remouchamps. Le reste de la meute suit ses traces. ▲

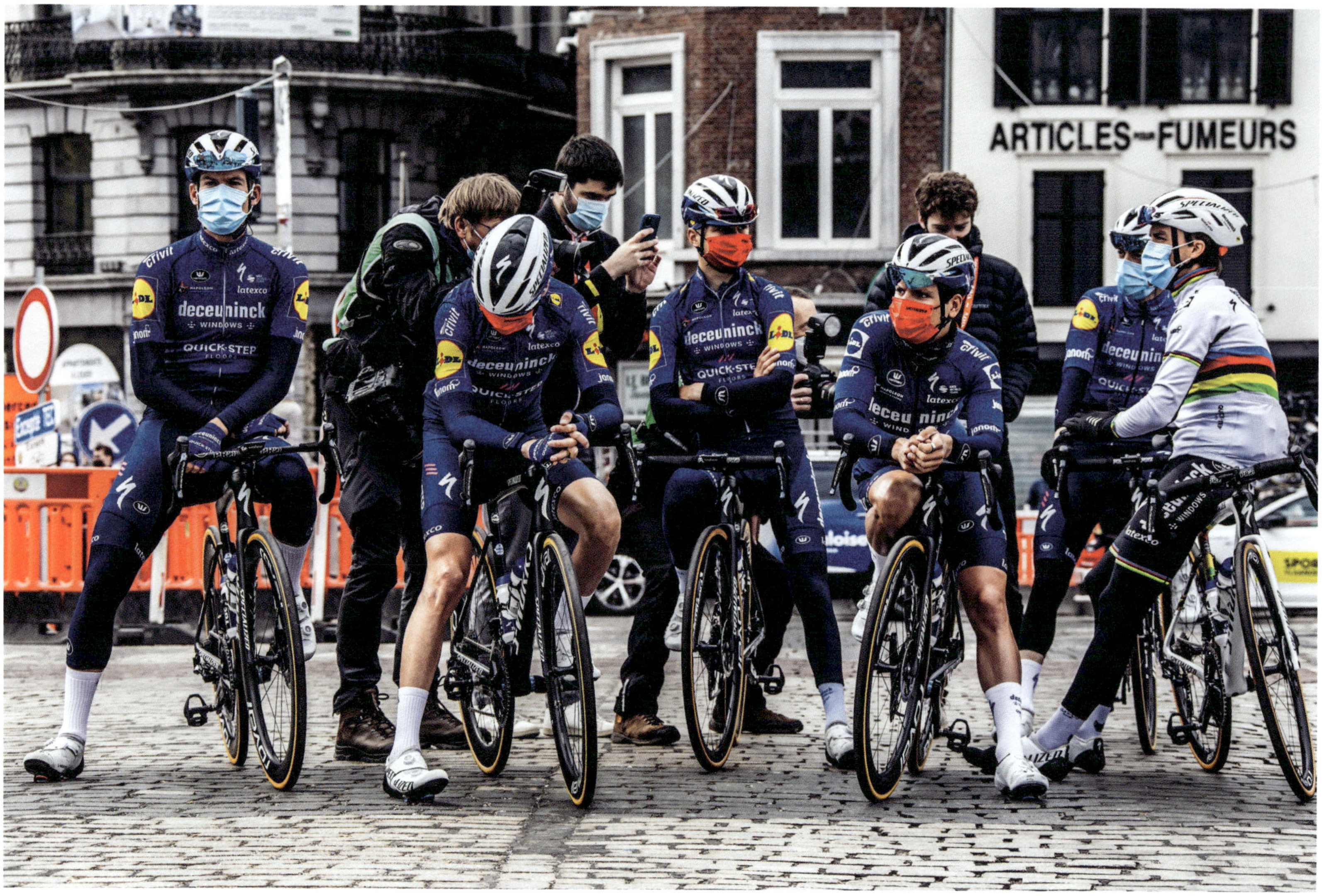
ARTICLES FUMEURS

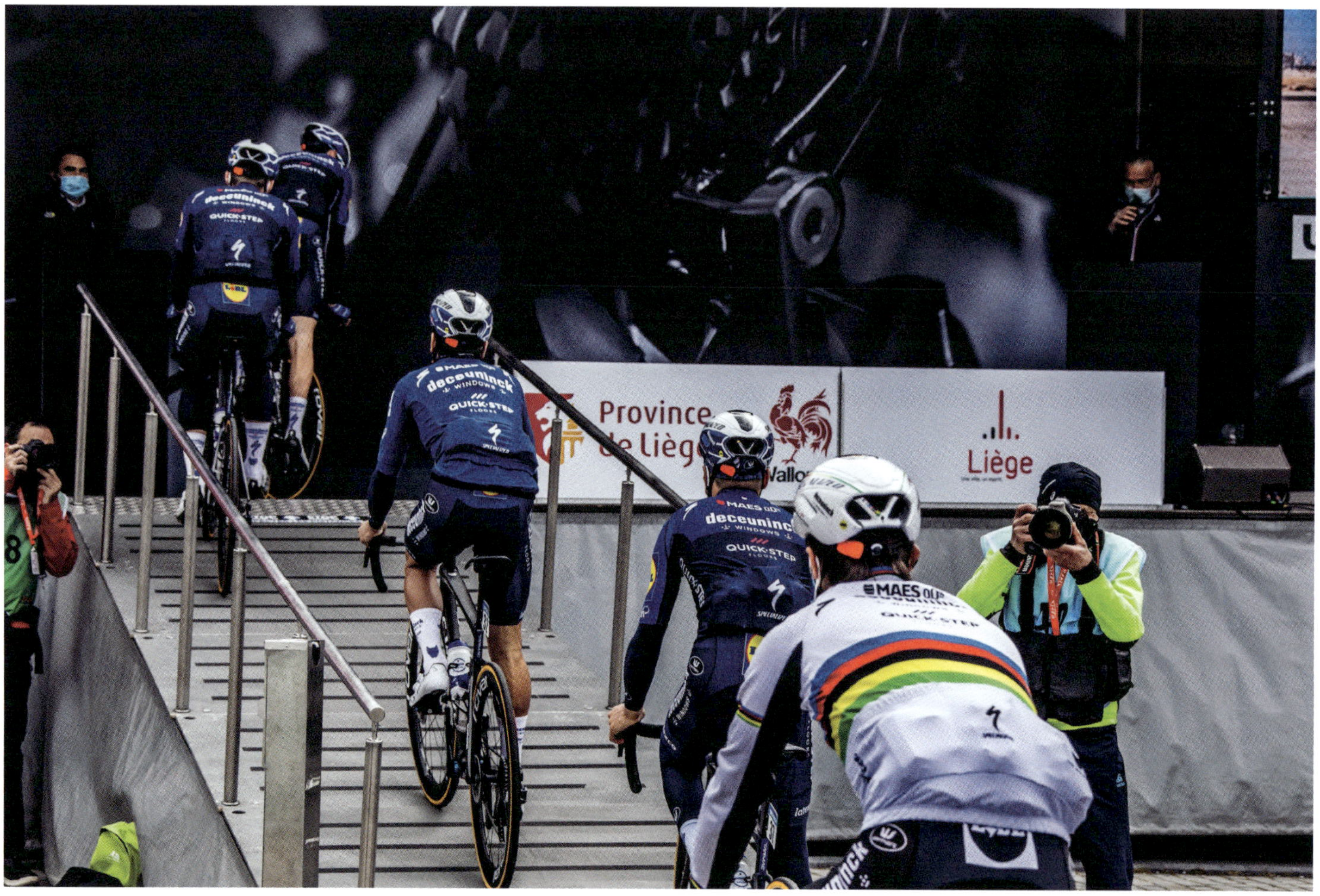
Province
de Liège
Liège

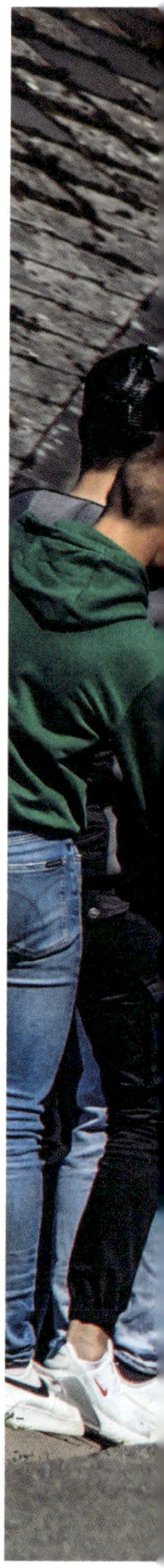

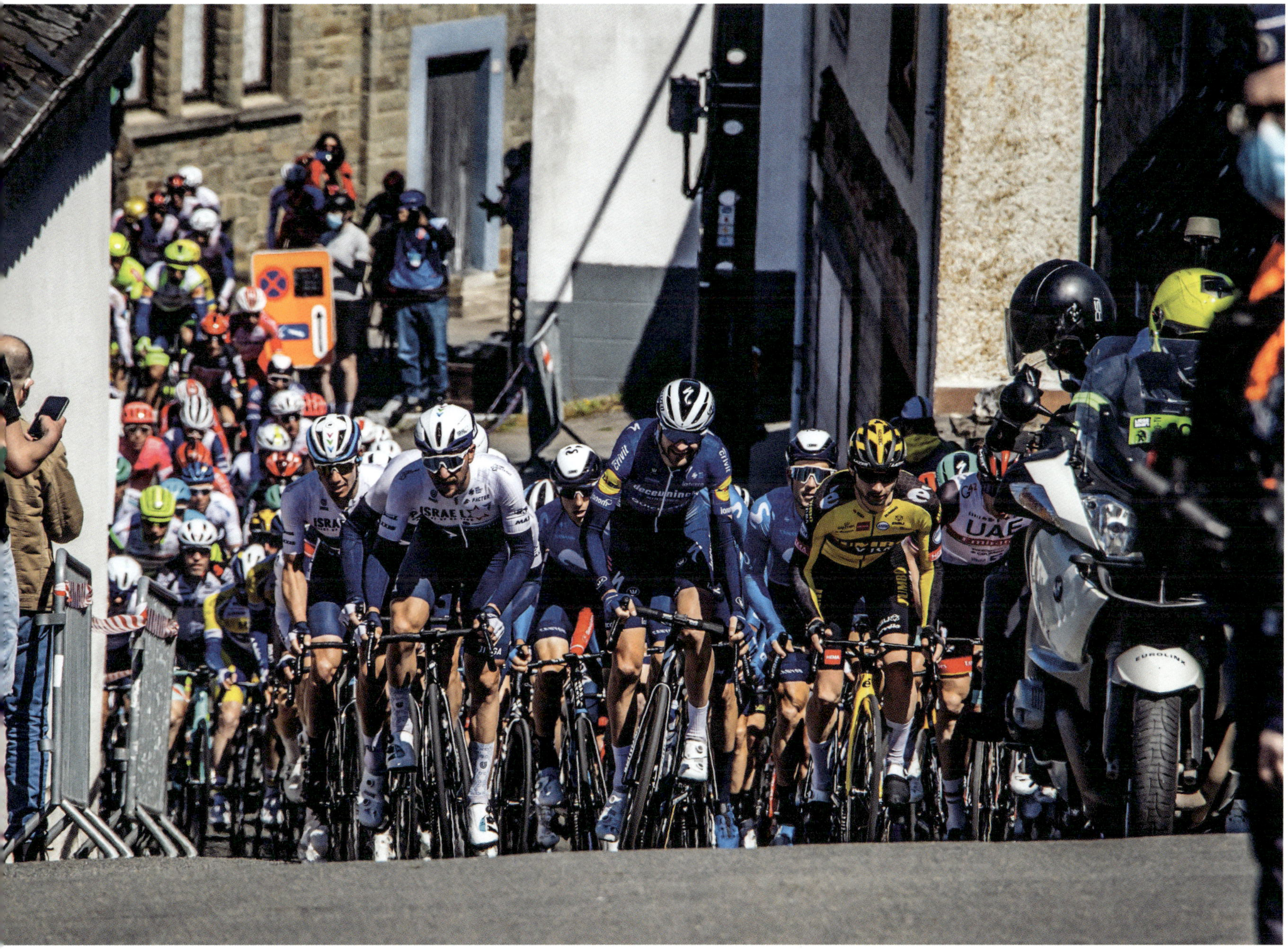
UAE

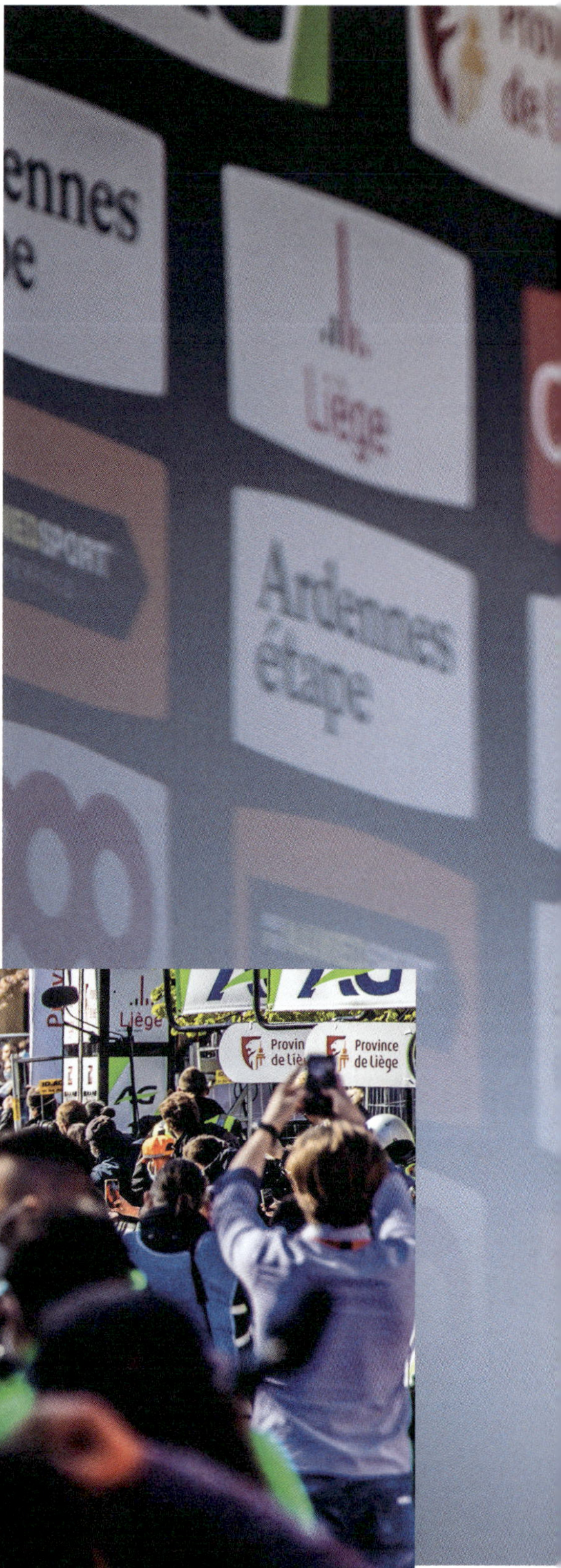
Liège
Ardennes
étape

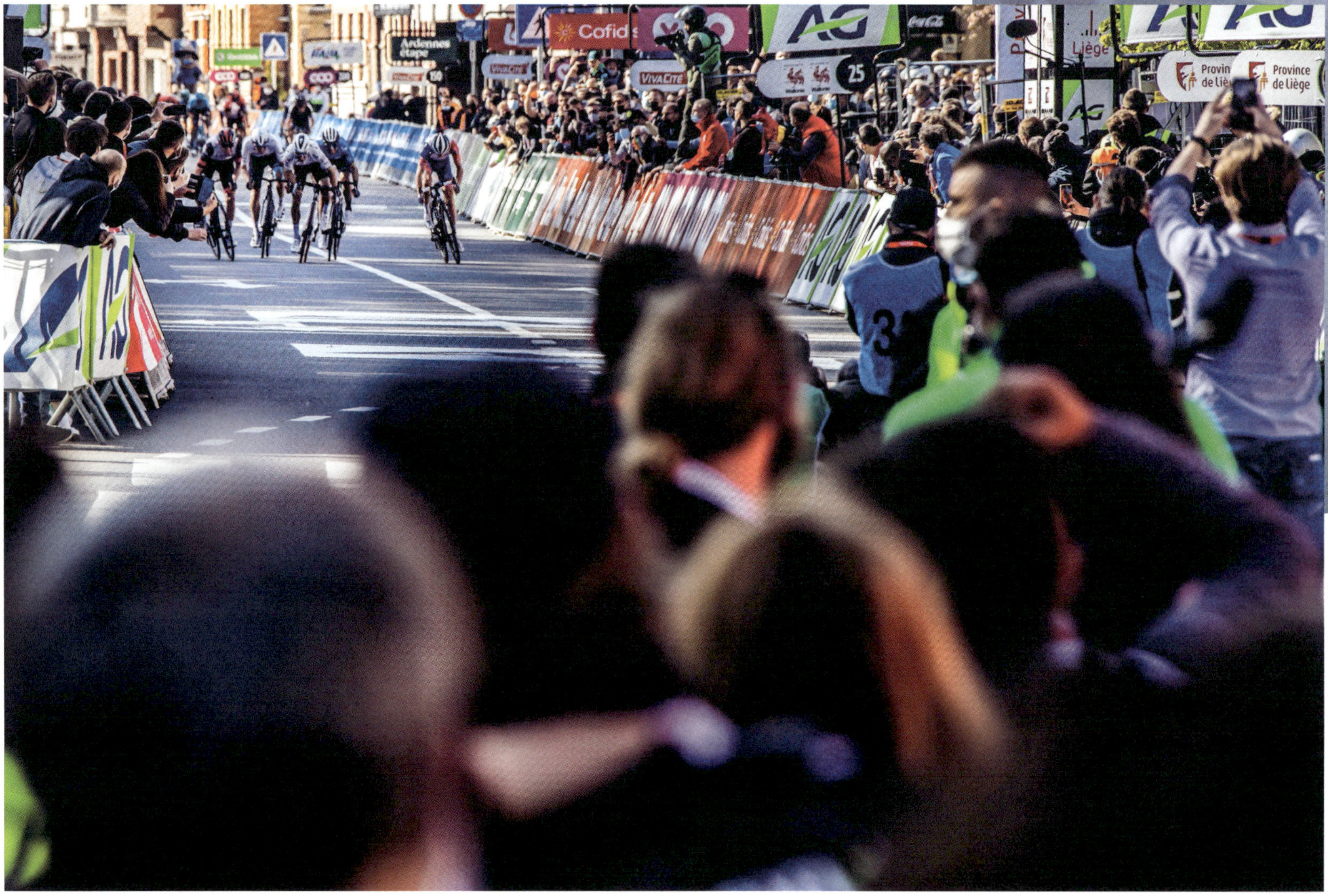
Province
de Liège
VivaCité

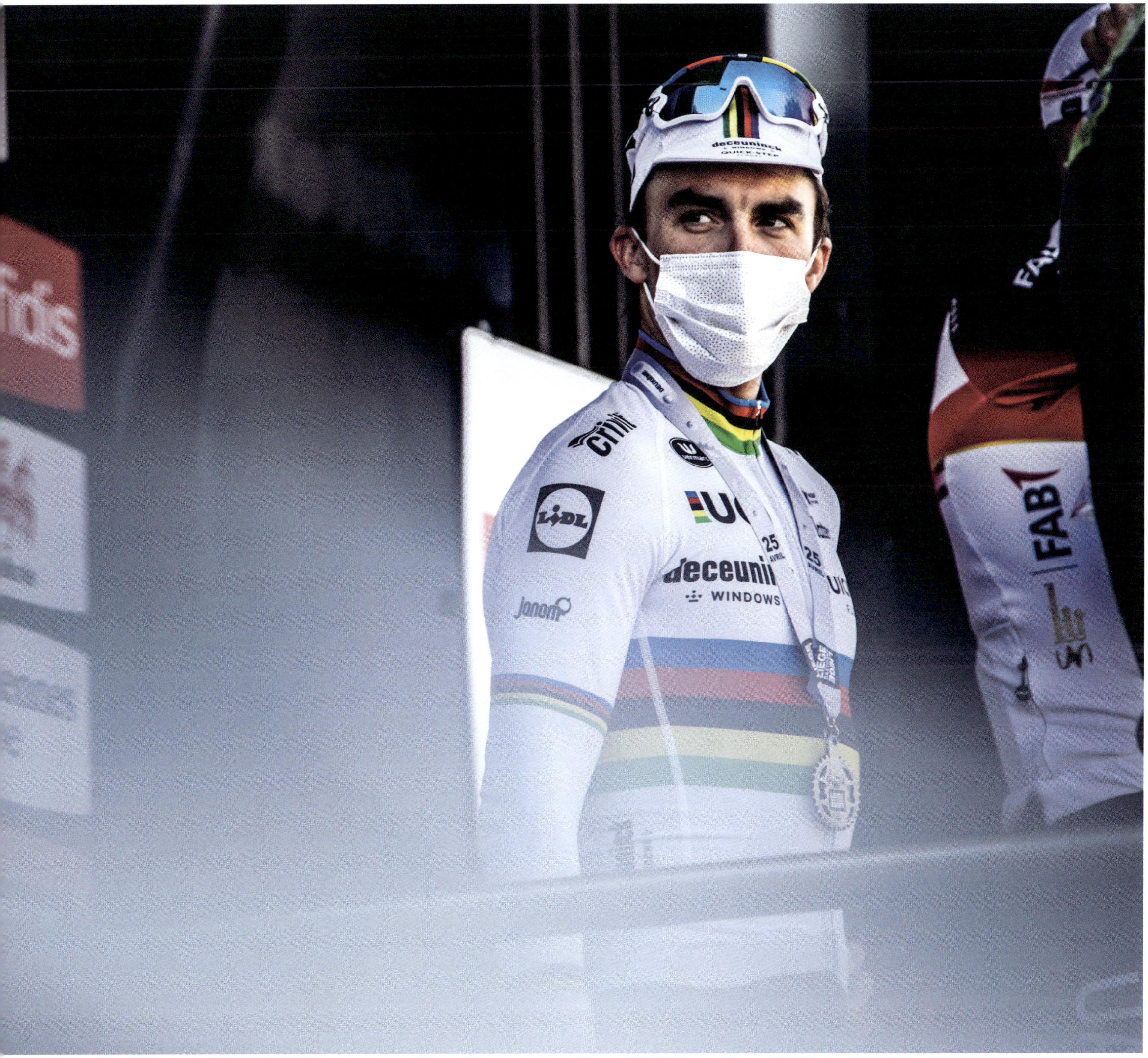

LIÈGE, 25.04.2021

Wereldkampioen Julian Alaphilippe verbijt de teleurstelling. Hij moet de duimen leggen voor Tadej Pogacar in de 107de editie van La Doyenne. Vorig jaar glipte de winst mysterieus door zijn handen, nu werd hij geklopt in een sprint met vijf.

World Champion Julian Alaphilippe is overcome with disappointment. He was beaten by Tadej Pogacar in the 107th edition of La Doyenne. Last year, the win mysteriously slipped through his fingers, and now he's been beaten in a five-man sprint.

Dépité, le Champion du Monde Julian Alaphilippe se remet de sa défaite à la 107e édition de la Doyenne des classiques. Il termine second, après le Slovène Tadej Pogacar. L'année dernière, la victoire lui a mystérieusement échappé, cette fois-ci, il a été battu dans un sprint à cinq.

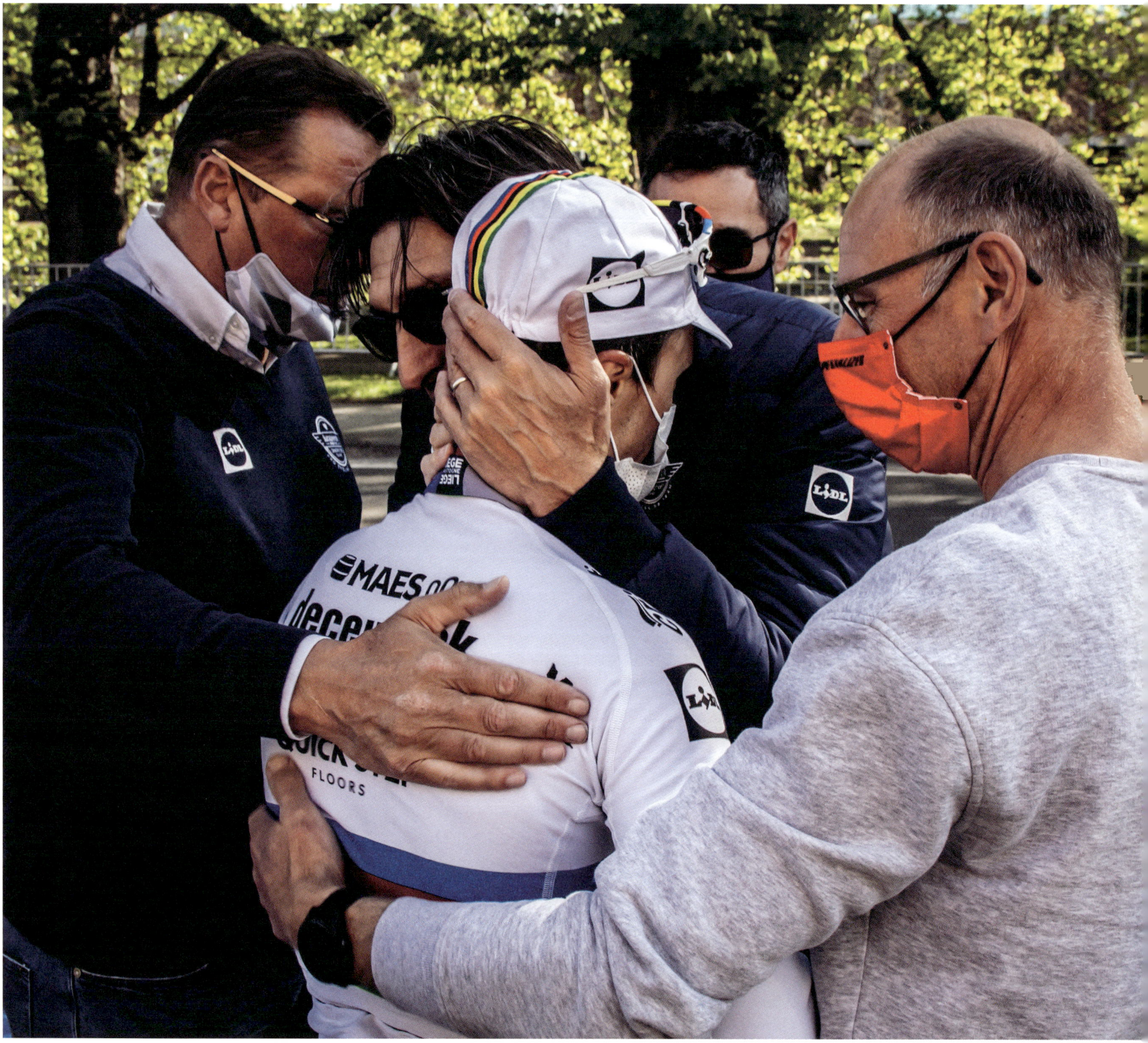

LIÈGE, 25.04.2021

Julian Alaphilippe wordt getroost door de sportdirecteurs Wilfried Peeters (links) en Davide Bramati (die Julian omhelst). Achteraan is technisch directeur Ricardo Scheidecker getuige en rechts zoekt masseur Marc Patry de juiste woorden.

Julian Alaphilippe is comforted by sports directors Wilfried Peeters (left) and Davide Bramati (hugging Julian). Technical director Ricardo Scheidecker witnesses the scene in the back, and on the left, masseur Marc Patry is trying to find the right words.

Julian Alaphilippe est réconforté par les directeurs sportifs Wilfried Peeters (à gauche) et Davide Bramati (qui prend Julian dans ses bras). À l'arrière, le directeur technique Ricardo Scheidecker est témoin de la scène et à gauche, le masseur Marc Patry cherche les mots justes.

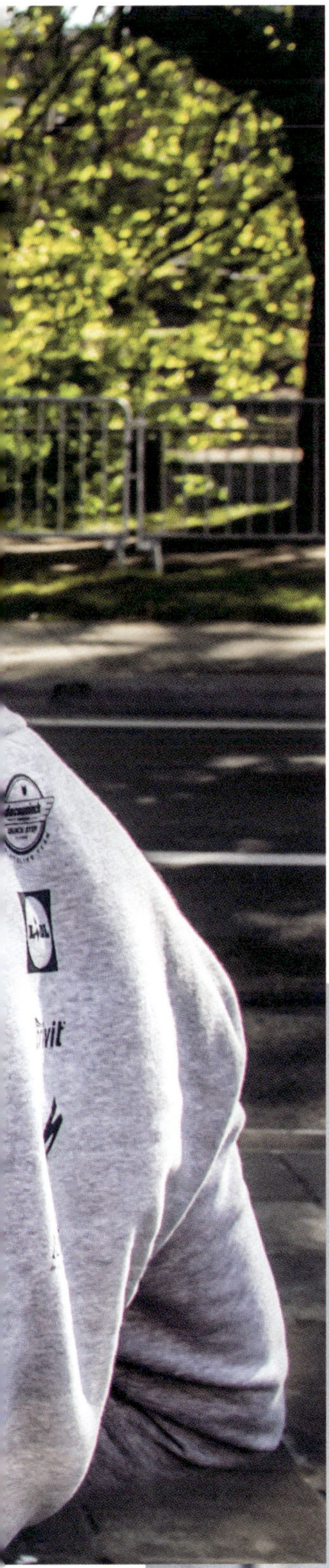

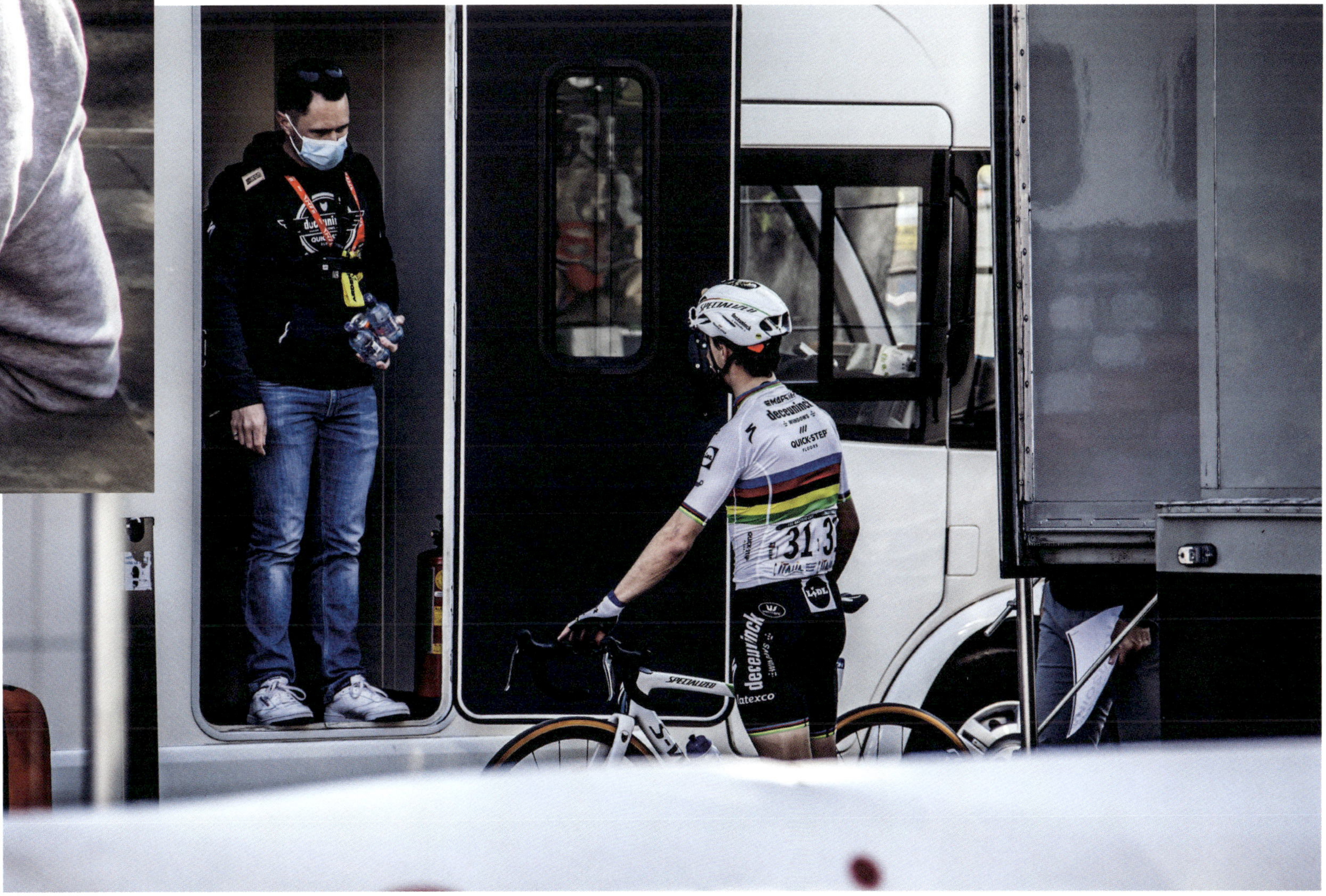
deceuninck
QUICK-STEP
latexco

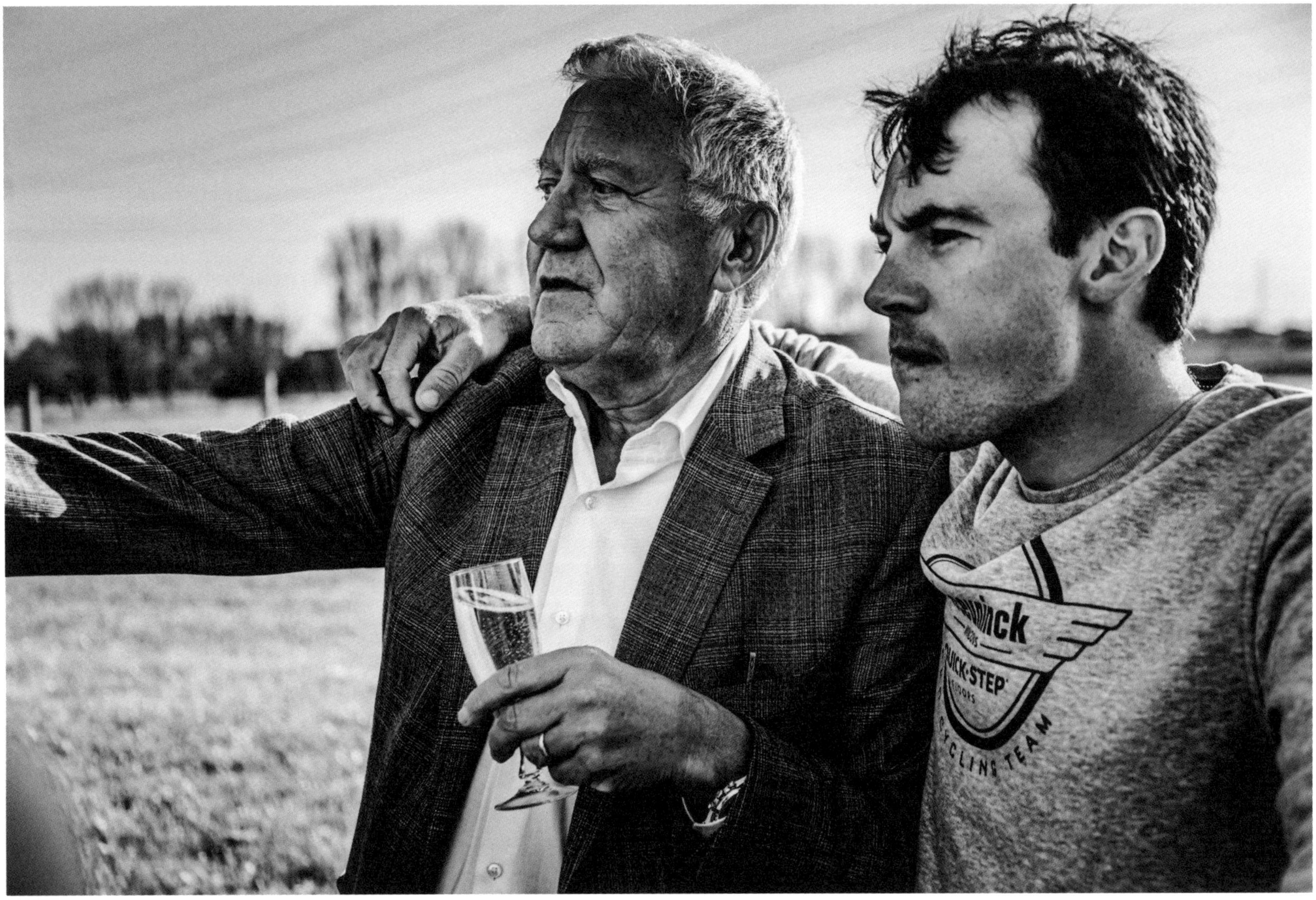

PATRICK LEFEVERE OVER WOLFPACK 2021

BIDDEN

'Het seizoen 2021 was behoorlijk moeilijk te voorspellen', zo kijkt CEO Patrick Lefevere terug op het voorbije jaar. 'Het is uiteindelijk een grand cru geworden, waar we trots op zijn. Maar dat kon niemand raden. Het enige wat we konden doen, was... bidden. Bidden dat corona niet weer stokken in de wielen zou steken, wensen dat zowel Fabio als Remco hun oude niveau weer zouden halen, hopen dat Julian zijn regenboogtrui eer zou aandoen en vertrouwen dat de transfer van Mark geen gok was.'

De coronapandemie was de grootste factor van onzekerheid voor Deceuninck – Quick-Step Team en bij uitbreiding voor de hele wielerwereld. Een tweede seizoen als in 2020 zou het hele bestel te gronde richten, zo werd gevreesd. En inderdaad, covid trok zich niks aan van de jaarwisseling. De eerste wedstrijden van het nieuwe seizoen werden alweer geschrapt, zowel in Australië en Nieuw-Zeeland als in Zuid-Amerika. Dat was al een eerste streep door de rekening. Toen ook beslist werd om wedstrijden als de Ronde van Valencia of de Ruta del Sol uit te stellen, koos de teamleiding ervoor om de competitie pas te hervatten in de Tour de la Provence, van 11 tot 14 februari. Davide Ballerini won de eerste twee ritten. Ook Sam Bennett toonde vroeg zijn goede vorm en won twee etappes in de UAE Tour.

Maar hoe zouden de traditionele wielerlanden omgaan met het hardnekkige coronabeestje? Organisatoren als Flanders Classics en Harelbeke bewezen hoe het kon. Met mondmaskers, in bubbels, geen publiek, zo weinig mogelijk entourage... Het Vlaamse wielerpubliek volgde *en masse* de oproep om de wedstrijden op televisie te volgen. Toen bleek dat de koers het openingsweekend, met de Omloop Het Nieuwsblad en Kuurne-Brussel-Kuurne, coronaproof had overleefd, was de trein ook in eigen land vertrokken. Overigens scoorde The Wolfpack onmiddellijk: Davide Ballerini verzilverde zijn goede benen met winst in Ninove in de Omloop, Andrea Bagioli won de Royal Bernard Drôme Classic en Mauri Vansevenant haalde in de GP Larciano zijn eerste profzege.

WINNEN WENT NOOIT

Als er weinig voorjaarskoersen zijn, dan moet je andere manieren zoeken om de manschappen klaar te stomen voor de maanden met de klassiekers, van midden maart tot eind april. Hoogtestages inlassen, bijvoorbeeld, en selecties maken met het oog op die klassieke periode.

Patrick Lefevere: 'Je hebt meer dan dertig profrenners in de rangen en meer dan vijftig stafleden. Die staan te popelen, allemaal! Dus moet je schaken, pionnen verzetten, nieuwe scenario's bedenken. En iedereen bij de les houden, want aan het einde van de rit heb je ze allemaal nodig.'

Julian Alaphilippe bewees al snel zijn waarde. Hij strandde op de tweede plek in de Strade Bianche, maar won de tweede rit in de Tirreno-Adriatico. Sam Bennett kon twee keer juichen in Parijs-Nice. Ook Vlaanderen was het team gunstig gezind. Bennet won de Oxyclean Classic Brugge-De Panne en Kasper Asgreen de E3 Harelbeke. De perfecte generale repetitie voor de Ronde van Vlaanderen, tien dagen later. Ook daar was het prijs. Onze Deense nationale Kampioen troefde Mathieu van der Poel af in een sprint met twee. Meesterlijk.

LIEFDE VOOR DE JEUGD

Zo tikte de teller snel aan. Als Mikkel Honoré op maandag 9 april de vijfde etappe wint in het Baskenland – een zware koers – is het al de vijftiende seizoenszege voor The Wolfpack. Met een mooi verhaaltje als bonus.

Lefevere: 'Mikkel Honoré rijdt samen met Josef Cerny naar de streep, twee Wolfpackers voor één zege. Bij het ingaan van de laatste honderden meters zegt Cerny op een onderkoelde manier: "Mikkel, you can win." (lacht) En zo geschiedt. En dan komt Mikkel naar mij toe: "Patrick, geef Josef maar de helft van mijn bonus!"' Ook dát is de Wolfpack!

'Iedereen die mij kent, weet dat de jeugd mij na aan het hart ligt. Overwinningen van Mauri Vansevenant en van Andrea Bagioli zijn in dat opzicht heel belangrijk. Ze doen me veel plezier.

Dat zijn kuikentjes die net komen piepen en die al direct meedoen voor winst. In zware, lastige koersen, én bij de profs. Niet onderschatten, hoor!'

'Winnen went nooit, neen. Dat geeft altijd een fantastisch gevoel. Uiteindelijk klokken we af op 65 zeges. Dat is waanzinnig veel. Maar of het er nu 62, 63, 64 of 65 zijn, voor de perceptie maakt dat niet zo veel uit, wel voor de bonussen die we betalen. (Lacht) En voor de sponsors, al durf ik te zeggen dat we er nu al jaren na elkaar toch zo goed als het maximum uit halen inzake sponsorreturn. Voor mij is het wel belangrijk dat we de zegekoning zijn, daar mik ik op. Eentje meer dan de concurrentie dus. (Lacht) En dat lukt. We zijn het voor het tiende seizoen op rij, sinds 2012! Daar ben ik trots op.'

CAVENDISH SHOW

Tussendoor kwam de Ronde van Turkije. Mét Mark Cavendish. Het was de vraag van één miljoen of hij nog kon winnen.

Op coronavlak was de Presidential Cycling Tour of Turkey een dubbeltje op zijn kant. De renners werden te slapen gelegd in toeristenhotels waarbij niet altijd duidelijk was hoe de coronaregels werden toegepast.

Patrick Lefevere: 'We hebben veel steun gehad van een lokale medewerkster van de Deceuninck-vestiging in Turkije. Die loodste ons door het Turkse avontuur. Dat was leuk. Dubbel leuk was het om te zien dat Mark Cavendish het winnen niet was verleerd.'

Na zijn derde plek in de Scheldeprijs mikte 'Cav' vier keer in de roos in Turkije. Vier keer! De vraag van één miljoen was snel beantwoord.

Voor Patrick Lefevere was Mark Cavendish een keuze van het hart én een berekend risico. Hij voelde aan dat de Brit fysiek nog steeds top is, ondanks de jaren op de teller. Het mentale luik was een grotere uitdaging.

'Het beeld van de ontredderde Cavendish na Gent-Wevelgem in 2020 kreeg ik niet uitgewist. Ik heb hem gebeld, uit bezorgdheid. Als mens, zonder plan. Ik kon het niet over mijn hart krijgen hem zo zijn carrière te zien beëindigen. Zo'n fantastische carrière. Turkije gaf me gelijk.'

Nog straffer is dat de Brit na Turkije op eigen houtje naar Griekenland trok voor een tiendaagse stage met DQT-trainer Vasilis Anastopoulos. Sprinttrainingen op de piste en op de weg. Vasilis bevestigde dat Cavendish de wattages duwde die hij vroeger haalde. Lefevere had het juist. En toen moest de Tour de France nog komen.

Er werd toen inderdaad al aan de Ronde van Frankrijk gedacht. Ontegensprekelijk was Sam Bennett de eerste keuze, na het groen in 2020. Sams voorjaar was sterk, hij had al zeven zeges geplukt. Maar net voor de Baloise Belgium Tour manifesteerde zich een hardnekkig knieprobleem bij de Ier. Geen Bennett dus. In allerijl, in de nacht vóór de start van de eerste rit in Beveren, werd Cavendish vanuit Londen ingevlogen per helikopter. De Brit onderstreept zijn stijgende vorm met een spurtzege in de vijfde rit. Remco Evenepoel wint de tijdrit en het eindklassement.

VRUCHTBARE NATIONALE KAMPIOENSCHAPPEN

The Wolfpack is een team voor de klassiekers. Een team met sprinters die semiklassiekers en puntentruien winnen. Een team met sterke troeven voor kleinere rittenwedstrijden. En dat is nog niet alles. The Wolfpack is ook een team van tijdrijders. Yves Lampaert pakte de Belgische TT-titel. Kasper Asgreen hernieuwde zijn Deense titel. Josef Cerny was de beste in Tsjechië en João Almeida boekte zijn eerste profzege in Portugal op zijn tijdritfiets. In Frankrijk pakte Rémi Cavagna de driekleur op de weg. De TGV de Clermont-Ferrand soleerde naar de zege.

OP NAAR HET DELIRIUM

De Baloise Belgium Tour eindigde op zondag 13 juni, geen volle twee weken voor de Tour de France. Sam Bennett bleef inactief en Mark Cavendish had zijn goede conditie bewezen. Dus werd de 36-jarige Manxman het speerpunt van The Wolfpack voor de sprintetappes in Frankrijk, met Michael Mørkøv en Davide Ballerini als lead-outkompanen. En of dat heeft gewerkt. Maar eerst legde Julian Alaphilippe zijn troeven op tafel, door de eerste rit te winnen en het eerste geel en groen binnen te halen. Met dank ook aan Dries Devenyns, die hem schitterend piloteerde. En in de Wolfpack-spirit werd ook Dries eerst naar die ideale plek geloodst.

Het groen bleef om de schouders van Julian tot de vierde rit, toen Cavendish zijn eerste zege behaalde en de puntentrui overnam. Hij zou die niet meer afstaan. Hij won ook de zesde, tiende en dertiende rit. Er was geen houden aan. Toen hij met zijn vierde zege ook het absolute zegerecord van Eddy Merckx evenaarde, spaarden de kranten de superlatieven niet.

Patrick Lefevere: 'Ook hier mogen we de verdienste van het team niet vergeten. Als je ziet hoe de makkers – Devenyns, Declercq, Mørkøv, Ballerini – Mark als het ware over de Pyreneeën hebben gedragen, met de tijdlimiet in het achterhoofd. Het ontroert me steeds weer. Natuurlijk zijn het profs, en Mark zorgt voor premies. Maar het zijn ook mensen. Het menselijke aspect speelt mee. Als ze het niet uit menselijk oogpunt doen, dan gebeurt het niet. Want het zijn ook ego's en individualisten, anders word je geen coureur. Maar het zijn ook wolven, natuurlijk. De roedel staat boven alles.'

DE KRACHT VAN FABIO JAKOBSEN

Natuurlijk moeten we het over Fabio Jakobsen hebben. Patrick Lefevere: ‘Wat Fabio heeft gedaan, is *hors catégorie*. Zijn herstel is fenomenaal. Noem het geen mirakel, hij heeft het zelf gedaan, en de ploeg heeft het mogelijk gemaakt.’

Fabio kreeg de kans om weer renner te worden in de Ronde van Turkije. Zonder verwachtingen. Weer wennen aan de competitie, rijden in een peloton… Hij zag dat het goed was. Zo ook in de Algarve en de Dauphiné. In de Ronde van Wallonië startte hij al met de ambitie om een rit te winnen. Al werd het een geamputeerde Waalse Ronde vanwege de rampspoed die het oosten van ons land trof. De tweede rit op 21 juli werd vervangen door een korte etappe van 120 kilometer op het autocircuit van Zolder. Die werd gewonnen door, jawel, Fabio Jakobsen. Zijn eerste winst, zo, goed als één jaar na zijn doodsmak in Polen, op 5 augustus 2020. Ook in de vijfde rit was het raak.

De Vuelta van Fabio was fenomenaal. Hij wint de vierde rit op een hellende aankomst. Niemand van de ploeg had dit zien aankomen. Hij is de beste in de achtste en zestiende rit, én pakt de puntentrui mee naar huis. Florian Sénéchal wint daarenboven de dertiende rit.

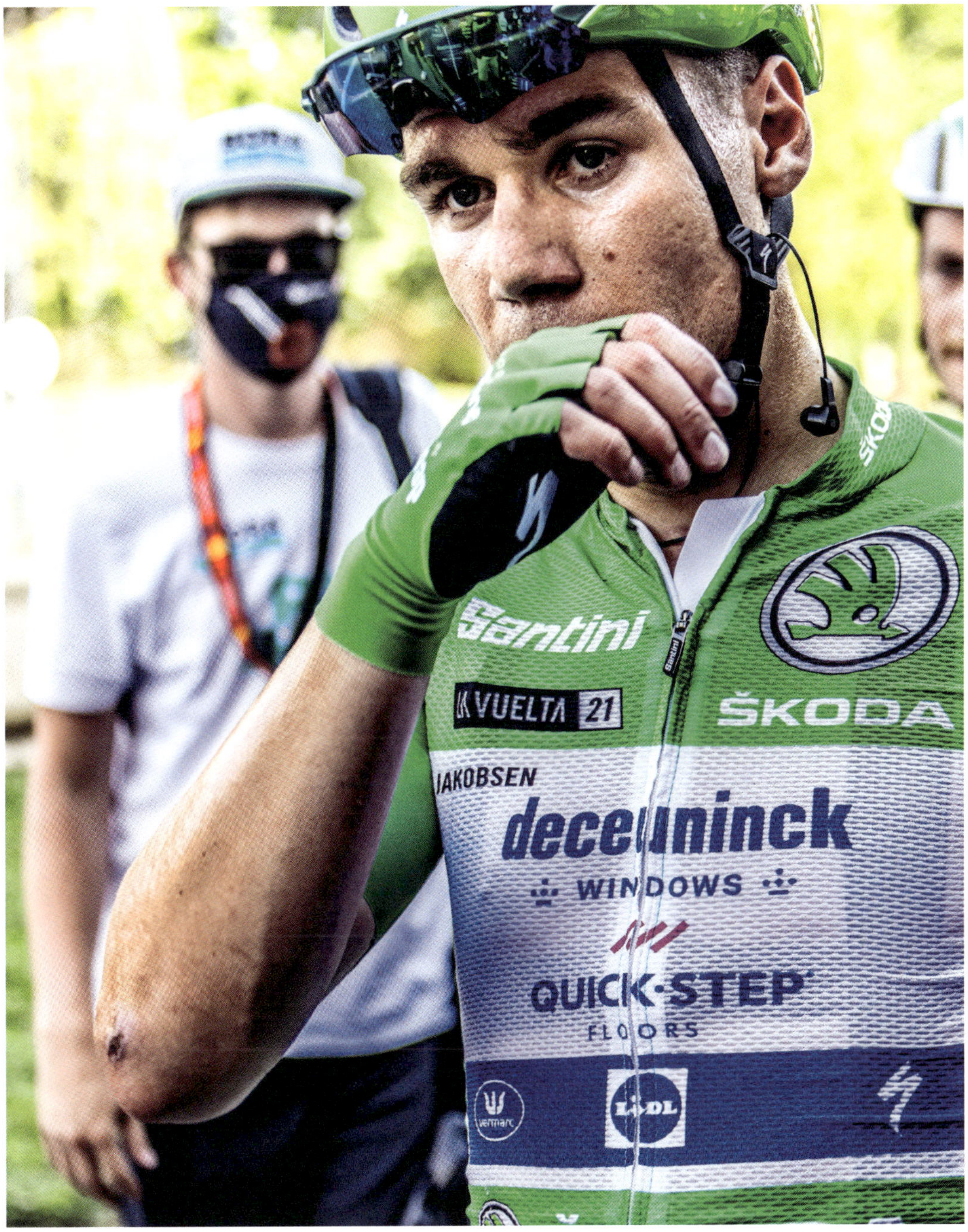

‘Het is duidelijk dat Fabio weer volwaardig coureur is’, zegt Lefevere. ‘Met alle kantjes die erbij horen. Ook frustratie nadat hij in de etappe die Sénéchal wint, de rol moest lossen in volle voorbereiding op de sprint.’

Zijn derde Vuelta-zege pakt Fabio op zijn 25ste verjaardag, op 31 augustus, in Santa Cruz de Bezana. Daar gebeurt iets dat ‘oldskool Lefevere’ is. Patrick stapt op Fabio af, feliciteert hem met zijn verjaardag en met zijn derde Vuelta-zege, maar tikt hem daarna op de vingers vanwege zijn kritiek op de lead-out van Sénéchal in de dertiende rit. ‘Weet je wat, vriend? Vergeet niet dat we je dertien maanden geleden voor dood hebben opgeraapt in Polen. Je hebt een fantastisch parcours gereden het voorbij jaar. Ook dankzij je ploeg! Vergeet dat niet. Dus, rustig aan! We zullen het seizoen uitdoen op een rustige manier, we maken dat je een goede winter hebt, en volgend jaar ben je nog 10 of 15% beter!’

Op de vraag of Lefevere overtuigd was dat Jakobsen er weer bovenop zou komen, antwoordt de CEO volmondig ja: ‘Eigenlijk wel, op voorwaarde dat wij als ploeg, en hij als renner, het strikt uitgestippelde parcours zouden volgen. Dat was niet gemakkelijk, ook met corona. Maar het bewijst vooral hoe krachtig Fabio als mens én atleet is.’

DE DUBBEL VAN JULIAN ALAPHILIPPE

Na de Vuelta stond de teller op 53 overwinningen voor The Wolfpack. Michael Mørkøv had goud behaald op de Olympische Spelen in de madison (samen met Lasse Norman Hansen) en DQT had de Ronde van Polen en de Ronde van Denemarken beheerst. Remco Evenepoel won in Denemarken de derde rit, de afsluitende tijdrit en het eindklassement.

De Ronde van Polen was nog indrukwekkender: Rémi Cavagna won de zesde rit (tegen de chrono), João Almeida de tweede en de vierde etappe, én het eindklassement.

Via zeges in Groot-Brittannië (Yves Lampaert), Slovakije (Jannik Steimle en Álvaro Hodeg), de Tour de Luxembourg (João Almeida en Mattia Cattaneo), de Gooikse Pijl (Fabio Jakobsen) en de Primus Classic (Florian Sénéchal) kwam het Wereldkampioenschap op de weg in het vizier.

Het WK in Leuven werd bijgewoond door zo'n 300.000 wielerliefhebbers. Corona leek een vergeten nachtmerrie. Het Kampioenschap mondde uit in een demonstratie van Julian Alaphilippe. Hij toonde vriend en vijand hoe je piekt naar één topmoment en wanneer je je laatste cartouche verschiet. Hij fietste zichzelf de geschiedenisboeken in en komt in een mooi rijtje terecht van dubbele wereldkampioenen, naast onder meer Rik Van Looy, Gianni Bugno, Paolo Bettini, Freddy Maertens en Briek Schotte.

HET INSTITUUT DECEUNINCK – QUICK-STEP

Vriend en vijand is het erover eens dat Patrick Lefevere in de voorbije jaren zijn team heeft uitgebouwd tot een 'instituut'. Met een vaste hiërarchie, een sterke structuur, een duidelijke filosofie en scherpe targets.

'Tuurlijk kon ik niet voorspellen dat mijn ploeg zo succesvol zou zijn. Maar het winnen zat al altijd in mij. Ik wilde en wil elke koers winnen. Wat als coureur niet echt lukte (lacht), streefde ik vanaf de eerste dag na als ploegleider. Bij mijn eerste jaar bij Marc Zeepcentrale was het direct bingo: we wonnen de Omloop Het Volk in 1980 met Joseph Bruyère, het was mijn eerste jaar als manager. En de Omloop had toen meer uitstraling dan nu, internationaal vooral.'

Situaties zorgen er vaak voor dat de middelen ontbreken om te scoren. 'Maar als de middelen er waren, dan was ik op het appel.' Inderdaad, we herinneren ons de Mapei-machine in de jaren 90. 'Ik heb veel geleerd. Zo is een goede voorbereiding primordiaal op logistiek vlak, zodat er rust is in de tent. En ploegsfeer is dat ook. Je moet jongens hebben die vrienden worden en voor elkaar vechten om te winnen. Ik heb geleerd om een entourage te creëren waarin het mogelijk is dat ze vrienden worden.'

'De merknaam Quick-Step is de rode draad in mijn carrière sinds 2003, de basis van het succes. Vanaf toen speelde ik in een hogere afdeling. De trein was vertrokken, om niet meer stil te vallen. Er was maar één dipje, in 2010. Maar wat voor ons een dipje was, daar zouden andere teams voor willen tekenen. In 2018 behaalden we zelfs 73 zeges. Wat wij ook dit jaar weer winnen, is uitzonderlijk, 65 overwinningen. En we doen het bijna jaar na jaar. Maar dit seizoen is sterk: groen in de Tour, vijf ritten in de Tour en één dag geel, Vuelta groen en vier zeges, jonge mannen die boven komen drijven... [Vansevenant, Bagioli, Ballerini, Almeida, Cavagna en anderen]. Jakobsen en Evenepoel die genezen zijn. We hebben de Franse kampioenstrui, olympisch goud, vier nationale tijdrittruien... en een fantastische Wolfpack-spirit."

Tot op vandaag blijft Patrick Lefevere de baas, de CEO. Geert Coeman is CFO, Ricardo Scheidecker is Technical & Development Director en Alessandro Tegner is Marketing & Communication Manager. Zij hebben de dagelijkse leiding en rapporteren aan Patrick. Omdat de ploeg op drie, soms vier fronten actief is, op vele plaatsen in de wereld en met renners die van overal komen, is een vrij strakke hiërarchie uitgetekend met horizontale niveaus en verticale rapporteringslijnen.

'Dat houdt ook in dat ik zelf niet meer elke dag in de weer ben, al blijf ik aansturen. Ik geniet nu meer, samen met de renners. Maar ik blijf de eindverantwoordelijke. Wat ik in handen hou, zijn de aanwervingen van personeel en renners. Ik volg alle uitslagen en ken alle jonge talenten, of ik word getipt. Ik onderhandel over het loon, en voor de bonussen overleg ik met Geert Coeman. De structuur staat er en kan nog jaren functioneren zoals hij dit jaar deed.'

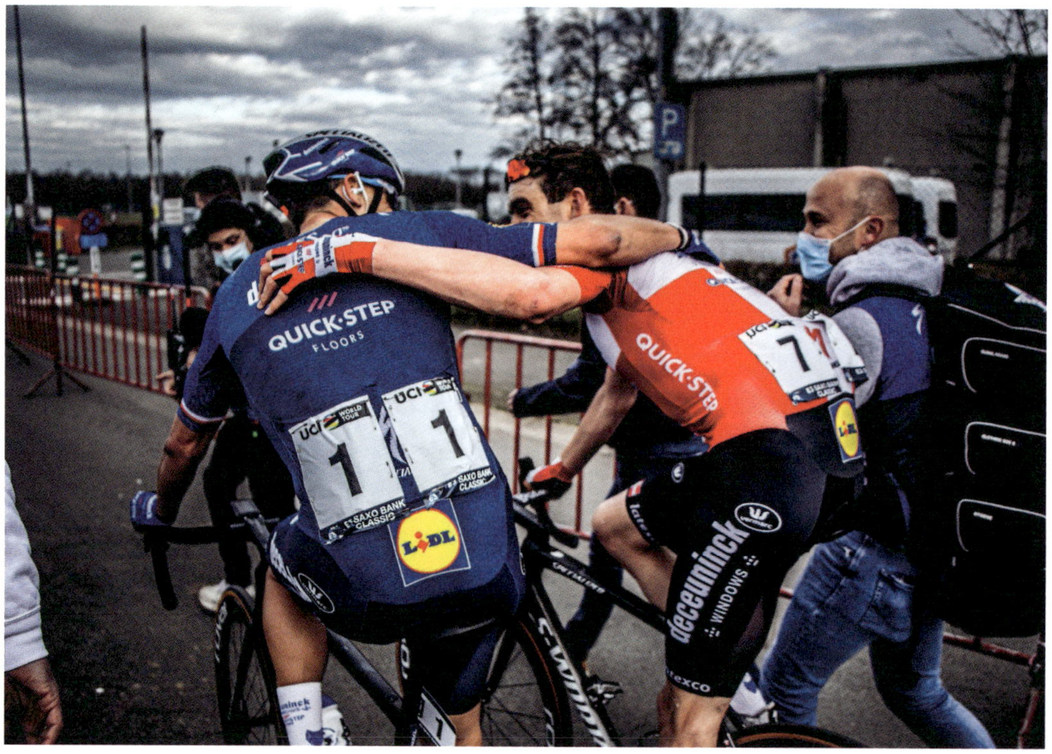

PATRICK LEFEVERE ABOUT WOLFPACK 2021

PRAYING

“The 2021 season was quite difficult to predict,” CEO Patrick Lefevere says as he looks back over the past year. “It turned out to be a grand cru, which we’re very proud of. But nobody could’ve guessed that. The only thing we could do was… pray. Pray that the coronavirus wouldn’t throw a wrench in the works again, wish that both Fabio and Remco would get back to their old level, hope that Julian would honor his rainbow jersey, and trust that Mark’s transfer wasn’t a gamble.”

The COVID-19 pandemic was the most important unknown quantity for the Deceuninck – Quick-Step Team, and for the entire cycling world. Everyone was afraid that a second season like the one in 2020 would completely destroy the system. And indeed, the virus didn’t care whether it was a new year. The first races of the new season were already cancelled, in Australia and New Zealand as well as in South America. That was the first blow. When the decision was made to postpone races like the Volta a la Comunitat Valenciana or the Ruta del Sol, the team management decided to resume the competition in the Tour de la Provence, from February 11 to 14. Davide Ballerini won the first two stages. Sam Bennett also showed good form early on and won two stages in the UAE Tour.

But how would the traditional cycling nations deal with the stubborn coronavirus? Organizers such as Flanders Classics and Harelbeke proved how it could be done. With masks, in social bubbles, no audience, as little entourage as possible… The Flemish cycling fans respected the call to follow the races on television. When it turned out that the race had survived the opening weekend, with the Omloop Het Nieuwsblad and Kuurne-Brussel-Kuurne pulled off with no coronavirus-related issues, the ball really got rolling. The Wolfpack scored immediately: Davide Ballerini cashed in on his good legs by winning the Omloop in Ninove, Andrea Bagioli won the Royal Bernard Drôme Classic, and Mauri Vansevenant nailed his first professional victory in the GP Larciano.

YOU NEVER GET USED TO WINNING

If there are only a few spring races planned, one has to find other ways to get the men ready for the months with the classics, from mid-March to the end of April. For example, you can have high-altitude training sessions and make selections with the classics in mind.

Patrick Lefevere: “We have more than 30 professional riders in the ranks and over 50 staff members. They’re eager to start, all of them! So you have to play chess, move the pawns, think up new scenarios. And keep everyone on their toes, because at the end of the day, they all play an important part.”

Julian Alaphilippe quickly proved his worth. He finished second in the Strade Bianche, but won the second stage in the Tirreno-Adriatico. Sam Bennett was able to cheer twice in Paris-Nice. Flanders was also favorable for the team. Bennett won the Oxyclean Classic Bruges-De Panne, and Kasper Asgreen won the E3 Harelbeke. The perfect dress rehearsal for the Ronde van Vlaanderen, ten days later. There too, success was on the horizon. Our Danish national champion trumped Mathieu van der Poel in a two-man sprint. Phenomenal.

LOVE FOR THE YOUTH

And so, the counter was ticking fast. When Mikkel Honoré won the fifth stage in the Basque Country on Monday April 9 – a tough race – it was already The Wolfpack’s 15th victory of the season. With a good story as a bonus.

Lefevere: “Mikkel Honoré rides together with Josef Cerny to the line, two Wolfpackers for one victory. As they enter the final meters, Cerny says coolly: “Mikkel, it’s yours.” (laughs) And so it happens. And then Mikkel comes to me: “Patrick, give Josef half of my bonus!” That’s also the Wolfpack!

“Everyone who knows me, knows that the young team members are very important to me. Mauri Vansevenant and Andrea Bagioli’s wins are vital in that respect. I truly enjoy it. These are chicks that have just hatched and are already competing for wins. In tough, difficult races, and with the pros. Don’t underestimate them!”

"You never get used to winning, no. It always feels fantastic. In the end, we racked up 65 victories. That's an incredible amount. But whether it's 62, 63, 64, or 65, it doesn't really matter in terms of perception. It does matter for the bonuses we pay," (he laughs). "And for the sponsors, although I dare say that for years in a row now, we've been getting the absolute maximum out of it in terms of sponsor return. For me, it's important that we're the victory kings – that's what I am aiming for. Better than the competition," (he laughs again). "And that works. We've done it for the tenth consecutive season, since 2012! I'm proud of that."

CAVENDISH SHOW

In between came the Tour of Turkey. With Mark Cavendish. It was a million-dollar question whether he could still win.

When it came to the coronavirus, the Presidential Cycling Tour of Turkey was touch and go. The riders were sleeping in hotels full of tourists, where it wasn't always clear how the rules were being applied.

Patrick Lefevere: "We received a lot of support from a local employee of the Deceuninck branch in Turkey. She guided us through the Turkish adventure. That was fun. It was also great to see that Mark Cavendish hadn't forgotten how to win."

After his third place in the Scheldeprijs, "Cav" hit the bull's eye four times in Turkey. Four times! The million-dollar question was quickly answered.

For Patrick Lefevere, Mark Cavendish was both an emotional choice and a calculated risk. He felt the Briton was still physically at the top of his game, despite the number of years on his odometer. The mental aspect was more challenging.

"I couldn't forget the image of the dejected Cavendish after Gent-Wevelgem in 2020. I called him, out of concern. As a human being, without a plan. I couldn't bear to see him end his career like that. Such a fantastic career. Turkey proved me right."

Even better, after Turkey the Brit went on his own to Greece for a ten-day internship with DQT trainer Vasilis Anastopoulos. Sprint training on the track and on the road. Vasilis confirmed that Cavendish was pushing the wattages he used to. Lefevere was right. And the Tour de France was yet to come.

Indeed, the Tour de France was already being factored in at the time. Undeniably, Sam Bennett was the first choice, after winning green in 2020. Sam's spring was strong, he had already picked up seven victories. But just before the Belgium Tour, the Irishman was experiencing a persistent knee problem. So Bennett was out. On the night before the start of the first stage in Beveren, Cavendish was quickly flown in from London by helicopter. He underscores his rising form with a sprint victory in stage five while Remco Evenepoel wins the time trial and the general classification.

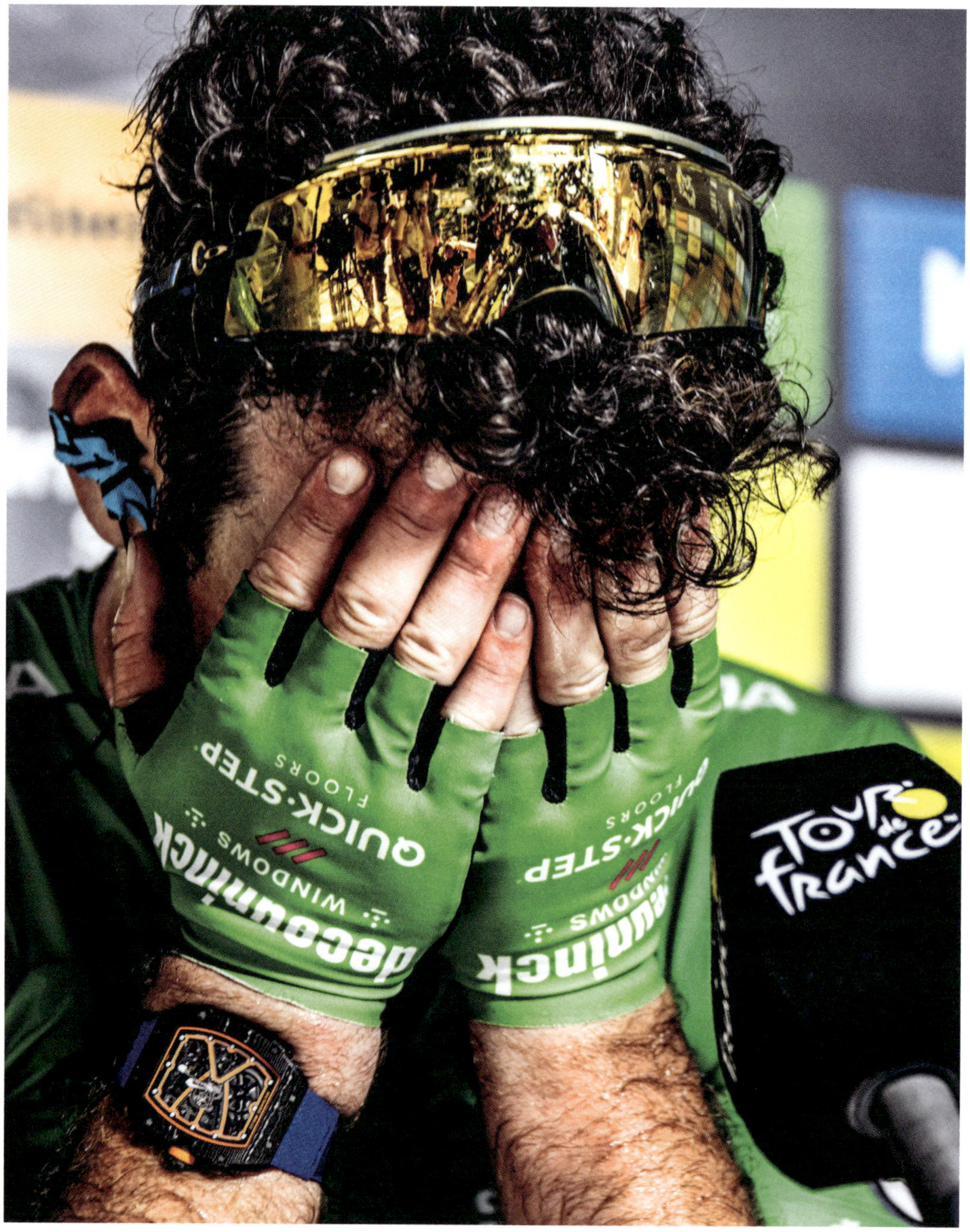

FRUITFUL NATIONAL CHAMPIONSHIPS

The Wolfpack is a team for the classics. A team with sprinters who win semi-classics and points jerseys. A team with strong assets for smaller stage races. And that's not all. The Wolfpack is also a team of time trialists. Yves Lampaert took the Belgian TT title. Kasper Asgreen retained his Danish title. Josef Cerny was the best in the Czech Republic, and João Almeida scored his first professional victory in Portugal on his time trial bike. In France, Rémi Cavagna took the national colors on the road. The TGV de Clermont-Ferrand soloed to victory.

ON TO DELIRIUM

The Belgium Tour ended on Sunday June 13, about two weeks before the Tour de France. Sam Bennett remained inactive, and Mark Cavendish had proven his good form. The 36-year-old Manxman became The Wolfpack's spearhead for the sprint stages in France, with Michael Mørkøv and Davide Ballerini as lead-out men. And that proved very successful. But first, Julian Alaphilippe showed his strengths by winning the first stage and getting the first yellow and green – also thanks to Dries Devenyns, who piloted him beautifully. And in the classic Wolfpack spirit, Dries was also guided to that ideal spot first.

The green jersey remained on Julian's shoulders until stage four, when Cavendish got his first win and took over the points jersey. He kept it. He also won stage six, stage ten, and stage thirteen. He was unstoppable! When he equaled Eddy Merckx' absolute victory record with his fourth win, the newspapers didn't spare the superlatives.

Patrick Lefevere: "Here again, we cannot forget the merit of the team. When you see how his teammates – Devenyns, Declercq, Mørkøv, Ballerini – have carried Mark over the Pyrenees, and with the time limit in mind. It moves me every time. Of course, they're pros, and Mark provides the premiums. But they're also people. The human aspect comes into play. If they don't do it from a human point of view, it won't happen. They're also egos and individualists, otherwise they wouldn't have become racers. But they're also wolves. The pack is above all else."

THE POWER OF FABIO JAKOBSEN

Of course, we have to talk about Fabio Jakobsen. Patrick Lefevere: "What Fabio has done is hors catégorie. His recovery is phenomenal. Don't call it a miracle: he did it himself, and the team made it possible."

Fabio got the chance to be a rider again at the Tour of Turkey. Without expectations. Getting used to the competition again, riding in a peloton... It proved successful. He did the same in the Algarve and the Dauphiné. In the Tour de Wallonie, he was already ambitious to win a stage. However, the race was cut short due to the disaster that hit the east of our country. The second stage on July 21 was replaced by a short 120-kilometre stage on the Zolder circuit. Fabio Jakobsen won it. His first win, almost one year after his crash in Poland, on August 5, 2020. The fifth stage was a success as well.

Fabio's Vuelta was phenomenal. He won the fourth stage on a sloping finish. Nobody on the team saw it coming. He was the best in the eighth and sixteenth stage, and took home the points jersey. Florian Sénéchal also won the thirteenth stage.

"It's clear that Fabio is a full-fledged rider again," Lefevere said. "With all the challenges that go with it. Including the frustration after he had to leave the role in the stage that Sénéchal won, in full preparation for the sprint."

Fabio took his third Vuelta victory on his 25th birthday, on August 31, in Santa Cruz de Bezana. There, something happens that's "old-school Lefevere". Patrick approaches Fabio, congratulates him on his birthday and on his third Vuelta victory, but then reprimands him for his criticism of Sénéchal's lead-out in stage thirteen. "You know what, friend? Don't forget that thirteen months ago, you could've died in Poland. You rode a fantastic race last year. In part thanks to your team! Don't forget that. So, take it easy! We'll finish the season calmly, we'll make sure you have a good winter, and next year, you'll be 10 or 15% better!"

When asked if Lefevere was convinced that Jakobsen would recover, the CEO responded with a resounding yes: "On the condition that we as a team, and he as a rider, strictly follow the course we've mapped out. That hasn't been easy, even with the coronavirus. But above all, it proves how powerful Fabio is both as a human being and as an athlete."

JULIAN ALAPHILIPPE'S DOUBLE

After the Vuelta, the counter stood at 53 victories for The Wolfpack. Michael Mørkøv had won gold at the Olympic Games in the Madison (together with Lasse Norman Hansen), and DQT had won the Tour de Pologne and the Danmark Rundt. Remco Evenepoel won the third stage in Denmark, the final time trial, and the general classification. The Tour de Pologne was even more impressive: Rémi Cavagna won stage six (against the clock), João Almeida won stage two and stage four as well as the overall classification.

With the victories in Great Britain (Yves Lampaert), Slovakia (Jannik Steimle and Álvaro Hodeg), the Tour de Luxembourg (João Almeida and Mattia Cattaneo), the Gooikse Pijl (Fabio Jakobsen), and the Primus Classic (Florian Sénéchal), the Road World Championships were on the horizon.

The World Championships in Leuven was attended by some 300,000 cycling fans. The coronavirus seemed to be a forgotten nightmare. The championship culminated in a demonstration by Julian Alaphilippe. He showed friend and foe how you peak at one top moment and give it your all. He cycled straight into the history books and ends up on a fine list of double World Champions, alongside Rik Van Looy, Gianni Bugno, Paolo Bettini, Freddy Maertens and Briek Schotte.

DECEUNINCK – QUICK-STEP: AN INSTITUTION

Friend and foe alike agree that Patrick Lefevere has developed his team into an "institution" in recent years. With a fixed hierarchy, a strong structure, a clear philosophy, and demanding targets.

"Naturally, I couldn't predict that my team would be this successful. But winning has always been a big part of who I am. I've always wanted, and still want, to win every race. What didn't really work out for me personally as a rider (laughs), I pursued from day one as a team leader. In my first year at Marc Zeepcentrale, we immediately achieved success: we won the Omloop Het Volk in 1980 with Joseph Bruyère. I'd only just started out as a manager. And the Omloop had more appeal then than now, especially on an international level."

Situations often result in a lack of means to score. "But if the resources were there, I'd take the call." Indeed, we remember the Mapei machine in the 1990s. "I learned a lot. For example, thorough preparation is paramount in terms of logistics, so that everyone can have some peace of mind. And so is team spirit. Everyone should become friends and fight for each other to win. I've learned to create an environment in which it's possible for them to become friends."

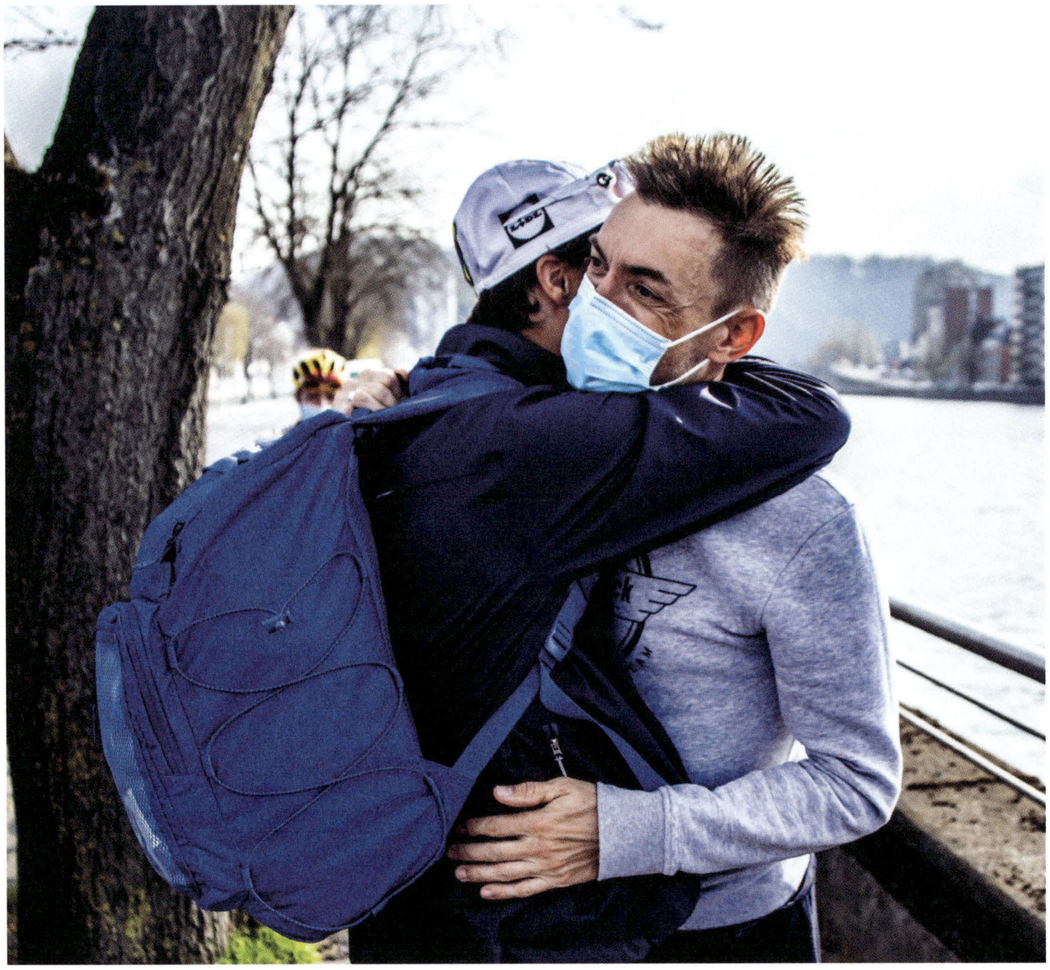

"The Quick-Step brand has been the focal point of my career since 2003 – the foundation of my success. From then on, I played in a higher division. The train had left the station, and it was unstoppable. There was only one slowdown, in 2010. But, what we experienced as a slowdown, was something other teams would've gladly signed up for. In 2018, we even achieved 73 victories. The number of wins we're chalking up again this year is exceptional: 65 victories. And we achieve this nearly year after year. This season has been exceptionally strong: green in the Tour, five stages in the Tour and one day of yellow, Vuelta green and four wins, young men coming out on top... [Vansevenant, Bagioli, Ballerini, Almeida, Cavagna, and others]. Jakobsen and Evenepoel have recovered. We've got the French Champion's jersey, Olympic gold, four national time trial jerseys... and a fantastic Wolfpack spirit."

Patrick Lefevere is still in charge, the CEO. Geert Coeman is CFO, Ricardo Scheidecker is Technical & Development Director, and Alessandro Tegner is Marketing & Communication Manager. They're in charge of the daily management and report to Patrick. As the team is active on three, sometimes four fronts, all over the world and with riders coming in from everywhere, a fairly strict hierarchy has been drawn up with horizontal levels and vertical reporting lines.

"That also means that I'm no longer busy with every aspect of our operations every day, although I still manage it all. I enjoy it more now, together with the riders. But, in the end, I'm still responsible. I handle the recruitment of staff and riders. I follow all the results and know all the young talents, or someone gives me a tip. I negotiate the wages, and I consult with Geert Coeman for the bonuses. The structure is there, and it can function for years to come as it did this year."

PATRICK LEFEVERE SUR WOLFPACK 2021

Patrick Lefevere : « Vous avez plus de trente coureurs professionnels à bord et plus de cinquante membres du staff. Ils sont impatients, tous autant qu'ils sont ! Vous devez donc jouer aux échecs, déplacer les pions, inventer de nouveaux scénarios. Et garder tout le monde au top et concentré, car à la fin de la journée, vous avez besoin de tout le monde.

PRIÈRE EXAUCÉE

« La saison 2021 était assez difficile à prévoir » le directeur général de l'équipe, Patrick Lefevere, revient sur l'année écoulée. « Mais elle s'est avérée être un grand cru exceptionnel, ce dont nous sommes fiers. C'était quelque chose que personne n'aurait pu deviner et tout ce qu'on pouvait faire était… prier. Nous avons prié pour que le Covid-19 ne vienne pas nous mettre des bâtons dans les roues, nous avons croisé les doigts pour que Fabio et Remco se rétablissent complètement, nous espérions sincèrement que Julian honore son maillot arc-en-ciel et que le transfert de Mark porte ses fruits. »

La pandémie a été la plus grande source d'incertitudes à laquelle l'équipe Deceuninck – Quick-Step, et par extension le monde du cyclisme, a dû faire face. La crainte était de voir la saison 2020 se reproduire cette année, ce qui aurait ruiné le système dans son ensemble. Et en effet, le Covid-19 n'a pas tenu compte du passage à la nouvelle année et les premières courses de la nouvelle saison ont vite été annulées, à savoir les courses en Australie et en Nouvelle-Zélande ainsi qu'en Amérique du Sud. Cela représentait un premier coup dur pour l'équipe. Et lorsqu'il a été annoncé que des courses telles que le Tour de Valence ou la Ruta del Sol ont également été reportées, la direction de l'équipe a pris la décision de ne reprendre la compétition qu'au Tour de la Provence, du 11 au 14 février. Davide Ballerini y a remporté les deux premières étapes. Sam Bennett a également démontré dès le début qu'il était au top de sa forme et a lui aussi remporté deux étapes lors de l'UAE Tour.

Mais comment les nations cyclistes traditionnelles peuvent-elles faire face au virus persistant qu'est le Covid-19 ? Eh bien, des organisateurs tels que Flanders Classics et ceux de l'E3 Classic ont prouvé que c'était tout à fait possible. Avec des masques, en bulles sociales, sans public, un entourage aussi restreint que possible… les Flamands adeptes du cyclisme ont suivi en masse l'appel à suivre les courses à la télévision. Lorsque le week-end d'ouverture, qui se composait de Omloop Het Nieuwsblad et de Kuurne-Bruxelles-Kuurne, a touché à sa fin sans accro, le monde de la compétition a poussé un soupir de soulagement et les choses sérieuses ont commencé. Le Wolfpack a immédiatement fait parler de lui : Davide Ballerini a remporté Omloop Het Nieuwsblad à Ninove grâce à ses jambes puissantes, Andrea Bagioli a gagné la Royal Bernard Drôme Classic et Mauri Vansevenant a obtenu sa première victoire professionnelle lors du GP de Larciano.

ON NE SE LASSE JAMAIS DE GAGNER

Comme le nombre de courses maintenues au printemps était plus que limité, il a fallu trouver d'autres moyens de préparer l'équipe pour les mois des classiques, de la mi-mars à la fin avril. Il est, par exemple, essentiel de s'entraîner en haute altitude et de faire les bons choix en vue des classiques.

Julian Alaphilippe a rapidement fait ses preuves. Il a terminé deuxième dans les Strade Bianche, mais a remporté la deuxième étape de la Tirreno-Adriatico. Sam Bennett s'est imposé à deux reprises lors de la Paris-Nice. La Flandre a également été un lieu de victoires pour l'équipe. Bennet a remporté l'Oxyclean Classic Bruges-De Panne et Kasper Asgreen a remporté l'E3 Classic à Harelbeke. C'était donc une excellente répétition générale pour le Ronde van Vlaanderen dix jours plus tard. Là aussi, la victoire est allée à la DQT puisque notre Champion national Danois a devancé Mathieu van der Poel dans un sprint à deux. Un final magistral.

L'AMOUR DE LA JEUNESSE

Tout allait si vite. Lorsque Mikkel Honoré a remporté la cinquième étape au Pays basque le lundi 9 avril – une course difficile –, c'était déjà la quinzième victoire de la saison pour le Wolfpack. Et en plus, c'était une belle victoire.

Lefevere : « Mikkel Honoré et Josef Cerny ont franchi la ligne d'arrivée ensemble, une victoire partagée par deux loups. Alors qu'ils étaient encore à une centaine de mètres de la ligne, Cerny s'est tourné vers son coéquipier pour lui dire : “Mikkel, tu peux gagner.” (rire) et c'est ce qui est arrivé. Ensuite, Mikkel est venu me voir et m'a dit : “Patrick, donne la moitié de mon bonus à Josef !” » C'est aussi ça le Wolfpack !

« Tous ceux qui me connaissent savent que la jeunesse est chère à mon cœur. Et à ce titre, les victoires de Mauri Vansevenant et Andrea Bagioli sont très importantes. Elles me remplissent de joie, car ils sont à peine sortis du nid et affrontent déjà les meilleurs talents sur les pistes. Ils participent à des courses difficiles, et avec les pros. Ne les sous-estimez pas ! »

Non, on ne se lasse jamais de gagner. C'est toujours un plaisir incroyable. En tout, nous avons remporté 65 victoires, ce qui est énorme ! Mais qu'on en soit maintenant à la n° 62, 63, 64 ou 65, cela n'a pas d'importance au niveau de la joie que cela nous procure. Les choses sont différentes pour les bonus que nous versons, cependant. (Rire) Et pour les sponsors même si j'ose dire que depuis plusieurs années consécutives, nous avons bien rentabilisé leurs investissements dans l'équipe. Pour moi, il est important que nous soyons rois des victoires et c'est ce que je vise. Une petite victoire de plus que la concurrence, en somme. (Rire) Et nous y arrivons. Et ce, pour la dixième saison consécutive depuis 2012 ! J'en suis très fier. »

CAVENDISH SHOW

Ensuite, il y a eu le Tour de Turquie. Avec Mark Cavendish. La question à un million était de savoir s'il pouvait encore gagner.

En ces temps de pandémie, le Tour présidentiel de Turquie a été doublement difficile pour les coureurs. Ils ont été hébergés dans des hôtels touristiques où l'application des mesures sanitaires n'était pas toujours claire.

Patrick Lefevere : « Nous avons vraiment pu compter sur l'aide d'une employée locale de la filiale turque de Deceuninck. Elle nous a guidés au cours de notre aventure turque. Cela fait plaisir. Et cela nous a fait doublement plaisir de voir que Mark Cavendish n'avait pas oublié comment décrocher la victoire. »

Après sa troisième place au Grand Prix de l'Escaut, « Cav » a été lauréat à quatre reprises en Turquie. Quatre victoires ! Cela apportait donc une réponse claire à la question à un million.

Mark Cavendish était un choix du cœur pour Patrick Lefevere et un risque calculé. Il a estimé que le Britannique était toujours au top physiquement, malgré les années au compteur. Ce qui restait un point d'interrogation, c'était la partie mentale.

« L'image de Cavendish dépité après la Gand-Wevelgem de 2020 restait gravée dans ma mémoire. Je l'ai appelé comme j'étais inquiet. Je n'avais aucune arrière-pensée, mais il est vrai que je ne supportais pas de le voir terminer sa carrière comme ça. Une si belle carrière. La Turquie m'a donné raison.

Et il ne s'est pas arrêté là. Après la Turquie, le Britannique s'est rendu seul en Grèce pour un stage de dix jours avec l'entraîneur de DQT, Vasilis Anastopoulos. Le but était de s'entraîner au sprint sur la piste et sur la route. Vasilis a confirmé que la puissance en watts de Cavendish n'avait pas diminué. Lefevere avait raison. Et cela, alors que le Tour de France approchait peu à peu.

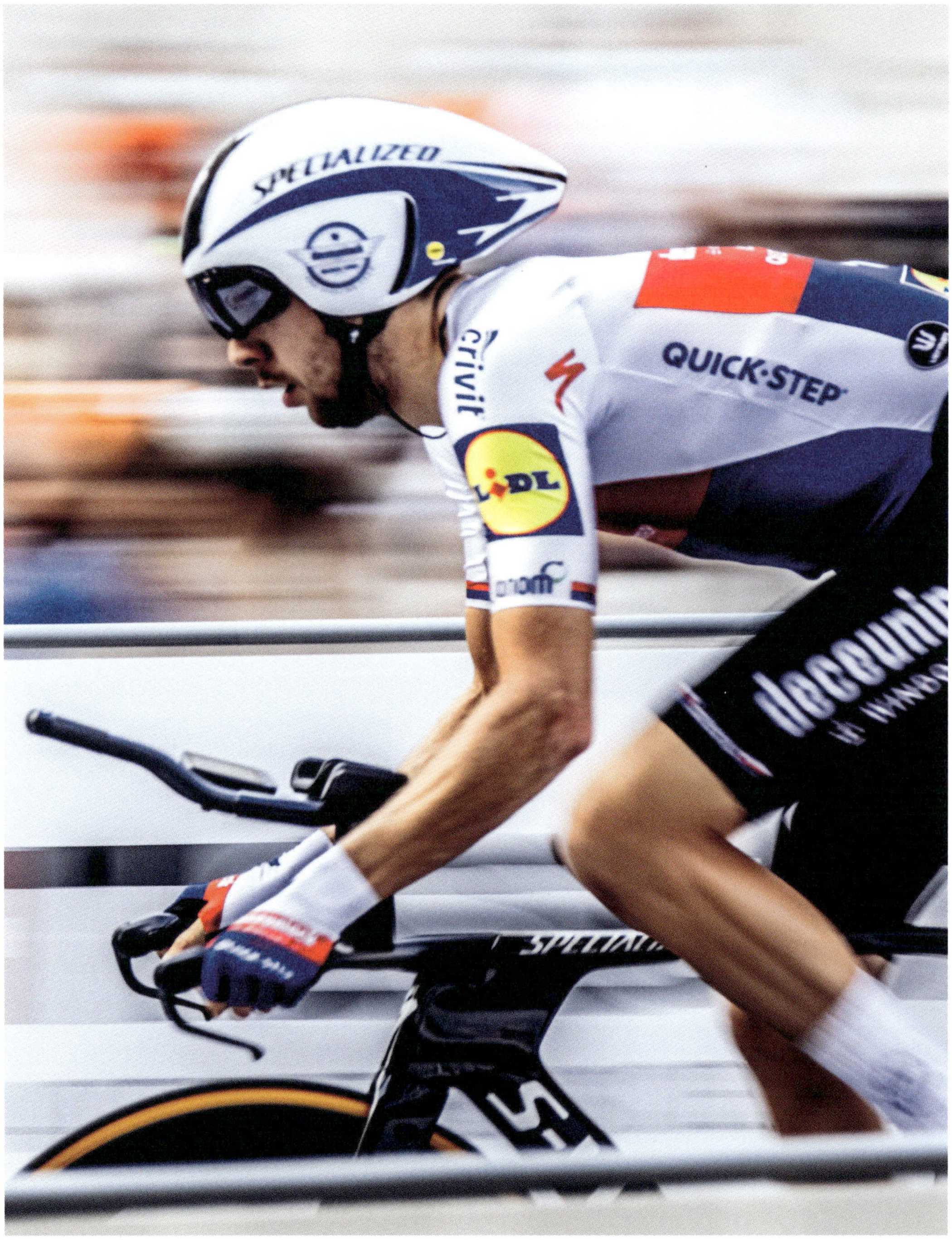

À l'époque, l'équipe réfléchissait déjà beaucoup à sa stratégie pour le Tour de France. Sans hésitation, Sam Bennett était le premier choix, après s'être adjugé le classement par points lors de la Grande Boucle en 2020. Sam avait déjà très bien commencé le printemps avec 7 victoires à son actif. Mais juste avant le Baloise Belgium Tour, il a dû déclarer forfait en raison d'une blessure au genou. Autrement dit, pas de Bennett. La nuit précédant le départ de la première étape à Beveren, Cavendish a fait d'urgence le trajet en hélicoptère depuis Londres. Le Britannique marque son grand retour en remportant une victoire éclatante dans la cinquième étape. Remco Evenepoel remporte le contre-la-montre et le classement général.

VICTOIRES AUX CHAMPIONNATS NATIONAUX

Le Wolfpack est une équipe pour les classiques. Une équipe constituée de sprinters qui gagnent des semi-classiques et des maillots à points. Une équipe aux atouts solides pour les petites courses à étapes. Mais cela ne s'arrête pas là. Le Wolfpack est aussi une équipe de champions du contre-la-montre. Yves Lampaert a remporté le titre champion CLM de Belgique. Kasper Asgreen a renouvelé son titre de Champion du Danemark. Josef Cerny a été le meilleur en République tchèque et João Almeida a remporté sa première victoire professionnelle au Portugal sur son vélo de contre-la-montre. En France, Rémi Cavagna a porté les couleurs nationales sur la route. Le « TGV de Clermont-Ferrand » a remporté la victoire en solitaire.

DE LA FOLIE

Le Baloise Belgium Tour s'est terminé le dimanche 13 juin, soit deux semaines avant le Tour de France. Sam Bennett était toujours à l'arrêt et Mark Cavendish a prouvé qu'il n'avait rien perdu. le 'Manxman' de 36 ans est donc devenu le fer de lance du Wolfpack pour les étapes de sprint en France, porté par Michael Mørkøv et Davide Ballerini. Et ça a porté ses fruits. Mais avant tout, Julian Alaphilippe a montré qu'il était plus qu'en forme en gagnant la première étape et en obtenant les premiers jaune et vert. Et c'est aussi grâce à Dries Devenyns, qui l'a superbement emmené au sprint. Et dans l'esprit Wolfpack, Dries a également été lui-même porté vers cette place de choix.

Le maillot vert est resté sur les épaules de Julian jusqu'à la quatrième étape, lorsque Cavendish a décroché sa première victoire et s'est hissé en tête du classement par points. Personne n'a pu lui arracher cette première place. Il a également remporté la sixième, la dixième et la treizième étape. Plus rien ne pouvait l'arrêter. Et lorsque, avec sa quatrièmewvictoire, il a égalé le record absolu de victoires d'Eddy Merck, son succès a fait couler beaucoup d'encre.

Patrick Lefevere : « Il est aussi important de souligner le mérite de l'équipe. Surtout quand on voit comment ses coéquipiers – Devenyns, Declercq, Mørkøv, Ballerini – ont porté Mark à travers les Pyrénées, pour ainsi dire, en tenant compte du temps imparti. Je ne pourrais pas être plus fier. Ce sont certes des cyclistes professionnels et Mark a remporté la victoire. Mais ce sont aussi des personnes. Et l'aspect humain est tout aussi important. Si certains de ces coureurs ne s'étaient pas dévoués pour l'équipe, cette victoire n'aurait pas été possible. Parce qu'une personne égoïste et individualiste n'est pas un bon coureur. Mais ils sont aussi des loups après tout. Et la meute passe en premier. »

LA FORCE DE FABIO JAKOBSEN

Nous devons bien sûr mentionner Fabio Jakobsen. Patrick Lefevere : « Ce que Fabio a réussi est du hors catégorie. Son rétablissement est phénoménal. Je ne dirais pas que c'est un miracle, car c'est un combat qu'il a livré lui-même, avec le soutien de l'équipe. »

Fabio a pu rejoindre le monde de la compétition lors du Tour de Turquie. Sans attentes particulières. Le but était pour lui de se réhabituer à la compétition, de rouler dans un peloton... et il a pu tester que tout allait bien. Il a fait la même chose dans l'Algarve et le Dauphiné. Lorsque est arrivé le Tour de Wallonie, il a participé avec l'ambition de gagner une étape. Malheureusement, le Tour a dû être altéré à la suite des inondations qui ont touché l'est de notre pays. La deuxième étape du 21 juillet a été remplacée par une courte étape de 120 kilomètres sur le circuit de Zolder, étape qui a été remportée par Fabio Jakobsen. Sa première victoire, près d'un an après son terrible accident en Pologne, le 5 août 2020. Il a vite décroché une autre victoire, lors de la cinquième étape.

La Vuelta de Fabio a été phénoménale. Il remporte la quatrième étape sur une arrivée en pente. Aucun des membres de l'équipe ne l'a vu venir. Il s'impose aussi dans la huitième et la seizième étape et termine en tête du classement par points. Florian Sénéchal remporte également la 13e étape.

« Il est clair que Fabio est à nouveau un coureur de haut niveau » a déclaré Lefevere. « Avec tout ce que cela implique. Il a bien sûr été frustré lorsqu'il a dû abandonner son rôle de sprinteur, en pleine préparation du sprint, au cours de l'étape qu'a remporté Sénéchal

Fabio a remporté sa troisième victoire sur la Vuelta le jour de son 25e anniversaire, le 31 août, à Santa Cruz de Bezana. Cela a donné lieu à un moment « typiquement Lefevere ». Patrick s'est approché de Fabio, lui a souhaité bon anniversaire et l'a félicité pour sa troisième victoire sur la Vuelta, mais l'a ensuite réprimandé pour sa critique de l'emmenée au sprint de Sénéchal dans la 13e étape. « Tu sais quoi, Fabio ? N'oublie pas qu'il y a treize mois, on t'a ramassé presque mort en Pologne. Tu as eu un parcours fantastique l'année dernière. Et tu le dois aussi à l'équipe ! Ne l'oublie pas. Alors, calme-toi. On va terminer calmement la saison, te faire passer un bon hiver et l'année prochaine, tu seras 10 à 15 % meilleur ! »

À la question de savoir si Jakobsen se rétablirait complètement, Lefevere a répondu par un oui catégorique : « J'en suis sûr, à condition que nous, en tant qu'équipe, et lui, en tant que coureur, suivions le parcours strictement tracé. Cela n'a pas été facile, surtout à cause du Covid-19. Mais cela nous a surtout démontré la force remarquable de Fabio en tant qu'homme et en tant qu'athlète. »

LE DOUBLÉ DE JULIAN ALAPHILIPPE

Après la Vuelta, le bilan était de 53 victoires pour le Wolfpack. Michael Mørkøv avait remporté l'or aux Jeux olympiques sur la Madison (avec Lasse Norman Hansen) et DQT avait dominé le Tour de Pologne et le Tour du Danemark. Remco Evenepoel a remporté la troisième étape au Danemark, le contre-la-montre final et le classement général. Le Tour de Pologne a été encore plus impressionnant : Rémi Cavagna a remporté le contre-la-montre de la 6e étape, João Almeida a remporté la 2e et la 4e étape, ainsi que le classement général.

Grâce à des victoires en Grande-Bretagne (Yves Lampaert), en Slovaquie (Jannik Steimle et Álvaro Hodeg), au Tour de Luxembourg (João Almeida et Mattia Cattaneo), à la Flèche de Gooik (Fabio Jakobsen) et à la Primus Classic (Florian Sénéchal), les Championnats du Monde s'annonçaient prometteurs.

Les Championnats du Monde à Louvain ont été suivis par quelque 300 000 fans de cyclisme. Le Covid-19 semblait être un cauchemar du passé. Les Championnats se sont achevés par une prouesse incroyable de Julian Alaphilippe. Il a montré à tout le monde, équipiers et concurrents, comment atteindre le sommet et placer une brillante accélération à 15 km. Il est entré dans les annales du cyclisme et a rejoint l'élite des doubles champions du monde, aux côtés de Rik Van Looy, Gianni Bugno, Paolo Bettini, Freddy Maertens et Briek Schotte.

L'INSTITUTION DECEUNINCK – QUICK-STEP

Amis et ennemis s'accordent à dire que ces dernières années, Patrick Lefevere a élevé son équipe au rang d'« instituton » du monde du cyclisme. Grâce à une hiérarchie fixe, une structure solide, une philosophie claire et des objectifs précis.

« Je ne pouvais bien entendu pas prévoir que mon équipe connaîtrait tel succès. Mais la victoire a toujours fait partie de moi. J'ai toujours voulu, et je veux toujours, gagner chaque course. Ce qui ne m'a pas vraiment réussi en tant que coureur (rire), j'en ai fait l'objectif dès le premier jour en tant que chef d'équipe. Lors de ma première année à la Marc Zeepcentrale, ma première en tant que directeur d'équipe, nous avons tout de suite tapé dans le mille et remporté le Omloop Het Volk en 1980 avec Joseph Bruyère. Et cette course avait plus d'attrait à l'époque qu'aujourd'hui, surtout au niveau international.

Souvent les conditions ne sont pas réunies pour remporter la victoire. « Mais quand il faut les réunir, je suis présent. » En effet, nous nous souvenons tous de la machine Mapei dans les années 1990. « J'ai beaucoup appris. Par exemple, une bonne préparation est primordiale en termes de logistique, afin que la paix règne dans le groupe. Et l'esprit d'équipe aussi. Il est important d'avoir des coureurs qui deviennent amis et qui se battent les uns pour les autres afin de remporter la victoire. J'ai appris à mettre en place un environnement dans lequel il est possible pour eux de devenir amis. »

« La marque Quick-Step est le fil rouge de ma carrière depuis 2003, la base de mon succès. Dès que j'ai pris les rênes de l'équipe, j'ai joué dans une division supérieure. Le train était lancé et rien ne pouvait l'arrêter. Il n'y a eu qu'une seule baisse de régime, en 2010. Mais ce qui était un creux dans notre parcours est ce dont rêvent d'autres équipes. En 2018, nous avons même obtenu un total de 73 victoires. Et cette année encore, nous avons décroché un nombre exceptionnel de 65 victoires. Nous connaissons victoire sur victoire presque chaque année. Mais cette saison a été remarquable : le vert sur le Tour, cinq étapes du Tour et un jour de jaune, le vert sur la Vuelta et quatre victoires, des jeunes qui s'imposent… [Vansevenant, Bagioli, Ballerini, Almeida, Cavagna et autres]. Jakobsen et Evenepoel qui ont récupéré. Nous détenons le maillot de Champion de France, l'or olympique, quatre maillots nationaux de contre-la-montre… et un fantastique esprit Wolfpack. »

À ce jour, Patrick Lefevere est toujours le grand patron, le directeur général, le CEO. Geert Coeman est directeur financier, Ricardo Scheidecker est directeur technique et du développement et Alessandro Tegner est directeur du marketing et de la communication. Ils sont chargés de la gestion quotidienne et en réfèrent à Patrick. Étant donné que l'équipe est active sur trois, parfois quatre, fronts, dans de nombreux endroits du monde et avec des coureurs venant d'un peu partout, une organisation hiérarchique assez claire et reposant sur différents niveaux a été mise en place.

« Cela signifie également que je ne suis plus impliqué dans la gestion quotidienne, même si je reste aux commandes. J'en profite davantage maintenant, avec les coureurs. Mais la responsabilité finale reste entre mes mains et je continue à décider du recrutement des membres du staff et des coureurs. Je suis tous les résultats, je connais tous les jeunes talents et si pas, je suis bien renseigné. Je négocie les salaires, et pour les bonus, je consulte Geert Coeman. La structure est en place et continuera à fonctionner aussi bien que cette année. »

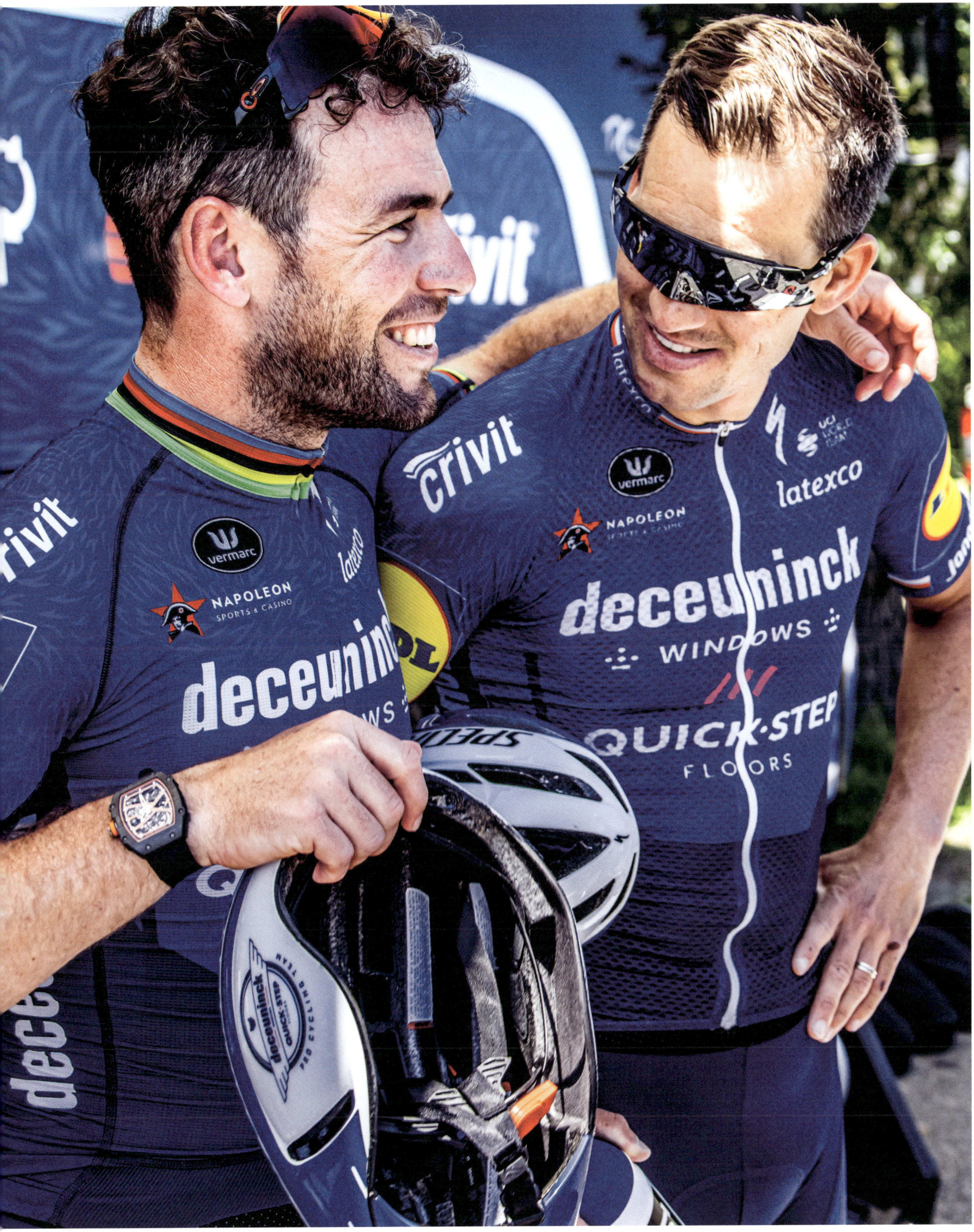
Crivit
vermarc
NAPOLEON
SPORTS & CASINO
latexco
deceuninck
WINDOWS
QUICK·STEP
FLOORS
deceuninck
QUICK·STEP
PRO CYCLING TEAM

GIRO D'ITALIA
08.05 - 30.05.2021

Als de lente openbloeit, is het tijd voor de kleinere ronden. Zowel in de Ronde van Romandië als in de Volta ao Algarve is het DQT Team succesvol. In Romandië wint Rémi Cavagna de vijfde etappe. Het was de afsluitende tijdrit en de Fransman klopt Stefan Bissegger en Geraint Thomas. Fausto Masnada wordt derde in het eindklassement, nadat hij op 1 mei in echt beestenweer vijfde geworden was in de koninginnenrit naar het skioord Thyon 2000.

Beter weer was het in de Algarve begin mei. Sam Bennett wint de enige twee massasprints – eerste en derde rit – en verovert de groene puntentrui. Kasper Asgreen wint de tijdrit.

Once spring shows its face, it's time for the smaller tours. The DQT Team is successful in both the Tour de Romandie and the Volta ao Algarve. In Romandy, Rémi Cavagna wins the fifth stage. It was the final time trial, and the Frenchman beats Stefan Bissegger and Geraint Thomas. Fausto Masnada finishes third in the general classification after taking fifth on the queen stage to the ski resort of Thyon 2000 on 1 May in dire weather conditions.

The weather was more favorable in the Algarve in early May. Sam Bennett wins the only two bunch sprints – first and third stage – and takes the green points jersey. Kasper Asgreen wins the time trial.

Le printemps, c'est aussi la période des courses plus courtes. L'équipe DQT rencontre le succès tant au Tour de Romandie qu'à la Volta ao Algarve. En Romandie, Rémi Cavagna gagne la 5e étape. Il s'agit du dernier contre-la-montre et le Français a devancé Stefan Bissegger et Geraint Thomas. Fausto Masnada arrive à la troisième place du classement général après avoir terminé cinquième de l'étape reine vers la station de ski de Thyon 2000 le 1er mai dans des conditions météorologiques très mauvaises.

Au début du mois de mai, le temps était bien meilleur en Algarve. Sam Bennett s'impose aux deux seuls sprints massifs, à savoir les première et troisième étapes, et remporte le maillot vert de classement. Kasper Asgreen gagne le contre-la-montre.

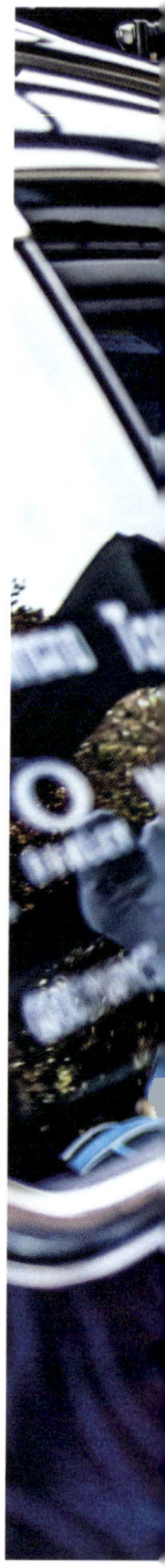

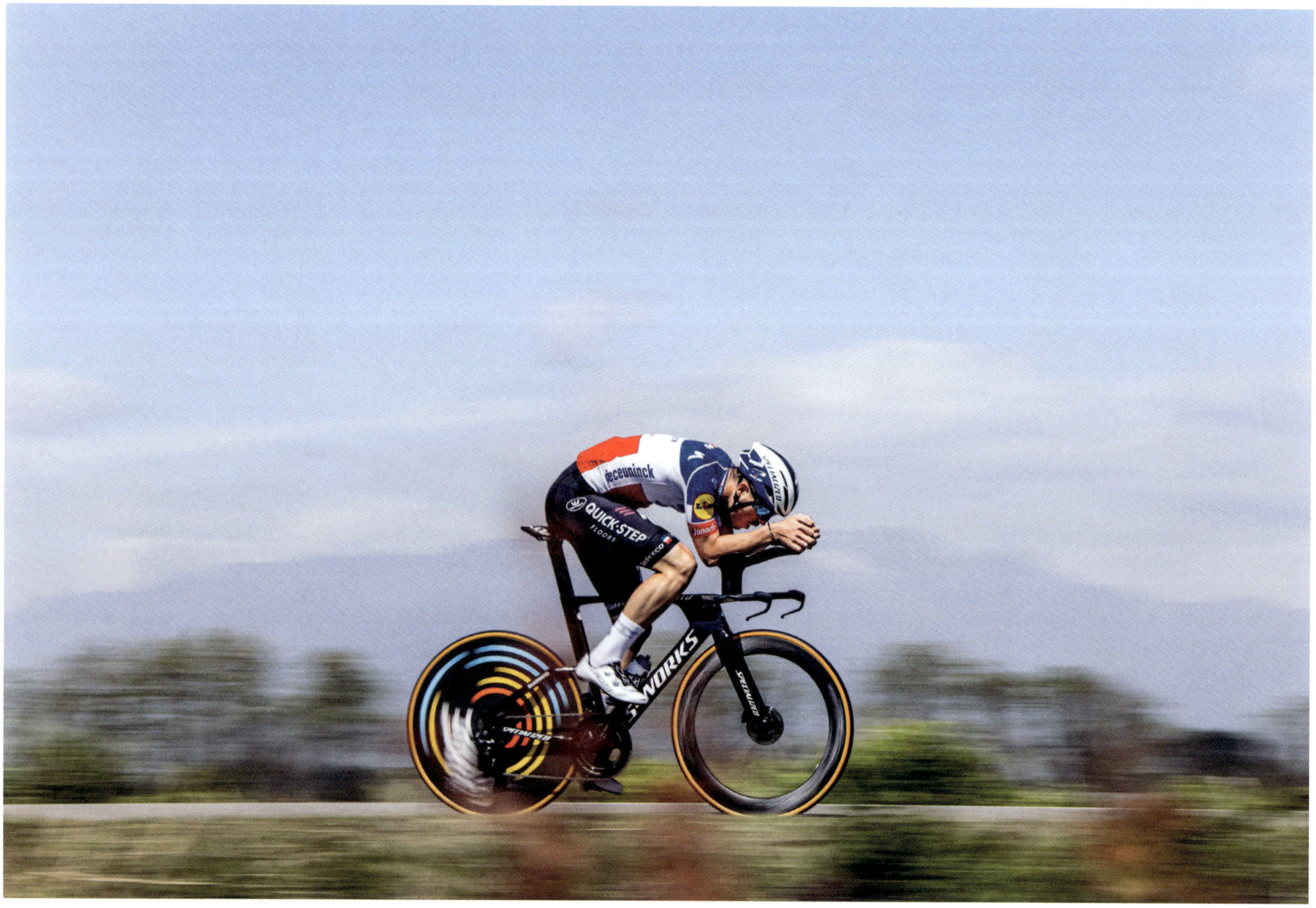

TORINO, 07.05.2021

Rémi Cavagna op training voor de proloog. Zoeken naar de perfecte houding. Steeds weer opnieuw.

Rémi Cavagna is training for the prologue. Searching for the perfect position. Over and over again.

Rémi Cavagna s'entraînant pour le prologue. Il travaille les moindres détails. Encore et encore.

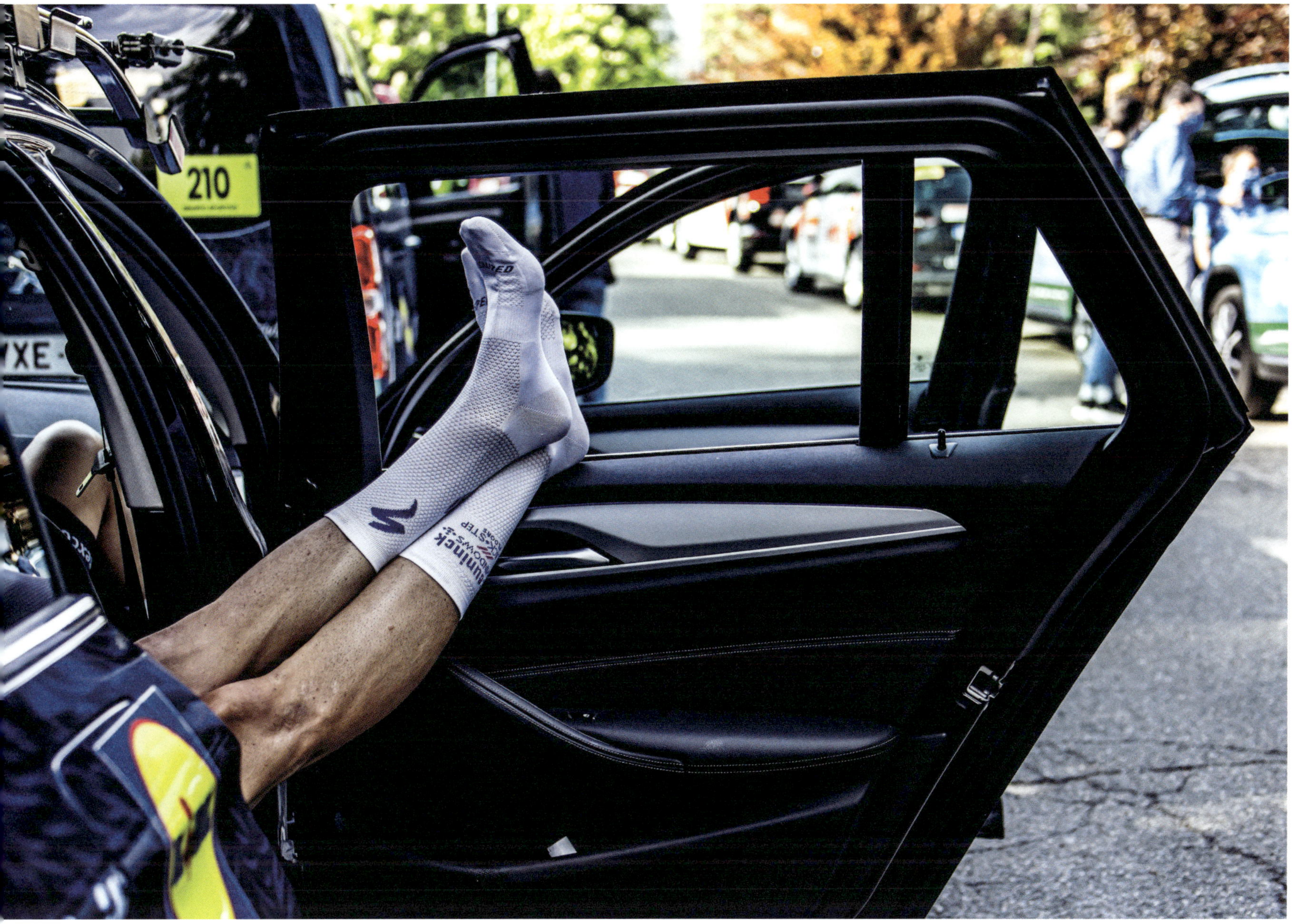

Op naar de Giro, waar alle zintuigen gericht zijn op Remco Evenepoel. Hij maakt er zijn comeback na 265 dagen inactiviteit. Hij start meer dan behoorlijk met een zevende stek in de proloog. Waarna REV langzaam naar voren schuift in het algemeen klassement. Hij houdt aardig stand en draagt gedurende enkele dagen de witte jongerentrui, weliswaar als vervanger van leider Attila Valter.

Dichter dan de tweede plek in het klassement komt hij niet. Hij wordt tweede op 11 seconden van Valter na de zesde (berg)etappe naar San Giacomo. Hij behoudt die tweede stek tot en met de tiende rit, dan is Egan Bernal al leider. Daarna wordt het moeilijker, ondanks de steun van zijn ploegmakkers en de volledige staf. De derde week wordt heel zwaar. Hij stapt uit de Giro op de ochtend van de achttiende etappe, na een dubbele valpartij in de zeventiende rit.

On to the Giro, where all eyes are on Remco Evenepoel. After 265 days of inactivity, he's able to make his comeback. He started well with a seventh place in the prologue. After that, he slowly moved up in the general classification. He'll be able to hold on and wear the white jersey for a few days, replacing leader Attila Valter.

He won't come closer than second in the general classification. After the sixth (mountain) stage to San Giacomo, he came second 11 seconds after Valter. He keeps second place until the tenth stage, when Egan Bernal is already the leader. After that, it gets harder, despite the support of his teammates and the entire staff. The third week will be very tough. He dropped out of the Giro on the morning of stage 18, after a double crash in stage 17.

En route pour le Giro, où tous les yeux sont rivés sur Remco Evenepoel. Il fait son retour après 265 jours d'inactivité. Il prend un excellent départ en terminant septième du prologue. Il se fait ensuite lentement une place dans le classement général et tient bon, portant le maillot blanc pendant plusieurs jours, derrière le Hongrois Attila Valter.

Il n'ira malheureusement pas plus haut que la deuxième place du classement général. Après la sixième étape (en montagne) vers San Giacomo, il prend la deuxième place à 11 secondes de Valter. Il conserve cette deuxième place jusqu'à la dixième étape, dauphin d'Egan Bernal. Après cela, les choses se compliquent, malgré le soutien de ses coéquipiers et de l'ensemble du staff. La troisième semaine sera très difficile pour lui et il quitte le Giro le matin de la 18e étape, après une double chute dans la 17e étape.

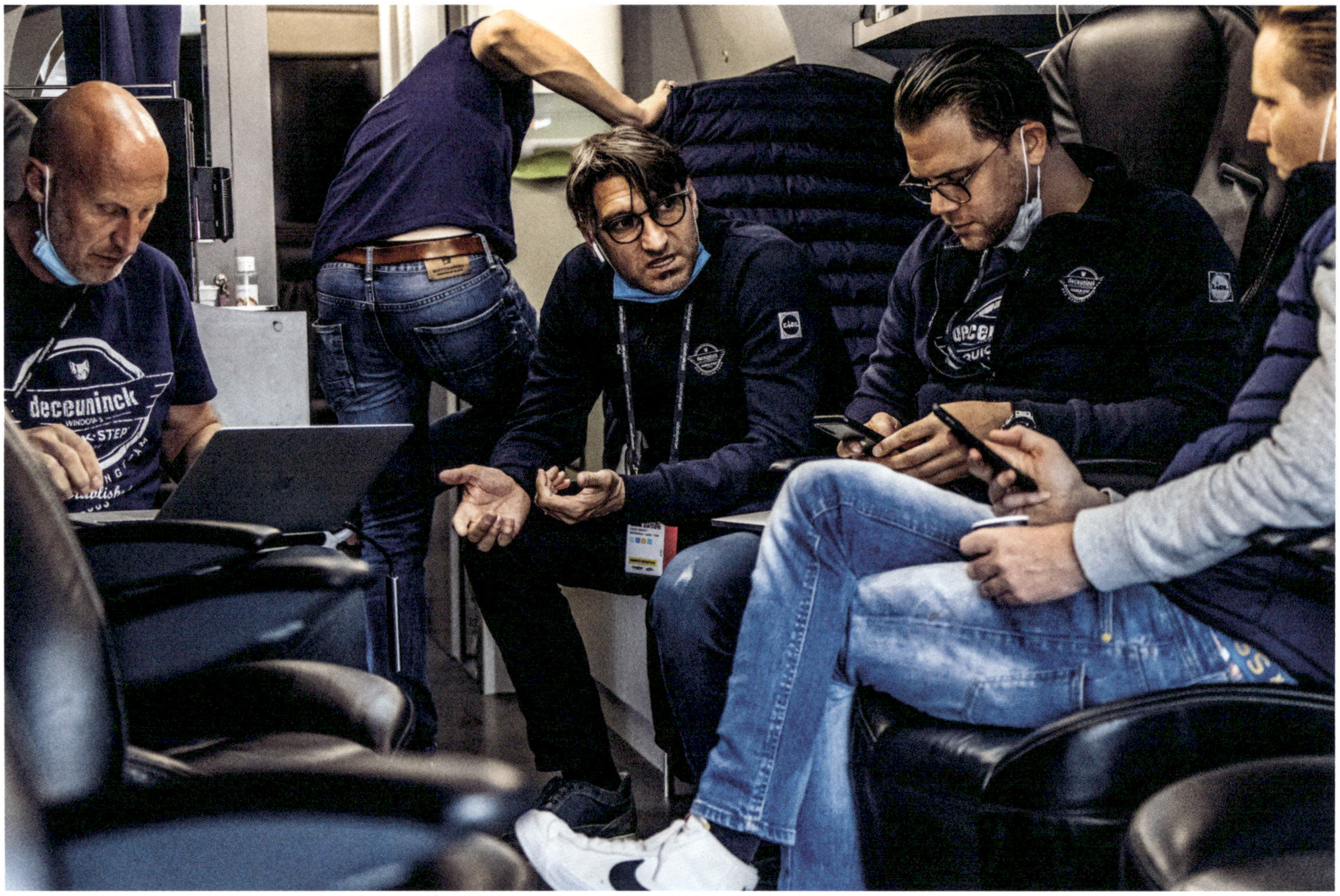

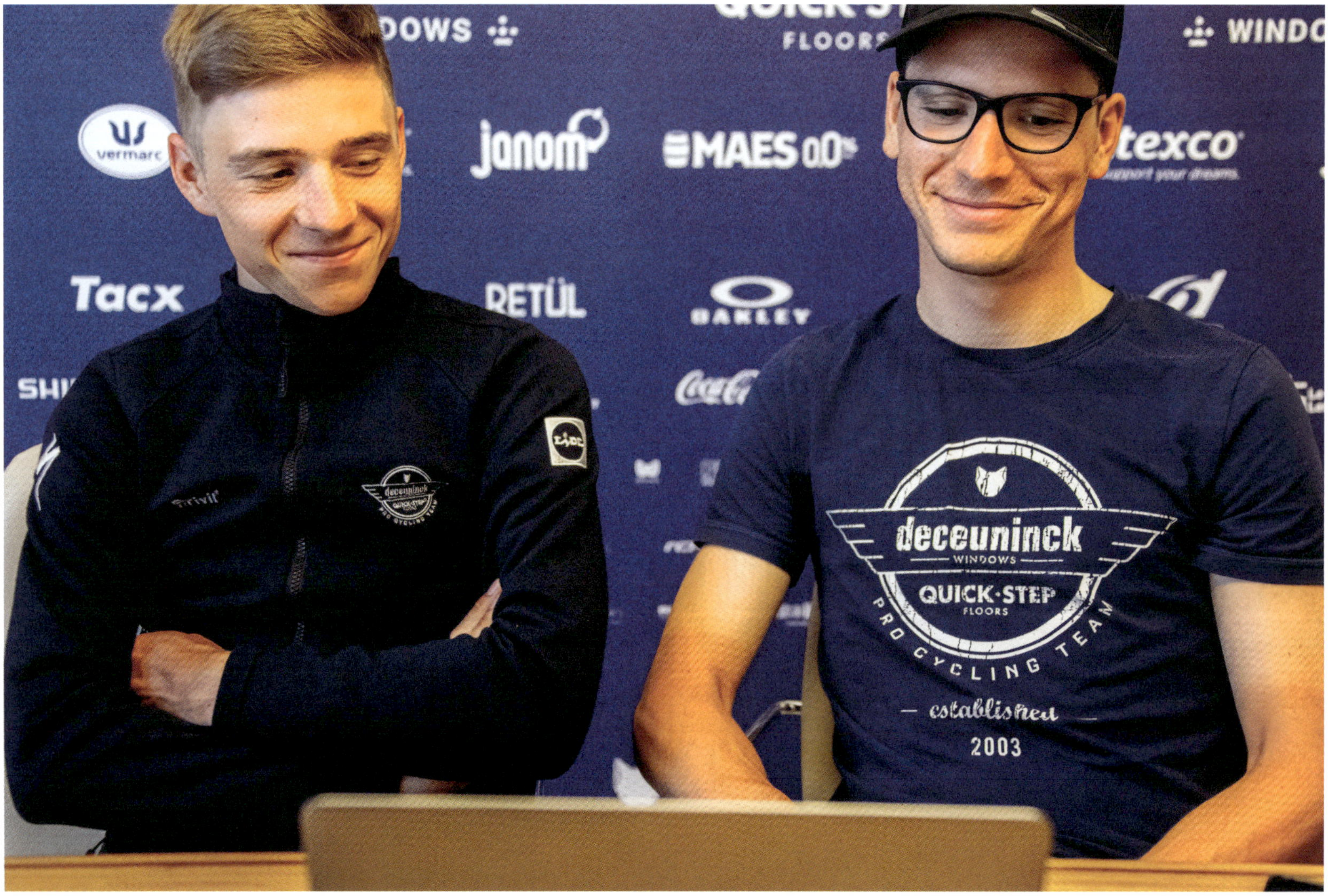
vermarc
janom
MAES 0.0%
texco
Tacx
RETÜL
OAKLEY
deceuninck
WINDOWS
QUICK·STEP
FLOORS
PRO CYCLING TEAM
established
2003

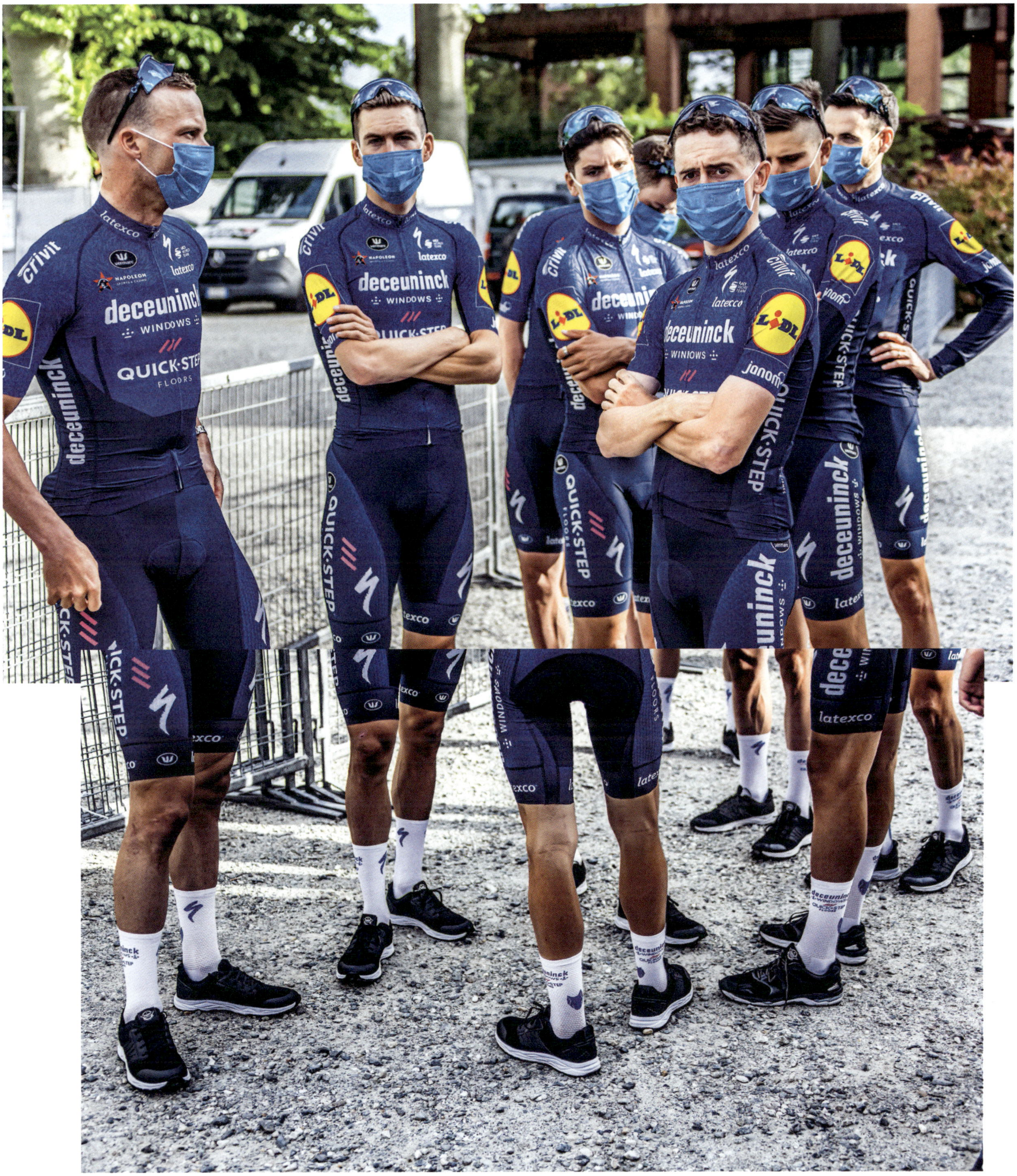

TORINO, 06.05.2021

Zeven van de acht Wolven voor de Giro 2021. V.l.n.r.: Iljo Keisse, Mikkel Honoré, João Almeida, Rémi Cavagna, James Knox, Fausto Masnada en Pieter Serry.

Seven of the eight wolves for the Giro 2021. FLTR: Iljo Keisse, Mikkel Honoré, João Almeida, Rémi Cavagna, James Knox, Fausto Masnada and Pieter Serry.

Sspt des huit loups pour le Giro 2021. Dgàd : Iljo Keisse, Mikkel Honoré, João Almeida, Rémi Cavagna, James Knox, Fausto Masnada et Pieter Serry.

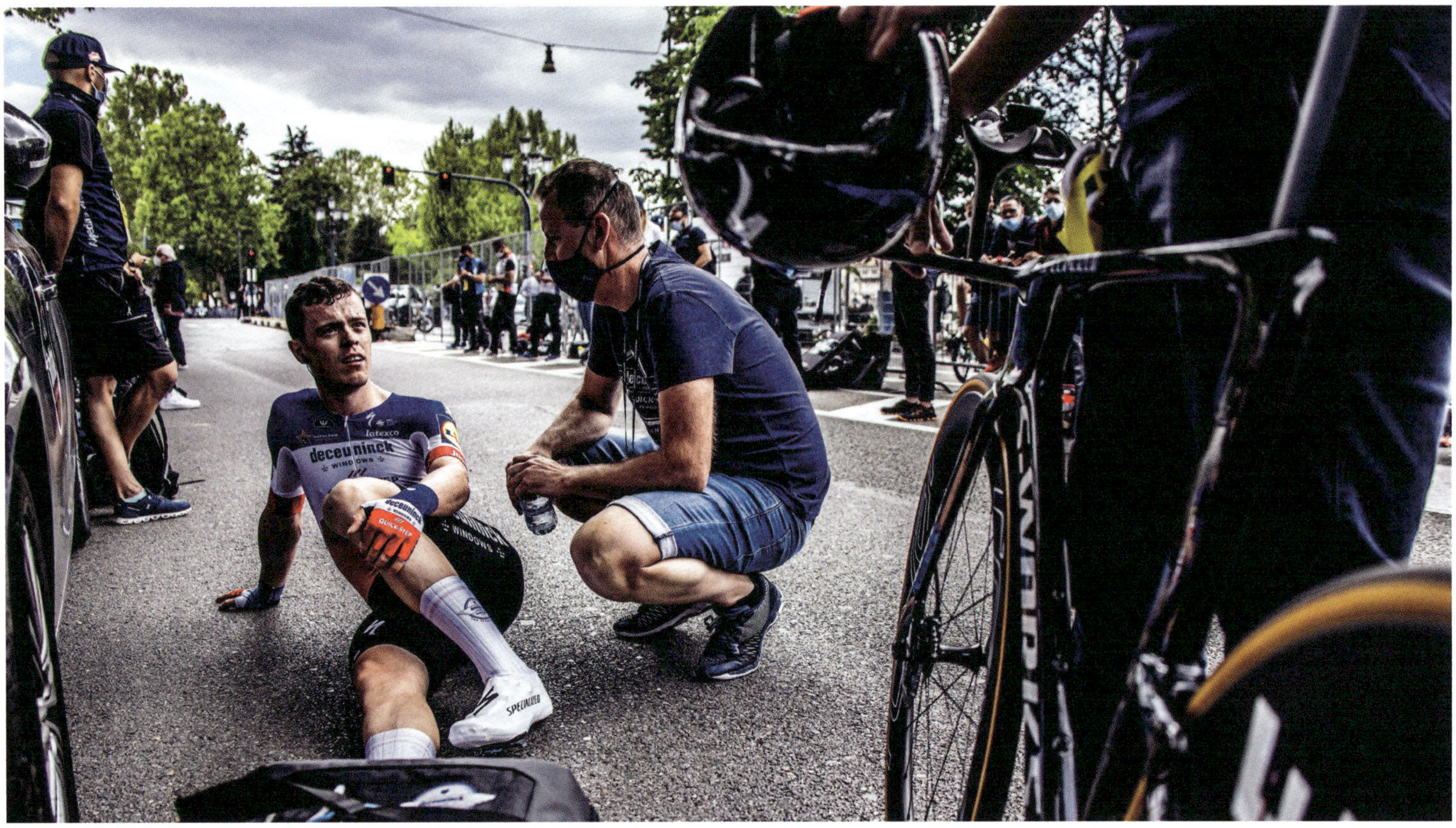
deceuninck

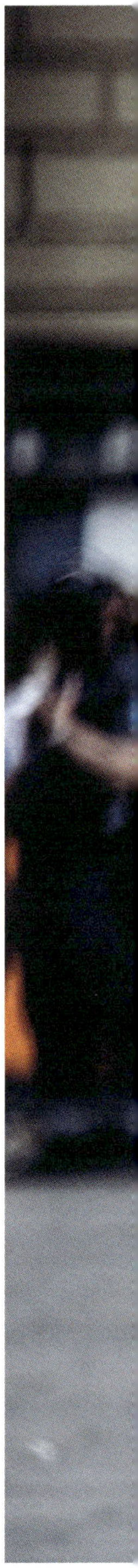

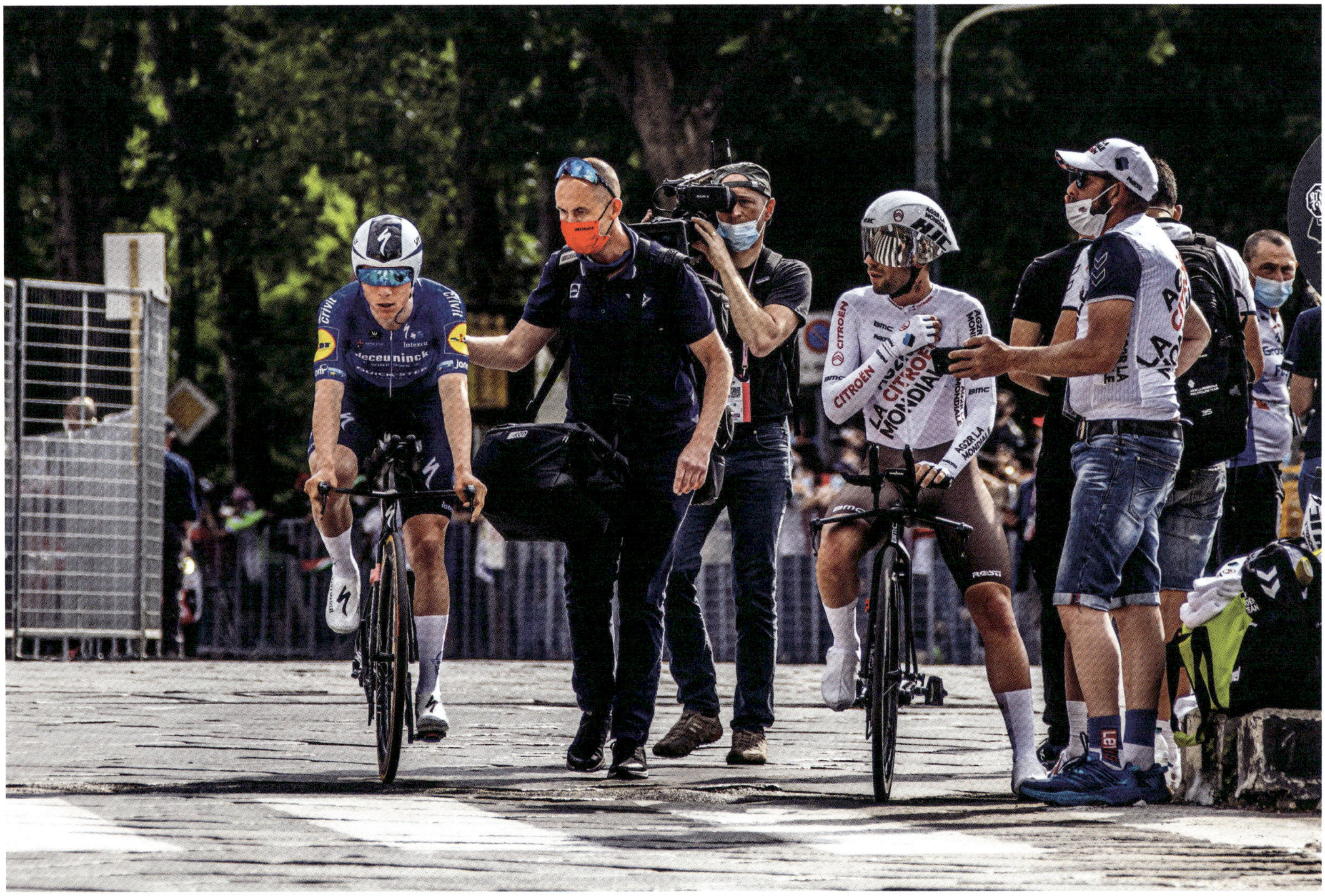
deceuninck
CITROËN
LA CITROËN
MONDIALE

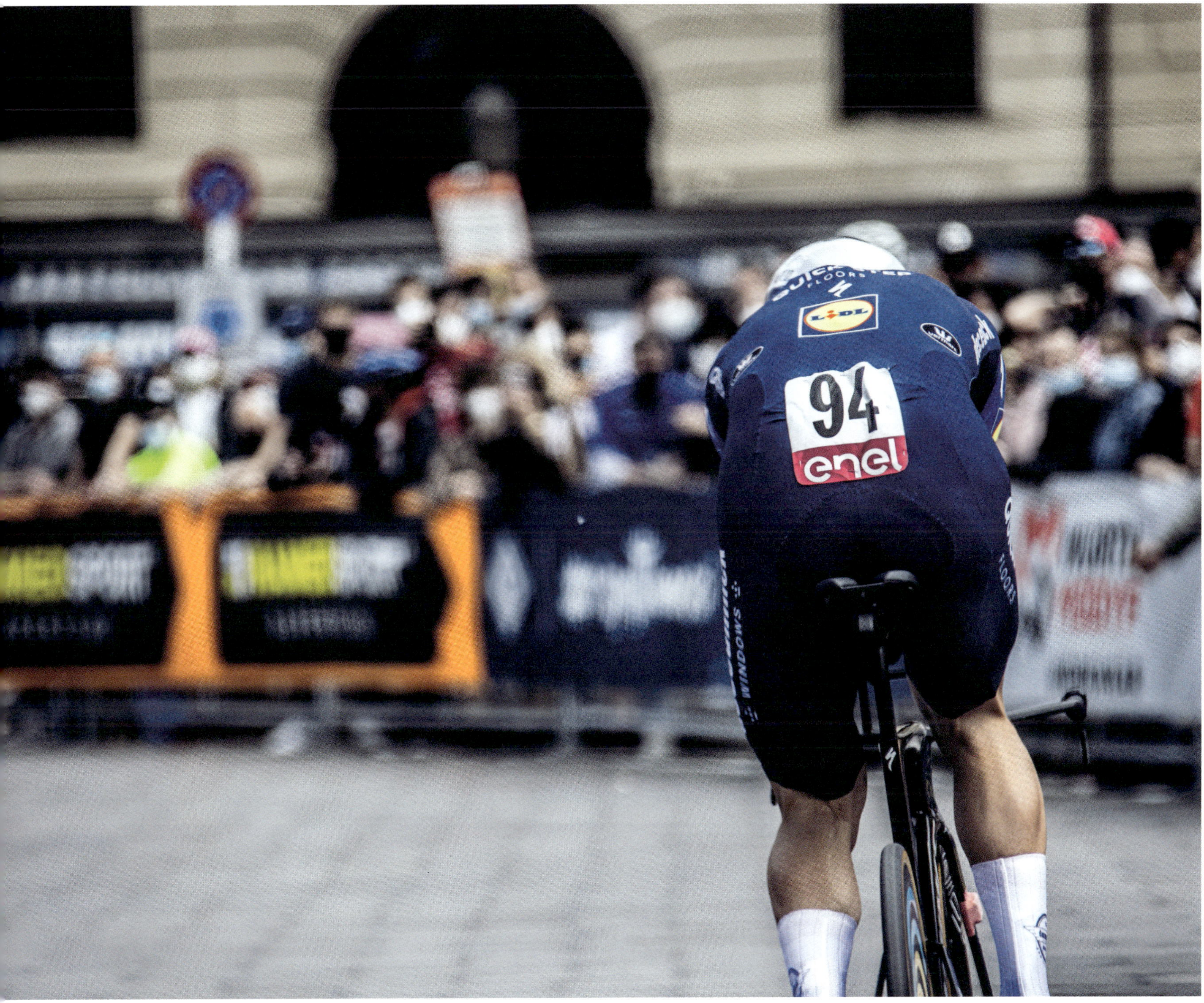

TORINO, 08.05.2021

Het echte werk. De proloog van de Giro 2021 op 8 mei in de straten van Turijn, 8,6 kilometer lang. Rémi Cavagna, met soigneur David Geeroms, is heel diep gegaan en eindigt vijfde.

Remco Evenepoel strandt op de negende stek in de proloog van de Giro. Fysiotherapeut Frederick Pollentier is de eerste om Remco op te vangen. Het was zijn eerste competitiedag sinds de val in Lombardije in 2020.

The real deal. The prologue of the Giro 2021 on 8 May in the streets of Turin, 8.6 km long. Rémi Cavagna, with soigneur David Geeroms, went all the way and finished fifth.

Remco Evenepoel finishes ninth in the prologue of the Giro. Physiotherapist Frederick Pollentier is the first to catch up with Remco. It was his first day of competition since the fall in Lombardy in 2020.

Ça, c'est de l'effort. Le prologue du Giro 2021 le 8 mai, long de 8,6 km, dans les rues de Turin. Rémi Cavagna, avec le soigneur David Geeroms, a vraiment tout donné et a terminé cinquième.

Remco Evenepoel termine en neuvième place lors du prologue du Giro. Frederick Pollentier, le kinésithérapeute, est le premier à rejoindre Remco. C'était son premier jour de compétition depuis sa chute en Lombardie en 2020.

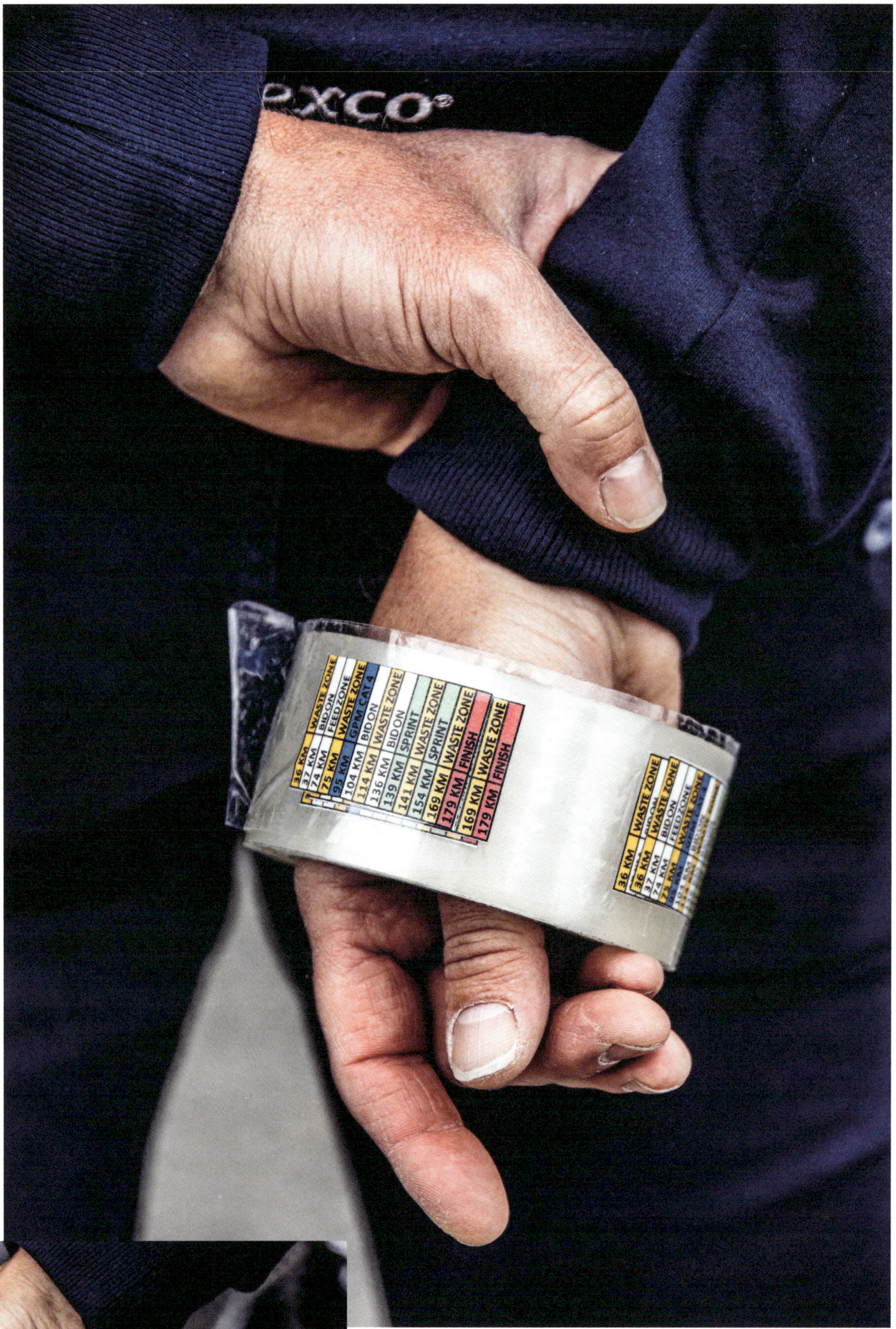
36 KM WASTE ZONE
37 KM BIDON
74 KM FEEDZONE
75 KM WASTE ZONE
95 KM GPM CAT 4
104 KM BIDON
114 KM WASTE ZONE
136 KM BIDON
139 KM SPRINT
141 KM WASTE ZONE
154 KM SPRINT
169 KM WASTE ZONE
179 KM FINISH
169 KM WASTE ZONE
179 KM FINISH

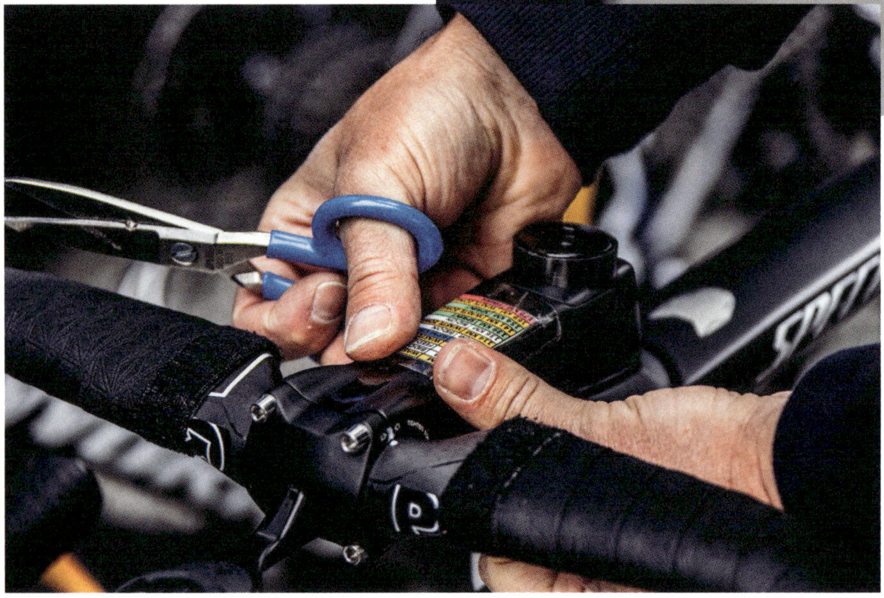

CANALE, 10.05.2021

De Giro is altijd een avontuur. Vaak een mooi avontuur, letterlijk. Door *la bella Italia*, langs begeesterende landschappen en door heerlijk leuke stadjes, zoals op dit beeld. De passage door Crescentino, na 41 kilometer in de derde rit, van Biella naar Canale, op de grens tussen Lombardije en Piemonte. Al heerste in de editie 2021 vooral de regen.

The Giro is always an adventure. Often a beautiful adventure – literally. Through *la bella Italia*, filled with inspiring landscapes and lovely little towns, like in this image: the passage through Crescentino, after 41 km in the third stage, from Biella to Canale, on the border between Lombardy and Piedmont. In the 2021 edition, the rain prevailed.

Le Giro est toujours une aventure. Bien souvent, c'est une très belle aventure. Dans *la bella Italia*, le long de paysages inspirants et à travers de charmantes petites villes, comme nous le voyons sur cette image. La traversée de Crescentino, un trajet de 41 km pendant la troisième étape de Biella à Canale, à la frontière entre la Lombardie et le Piémont. Cependant, cette étape de l'édition 2021 s'est faite sous la pluie.

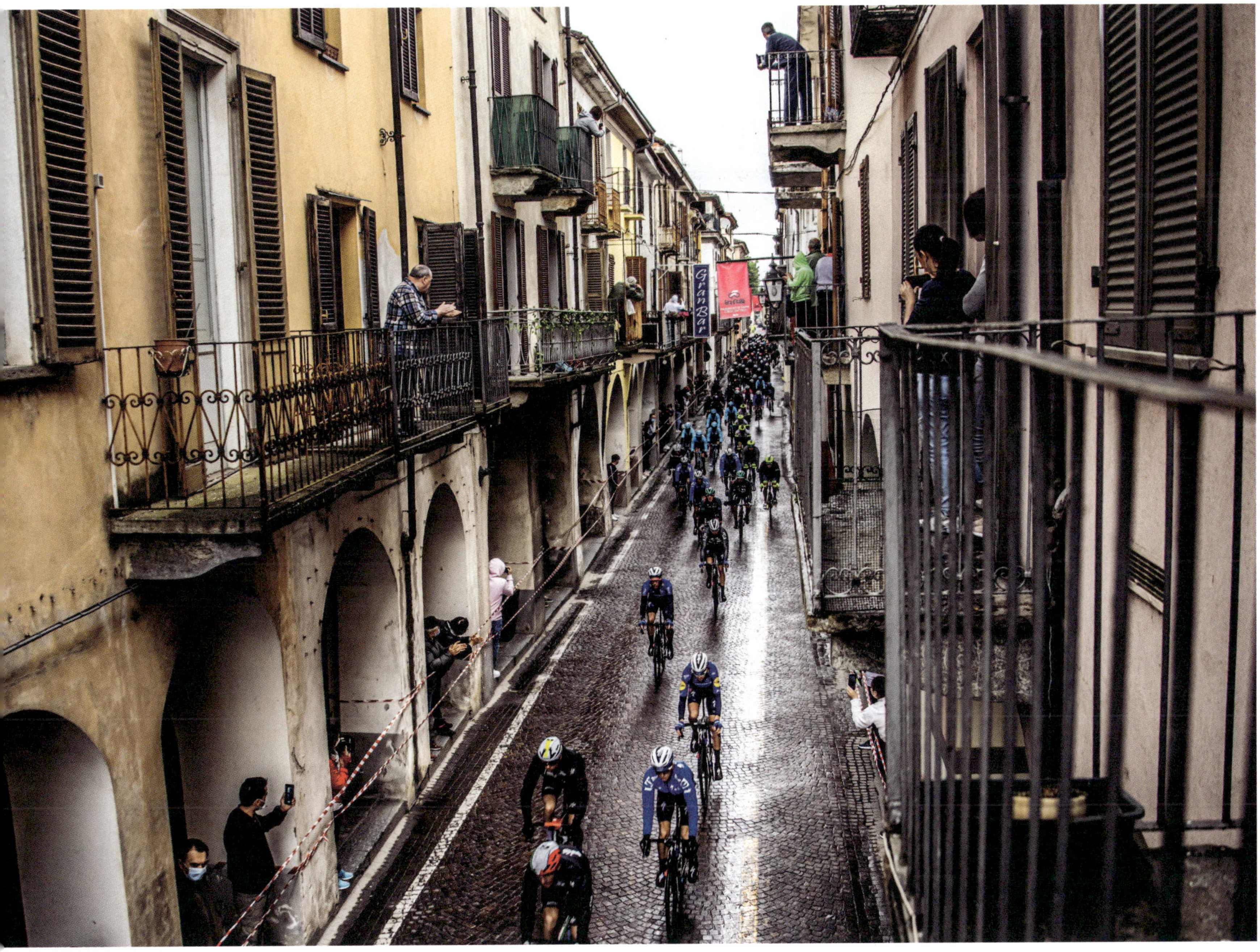

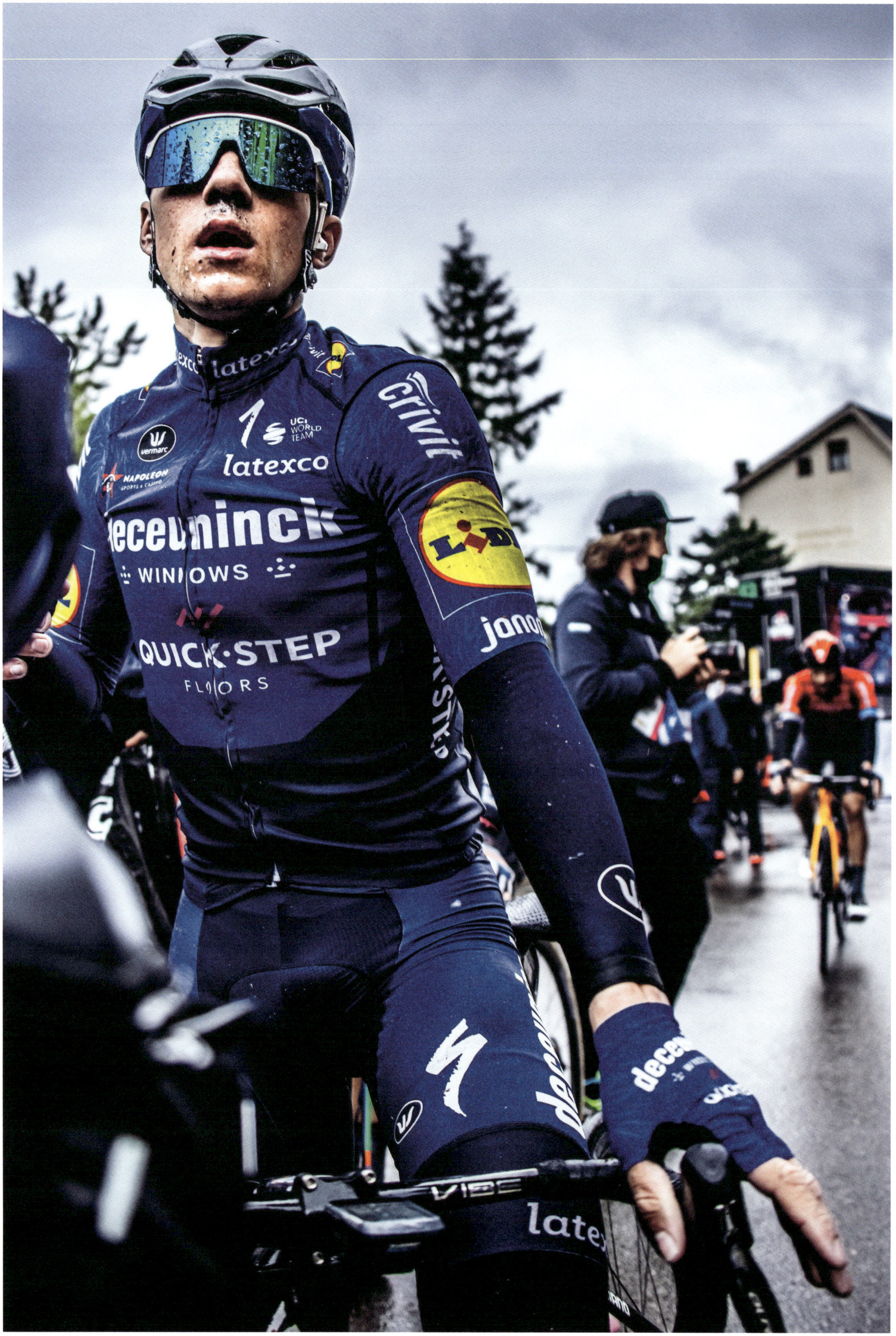
latexco
UCI WORLD TEAM
QUICK·STEP
crivit
VIBE

SESTOLA, 11.05.2021

Remco Evenepoel aan het einde van de vierde rit in de Giro. Met aankomst op de Colle Passerino in Sestola.

Remco Evenepoel at the end of the fourth stage of the Giro. Arrival at the Colle Passerino in Sestola.

Remco Evenepoel à l'issue de la quatrième étape du Giro. Avec arrivée sur le Colle Passerino à Sestola.

SAN GIACOMO, 13.05.2021

Remco Evenepoel is diep gegaan, zeer diep, aan het einde van de zesde rit naar San Giacomo. Tegen de kou en de regen, in het gezelschap van Egan Bernal en Dan Martin onder meer. Hij werd vierde en klom in het klassement naar de tweede plaats. En dat verdient een warme aanmoediging van João Almeida.

At the end of the sixth stage to San Giacomo, Remco Evenepoel gave everything – truly his all. Through the cold and the rain, in the company of Egan Bernal and Dan Martin, among others. He finished fourth and climbed to second place in the general classification. That deserves a warm cheer from João Almeida.

Remco Evenepoel a vraiment tout donné à la fin de la sixième étape vers San Giacomo. Il a bravé froid et pluie, en compagnie notamment d'Egan Bernal et de Dan Martin. Il a terminé quatrième et s'est hissé à la deuxième place du classement général. Et cela mérite des félicitations chaleureuses de la part de João Almeida.

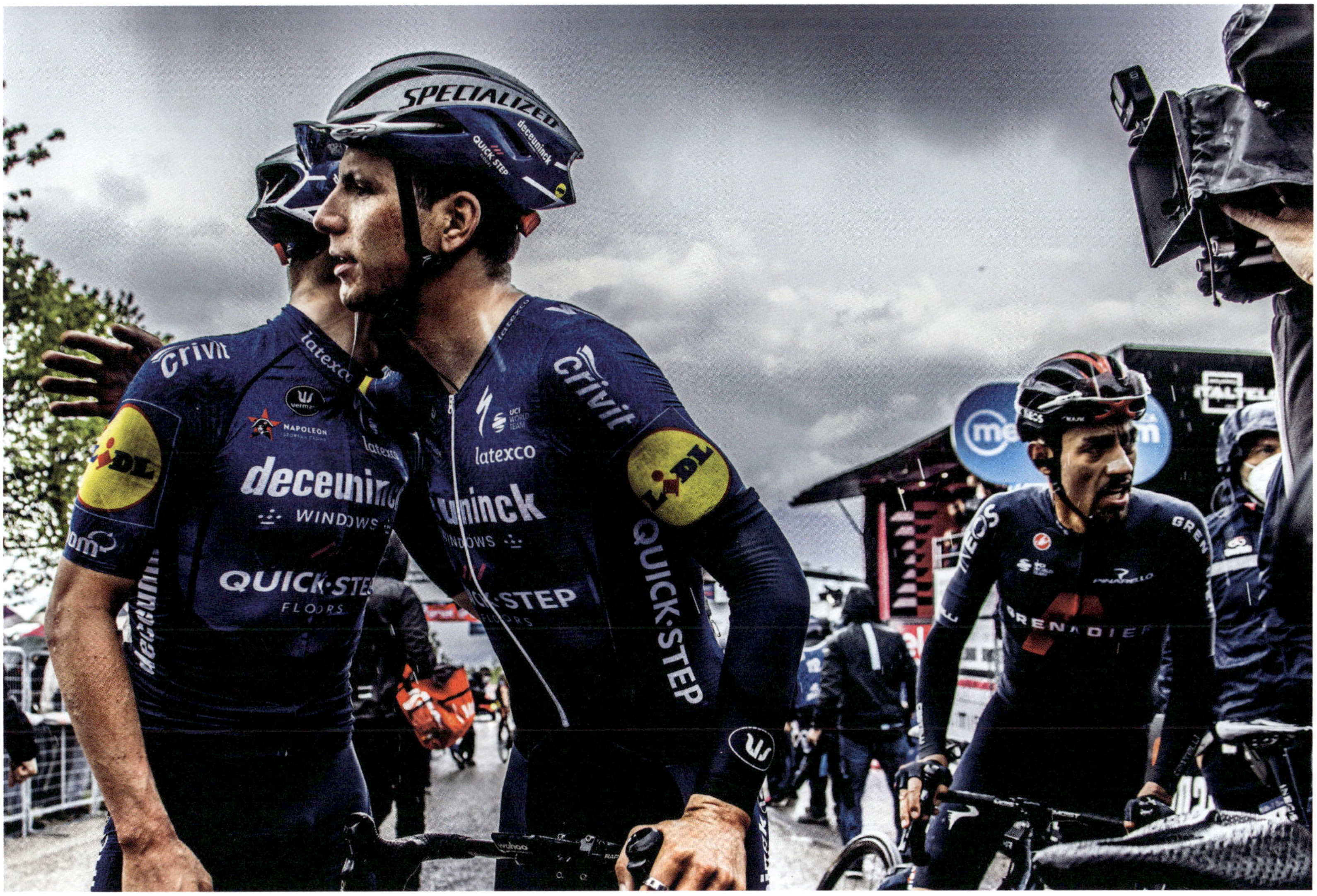

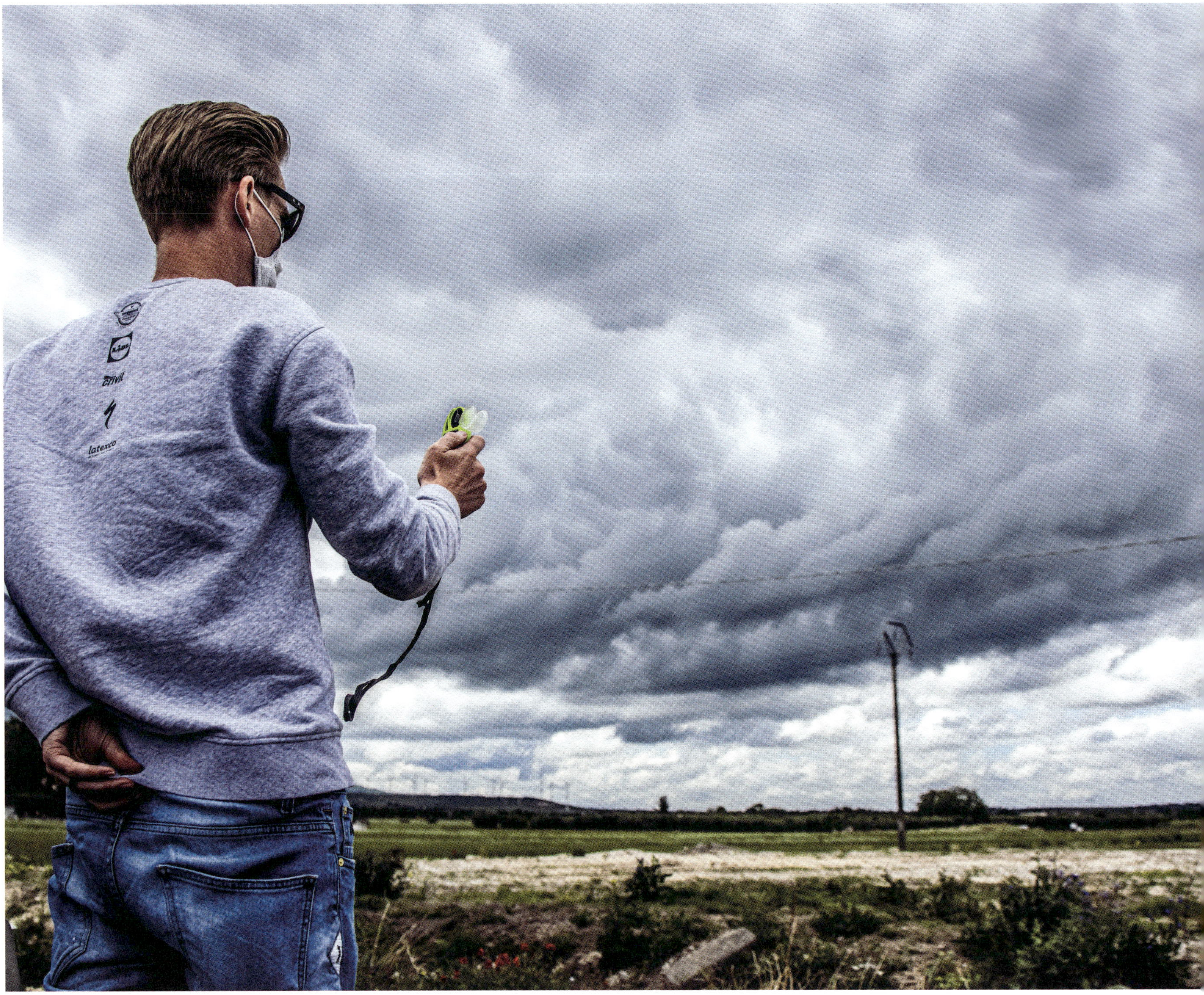

FOGGIA, 15.05.2021

Meten is weten. Trainer Koen Pelgrim is de verkenner van dienst. Hij rijdt een kwartier vóór het peloton het parcours op en... meet de wind. De snelheid, de richting, de wispelturigheid... Niets wordt aan het toeval overgelaten. Dit is topsport. David Bowie zong het al: *'Wild is the wind'*. Dat was niet anders tijdens de achtste rit van de Giro, van Foggia naar Guardia Sanframondi, net boven Napels. Het was de zuidelijkste rit van de Ronde van Italië dit jaar.

To measure is to know. Trainer Koen Pelgrim is the scout on duty. He rides onto the course 15 minutes before the peloton and measures the wind. The speed, the direction, its twists and turns... Nothing is left to chance. This is top-class sport. As David Bowie sang: "Wild is the wind". It was no different on the eighth stage of the Giro, from Foggia to Guardia Sanframondi, just above Naples. It was the southernmost stage of this year's Giro.

Mieux vaut prévenir que guérir. Koen Pelgrim, entraîneur de l'équipe est toujours vigilant. Il se rend sur la piste quinze minutes avant le peloton et... mesure le vent. Sa vitesse, sa direction, ses caprices... Rien n'est laissé au hasard. C'est du sport de haut niveau, après tout. Comme le chantait David Bowie : « *Wild is the wind* ». Il n'en a pas été autrement lors de la huitième étape du Giro, de Foggia à Guardia Sanframondi, un peu au nord de Naples. C'était l'étape la plus au sud du Tour d'Italie de cette année.

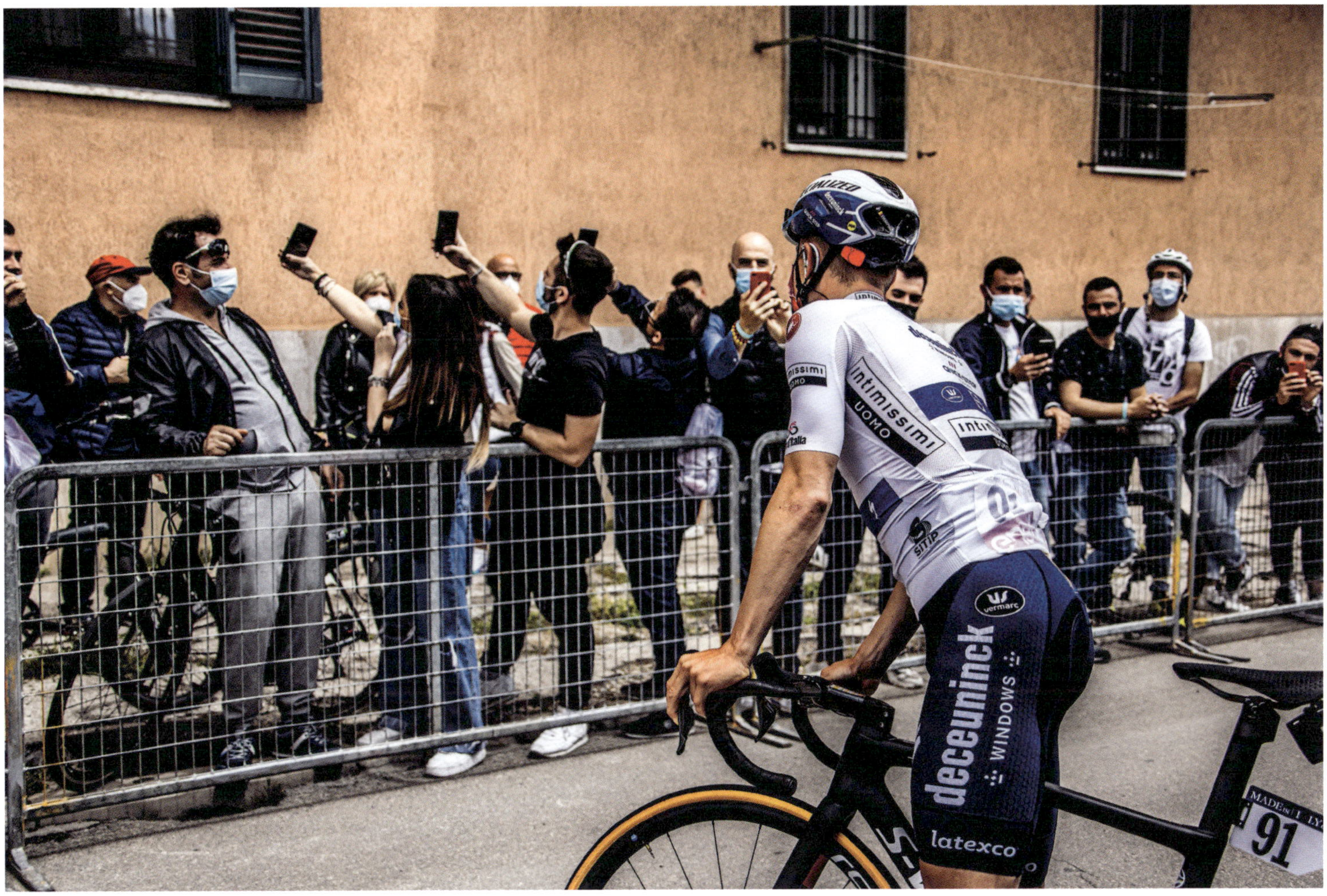
intimissimi
UOMO
deceuninck
WINDOWS
latexco
91

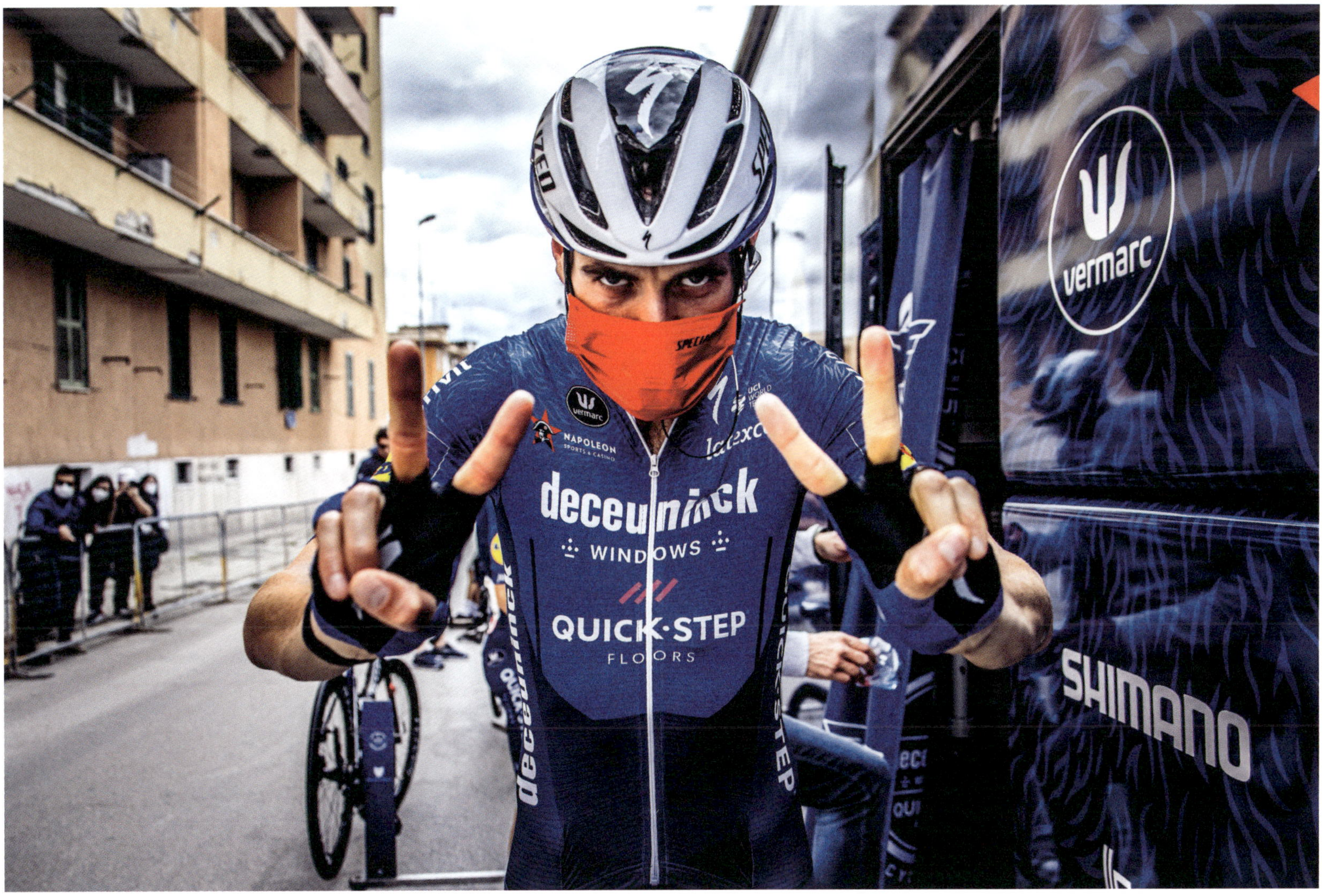
vermarc
deceuninck
WINDOWS
QUICK·STEP
FLOORS
SHIMANO

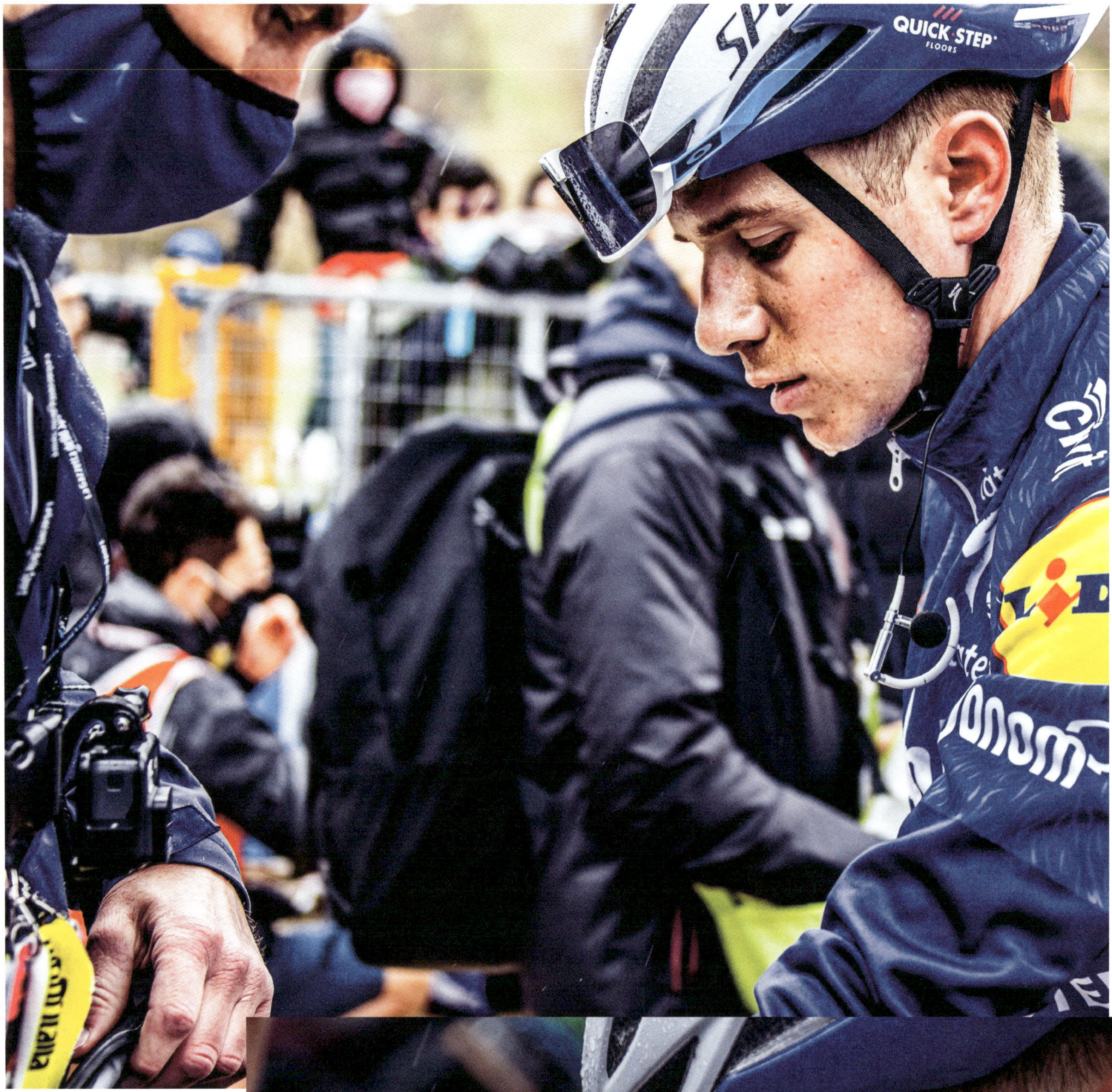
QUICK STEP
FLOORS

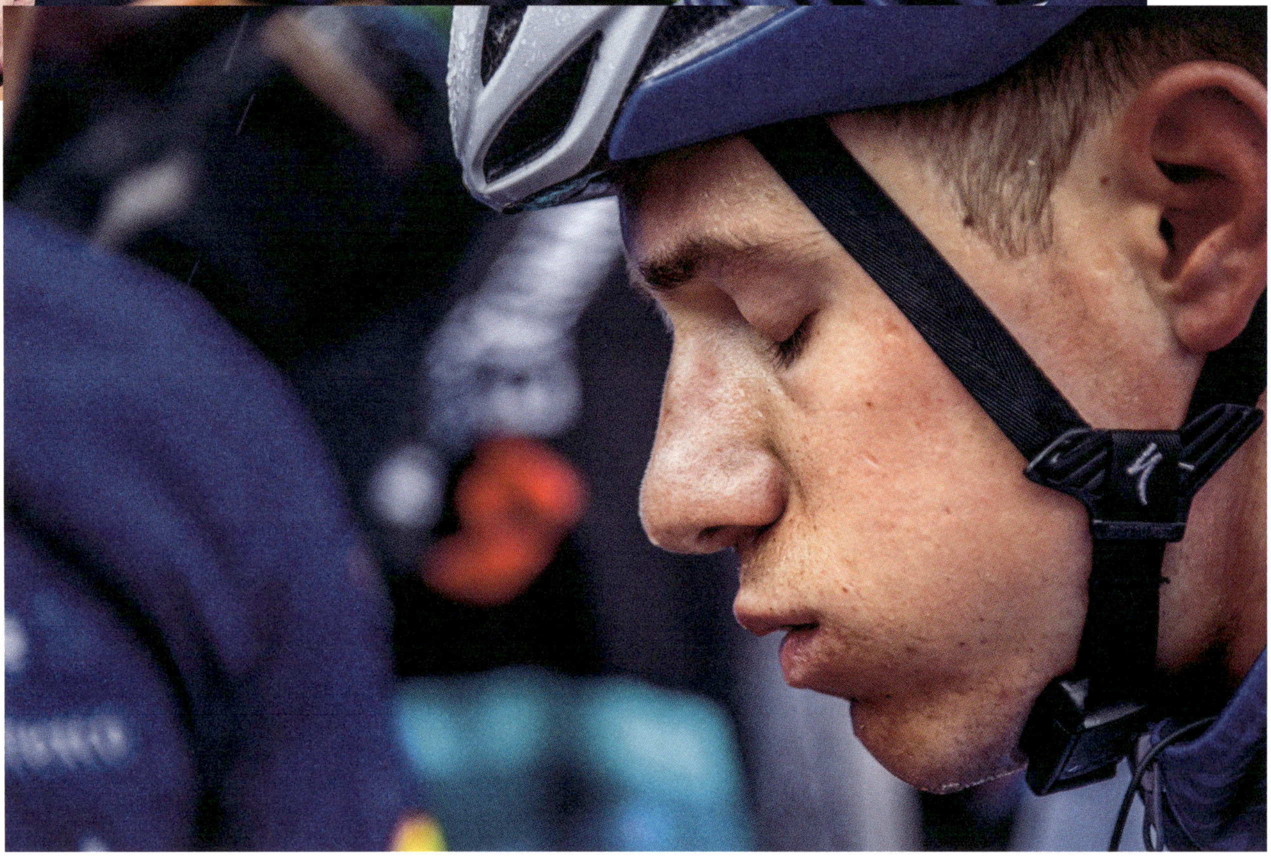

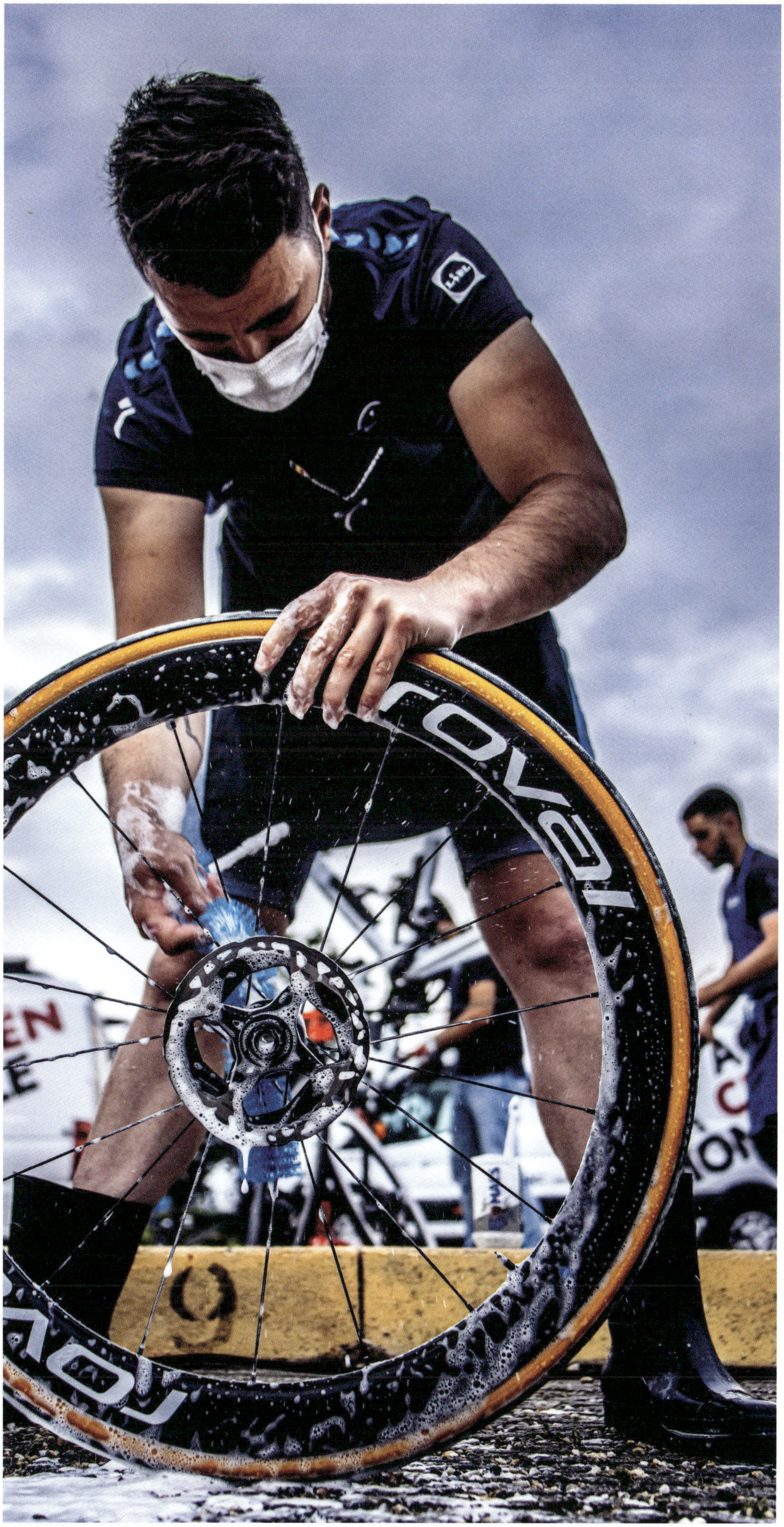

Elke dag opnieuw, een hele karwei. Elke koersdag van het jaar, en dat zijn er veel. Het hoort bij een professionele wielerploeg. Uit respect voor elkaar, uit respect voor de renners, én uit respect voor de sponsors. Elke dag opnieuw wordt elke fiets tot het kleinste onderdeel gereinigd, elke wagen gewassen en gestofzuigd, technisch gecontroleerd en netjes opgesteld. Voorwaar een stevig karwei, zoals mecanicien Lounes Verschaeve hier pittig illustreert.

Every day is a new challenge. Every race day of the year pushes the team further. It's part of being in a professional cycling team. Out of respect for each other, for the riders, and for the sponsors. Each day, all of the bikes are meticulously cleaned, down to the last detail; every car is washed and vacuumed, technically checked, and neatly set up. A tough job indeed, as mechanic Lounes Verschaeve vividly illustrates.

Un travail difficile, jour après jour. Course après course, et il y en a beaucoup. Il fait partie d'une équipe cycliste professionnelle. Par respect pour les autres, par respect pour les coureurs et par respect pour les sponsors. Chaque jour, l'équipe nettoie soigneusement chacun de vélos, passe l'aspirateur dans les voitures, les nettoie et vérifie que tout est en ordre. C'est un travail minutieux et très difficile, comme nous le montre ici le mécanicien Lounes Verschaeve.

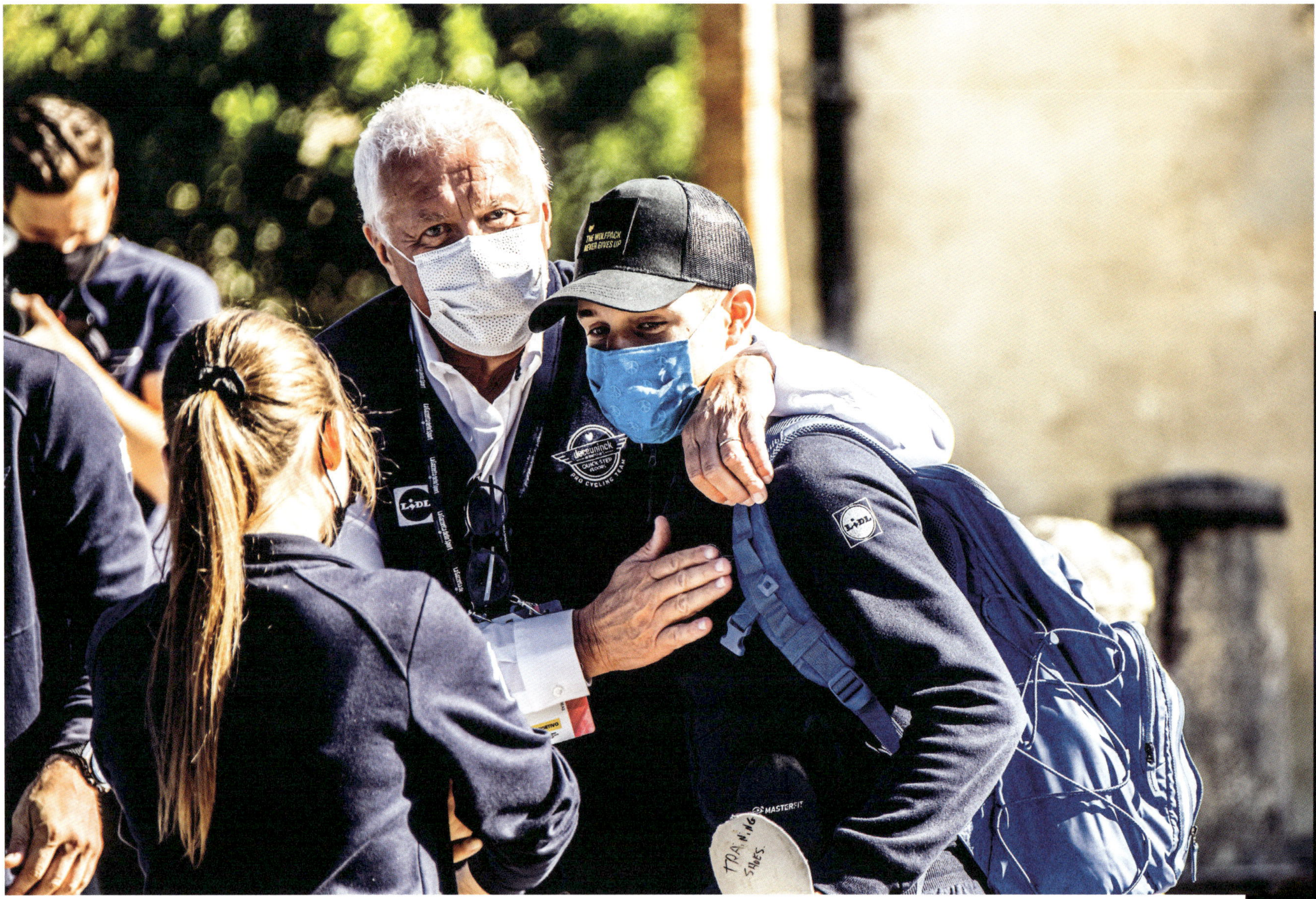

POGGIBONSI, 20.05.2021

Patrick Lefevere ontfermt zich over Remco Evenepoel aan de ochtend van de twaalfde rit, van Siena naar Bagno di Romana. Patrick nuanceert: 'Remco staat zevende. Eddy Merckx is in zijn eerste Giro in 1967 ook pas negende geworden.' Met de rug naar de camera, persverantwoordelijke Pauline Farazijn.

Patrick Lefevere takes care of Remco Evenepoel the morning before the 12th stage, from Siena to Bagno di Romana. He gives some perspective: "Remco came in seventh. Eddy Merckx also only finished ninth in his first Giro in 1967." Shown with her back to the camera is press officer Pauline Farazijn.

Patrick Lefevere est aux côtés de Remco Evenepoel, le matin avant la douzième étape, de Siena à Bagno di Romana. Il relative: « Remco est septième. Eddy Merckx n'a terminé que neuvième lors de son premier Giro en 1967 ». Dos à la caméra, Pauline Farazijn, attachée de presse.

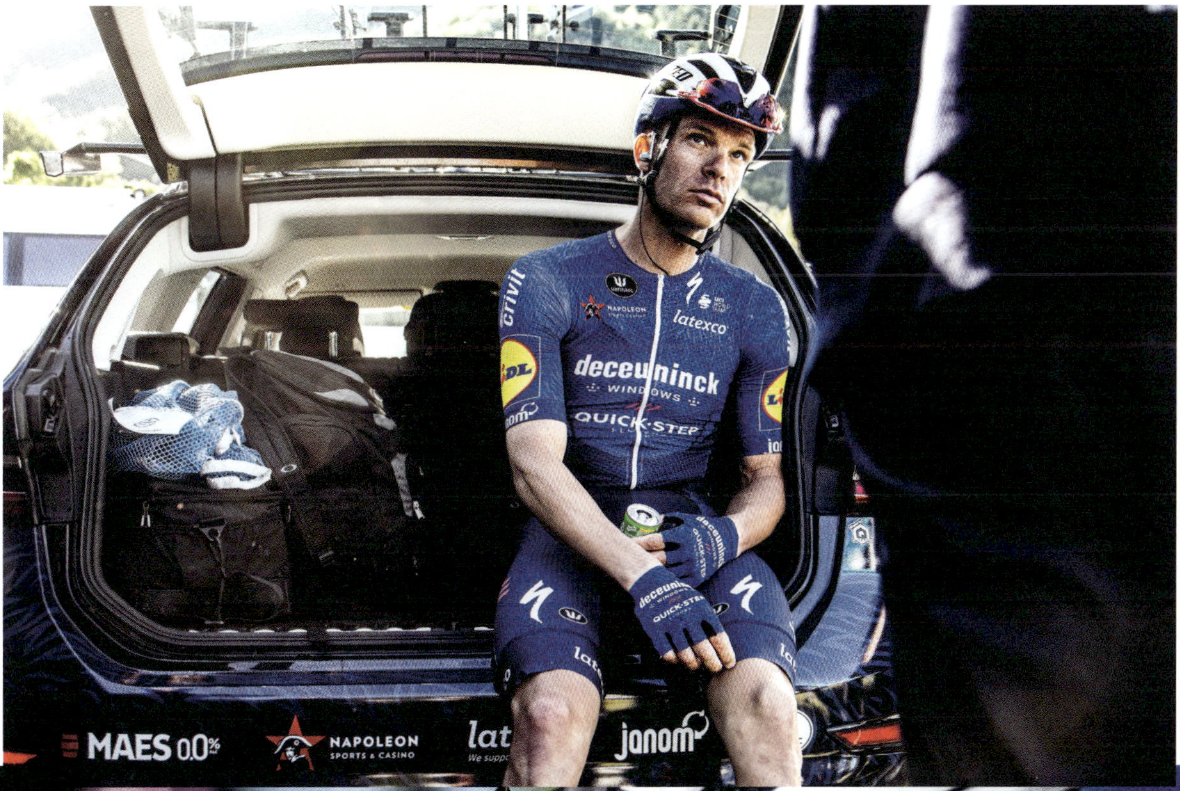
crivit
latexco
deceuninck
WINDOWS
QUICK-STEP
MAES 0.0%
NAPOLEON
SPORTS & CASINO
janom

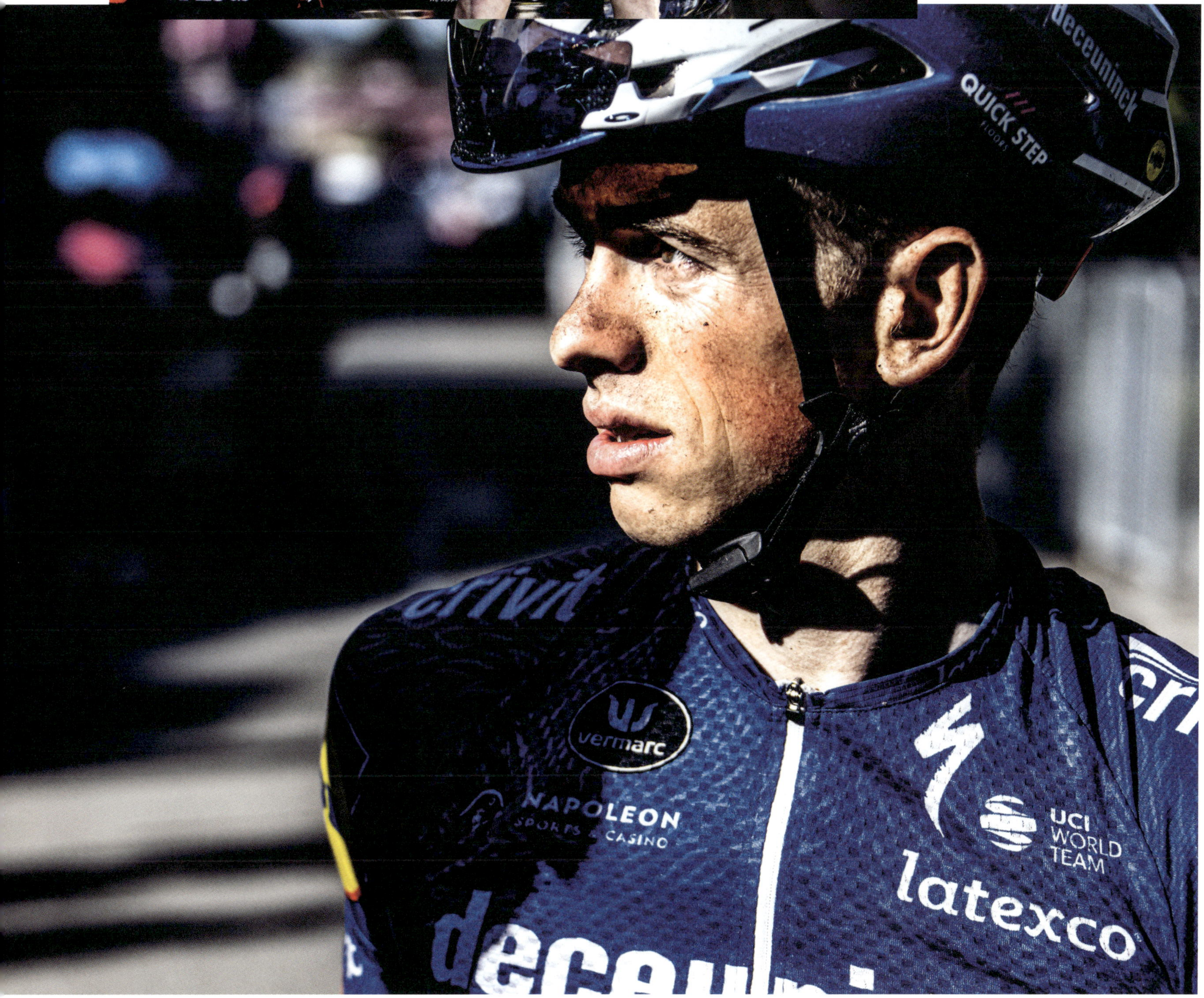
deceuninck
QUICK STEP
crivit
vermarc
NAPOLEON
SPORTS & CASINO
UCI
WORLD
TEAM
latexco

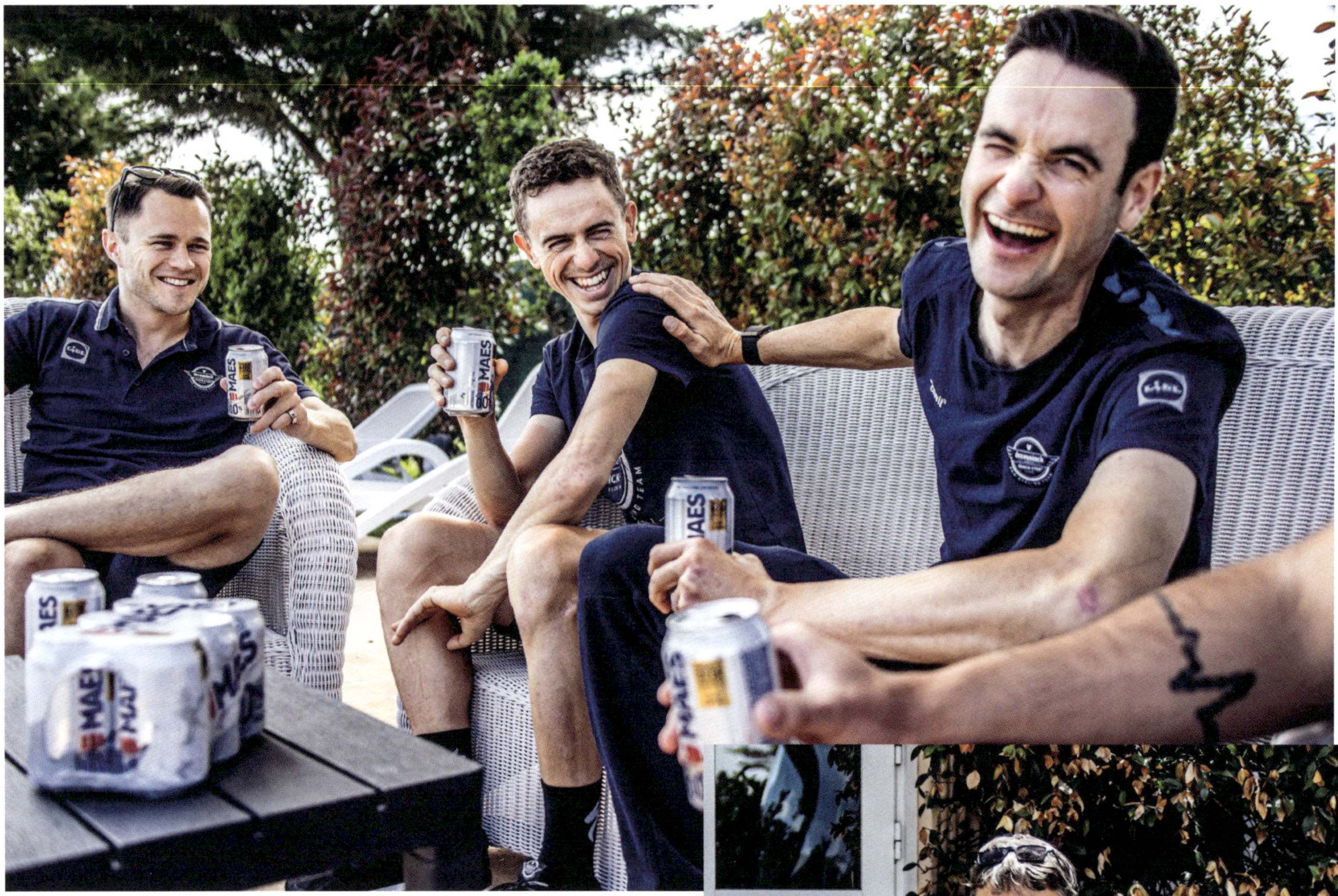
MAES

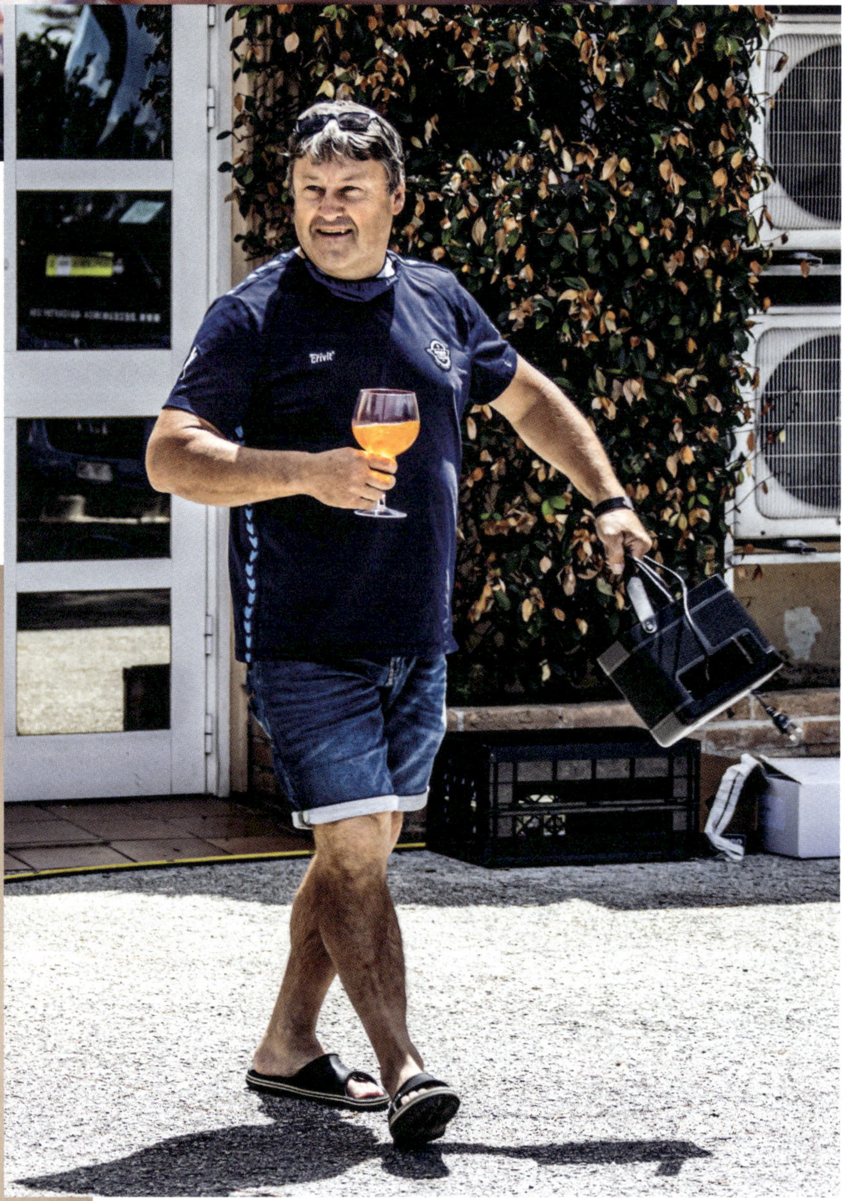

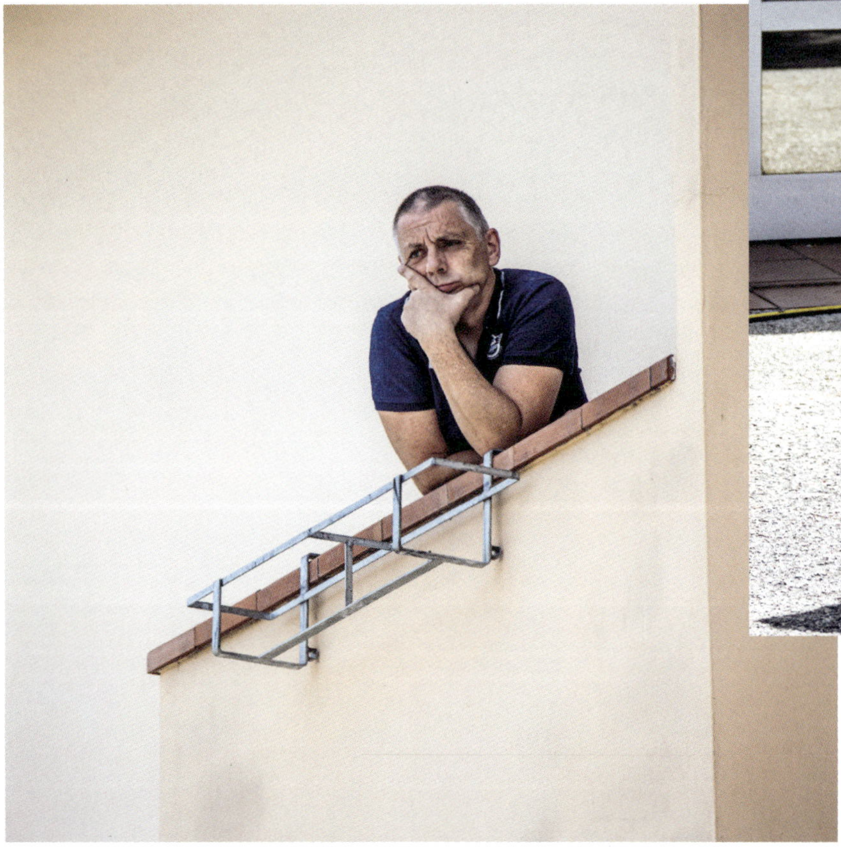

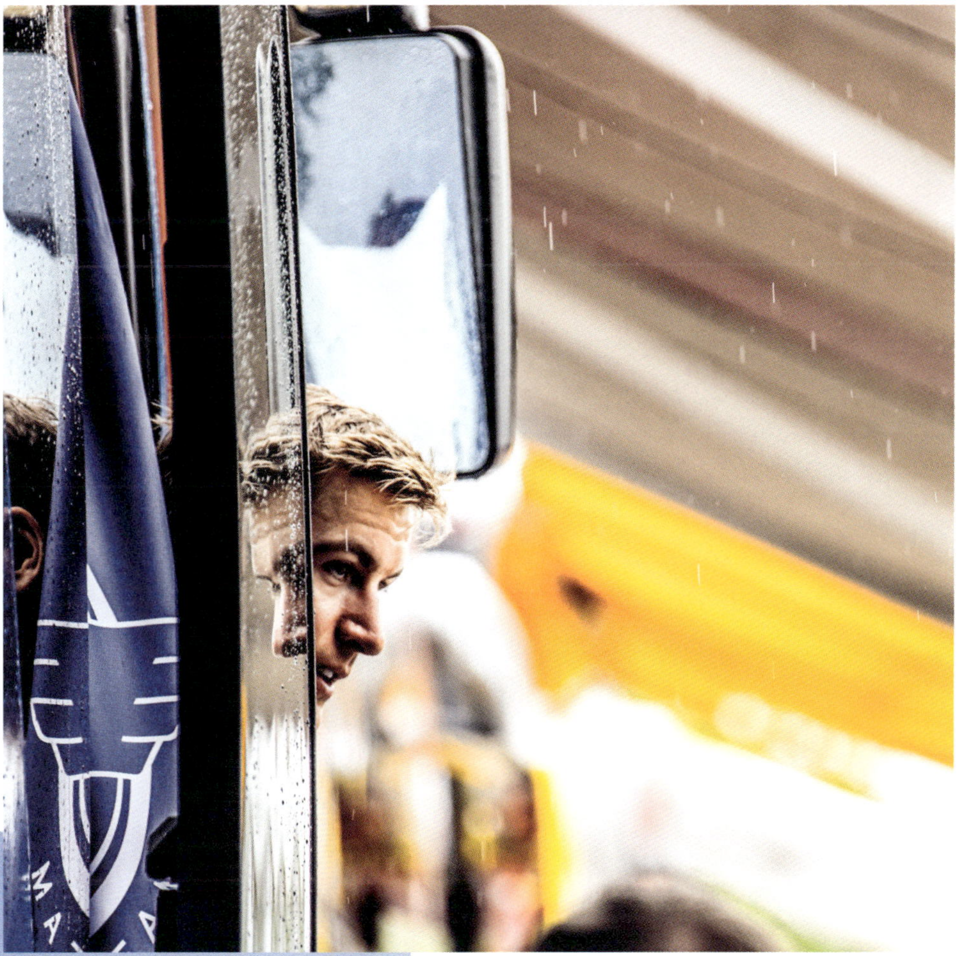

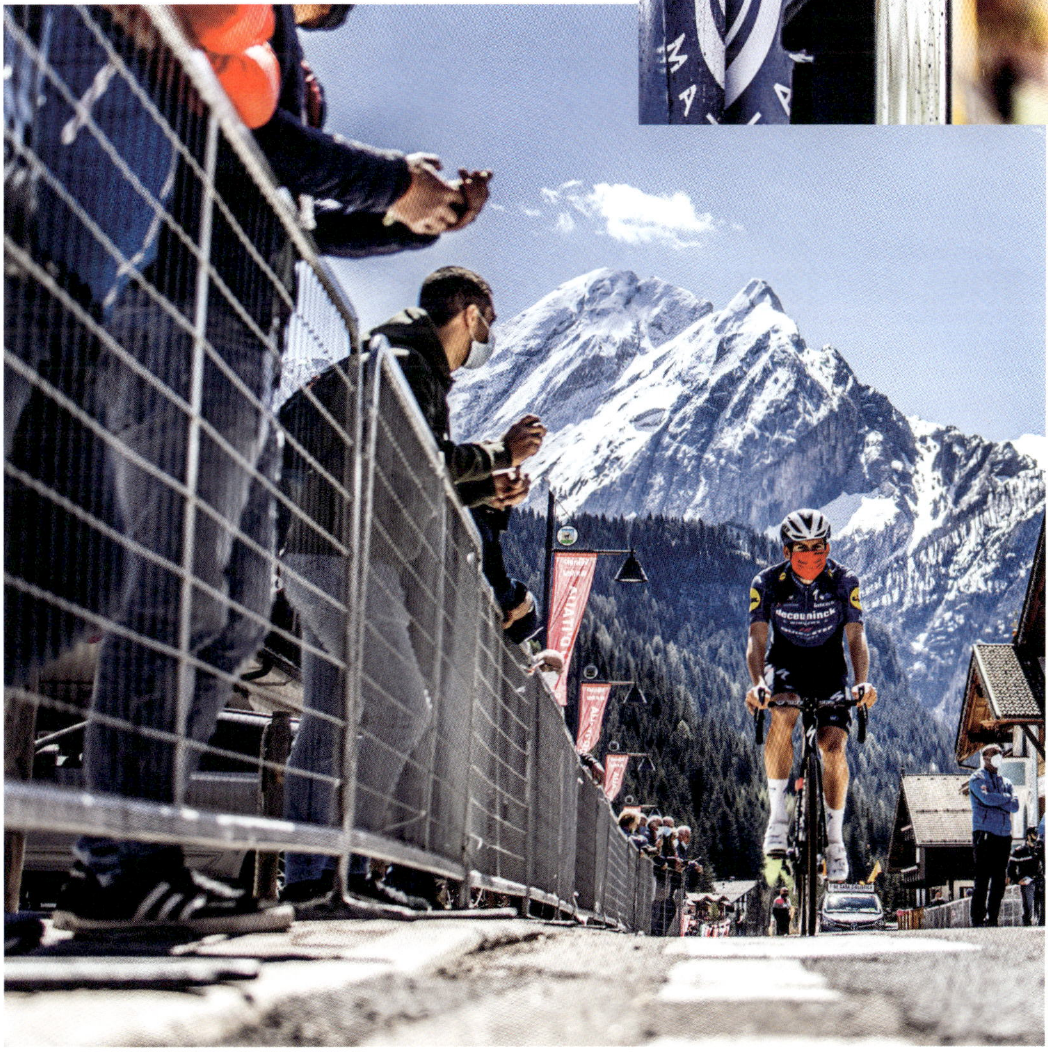

CANAZEI, 26.05.2021

Mikkel Honoré, op weg naar de startpresentatie van de zeventiende rit in Canazei. De karavaan trekt naar de aankomst, 195 kilometer verder, boven op de Sega di Ala. In de achtergrond de Italiaanse Alpen.

Mikkel Honoré on his way to the start presentation of the 17th stage in Canazei. The group moves towards the finish, 195 km away, on top of the Sega di Ala. The Italian Alps are shown in the background.

Mikkel Honoré, sur le chemin de la présentation du départ de la 17e étape à Canazei. La caravane progresse vers l'arrivée, 195 km plus loin, au sommet de la Sega di Ala. En arrière-plan, les Alpes italiennes.

SEGA DI ALA, 26.05.2021

João Almeida eindigt tweede in de rit, op 13 seconden van Dan Martin.

Iljo Keisse (links) en Mikkel Honoré (rechts) ontfermen zich over Remco Evenepoel. Ze bereiken samen de eindstreep van de zeventiende rit, in de buik van het grote peloton. Daar zou voor Remco ook de eindstreep liggen van de Giro. Veel ervaring rijker.

De mooie kant van het leven van een renner en een masseur. Rudy Pollet kneedt de spieren van Mikkel Honoré na de zeventiende etappe van de Giro. Vandaag geen donker hotelletje, maar een prachtig panorama op de wijnranken van de Trentino-regio.

João Almeida finished second in that stage, 13 seconds behind Dan Martin.

Iljo Keisse (left) and Mikkel Honoré (right) take care of Remco Evenepoel. They reached the finish line of the 17th stage together, in the middle of the peloton. Remco would also reach the finish line of the Giro there. The Giro offers so much experience.

The beautiful side of the life of a rider and a masseur. Rudy Pollet massages Mikkel Honoré's muscles after the 17th stage of the Giro. No dark hotel this time, but a beautiful panorama on the vineyards of the Trentino region.

João Almeida a terminé deuxième de cette étape, 13 secondes derrière Dan Martin.

Iljo Keisse (à gauche) et Mikkel Honoré (à droite) encadrent Remco Evenepoel. Ils atteignent la ligne d'arrivée de la 17e étape ensemble, au milieu du peloton. Pour Remco, cela s'avérait également être la dernière ligne d'arrivée du Giro. Une expérience beaucoup plus riche.

La belle vie d'un cycliste et d'un masseur. Rudy Pollet aide les muscles de Mikkel Honoré à se remettre de la 17e étape du Giro. Plutôt que dans une pièce sombre d'un hôtel, le massage se fait à ciel ouvert, avec un beau panorama sur les vignobles de la région du Trentin.

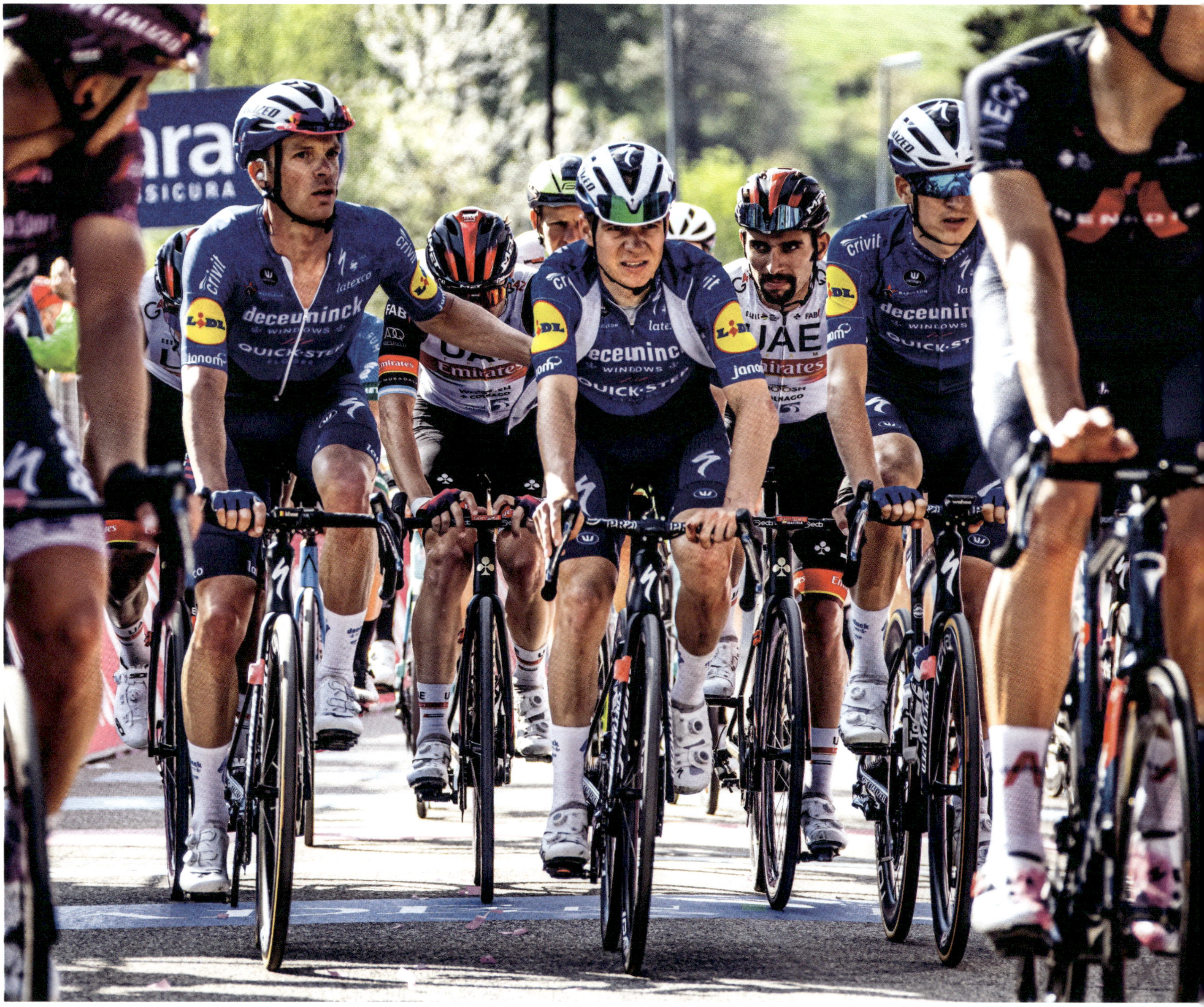

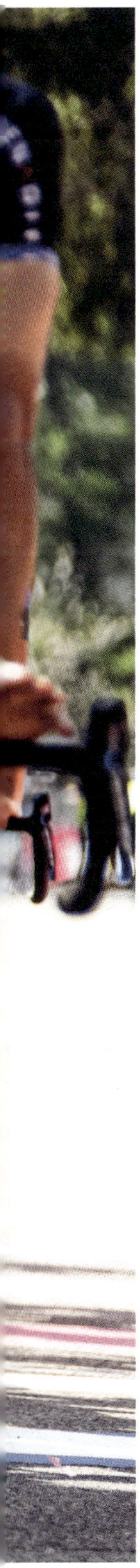

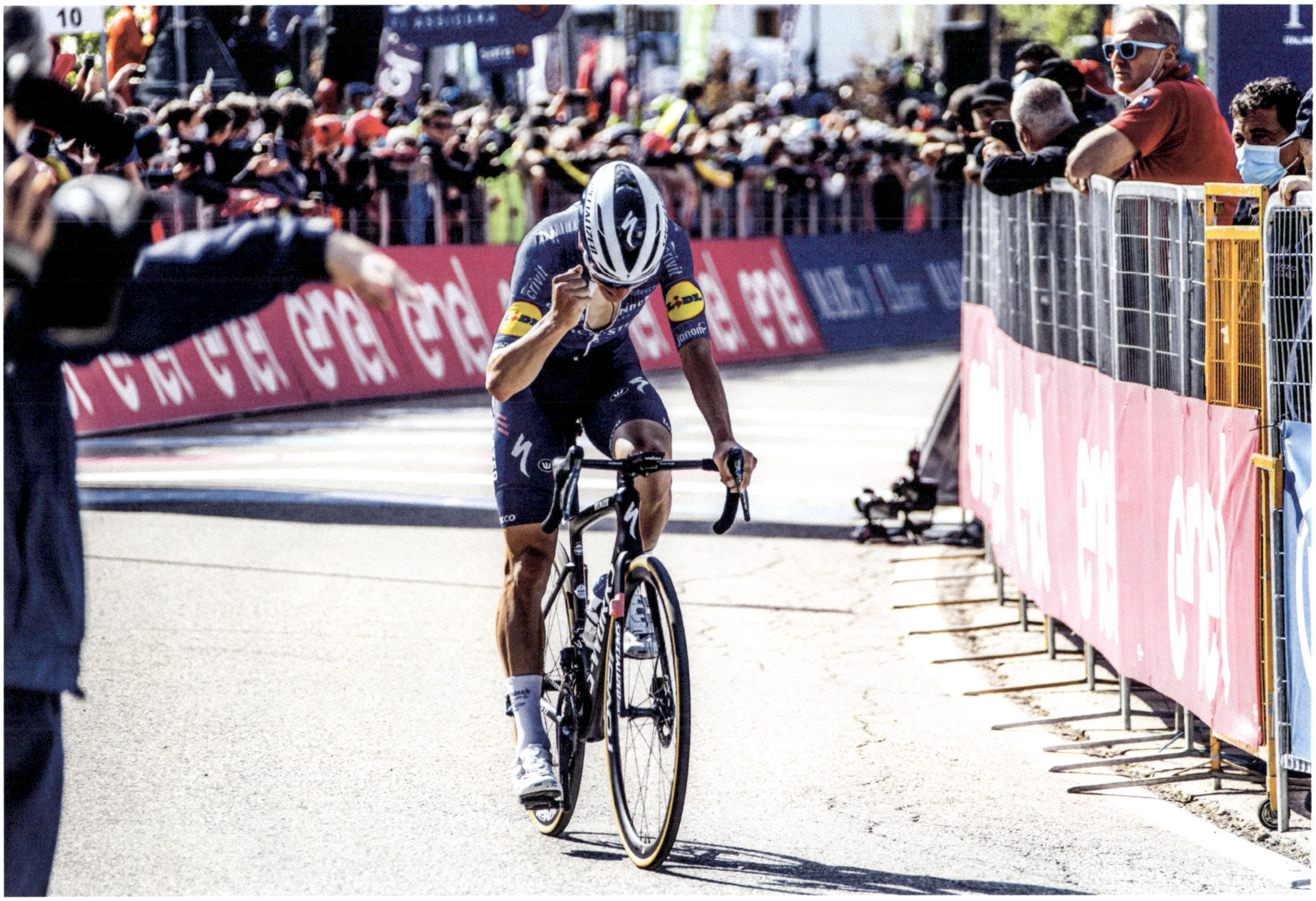
10
enel
LIDL

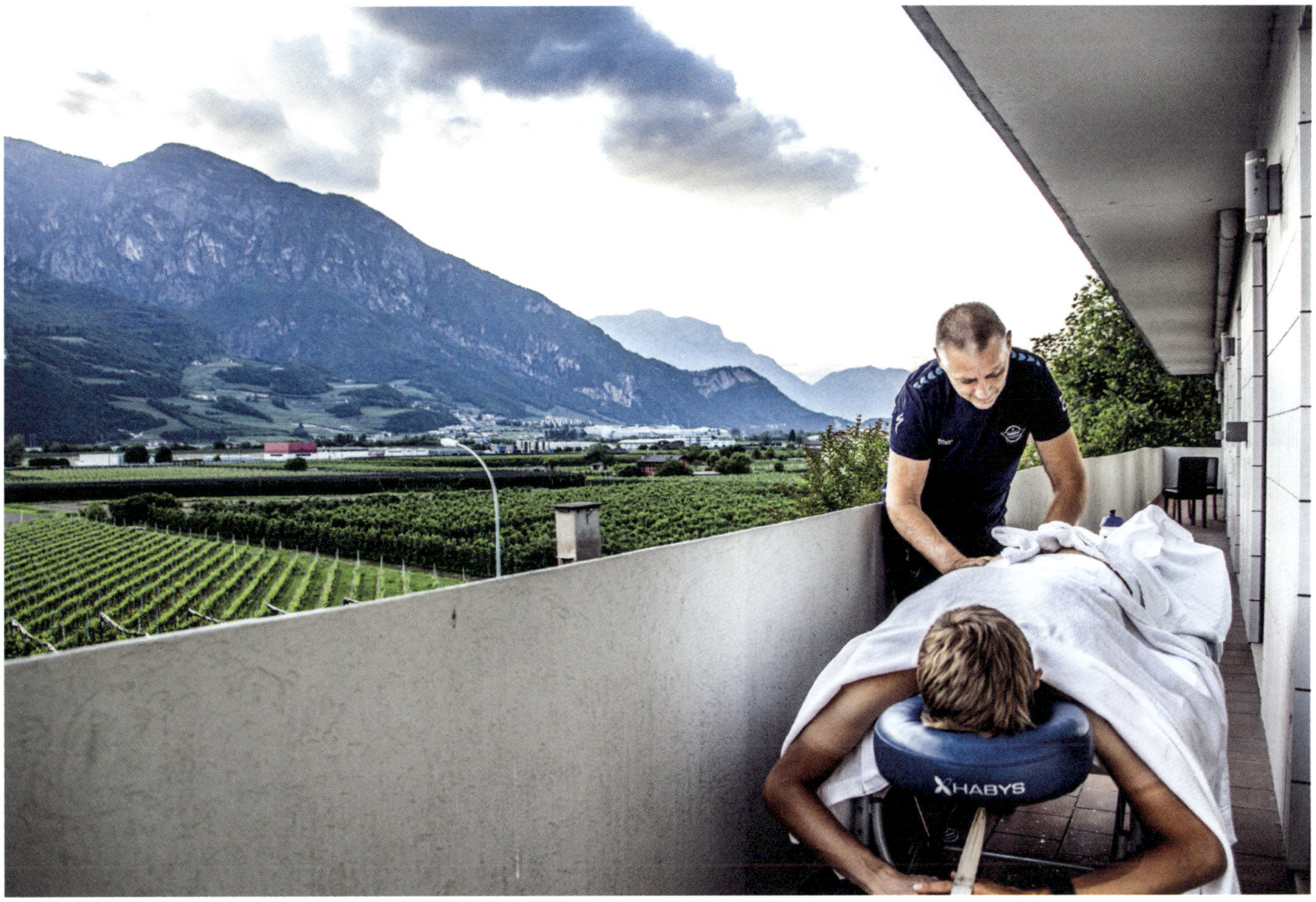
HABYS

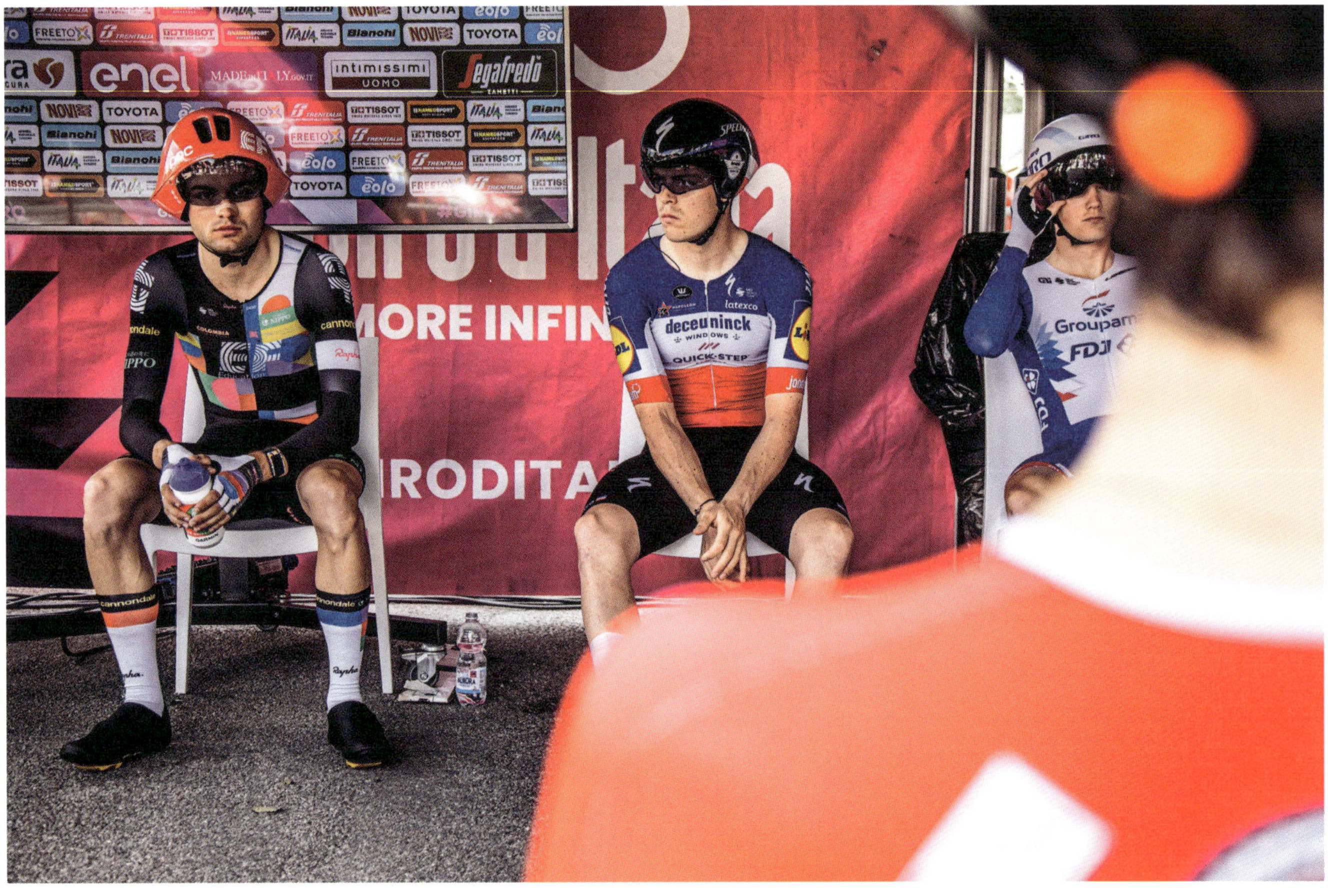
enel
TOYOTA
Bianchi
intimissimi
UOMO
Segafredo
MORE INFIN
IRODITA
deceuninck
WINDOWS
QUICK-STEP
Groupama
FDJ

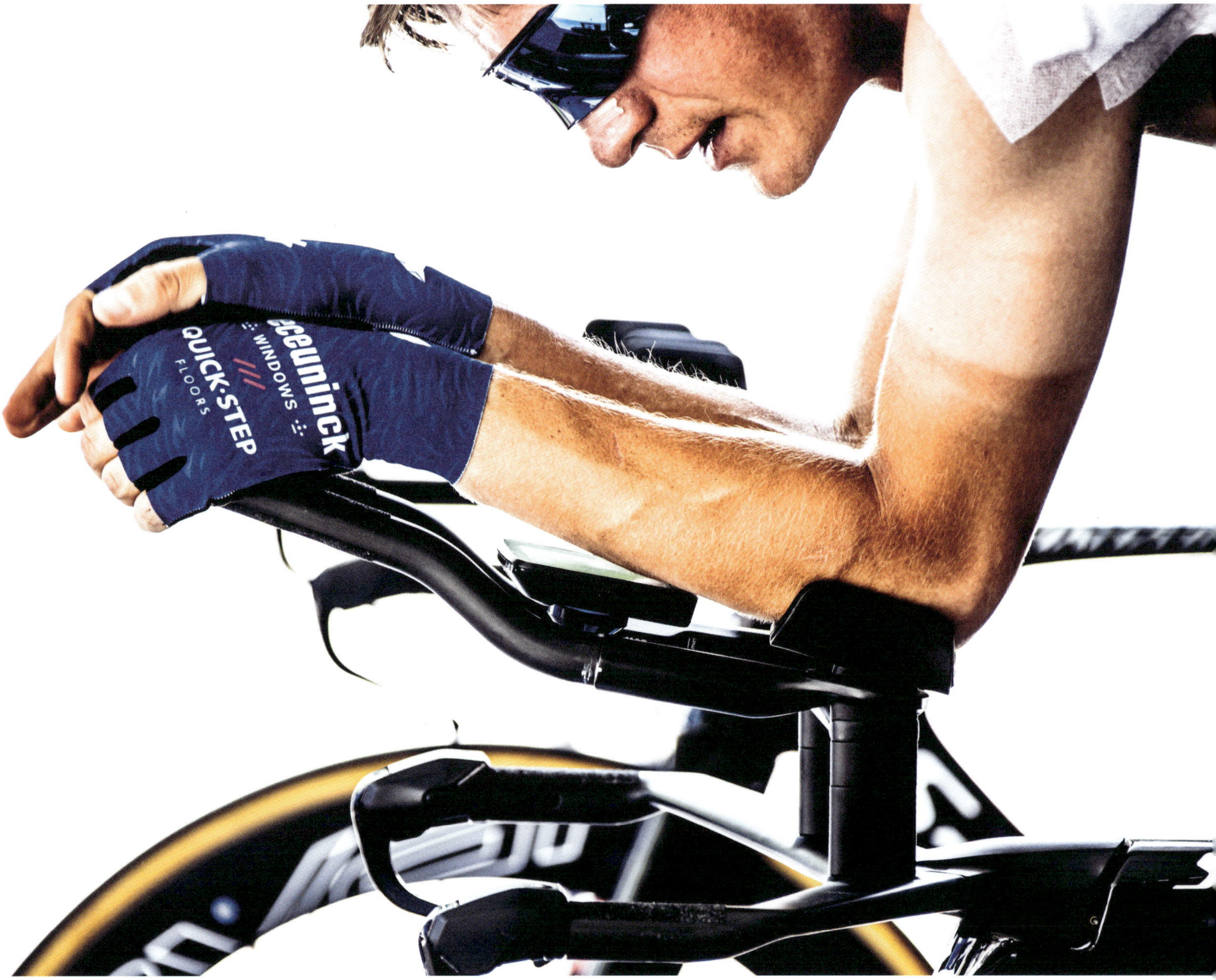
deceuninck
WINDOWS
QUICK-STEP
FLOORS

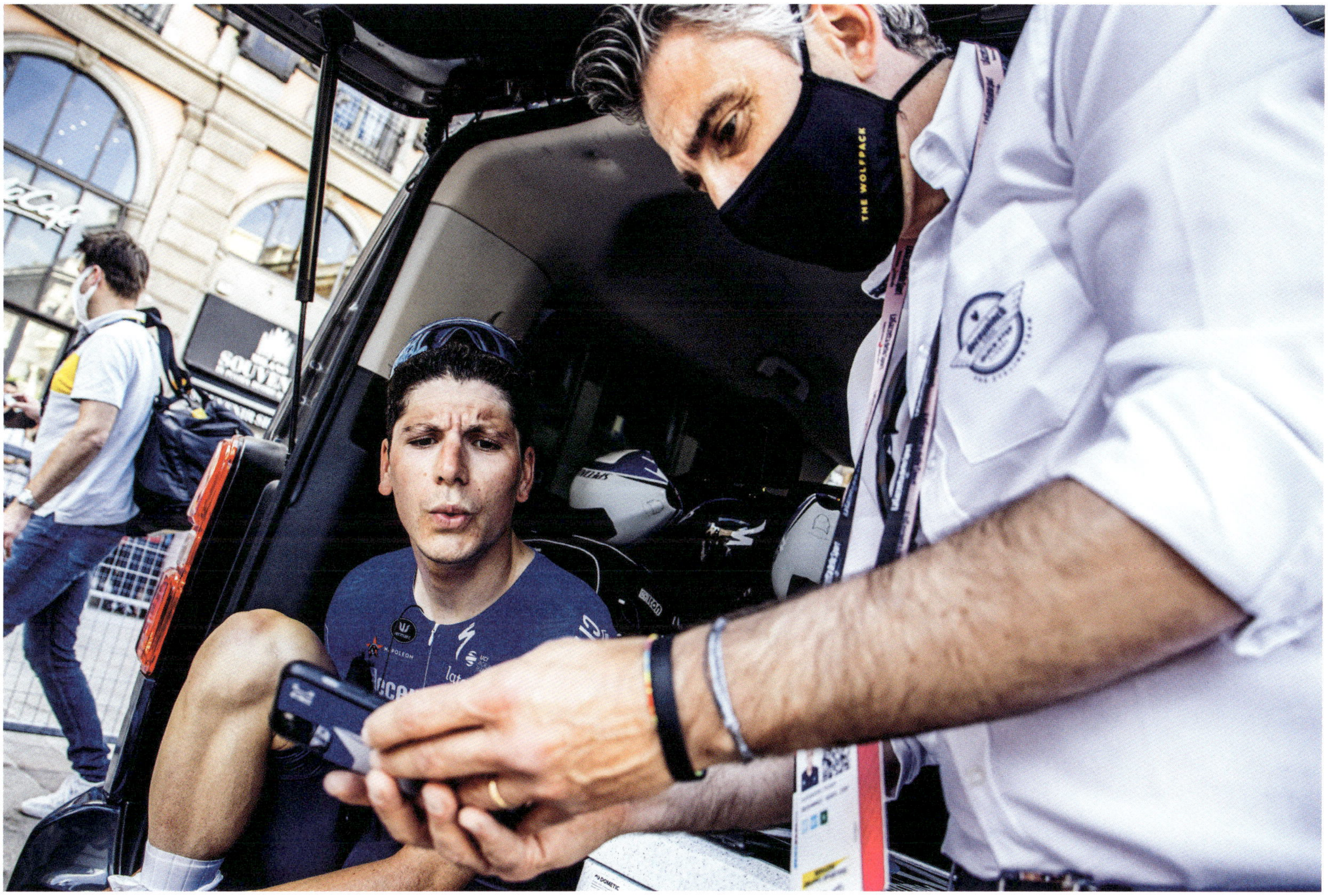

MILANO, 30.05.2021

João Almeida eindigde vijfde in de tijdrit naar Milaan. Hij wint nog twee plaatsen in het eindklassement en eindigt de Ronde van Italië als zesde.

João Almeida finished fifth in the Milan time trial. He gained two more places in the final classification and concluded the Giro d'Italia in sixth place.

João Almeida a terminé cinquième dans le contre-la-montre de Milan. Il gagne deux autres places au classement final et termine le Tour d'Italie en sixième position. ▲

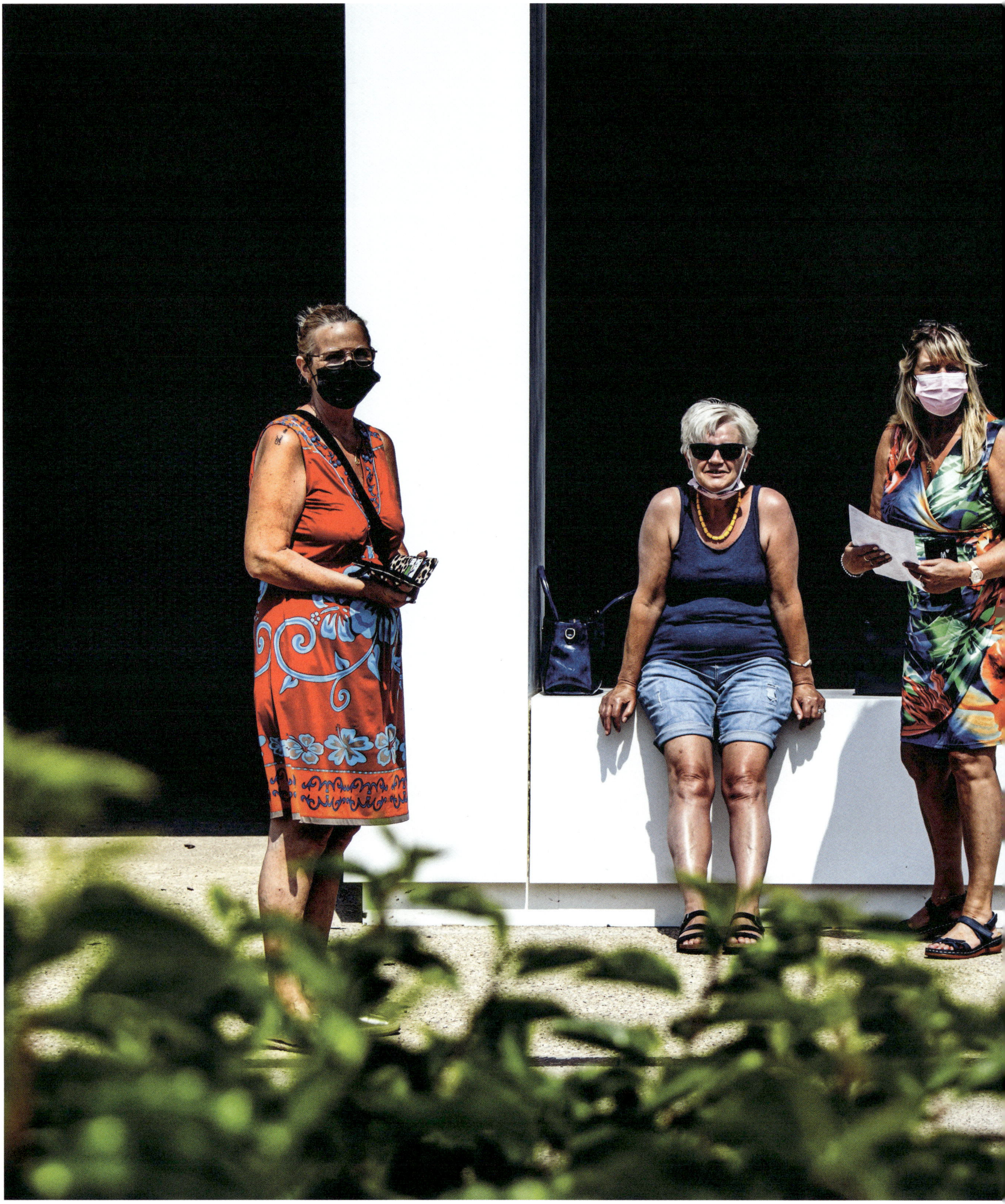

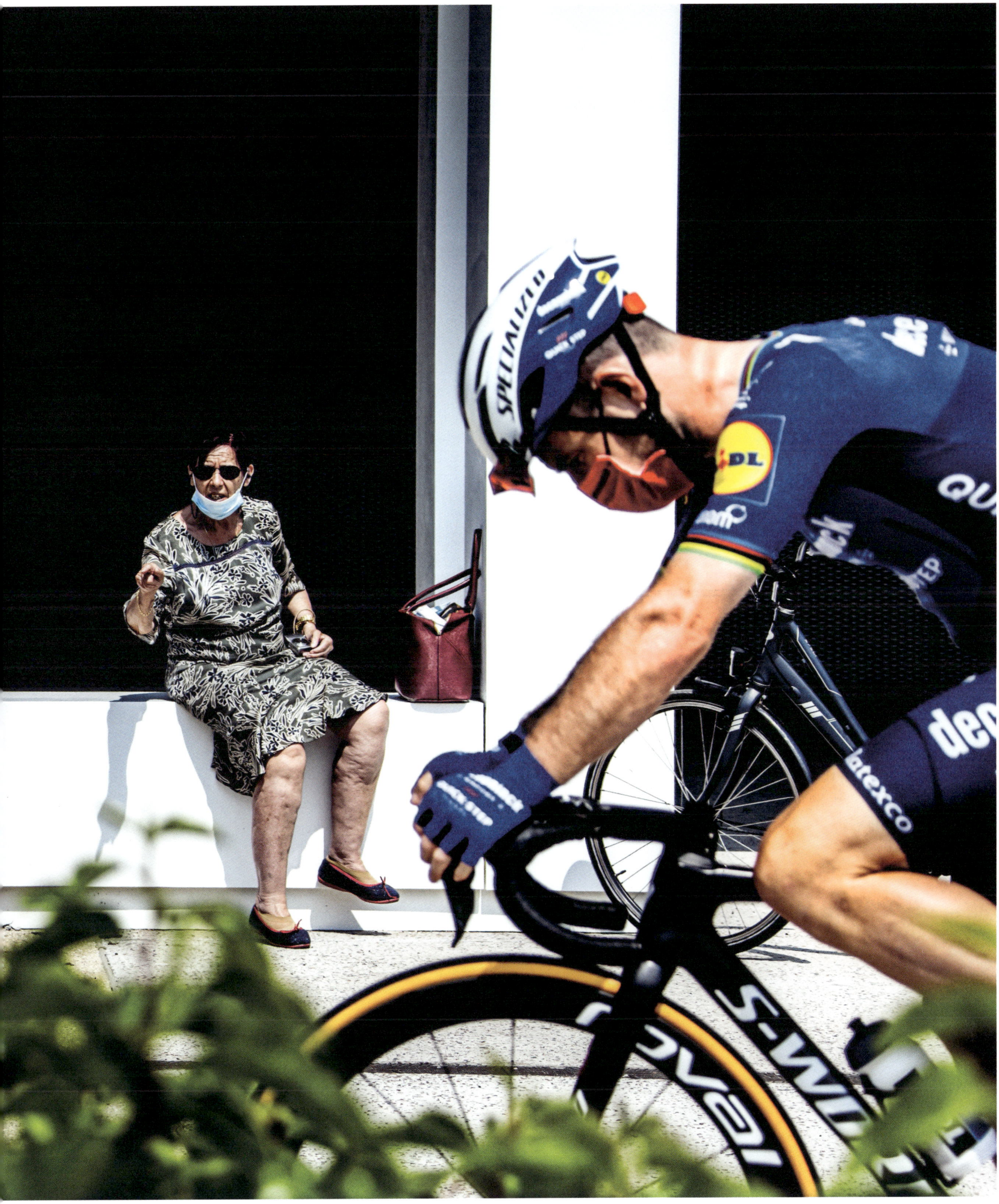
SPECIALIZED
latexco

MAARKEDAL, 09.06.2021

Remco Evenepoel heeft de Giro verteerd, zijn conditie groeit naar het beste niveau. Hij keurt zijn collega's in de jacht op Robbe Ghys. Links Remco, centraal Victor Campenaerts met Caleb Ewan tussen beide heren in.

Remco Evenepoel has digested the Giro, his fitness is improving to its optimal level. He pushes his companions in the hunt for Robbe Ghys. Remco on the left, Victor Campenaerts in the center with Caleb Ewan between them.

Remco Evenepoel s'est bien remis du Giro et il est au top de sa forme. Il teste ses coéquipiers lors de la poursuite de Robbe Ghys. Remco à gauche, Victor Campenaerts à droite, et Caleb Ewan entre les deux.

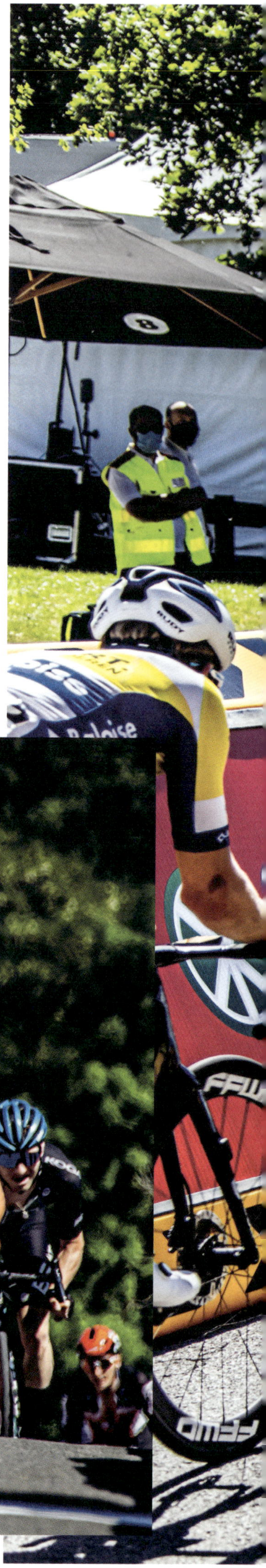

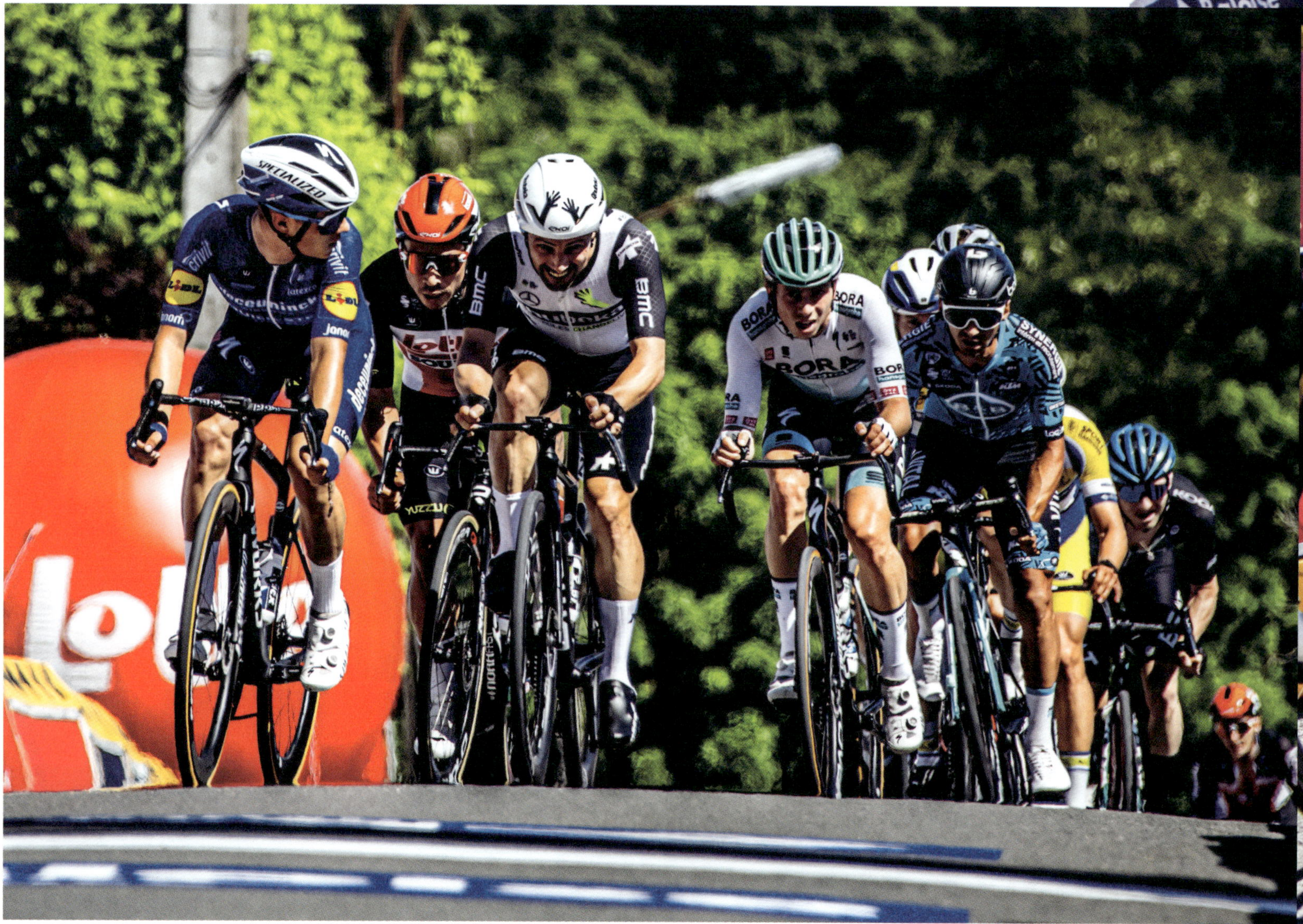

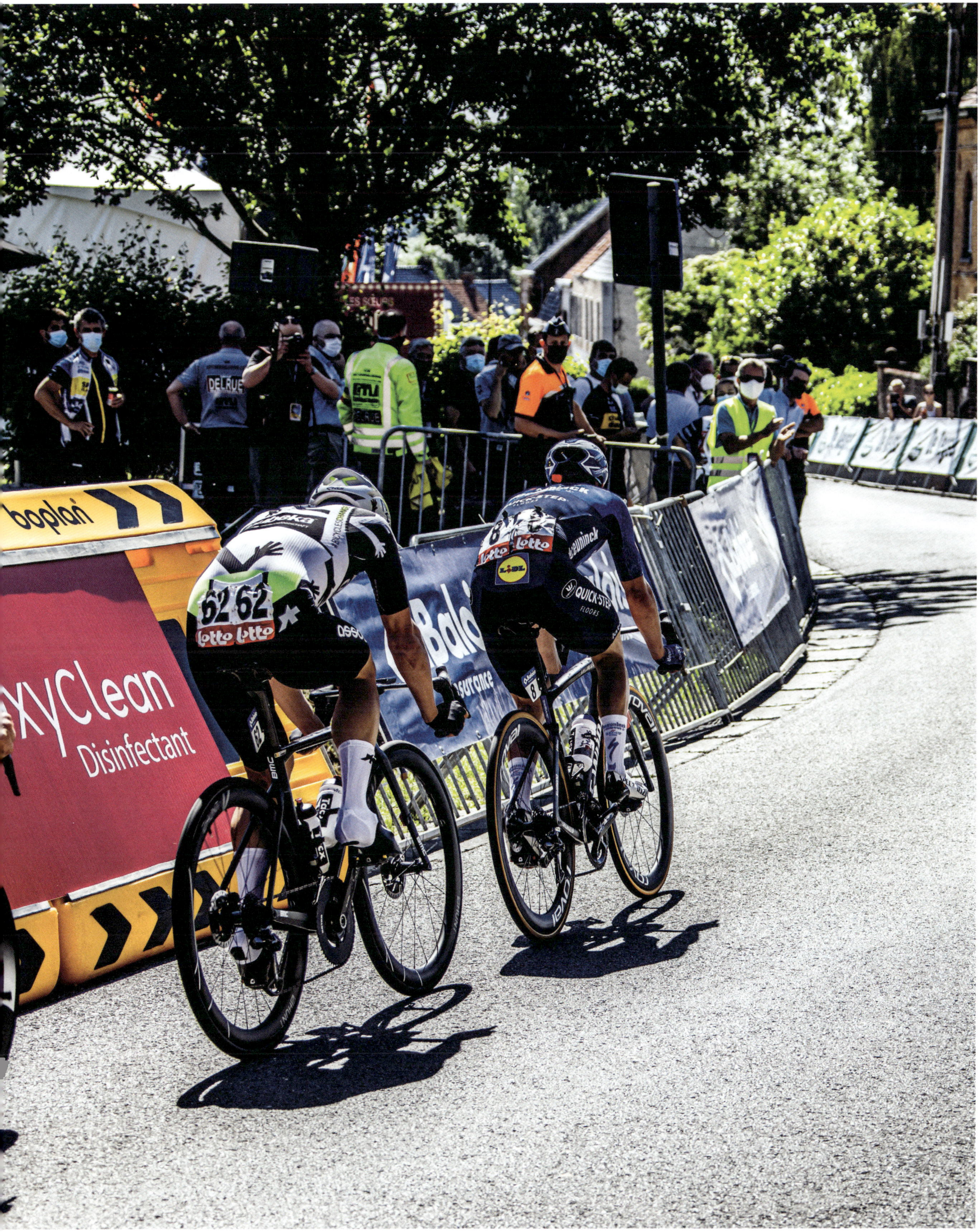
boplan
xyClean
Disinfectant

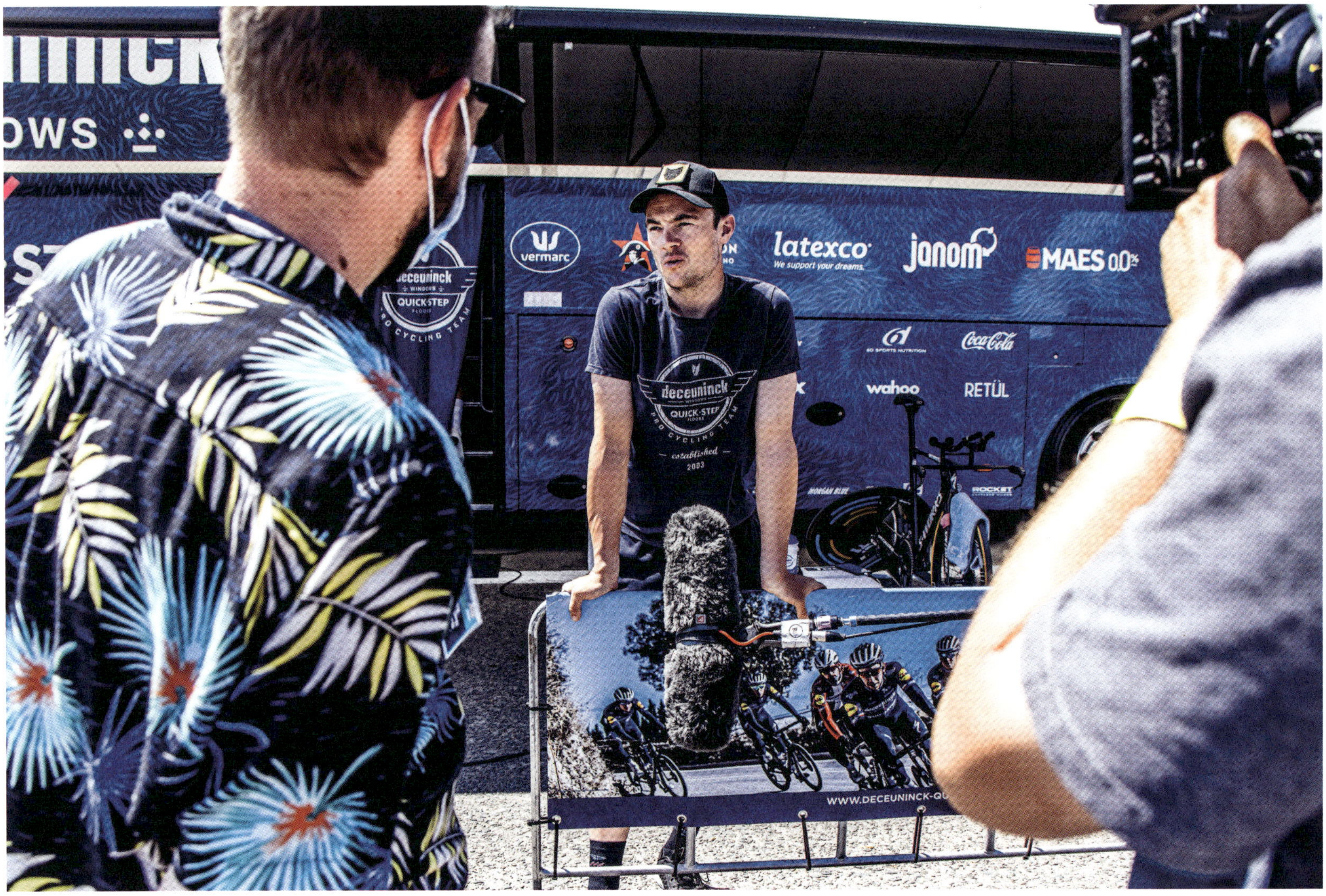
vermarc
latexco
We support your dreams.
janom
MAES 0.0%
Coca-Cola
wahoo
RETÜL
deceuninck
QUICK-STEP
PRO CYCLING TEAM
established
2003
WWW.DECEUNINCK-QU

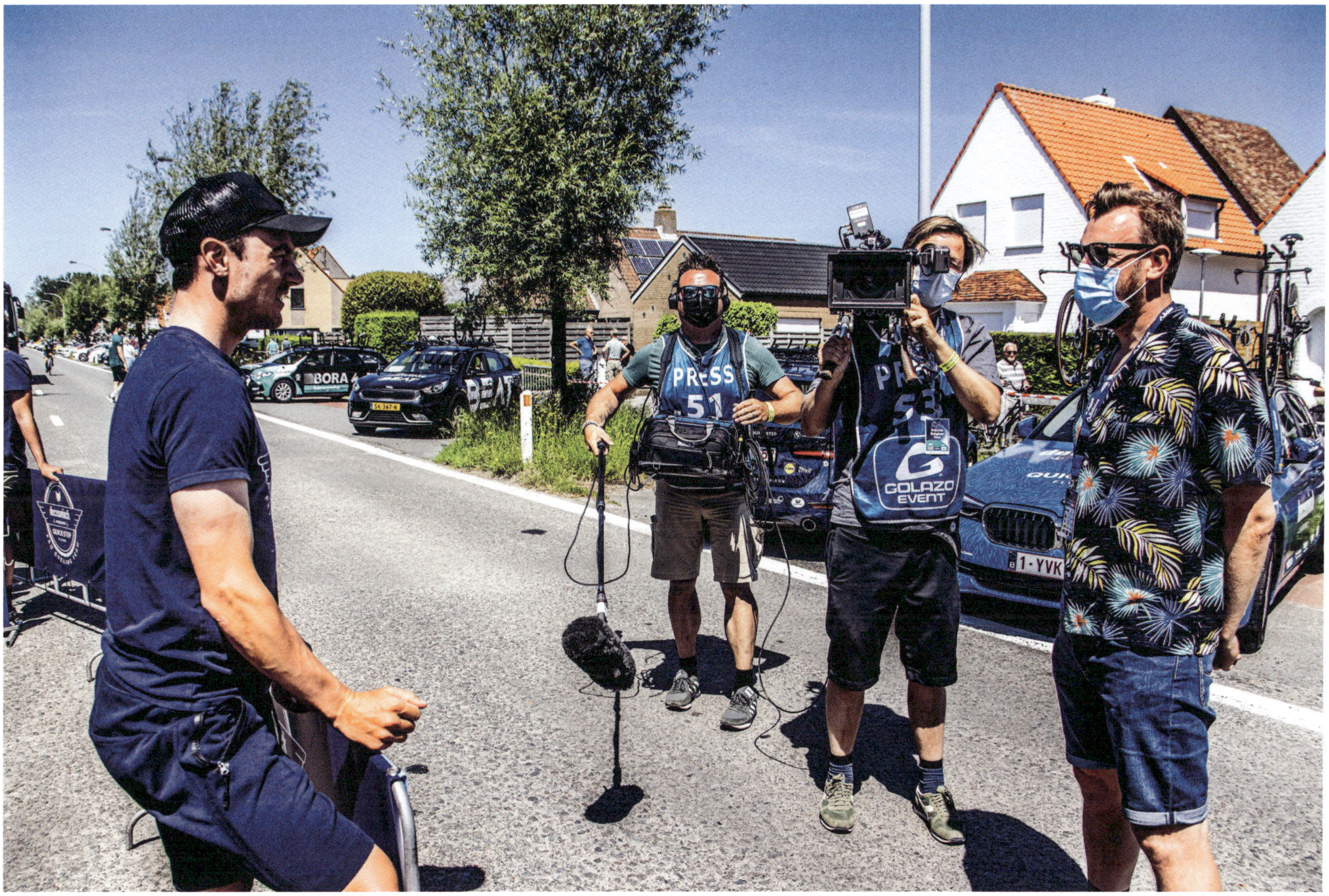

KNOKKE-HEIST, 10.06.2021

Na de tijdrit maakt Yves Lampaert tijd voor de cameraploeg van *Iedereen Beroemd* (VRT), die een realityreeks maakt rond zijn persoon, met de sprekende titel 'De weg naar Roubaix'. Dit jaar is die weg langer, want Parijs-Roubaix wordt pas op zondag 3 oktober gereden.

After the time trial, Yves Lampaert makes time for the camera crew of TV show *Iedereen Beroemd* (Belgium, VRT) and the reality show about his life, with the striking title De weg naar Roubaix (The road to Roubaix). This year, that road is longer, as Paris-Roubaix was only ridden on Sunday 3 October.

Après le contre-la-montre, Yves Lampaert accorde un moment à l'équipe de tournage de *Iedereen Beroemd* (VRT), qui réalise une émission de télé-réalité sur le coureur et qui s'appelle « De weg naar Roubaix » (En route vers Roubaix). Cette année, cette route est plus longue, car Paris-Roubaix ne sera couru que le dimanche 3 octobre.

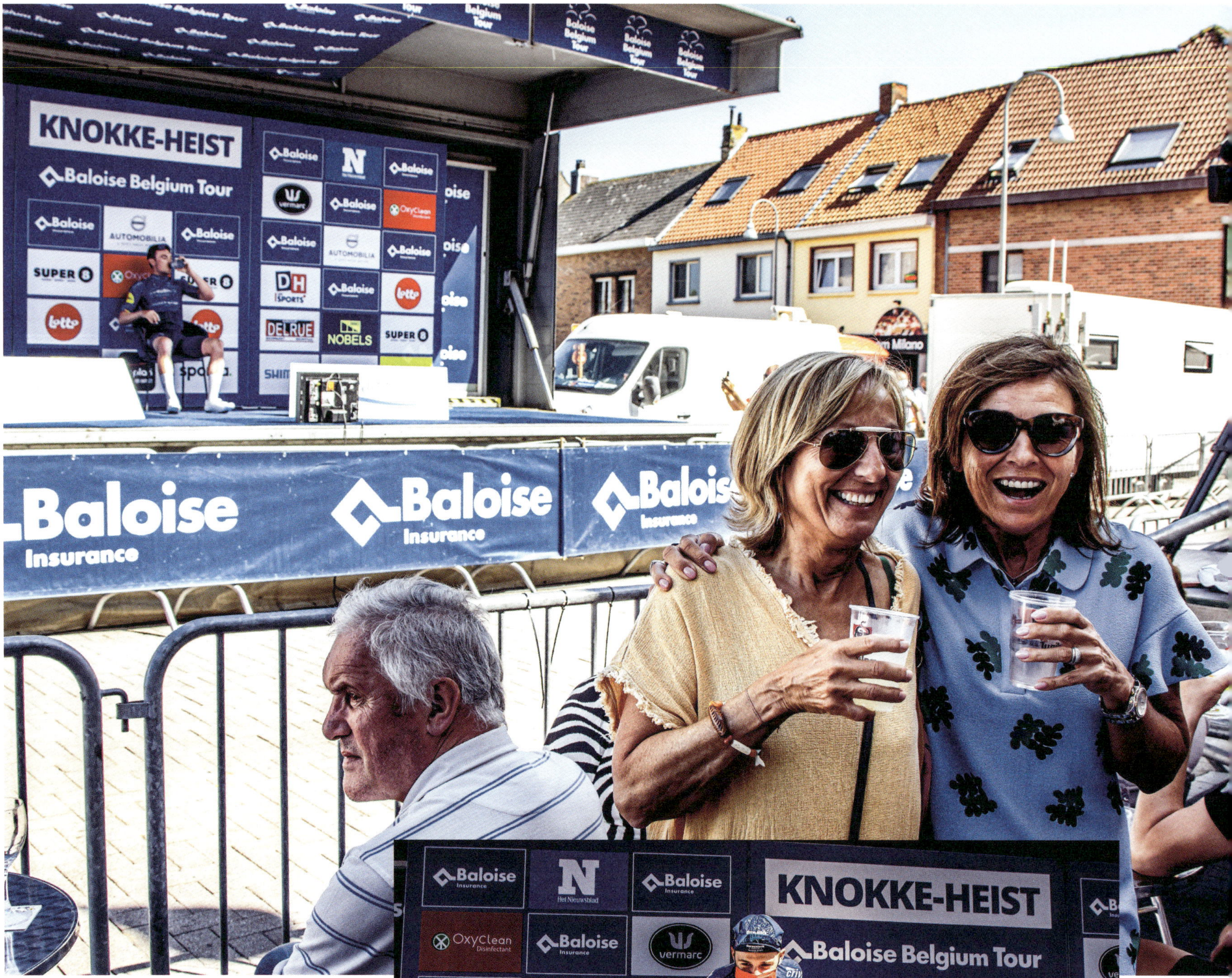
KNOKKE-HEIST
Baloise Belgium Tour
Baloise Insurance

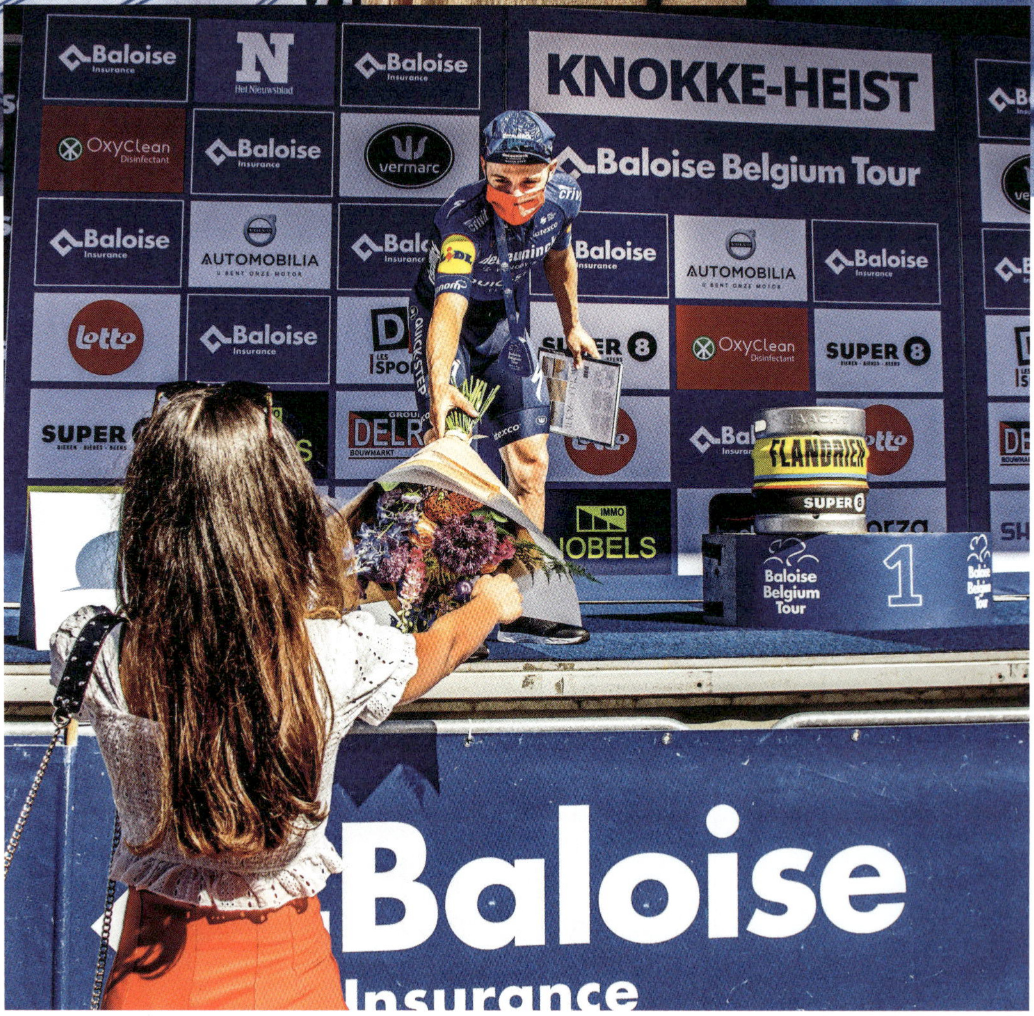
KNOKKE-HEIST
Baloise Belgium Tour
AUTOMOBILIA
OxyClean
SUPER 8
FLANDRIEN
Baloise Belgium Tour
1
Baloise Insurance

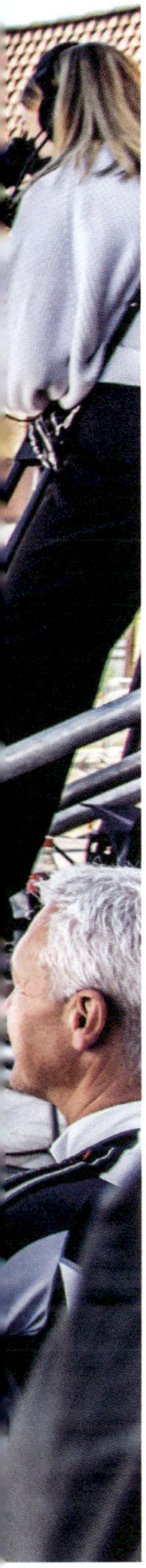

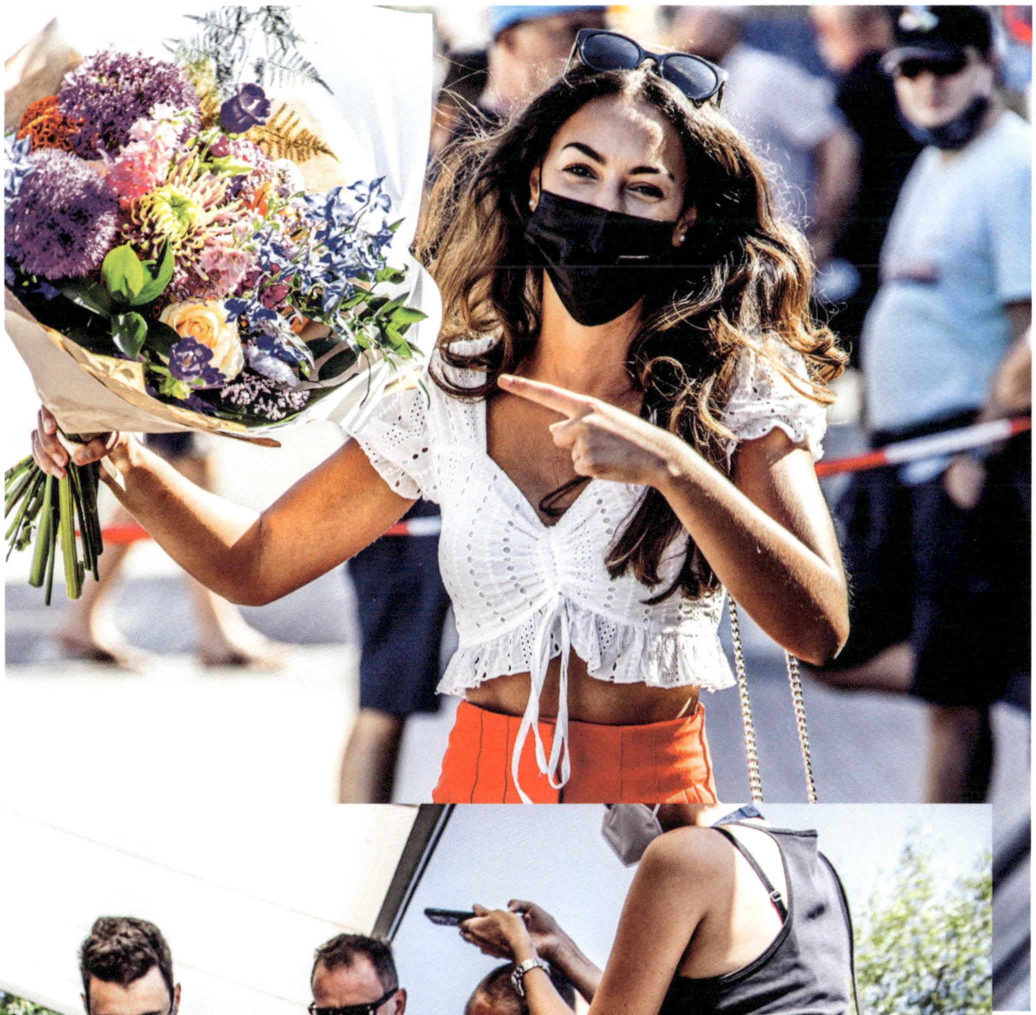

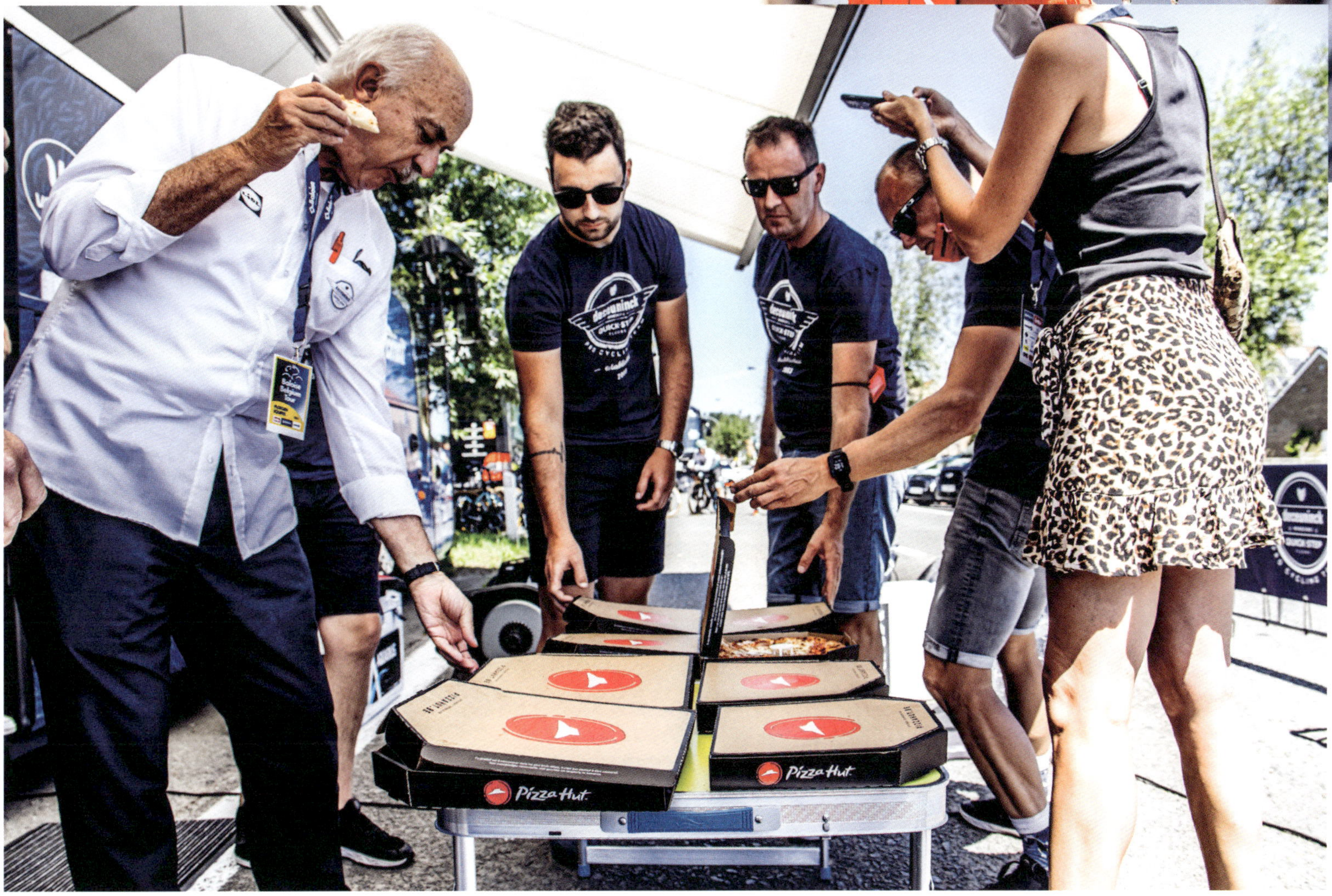

KNOKKE-HEIST, 10.06.2021

Yves Lampaert in de hot seat. Hij rijdt 16 seconden sneller dan Finn Fisher-Black, maar Remco Evenepoel is nog onderweg.

And the winner is... Remco Evenepoel. Hij wint de 11 kilometer lange tijdrit in Knokke en klopt Yves Lampaert met 2 seconden.

Yves Lampaert in the hot seat. He is 16 seconds faster than Finn Fisher-Black, but Remco Evenepoel is still on the move.

And the winner is... Remco Evenepoel. He wins the 11 km time trial in Knokke and beats Yves Lampaert by two seconds.

Yves Lampaert dans son nouveau trône. Il devance Finn Fisher-Black de 16 secondes, mais termine en deuxième place après Remco Evenepoel. ◤

And the winner is... Remco Evenepoel. Il a remporté le contre-la-montre de 11 km à Knokke, battant Yves Lampaert de 2 secondes. ◀

Het Deceuninck – Quick-Step Team mocht dit jaar vier nationale tijdritkampioenen vieren: João Almeida in Portugal, Josef Cerny in Tsjechië, Kasper Asgreen in Denemarken en Yves Lampaert in België.

The Deceuninck – Quick-Step Team celebrated four national time trial champions this year. João Almeida in Portugal, Josef Cerny in the Czech Republic, Kasper Asgreen in Denmark, and Yves Lampaert in Belgium.

L'équipe Deceuninck - Quick-Step a couronné quatre champions nationaux du contre-la-montre cette année : João Almeida au Portugal, Josef Cerny en République tchèque, Kasper Asgreen au Danemark et Yves Lampaert en Belgique.

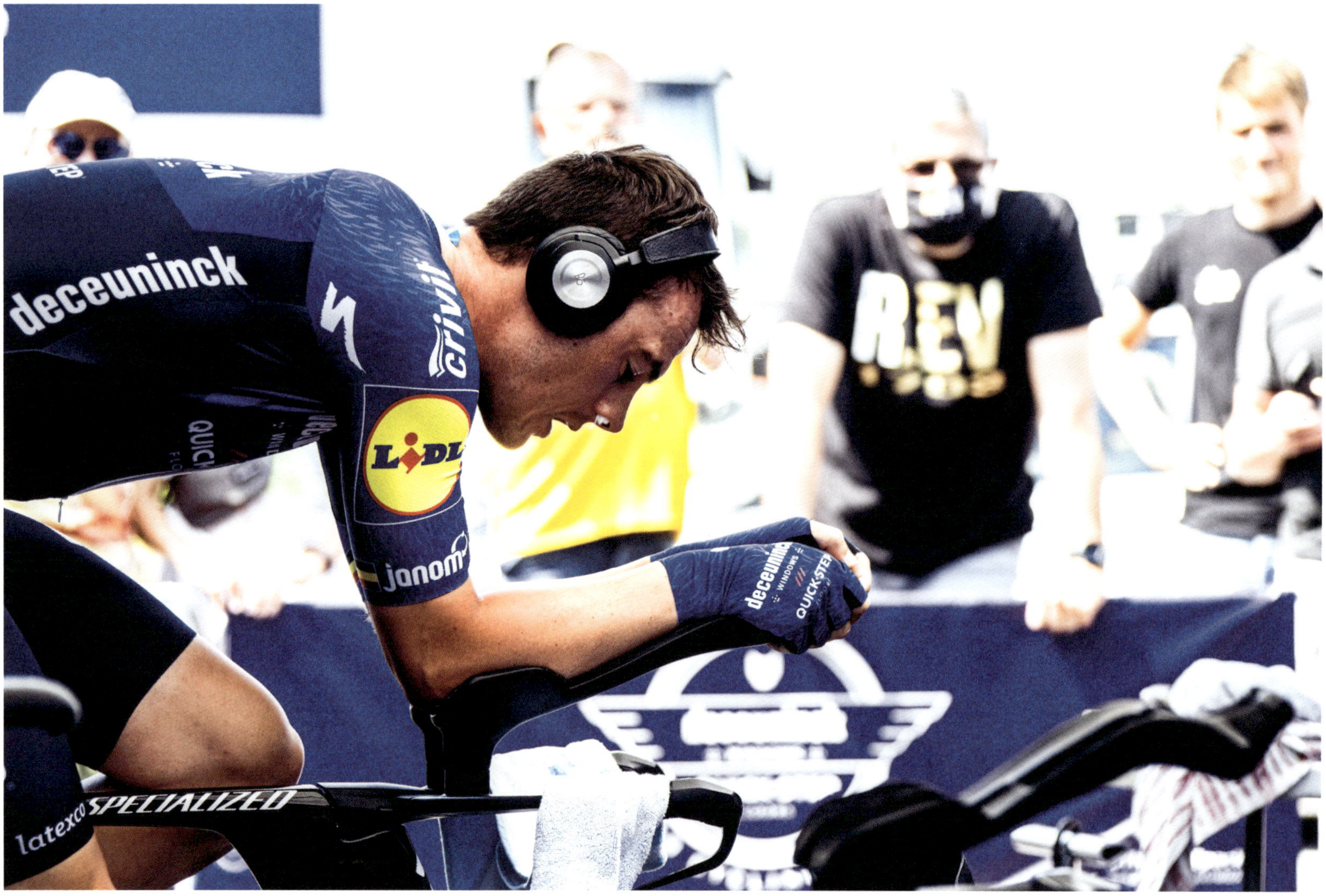

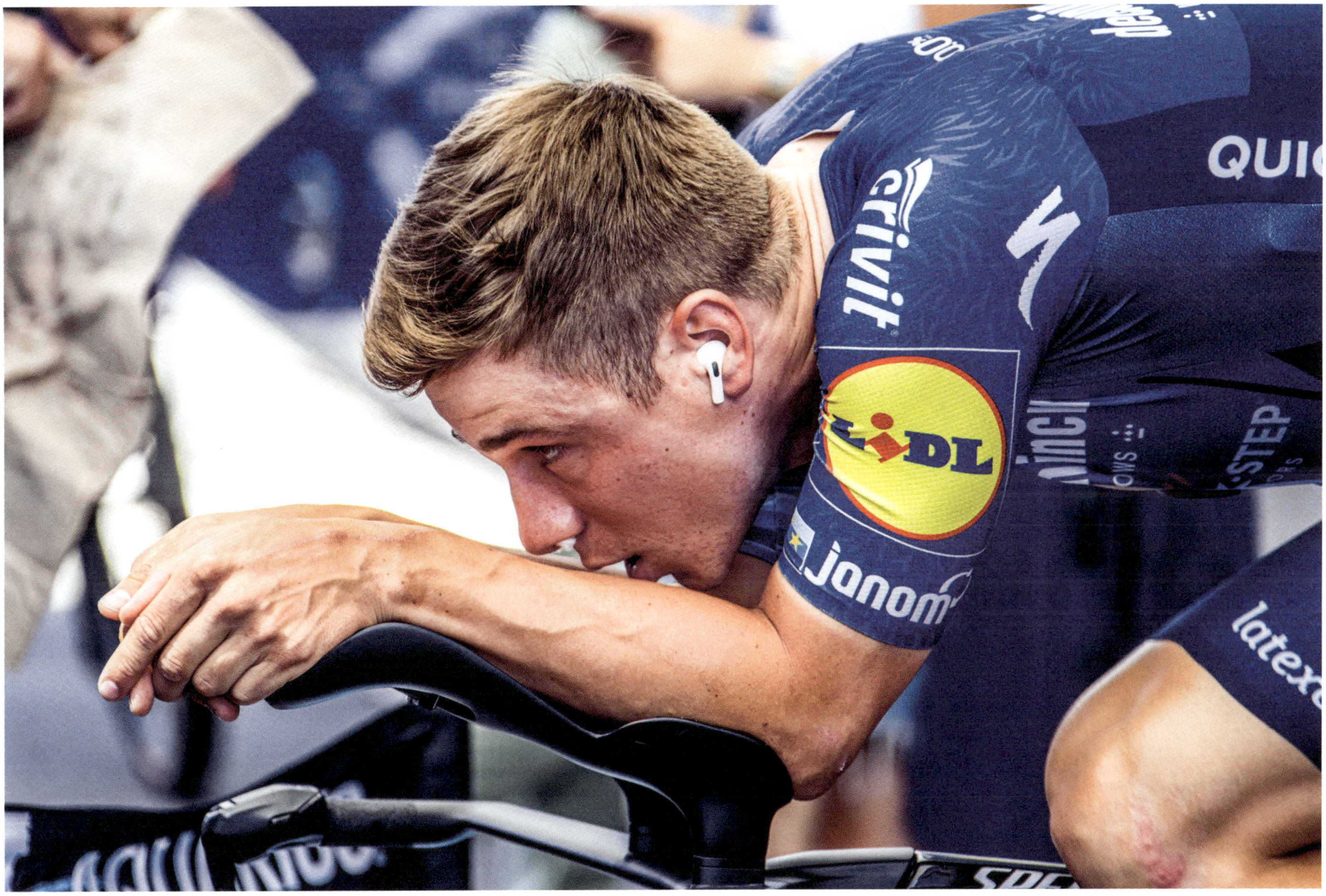

INGELMUNSTER, 16.06.2021

Voor eigen publiek in Ingelmunster kan Yves Lampaert altijd een tikje meer. Ingelmunster zal het op woensdag 16 juni geweten hebben. En ook Evenepoel zal het geweten hebben. Yves klopt Remco in het Belgisch Kampioenschap Tijdrijden en mag de gouden medaille en de tricolore trui in ontvangst nemen.

In front of the home crowd, Yves Lampaert can always give that bit more. Ingelmunster gets the full experience on Wednesday 16 June, and Remco Evenepoel too. Yves beats Remco in the Belgian Time Trial Championships to take the gold medal and the tri-color jersey.

Yves Lampaert est toujours déchainé devant le public de sa ville natale d'Ingelmunster. Il démontre sa rage de vaincre le 16 juin à Ingelmunster. Evenepoel aussi s'en souviendra. Yves bat Remco lors des Championnats de Belgique du contre-la-montre et décroche la médaille d'or et le maillot tricolore. ▶▶

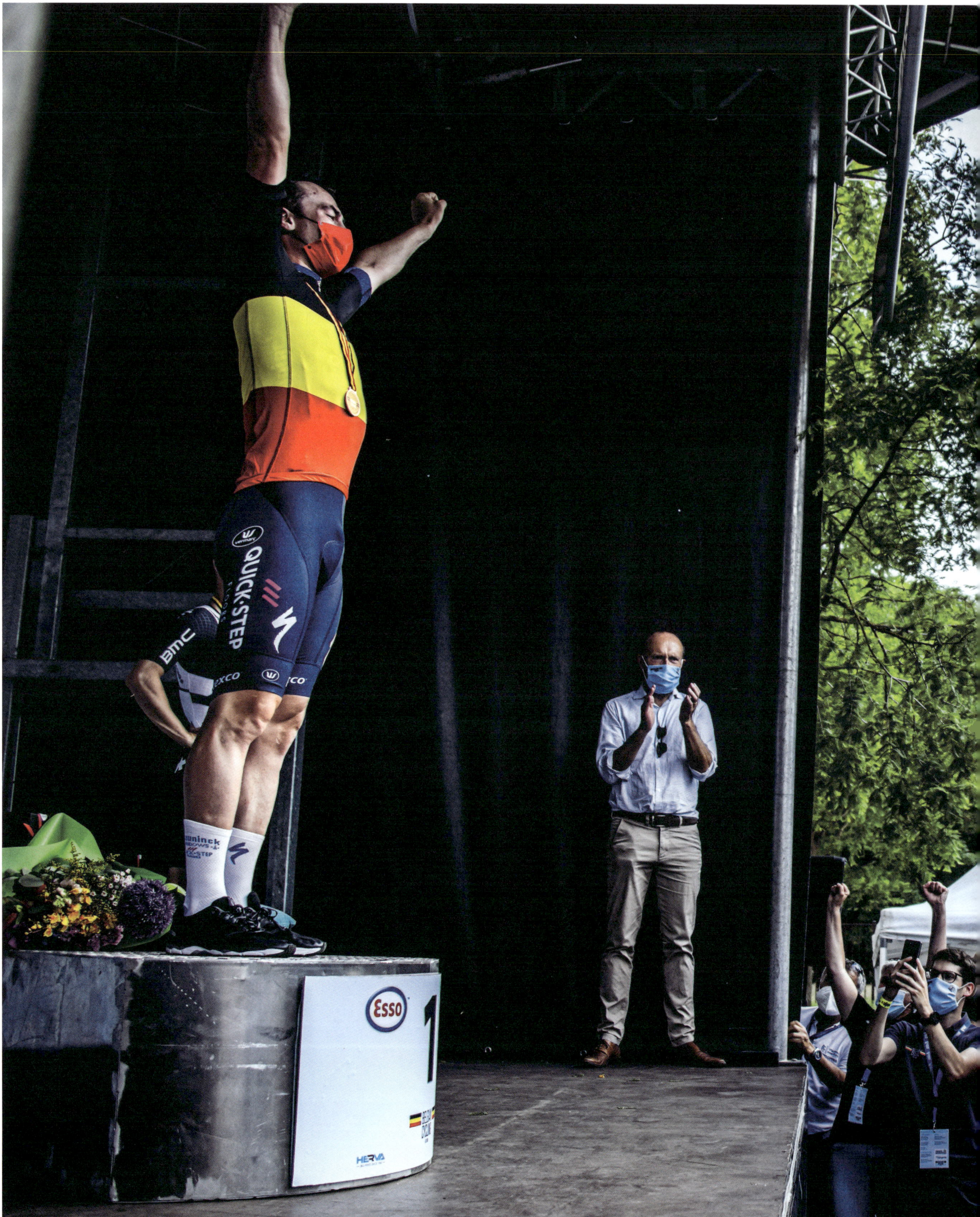
QUICK·STEP
BMC
Esso
1

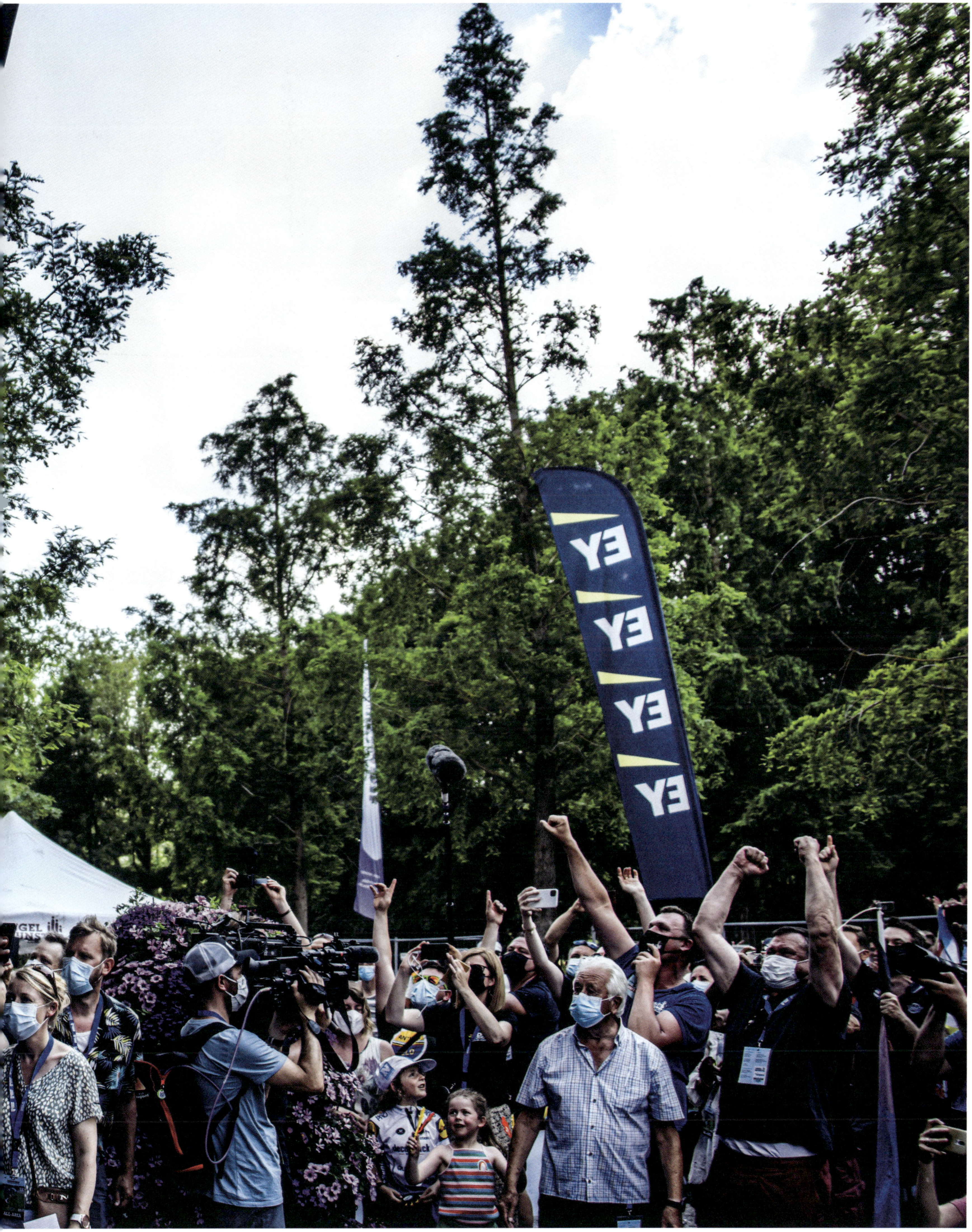

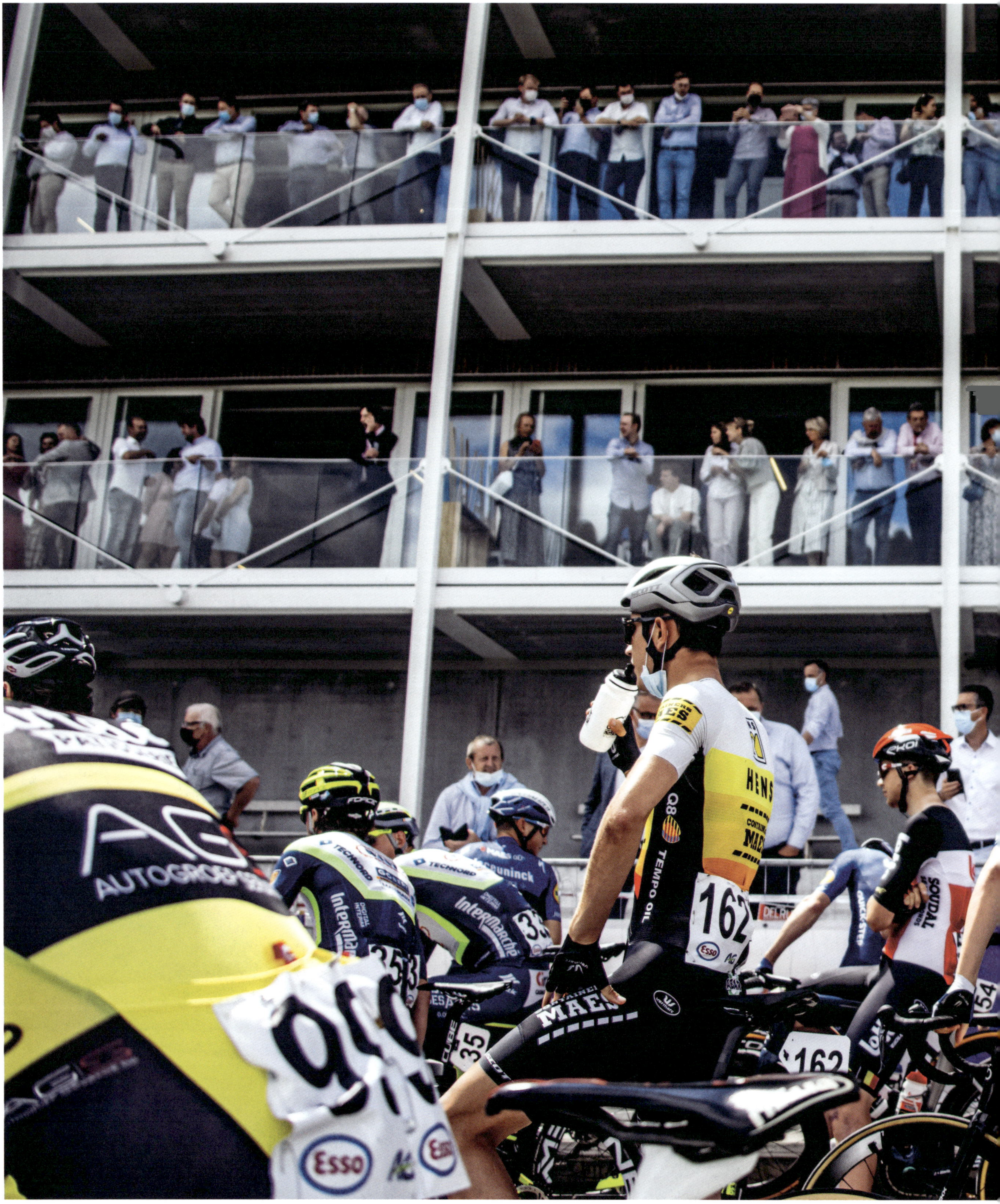
AUTOGROEP
HENS
TEMPO OIL
162
Esso
SOUDAL
Esso

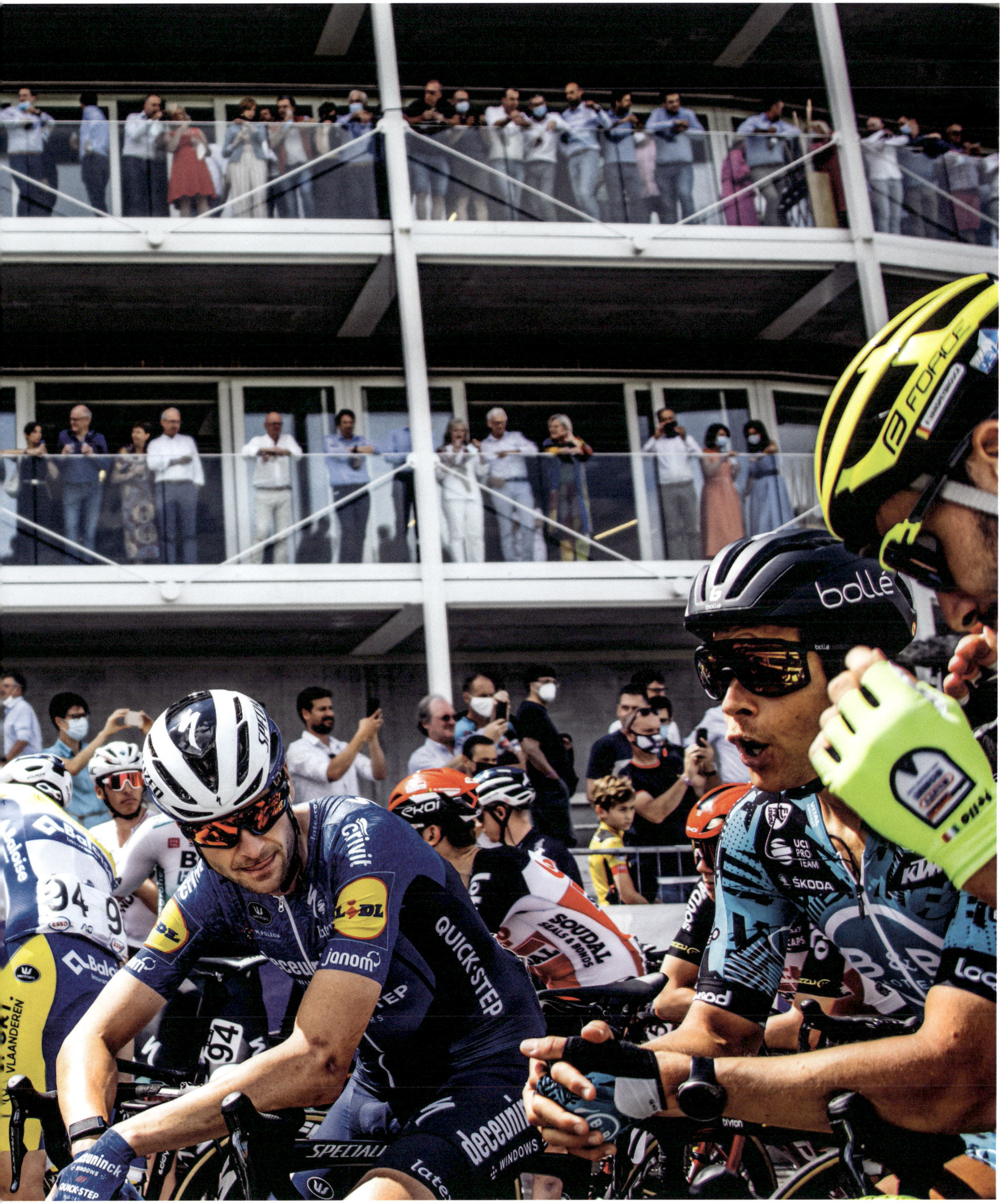

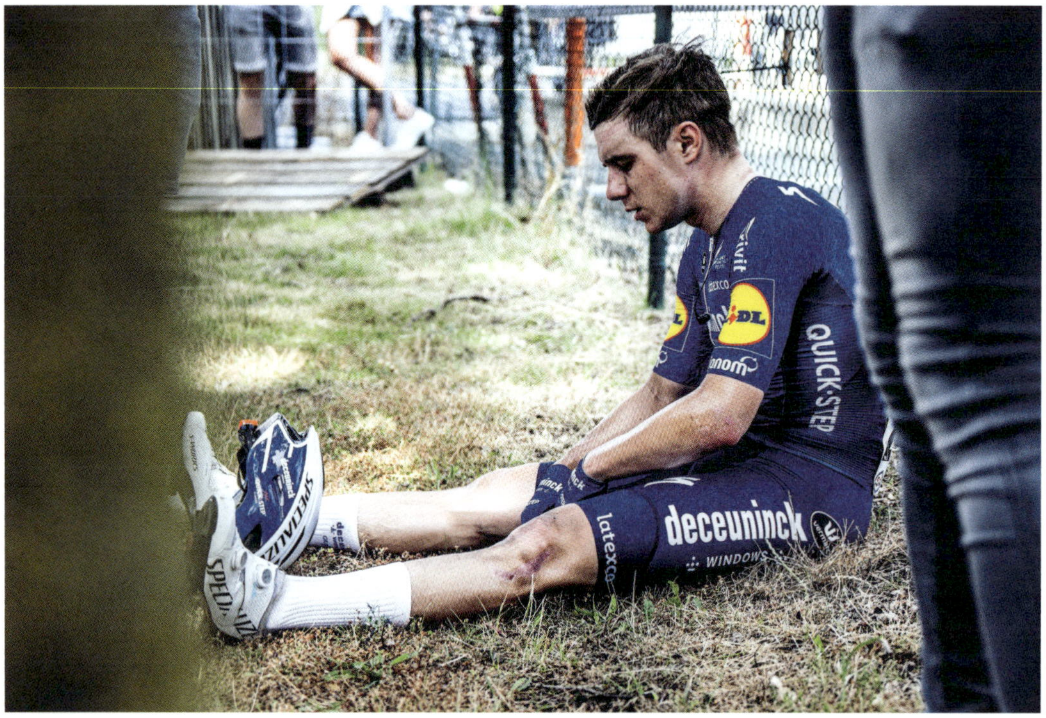
QUICK-STEP
deceuninck

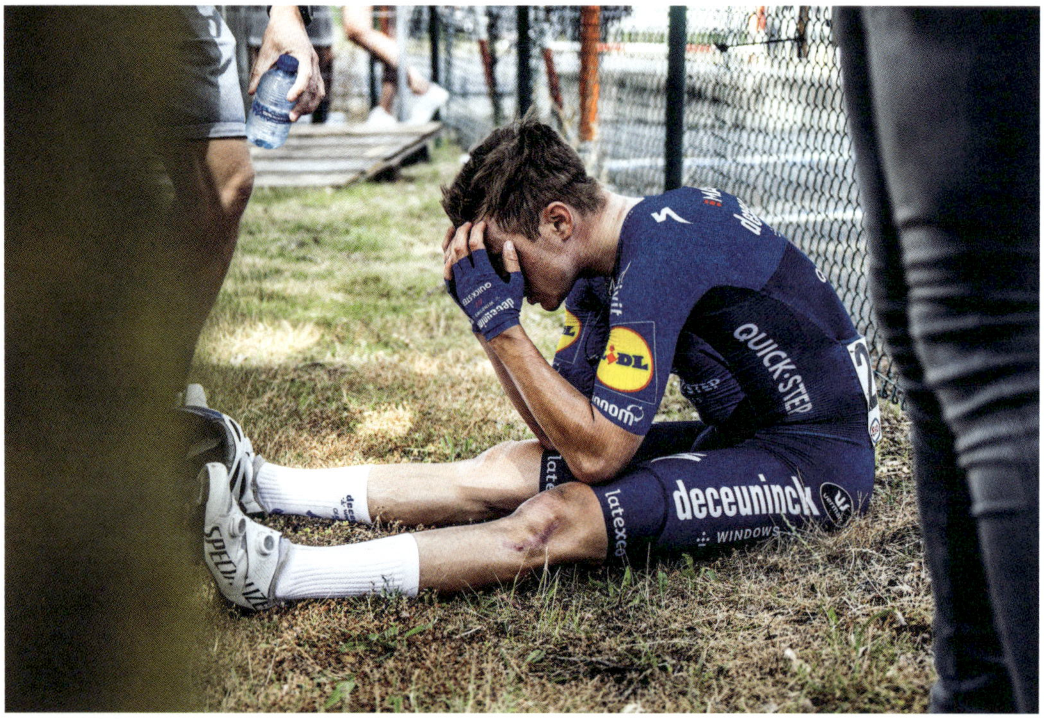
QUICK-STEP
deceuninck

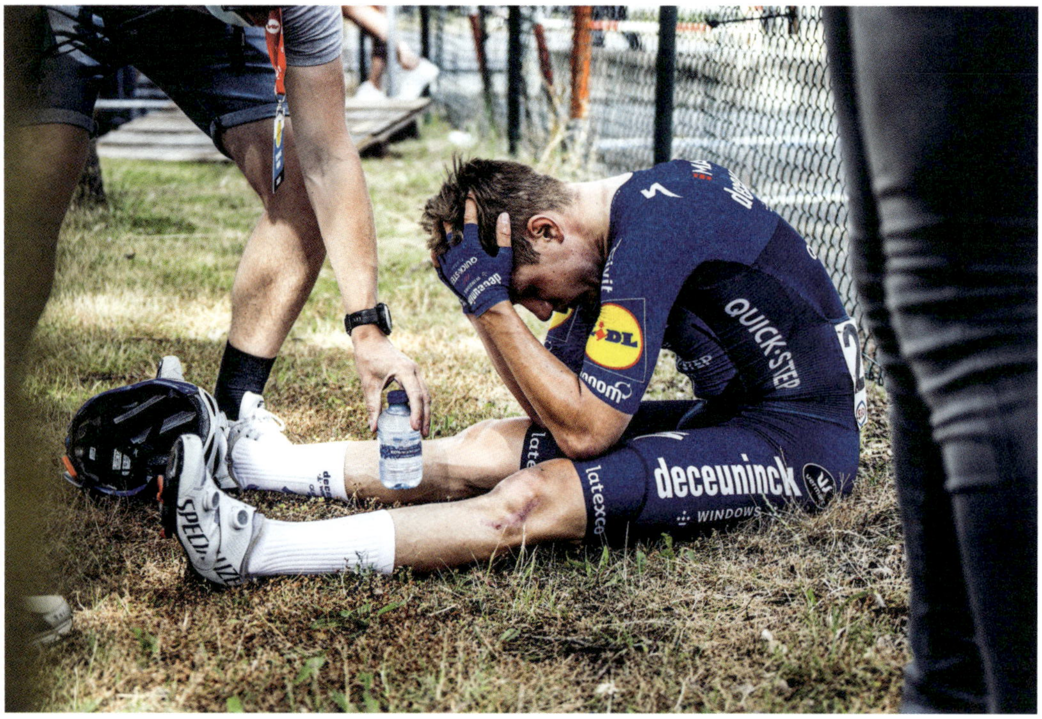
QUICK-STEP
deceuninck

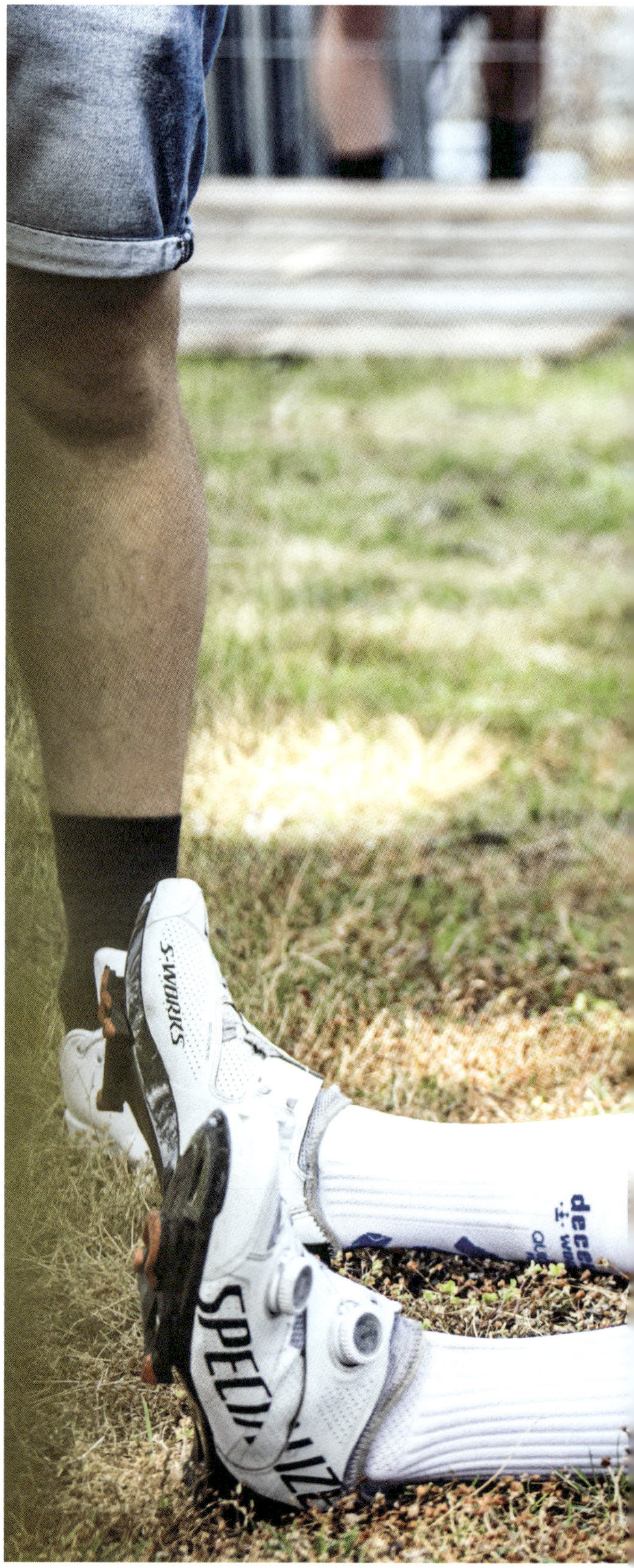
S-WORKS

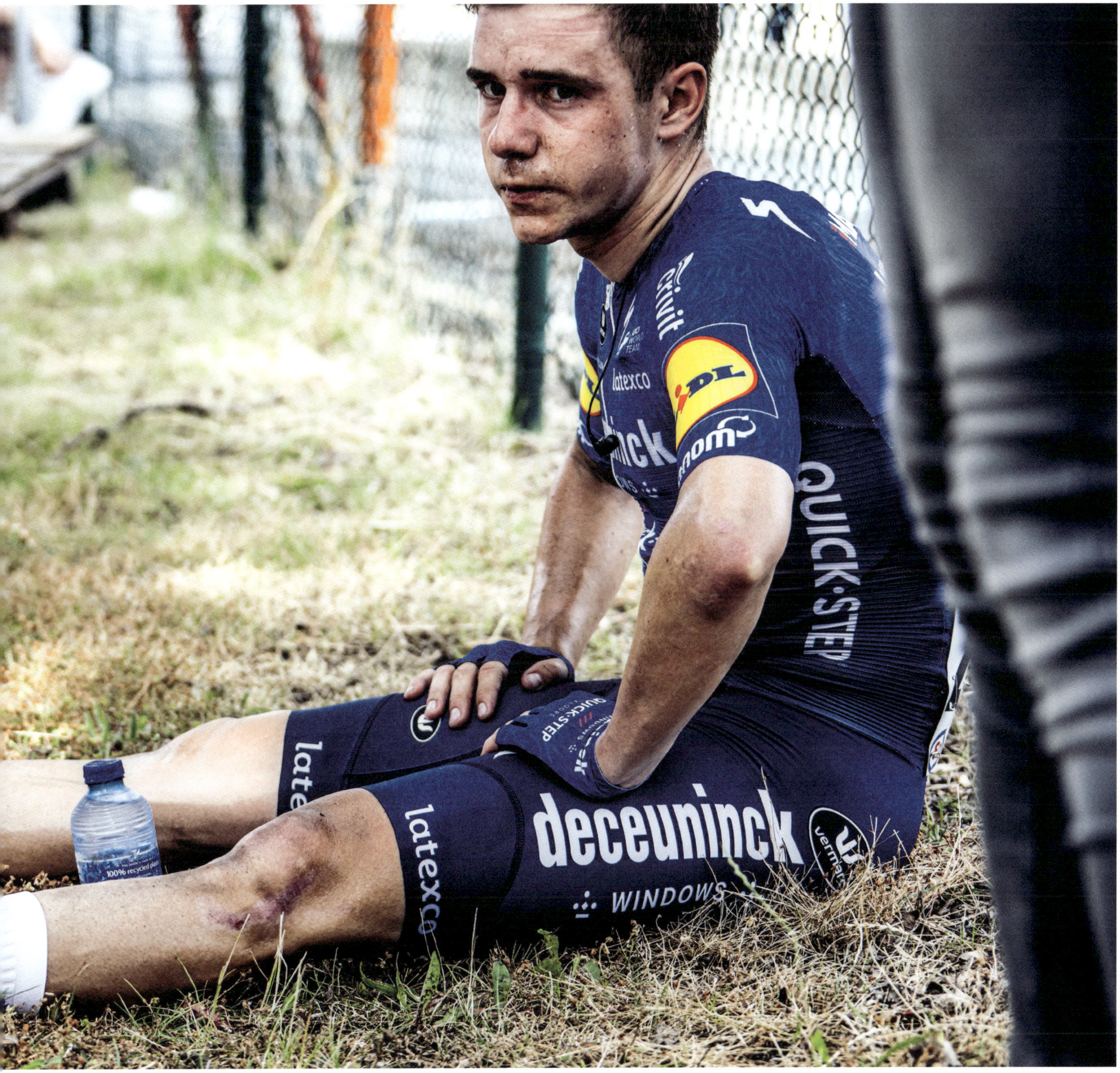

Op zondag 20 juni stond het Belgisch Kampioenschap op de weg geprogrammeerd. Remco Evenepoel kan zijn ontgoocheling niet verbergen. Hij wordt derde na Wout van Aert en Edward Theuns.

On Sunday 20 June, the Belgian National Road Race Championship was on the agenda. Remco Evenepoel can't hide his disappointment. He finished third after Wout van Aert and Edward Theuns.

Les Championnats de Belgique de cyclisme sur route 2021 se sont disputés le dimanche 20 juin. Remco Evenepoel n'a pas pu cacher sa déception. Il a terminé troisième derrière Wout van Aert et Edward Theuns.

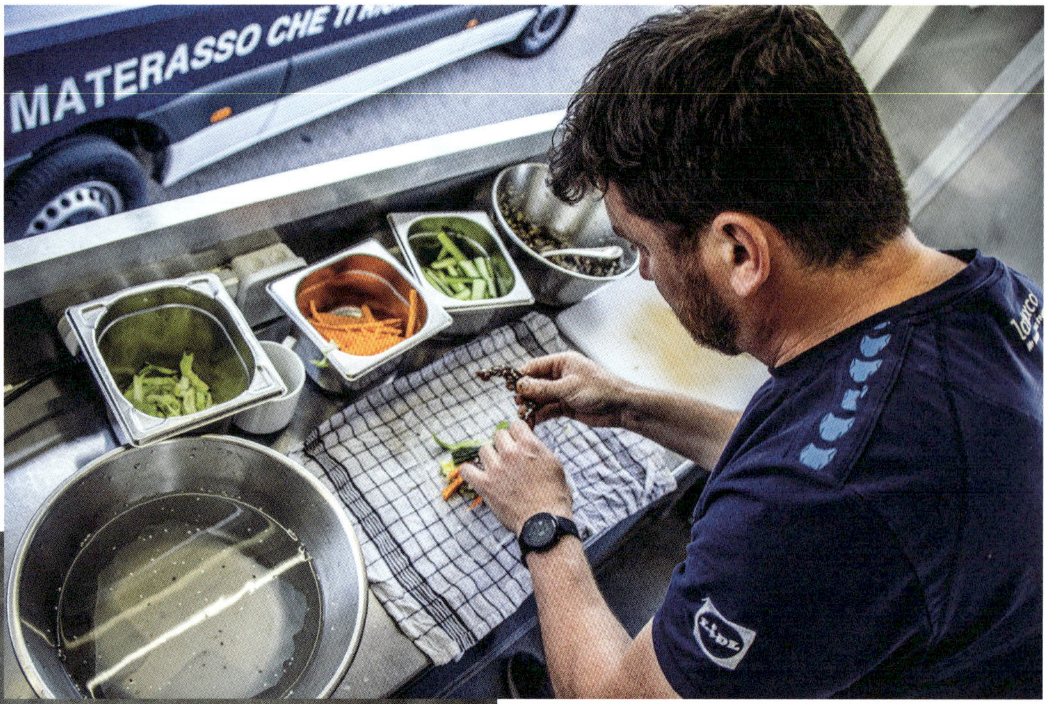
MATERASSO CHE

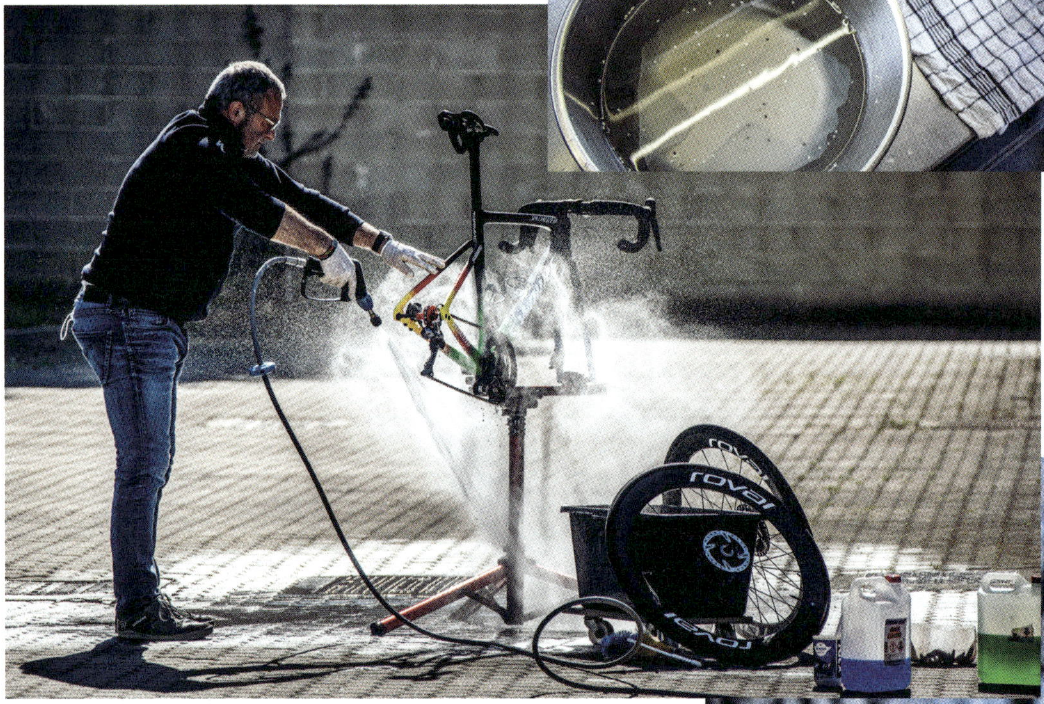
rovai

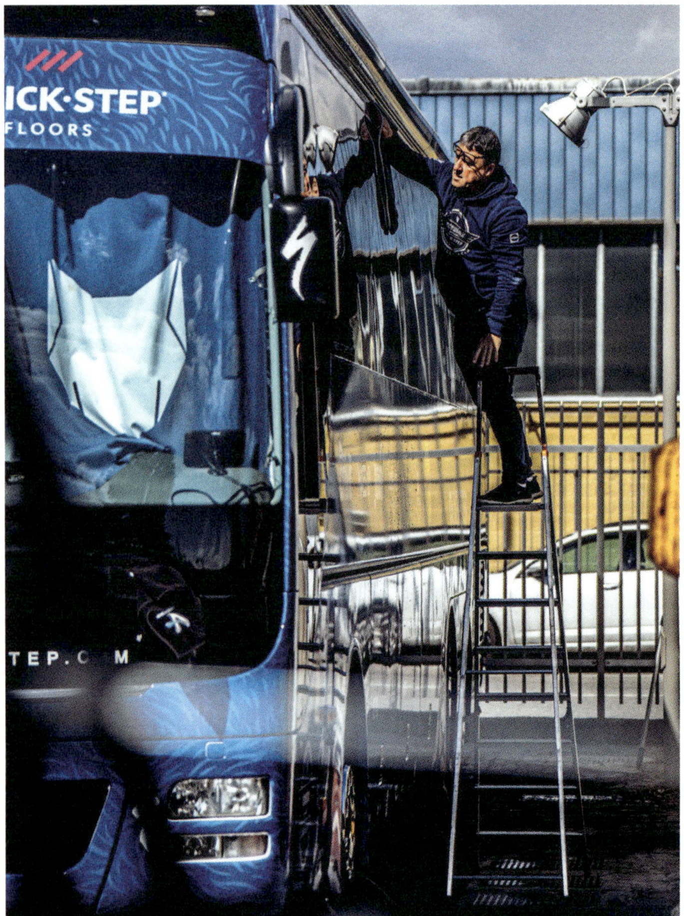
ICK·STEP
FLOORS
TEP.COM

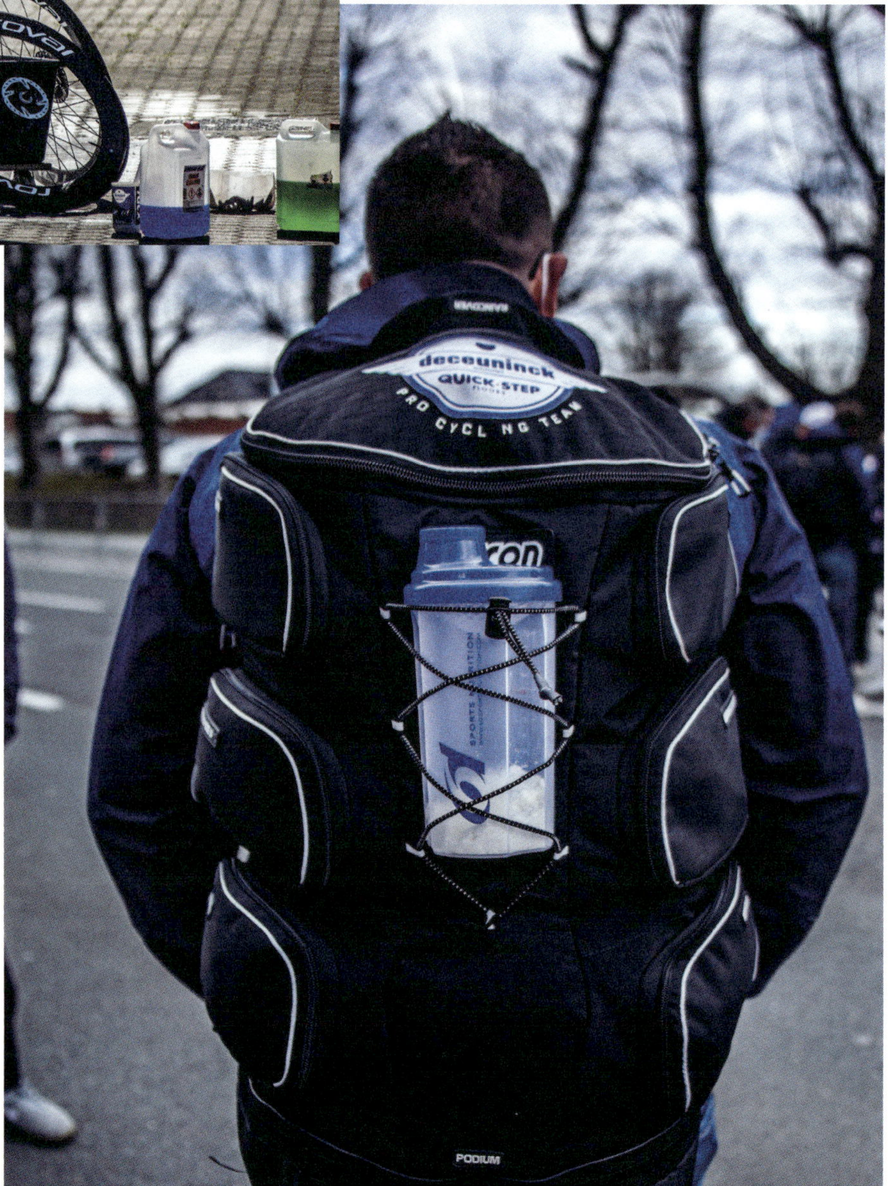
deceuninck
QUICK STEP
PRO CYCL NG TEAM
PODIUM

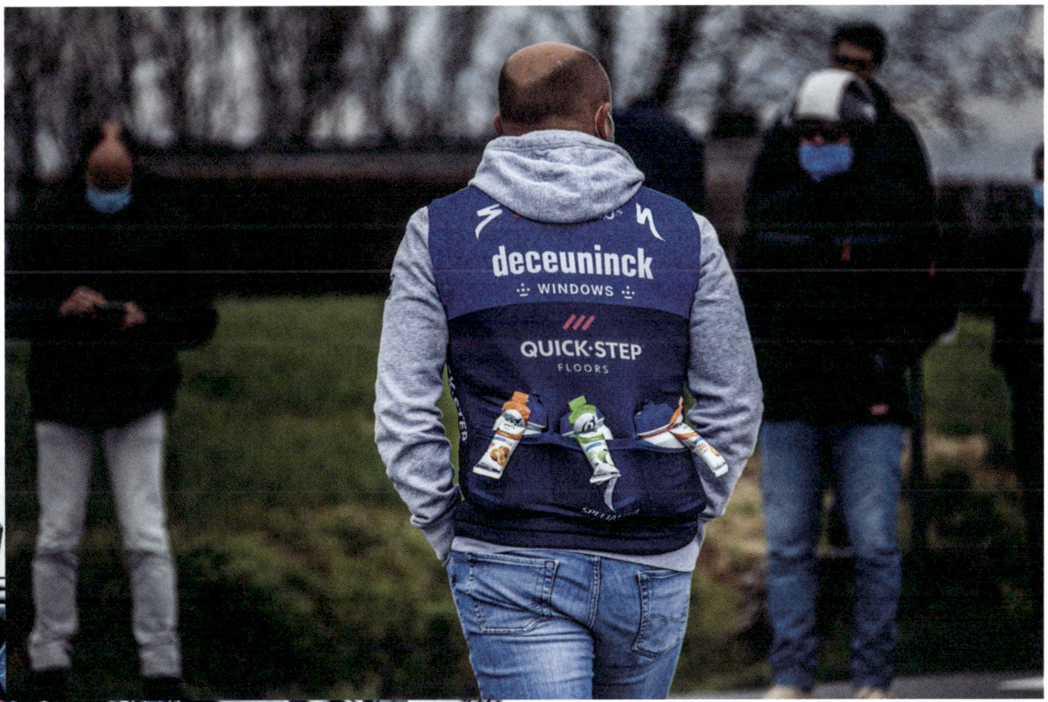

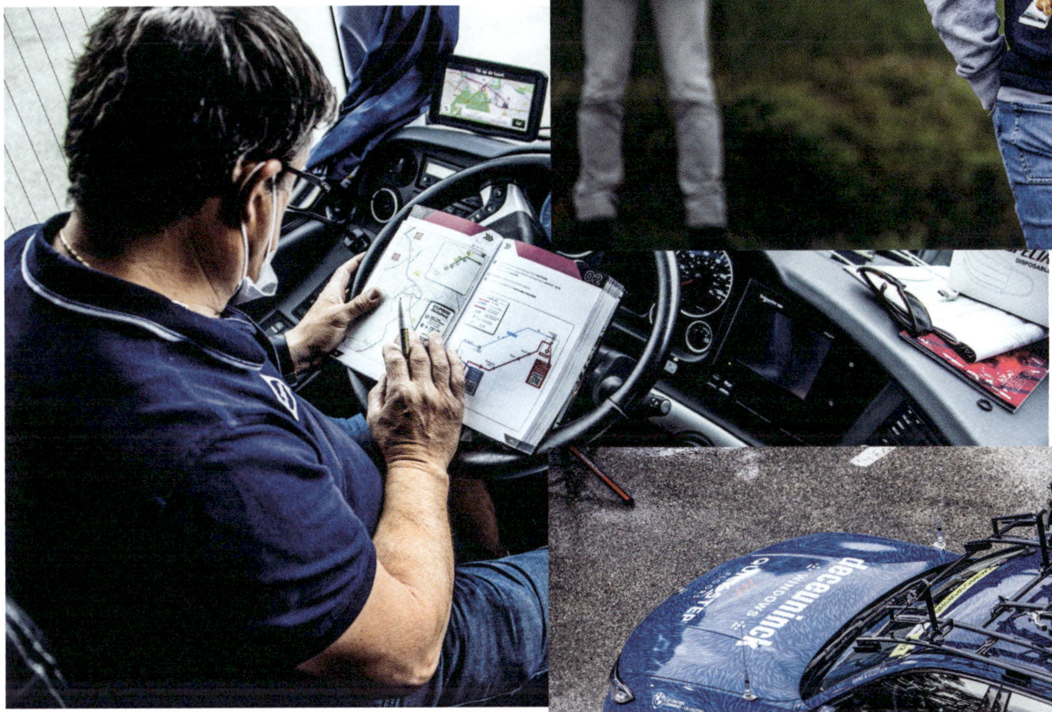

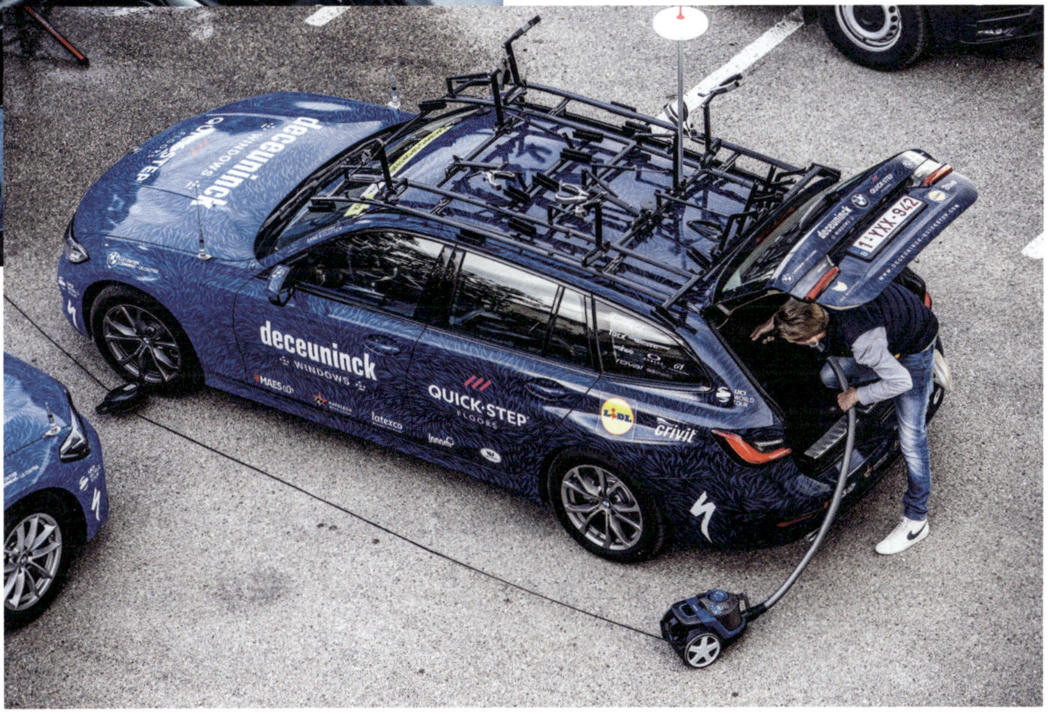

Stille krachten. Stille krachten zijn schaduwfiguren, maar ook o zo belangrijke schakels in het team. Dat is bij The Wolfpack niet anders. Een 'stille kracht' is rustig en zal niet in de spotlight staan. Toch is hij of zij niet het muurbloempje. Ook al zie je ze niet, als ze er niet zijn, stokt de machine. Onmisbaar zijn ze. Als tandwielen op een fiets, als olie op de ketting. Hun motto: 'Alles voor het team'. Of nog: `Doe je job, elke dag, elk uur, elke minuut. En waar het kan, doe je iets extra's.'

Stille krachten. Al is de een wel stiller dan de andere. Ook bij The Wolfpack.

Silent strength. All of the people working behind the scenes, who are nonetheless essential, are a team's silent strength. This is no different for The Wolfpack. This silent strength doesn't take center stage and isn't in the spotlight. Still, they're certainly not wallflowers. If they're not working, nothing is working. Their contribution is indispensable. Like sprockets on a bicycle, or oil on a chain. Their motto: "Everything for the team". Or: "Do your job, every day, every hour, every minute. And wherever you can, give a little extra."

Silent strength. Although some are quieter than others, even in The Wolfpack.

Les forces silencieuses travaillent dans l'ombre et sont des maillons très importants de la chaîne. Cela vaut aussi pour le Wolfpack. Une « force silencieuse » n'apparaît pas sous le feu des projecteurs. Et pourtant, elle ne fait pas tapisserie. On ne les voit pas, mais la machine ne tournerait pas sans elles. Tels les pignons d'un vélo, ou l'huile sur une chaîne. Leur devise : « Tout pour l'équipe ». Ou encore : « Faites votre travail chaque minute de chaque heure de chaque jour. Et quand c'est possible, faites quelque chose en plus. »

Les forces silencieuses. Même si certains sont plus silencieux que d'autres. Cela s'applique aussi au Wolfpack.

Voor het team van Patrick Lefevere was de Tour de France een dubbeltje op zijn kant. Sprinter Sam Bennett bleek out met een aanslepende knieblessure en het was de vraag van één miljoen of Mark Cavendish een rittenwedstrijd van drie weken aankon. Fysiek en mentaal. Al moet gezegd: zijn trainingswaarden bleven top en Mark kan zich nog focussen als de beste. Vertrouwen was er zeer zeker.

Dat dubbeltje viel uiteindelijk aan de goede kant. Het werd een Ronde van Frankrijk om in te kaderen voor de ploeg van Lefevere. Met vijf ritzeges en elke dag op het podium met geel of groen. Van dag één tot op de Champs Élysées. Wat een prestatie!

For the team of Patrick Lefevere, the Tour de France was a close call. Sprinter Sam Bennett was out with a lingering knee injury, and it remained to be seen if Mark Cavendish could handle a three-week Tour de France both physically and mentally. Still, his training values remained optimal, and Mark's focus was on point. There was certainly confidence.

In the end, the team was on the winning side. It became a Tour de France to remember for the Lefevere team, with five stage wins and a spot on the podium in yellow or green every day. From day one up until the Champs Elysées. What an achievement!

Au départ du Tour de France, deux problèmes se posaient pour l'équipe. Tout d'abord, Sam Bennett, blessé au genou, a dû renoncer à la course. Ensuite, il fallait voir si Mark Cavendish était capable d'affronter une course de trois semaines. Physiquement et mentalement. Mais les talents qu'il a démontrés à l'entraînement étaient bien au rendez-vous et il est capable de rester aussi concentré que les meilleurs. Il avait confiance en ses capacités, ça, c'était sûr.

Au final, cela s'est révélé être un bon Tour de France pour l'équipe de Lefevere. Le Wolfpack s'en est bien sorti, avec cinq victoires d'étape et tous les jours sur le podium en jaune ou en vert, du premier jour jusqu'aux Champs Élysées. Quel exploit !

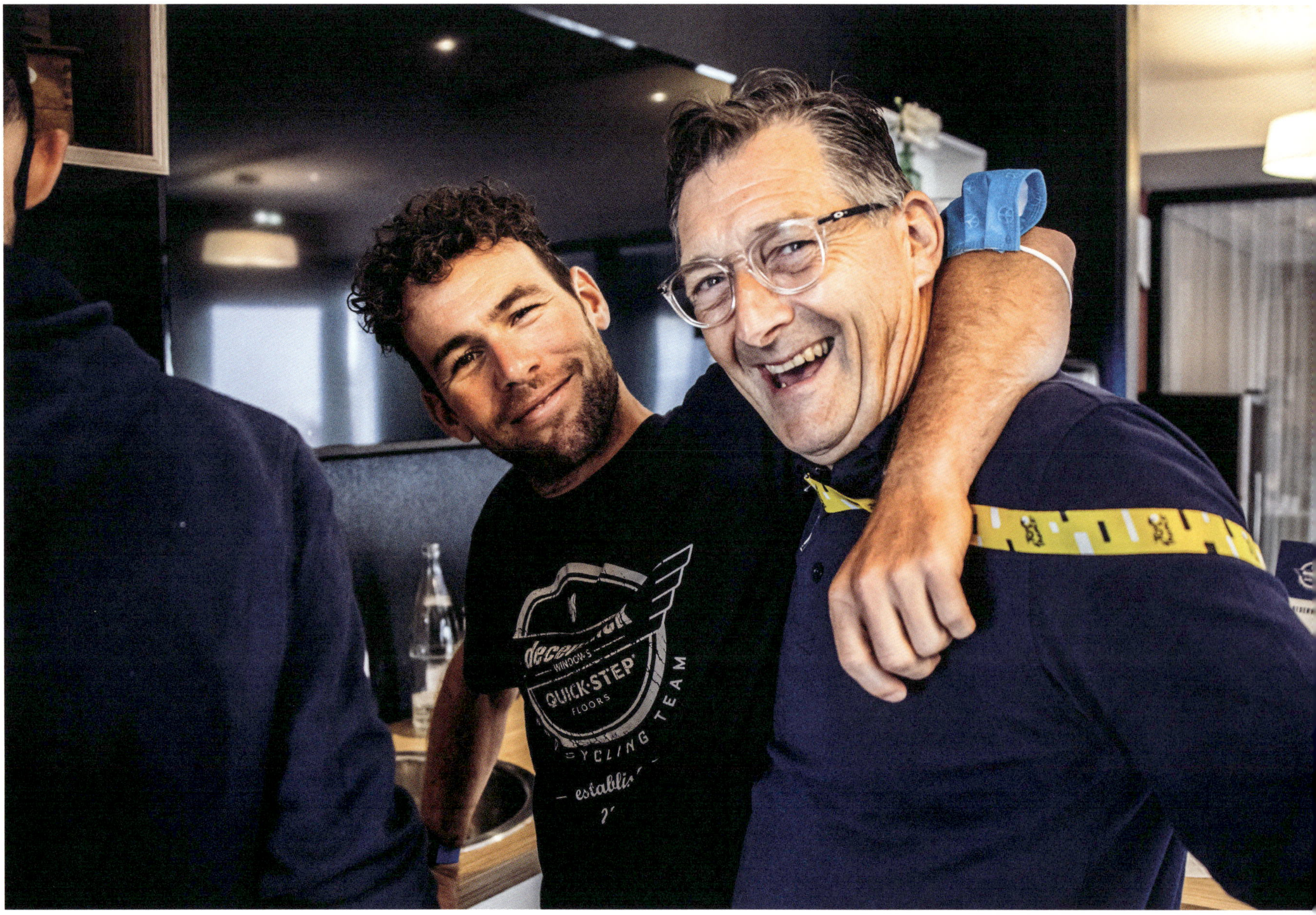

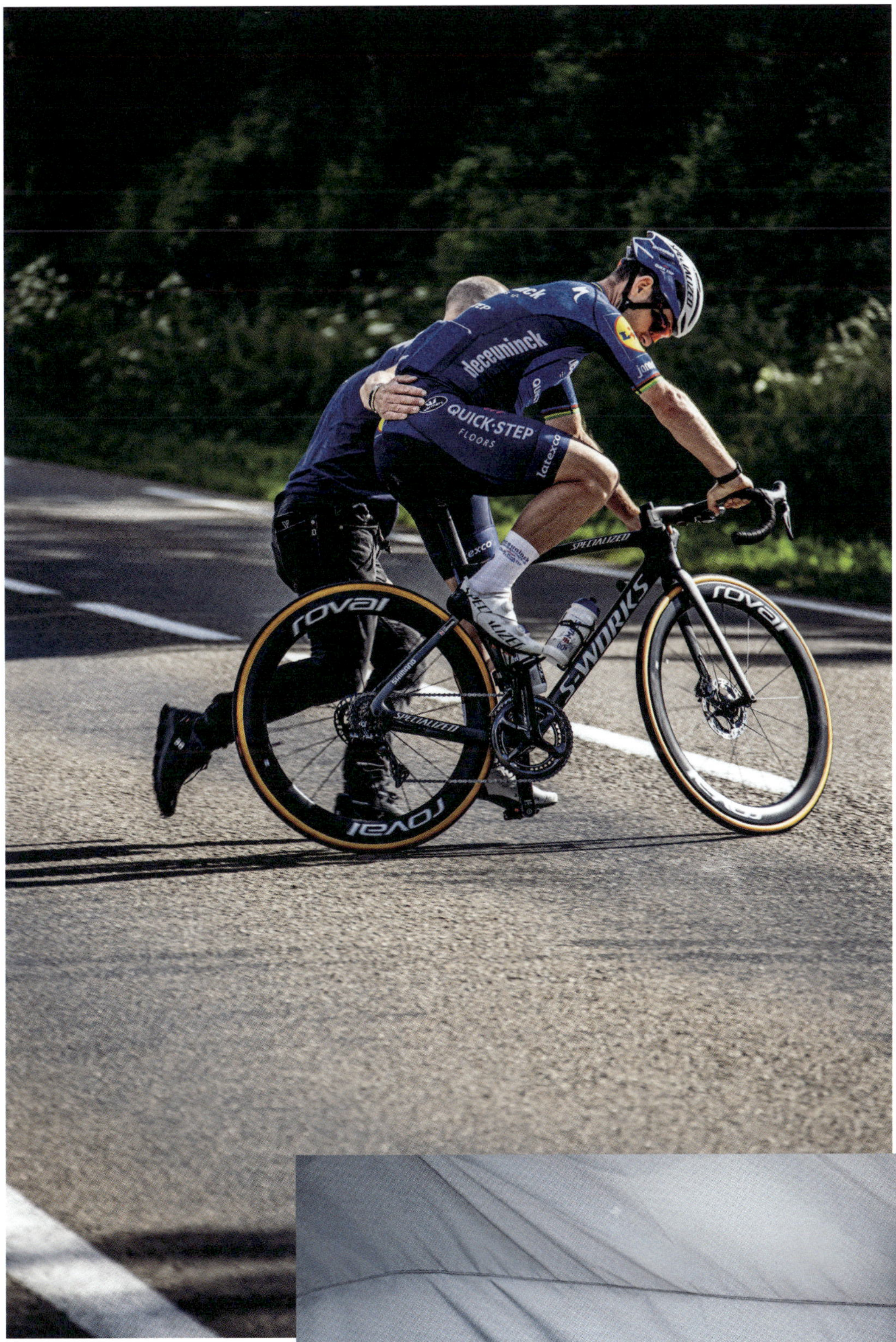

BREST, 23.06.2021

Mental coach Michaël Verschaeve geniet van de rust, voordat de Tour-gekte losbarst. In topsport wordt steeds meer aandacht besteed aan geestelijke gezondheid en dat is bij DQT niet anders. Stabiliteit in het hoofd zorgt voor geloof in eigen kunnen.

Mental coach Michaël Verschaeve enjoys the rest before the Tour madness breaks loose. In top sport, more and more attention is paid to mental health. That's also true for DQT. Mental stability ensures belief in one's own abilities.

Michaël Verschaeve, le coach mental de l'équipe, profite d'un peu de repos avant que la folie du Tour n'éclate. La préparation mentale est de plus en plus importante dans les sports de haut niveau et ce n'est pas différent pour la DQT. Force mentale et stabilité de l'esprit son essentiels pour croire en ses propres capacités. ▼

Teamspirit in de gedaante van twee gelukkige gezichten: Mark Cavendish en sportdirecteur Rik Van Slycke.

Team spirit shines through in two happy faces: Mark Cavendish and sports director Rik Van Slycke.

L'esprit d'équipe sous la forme de deux visages heureux : Mark Cavendish et Rik Van Slycke, directeur sportif. ◀◀

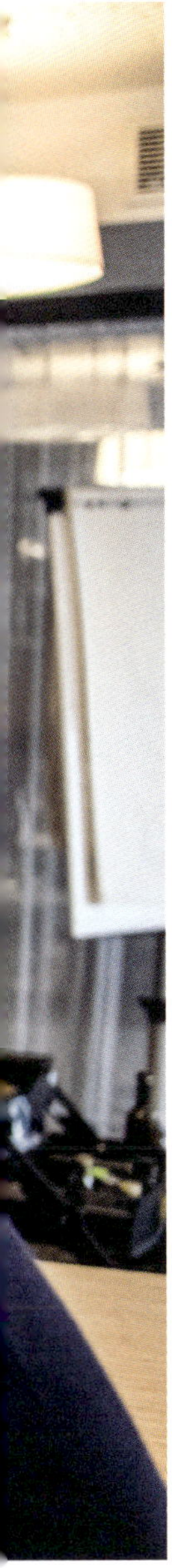

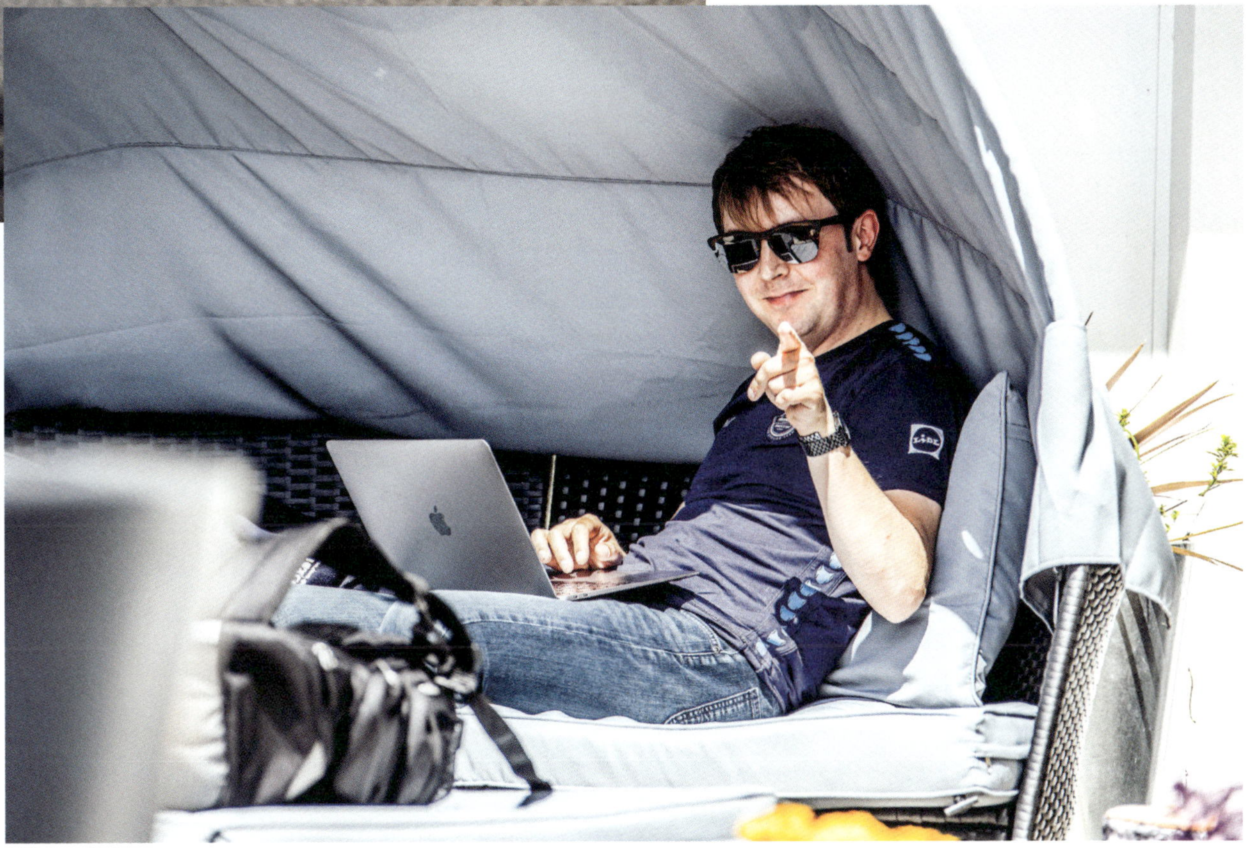

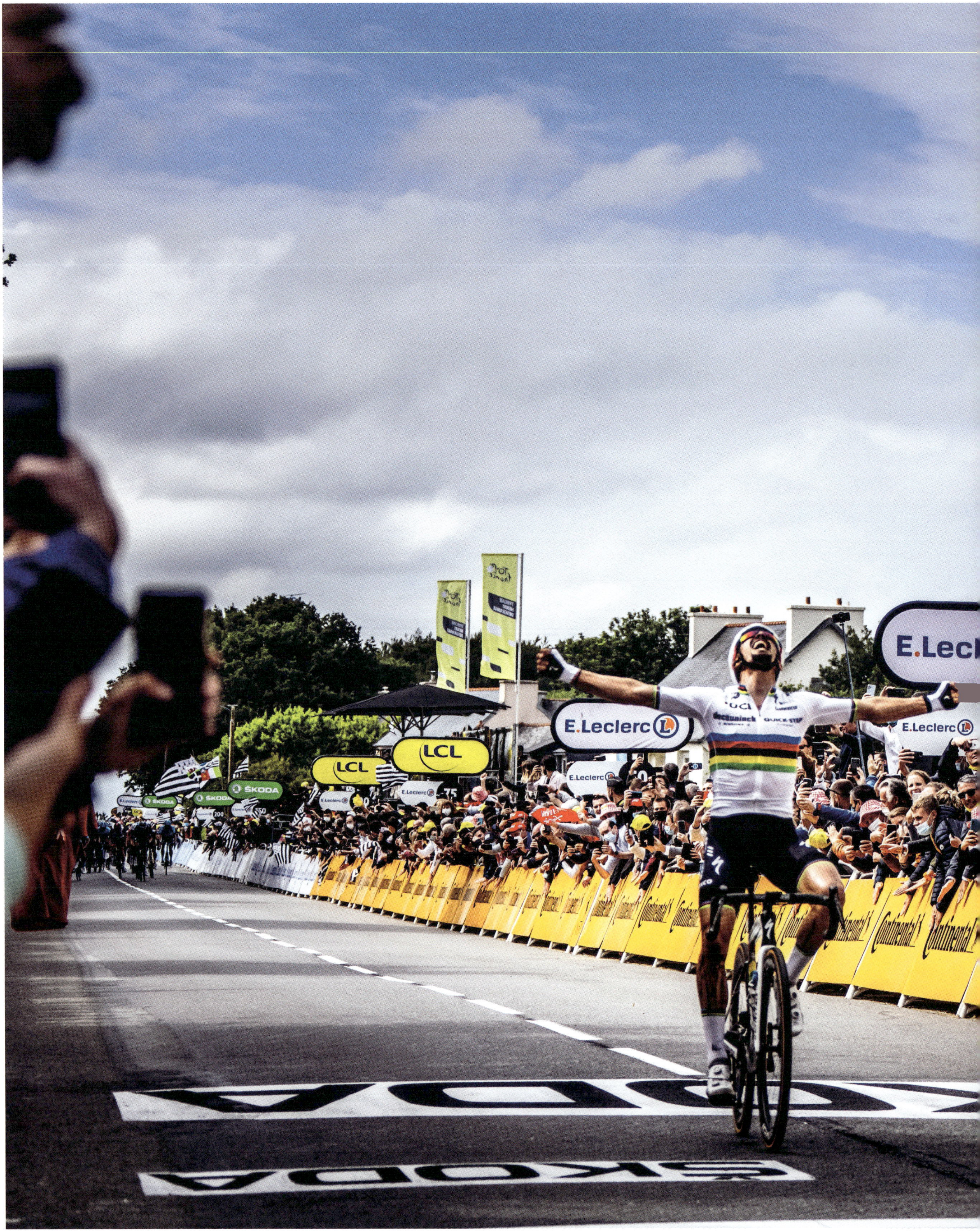
E.Leclerc
LCL
ŠKODA
Continental

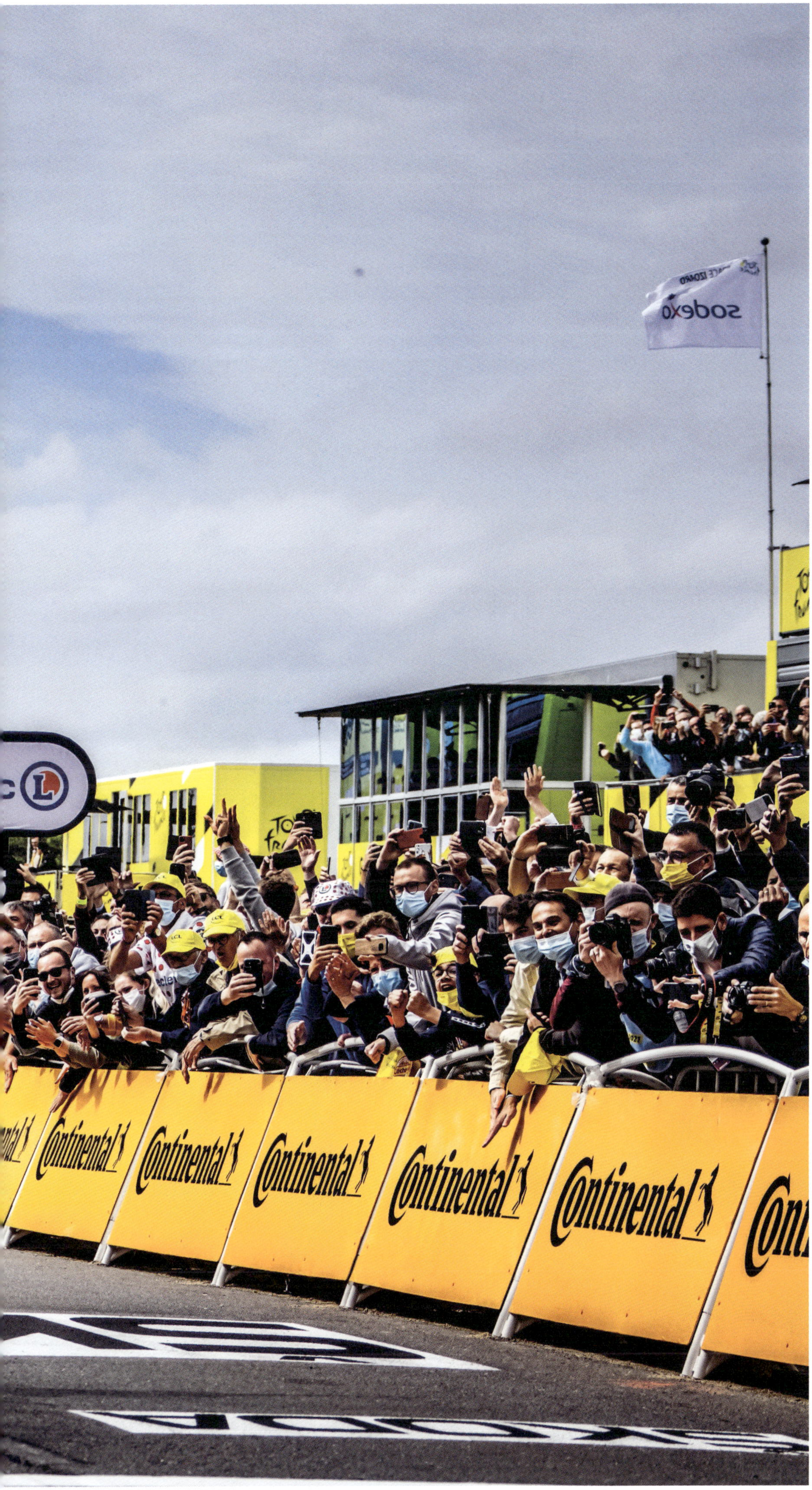

BREST, 26.06.2021

Bingo vanaf dag één. Julian Alaphilippe verrast zichzelf en het hele pak in Landerneau (Bretagne). Hij wordt uitstekend gepiloteerd door Dries Devenyns en schiet meteen raak. Winst in de Tour, op dag één. Met *le maillot jaune* erbovenop. Sterk. Heel sterk.

Winning from day one. Julian Alaphilippe surprises himself and the whole pack in Landerneau (Brittany). He was well piloted by Dries Devenyns and immediately hit the mark. Victory in the Tour, on day one. With le maillot jaune on top. Fantastic job.

Une réussite dès le premier jour. Julian Alaphilippe se surprend lui-même et surprend tout le peloton à Landerneau, en Bretagne. Il a été parfaitement lancé par Dries Devenyns et s'est immédiatement imposé. Une victoire pour l'équipe au premier jour du tour et avec le maillot jaune en plus. C'est fort. Très fort.

MÛR-DE-BRETAGNE, 27.06.2021

Mathieu van der Poel wint de tweede rit en neemt het geel over van Alaphilippe. Een prestatie die zijn grootvader Raymond Poulidor nooit heeft kunnen realiseren. Een mooi moment na de finish van de rit naar de Mûr-de-Bretagne. MVDP komt bij na zijn ultieme inspanning en krijgt de eerste felicitaties van Julian Alaphilippe. *Un grand champion, un grand monsieur.*

Mathieu van der Poel won the second stage and took over the yellow jersey from Alaphilippe. A feat that his grandfather Raymond Poulidor never managed to pull off. A beautiful moment after the finish of the stage to the Mûr-de-Bretagne. MVDP recovers after his ultimate effort and receives the first congratulations from Julian Alaphilippe. *Un grand champion, un grand monsieur.*

Mathieu van der Poel remporte la deuxième étape et prend le maillot jaune à Alaphilippe. Une prouesse que son grand-père Raymond Poulidor n'a jamais pu réaliser. Un beau moment après l'arrivée de l'étape de Mûr-de-Bretagne. MVDP reprend ses esprits après son immense effort et reçoit ses premières félicitations de la part de Julian Alaphilippe. *Un grand champion, un grand monsieur.* ▶

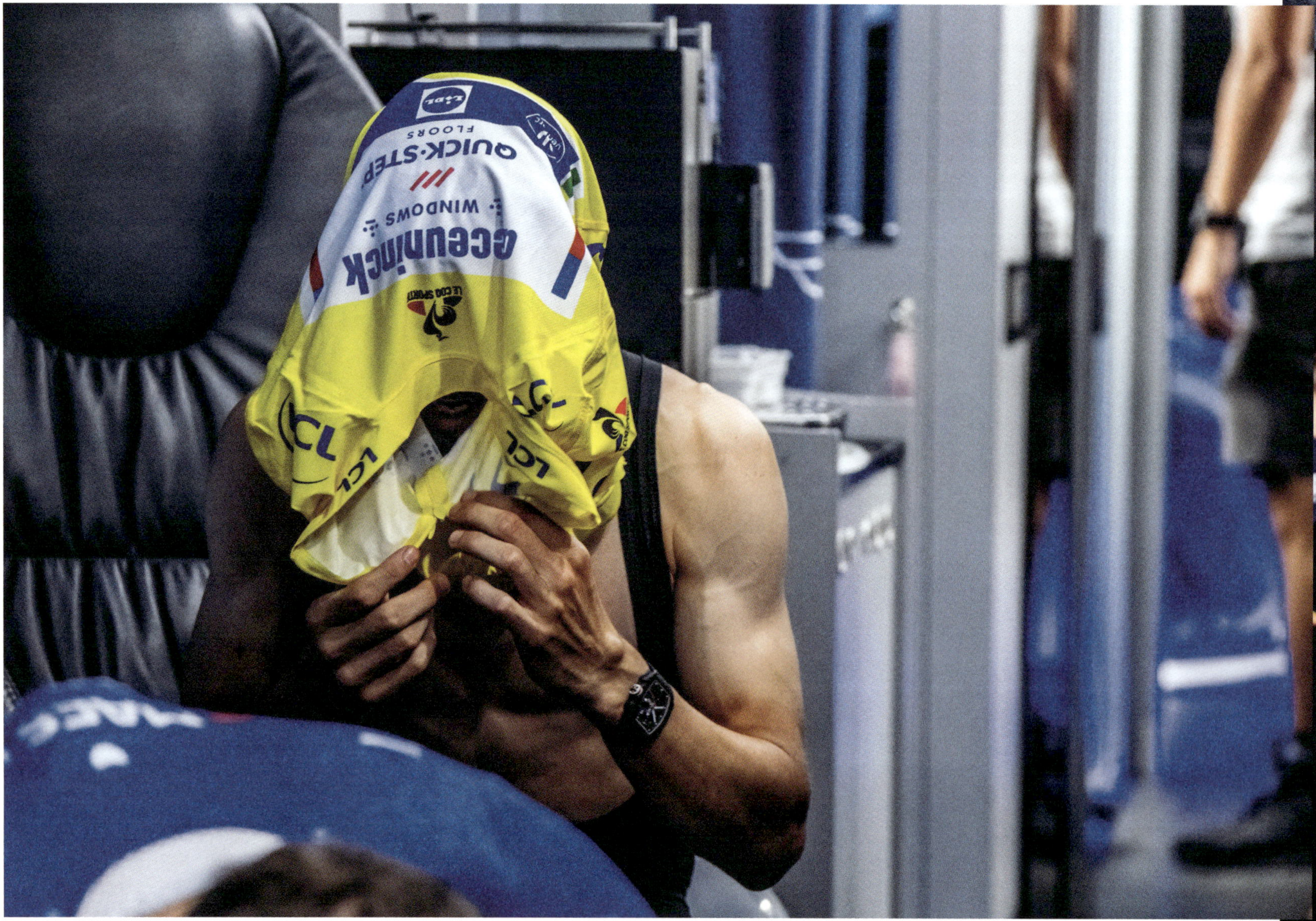

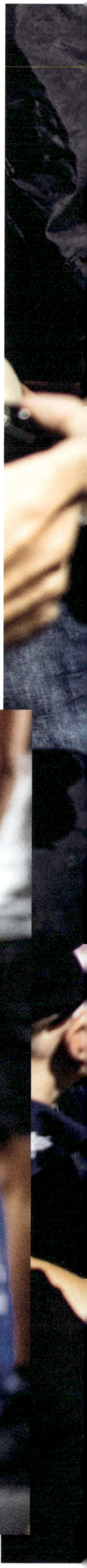

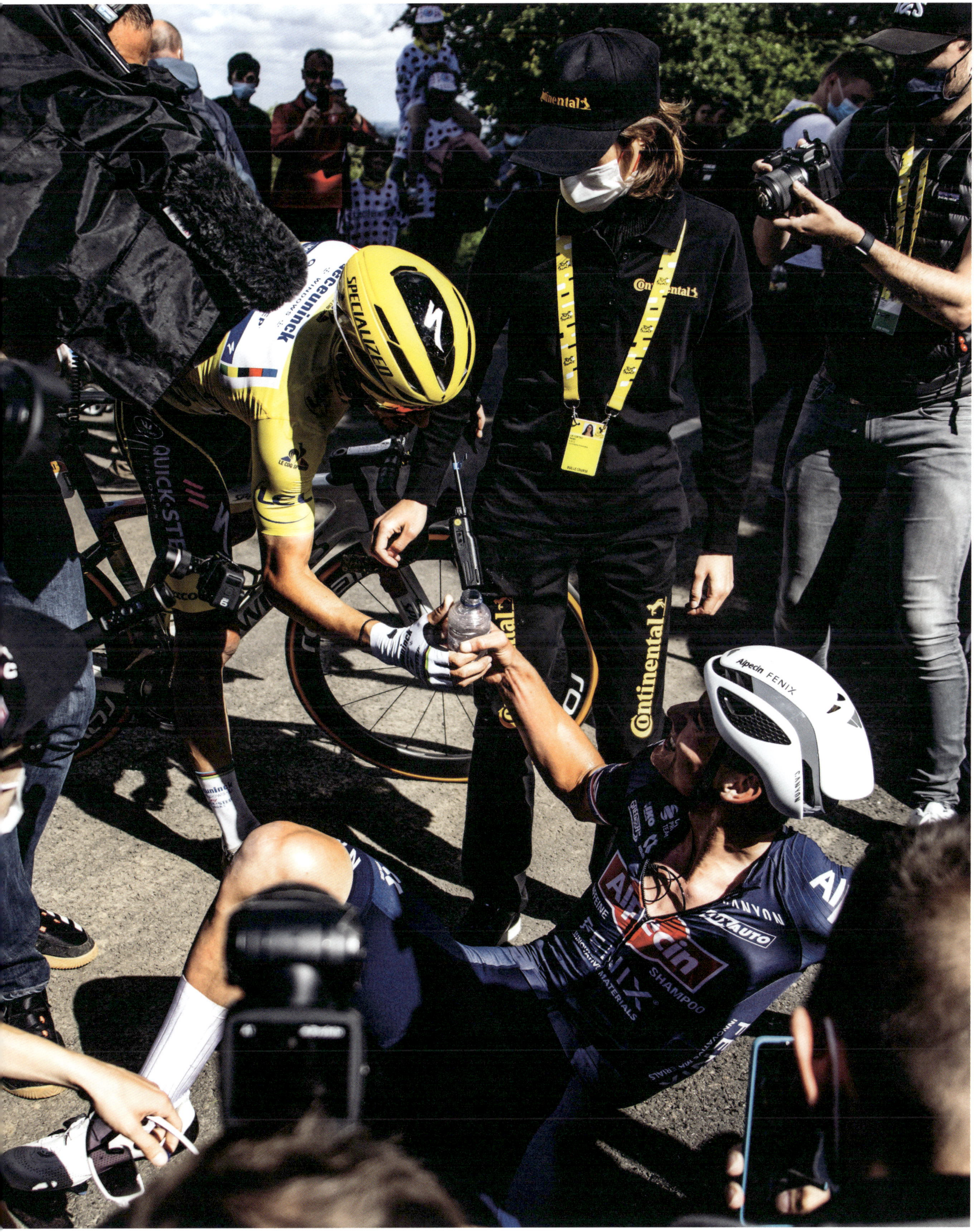
Continental
SPECIALIZED
Continental
Alpecin FENIX
CANYON
SHAMPOO

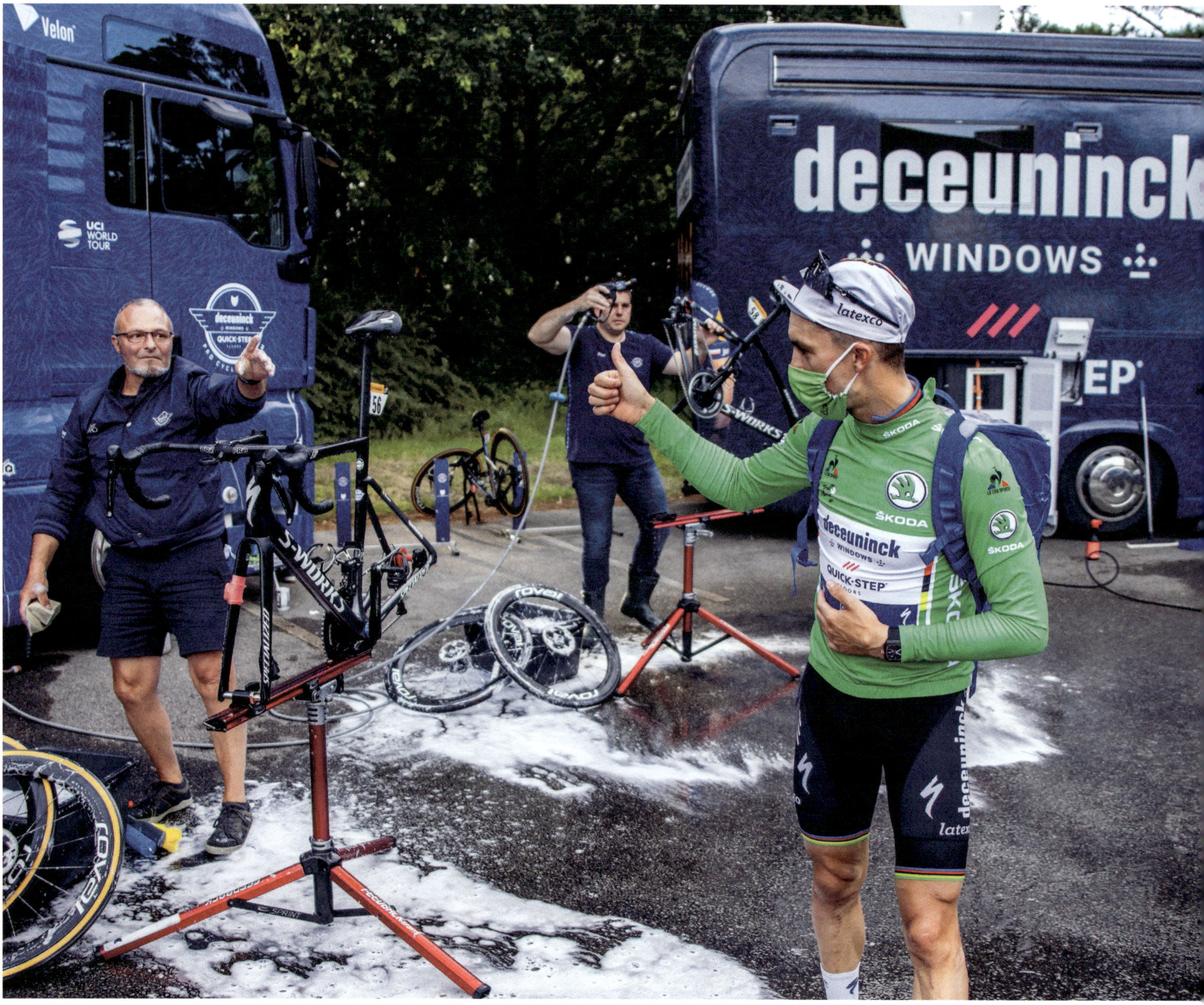

MÛR-DE-BRETAGNE, 27.06.2021

Julian Alaphilippe heeft het geel geruild voor het groen. Vanaf rit 1 blijft het groen in de ploeg. Minzaam groet hij de harde werkers achter de schermen. Een mooi gebaar. Links Dirk Tyteca, achteraan Stijn Vandenberghe.

De eerste van Mark Cavendish in de Tour de France van dit jaar, de vierde rit in Fougères. En of hij het nog kan! Mark doet het nu ook in de Tour de France! Julian Alaphilippe (in het groen) geniet mee, evenals Kasper Asgreen achteraan. Masseur Kevin Verstaen geeft hem een stevige knuffel.

Julian Alaphilippe traded yellow for green. From stage 1, the green stayed with the team. From stage 4, Mark Cavendish wore it. He gives a friendly greeting to the hard workers behind the scenes. A nice gesture. Dirk Tyteca on the left, Stijn Vandenberghe at the back.

Mark Cavendish's first in this year's Tour de France, stage 4 in Fougères. He still got it! Mark pulls it off in the Tour de France! Julian Alaphilippe (in green) enjoys it, as does Kasper Asgreen at the back. Masseur Kevin Verstaen gives him a strong hug.

Julian Alaphilippe a échangé le jaune contre le vert. Le vert appartient à l'équipe dès la première étape. À partir de la quatrième étape, il est porté par Mark Cavendish. Affable il salue les travailleurs de l'ombre. Un beau geste. À gauche Dirk Tyteca, à l'arrière Stijn Vandenberghe. ▲

La première victoire de Mark Cavendish dans le Tour de France de cette année, la quatrième étape à Fougères. Après un beau sprint, il y est arrivé ! Julian Alaphilippe (en vert) partage sa joie, tout comme Kasper Asgreen à l'arrière. Kevin Verstaen, le masseur, le serre (bien fort) dans ses bras. ▶

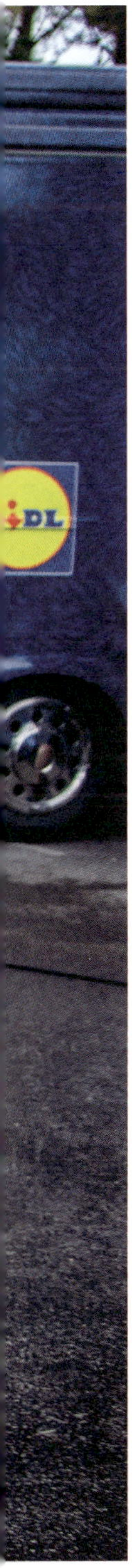
iDL

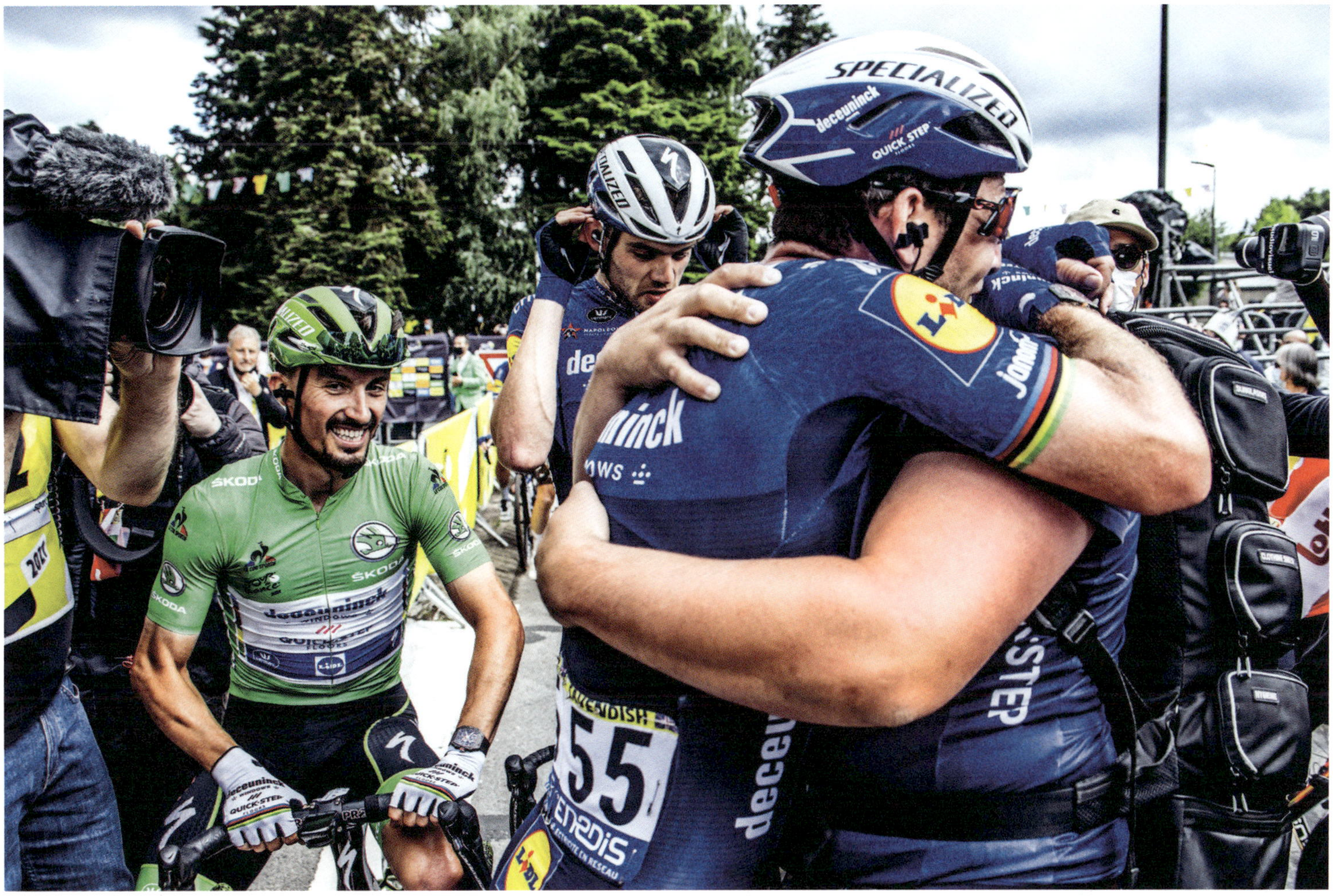
SPECIALIZED
deceuninck
QUICK STEP
55
ENEDIS
SKODA

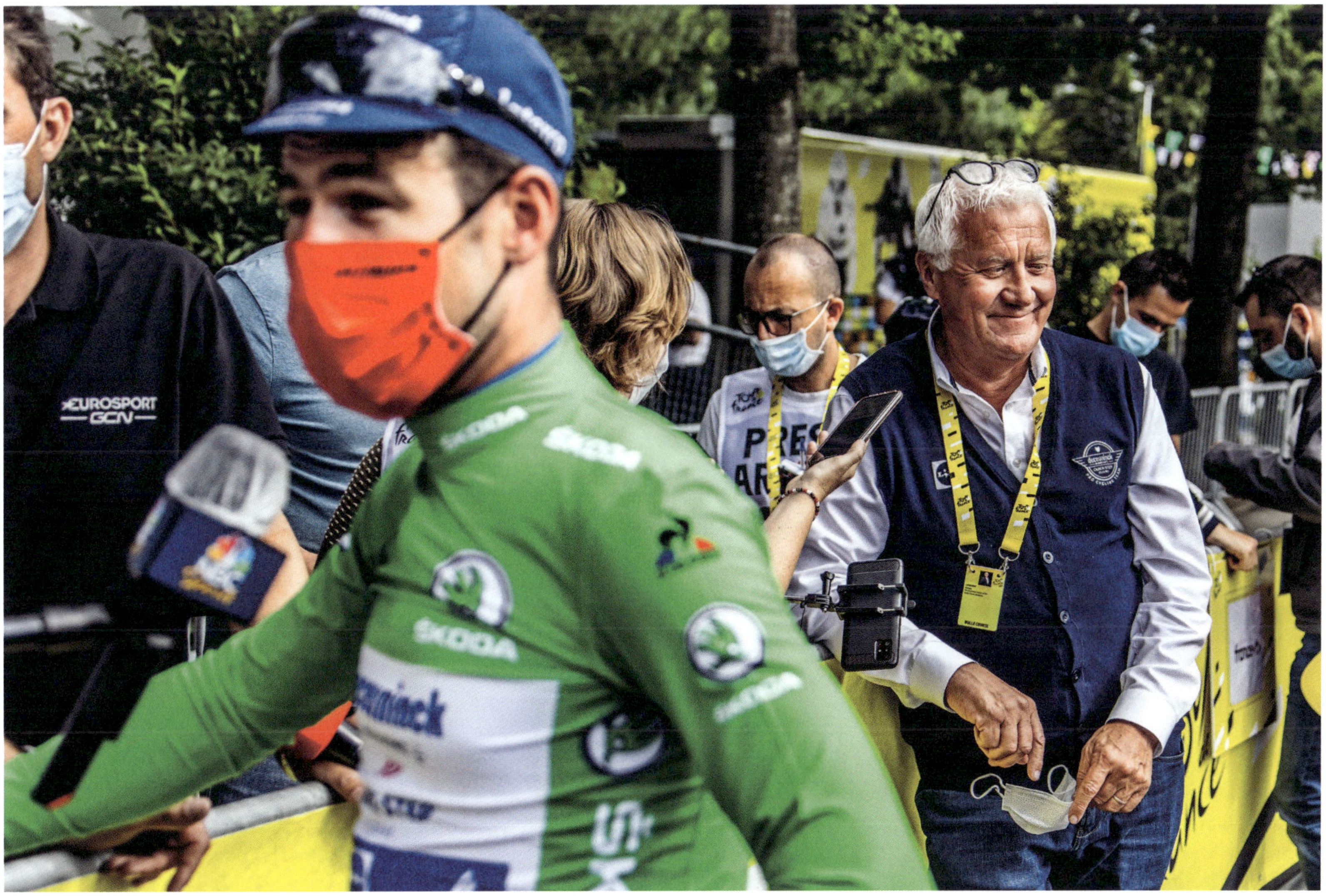
EUROSPORT
GCN
SKODA

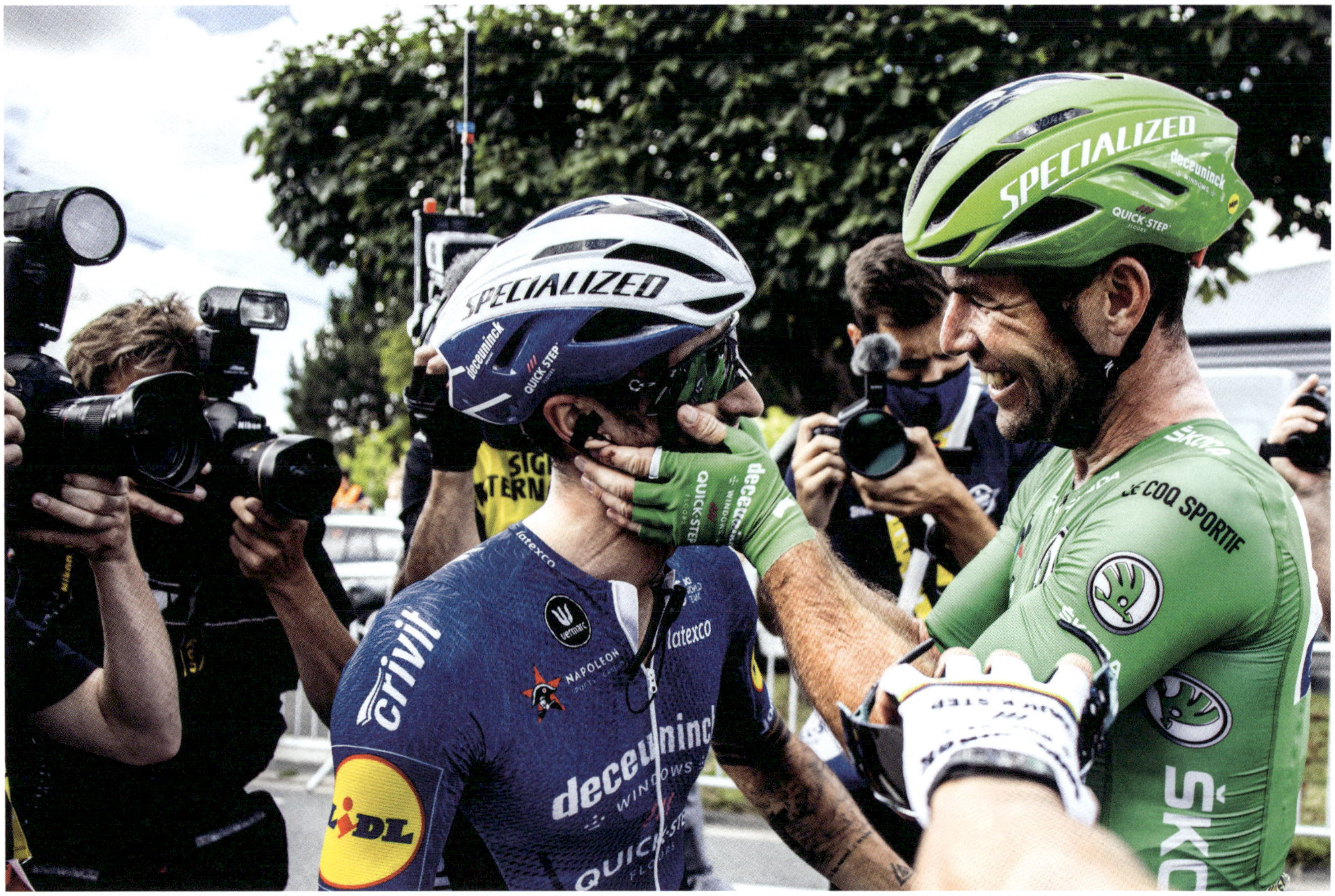
SPECIALIZED
deceuninck
QUICK-STEP
SPECIALIZED
deceuninck
QUICK-STEP
LE COQ SPORTIF
crivit
latexco
NAPOLEON
deceuninck
WINDOWS
QUICK-STEP
LIDL

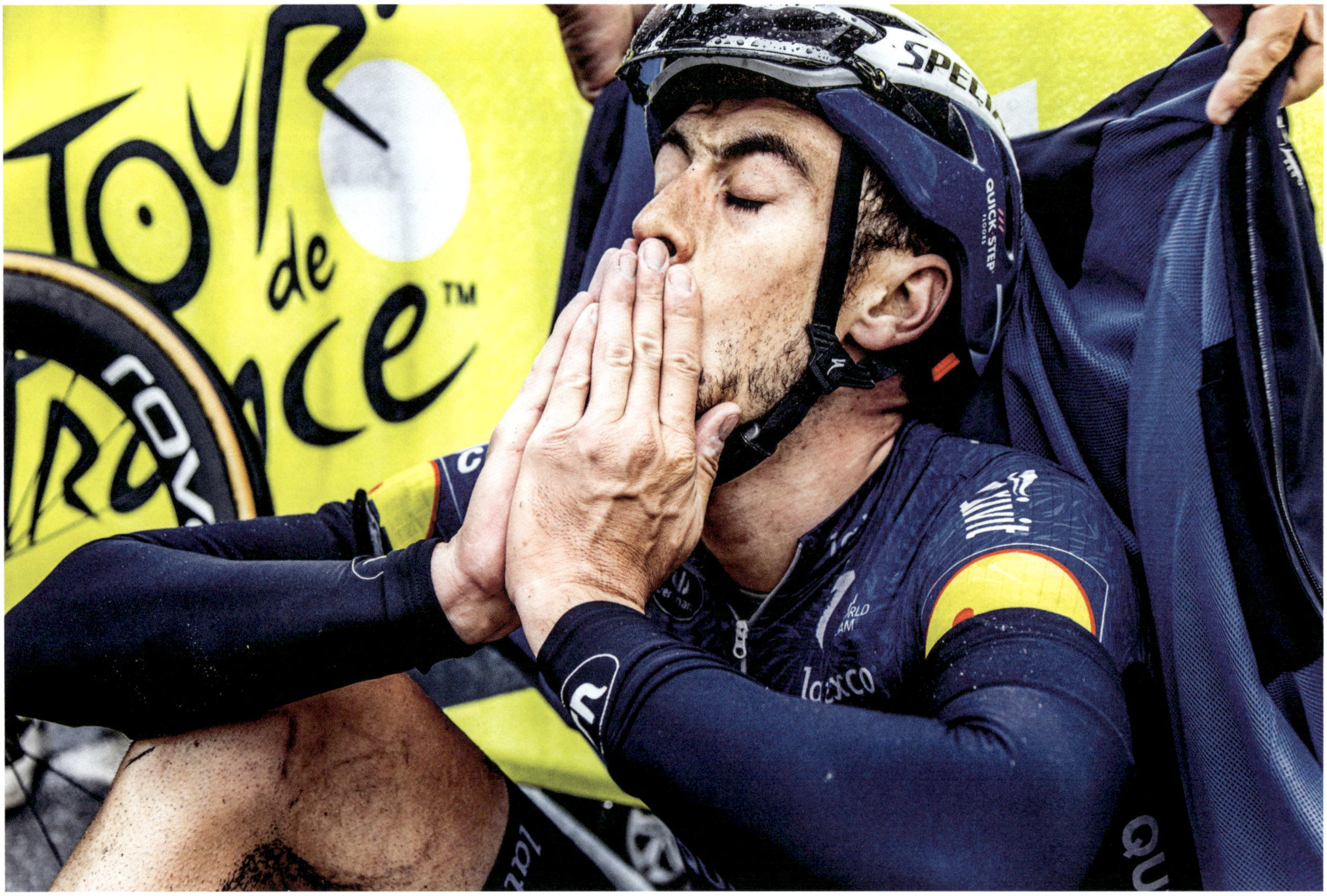
Tour de France™
QUICK-STEP
latexco

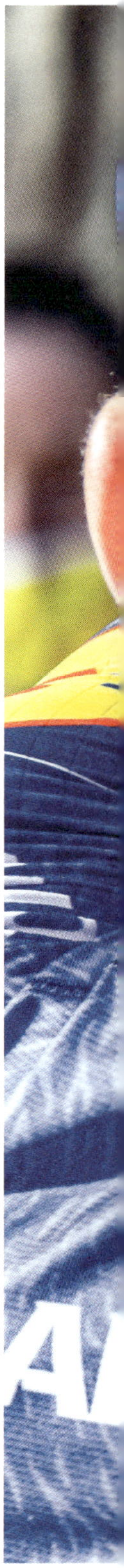

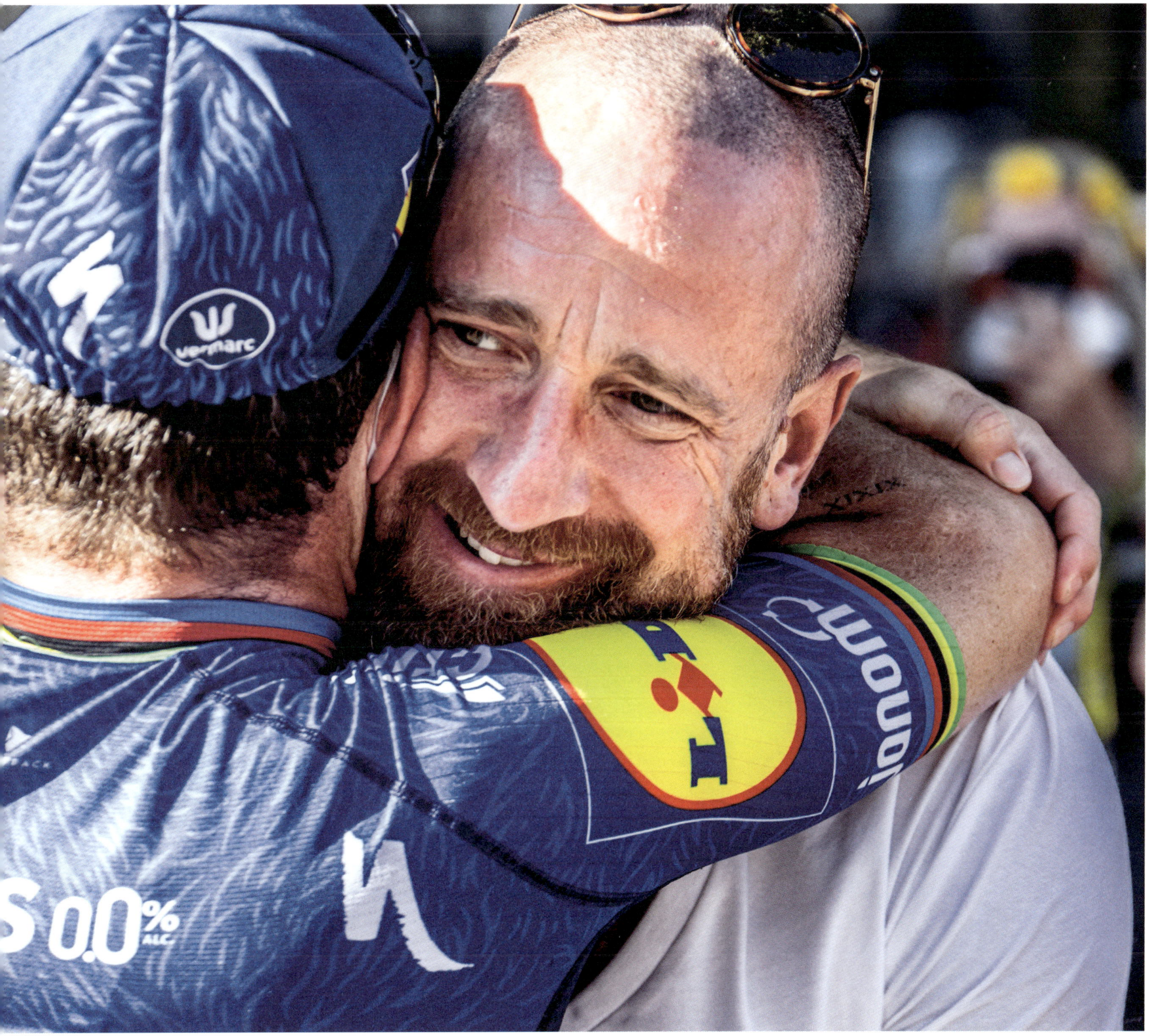

FOUGÈRES, 29.06.2021

De dankbaarheid straalt van het gezicht van Mark Cavendish. Mattia Cattaneo neemt de lof graag in ontvangst en was er zelf heel dicht bij. In de negende etappe, de bergrit naar de Montée de Tignes, strandt Mattia op de tweede plaats.

Een stevige `hug' van sir Bradley Wiggins voor Mark Cavendish na zijn eerste Tourzege in Fougères.

Mark Cavendish's face is beaming with gratitude. Mattia Cattaneo is happy to accept the praise. In the mountainous stage 9 to Montée de Tignes, Mattia finished in second place. He would also finish fourth in the 14th stage.

A big hug from Sir Bradley Wiggins for Mark Cavendish after his first Tour victory in Fougères.

La gratitude illumine le visage de Mark Cavendish. Mattia Cattaneo est heureux d'accepter ses éloges. Pour la neuvième étape, l'étape de la montée de Tignes, Mattia a dû se contenter de la deuxième place. Il a également terminé quatrième lors de la quatorzième étape. ◤

Un énorme « hug » de Sir Bradley Wiggins pour Mark Cavendish après sa première victoire sur le Tour, à Fougères. ▲

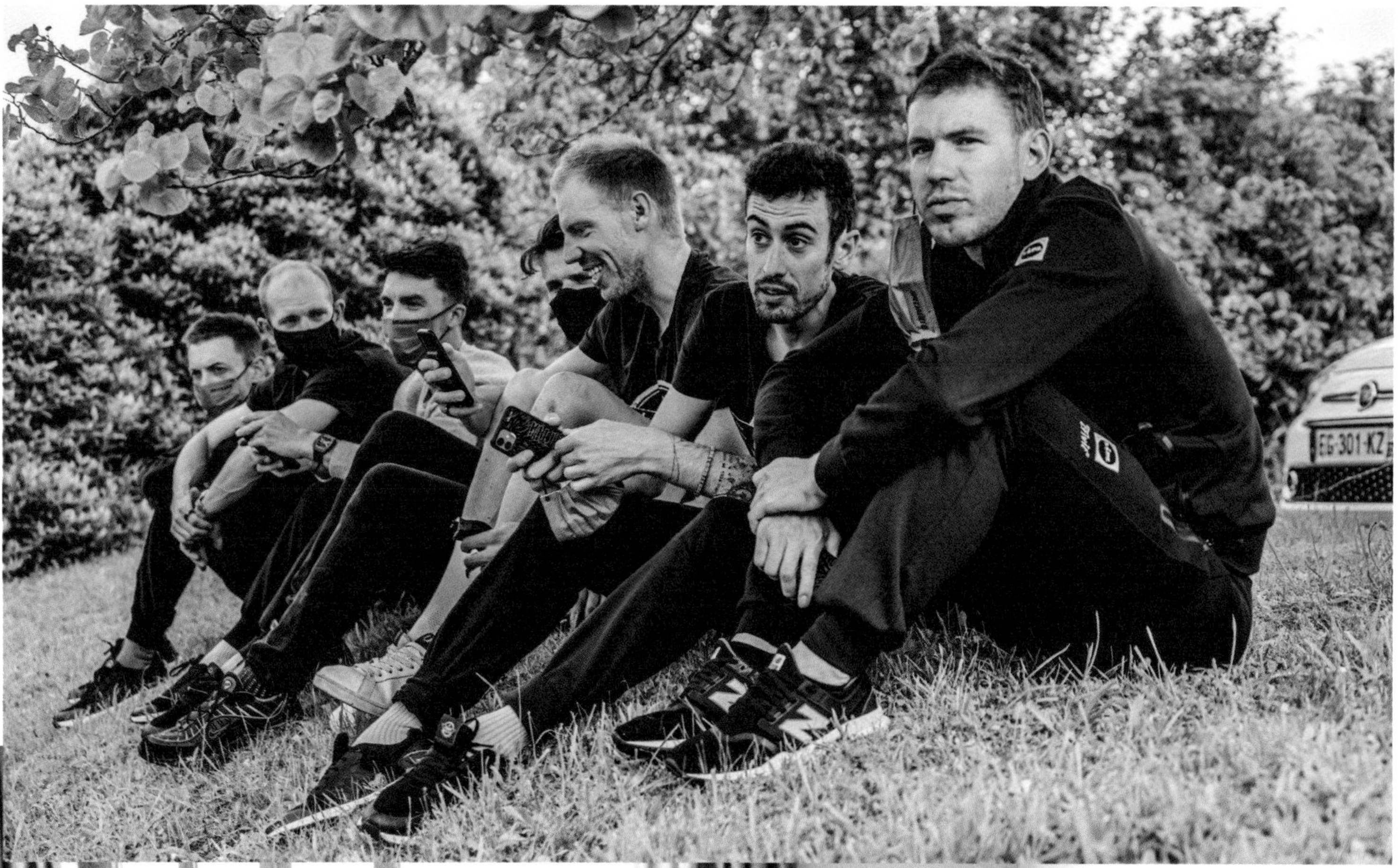
EG-301-KZ

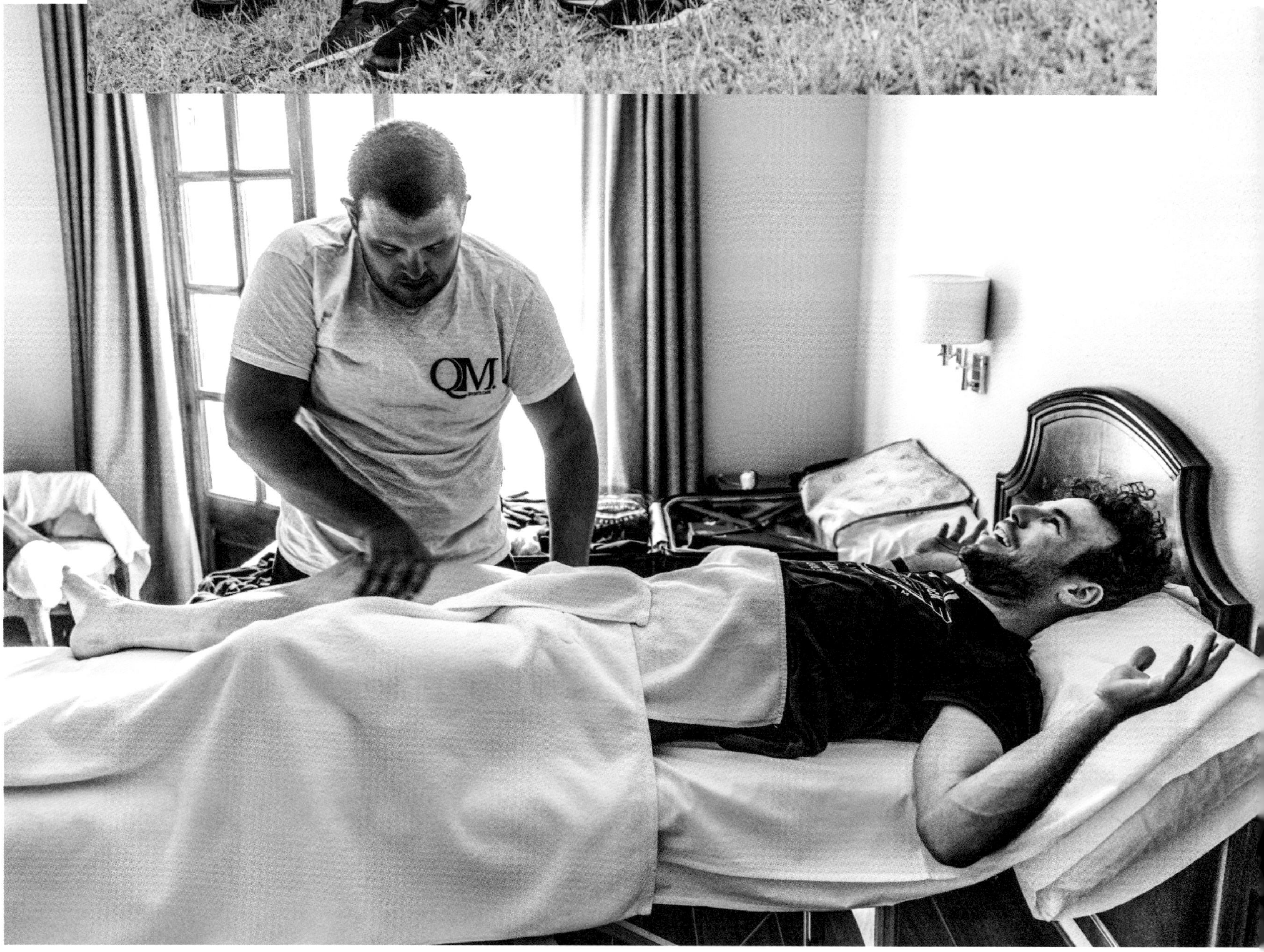
QM

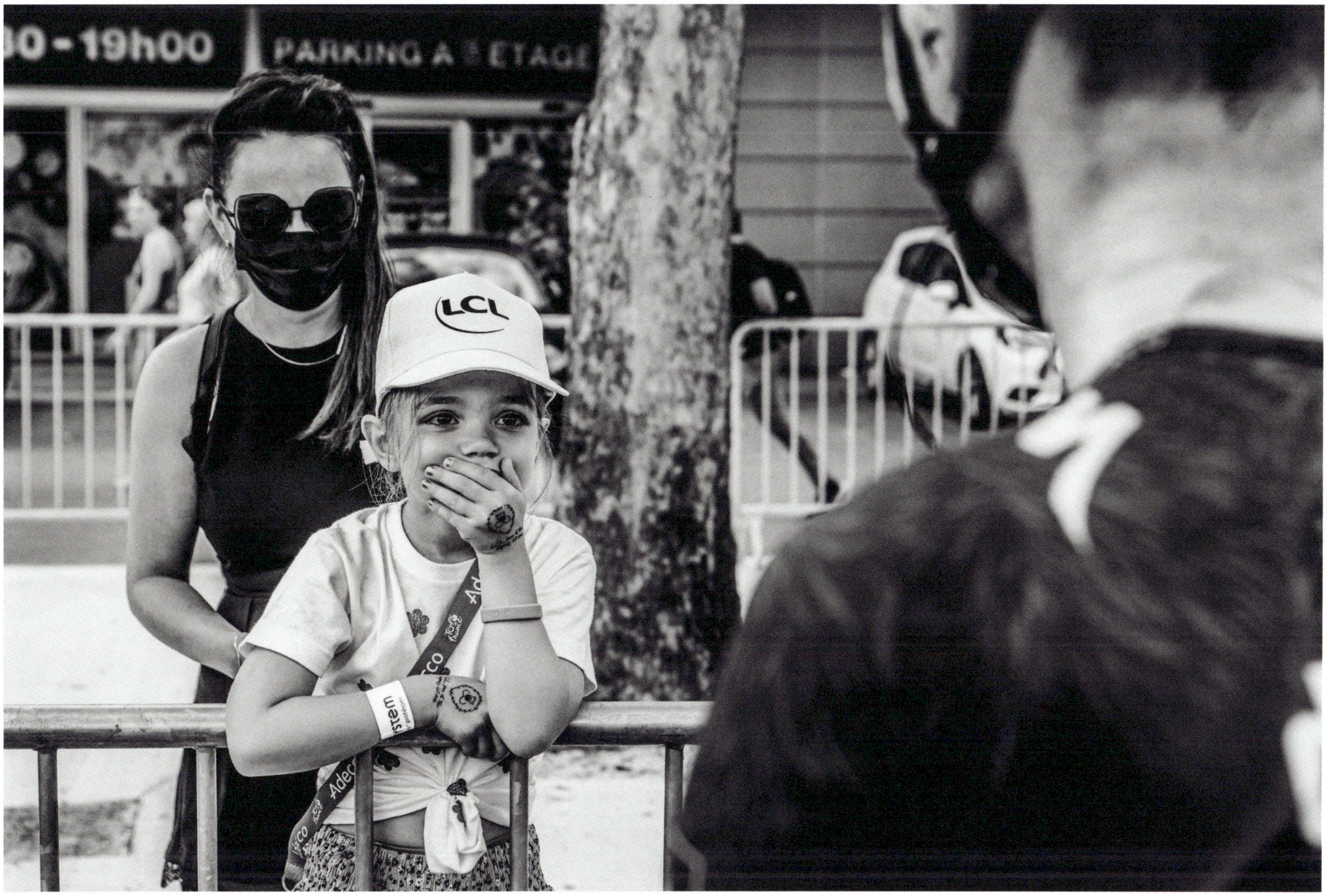

SAINT-PAUL-TROIS-CHÂTEAUX, 08.07.2021

Belangrijke gasten voor Dries Devenyns, na de twaalfde etappe in Nîmes, op 8 juli: vrouwlief en dochtertje op bezoek. Maar in coronatijden nog steeds op een opgelegde afstand. Doodjammer, en lastig vooral. De Tour is zwaar, een innig moment met familie is zo opbeurend. Hopen dat het volgend jaar weer volop kan.

Important visitors for Dries Devenyns after the 12th stage in Nîmes on 8 July. His wife and daughter are visiting, though at the necessary distance during the time of the pandemic. A great pity, and above all, an inconvenience. The Tour is tough, and an intimate moment with family is so comforting. We hope there'll be plenty of that next year.

Des invitées d'honneur pour Dries Devenyns, après la douzième étape à Nîmes, le 8 juillet : sa femme et sa fille sont au rendez-vous. Mais elles gardent leur distance, Covid-19 oblige. Des conditions assez difficiles. Le Tour est une épreuve de taille et un moment intime avec la famille, ça aide. En espérant que les choses iront mieux l'année prochaine. ▲

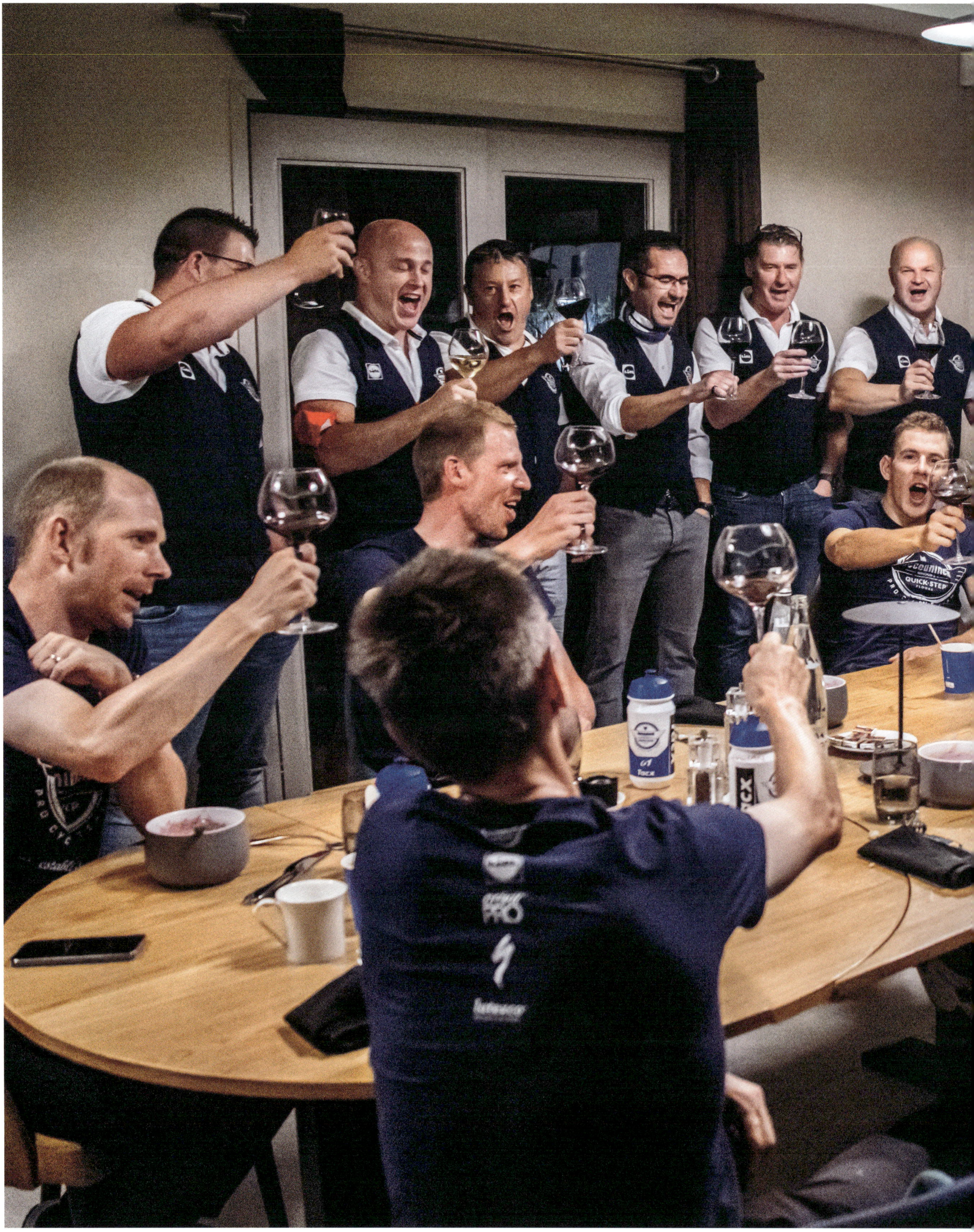
QUICK-STEP
PRO

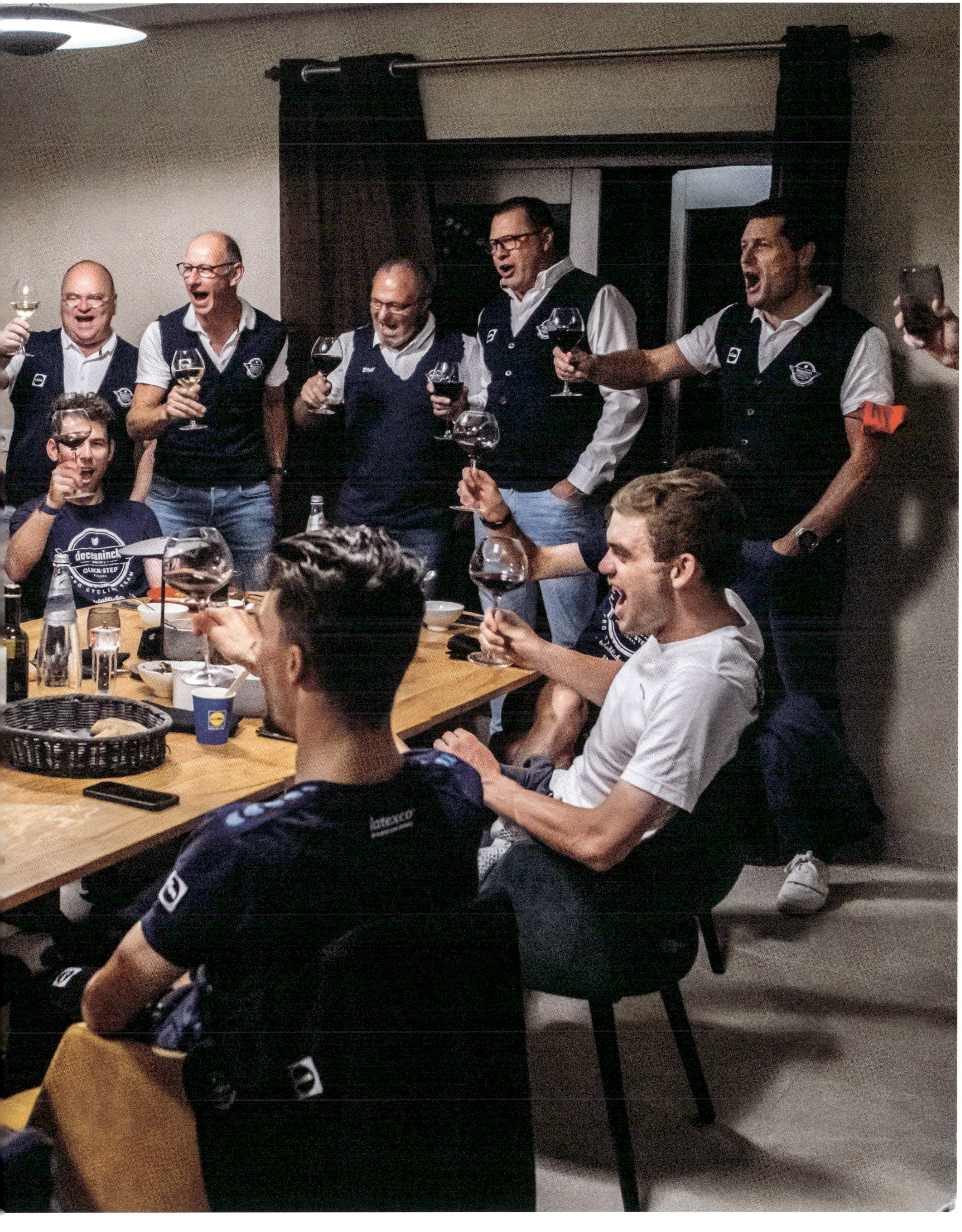
QUICK-STEP
latexco

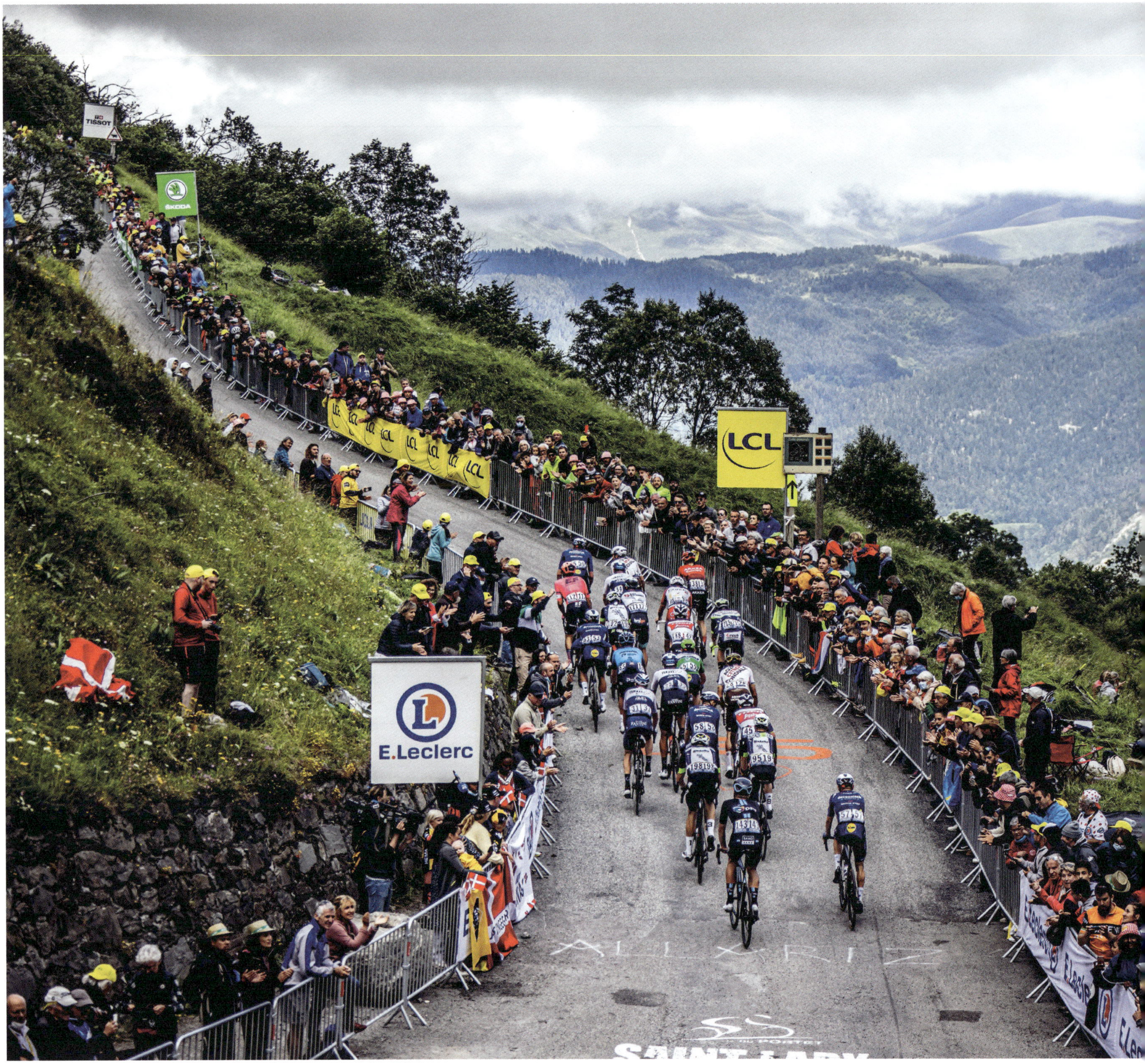

LUZ ARDIDEN, 15.07.2021

Samen strijden, in goede en kwade dagen. Groene trui Mark Cavendish wordt over de Pyreneeën 'gedragen' door vier ploegmaten: Dries Devenyns, Tim Declercq, Davide Ballerini en Michael Mørkøv. Missie geslaagd. De 'gruppetto' beëindigde de zeventiende rit naar Col du Portet binnen de tijdslimiet.

It's a team effort, on good and bad days. Green jersey Mark Cavendish is "carried" across the Pyrenees by four teammates: Dries Devenyns, Tim Declercq, Davide Ballerini, and Michael Mørkøv. Mission accomplished. The "gruppetto" finished the 17th stage to Col du Portet inside the time limit.

Rester soudés, dans les bons jours comme les mauvais. Le maillot vert Mark Cavendish est « porté » à travers les Pyrénées par quatre coéquipiers : Dries Devenyns, Tim Declercq, Davide Ballerini et Michael Mørkøv. Mission accomplie. Le « gruppetto » a terminé la dix-septième étape au col du Portet dans le délai imparti. ▶

eclerc

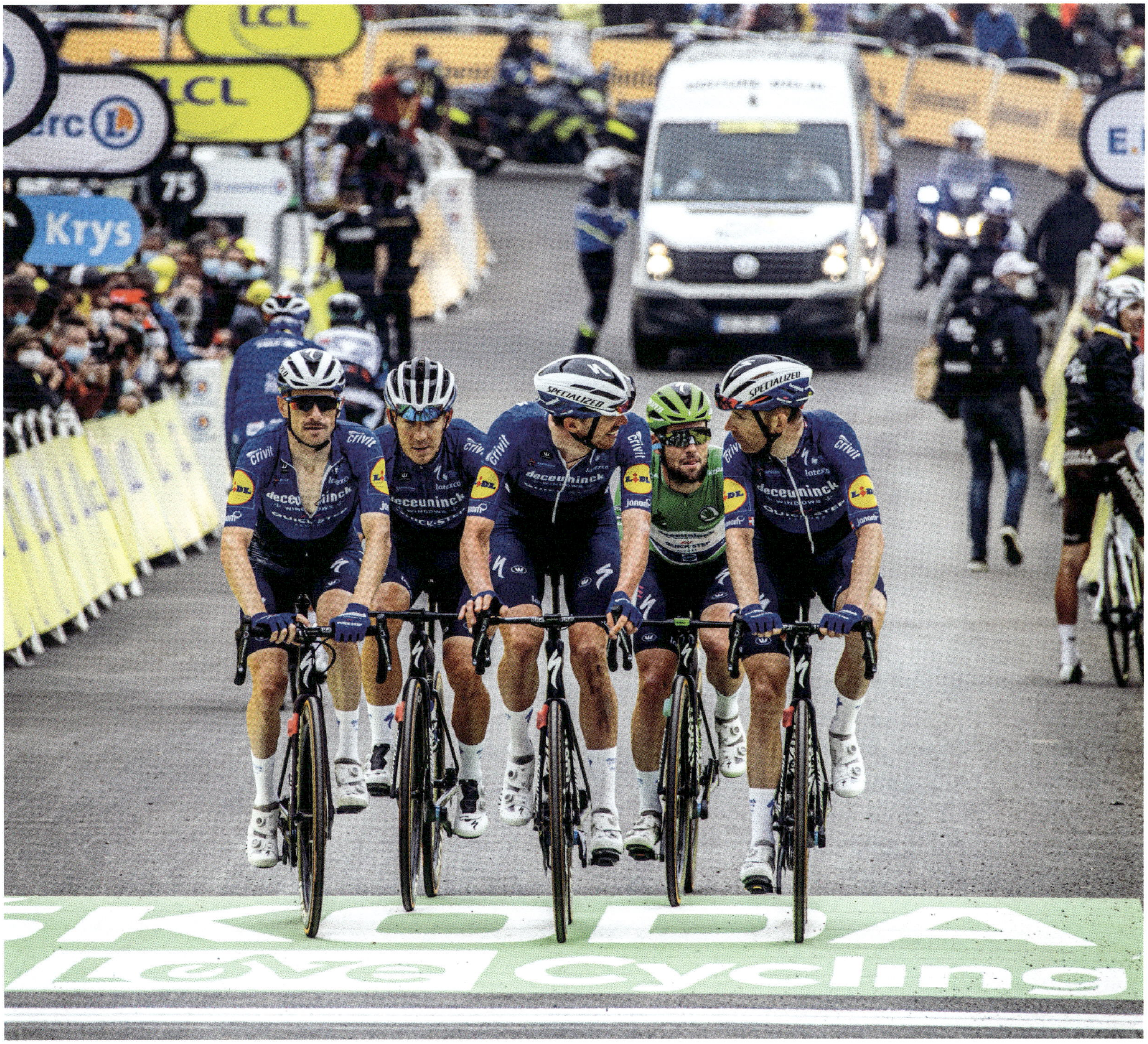
LCL
LCL
Krys
75
deceuninck
Love Cycling

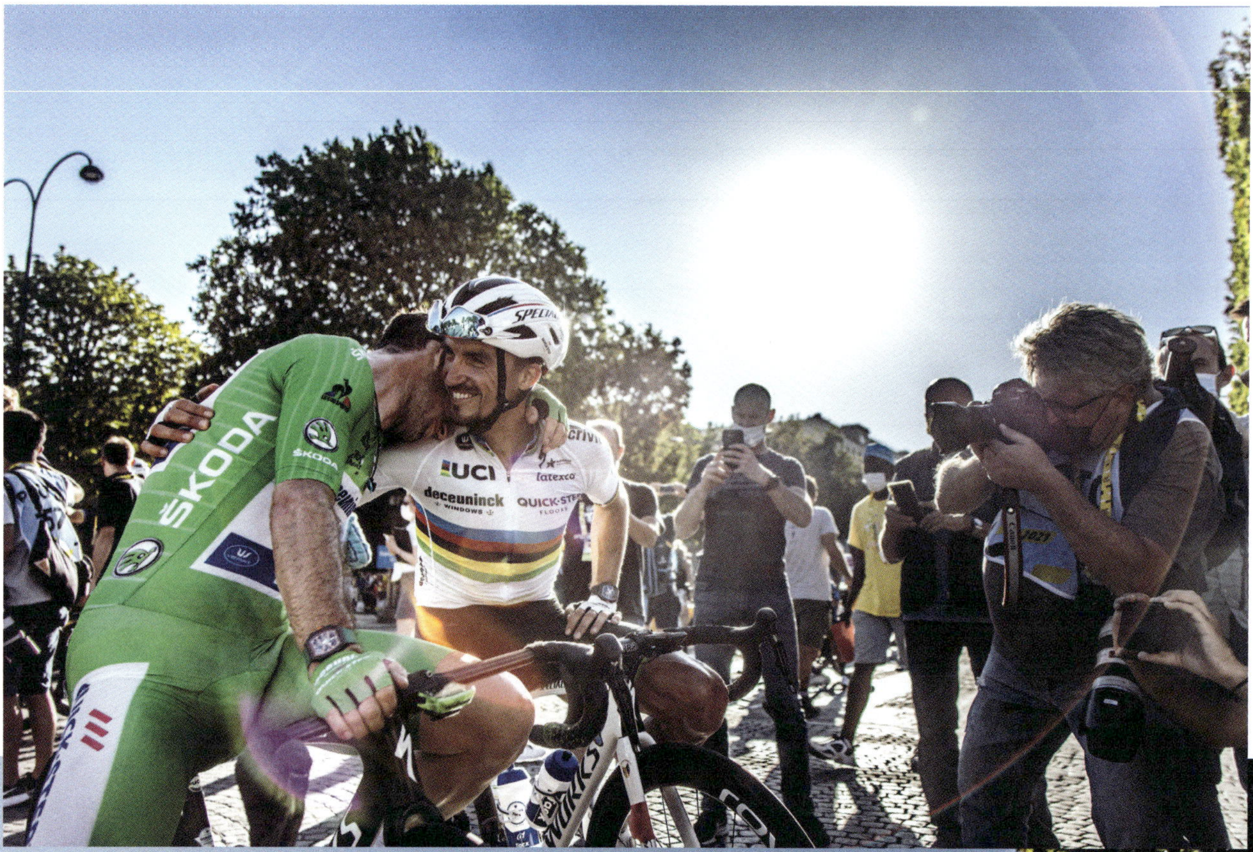
ŠKODA
UCI
deceuninck

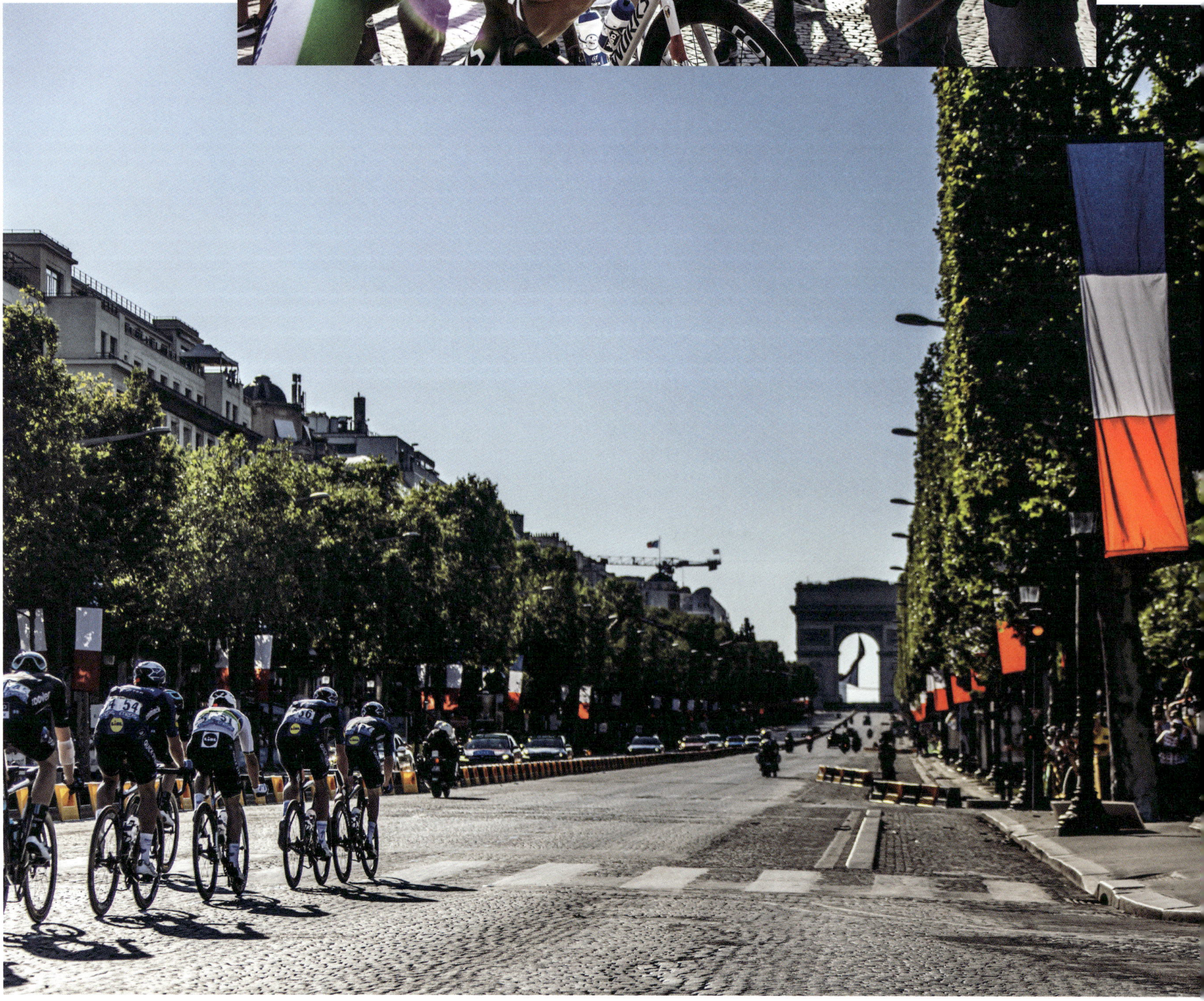

PARIS, 18.07.2021

Mark Cavendish wordt derde in de slotetappe, maar mag zijn groene trui showen aan Parijs en de wereld. En aan vrouw en zoontje. Het groen was al sinds dag één in het bezit van de ploeg.

Mark Cavendish finished third in the final stage, but was able to show off his green jersey to Paris and the world. And to his wife and son. The team had held onto the green jersey since day one.

Mark Cavendish termine troisième dans la dernière étape, mais peut brandir son maillot vert à Paris et pour le monde entier. Et pour sa femme et son fils. Le maillot vert était en possession de l'équipe depuis le premier jour.

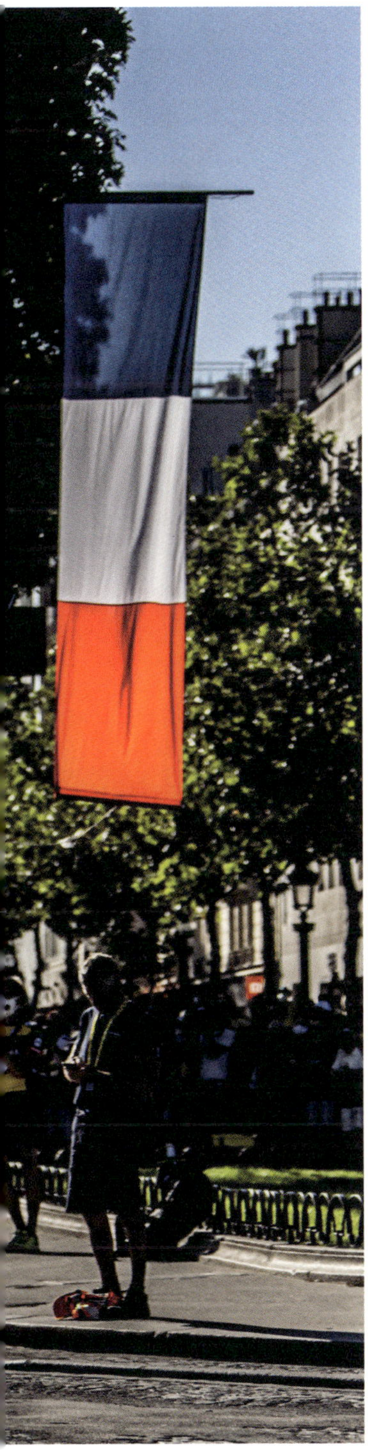

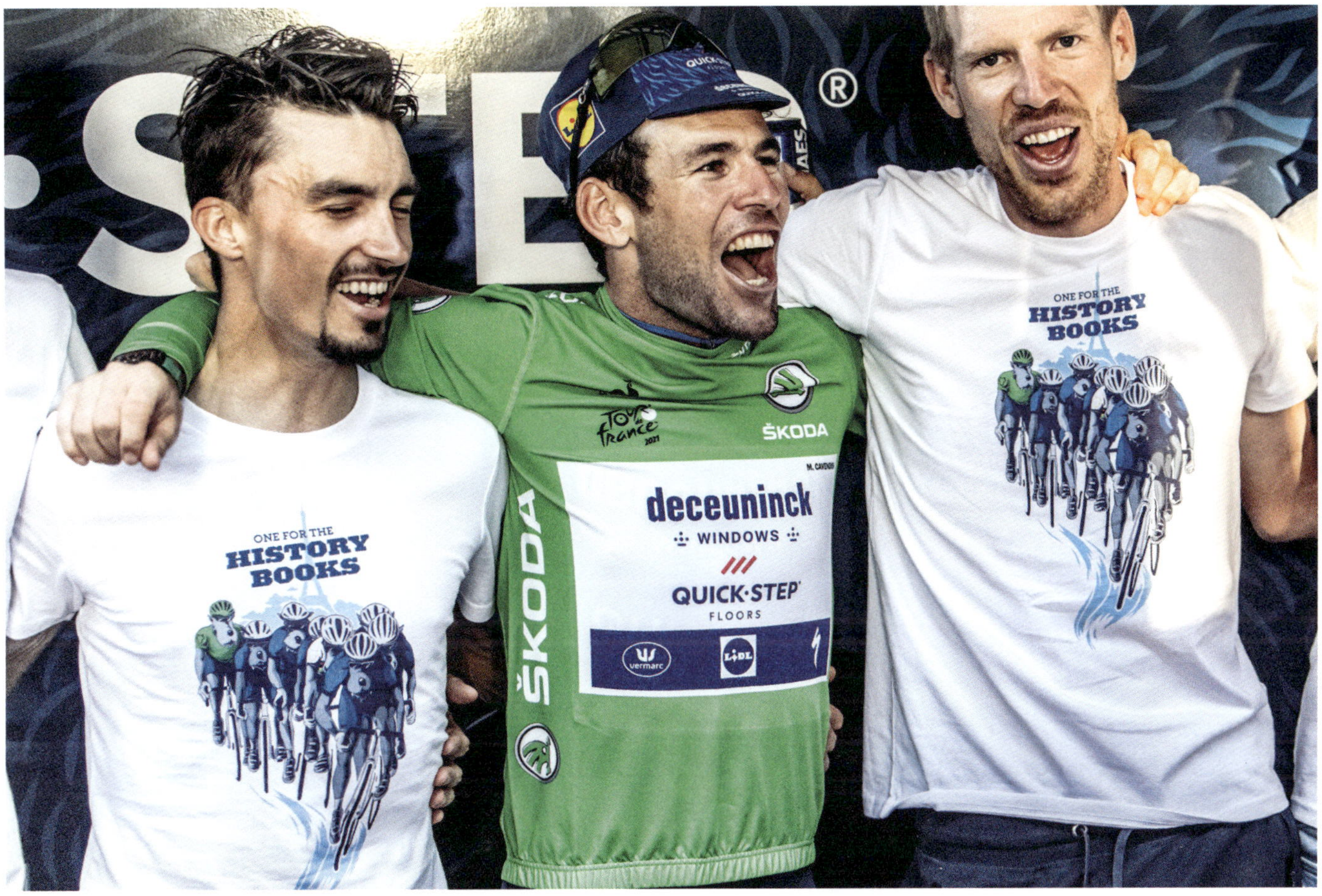

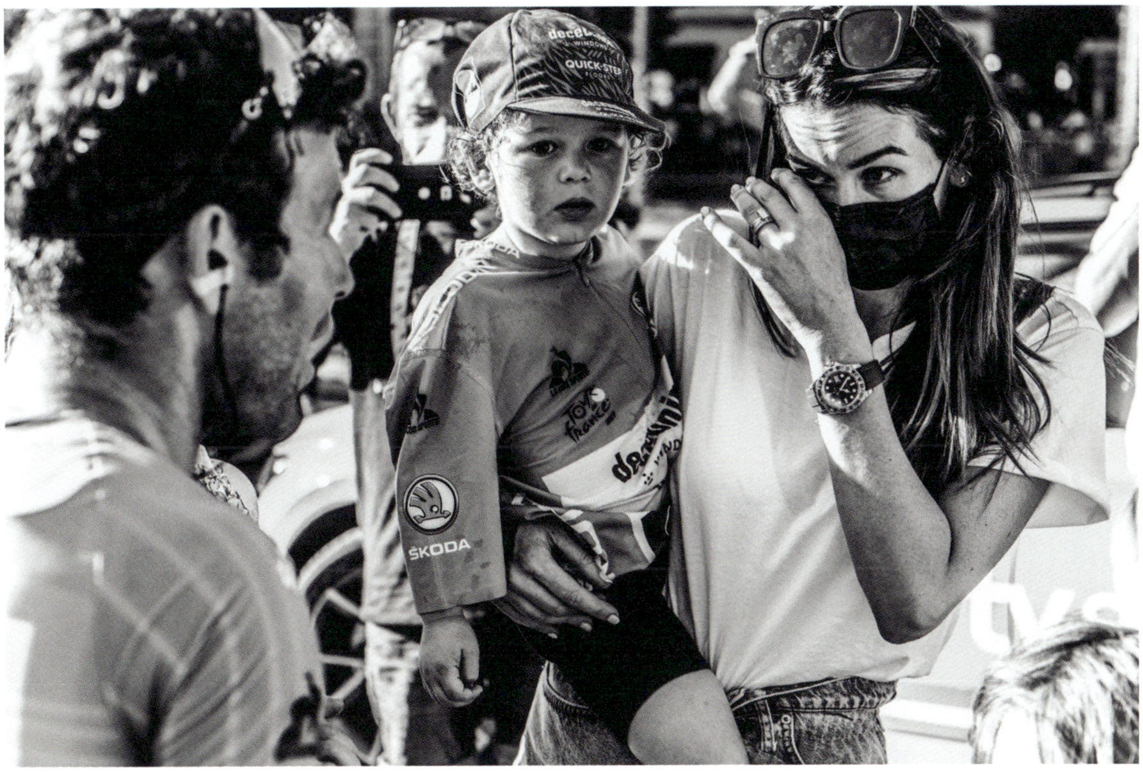

TOUR DE POLOGNE
09.08 - 15.08.2021

Nog maar eens een succesweek voor DQT. Op twee fronten nog wel. João Almeida is de sterkste in de Ronde van Polen. Hij wint twee ritten en ook Rémi Cavagna pikt er eentje mee.

Another successful week for DQT. On two fronts. João Almeida proves to be the strongest in the Tour de Pologne. He won two stages, and Rémi Cavagna also won one.

Une autre semaine réussie pour la DQT. Sur deux fronts. João Almeida s'impose sur le Tour de Pologne. Il a remporté deux étapes et Rémi Cavagna en a également remporté une.

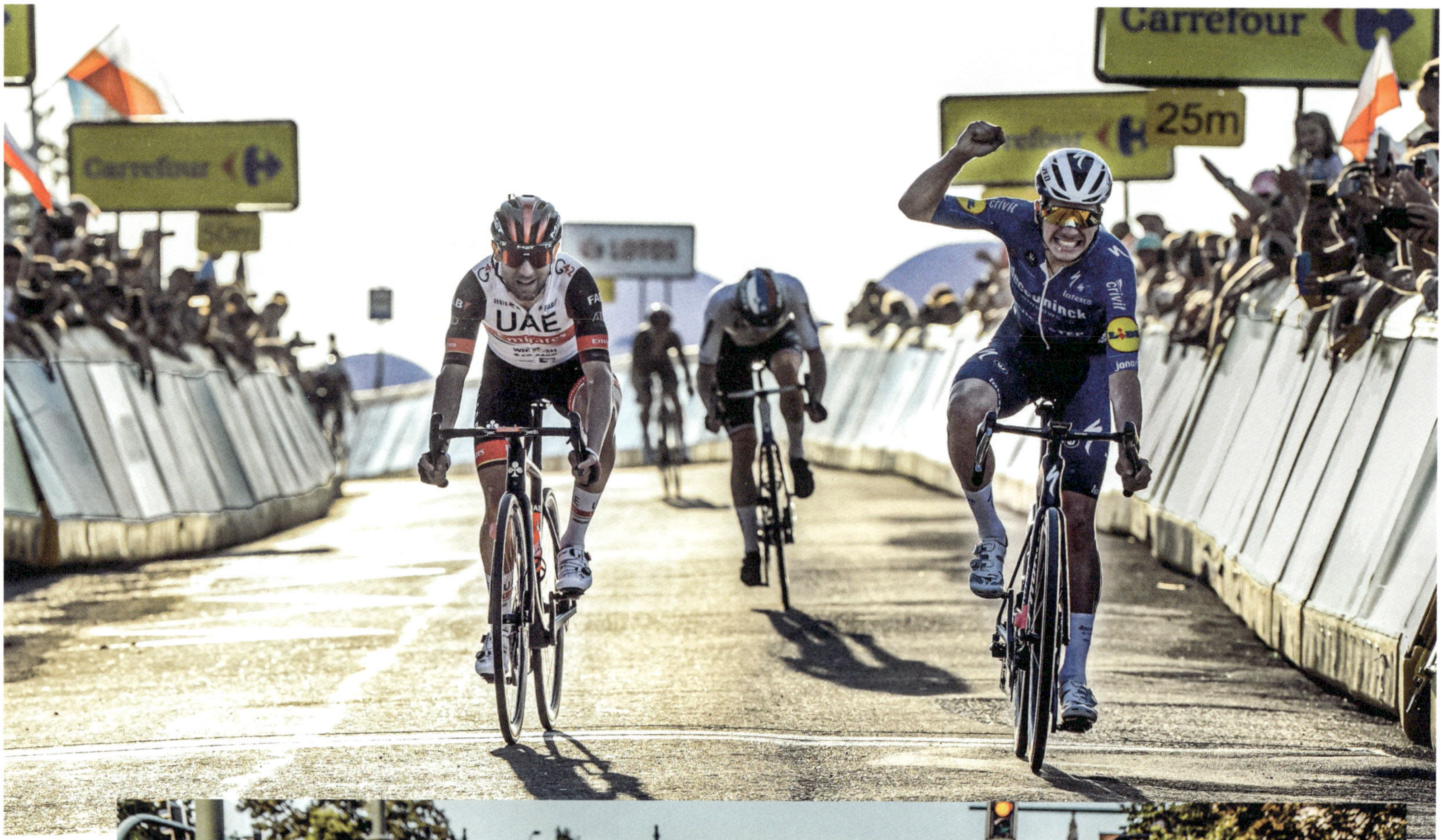

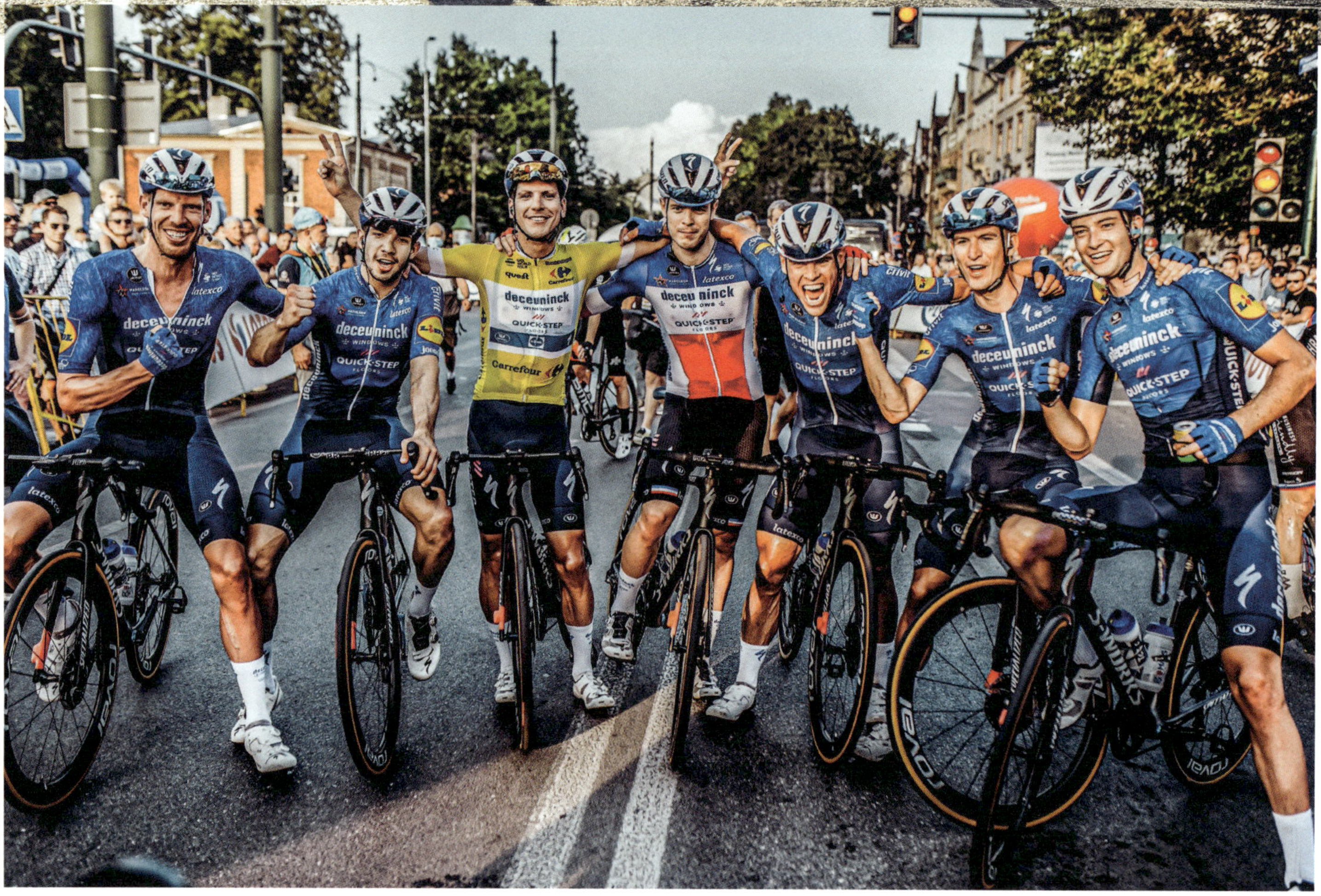

POSTNORD DANMARK RUNDT
10.08 - 14.08.2021

Remco Evenepoel wint de derde etappe van de Ronde van Denemarken. Hij wint ook de slottijdrit en wordt eindwinnaar.

Remco Evenepoel wins the third stage of the Danmark Rundt. He also wins the final time trial and comes out as the overall winner.

Remco Evenepoel remporte la troisième étape du Tour du Danemark. Il a également remporté le contre-la-montre final et se hisse au sommet du classement général.

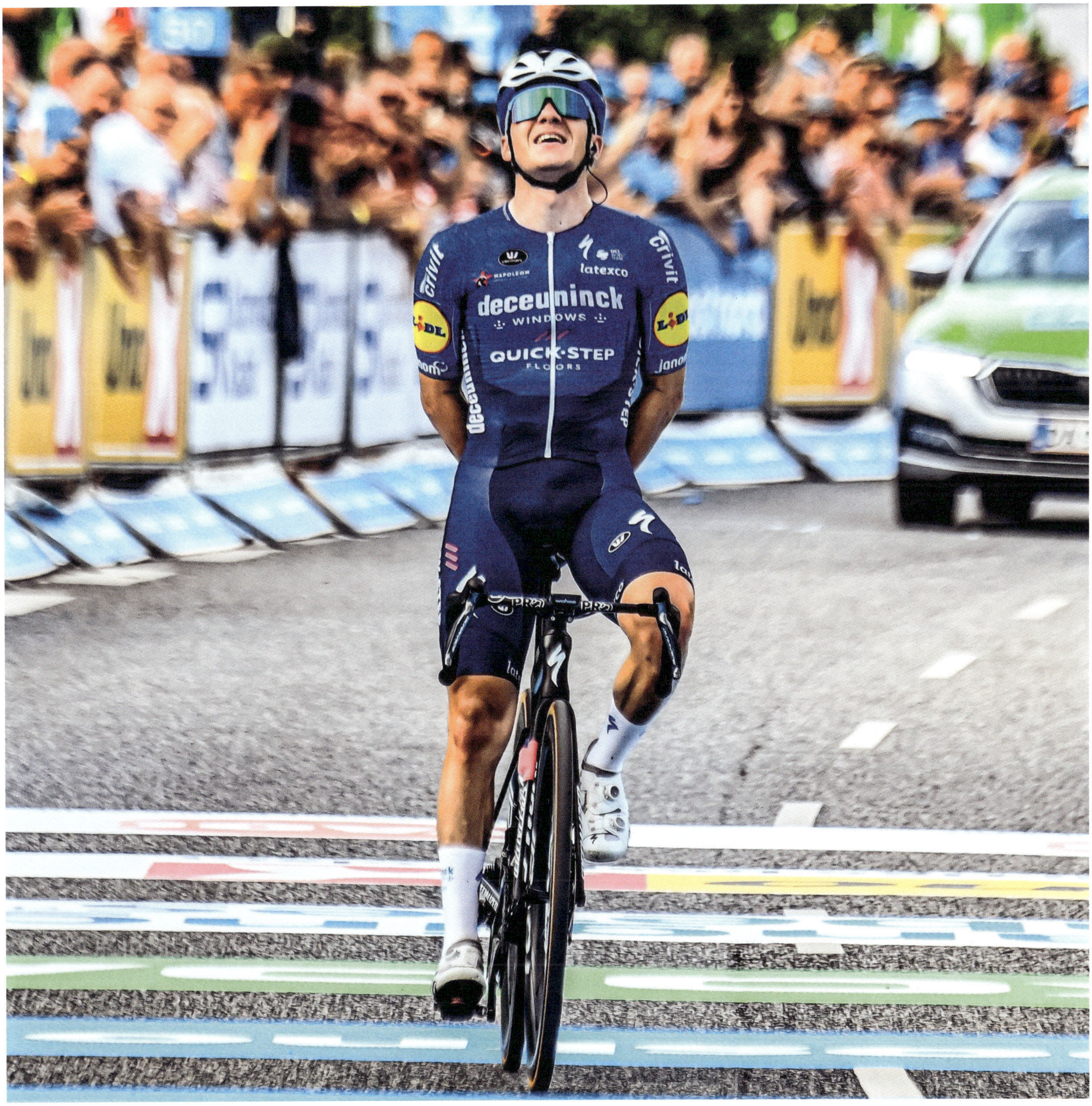

BRUSSELS CYCLING CLASSIC
28.08.2021

In de Brussels Cycling Classic verpulvert Remco Evenepoel de tegenstand en soleert hij naar de zege. De Houba de Strooperlaan werd op 20 augustus de Remco Evenepoellaan.

In the Brussels Cycling Classic, Remco Evenepoel defeated the opposition and soloed to victory. On 20 August, the Houba de Strooperlaan became the Remco Evenepoellaan.

Sur la Brussels Cycling Classic, Remco Evenepoel pulvérise l'opposition et s'impose en solitaire. Le 20 août, l'Avenue Houba de Strooper est devenue l'Avenue Houba d'Evenepoel.

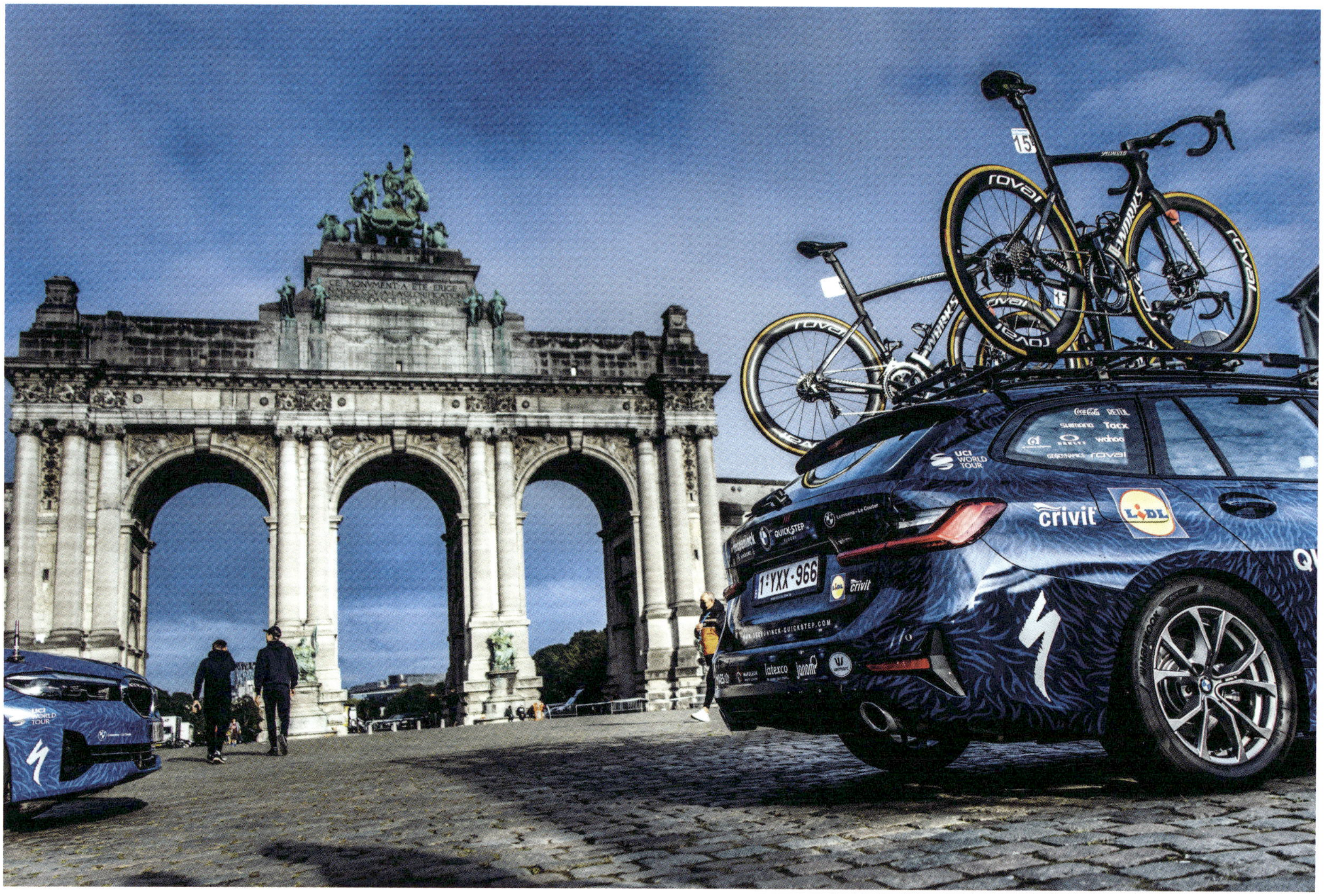

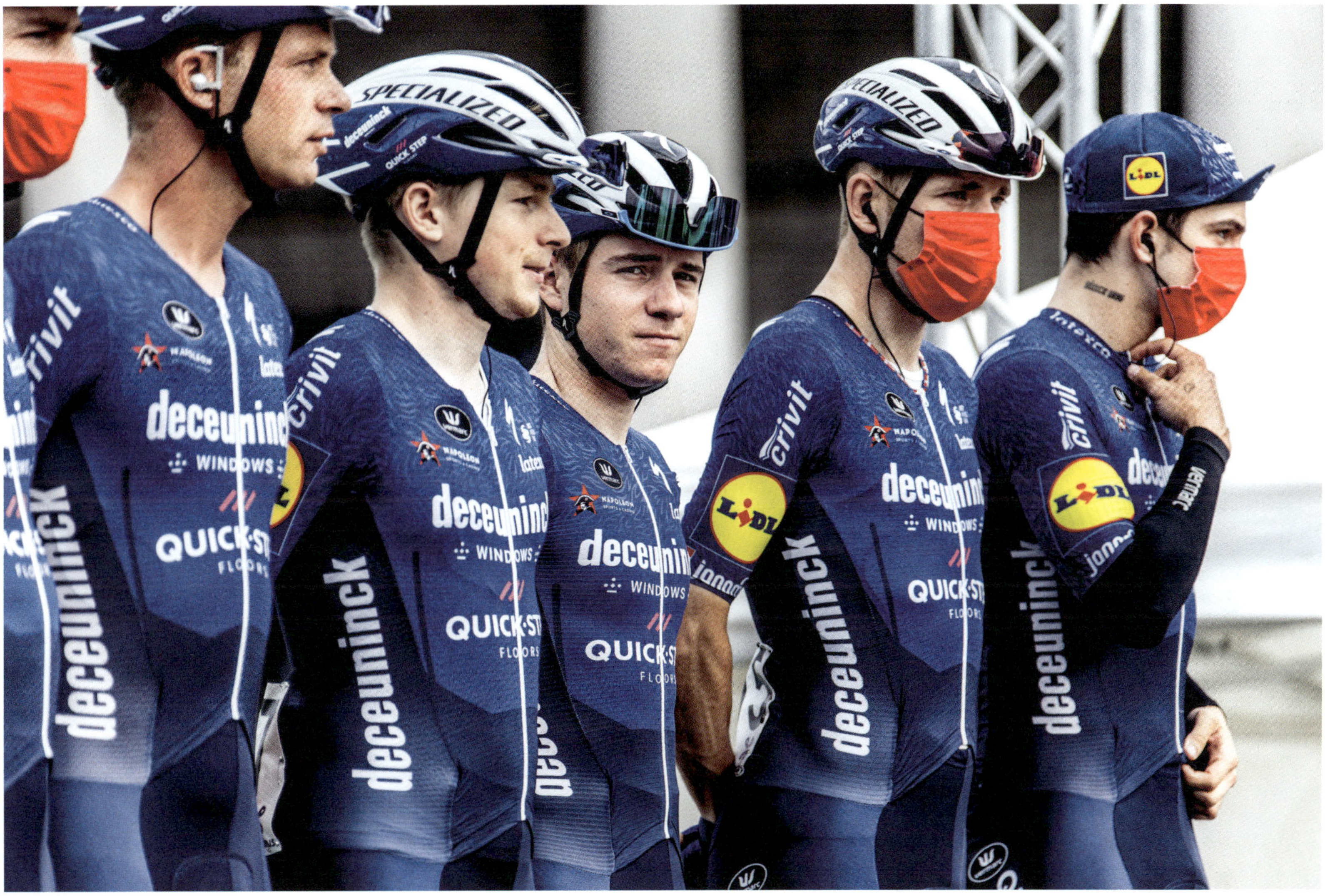
SPECIALIZED
deceuninck
WINDOWS
crivit
LIDL

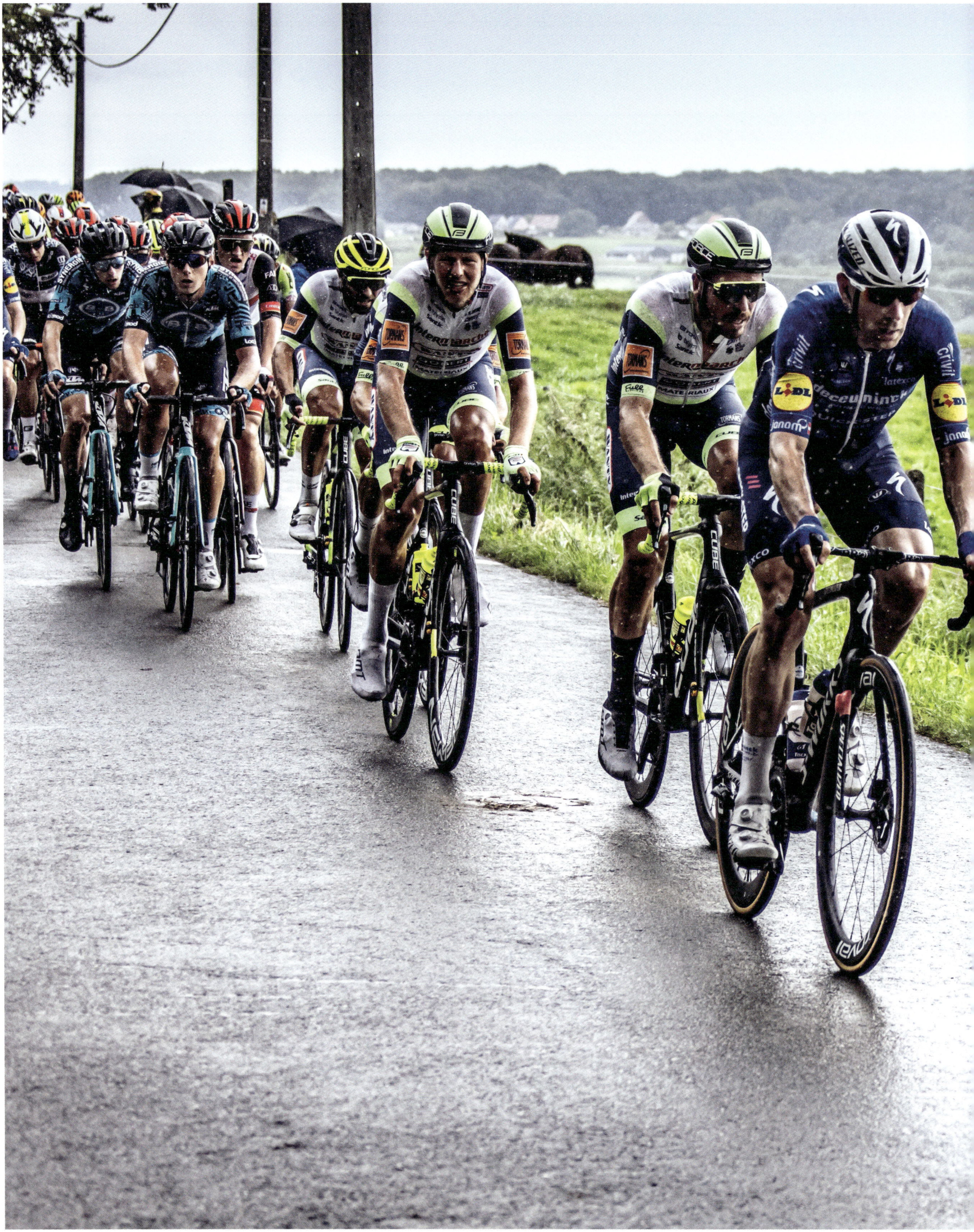
deceuninck
CUBE

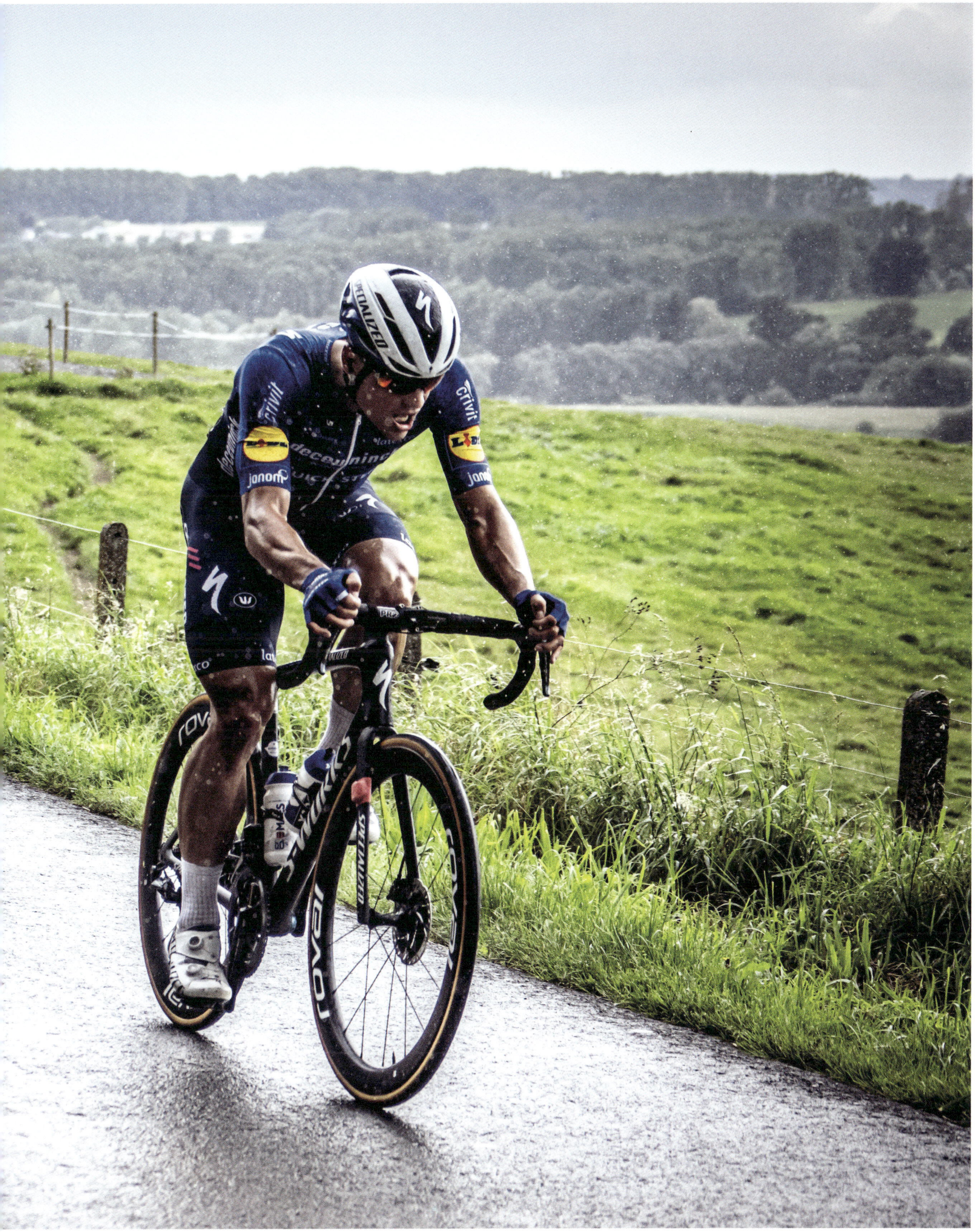
crivit
janom
crivit
janom
roval
roval

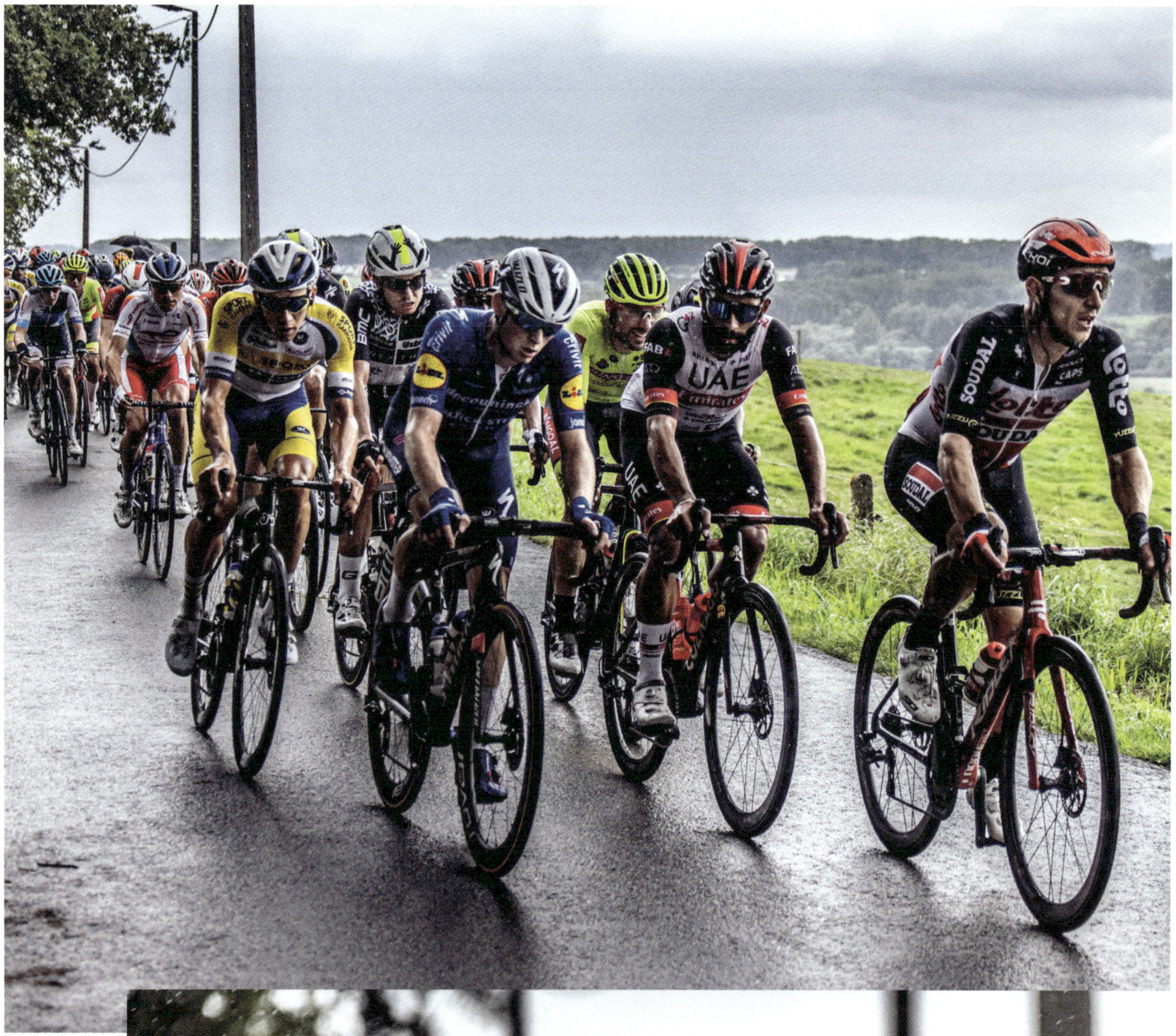

Stagiair Stan Van Tricht stapte de DQT-wereld binnen op 1 augustus 2021 en won al op 7 september Gullegem Koerse. Onder het goedkeurende oog van Patrick Lefevere.

Rider Stan Van Tricht entered the world of DQT on 1 August 2021 and already won Gullegem Koerse on 7 September, all under the approving eye of Patrick Lefevere.

Stan Van Tricht, le jeune stagiaire, a fait ses débuts dans le monde de la DQT le 1er août 2021 et a remporté Gullegem Koerse le 7 septembre. Sous le regard approbateur de Patrick Lefevere.

◀

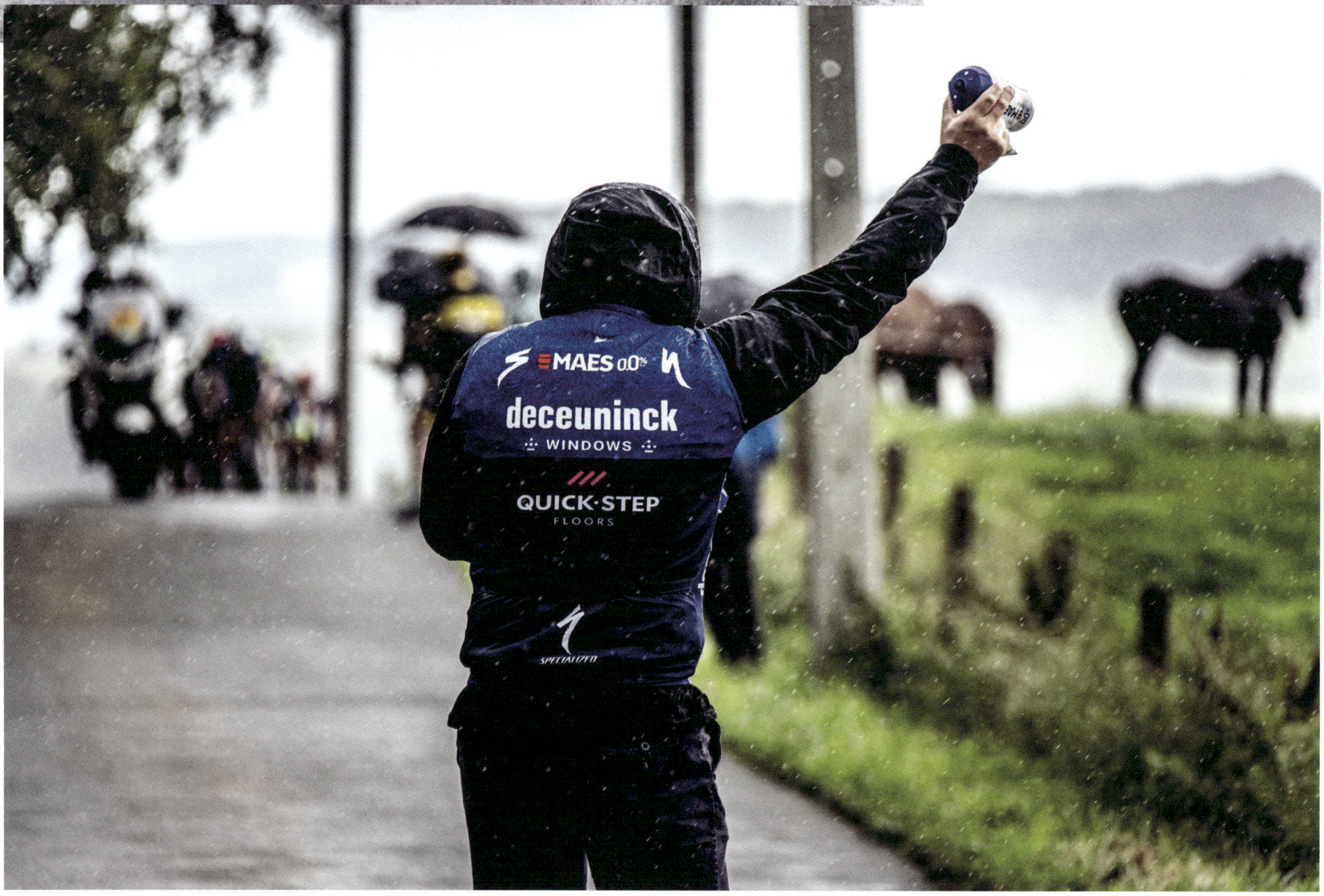

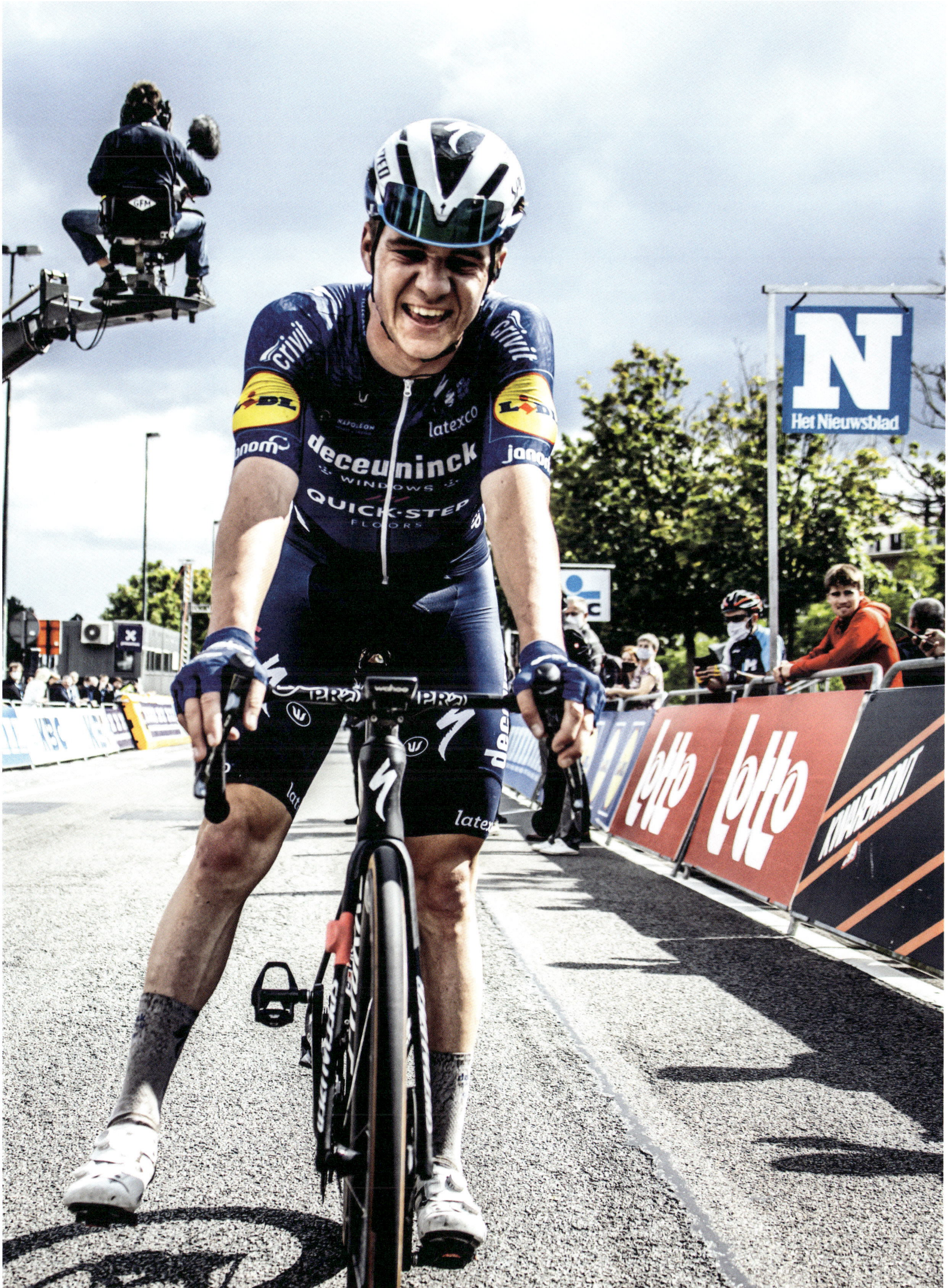
N
Het Nieuwsblad
deceuninck
WINDOWS
QUICK-STEP
FLOORS
latexco
crivit
lotto
lotto
KBC

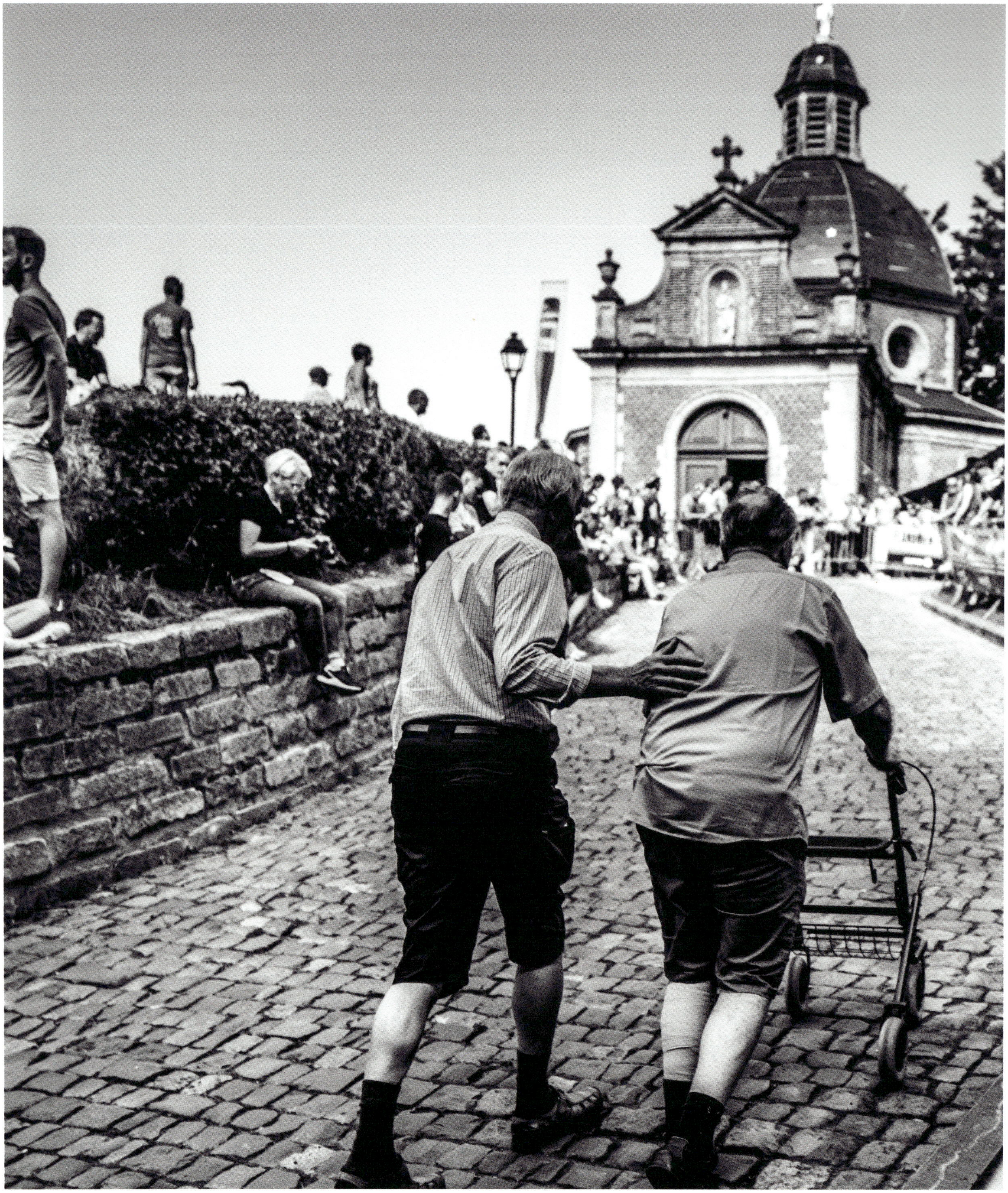

GERAARDSBERGEN, 05.09.2021

Kasper Asgreen leidt Matej Mohoric en Brandon McNulty naar de kapel bovenop de Muur van Geraardsbergen.

Kasper Asgreen leads Matej Mohoric and Brandon McNulty to the chapel on top of the Muur van Geraardsbergen.

Kasper Asgreen devant Matej Mohoric et Brandon McNulty sur les pavés du Mur de Grammont. ▶

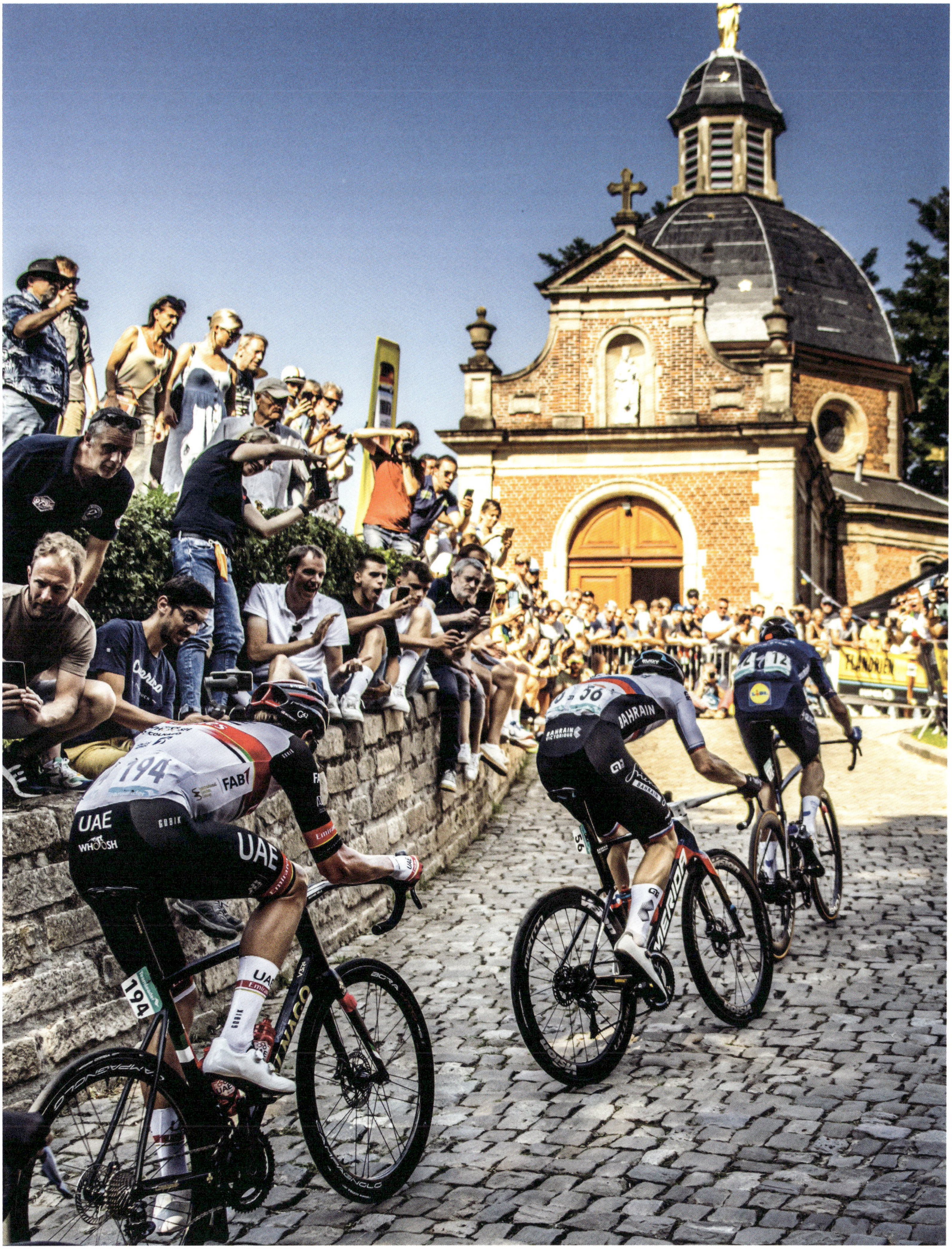
194
FAB
UAE
UAE
56
BAHRAIN
12

Na het succesrijke voorjaar en de uitmuntende Tour de France, tijd voor de Ronde van Spanje. En ook in de Vuelta verbluftte DQT de wielerwereld. In het bijzonder Fabio Jakobsen toonde dat de mens een bijzonder sterk wezen is.

Dat Fabio hersteld was, zijn conditie groeide en hij nog steeds over alle capaciteiten van een topsprinter beschikte, had hij al bewezen in de Tour de Wallonie. Hij won er twee ritten.

Zo goed als dag op dag één jaar na zijn gruwelijk ongeval in de Ronde van Polen knoopte hij ook aan met winst in een grote ronde. Hij werd tweede in Burgos (tweede rit) en won op koninklijke wijze de klimsprint van de vierde rit in Molina de Aragón. Hij schreef ook de achtste en de zestiende rit op zijn naam. En trok met de puntentrui huiswaarts. Wat een knaller!

After the successful spring and the excellent Tour de France, it's time for La Vuelta a España. DQT also astonished the cycling world in the Vuelta. Fabio Jakobsen in particular showed what human beings are capable of.

The fact that Fabio had recovered, that his condition was improving, and that he still showed all the capabilities of a top sprinter, had already been proven in the Tour de Wallonie when he won two stages there.

Almost one year after his horrific accident in the Tour de Pologne, he also started winning in a Grand Tour. He came second in Burgos (second stage) and won the slightly uphill finish of the fourth stage in Molina de Aragón in majestic fashion. He also won stage eight and stage sixteen. He eventually went home with the points jersey. What an achievement!

Après un printemps réussi et l'excellent Tour de France, place au Tour d'Espagne. Et une fois de plus, les performances de la DQT dans la Vuelta ont impressionné le monde du cyclisme. Fabio Jakobsen, en particulier, nous a montré à quel point l'être humain était capable de prouesses incroyables.

Fabio avait déjà prouvé lors du Tour de Wallonie qu'il s'était bien remis, que sa condition physique s'améliorait et qu'il avait encore toutes les capacités d'un sprinter de haut niveau. Il y a gagné deux étapes.

Presque un an après son horrible accident au Tour de Pologne, il est bien reparti… vers la victoire. Il commence à gagner dans un grand tour : il s'est classé deuxième à Burgos (deuxième étape) et a brillamment remporté le sprint de montée de la quatrième étape à Molina de Aragón. Il a également remporté les huitième et seizième étapes et rentre chez lui en tête du classement par points. Quel exploit !

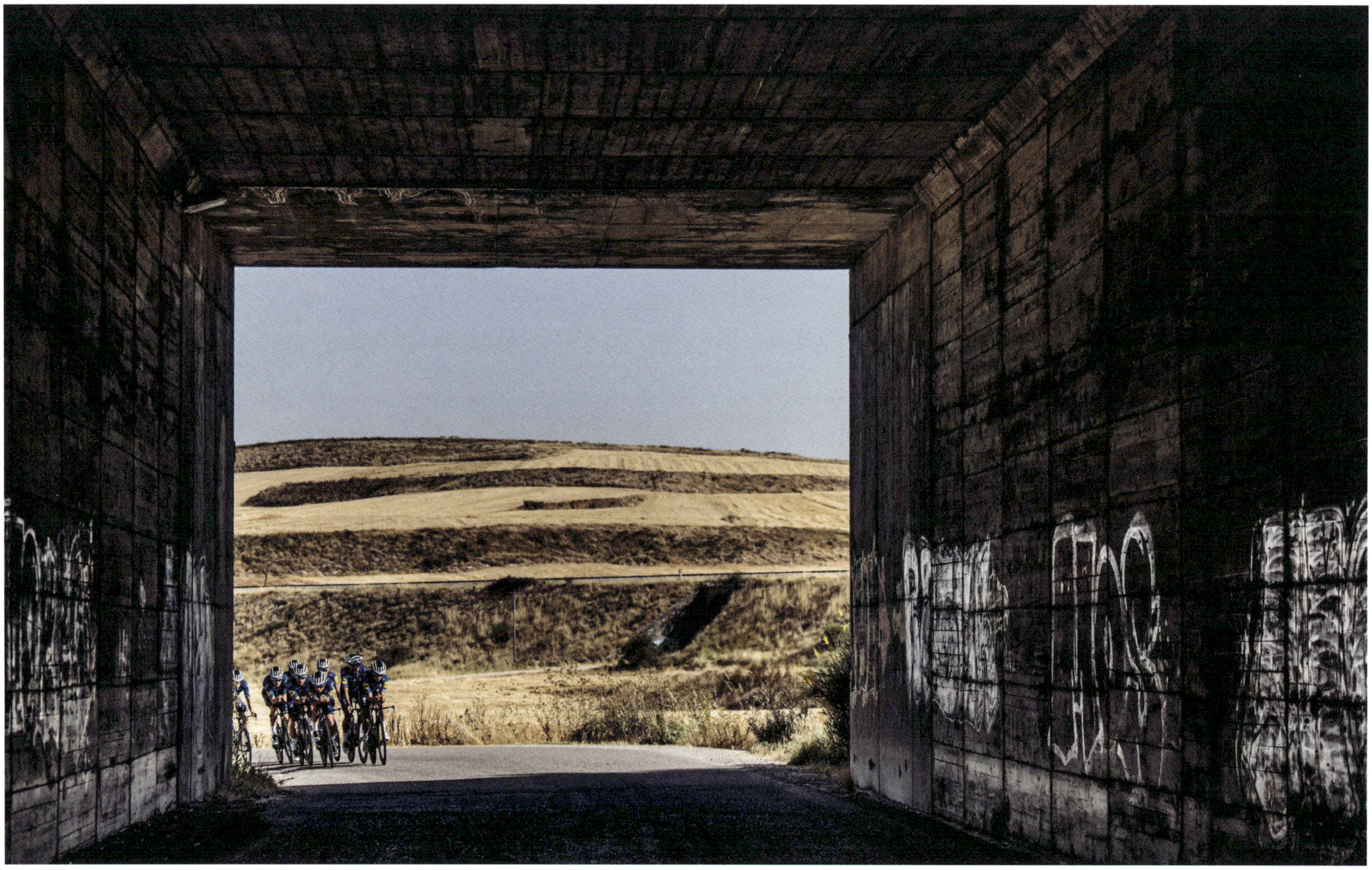

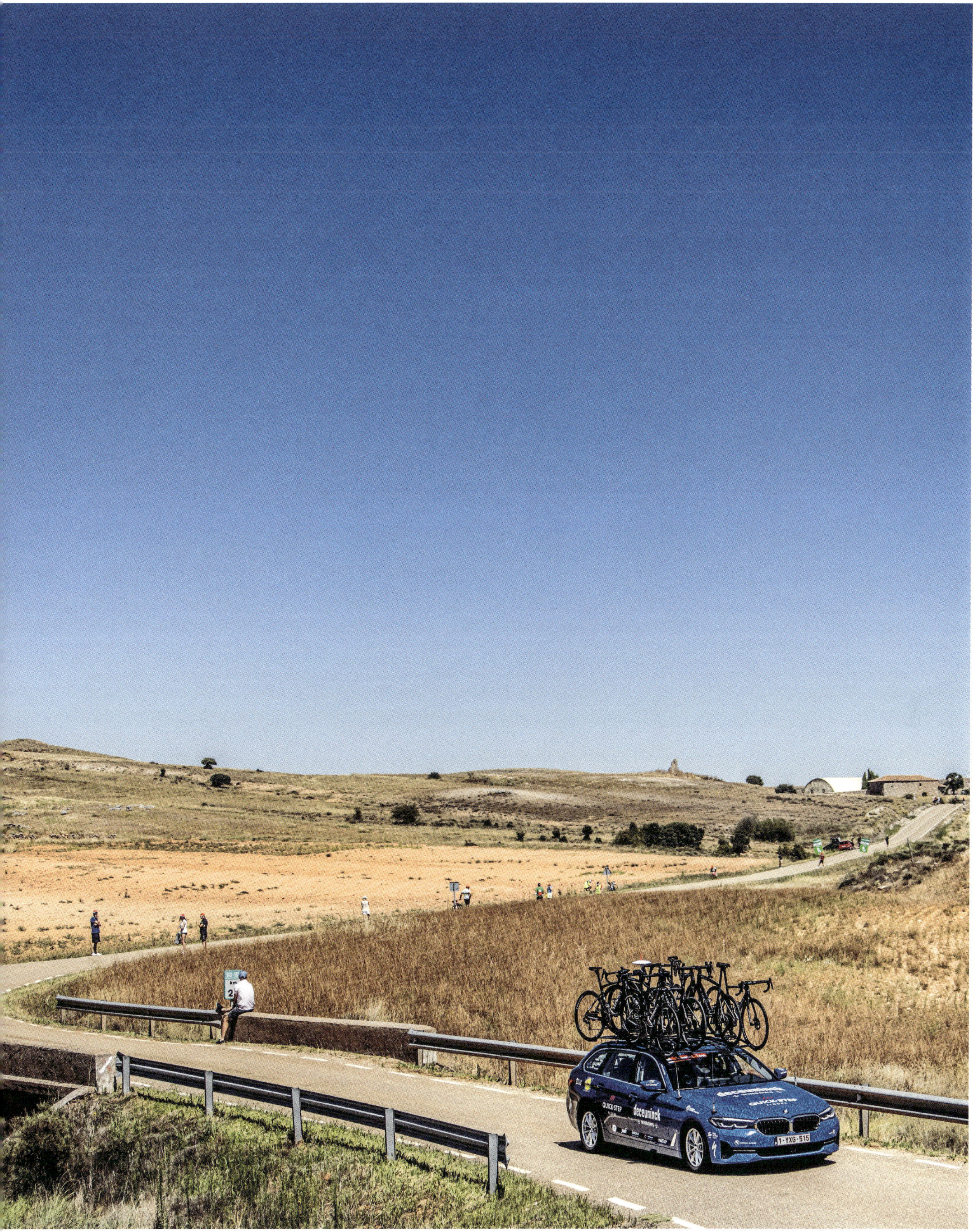
QUICK-STEP
deceuninck
WINDOWS
1-YXG-515

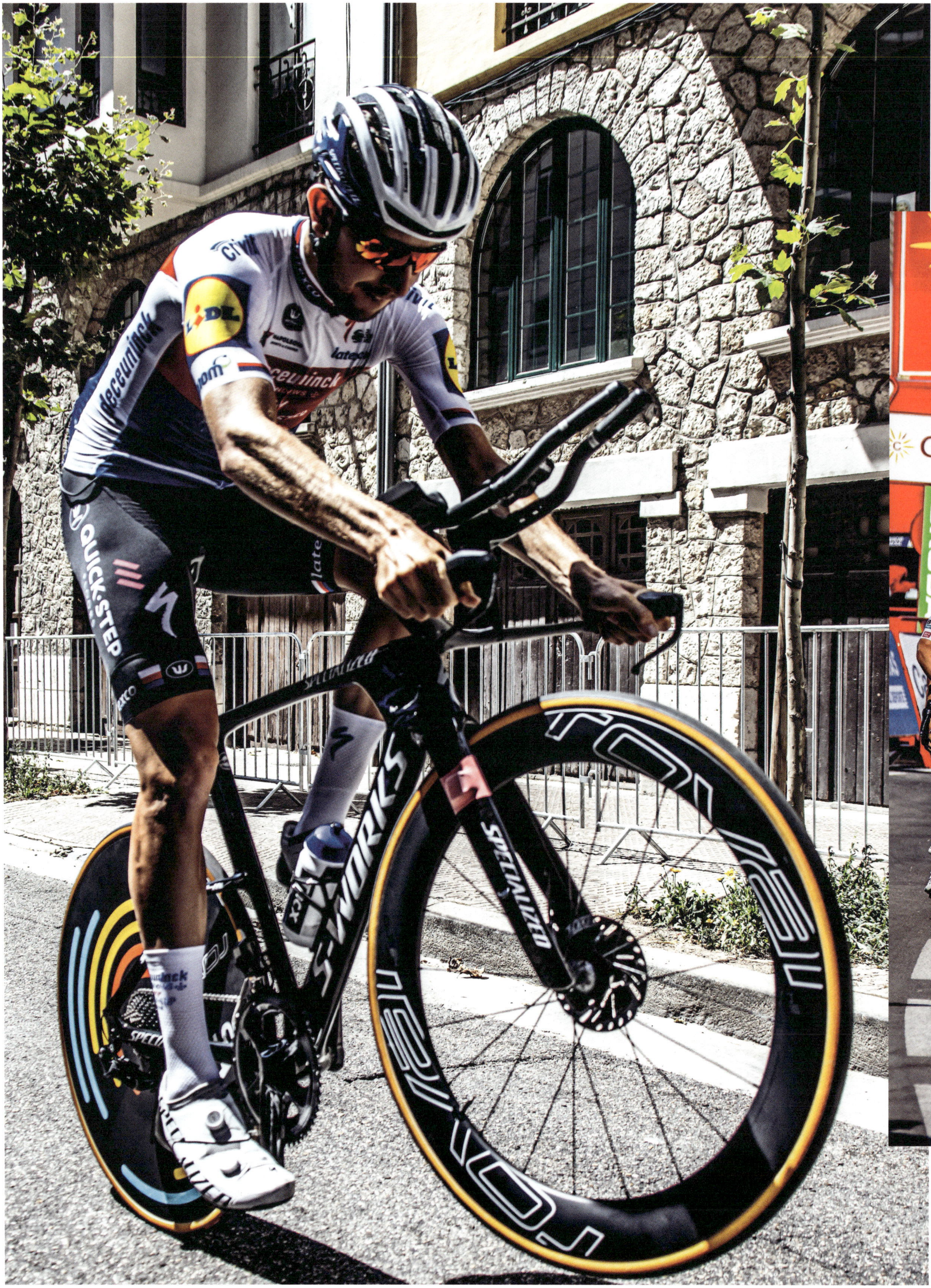
QUICK-STEP
S-WORKS
SPECIALIZED

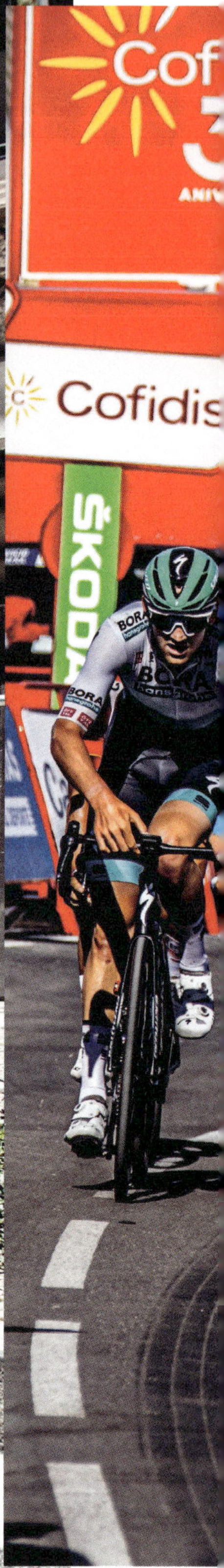
Cofidis
ŠKODA

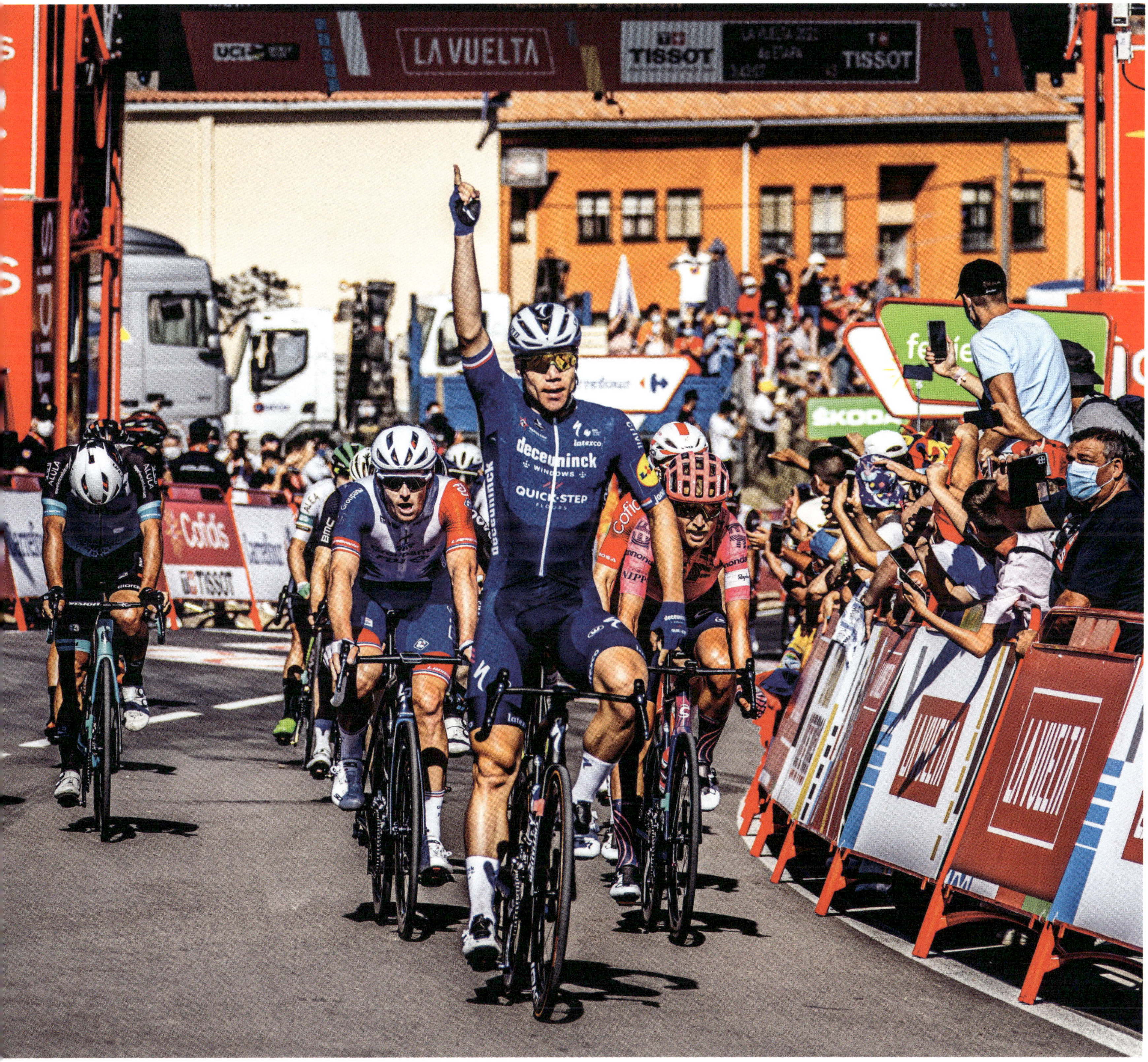

MOLINA DE ARAGÓN, 17.08.2021

Fabio Jakobsen verrast zichzelf en de hele bende. Hij komt op 17 augustus als eerste uit het pak in de vierde rit, op de hellende aankomst in Molina de Aragón.

Fabio Jakobsen surprises himself and the whole crew. He comes out of the pack first in the fourth stage on 17 August, on the challenging finish in Molina de Aragón.

Fabio Jakobsen se surprend lui-même et surprend toute l'équipe. Il franchit premier la ligne d'arrivée en pente à Molina de Aragón lors de la quatrième étape du 17 août.

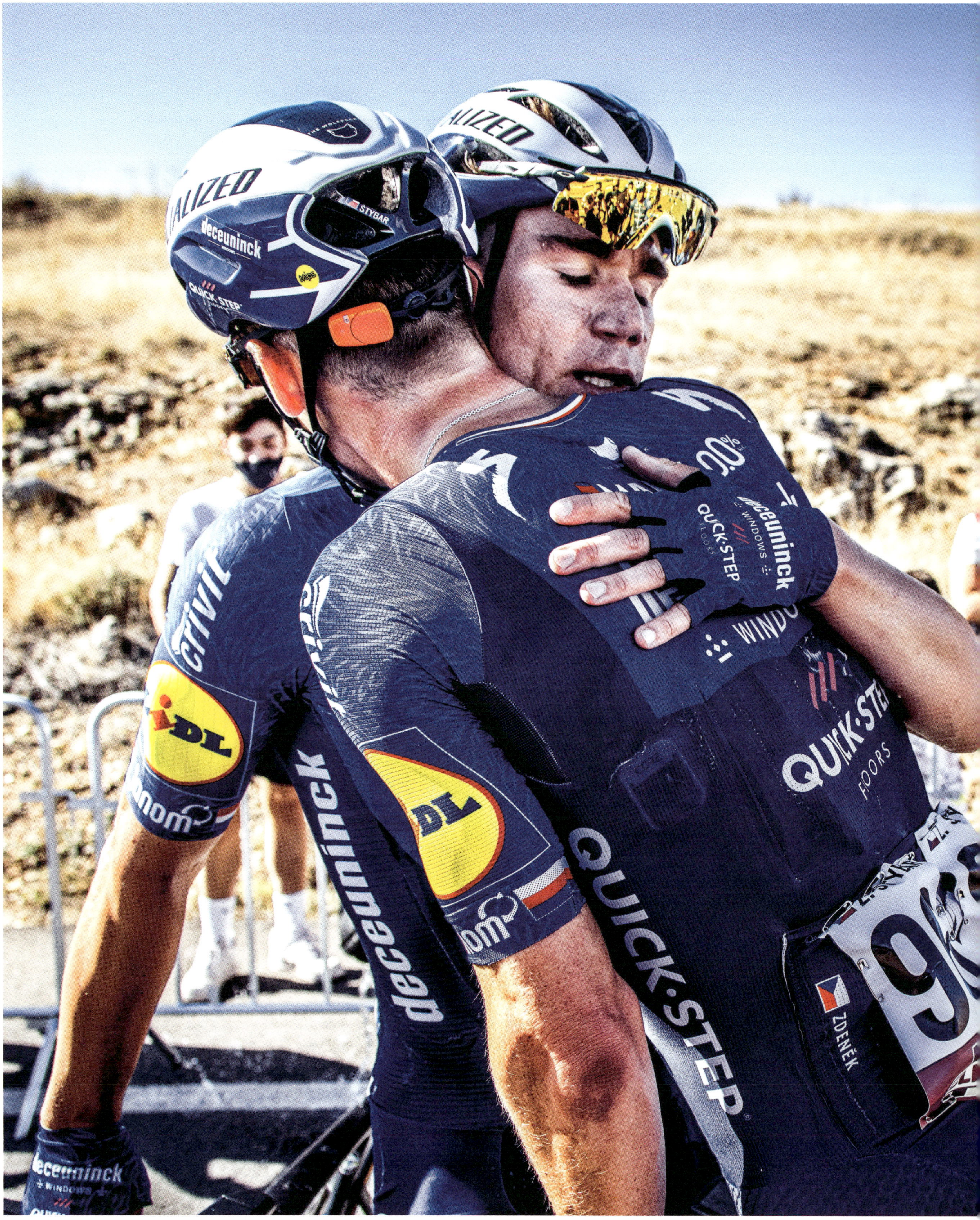
STYBAR
deceuninck
QUICK-STEP
crivit
deceuninck
QUICK·STEP
WINDOWS
QUICK·STEP
FLOORS
QUICK·STEP
ZDENĚK
deceuninck

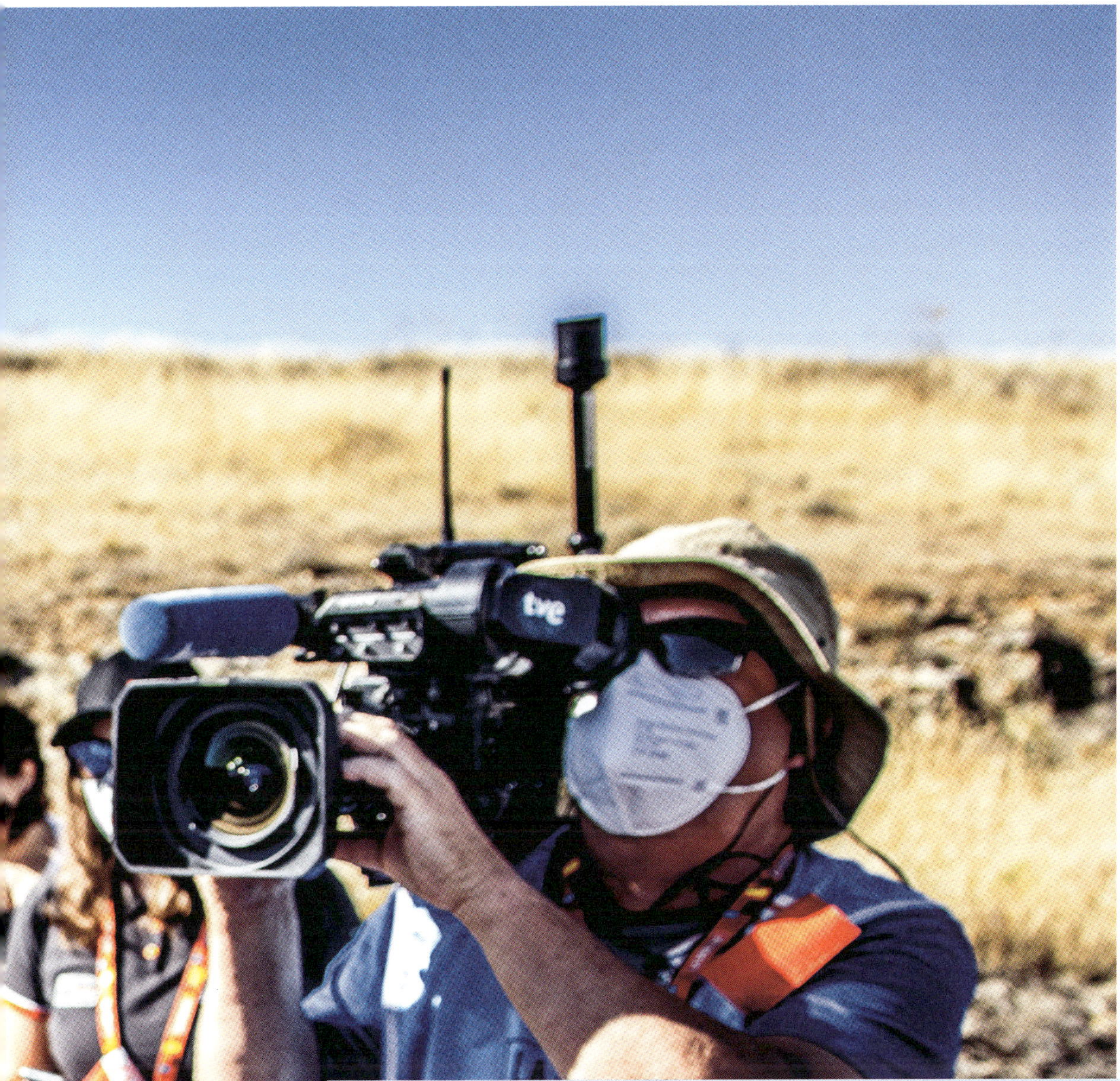
tve
LIDL

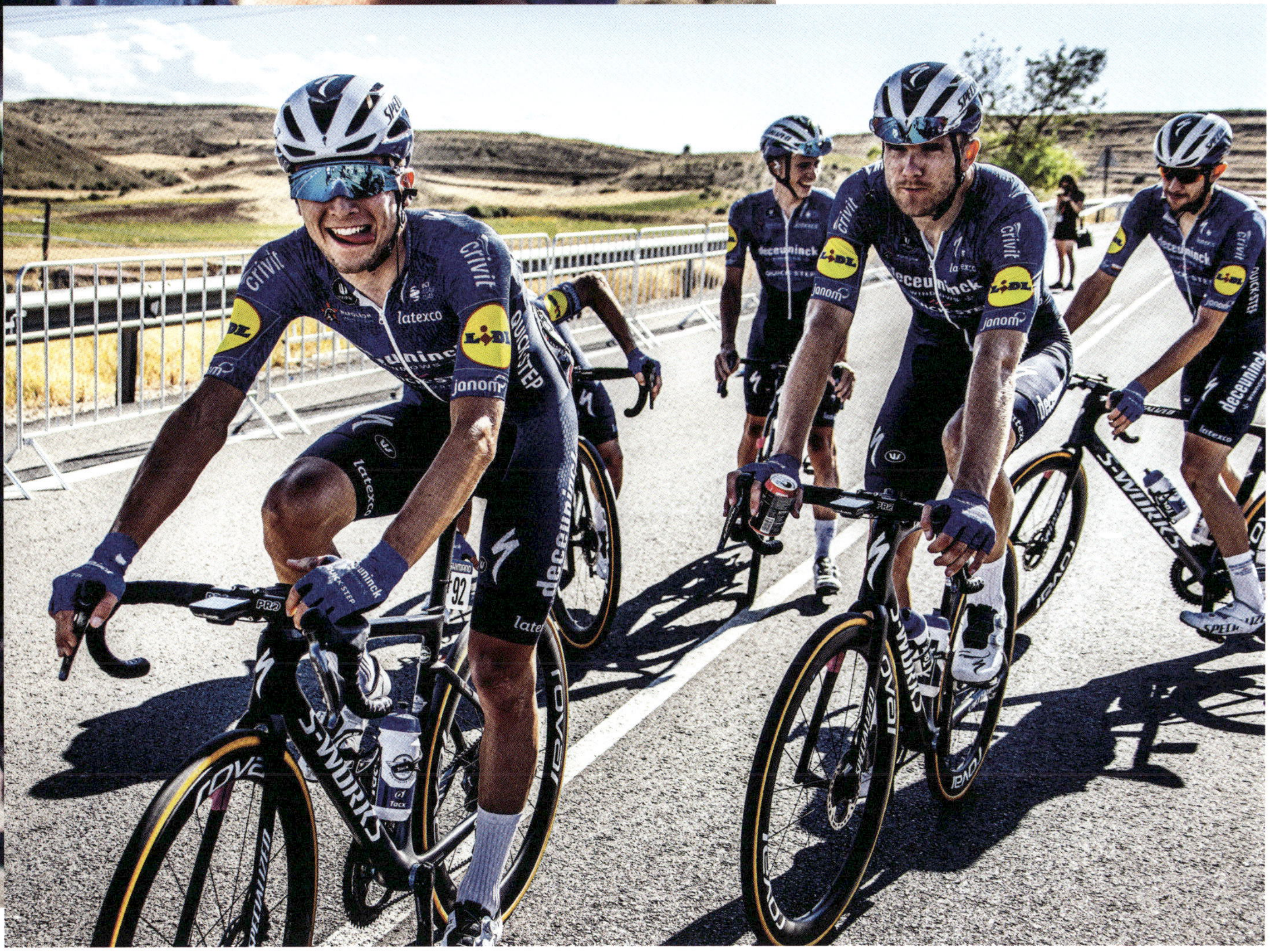
crivit
latexco
LIDL
deceuninck
S-WORKS

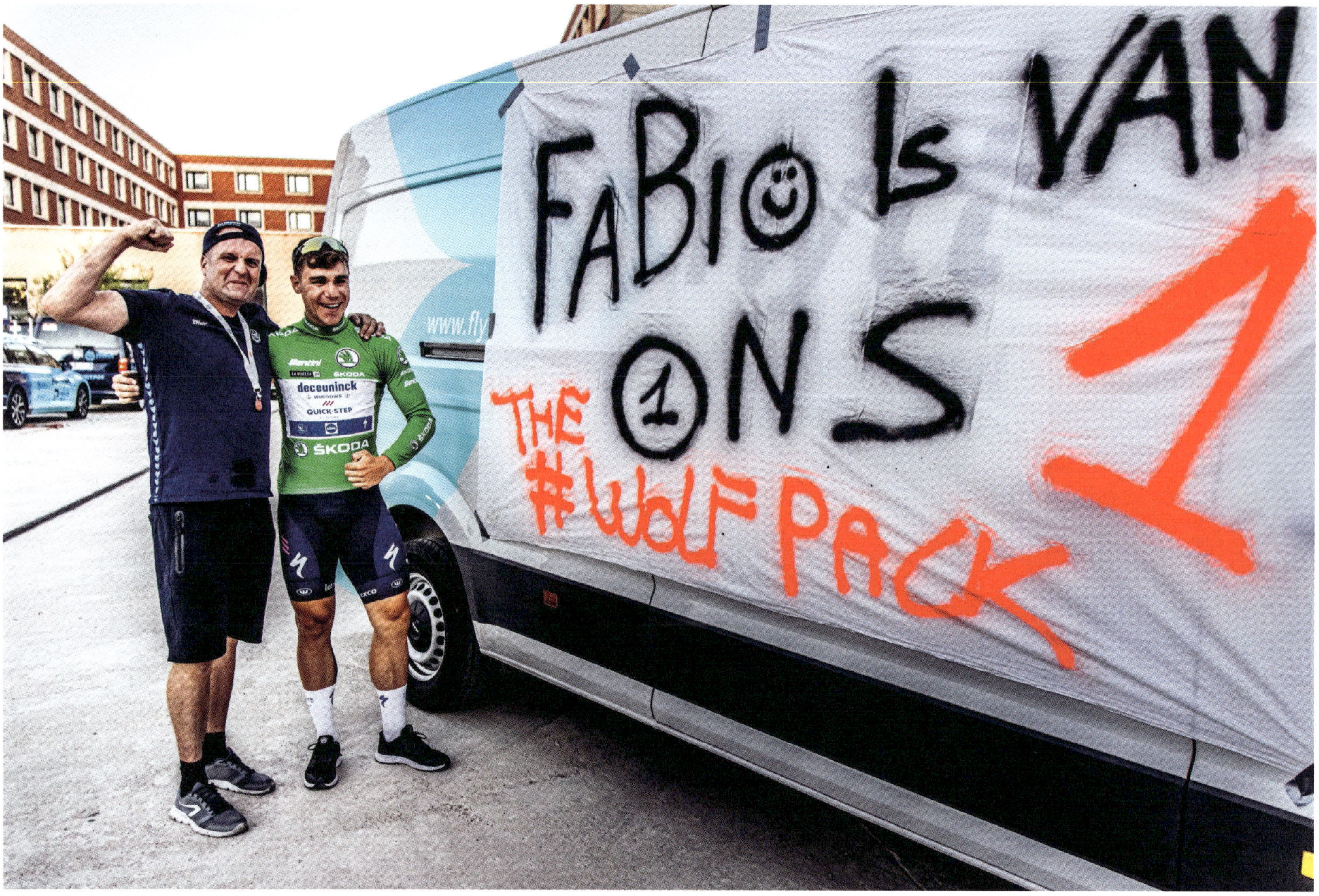
FABIO IS VAN
ONS
THE #WOLFPACK
1

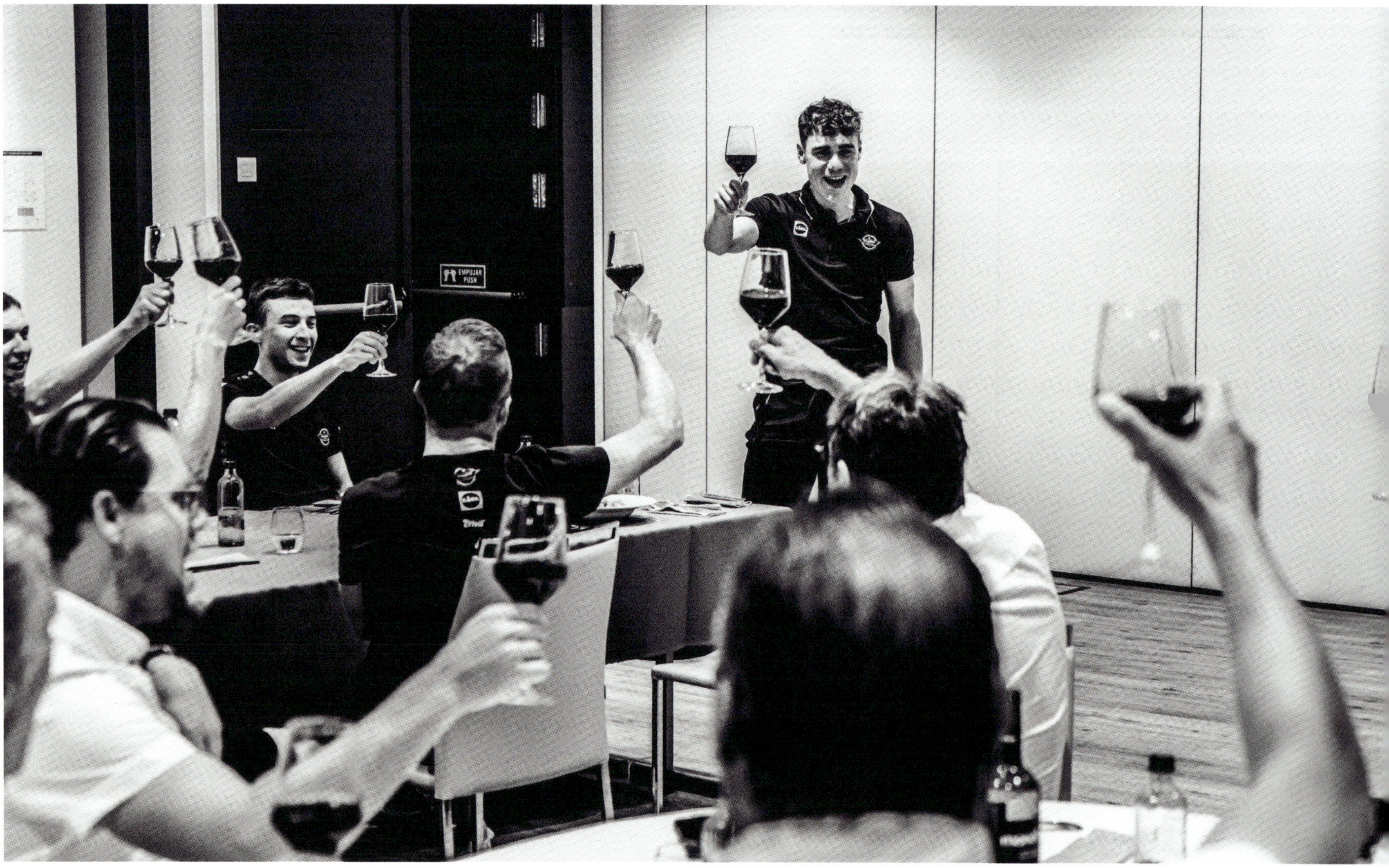

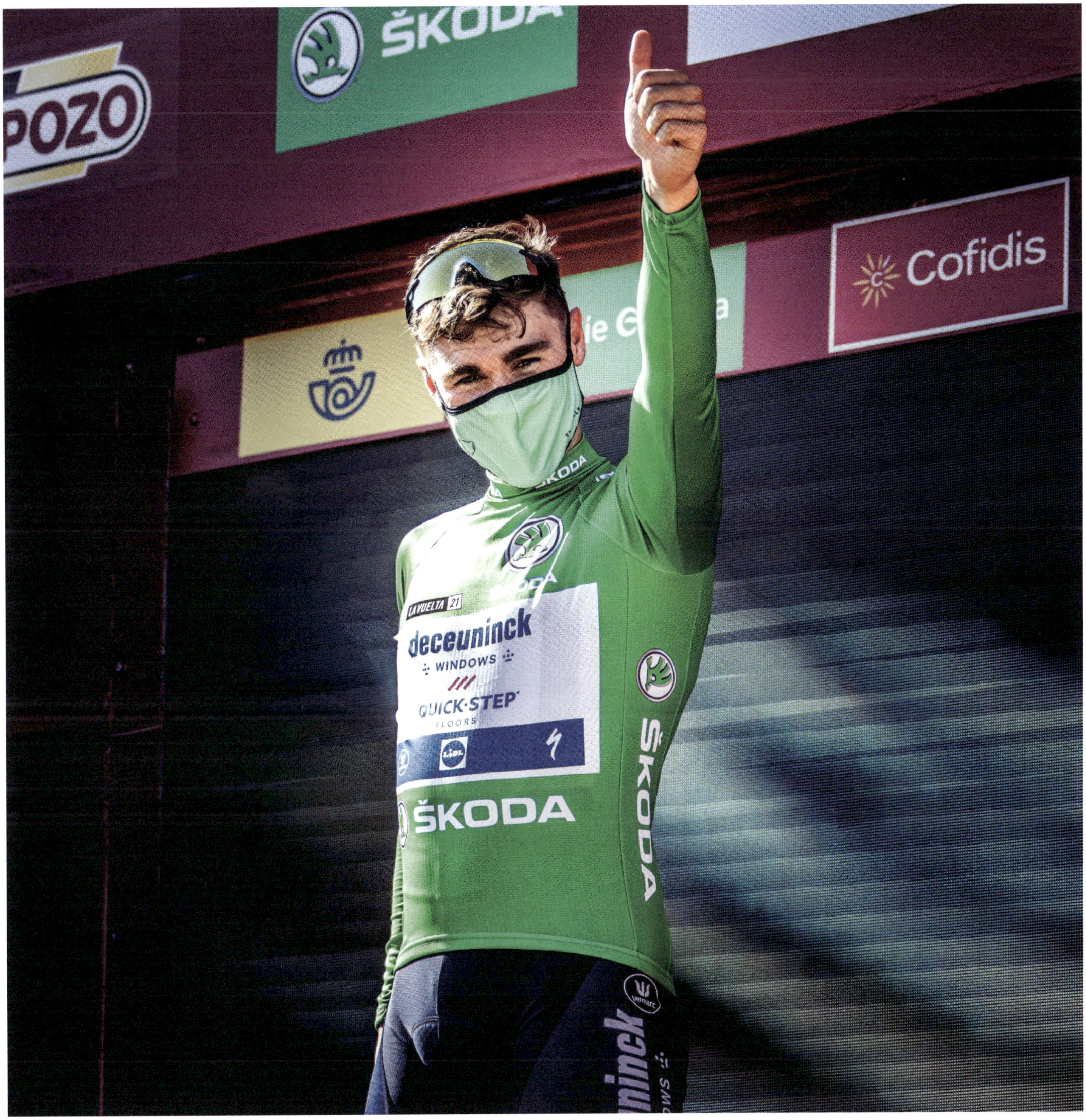

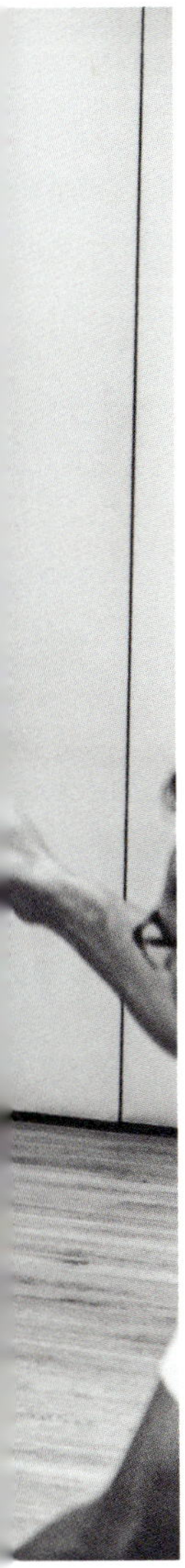

MOLINA DE ARAGÓN, 17.08.2021

De eerste zege van Fabio Jakobsen tijdens de Vuelta van 2021. Daar hoort een goed glas rode wijn bij, zo wil de traditie het. Rond de tafel, achteraan: Mauri Vansevenant, Andrea Bagioli en Fabio Jakobsen. Vooraan v.l.n.r.: Klaas Lodewyck, Wilfried Peeters en Davide Bramati.

The first victory of Fabio Jakobsen at this year's Vuelta. A fine glass of red wine to go with it, in keeping with tradition. Around the table, in the back: Mauri Vansevenant, Andrea Bagioli, and Fabio Jakobsen. In the front, FLTR: Klaas Lodewyck, Wilfried Peeters, and Davide Bramati.

La première victoire de Fabio Jakobsen sur la Vuelta de 2021. Un bon verre de vin rouge pour célébrer ça, comme le veut la tradition. Autour de la table, au fond : Mauri Vansevenant, Andrea Bagioli et Fabio Jakobsen. Devant, dgàd : Klaas Lodewyck, Wilfried Peeters et Davide Bramati.

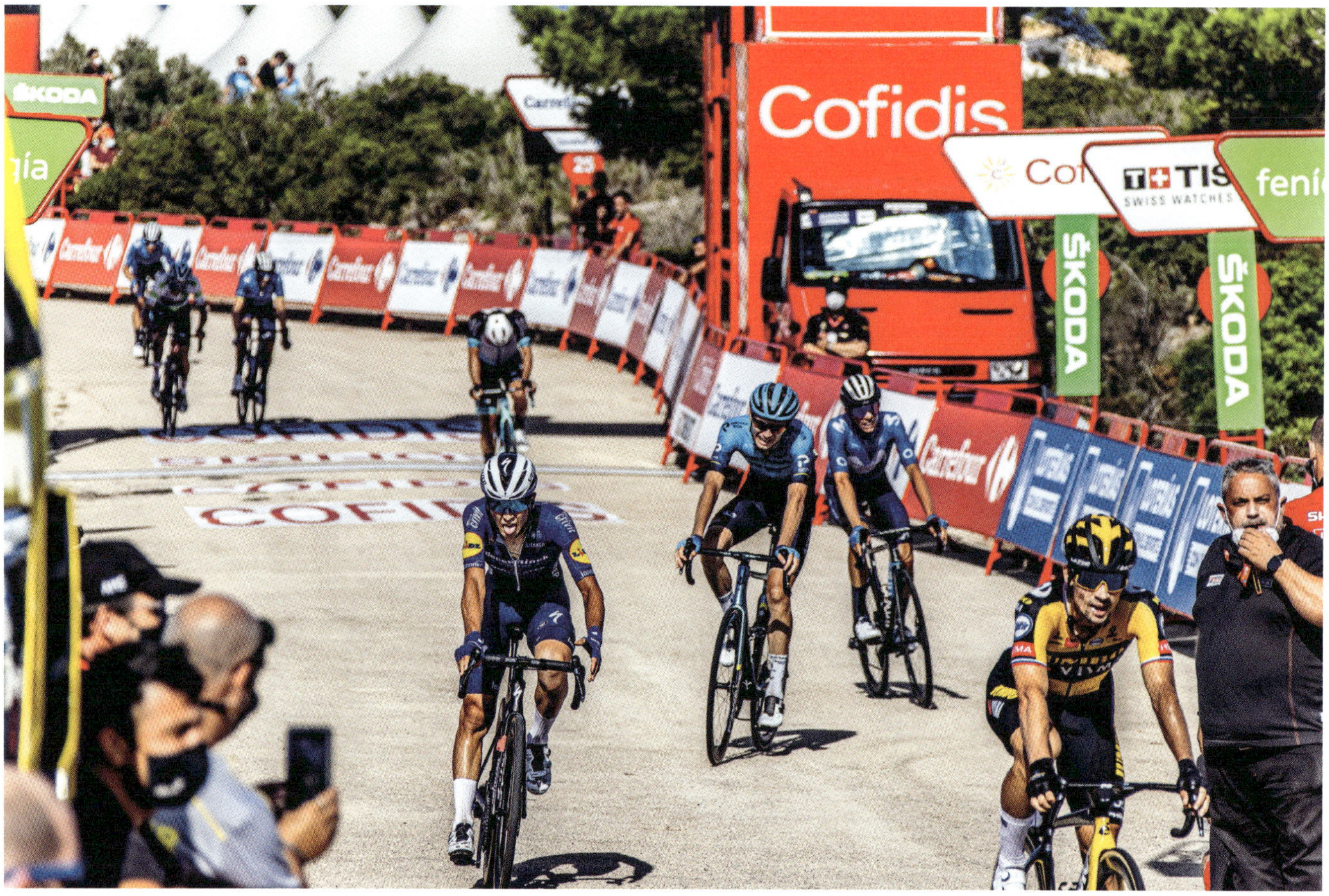
Cofidis
ŠKODA
ŠKODA
SWISS WATCHES

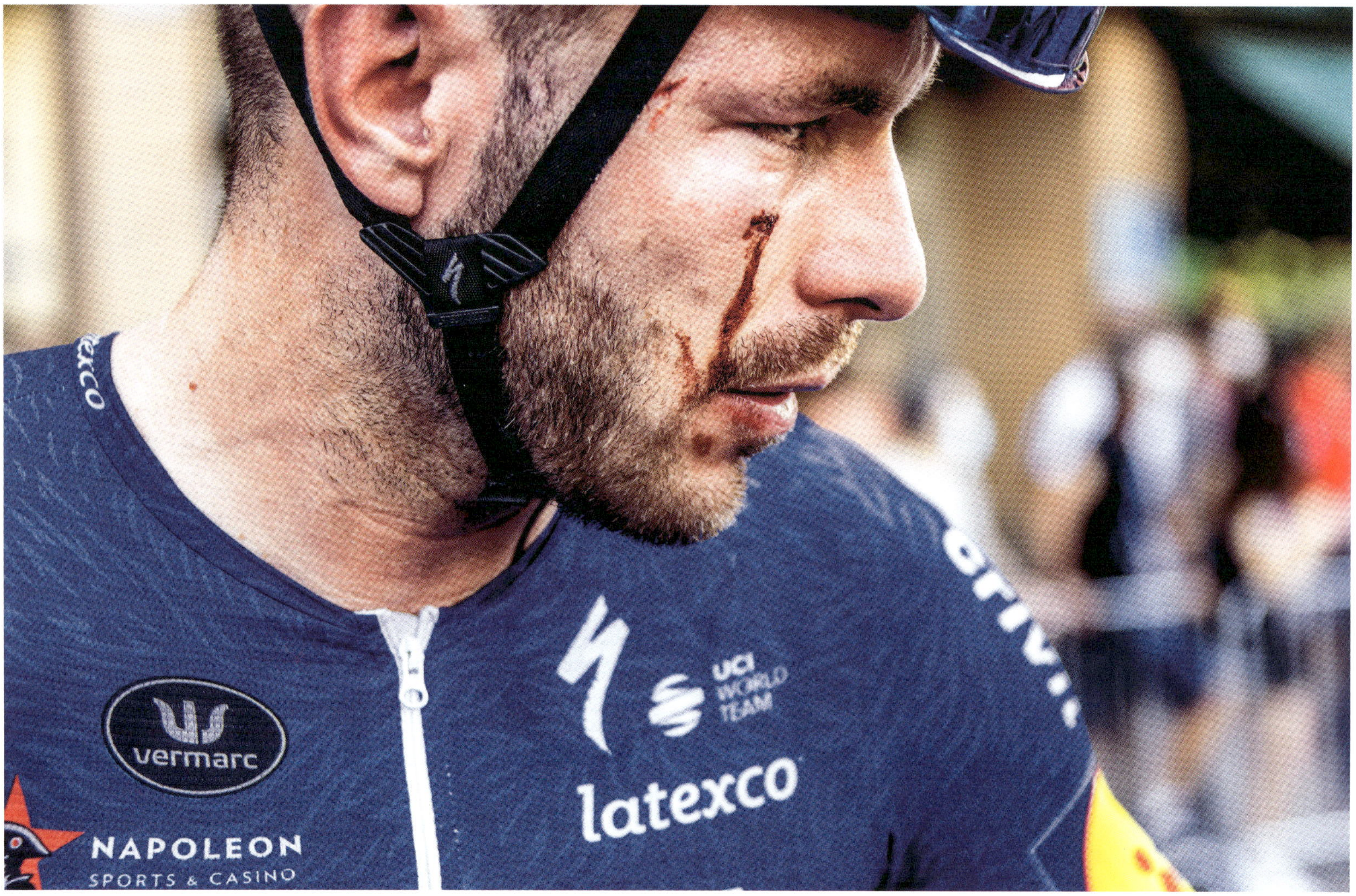
vermarc
NAPOLEON
SPORTS & CASINO
UCI
WORLD
TEAM
latexco

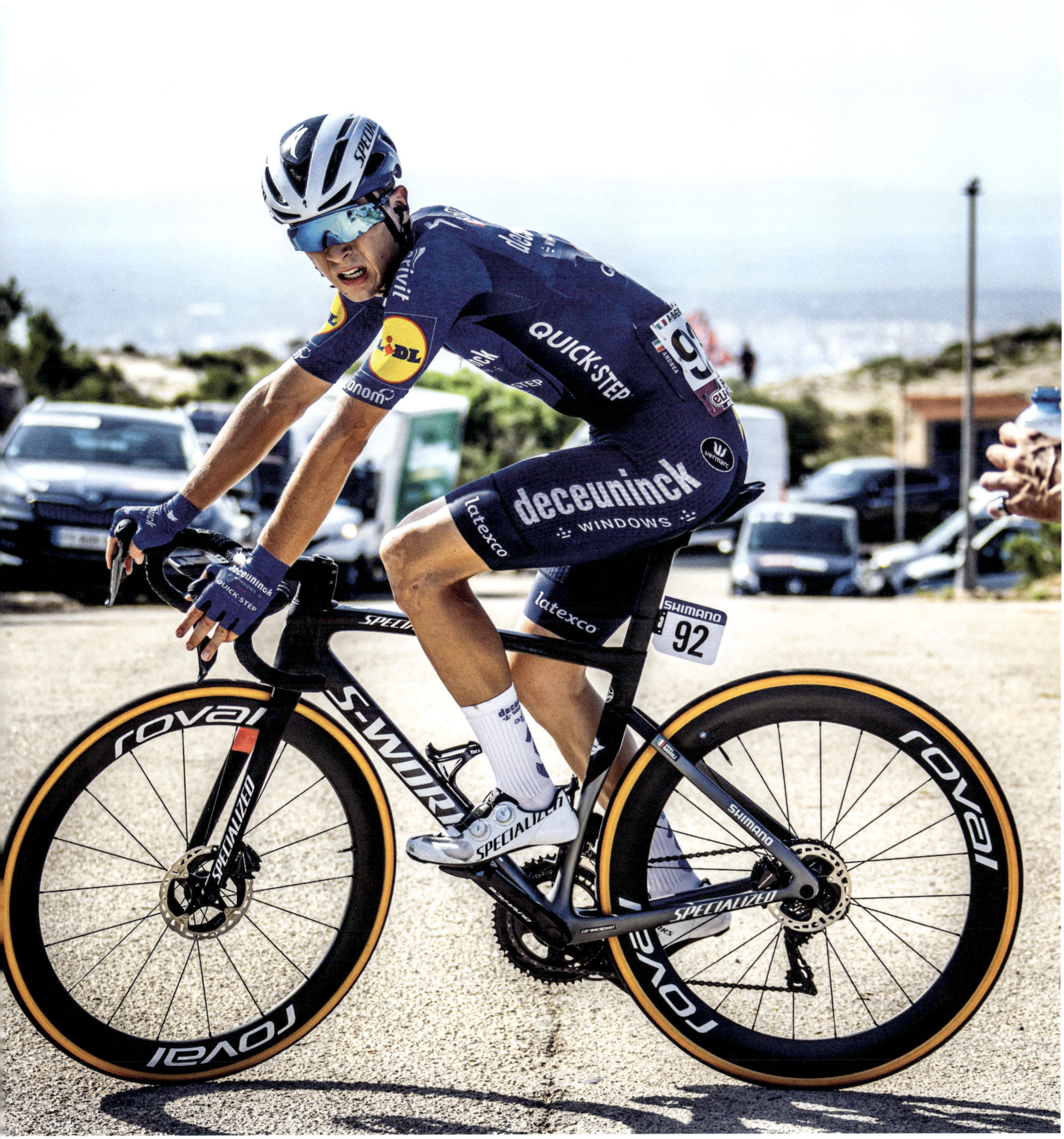

ALTO DE LA MONTAÑA DE CULLERA, 19.08.2021

De zesde rit in de Vuelta, naar de Alto de la Montaña de Cullera. Andrea Bagioli wordt derde na Magnus Cort en Primoz Roglic.

The sixth stage in the Vuelta, to the Alto de la Montaña de Cullera. Andrea Bagioli finishes third after Magnus Cort and Primoz Roglic.

La sixième étape de la Vuelta, vers l'Alto de la Montaña de Cullera. Andrea Bagioli termine troisième derrière Magnus Cort et Primoz Roglic.

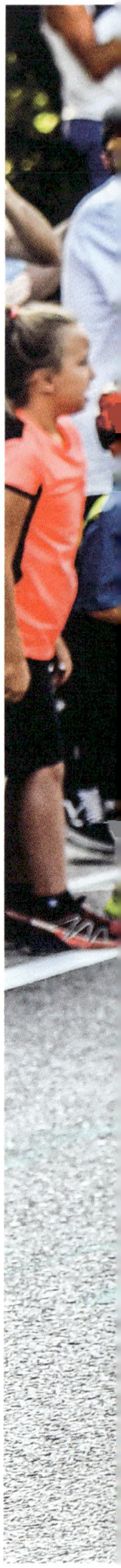

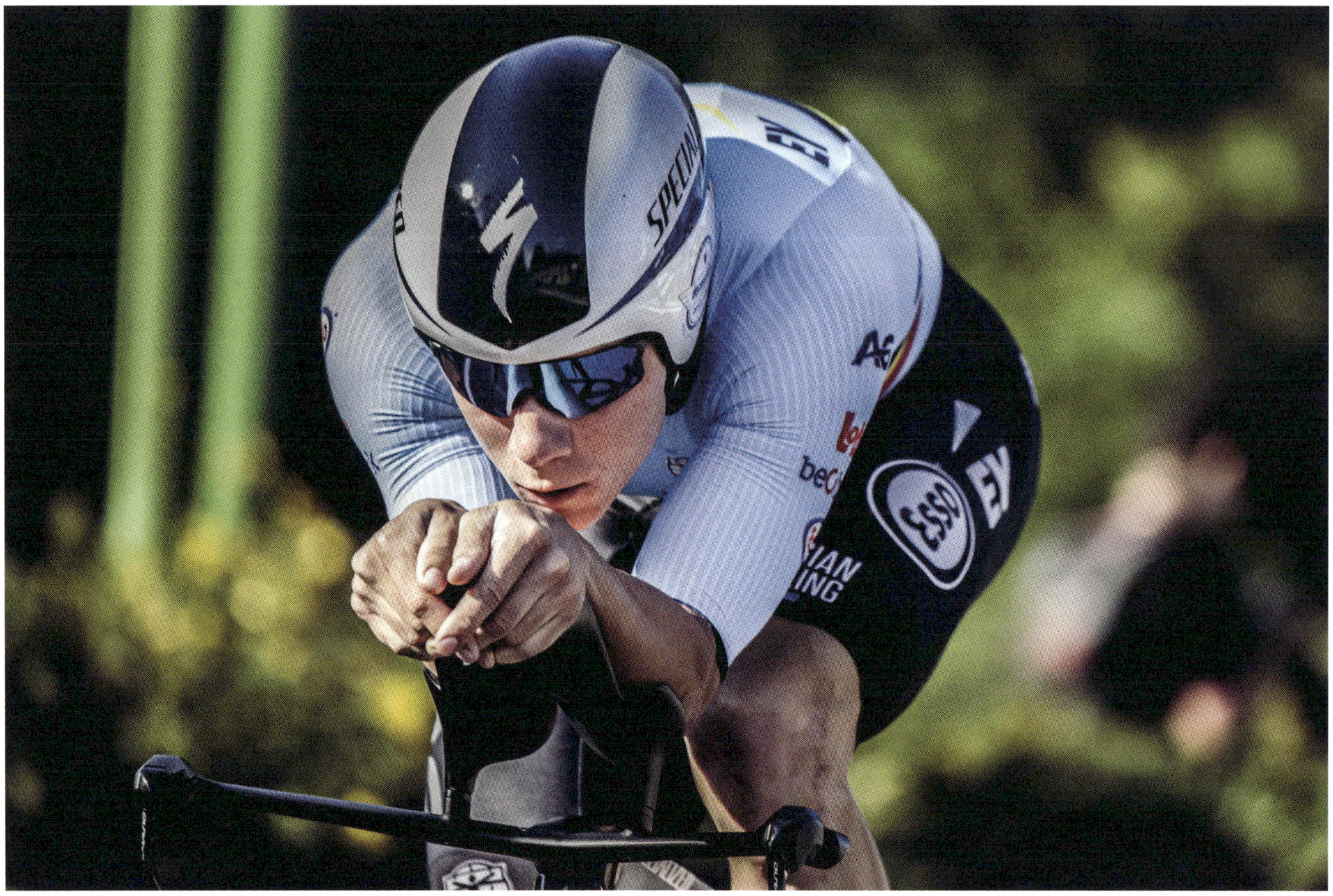

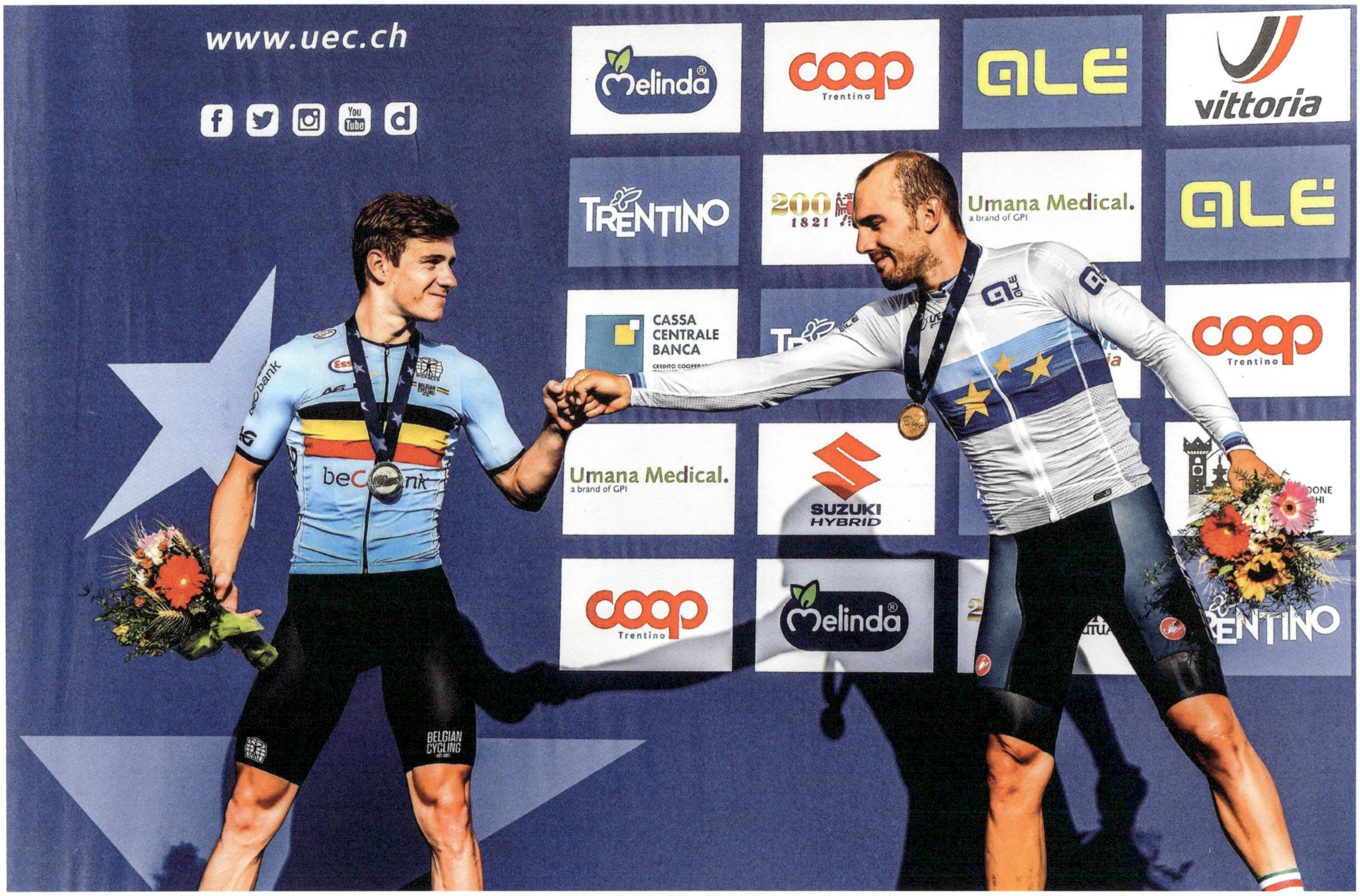
www.uec.ch
Melinda
coop
Trentino
ALÉ
vittoria
TRENTINO
Umana Medical.
a brand of GPI
CASSA
CENTRALE
BANCA
SUZUKI
HYBRID

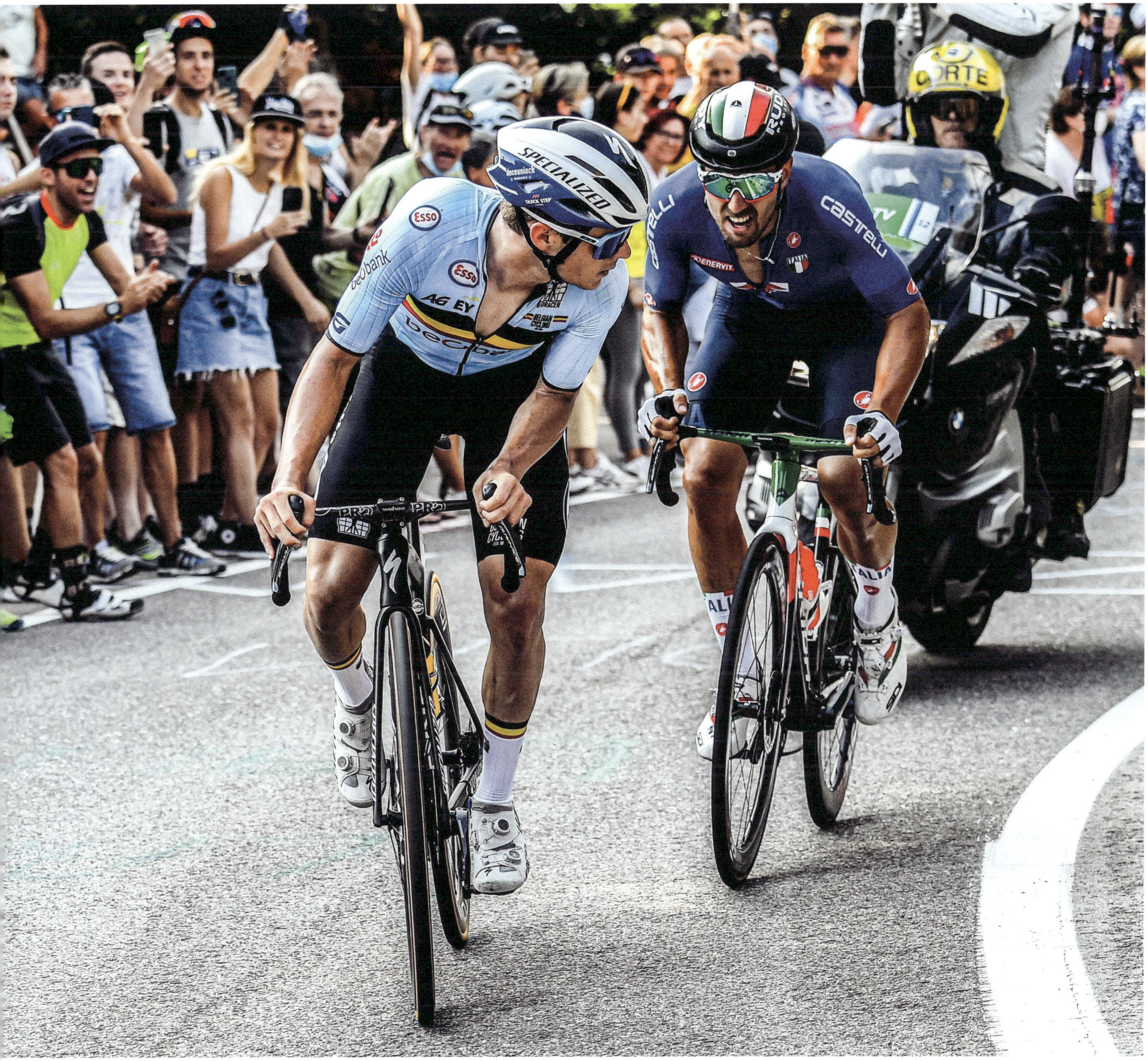

TRENTO, 12.09.2021

Remco Evenepoel pakt zilver en brons op het EK in Italië. Hij behaalt de derde plaats in de tijdrit en strand op stek twee in de wegrit, na Sonny Colbrelli.

Remco Evenepoel wins silver and bronze at the European Championships in Italy. He finished third in the time trial and second in the road race, behind Sonny Colbrelli.

Remco Evenepoel remporte l'argent et le bronze aux Championnats d'Europe en Italie. Il a terminé troisième lors du contre-la-montre et deuxième dans la course en ligne derrière Sonny Colbrelli.

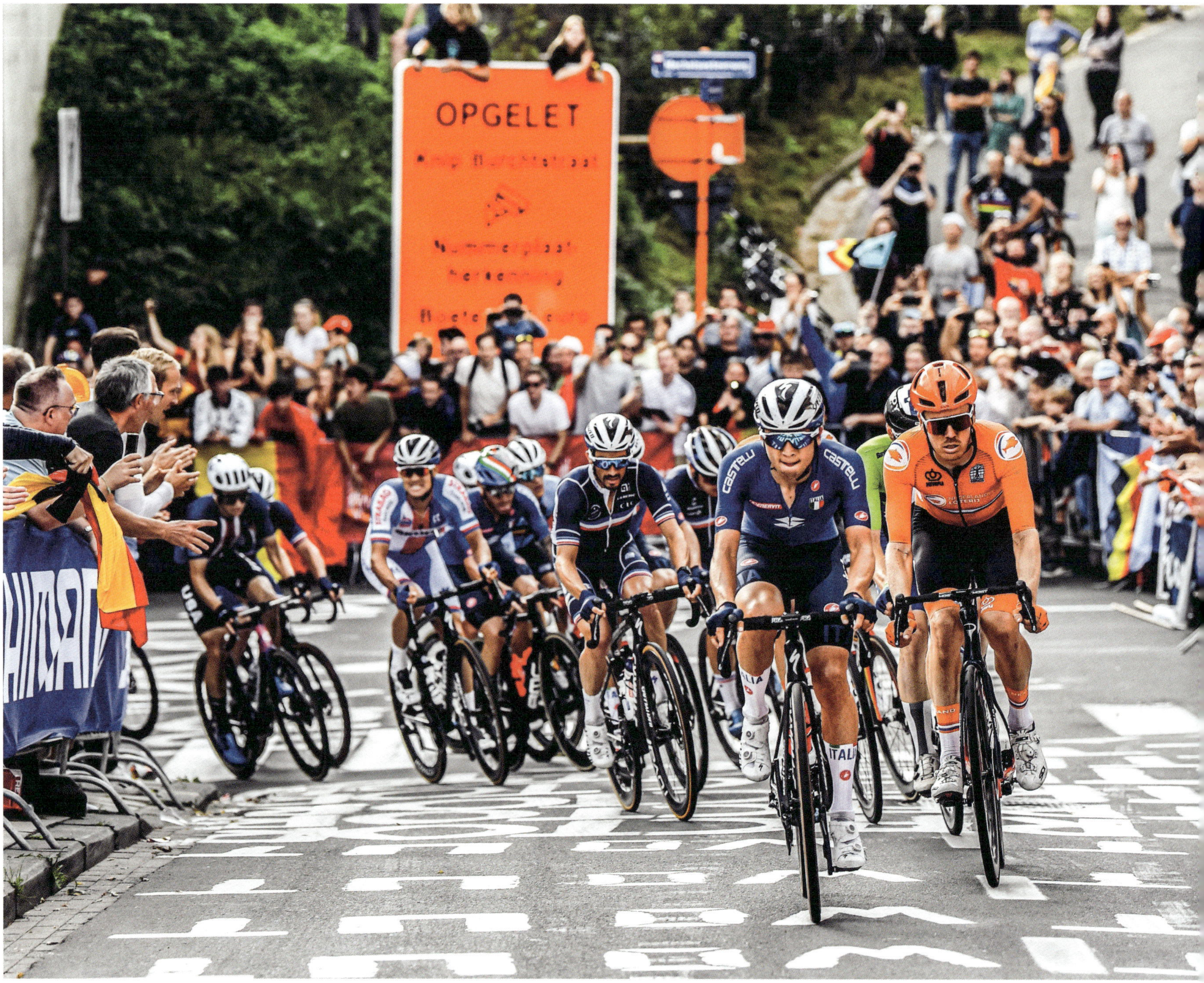

LEUVEN, 26.09.2021

Feestdag voor Vlaanderen, hoogdag voor The Wolfpack. Remco Evenepoel rijdt een beresterke koers, Julian Alaphilippe triomfeert in Leuven. Zijn tweede regenboogtrui in twee jaar tijd. Julian is pas de zevende renner die zichzelf als Wereldkampioen kan opvolgen. Wat een stunt!

A day of celebration for Flanders, and for The Wolfpack. Remco Evenepoel rides a very strong race, Julian Alaphilippe triumphs in Leuven. His second rainbow jersey in two years. Julian is only the seventh rider to be World Champion twice in a row. What a performance!

Un jour de fête pour la Flandre, un jour de fête pour le Wolfpack. Remco Evenepoel réalise une très bonne performance et Julian Alaphilippe triomphe à Louvain. Son deuxième maillot arc-en-ciel en deux ans. Il devient le septième coureur dans l'histoire à conserver son titre mondial. Quel exploit incroyable !

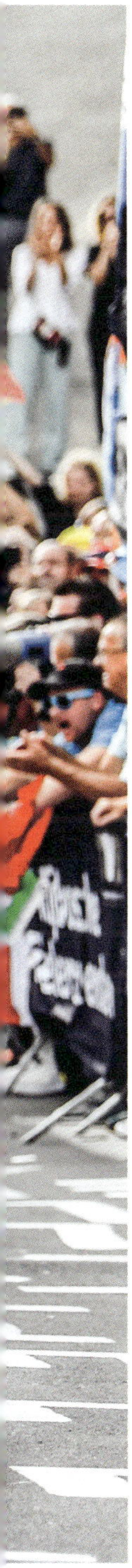

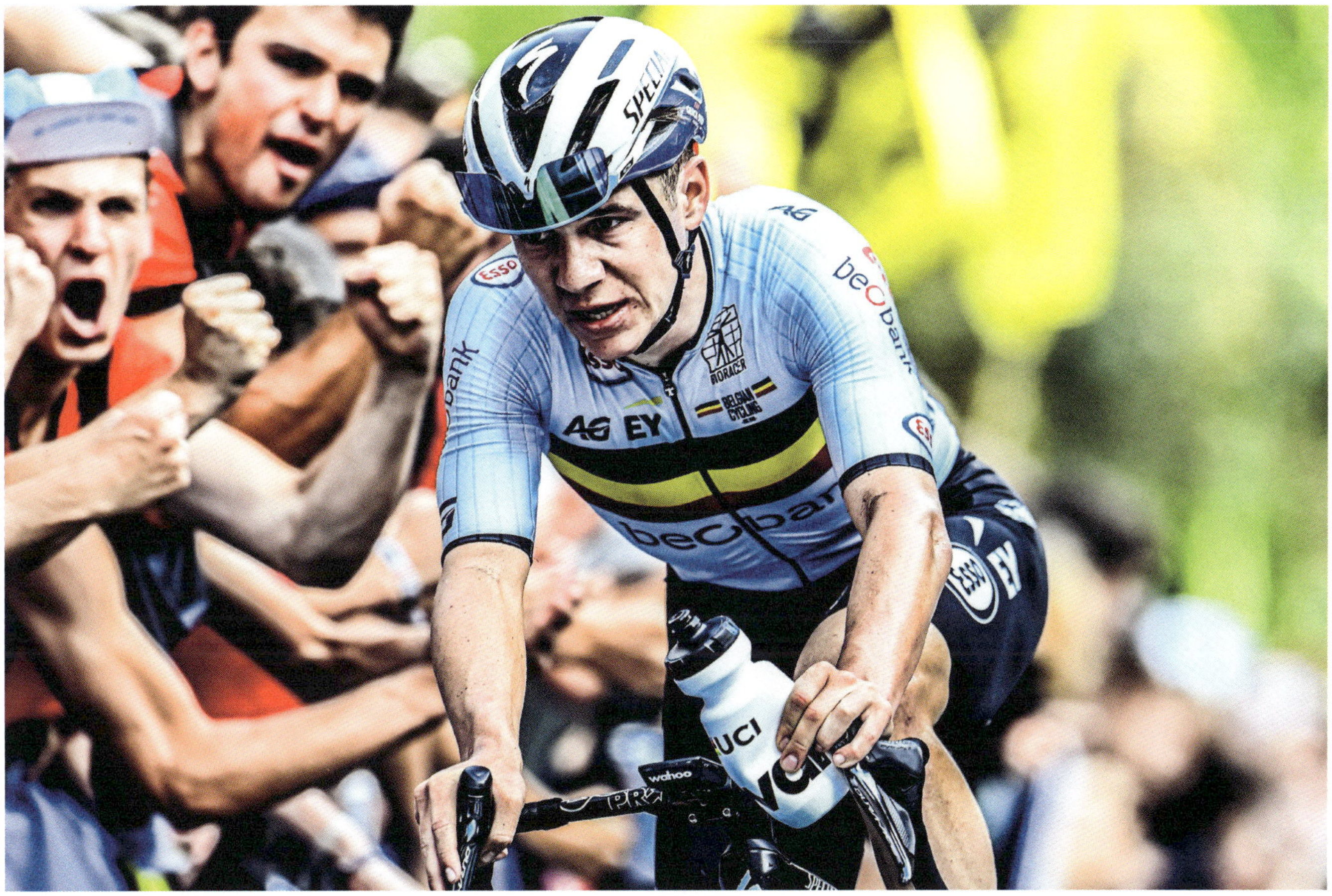
AG EY
UCI
wahoo

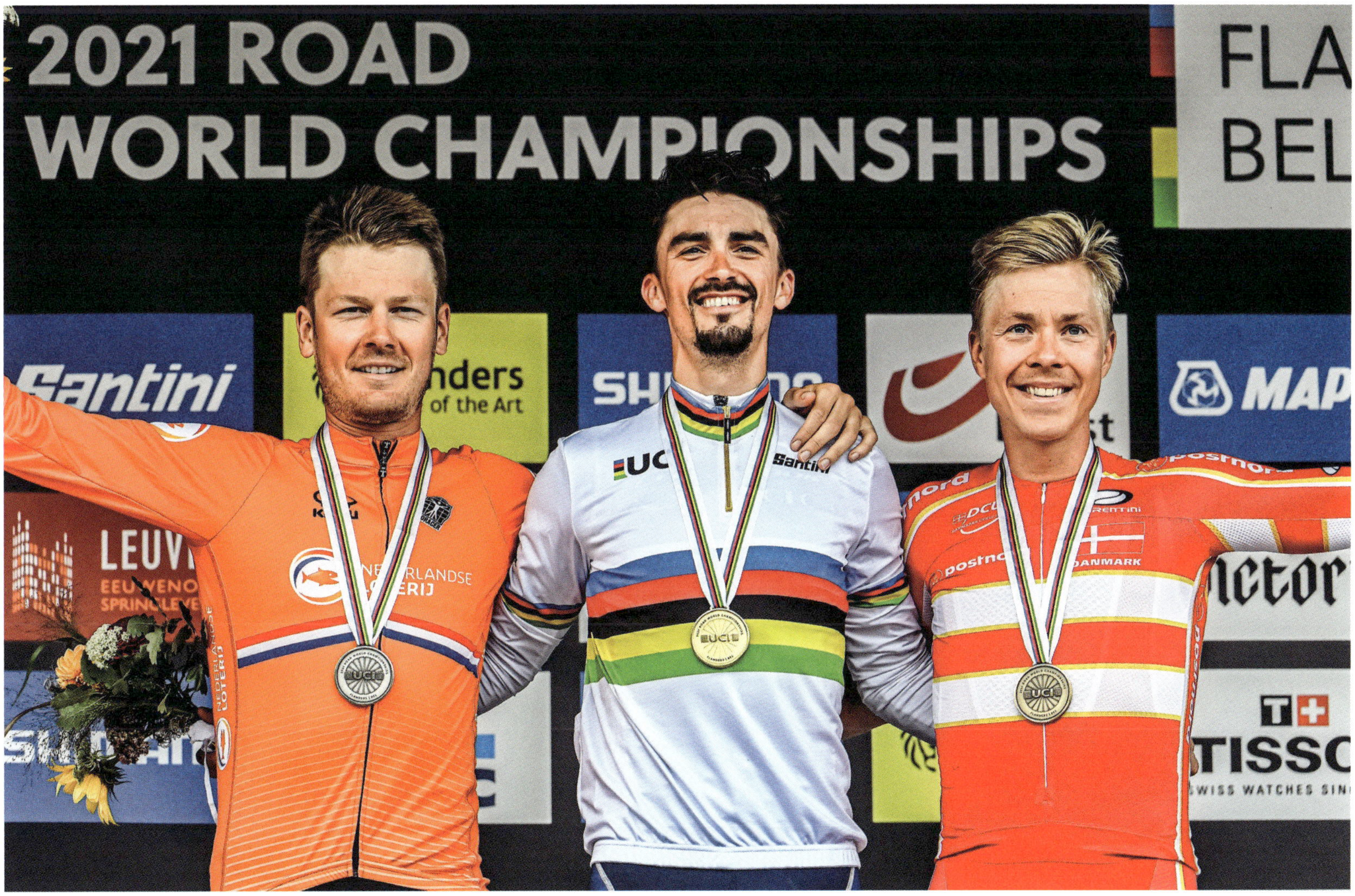
2021 ROAD
WORLD CHAMPIONSHIPS
Santini
of the Art
TISSO
SWISS WATCHES SIN

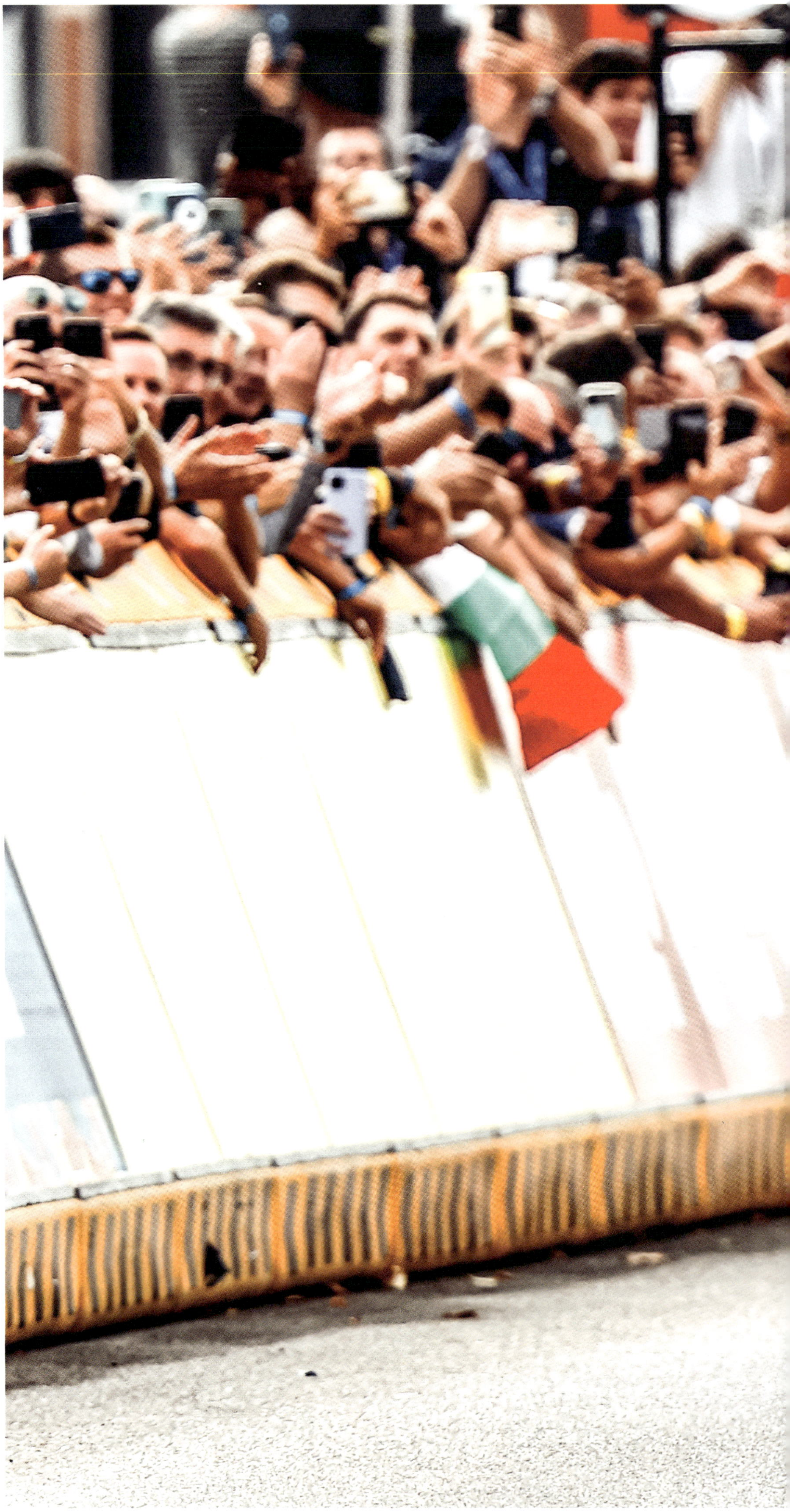

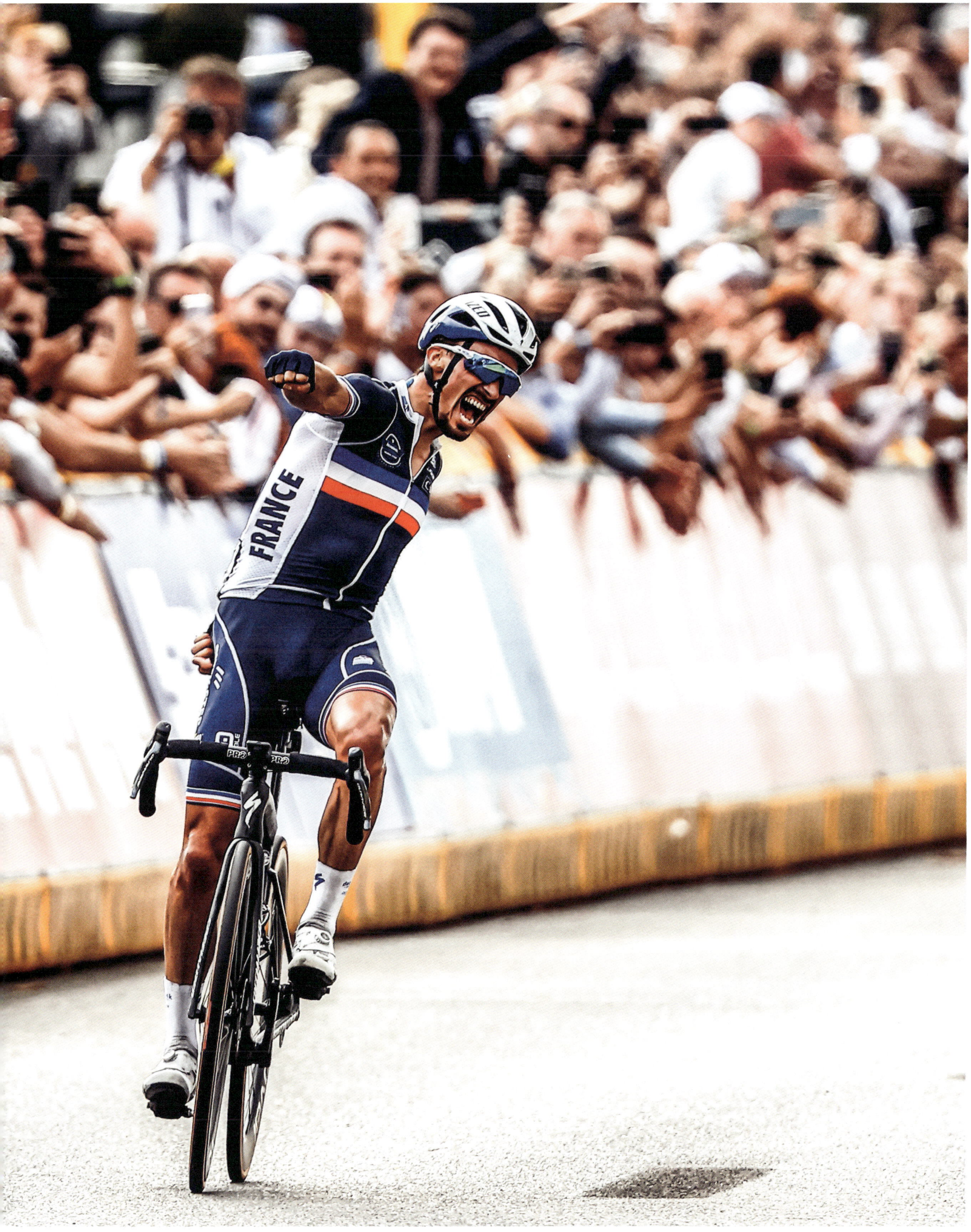
FRANCE

PARIS - ROUBAIX
03.10.2021

Het grote monument Parijs-Roubaix sneuvelde onder de coronadruk. De wedstrijd vlot en veilig laten verlopen op zondag 11 april leek lange tijd mogelijk, maar de coronadruk was te groot in Noord-Frankrijk. Geen Parijs-Roubaix dus, voor het tweede jaar op rij. Er werd beslist om uit te wijken naar het najaar. Naar zondag 3 oktober. Eén week na het WK in Vlaanderen, zes dagen voor Il Lombardia. Yves Lampaert werd vijfde.

The monumental Paris-Roubaix event fell under the pressure of the COVID-19 virus. Allowing the race to be run smoothly and safely on Sunday 11 April seemed possible for a long time, but the pressure of the virus was to big in Northern France. So, for the second year in a row, Paris-Roubaix was called off. The decision was made to postpone the event until Sunday 3 October: one week after the World Championships in Flanders and six days before Il Lombardia. Yves Lampaert finished fifth.

Seul le Paris-Roubaix, le monument classique, a cédé à la pression du Covid-19. On a longtemps cru qu'il était possible d'organiser la course sans incident et en toute sécurité le dimanche 11 avril, mais la pression du Covid-19 était trop grande dans le nord de la France. Autrement dit, pas de Paris-Roubaix, pour la deuxième année consécutive. La décision a été prise et la course a été reportée à l'automne, le dimanche 3 octobre. Une semaine après les Championnats du Monde en Flandre, six jours avant Il Lombardia. Yves Lampaert a terminé cinquième.

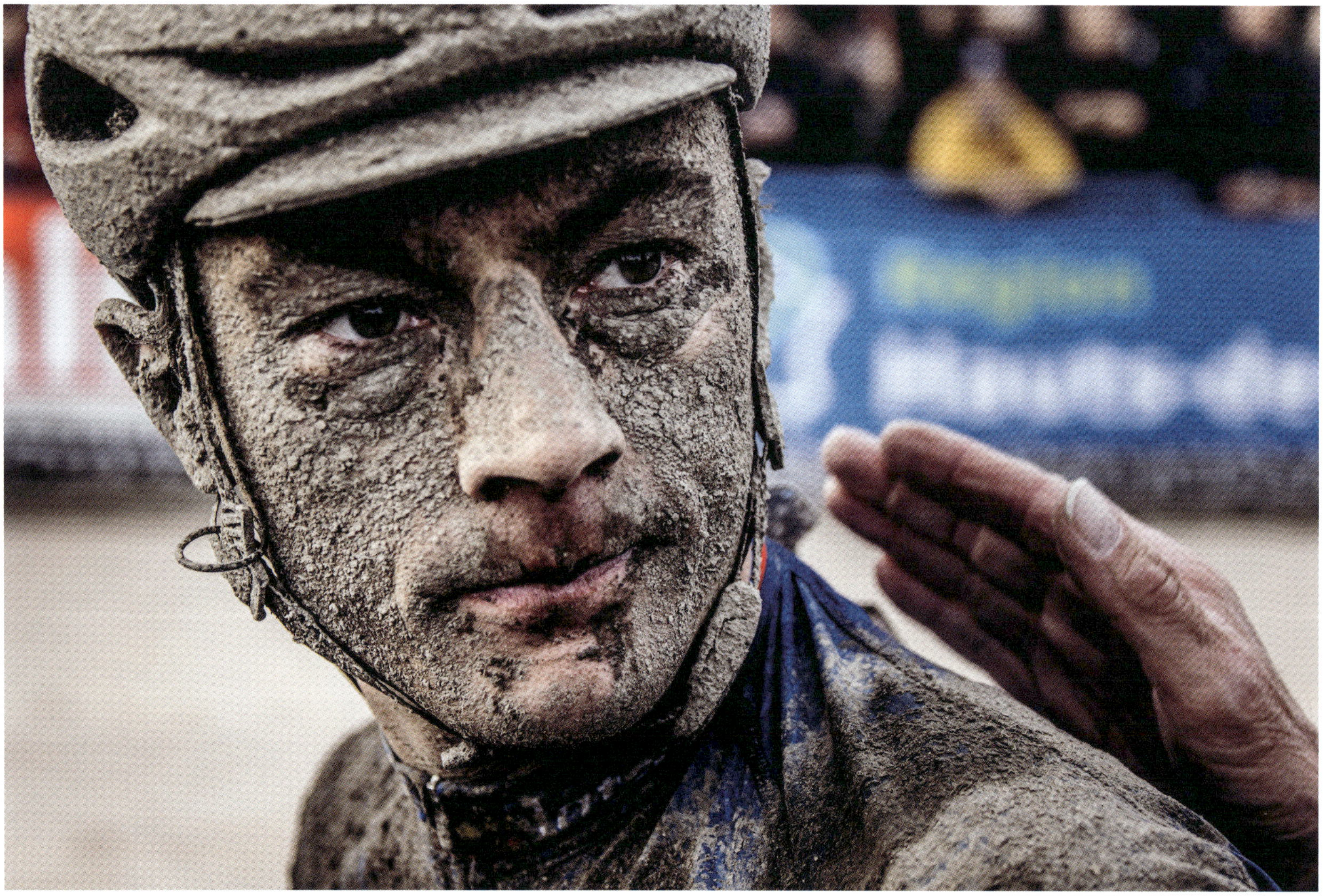

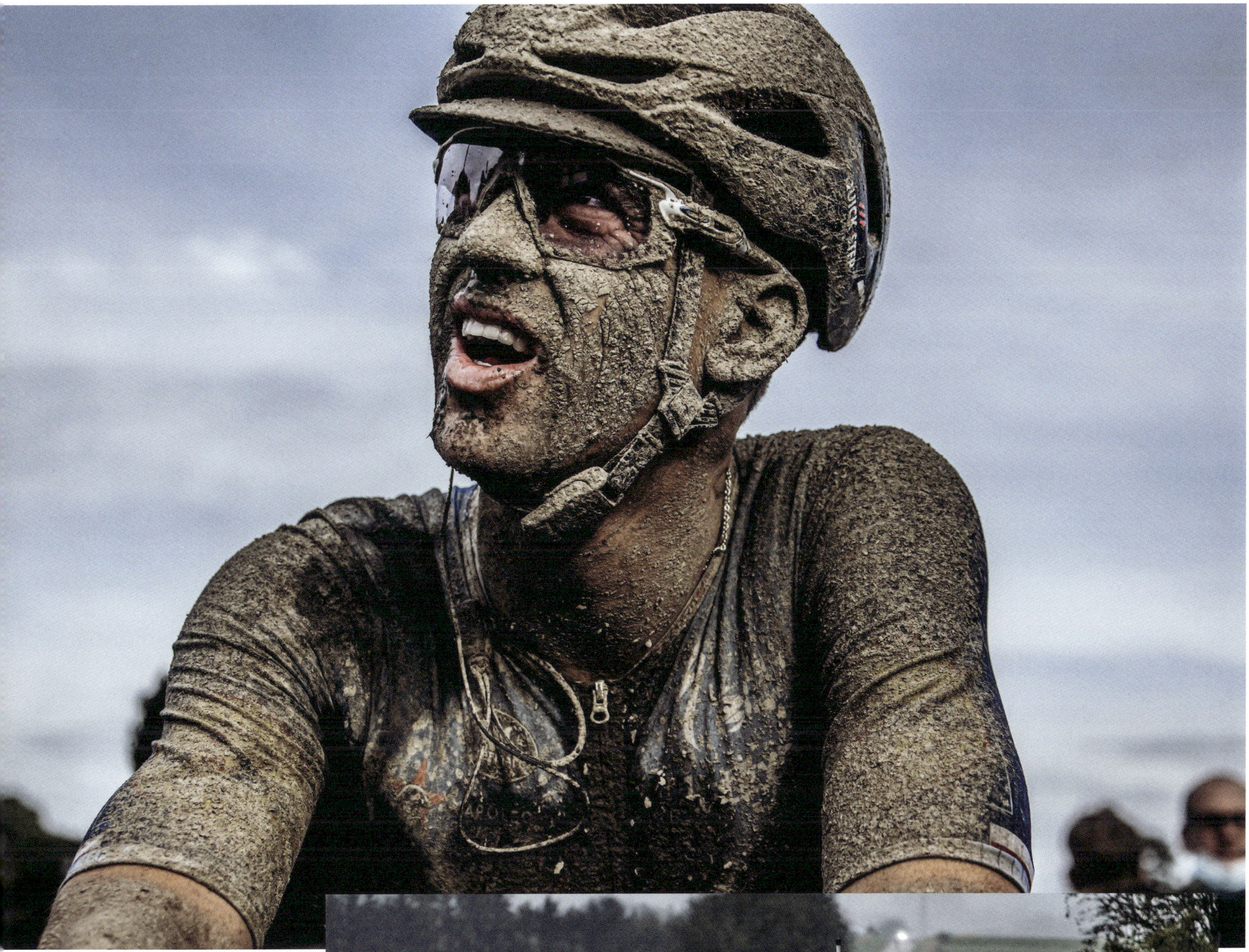

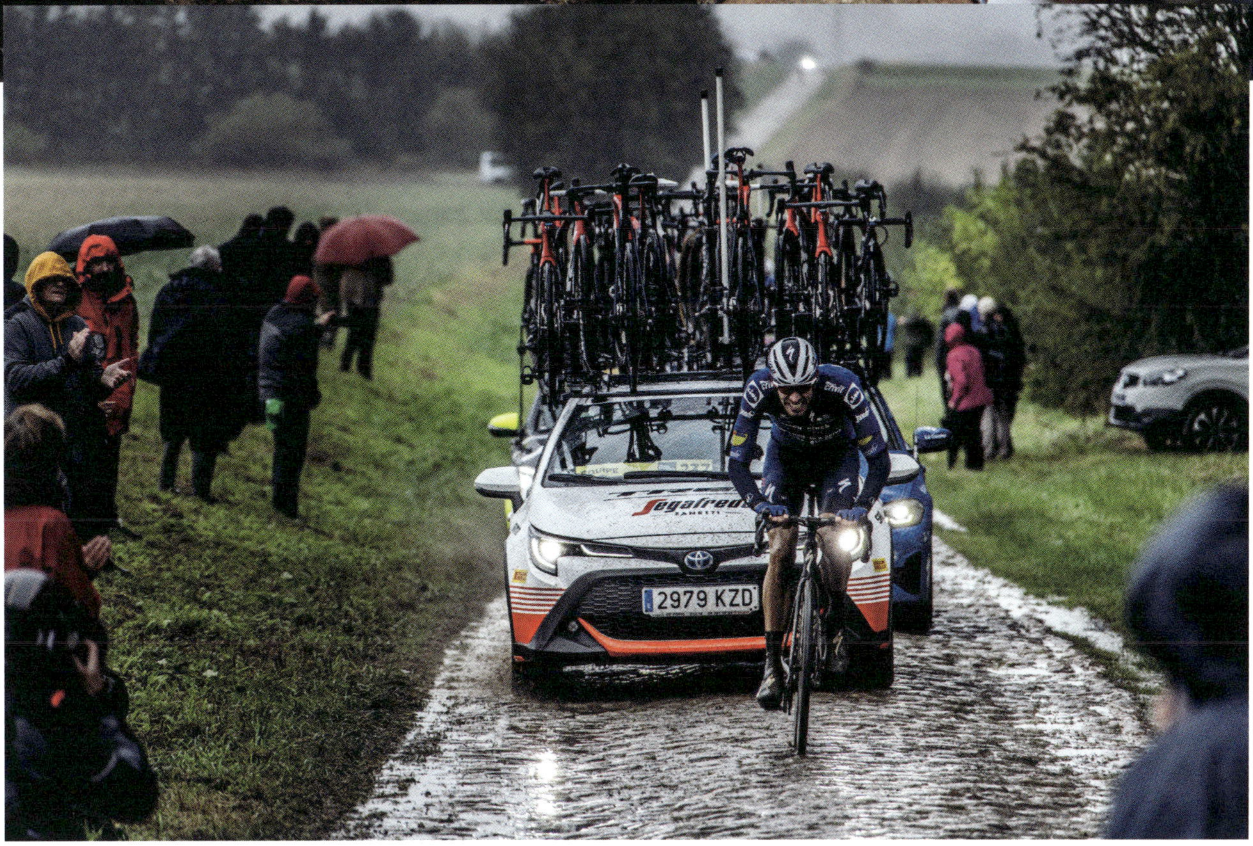
2979 KZD

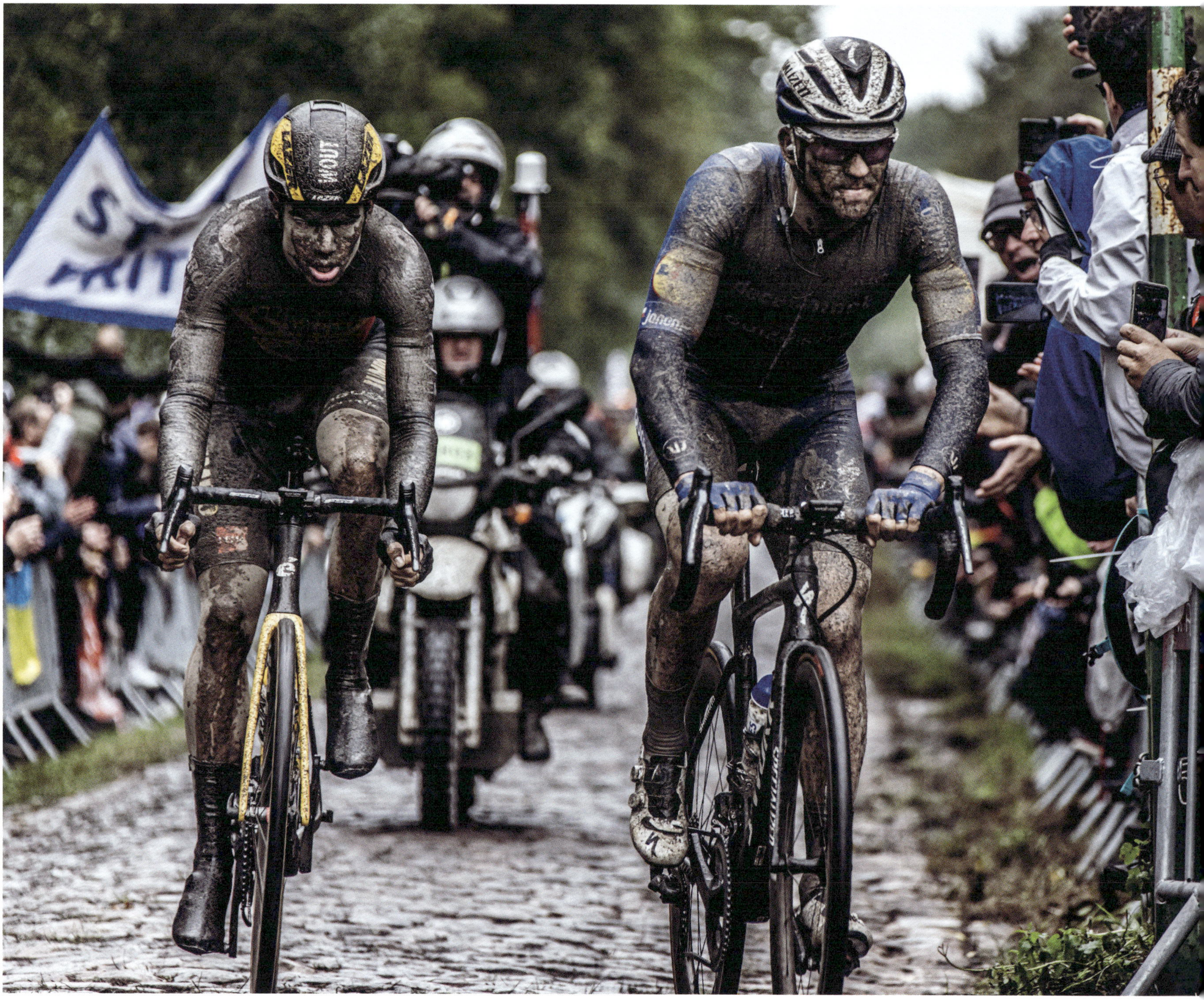

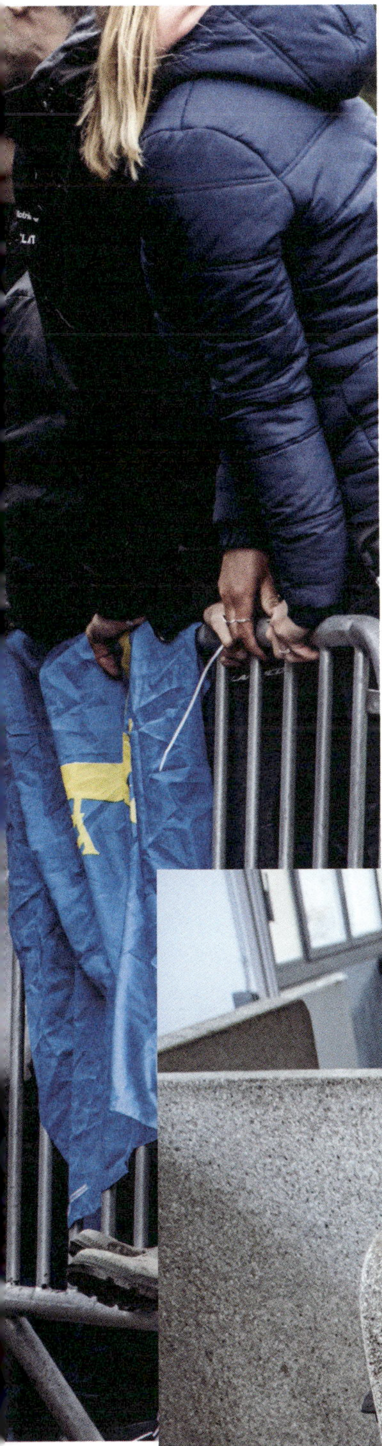

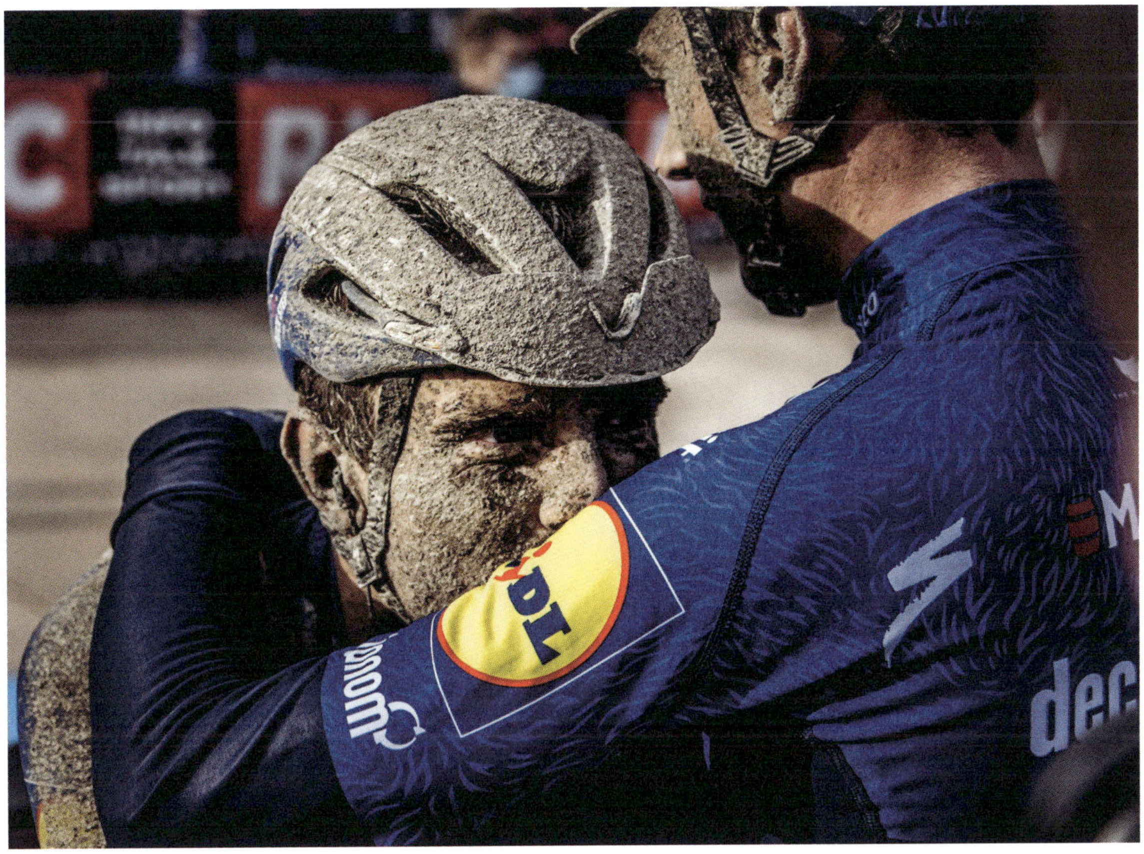

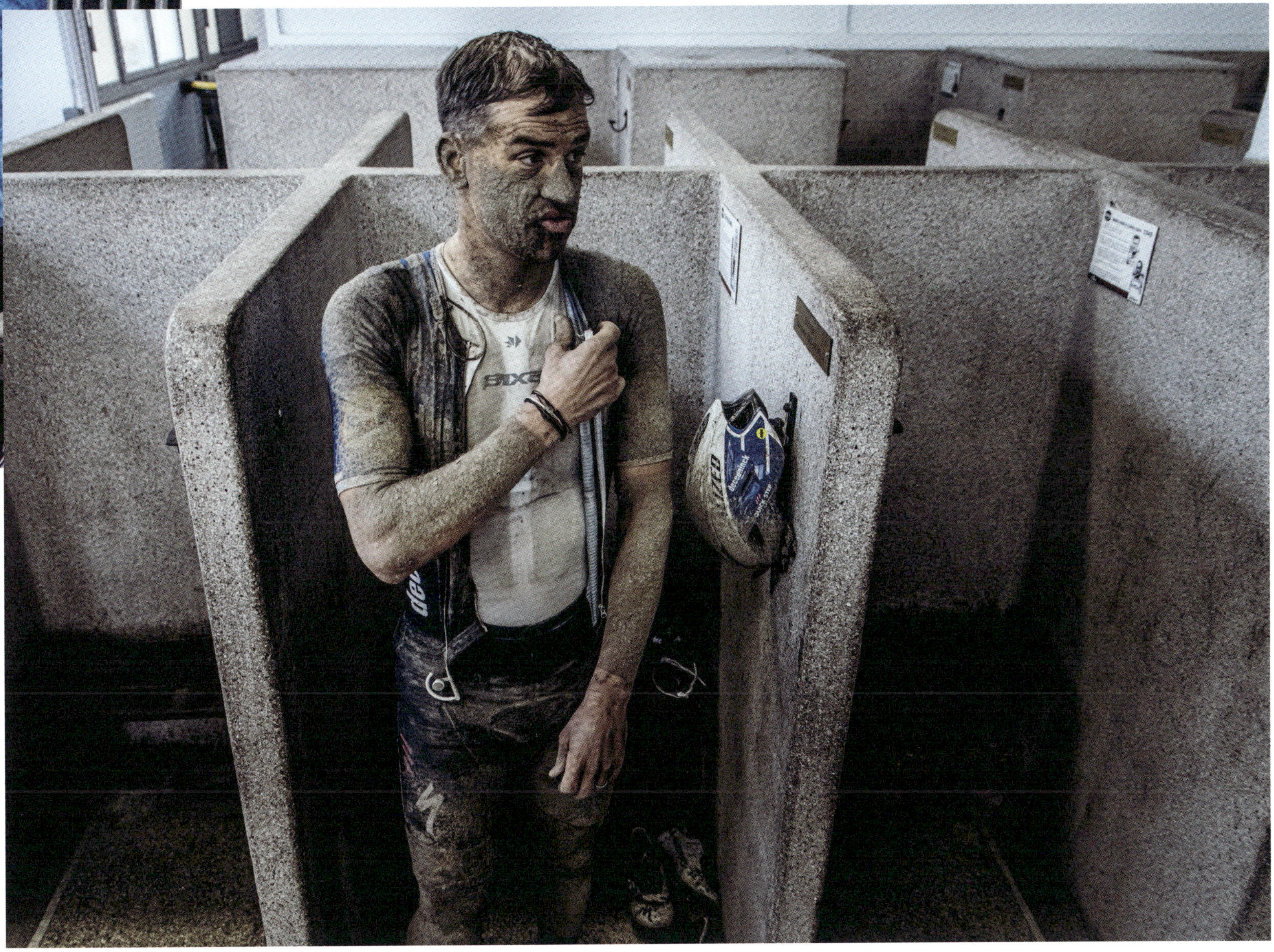

COPPA BERNOCCHI 04.10.2021

Van de Tour de la Provence in februari tot Il Lombardia op 9 oktober. Dit was de arena voor The Wolfpack in 2021. Na de regenboogtrui van Julian Alaphilippe was ook de laatste competitieweek succesvol. Fabio Jakobsen won de Eurométropole Tour op 29 september, Mark Cavendish was de snelste in Münsterland Giro op 3 oktober en Remco Evenepoel tekende op 4 oktober voor de 65ste jaarzege van de ploeg in de Coppa Bernocchi.

From the Tour de la Provence in February to Il Lombardia on 9 October. This was the arena for The Wolfpack in 2021. After Julian Alaphilippe's rainbow jersey, the final week of competition was also successful. Fabio Jakobsen won the Eurométropole Tour on 29 September, Mark Cavendish was the fastest in Münsterland Giro on 3 October, and Remco Evenepoel secured the team's 65th annual victory in the Coppa Bernocchi on 4 October.

Du Tour de la Provence en février à Il Lombardia le 9 octobre, le Wolfpack a encore fait parler de lui en 2021. Après le maillot arc-en-ciel de Julian Alaphilippe, la dernière semaine de compétition a également été couronnée de succès. Fabio Jakobsen a remporté le Tour de l'Eurométropole le 29 septembre, Mark Cavendish a été le plus rapide au Giro de Münsterland le 3 octobre et Remco Evenepoel a décroché la 65e victoire annuelle de l'équipe à la Coppa Bernocchi le 4 octobre.

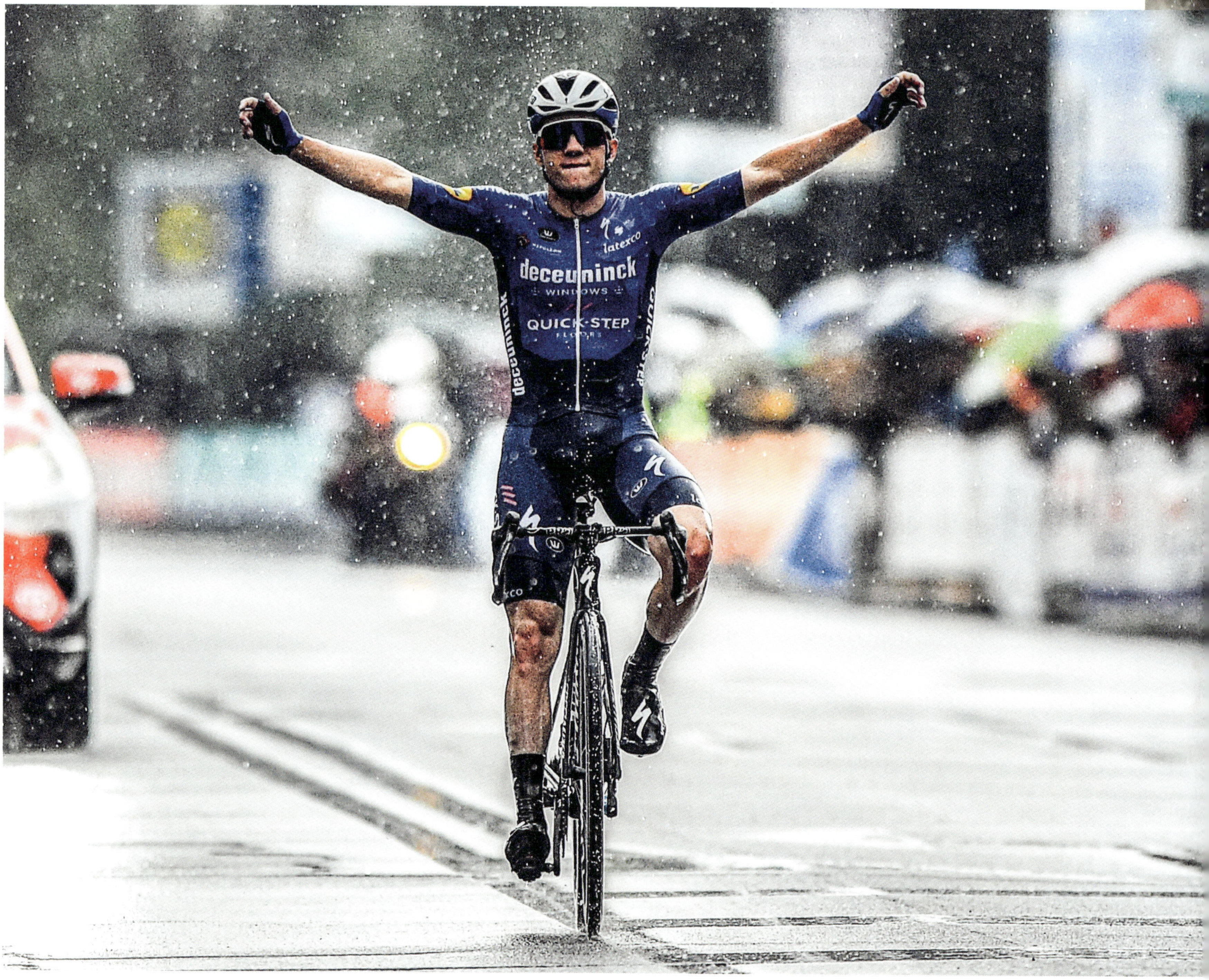

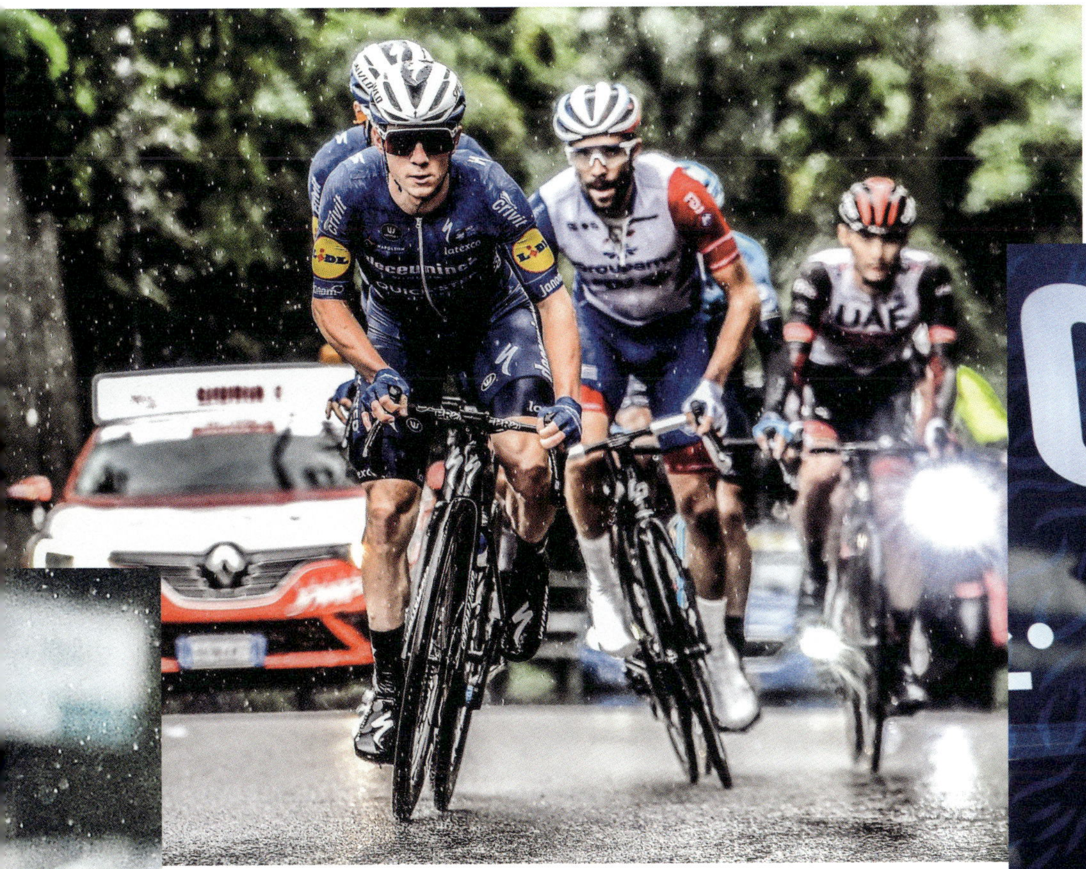

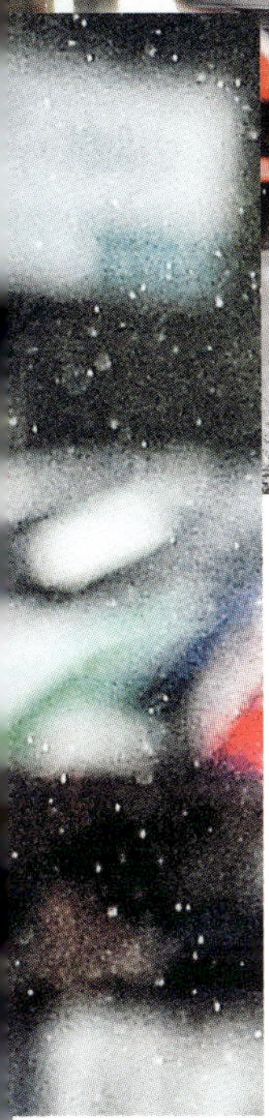

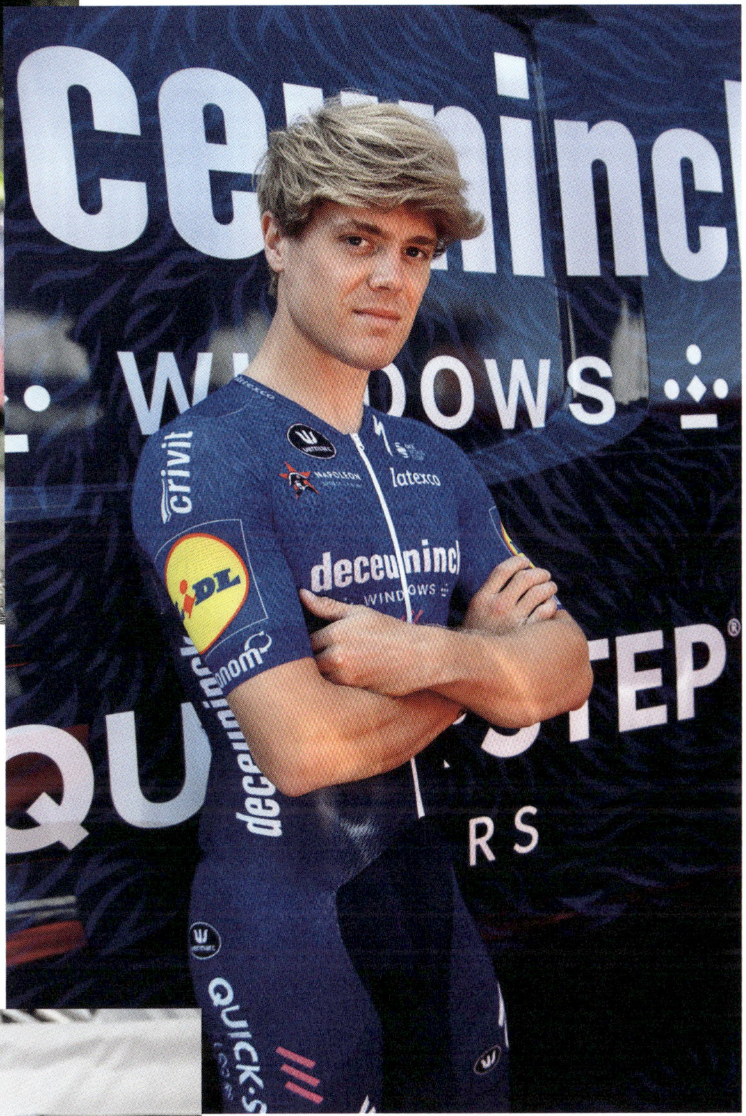

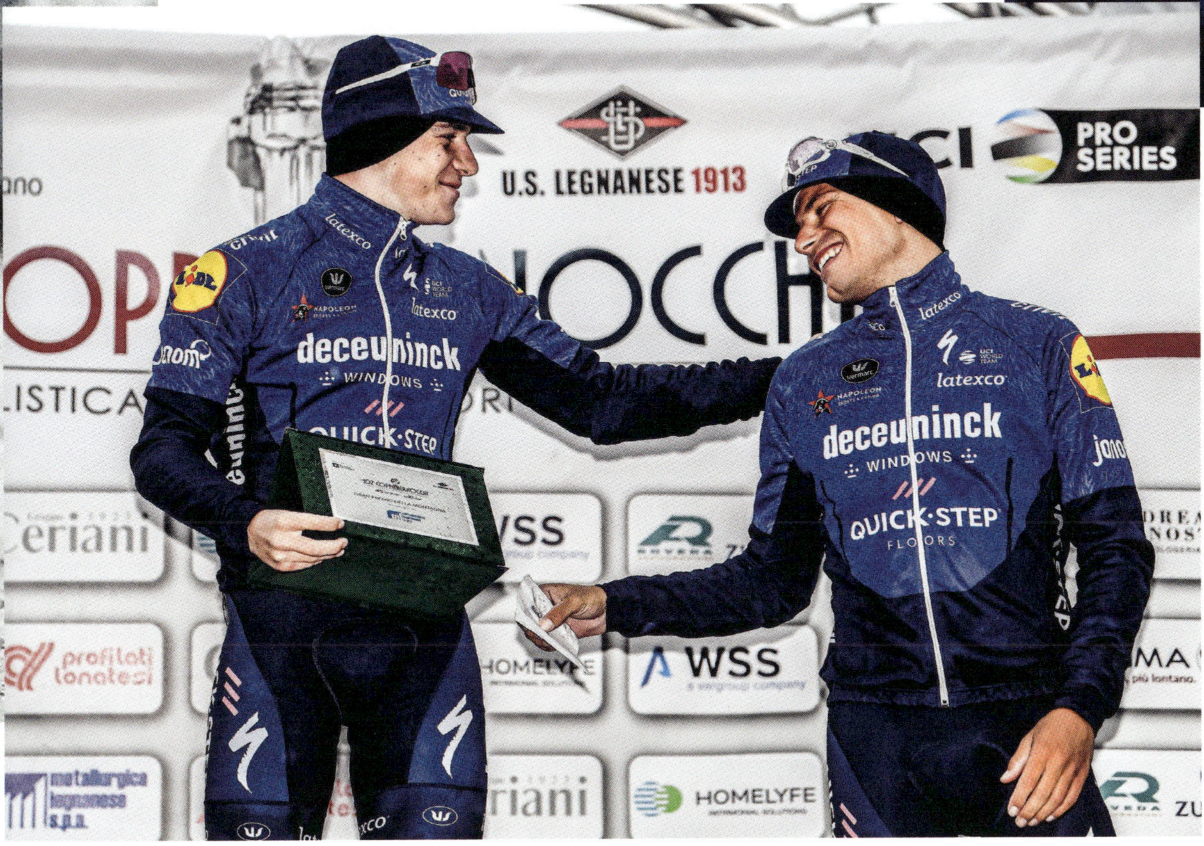

Toproeier Jason Osborne zag fietsen gewoon als training, tot hij het Zwift-ESports Cycling WK eind 2020 won. Amper zes weken na zijn zilveren medaille in de 'lichte dubbel-twee' op de Spelen in Tokyo startte zijn seizoen in Gullegem op 7 september.

Top rower Jason Osborne just saw cycling as training, until he won the Zwift-ESports Cycling World Championship at the end of 2020. Barely six weeks after his silver medal in the 'light doubles' at the Tokyo Games, his season started in Gullegem on September 7.

Rameur Jason Osborne a considéré le cyclisme comme un entraînement, jusqu'à ce qu'il remporte le championnat du monde de cyclisme Zwift-ESports fin 2020. À peine six semaines après sa médaille d'argent en « double léger » aux Jeux de Tokyo, sa saison a débuté à Gullegem le 7 septembre. ▲

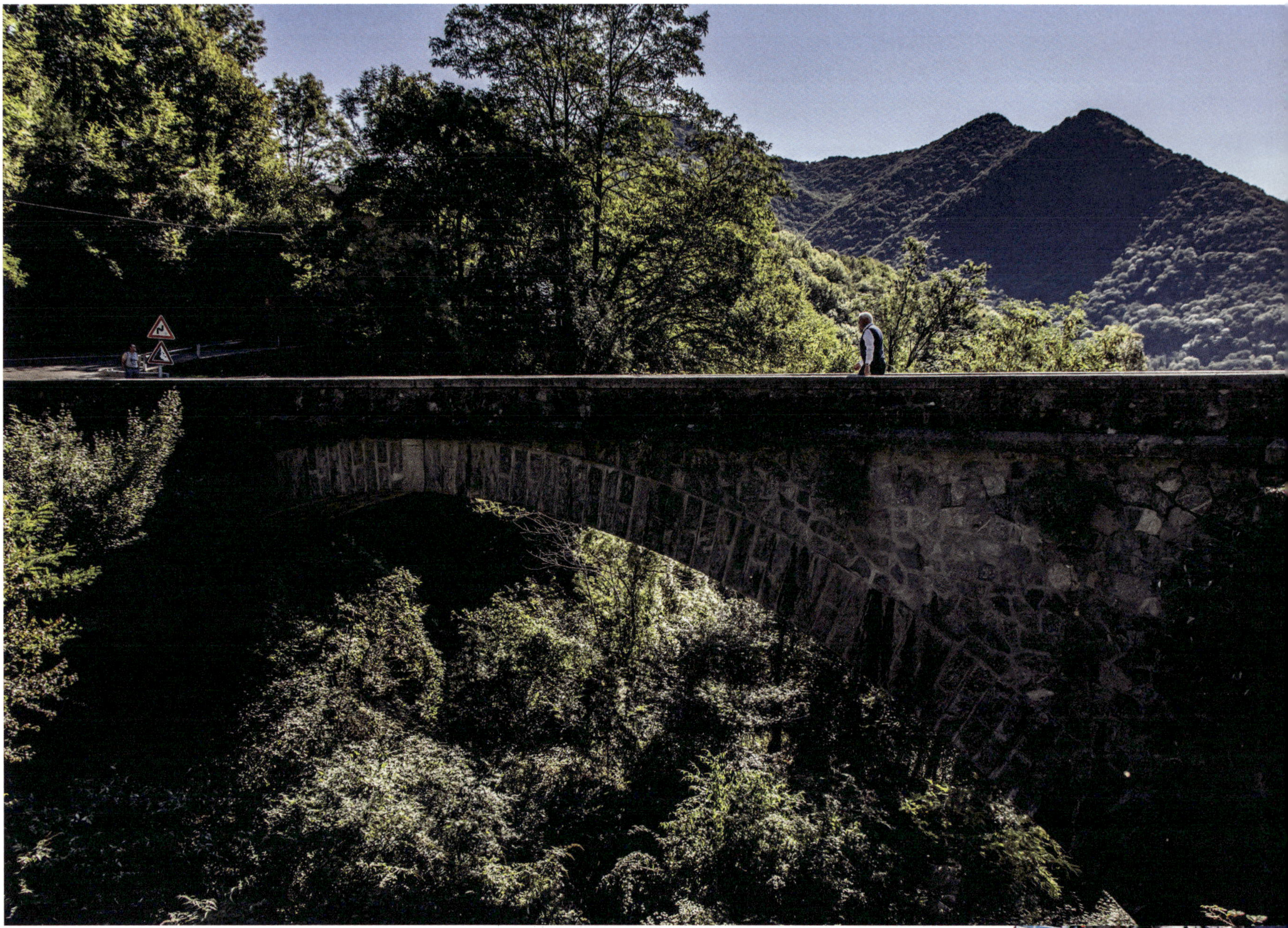

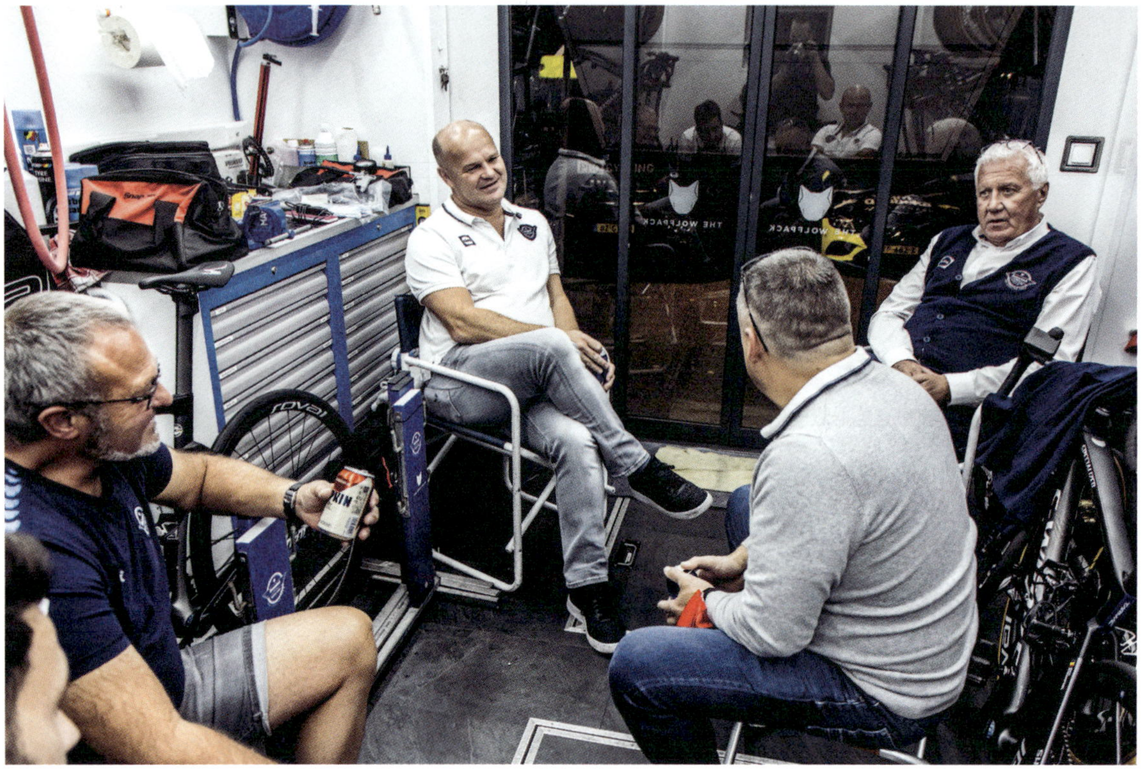

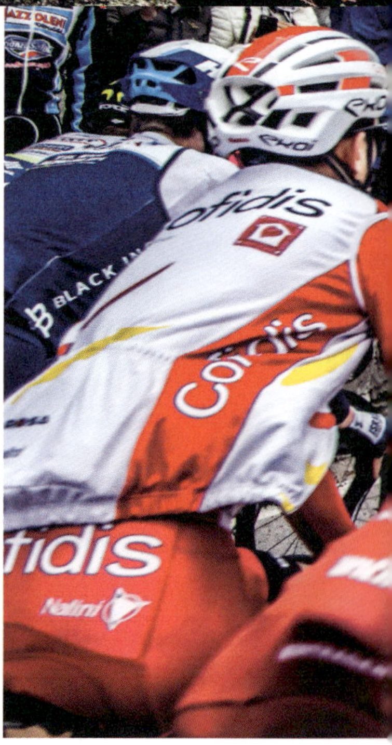
ofidis
Cofidis
fidis

SORMANO, 08.10.2021

Even tijd voor bezinning. Patrick Lefevere steekt de brug over waar Remco Evenepoel op 15 augustus 2020 zijn horrormoment beleefde. Zijn crash in de afzink van de Muro di Sormano staat voor altijd op ons netvlies gebrand. Een jaar later is Remco weer topatleet.

A moment for reflection. Patrick Lefevere crosses the bridge where Remco Evenepoel experienced the horror on 15 August 2020. His crash on the descent of Muro di Sormano will be imprinted in our memory forever. One year later, Remco made his comeback as a top athlete.

Un moment de réflexion. Patrick Lefevere traverse le pont où Remco Evenepoel a vécu son terrible accident le 15 août 2020. Sa chute dans la descente du Mur de Sormano est quelque chose qu'aucun d'entre nous ne pourra oublier. Un an plus tard, Remco est redevenu un athlète de haut niveau. ◀

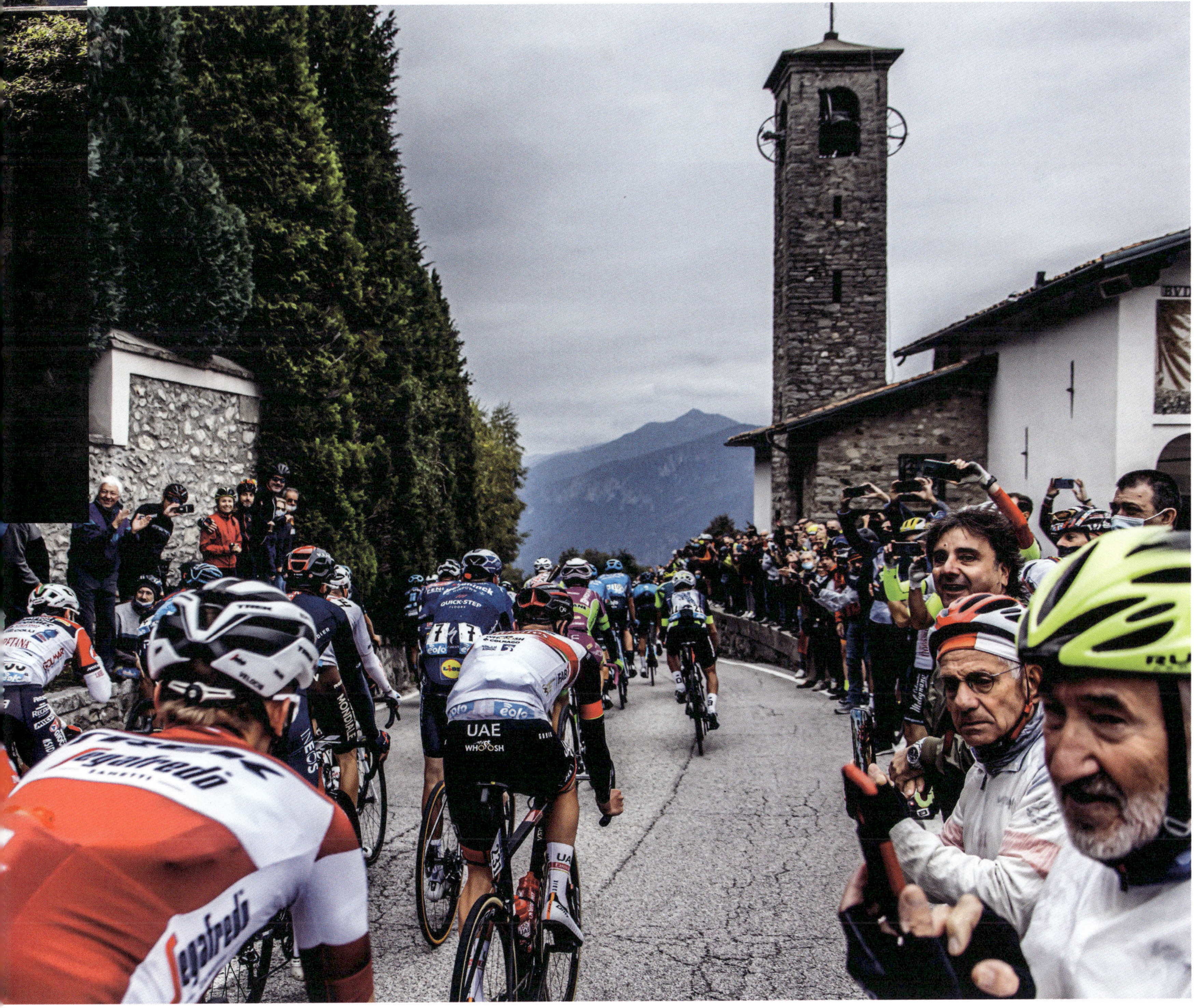

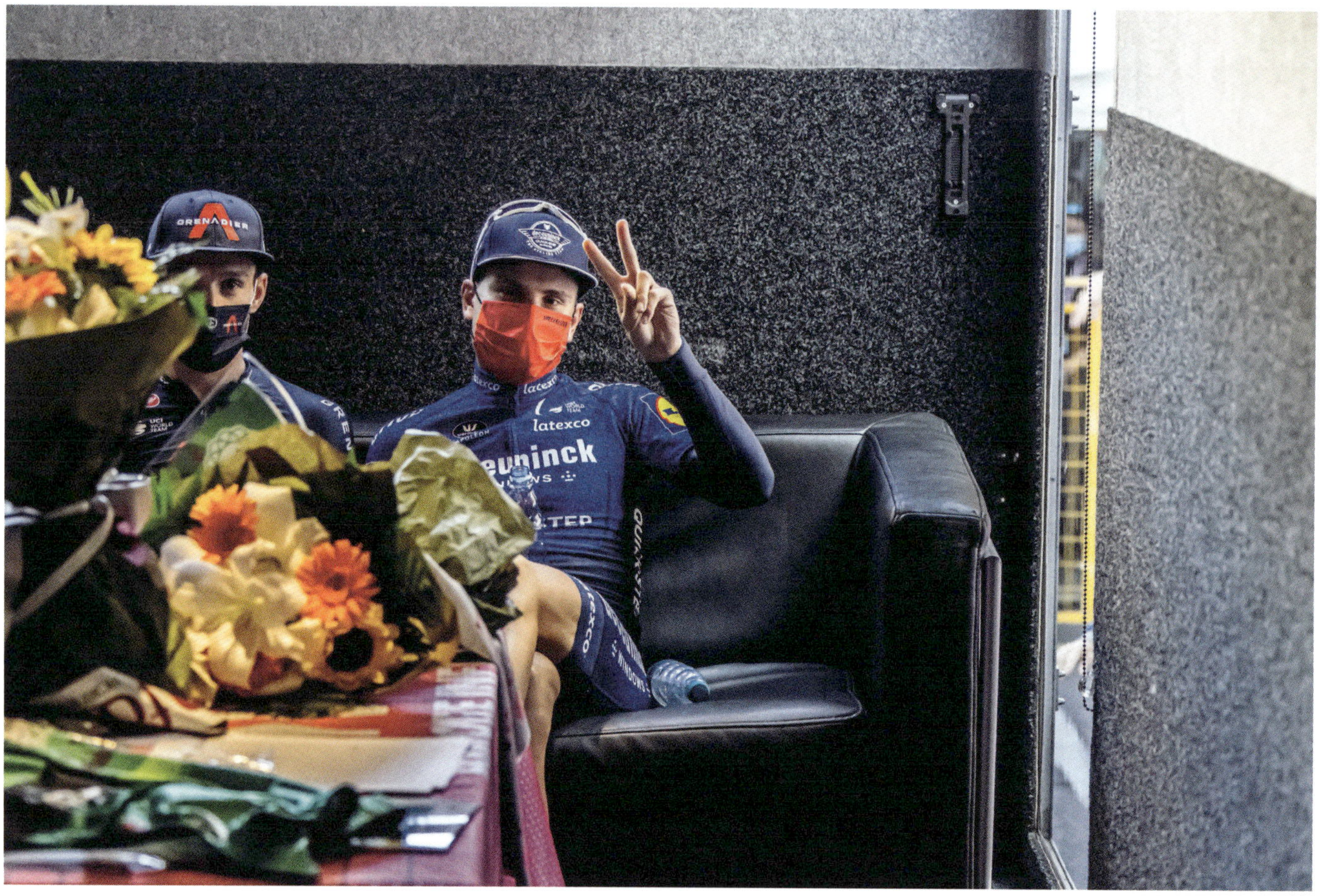
GRENADIER
latexco

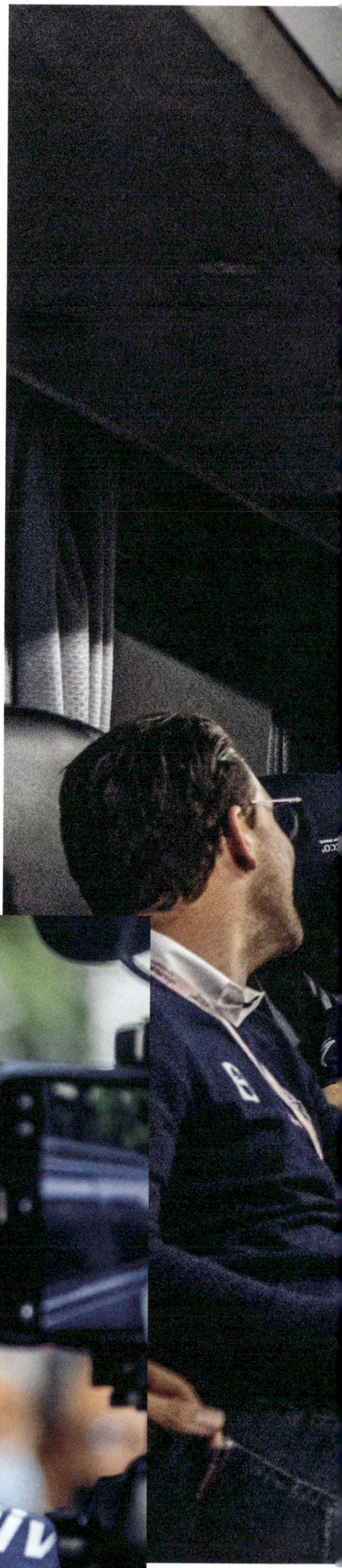

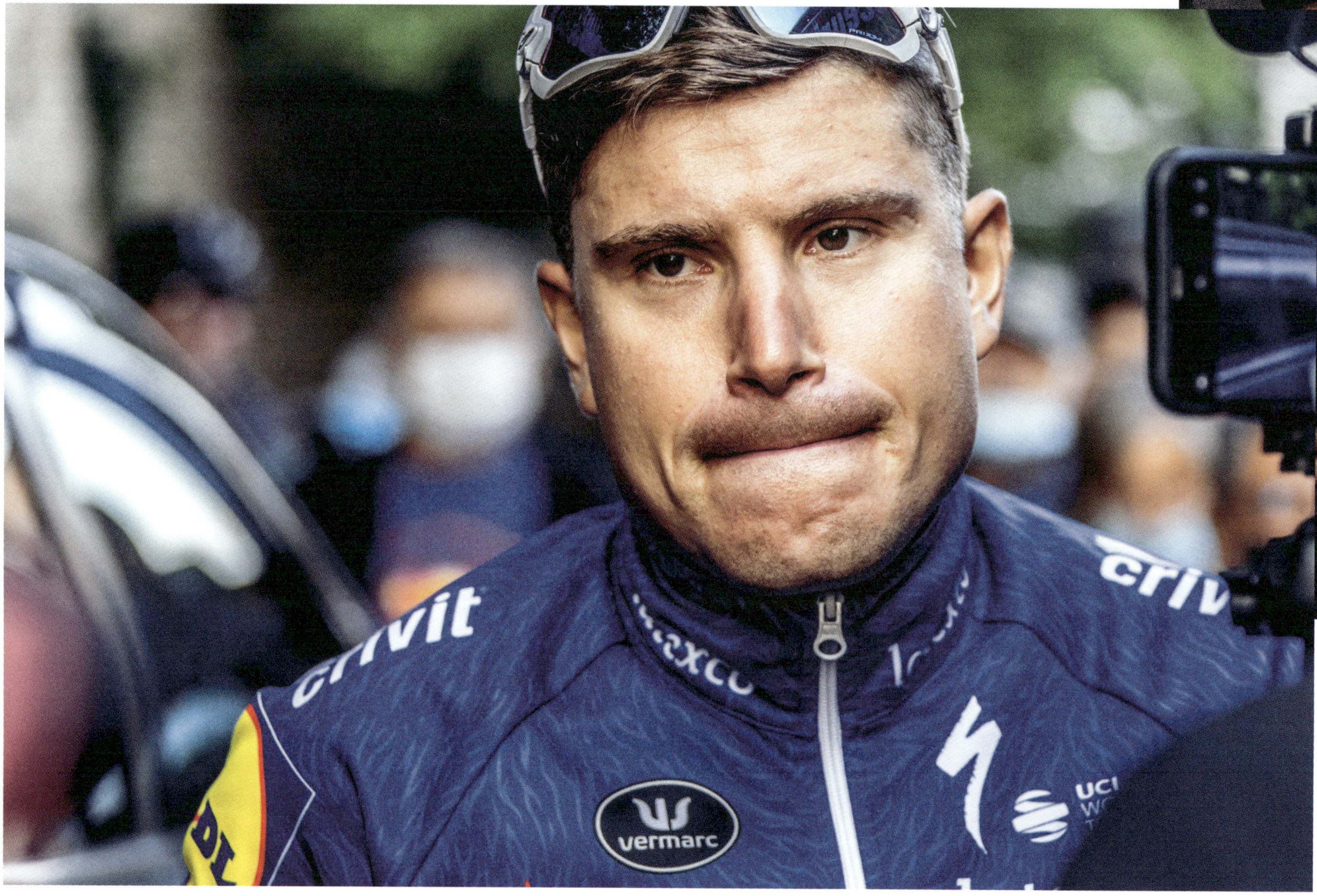
crivit
vermarc

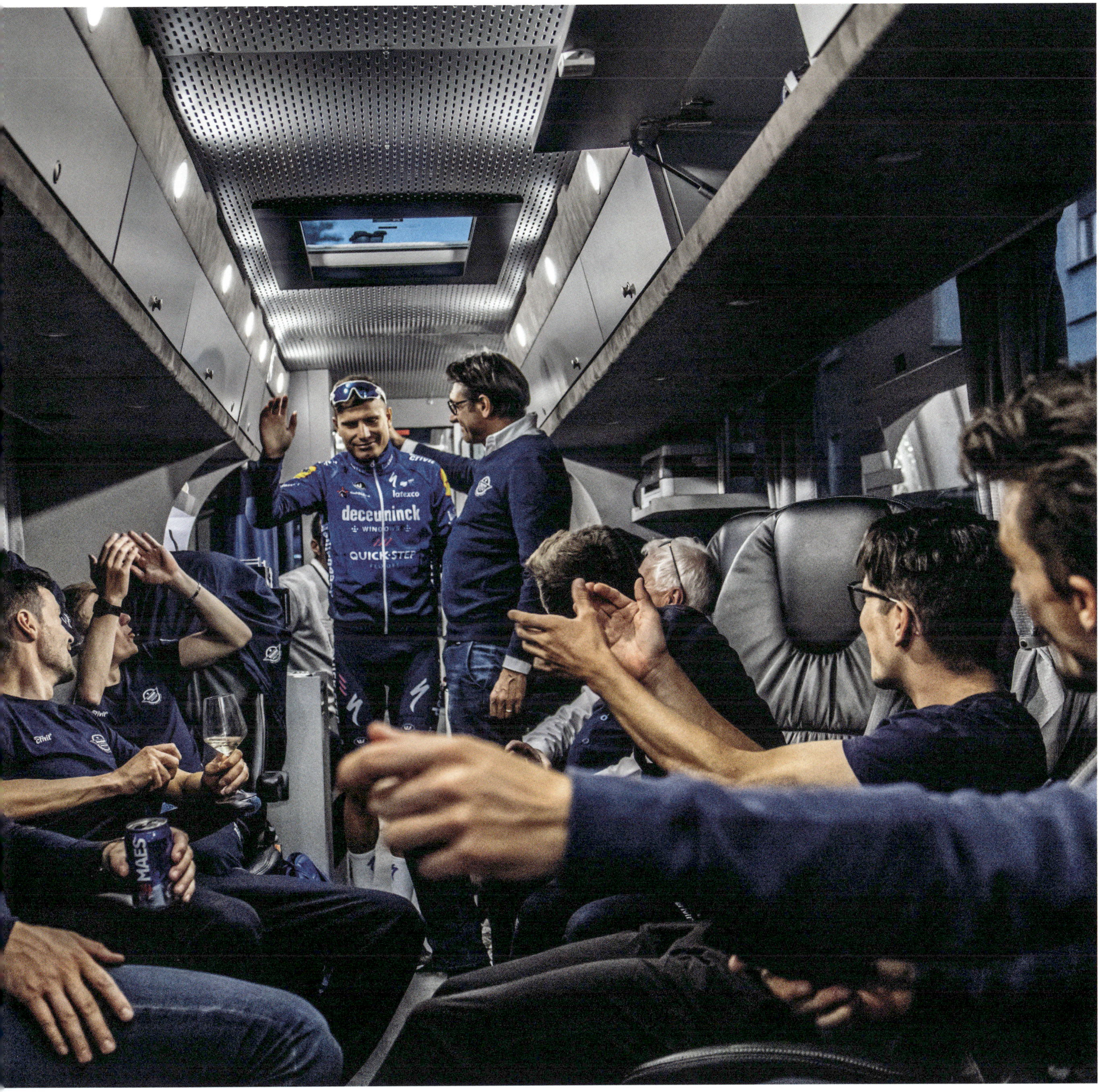
deceuninck
QUICK-STEP
latexco
MAES

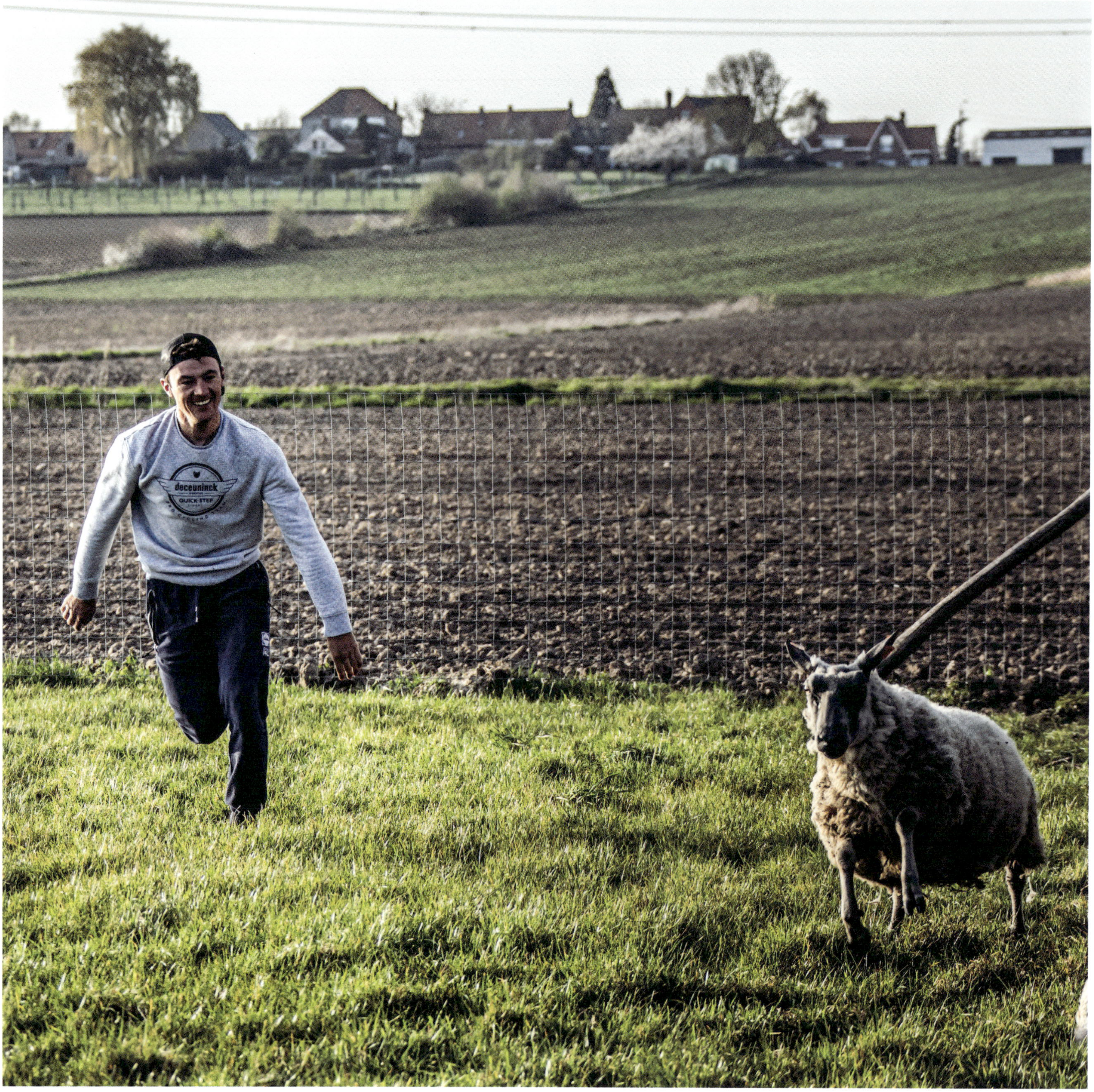
deceuninck
QUICK STEP

WWW.LANNOO.COM

Registreer u op onze website en we sturen u regelmatig een nieuwsbrief met informatie over nieuwe boeken en met interessante, exclusieve aanbiedingen.

Register on our web site and we will regularly send you a newsletter with information about new books and interesting, exclusive offers.

En vous enregistrant sur notre site, vous recevrez régulièrement une newsletter qui vous informera de nos nouvelles parutions et vous proposera des offres exclusives.

Photography: Wout Beel,
Photonews: p. 202-203, 222-227, 232, 233 boven,
Getty Images: p. 233 onder

Text: Geert Vandenbon

Graphic design: Wim Esteban De Dobbeleer @ Bataia.cc

Als u opmerkingen of vragen heeft, dan kunt u contact nemen met onze redactie: redactielifestyle@lannoo.com

If you have observations or questions, please contact our editorial office: redactielifestyle@lannoo.com

Si vous avez des remarques ou des questions, n'hésitez pas à prendre contact avec notre rédaction : redactielifestyle@lannoo.com

© Wout Beel, Uitgeverij Lannoo nv, Tielt, 2021
D/2021/45/615 – NUR 480, 489 – ISBN 978 94 014 8219 6

All rights reserved. Nothing from this publication may be copied, stored in an automated database and/or be made public in any form or in any way, either electronic, mechanical or in any other manner without the prior written consent of the publisher.